ACCA

Strategic Business Reporting
Practice & Revision Kit

BPP Learning Media is an **ACCA Approved Content Provider** for the ACCA qualification. This means we work closely with ACCA to ensure our products fully prepare you for your ACCA exams.

In this Practice & Revision Kit, which has been reviewed by the **ACCA examining team**, we:

- Discuss the **best strategies** for revising and taking your ACCA exams

- Ensure you are well **prepared** for your exam

- Provide you with **lots of great guidance** on tackling questions

- Provide you with **five** mock exams

For exams in September 2018, December 2018, March 2019 and June 2019

First edition 2018

ISBN 9781 5097 1547 3

e-ISBN: 9781 5097 1557 2

British Library Cataloguing-in-Publication Data
A catalogue record for this book is available
from the British Library

Published by

BPP Learning Media Ltd
BPP House, Aldine Place
142–144 Uxbridge Road
London W12 8AA

www.bpp.com/learningmedia

Printed in the United Kingdom

Your learning materials, published by BPP Learning Media Ltd, are
printed on paper obtained from traceable, sustainable sources.

Contents

Finding Questions

Question index

The headings in this checklist/index indicate the main topics of questions, but questions often cover several different topics.

Questions set under the previous syllabi *Advanced Corporate Reporting (ACR)* and *Corporate Reporting* (P2) are included because their content is similar to those which appear in the *Strategic Business Reporting* (SBR) exam.

Topic index

Listed below are the key SBR syllabus topics and the numbers of the questions in this Kit covering those topics.

If you need to concentrate your practice and revision on certain topics or if you want to attempt all available questions that refer to a particular subject, you will find this index useful.

Syllabus topic	Question numbers	Workbook chapter
Agriculture (IAS 41)	56, 63	3
Accounting policies (IAS 8)	31, 61, 62, 64	1
Borrowing costs (IAS 23)	33, 62	3
Changes in group structure and group reorganisations	73, 74	12
Conceptual Framework	24, 25, 26, 30, 77	1
Consolidated statement of financial position	10, 14, 48, 64, 65, 66, 67, 70, 73	10
Consolidated statement of profit or loss and other comprehensive income	12, 13, 48, 64	10
Consolidated statement of cash flows	10, 15, 16, 20, 21, 64, 68, 69, 79	16
Corporate responsibility	19, 77	17
Current issues	23, 24, 25, 77, 79	19
Disclosure initiative	20, 24, 25	19
Deferred tax (IAS 12)	36, 46, 47, 48, 58, 63, 64, 72	6
Disposals of investments	7, 13, 49, 65, 66, 69	12
Employee benefits (pensions)	3, 4, 13, 30, 45, 48, 51, 52	4
Ethics	17–22, 29, 30, 49, 67, 69	2
Events after the reporting period (IAS 10)	24, 37, 49	5
Fair value (IFRS 13)	13, 18, 34, 40, 45, 55, 56, 57, 59	7
Financial instruments (IFRS 9)	1, 4, 12, 24, 34, 36, 37, 40, 41, 42, 43, 44, 48, 58, 67, 77	7
Foreign currency (IAS 21)	9, 14, 63, 64, 73, 74	15
Global reporting initiative	17	17
Government grants (IAS 20)	31, 64, 68	3
Impairment (IAS 36)	30, 32, 33, 34, 35, 38, 49, 57, 58	3

Syllabus topic	Question numbers	Workbook chapter
Intangible assets (IAS 38)	17, 28, 33, 34, 48, 57	3
Integrated reporting	17, 20, 77, 79	17
Interpretation of financial statements	75–78	17
Interim reporting (IAS 34)	28	1
Investment property (IAS 40)	36, 38, 57, 58	3
Joint arrangements (IFRS 11)	12, 37	14
Leasing (IFRS 16)	2, 18, 29, 38, 44, 46, 52, 53	8
Non-current assets held for sale and discontinued operations (IFRS 5)	12, 28, 29, 32, 36, 48, 49, 63	13
Property, plant and equipment (IAS 16)	27, 28, 31, 36, 37, 57, 70, 77	3
Provisions and contingencies (IAS 37)	31, 37, 38, 39, 45, 50, 51, 52, 74	5
Related party transactions (IAS 24)	22, 30, 33, 40	2
Revenue recognition (IFRS 15)	13, 26, 27, 28, 29, 30, 31, 44, 51	1
Segment reporting (IFRS 8)	19, 31, 67	17
Share-based payment (IFRS 2)	46, 49, 51, 52, 53, 56, 65	9
Small and medium-sized entities	59, 60	18
Social and environmental reporting	17, 19	17
Step acquisitions	8, 14, 65, 67	11

Helping you with your revision

BPP Learning Media – ACCA Approved Content Provider

As an ACCA **Approved Content Provider**, BPP Learning Media gives you the **opportunity** to use revision materials reviewed by the ACCA examining team. By incorporating the ACCA examining team's comments and suggestions regarding the depth and breadth of syllabus coverage, the BPP Learning Media Practice & Revision Kit provides excellent, **ACCA-approved** support for your revision.

These materials are reviewed by the ACCA examining team. The objective of the review is to ensure that the material properly covers the syllabus and study guide outcomes, used by the examining team in setting the exams, in the appropriate breadth and depth. The review does not ensure that every eventuality, combination or application of examinable topics is addressed by the ACCA Approved Content. Nor does the review comprise a detailed technical check of the content as the Approved Content Provider has its own quality assurance processes in place in this respect.

The structure of this Practice & Revision Kit

This Practice & Revision Kit is divided into three sections. The questions in Section 1 are preparation questions to help develop your knowledge. Section 2 provides a number of questions focused on the preparation of full consolidated financial statements. It is highly unlikely that you will be required to prepare full consolidated financial statements in the exam, it is more likely that extracts will be required, so the aim of this section is to help develop your consolidation knowledge and technique. Section 3 contains a number of exam standard questions which are of appropriate complexity and format to mimic the style of the final exam. There are also five mock exams which provide sufficient opportunity to refine your knowledge and skills as part of your final exam preparations.

Approach to examining the syllabus

The Strategic Business Reporting syllabus is assessed by a 3 hour 15 minute exam. The pass mark is **50%**. All questions in the exam are **compulsory**.

At the revision stage, we advise students to revisit the following main syllabus requirements so that you have a good understanding of the overall objectives of this exam. Remember, ACCA's examining team expect you to be able to:

- Demonstrate **professional competences** within the business reporting environment. You will be examined on concepts, theories, and principles, and on your ability to question and comment on proposed accounting treatments.

- Relate professional issues to relevant concepts and practical situations. The **evaluation of alternative accounting practices** and the **identification and prioritisation** of issues will be a key element of the exam.

- Exercise **professional** and **ethical judgement**, and **integrate technical knowledge** when addressing business reporting issues in a business context.

- Adopt **either a stakeholder or an external focus** in answering questions and demonstrate personal skills such as **problem solving**, **dealing with information** and **decision making**. You will also have to demonstrate **communication skills** appropriate to the scenario.

- Demonstrate specific professional knowledge appropriate to the **preparation and presentation of consolidated and other financial statements** from accounting data, to conform with relevant accounting standards. Here, you may be required to interpret financial statements for different stakeholders and/or communicate the impact of changes in accounting regulation on financial reporting.

Format of the exam

100 marks, two sections, each section 50 marks		Marks
Section A	Two compulsory scenario-based questions, totalling 50 marks Question 1: • Based on the financial statements of group entities, or extracts thereof (syllabus area D) • Also likely to require consideration of some financial reporting issues (syllabus area C) • Numerical aspects of group accounting will be a maximum of 25 marks • Discussion and explanation of numerical aspects will be required Question 2: • Consideration of the reporting implications and the ethical implications of specific events in a given scenario Two professional marks will be awarded to the ethical issues question.	50 (incl. 2 professional marks)
Section B	Two compulsory 25-mark questions Questions: • May be scenario, case-study, or essay based • Will contain both discursive and computational elements • Could deal with any aspect of the syllabus • Will always include either a full or part question that requires the appraisal of financial and/or non-financial information from either the preparer's or another stakeholder's perspective Two professional marks will be awarded to the question that requires analysis.	50 (incl. 2 professional marks)

Current issues

The current issues element of the syllabus (Syllabus area F) may be examined in Section A or B but will not be a full question. It is more likely to form part of another question.

(handwritten annotations):
Q1 ⎤
Q2 ⎦ 50
① extracts or Discussions
Q3-25
Q4-25
Current issues 10 marks

Essential skills areas to be successful in Strategic Business Reporting

There are three areas you should develop in order to achieve exam success in Strategic Business Reporting. As a reminder, these are:

(1)   Knowledge application
(2)   Specific Strategic Business Reporting skills
(3)   Exam success skills

At the revision and final exam preparation phases **these should be developed together as part of a comprehensive study plan of focused question practice**.

Take some time to revisit the Specific **Strategic Business Reporting skills** and **Exam success skills**. These are shown in the diagram below and followed by tutorial guidance of how to apply them.

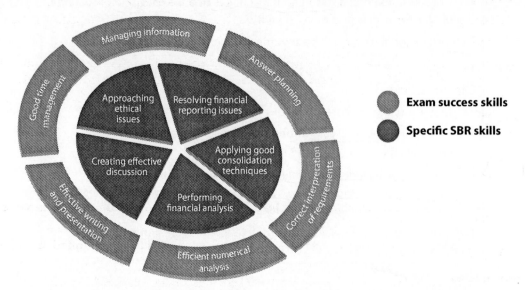

Specific Strategic Business Reporting skills – reminder

These are the skills specific to SBR that we think you need to develop in order to pass the exam.

In the BPP Strategic Business Reporting Workbook, there are five **Skills Checkpoints** which define each skill and show how it is applied in answering a question. A brief summary of each skill is given below.

Skill 1: Approaching ethical issues

Question 2 in Section A of the exam will require you to consider the **reporting implications** and the **ethical implications** of specific events in a given scenario. The two Section B questions could deal with any aspect of the syllabus. Therefore, ethics could feature in this part of the exam too.

Given that ethics will feature in every exam, it is essential that you master the appropriate technique for approaching ethical issues in order to maximise your mark.

BPP recommends a step-by-step technique for approaching questions on ethical issues:

STEP 1   Work out how many minutes you have to answer the question.

STEP 2   Read the requirement and analyse it.

BPP LEARNING MEDIA

STEP 3 Read the scenario, identify which IAS or IFRS may be relevant, whether the proposed accounting treatment complies with that IAS or IFRS and whether there are any threats to the fundamental ethical principles.

STEP 4 Prepare an answer plan using key words from the requirements as headings.

STEP 5 Write up your answer using key words from the requirements as headings.

Skills Checkpoint 1 in the BPP Workbook for Strategic Business Reporting covers this technique in detail through application to an exam-standard question. Consider revisiting Skills Checkpoint 1 and completing the scenario-based question to specifically improve this skill.

Skill 2: Resolving financial reporting issues

Financial reporting issues are highly likely to be tested in both sections of your Strategic Business Reporting exam, so it is essential that you master the skill for resolving financial reporting issues in order to maximise your chance of passing the exam.

The basic approach BPP recommends for resolving financial reporting issues is very similar to the one for ethical issues. This consistency is important because in Question 2 of the exam, both will be tested together.

STEP 1 Work out how many minutes you have to answer the question.

STEP 2 Read the requirement and analyse it, identifying sub-requirements.

STEP 3 Read the scenario, identifying relevant IASs or IFRSs and their application to the scenario.

STEP 4 Prepare an answer plan ensuring that you cover each of the issues raised in the scenario.

STEP 5 Write up your answer, using separate headings for each item in the scenario.

Skills Checkpoint 2 in the BPP Workbook for Strategic Business Reporting covers this technique in detail through application to an exam-standard question. Consider revisiting Skills Checkpoint 2 and completing the scenario based question to specifically improve this skill.

Skill 3: Applying good consolidation techniques

Question 1 of Section A of the exam will be based on the financial statements of group entities, or extracts thereof. Section B of the exam could deal with any aspect of the syllabus so it is also possible that groups feature in Question 3 or 4.

Good consolidation techniques are therefore essential when answering both written and numerical aspects of group questions.

Skills Checkpoint 3 focuses on the more challenging technique for correcting errors in group financial statements that have already been prepared.

A step-by-step technique for applying good consolidation techniques is outlined below.

STEP 1 Work out how many minutes you have to answer the question.

STEP 2 Read the requirement for each part of the question and analyse it, identifying sub-requirements.

STEP 3 Read the scenario, identify exactly what information has been provided and what you need to do with this information. Identify which consolidation workings/adjustments may be required.

STEP 4 Draw up a group structure. Make notes in the margins of the question as to which consolidation working, adjustment or correction to error is required. Do not perform any detailed calculations at this stage.

STEP 5 Write up your answer using key words from the requirements as headings (if preparing narrative). Perform calculations first, then explain. Remember that marks will be available for a discussion of the principles underpinning any calculations.

Skills Checkpoint 3 in the BPP Workbook for Strategic Business Reporting covers this technique in detail through application to an exam-standard question. Consider revisiting Skills Checkpoint 3 and completing the scenario based question to specifically improve this skill.

Skill 4: Performing financial analysis

Section B of the SBR exam will contain two questions, which may be scenario or case-study or essay based and will contain both discursive and computational elements. Section B could deal with any aspect of the syllabus but will always include either a full question, or part of a question that requires appraisal of financial or non-financial information from either the preparer's and/or another stakeholder's perspective. Two professional marks will be awarded to the question in Section B that requires analysis.

Given that appraisal of financial and/or non-financial information will feature in Section B of every exam, it is essential that you have mastered the appropriate technique in order to maximise your chance of passing the SBR exam.

A step-by-step technique for performing financial analysis is outlined below.

STEP 1 Work out how many minutes you have to answer the question

STEP 2 Read and analyse the requirement

STEP 3 Read and analyse the scenario

STEP 4 Prepare an answer plan

STEP 5 Write up your answer

Skills Checkpoint 4 in the BPP Workbook for Strategic Business Reporting covers this technique in detail through application to an exam-standard question. Consider revisiting Skills Checkpoint 4 and completing the scenario based question to specifically improve this skill.

Skill 5: Creating effective discussion

Significantly more marks in the Strategic Business Reporting exam will relate to written answers than numerical answers. It is very tempting to only practise numerical questions as they are easy to mark because the answer is right or wrong, whereas written questions are more subjective and a range of different answers will be given credit. Even when attempting written questions, it is tempting to write a brief answer plan and then look at the answer rather than writing a full answer to plan. Unless you practise written questions in full to time, you will never acquire the necessary skills to tackle discussion questions.

The basic five steps adopted in Skills Checkpoint 4 should also be used in discussion questions.

Steps 2 and 4 are particularly important for discussion questions. You will definitely need to spend a third of your time reading and planning. Generating ideas at the planning stage to create a comprehensive answer plan will be the key to success in this style of question. Consideration of the *Conceptual Framework*, ethical principles and the perspective of stakeholders will often help with discursive questions in SBR.

Skills Checkpoint 5 in the BPP Workbook for Strategic Business Reporting covers this technique in detail through application to an exam-standard question. Consider revisiting Skills Checkpoint 5 and completing the scenario based question to specifically improve this skill.

Exam success skills

Passing the SBR exam requires more than applying syllabus knowledge and demonstrating the Specific SBR skills; it also requires the development of excellent exam technique through question practice.

We consider the following six skills, or exam techniques, to be vital for exam success. These skills were introduced in the BPP Workbook and you can revisit the five Skills Checkpoints in the BPP Workbook for tutorial guidance of how to apply each of the six Exam success skills in your question practice and in the exam.

Aim to consider your performance in all six Exam success skills during your revision stage question practice and reflect on your particular strengths and weaker areas which you can then work on.

Exam success skill 1

Managing information

Questions in the exam will present you with a lot of information. The skill is how you handle this information to make the best use of your time. The key is determining how you will approach the exam and then actively reading the questions.

Advice on Managing information

Approach

The exam is 3 hours 15 minutes long. There is no designated 'reading' time at the start of the exam, however, one approach that can work well is to start the exam by spending 10–15 minutes carefully reading through all of the questions to familiarise yourself with the exam.

Once you feel familiar with the exam, consider the order in which you will attempt the questions; always attempt them in your order of preference – for example, you may want to leave to last the question you consider to be the most difficult.

If you do take this approach, remember to adjust the time available for each question appropriately – see Exam success skill 6: Good time management.

If you find that this approach doesn't work for you, don't worry – you can develop your own technique.

Active reading

You must take an active approach to reading each question. Focus on the requirement first, underlining key verbs, for example, prepare, comment, explain or discuss, to ensure you answer the question properly. Then read the rest of the question, underlining and annotating important and relevant information, and making notes of any relevant technical information you think you will need.

Exam success skill 2

Correct interpretation of the requirements

The active verb used often dictates the approach that written answers should take (eg 'explain', 'discuss', 'evaluate'). It is important you identify and use the verb to define your approach. The **Correct interpretation of the requirements** skill is correctly producing only what is being asked for by a requirement. Anything not required will not earn marks.

Advice on Correct interpretation of the requirements

This skill can be developed by analysing question requirements and applying this process:

Step 1   **Read the requirement**

Firstly, read the requirement a couple of times slowly and carefully and highlight the active verbs. Use the active verbs to define what you plan to do. Make sure you identify any sub-requirements.

Step 2   **Read the rest of the question**

By reading the requirement first, you will have an idea of what you are looking out for as you read through the case overview and exhibits. This is a great time saver and means you don't end up having to read the whole question in full twice. You should do this in an active way – see Exam success skill 1: Managing information.

Step 3   **Read the requirement again**

Read the requirement again to remind yourself of the exact wording before starting your written answer. This will capture any misinterpretation of the requirements or any requirements missed entirely. This should become a habit in your approach and, with repeated practice, you will find the focus, relevance and depth of your answer plan will improve.

Exam success skill 3

Answer planning: Priorities, structure and logic

This skill requires the planning of the key aspects of an answer which accurately and completely responds to the requirement.

Advice on Answer planning: Priorities, structure and logic

Everyone will have a preferred style for an answer plan. For example, it may be a mind map, bullet-pointed lists or simply annotating the question. Choose the approach that you feel most comfortable with or if you are not sure, try out different approaches for different questions until you have found your preferred style.

For a discussion question, annotating the question is likely to be insufficient. It would be better to draw up a separate answer plan in the format of your choosing (eg a mind map or bullet-pointed lists). For a groups question, you will typically spend less time planning than for a discussion type question. You should aim to draw up the group structure. Then, rather than drawing up a formal plan, the best use of your time is to annotate the question margins noting which group working, adjustment or correction of error will be required.

Exam success skill 4

Efficient numerical analysis

This skill aims to maximise the marks awarded by making clear to the marker the process of arriving at your answer. This is achieved by laying out an answer such that, even if you make a few errors, you can still score subsequent marks for follow-on calculations. It is vital that you do not lose marks purely because the marker cannot follow what you have done.

Advice on Efficient numerical analysis

This skill can be developed by applying the following process:

Step 1   **Use a standard proforma working where relevant**

If answers can be laid out in a standard proforma then always plan to do so. This will help the marker to understand your working and allocate the marks easily. It will also help you to work through the figures in a methodical and time-efficient way.

Step 2   **Show your workings**

Keep your workings as clear and simple as possible and ensure they are cross-referenced to the main part of your answer. Where it helps, provide brief narrative explanations to help the marker understand the steps in the calculation. This means that if a mistake is made then you do not lose any subsequent marks for follow-on calculations.

Step 3   **Keep moving!**

It is important to remember that, in an exam situation, it is difficult to get every number 100% correct. The key is therefore ensuring you do not spend too long on any single calculation. If you are struggling with a solution then make a sensible assumption, state it and move on.

Exam success skill 5

Effective writing and presentation

Written answers should be presented so that the marker can clearly see the points you are making, presented in the format specified in the question. The skill is to provide efficient written answers with sufficient breadth of points that answer the question, in the right depth, in the time available.

Advice on Effective writing and presentation

Step 1   **Use headings**

Using the headings and sub-headings from your answer plan will give your answer structure, order and logic. This will ensure your answer links back to the requirement and is clearly signposted, making it easier for the marker to understand the different points you are making. Underlining your headings will also help the marker.

Step 2   **Write your answer in short, but full, sentences**

Use short, punchy sentences with the aim that every sentence should say something different and generate marks. Write in full sentences, ensuring your style is professional.

Step 3   **Do your calculations first, explanation second**

Questions often ask for an explanation with suitable calculations, the best approach is to prepare the calculation first but present it on the bottom half of the page of /next page to your answer. Then add the explanation before the calculation. Performing the calculation first should enable you to explain what you have done.

Good time management

This skill means planning your time across all the requirements so that all tasks have been attempted at the end of the 3 hours 15 minutes available and actively checking on time during your exam. This is so that you can flex your approach and prioritise requirements which, in your judgement, will generate the maximum marks in the available time remaining.

Advice on Good time management

The exam is 3 hours 15 minutes long, which translates to 1.95 minutes per mark. Therefore a 10-mark requirement should be allocated a maximum of 20 minutes to complete your answer before you move on to the next task. At the beginning of a question, work out the amount of time you should be spending on each requirement and write the finishing time next to each requirement on your exam. If you take the approach of spending 10–15 minutes reading and planning at the start of the exam, adjust the time allocated to each question accordingly, eg if you allocate 15 minutes to reading, then you will have 3 hours remaining which is 1.8 minutes per mark.

Keep an eye on the clock

Aim to attempt all requirements, but be ready to be ruthless and move on if your answer is not going as planned. The challenge for many is sticking to planned timings. Be aware this is difficult to achieve in the early stages of your studies and be ready to let this skill develop over time.

If you find yourself running short on time and know that a full answer is not possible in the time you have, consider recreating your plan in overview form and then add key terms and details as time allows. Remember, some marks may be available, for example, simply stating a conclusion which you don't have time to justify in full.

Further advice for revising for Strategic Business Reporting

Question practice

Question practice under timed conditions is absolutely vital. We strongly advise you to create a revision study plan which focuses on question practice. This is so that you can get used to the pressures of answering exam questions in limited time, develop proficiency in the Specific SBR skills and the Exam success skills. Ideally, you should aim to cover all questions in this Kit, and very importantly, all five mock exams.

Selecting questions

To help you plan your revision, we have provided a full **topic index** which maps the questions to topics in the syllabus.

Making the most of question practice

At BPP Learning Media we realise that you need more than just questions and model answers to get the most from your question practice.

- Our **Top tips** included for certain questions provide essential advice on tackling questions, presenting answers and the key points that answers need to include

- We show you how you can pick up **Easy marks** on some questions, as we know that picking up all readily available marks often can make the difference between passing and failing

- We include **marking guides** to show you what the examining team rewards

Attempting mock exams

This Kit has five mock exams, including the ACCA Specimen Exam, which provide practice at coping with the pressures of the exam day. We strongly recommend that you attempt them under exam conditions. All the mock exams reflect the question styles and syllabus coverage of the exam.

The ACCA examining team consistently warn very strongly against question-spotting and trying to predict the topics that will be included in the exam. Students should not be surprised if the same topic area is examined in two successive sittings. ACCA's examining team regards few areas as off-limits for questions, and all of the syllabus can be tested.

That said, the following areas of the syllabus are very important, and your revision therefore needs to cover them particularly well.

- **Group accounts**: Group accounts will always be examined as part of Section A but may also feature in Section B. You are unlikely to be asked to prepare full consolidated financial statements in SBR but do need to be able to prepare extracts from them or key calculations within. You must also be able to explain the accounting treatment, as the marks for numerical aspects will be limited.

- **Ethical issues**: Ethical issues will feature in Section A of every exam and may also be examined in Section B. It is important that you can analyse ethical issues with regards to the fundamental principles of ACCA's *Code of Ethics and Conduct*.

- **Analysis and appraisal of information** will be tested in Section B. You should not focus only on 'traditional' financial analysis such as ratios. You will need to appraise companies using a range of financial and non-financial information, and from the perspective of different stakeholders.

- An in-depth **knowledge of the Conceptual Framework** is required. You will be expected to discuss the consistency of the Conceptual Framework (and revised Conceptual Framework), with each IFRS that is examined.

- **Developments in Financial Reporting**: You need to be able to assess the impact of a change or proposed change in accounting standards, such as the impact of IFRS 16 *Leases* on the financial statements, and on how stakeholders will analyse the financial statements. You need to read widely to develop your knowledge of current issues, including reading articles published on ACCA's website and looking at real published annual reports.

- More complex IFRSs such as IFRS 15 *Revenue from Contracts with Customers,* as there is significant scope for discussion and justification in more complex standards.

Examinable documents

The following documents are examinable for sittings up from September 2018 to June 2019. Knowledge of new examinable regulations issued by 31 August will be required in examination sessions being held in the following exam year. Documents may be examinable even if the effective date is in the future.

ACCA's Study Guide for Strategic Business Reporting offers more detailed guidance on the depth and level at which the examinable documents will be examined and this is available on accaglobal.com.

	International Accounting Standards (IASs)/International Financial Reporting Standards (IFRSs)
IAS 1	Presentation of Financial Statements
IAS 2	Inventories
IAS 7	Statement of Cash Flows
IAS 8	Accounting Policies, Changes in Accounting Estimates and Errors
IAS 10	Events After the Reporting Period
IAS 12	Income Taxes
IAS 16	Property, Plant and Equipment
IAS 19	Employee Benefits
IAS 20	Accounting for Government Grants and Disclosure of Government Assistance
IAS 21	The Effects of Changes in Foreign Exchange Rates
IAS 23	Borrowing Costs
IAS 24	Related Party Disclosures
IAS 27	Separate Financial Statements
IAS 28	Investments in Associates and Joint Ventures
IAS 32	Financial Instruments: Presentation
IAS 33	Earnings per Share
IAS 34	Interim Financial Reporting
IAS 36	Impairment of Assets
IAS 37	Provisions, Contingent Liabilities and Contingent Assets
IAS 38	Intangible Assets
IAS 40	Investment Property
IAS 41	Agriculture
IFRS 1	First-time Adoption of International Financial Reporting Standards
IFRS 2	Share-based Payment
IFRS 3	Business Combinations
IFRS 5	Non-current Assets held for Sale and Discontinued Operations
IFRS 7	Financial Instruments: Disclosures
IFRS 8	Operating Segments
IFRS 9	Financial Instruments
IFRS 10	Consolidated Financial Statements
IFRS 11	Joint Arrangements

IFRS 12	Disclosure of Interests in other Entities
IFRS 13	Fair Value Measurement
IFRS 15	Revenue from Contracts with Customers
IFRS 16	Leases
IFRS SMEs	IFRS for Small and Medium-sized Entities
Other Statements	
	Conceptual Framework for Financial Reporting
Practice St	Practice Statement: Management Commentary
	The International <IR> Framework
EDs, Discussion Papers and Other Documents	
ED/2016/1	Definition of a Business and Accounting for Previously Held Interests
ED/2015/8	IFRS Practice Statement Application of Materiality to Financial Statements
ED 2015/3	Conceptual Framework for Financial Reporting

Important note for UK students who are sitting the UK variant of Strategic Business Reporting

If you are sitting the UK variant of the Strategic Business Reporting exam you will be studying under International standards, but between 15 and 20 marks will be available for comparisons between International and UK GAAP. ACCA have provided the following advice:

> "The UK syllabus of Strategic Business Reporting will assess the differences between full IFRS and FRS 102. This means that the UK syllabus will be much more relevant than it is at present. It would also provide ACCA with a unique selling point where candidates that pass the UK syllabus are qualified in both UK GAAP and IFRS.

Effect on the exam

> Part of one of the Section B questions will be adapted to assess the differences between UK GAAP, UK legal requirements and full IFRS. This question may be based on either a single entity or a group. This question will test some of the specific differences between FRS 102 and full IFRS (listed in the examinable documents). It may also test certain aspects of the UK statutory requirements; for example those relating to group accounting or the use of the true and fair override where compliance with the standards does not result in a true and fair presentation. Alternatively, it may assess the changes to the recognition and measurement requirements introduced by the statutory instrument or the impact of the changes in the thresholds and eligibility criteria."

(ACCA SBR UK Syllabus and Study Guide September 2018 to June 2019)

This Practice & Revision Kit is based on International Financial Reporting Standards **only**. An online supplement will be available at www.bpp.com/learning-media, covering the additional UK issues and providing additional illustrations and examples.

Question Bank

Section 1 – Preparation questions

1 Financial instruments   12 mins

(a) Graben Co purchases a bond for $441,014 on 1 January 20X1. It will be redeemed on 31 December 20X4 for $600,000. The bond is held at amortised cost and carries no coupon.

Required

Calculate the valuation of the bond for the statement of financial position as at 31 December 20X1 and the finance income for 20X1 shown in profit or loss.   **(3 marks)**

Compound sum of $1: $(1 + r)^n$

Year	2%	4%	6%	8%	10%	12%	14%
1	1.0200	1.0400	1.0600	1.0800	1.1000	1.1200	1.1400
2	1.0404	1.0816	1.1236	1.1664	1.2100	1.2544	1.2996
3	1.0612	1.1249	1.1910	1.2597	1.3310	1.4049	1.4815
4	1.0824	1.1699	1.2625	1.3605	1.4641	1.5735	1.6890
5	1.1041	1.2167	1.3382	1.4693	1.6105	1.7623	1.9254

(b) Baldie Co issues 4,000 convertible bonds on 1 January 20X2 at par. The bonds are redeemable three years later at a par value of $500 per bond, which is the nominal value.

The bonds pay interest annually in arrears at an interest rate (based on nominal value) of 5%. Each bond can be converted at the maturity date into 30 $1 shares.

The prevailing market interest rate for three year bonds that have no right of conversion is 9%.

Required

Show how the convertible bond would be presented in the statement of financial position at 1 January 20X2.   **(3 marks)**

Cumulative three year annuity factors:

5%   2.723
9%   2.531   use on interest.

(Total = 6 marks)

$$\frac{1}{(1+r)^n} \longrightarrow principal.$$

2 Leases

Sugar Co leased a machine from Spice Co. The terms of the lease are as follows:

Inception of lease	1 January 20X1
Lease term	4 years at $78,864 per annum payable in arrears
Present value of future lease payments	$250,000
Useful life of asset	4 years

Required

(a) Calculate the interest rate implicit in the lease, using the table below. **(3 marks)**

This table shows the cumulative present value of $1 per annum, receivable or payable at the end of each year for n years.

Years		Interest rates	
(n)	6%	8%	10%
1	0.943	0.926	0.909
2	1.833	1.783	1.736
3	2.673	2.577	2.487
4	3.465	3.312	3.170
5	4.212	3.993	3.791

(b) Explain, with suitable workings and extracts from the financial statements, how Sugar Co should account for the lease for the year ended 31 December 20X1. Notes to the accounts are not required. **(7 marks)**

(Total = 10 marks)

3 Defined benefit plan

> **BPP note:** In this question, proforma are given to you to help you get used to setting out your answer. You may wish to transfer them to a separate sheet, or alternatively to use a separate sheet for your workings.

Brutus operates a defined benefit pension plan for its employees. The present value of the future benefit obligations and the fair value of its plan assets on 1 January 20X1 were $110 million and $150 million respectively.

The pension plan received contributions of $7 million and paid pensions to former employees of $10 million during the year.

Extracts from the most recent actuarial report shows the following:

Present value of pension plan obligation at 31 December 20X1	$116m
Fair value of plan assets at 31 December 20X1	$140m
Present cost of pensions earned in the period	$11m
Yield on high quality corporate bonds at 1 January 20X1	10%

On 1 January 20X1, the rules of the pension plan were changed to improve benefits for plan members. The actuary has advised that this will cost $10 million.

Required

Prepare extracts from the notes to Brutus' financial statements for the year ended 31 December 20X1 which show how the pension plan should be accounted for. **(10 marks)**

Note. Assume contributions and benefits were paid on 31 December.

NOTES TO THE STATEMENT OF PROFIT OR LOSS AND OTHER COMPREHENSIVE INCOME

Defined benefit expense recognised in profit or loss

	$m
Current service cost	~~20~~ 10 10
Past service cost	10
Net interest on the net defined benefit asset	12

Other comprehensive income (items that will not be reclassified to profit or loss)
Remeasurement of defined benefit plans

	$m
Remeasurement gain on defined benefit obligation	7
Remeasurement loss on plan assets	(2)
	5

NOTES TO THE STATEMENT OF FINANCIAL POSITION

Net defined benefit asset recognised in the statement of financial position

	31 December 20X1 $m	31 December 20X0 $m
Present value of pension obligation	116	110
Fair value of plan assets	140	150
Net asset	(24)	(40)

Changes in the present value of the defined benefit obligation

	$m
Opening defined benefit obligation	110
Interest on obligation 110x	11
Current service cost	
Past service cost	10
Benefits paid	
Gain on remeasurement of obligation (balancing figure)	___
Closing defined benefit obligation	116

Changes in the fair value of plan assets

	$m
Opening fair value of plan assets	150
Interest on plan assets	15
Contributions	7
Benefits paid	
Loss on remeasurement of assets (balancing figure)	___
Closing fair value of plan assets	140

4 Sundry standards

59 mins

(a) Penn has a defined benefit pension plan.

Required

Using the information below, prepare extracts from the statement of financial position and the statement of profit or loss and other comprehensive income for the year ended 31 January 20X8. Ignore taxation. **(10 marks)**

(i) The opening plan assets were $3.6m on 1 February 20X7 and plan liabilities at this date were $4.3m.

(ii) Company contributions to the plan during the year amounted to $550,000. The contributions were paid at the start of the year.

(iii) Pensions paid to former employees amounted to $330,000. These were paid at the start of the year.

(iv) The yield on high quality corporate bonds was 8% at 1 February 20X7.

(v) On 31 January 20X8, five staff were made redundant, and an extra $58,000 in total was added to the value of their pensions.

(vi) Current service costs as provided by the actuary are $275,000.

(vii) At 31 January 20X8, the actuary valued the plan liabilities at $4.64 million and the plan assets at $4.215 million.

(b) Sion operates a defined benefit pension plan for its employees. Sion has a 31 December year end. The following details relate to the plan.

	$'000
Present value of obligation at 1 January 20X8	40,000
Market value of plan assets at 1 January 20X8	40,000

	20X8	20X9
	$'000	$'000
Current service cost	2,500	2,860
Benefits paid out	1,974	2,200
Contributions paid by entity	2,000	2,200
Present value of obligation at end of the year	46,000	40,800
Market value of plan assets at end of the year	43,000	35,680
Yield on corporate bonds at start of the year	8%	9%

During 20X8, the benefits available under the plan were improved. The resulting increase in the present value of the defined benefit obligation was $2 million as at 31 December 20X8.

Contributions were paid into the plan and benefits were paid out of the plan on the final day of each accounting period.

On 31 December 20X9, Sion divested of part of its business, and as part of the sale agreement, transferred the relevant part of its pension fund to the buyer. The present value of the defined benefit obligation transferred was $11.4 million and the fair value of plan assets transferred was $10.8 million. Sion also made a cash payment of $400,000 to the buyer in respect of the plan.

6

Required

(i) Calculate the net defined benefit liability as at the start and end of 20X8 and 20X9 showing clearly any remeasurement gain or loss on the plan each year.

(ii) Show amounts to be recognised in the financial statements in each of the years 20X8 and 20X9 in respect of the plan. **(15 marks)**

(c) Bed Investment Co entered into a contract on 1 July 20X7 with Em Bank. The contract consisted of a deposit of a principal amount of $10 million, carrying an interest rate of 2.5% per annum and with a maturity date of 30 June 20X9. Interest will be receivable at maturity together with the principal. In addition, a further 3% interest per annum will be payable by Em Bank if the exchange rate of the dollar against the Ruritanian kroner (RKR) exceeds or is equal to $1.15 to RKR 1.

Bed's functional currency is the dollar.

Required

Explain how Bed should account for the above investment in the financial statements for the year ended 31 December 20X7 (no calculations are required). **(5 marks)**

(Total = 30 marks)

5 Control   23 mins

(a) IFRS 10 *Consolidated Financial Statements* was published in 2011. It focuses on control as the key concept underlying the parent/subsidiary relationship but it broadened the definition and clarified its application.

Required

Explain the circumstances in which an investor controls an investee according to IFRS 10. **(3 marks)**

(b) Twist holds 40% of the voting rights of Oliver and 12 other investors each hold 5% of the voting rights of Oliver. A shareholder agreement grants Twist the right to appoint, remove and set the remuneration of management responsible for directing the relevant activities. To change the agreement, a two-thirds majority vote of the shareholders is required. To date, Twist has not exercised its rights with regard to the management or activities of Oliver.

Required

Explain whether Twist should consolidate Oliver in accordance with IFRS 10. **(3 marks)**

(c) Copperfield holds 45% of the voting rights of Spenlow. Murdstone and Steerforth each hold 26% of the voting rights of Spenlow. The remaining voting rights are held by three other shareholders, each holding 1%. There are no other arrangements that affect decision-making.

Required

Explain whether Copperfield should consolidate Spenlow in accordance with IFRS 10. **(3 marks)**

(d) Scrooge holds 70% of the voting rights of Cratchett. Marley has 30% of the voting rights of Cratchett. Marley also has an option to acquire half of Scrooge's voting rights, which is exercisable for the next two years, but at a fixed price that is deeply out of the money (and is expected to remain so for that two-year period).

Required

Explain whether either of Scrooge or Marley should consolidate Cratchett in accordance with IFRS 10. **(3 marks)**

(Total = 12 marks)

6 Associate 39 mins

The statements of financial position of J Co and its investee companies, P Co and S Co, at 31 December 20X5 are shown below.

STATEMENTS OF FINANCIAL POSITION AS AT 31 DECEMBER 20X5

	J Co $'000	P Co $'000	S Co $'000
Assets			
Non-current assets			
Freehold property	1,950	1,250	500
Plant and equipment	795	375	285
Investments	1,500	–	–
	4,245	1,625	785
Current assets			
Inventories	575	300	265
Trade receivables	330	290	370
Cash	50	120	20
	955	710	655
	5,200	2,335	1,440
Equity and liabilities			
Equity			
Share capital ($1 ordinary shares)	2,000	1,000	750
Retained earnings	1,460	885	390
	3,460	1,885	1,140
Non-current liabilities			
12% debentures	500	100	–
Current liabilities			
Bank overdraft	560		
Trade payables	680	350	300
	1,240	350	300
	5,200	2,335	1,440

Additional information

(a) J Co acquired 600,000 ordinary shares in P Co on 1 January 20X0 for $1,000,000 when the accumulated retained earnings of P Co were $200,000.

(b) At the date of acquisition of P Co, the fair value of its freehold property was considered to be $400,000 greater than its value in P Co's statement of financial position. P Co had acquired the property ten years earlier and the buildings element (comprising 50% of the total value) is depreciated on cost over 50 years.

(c) J Co acquired 225,000 ordinary shares in S Co on 1 January 20X4 for $500,000 when the retained profits of S Co were $150,000.

(d) P Co manufactures a component used by J Co only. Transfers are made by P Co at cost plus 25%. J Co held $100,000 of these components in inventories at 31 December 20X5.

(e) It is the policy of J Co to review goodwill for impairment annually. The goodwill in P Co was written off in full some years ago. An impairment test conducted at the year end revealed impairment losses on the investment in S Co of $92,000.

(f) It is the group's policy to value the non-controlling interest at acquisition at fair value. The market price of the shares of the non-controlling shareholders just before the acquisition was $1.65.

Required

Prepare, in a format suitable for inclusion in the annual report of the J Group, the consolidated statement of financial position at 31 December 20X5. **(20 marks)**

7 Part disposal   49 mins

> **BPP note:** In this question, proforma are given to you to help you get used to setting out your answer. You may wish to transfer them to a separate sheet or to use a separate sheet for your workings.

Angel Co bought 70% of the share capital of Shane Co for $120,000 on 1 January 20X6. At that date Shane Co's retained earnings stood at $10,000.

The statements of financial position at 31 December 20X8, summarised statements of profit or loss and other comprehensive income to that date and movement on retained earnings are given below.

	Angel Co $'000	Shane Co $'000
STATEMENTS OF FINANCIAL POSITION		
Non-current assets		
Property, plant and equipment	200	80
Investment in Shane Co	120	–
	320	80
Current assets	890	140
	1,210	220
Equity		
Share capital – $1 ordinary shares	500	100
Retained reserves	400	90
	900	190
Current liabilities	310	30
	1,210	220

SUMMARISED STATEMENTS OF PROFIT OR LOSS AND OTHER COMPREHENSIVE INCOME

	$'000	$'000
Profit before interest and tax	100	20
Income tax expense	(40)	(8)
Profit for the year	60	12
Other comprehensive income (not reclassified to P/L), net of tax	10	6
Total comprehensive income for the year	70	18

MOVEMENT IN RETAINED RESERVES

Balance at 31 December 20X7	330	72
Total comprehensive income for the year	70	18
Balance at 31 December 20X8	400	90

Angel Co sells one half of its holding in Shane Co for $120,000 on 30 June 20X8. At that date, the fair value of the 35% holding in Shane was slightly more at $130,000 due to a share price rise. The remaining holding is to be dealt with as an associate. This does not represent a discontinued operation.

No entries have been made in the accounts for the above transaction.

Assume that profits accrue evenly throughout the year.

9

It is the group's policy to value the non-controlling interest at acquisition fair value. The fair value of the non-controlling interest on 1 January 20X6 was $51.4 million.

Required

(a) Prepare the consolidated statement of financial position, statement of profit or loss and other comprehensive income and a reconciliation of movement in retained reserves for the year ended 31 December 20X8. **(20 marks)**

Ignore income taxes on the disposal. No impairment losses have been necessary to date.

PART DISPOSAL PROFORMA

ANGEL GROUP
CONSOLIDATED STATEMENT OF FINANCIAL POSITION
AS AT 31 DECEMBER 20X8 $'000
Non-current assets
Property, plant and equipment
Investment in Shane
                                                           _____

Current assets   _____
                                                           _____
                                                           ========

Equity attributable to owners of the parent
Share capital
Retained earnings   _____

                                                           _____
Current liabilities   _____
                                                           _____
                                                           ========

CONSOLIDATED STATEMENT OF PROFIT OR LOSS AND OTHER COMPREHENSIVE INCOME FOR THE YEAR ENDED 31 DECEMBER 20X8

                                                           $'000
Profit before interest and tax
Profit on disposal of shares in subsidiary
Share of profit of associate   _____
Profit before tax
Income tax expense   _____
Profit for the year   _____

Other comprehensive income (not reclassified to P/L) net of tax:
Share of other comprehensive income of associate
Other comprehensive income for the year
Total comprehensive income for the year

Profit attributable to:
   Owners of the parent
   Non-controlling interests   _____

                                                           _____
Total comprehensive income attributable to:
   Owners of the parent
   Non-controlling interests   _____
                                                           ========

CONSOLIDATED RECONCILIATION OF MOVEMENT IN RETAINED RESERVES

$'000

Balance at 31 December 20X7
Total comprehensive income for the year
Balance at 31 December 20X8

_____

=======

(b) Explain the accounting treatment that would be required if Angel had disposed of 10% of its
holding in Shane. **(5 marks)**

(Total = 25 marks)

8 Step acquisition   PBR   ~~date of control~~   29 mins

SD acquired 60% of the 1 million $1 ordinary shares of KL on 1 July 20X0 for $3,250,000 when
KL's retained earnings were $2,760,000. The group policy is to measure non-controlling interests at
fair value at the date of acquisition. The fair value of non-controlling interests at 1 July 20X0 was
$1,960,000. There has been no impairment of goodwill since the date of acquisition.

NCI FV

SD acquired a further 20% of KL's share capital on 1 March 20X1 for $1,000,000.

The retained earnings reported in the financial statements of SD and KL as at 30 June 20X1 are
$9,400,000 and $3,400,000 respectively.

KL sold goods for resale to SD with a sales value of $750,000 during the period from
1 March 20X1 to 30 June 20X1. 40% of these goods remain in SD's inventories at the year-end. KL
applies a mark-up of 25% on all goods sold.

Profits of both entities can be assumed to accrue evenly throughout the year.

Required

(a) Explain the impact of the additional 20% purchase of KL's ordinary share capital by SD on the
consolidated financial statements of the SD Group for the year ended 30 June 20X1.

(5 marks)

(b) Calculate the amounts that will appear in the consolidated statement of financial position of
the SD Group as at 30 June 20X1 for:

(i) Goodwill;
(ii) Consolidated retained earnings; and
(iii) Non-controlling interests. **(10 marks)**

(Total = 15 marks)

9 Foreign operation   49 mins

> **BPP note:** In this question, proformas for the translation workings are given to assist you with the approach. You will need to also need to draw up proformas for the consolidated financial statements and the remaining group workings.

Standard acquired 80% of Odense SA for $520,000 on 1 January 20X5 when the retained reserves of Odense were 2,500,000 Danish krone.

The financial statements of Standard and Odense for the year ended 31 December 20X6 are as follows:

STATEMENTS OF FINANCIAL POSITION AT 31 DECEMBER 20X6

	Standard	Odense
	$'000	Kr'000
Property, plant and equipment	1,285	4,400
Investment in Odense	520	–
	1,805	4,400
Current assets	410	2,000
	2,215	6,400
Share capital	500	1,000
Retained earnings	1,115	4,300
	1,615	5,300
Loans	200	300
Current liabilities	400	800
	600	1,100
	2,215	6,400

STATEMENT OF PROFIT OR LOSS AND OTHER COMPREHENSIVE INCOME FOR YEAR ENDED 31 DECEMBER 20X6

	Standard	Odense
	$'000	Kr'000
Revenue	1,125	5,200
Cost of sales	(410)	(2,300)
Gross profit	715	2,900
Other expenses	(180)	(910)
Dividend from Odense	40	–
Profit before tax	575	1,990
Income tax expense	(180)	(640)
Profit/Total comprehensive income for the year	395	1,350

STATEMENTS OF CHANGES IN EQUITY FOR THE YEAR 31 DECEMBER 20X6 (EXTRACT FOR RETAINED EARNINGS)

	Standard	Odense
	$'000	Kr'000
Balance at 1 January 20X6	915	3,355
Dividends paid on 31 December 20X6	(195)	(405)
Total comprehensive income for the year	395	1,350
Balance at 31 December 20X6	1,115	4,300

In the year ended 31 December 20X5, Odense's total comprehensive income was 1,200,000 Danish krone. On 31 December 20X5, Odense paid dividends of 345,000 Danish krone.

An impairment test conducted at 31 December 20X6 revealed impairment losses of 148,000 Danish krone relating to Odense's goodwill. No impairment losses had previously been recognised. It is group policy to translate impairment losses at the closing rate.

At the date of acquisition, Standard chose to measure the non-controlling interest in Odense at the proportionate share of the fair value of net assets.

Exchange rates were as follows:

	Kr to $1
1 January 20X5	9.4
31 December 20X5	8.8
Average 20X5	9.1
31 December 20X6	8.1
Average 20X6	8.4

Required

Prepare the consolidated statement of financial position and consolidated statement of profit or loss and other comprehensive income of the Standard Group for the year ended 31 December 20X6 (round your answer to the nearest $'000). **(25 marks)**

TRANSLATION OF ODENSE – STATEMENT OF FINANCIAL POSITION

	Kr'000	Rate	$'000
Property, plant and equipment		X6 CR	
Current assets		X6 CR	
Share capital		HR	
Pre-acquisition retained earnings		HR	
Post-acquisition retained earnings:			
20X5 profit		X5 AR	
20X5 dividend		X5 Actual	
20X6 profit		X6 AR	
20X6 dividend		X6 Actual	
Exchange difference on net assets		Bal. fig.	
Loans		X6 CR	
Current liabilities		X6 CR	

TRANSLATION OF ODENSE – STATEMENT OF PROFIT OR LOSS AND OTHER COMPREHENSIVE INCOME

	Odense Kr'000	Rate (AR)	Odense $'000
Revenue			
Cost of sales			
Gross profit			
Other expenses			
Profit before tax			
Income tax expense			
Profit/Total comprehensive income for the year			

10 Consolidated statement of cash flows

> **BPP note:** In this question, proformas are given to you to help you get used to setting out your answer. You may wish to transfer them to a separate sheet, or alternatively to use a separate sheet for your workings.

On 1 September 20X5 Swing Co acquired 70% of Slide Co for $5,000,000 comprising $1,000,000 cash and 1,500,000 $1 shares.

The statement of financial position of Slide Co at acquisition was as follows:

	$'000
Property, plant and equipment	2,700
Inventories	1,600
Trade receivables	600
Cash	400
Trade payables	(300)
Income tax payable	(200)
	4,800

The consolidated statement of financial position of Swing Co as at 31 December 20X5 was as follows:

	20X5	20X4
	$'000	$'000
Non-current assets		
Property, plant and equipment	35,500	25,000
Goodwill	1,400	–
	36,900	25,000
Current assets		
Inventories	16,000	10,000
Trade receivables	9,800	7,500
Cash	2,400	1,500
	28,200	19,000
	65,100	44,000
Equity attributable to owners of the parent		
Share capital	12,300	10,000
Share premium	5,800	2,000
Revaluation surplus	350	–
Retained earnings	32,100	21,900
	50,550	33,900
Non-controlling interest	1,750	–
	52,300	33,900
Current liabilities		
Trade payables	7,600	6,100
Income tax payable	5,200	4,000
	12,800	10,100
	65,100	44,000

W4
oPA

W

The consolidated statement of profit or loss and other comprehensive income of Swing Co for the year ended 31 December 20X5 was as follows:

	20X5 $'000
Profit before tax	16,500 → oP Acc
Income tax expense	(5,200)
Profit for the year	11,300
Other comprehensive income (not reclassified to P/L)	
Revaluation surplus W → PDₗₑ	500
Total comprehensive income for the year	11,800
Profit attributable to:	
Owners of the parent RE	11,100
Non-controlling interest	200
	11,300
Total comprehensive income for the year attributable to:	
Owners of the parent	11,450
Non-controlling interest 200 + (500 × 30%) Ncɪ w.	350
	11,800

OPA   PPEW.

Notes

1 Depreciation charged for the year was $5,800,000. The group made no disposals of property, plant and equipment.

2 Dividends paid by Swing Co amounted to $900,000.

It is the group's policy to value the non-controlling interest at its proportionate share of the fair value of the subsidiary's identifiable net assets.

Required

Prepare the consolidated statement of cash flows of Swing Co for the year ended 31 December 20X5. No notes are required. **(20 marks)**

CONSOLIDATED STATEMENT OF CASH FLOWS PROFORMA
STATEMENT OF CASH FLOWS FOR THE YEAR ENDED 31 DECEMBER 20X5

	$'000	$'000
Cash flows from operating activities		
Profit before tax		
Adjustments for:		
Depreciation		
Impairment losses		
Increase in trade receivables (W4)	_____	
Increase in inventories (W4)		
Increase in trade payables (W4)	_____	
Cash generated from operations		
Income taxes paid (W3)	_____	
Net cash from operating activities		
Cash flows from investing activities		
Acquisition of subsidiary, net of cash acquired (W2)		
Purchase of property, plant & equipment (W1)	_____	
Net cash used in investing activities		

	$'000	$'000
Cash flows from financing activities		
Proceeds from issue of share capital		
Dividends paid		
Dividends paid to non-controlling interest (W2)	————	
Net cash used in financing activities		————
Net increase in cash and cash equivalents		
Cash and cash equivalents at the beginning of the period		
Cash and cash equivalents at the end of the period		

Workings

1   *Assets*

	Property, plant and equipment $'000	Goodwill $'000
b/d		–
OCI (revaluation)		
Depreciation/ Impairment		**(X)** β
Acquisition of sub/associate		(W5)
Cash paid/(rec'd) β	X	–
c/d	═	═

2   *Equity*

	Share capital $'000	Share premium $'000	Retained earnings $'000	Non-controlling interest $'000
b/d				–
P/L				
Acquisition of subsidiary				(W5)
Cash (paid)/rec'd β	X	X	(X)*	X
c/d	═	═	═	═

*Dividend paid is given in question but working shown for clarity.

3   *Liabilities*

	Tax payable $'000
b/d	
P/L	
Acquisition of subsidiary	
Cash (paid)/rec'd	(X) β
c/d	═

4   *Working capital changes*

	Inventories $'000	Receivables $'000	Payables $'000
Balance b/d			
Acquisition of subsidiary			
Increase/(decrease) (balancing figure)	X	X	X
Balance c/d	═	═	═

5   *Purchase of subsidiary*

                                                                                    $'000

Cash received on acquisition of subsidiary
Less cash consideration   ___
Cash outflow   **(X)**

Note. Only the **cash** consideration is included in the figure reported in the statement of cash flows. The **shares** issued as part of the consideration are reflected in the share capital working (W2) above.

Goodwill on acquisition (to show no impairment):

                                                                                    $'000

Consideration
Non-controlling interest
Net assets acquired   ___
Goodwill   ===

11 Current issues   **49 mins**

> **BPP note:** Current developments in financial reporting such as the IASB Disclosure Initiative, proposals relating to materiality, amendments to IAS 1 and the *Conceptual Framework* are covered in Chapter 19 of the SBR Workbook. Recently issued standards are covered within individual topics; for example, the recent standard IFRS 16 *Leases* is covered in Chapter 8 and IFRS 15 *Revenue from Contracts with Customers* is covered in Chapter 1.

(a)   In January 2016, the IASB published IFRS 16 *Leases*.

Required

(i)   Briefly list the key changes.
(ii) Briefly suggest the main likely effects of the new standard.   **(5 marks)**

(b)   On-Ice Co, a retailer of frozen food, leases freezers from Icicle Co for ten years at $30,000 per year. This payment includes servicing costs.

On-Ice could lease the same make and model of freezers from Icicle for $27,000 per year without the servicing, and get the servicing done by another company for $5,000 per year.

Required

How should On-Ice account for the payments to Icicle?   **(2 marks)**

(c)   Briefly discuss the classification of liabilities under the proposed amendments to IAS 1 *Presentation of Financial Statements* (ED 2015/1).   **(3 marks)**

(d)   Explain the types of and significance of additional performance measures, and suggest potential problems with such measures.   **(5 marks)**

(e)   (i)   Explain what is meant by the IASB 'Disclosure Initiative'.
      (ii) Briefly summarise its proposals relating to materiality.   **(5 marks)**

(f)   The existing IASB *Conceptual Framework for Financial Reporting,* issued in 2010, has been criticised for being incomplete. As a result, an Exposure Draft (ED) was issued in May 2015 which proposes a new *Conceptual Framework* chapter on presentation and disclosure.

Required

Briefly discuss the ED's guidance on the presentation of the statement of profit and loss.

                                                                             (5 marks)

                                                                      (Total = 25 marks)

Section 2 – Groups preparation questions

12 Ejoy

ACR, 6/06, amended

Ejoy, a public limited company, has acquired two subsidiaries. The details of the acquisitions are as follows:

Company	Date of acquisition	Ordinary share capital of $1 $m	Reserves at acquisition $m	Fair value of net assets at acquisition $m	Cost of investment $m	Ordinary share capital of $1 acquired $m
Zbay	1 June 20X4	200	170	600	520	160
Tbay	1 December 20X5	120	80	310	192	72

Any fair value adjustments relate to non-depreciable land. The draft statements of profit or loss and other comprehensive income for the year ended 31 May 20X6 are:

	Ejoy $m	Zbay $m	Tbay $m
Revenue	2,500	1,500	800
Cost of sales	(1,800)	(1,200)	(600)
Gross profit	700	300	200
Other income	70	10	–
Distribution costs	(130)	(120)	(70)
Administrative expenses	(100)	(90)	(60)
Finance costs	(50)	(40)	(20)
Profit before tax	490	60	50
Income tax expense	(200)	(26)	(20)
Profit for the year	290	34	30
Other comprehensive for the year (not reclassified to profit or loss):			
Gain on property revaluation net of tax	80	10	8
Total comprehensive income for the year	370	44	38
Total comprehensive income for year to 31 May 20X5	190	20	15

The following information is relevant to the preparation of the group financial statements.

(a) Tbay was acquired exclusively with a view to sale and at 31 May 20X6 meets the criteria of being a disposal group. The fair value of Tbay at 31 May 20X6 is $344 million and the estimated selling costs of the shareholding in Tbay are $5 million.

(b) Ejoy entered into a joint arrangement with another company on 31 May 20X6, which met the IFRS 11 definition of a joint venture. The joint venture is a limited company and Ejoy has contributed assets at fair value of $20 million (carrying amount $14 million). Each party will hold five million ordinary shares of $1 in the joint venture. The gain on the disposal of the assets ($6 million) to the joint venture has been included in 'other income'.

(c) On 31 May 20X5, Zbay made a loan of $100m to a customer with a similar credit risk to Zbay. Interest payable on this loan was 4.5% per annum. On 31 May 20X5 the initial present value of expected credit losses over the life of the loan, using a discount factor of 4%, was $25 million. At that date, the probability of default over the next 12 months was 10%. An allowance of 12 months' expected credit losses had been recognised at 31 May 20X5 in accordance with IFRS 9 *Financial Instruments*.

By 31 May 20X6 it became clear that the customer was in serious financial difficulties, and the directors of Zbay believed that there was objective evidence of impairment. The present value of expected credit losses was revised to $48.1 million.

No entries have been made in respect of the loan in the year ending 31 May 20X6.

(d)   On 1 June 20X5, Ejoy purchased a five year bond with a principal amount of $50 million and a fixed interest rate of 5% which was the current market rate. The bond is classified as at fair value through profit or loss. Because of the size of the investment, Ejoy has entered into a floating interest rate swap. Ejoy has designated the swap as a fair value hedge of the bond. At 31 May 20X6, market interest rates were 6%. As a result, the fair value of the bond has decreased to $48.3 million. Ejoy has received $0.5 million in net interest payments on the swap at 31 May 20X6. You should assume that the IFRS 9 hedge effectiveness criteria have been met and that any gain/loss on the swap is the same as the opposite loss/gain on the bond. No entries have been made in the statement of profit or loss and other comprehensive income to account for the bond or the hedge.

(e)   No impairment of the goodwill arising on the acquisition of Zbay had occurred at 1 June 20X5. The recoverable amount of Zbay was $630 million and the value in use of Tbay was $334 million at 31 May 20X6. Impairment losses on goodwill are charged to cost of sales.

(f)   Assume that profits accrue evenly throughout the year and ignore any taxation effects.

(g)   It is the group's policy to value the non-controlling interest at its proportionate share of the fair value of the subsidiary's identifiable net assets.

Required

Prepare a consolidated statement of profit or loss and other comprehensive income for the Ejoy Group for the year ended 31 May 20X6 in accordance with International Financial Reporting Standards. **(30 marks)**

13 Zippy

59 mins

P2 Sep/Dec 16, amended

The following draft financial statements relate to Zippy, a public limited company. Zippy is a manufacturing company but also has a wide portfolio of investment properties. Zippy has investments in Ginny and Boo, both public limited companies.

DRAFT STATEMENTS OF PROFIT OR LOSS AND OTHER COMPREHENSIVE INCOME FOR THE YEAR ENDED 30 JUNE 20X6

	Zippy $m	Ginny $m	Boo $m
Revenue	420	132	90
Cost of sales	(304)	(76)	(72)
Gross profit	116	56	18
Investment income	36	19	5
Administrative costs	(22)	(12)	(18)
Other expenses	(31)	(18)	(15)
Operating profit/(loss)	99	45	(10)
Net finance costs	(2)	(6)	(9)
Profit/(loss) before tax	97	39	(19)
Income tax expense	(30)	(7)	3
Profit/(loss) for the year	67	32	(16)
Other comprehensive income			
Items that will not be reclassified to profit or loss:			
Gain on property revaluation	14	16	–
Total comprehensive income for year	81	48	(16)

The following information is relevant to the preparation of the group statement of profit or loss and other comprehensive income.

(i)   On 1 July 20X4, Zippy acquired 60% of the equity interests of Ginny, a public limited company. The purchase consideration comprised cash of $90 million and the fair value of the identifiable net assets acquired was $114 million at that date. Zippy uses the 'full goodwill' method for all acquisitions and the fair value of the non-controlling interest (NCI) in Ginny was $50 million on 1 July 20X4. Goodwill had been reviewed annually for impairment and no impairment was deemed necessary.

(ii)   Zippy disposed of a 20% equity interest in Ginny on 31 March 20X6 for a cash consideration of $44 million. The remaining 40% holding had a fair value of $62 million and Zippy exercised significant influence over Ginny following the disposal. Zippy accounts for investments in subsidiaries at cost and has included a gain in investment income of $14 million within its individual financial statements to reflect the disposal. The net assets of Ginny had a fair value of $118 million at 1 July 20X5 and this was reflected in the carrying amounts of the net assets. All gains and losses of Ginny have accrued evenly throughout the year. The disposal is not classified as a separate major line of business or geographical operation.

(iii)   Zippy acquired 80% of the equity interests of Boo, a public limited company, on 30 June 20X4. The purchase consideration was cash of $60 million. The fair value of the NCI was calculated as $12 million at this date. Due to a tight reporting deadline, the fair value of the identifiable net assets at acquisition had not been finalised by the time the financial statements for the year ended 30 June 20X4 were published. Goodwill of $28 million was calculated using the carrying amount of the net assets of Boo. The fair value of the identifiable net assets of Boo was finalised on 31 December 20X4 as $54 million. The excess of the fair value of the identifiable net assets at acquisition is due to plant which had a remaining useful life of five years at the acquisition date. Depreciation is charged to cost of sales.

        Due to the losses of Boo, an impairment review was undertaken at 30 June 20X6. It was decided that goodwill had reduced in value by 10%. Goodwill impairments are charged to other expenses.

(iv)   Zippy holds properties for investment purposes. At 1 July 20X5, Zippy held a 10-floor office block at a fair value of $90 million with a remaining useful life of 15 years. The first floor was occupied by Zippy's staff and the second floor was let to Boo free of charge. The other eight floors were all let to unconnected third parties at a normal commercial rent. It was estimated that the fair value of the office block was $96 million at 30 June 20X6. Zippy has a policy of restating all land and buildings to fair value at each reporting date. The only accounting entries for the year ended 30 June 20X6 in relation to this office block have been to correctly include the rental income in profit or loss. It can be assumed that each floor is of equal size and value. Depreciation is charged to administrative costs.

(v)   The following information relates to Zippy's defined benefit pension scheme:

	$m
Net plan obligation at 30 June 20X5	(14)
Service cost for year ended 30 June 20X6	10
Contributions paid into the scheme on 30 June 20X6	8
Discount rate at 1 July 20X5	10%
Discount rate at 30 June 20X6	12%
Remeasurement gains in year ended 30 June 20X6	4

        No entries have been entered in the financial statements except that the contributions into the scheme have been correctly added to the pension scheme's assets.

(vi)   On 1 January 20X6, Zippy entered into a contract to sell 10,000 units of a new product, the Whizoo, to a customer for $1,000 per unit. It was agreed that if the customer ordered an additional 5,000 units, a volume discounted price of $950 per unit would apply. 6,000 units

were manufactured and delivered in the four months to 30 April 20X6. The customer placed the order for another 5,000 units on 31 March 20X6.

Minor defects were discovered in the first 6,000 units due to an error in the manufacturing process and it was agreed that a credit note of $40 per unit would be issued as compensation. Zippy and the customer agreed to net this amount off against subsequent payments for future orders. A further 7,000 units had been manufactured and delivered by 30 June 20X6 without any defects. Zippy has included $6 million in revenue (6,000 × $1,000) for the first 6,000 units but has not recorded any additional revenue, as the directors are unsure of the correct accounting treatment.

Required

Prepare the consolidated statement of profit or loss and other comprehensive income for the Zippy Group for the year ended 30 June 20X6. **(30 marks)**

14 Bravado   59 mins

P2 6/09, amended

Bravado, a public limited company, has acquired two subsidiaries and an associate. The draft statements of financial position are as follows at 31 May 20X9:

	Bravado $m	Message $m	Mixted $m
Assets			
Non-current assets			
Property, plant and equipment	265	230	161
Investments in subsidiaries:			
Message	300		
Mixted	133		
Investment in associate: Clarity	20		
Investment in equity instruments	51	6	5
	769	236	166
Current assets			
Inventories	135	55	73
Trade receivables	91	45	32
Cash and cash equivalents	102	100	8
	328	200	113
Total assets	1,097	436	279
Equity and liabilities			
Share capital	520	220	100
Retained earnings	240	150	80
Other components of equity	17	4	7
Total equity	777	374	187
Non-current liabilities			
Long-term borrowings	120	15	5
Deferred tax	25	9	3
Total non-current liabilities	145	24	8

	Bravado $m	Message $m	Mixted $m
Current liabilities			
Trade and other payables	115	30	60
Current tax	60	8	24
Total current liabilities	175	38	84
Total liabilities	320	62	92
Total equity and liabilities	1,097	436	279

The following information is relevant to the preparation of the group financial statements.

(i) On 1 June 20X8, Bravado acquired 80% of the equity interests of Message, a private entity. The purchase consideration comprised cash of $300 million. The fair value of the identifiable net assets of Message was $400 million, including any related deferred tax liability arising on acquisition. The owners of Message had to dispose of the entity for tax purposes by a specified date, and therefore sold the entity to the first company to bid for it, which was Bravado. An independent valuer has stated that the fair value of the non-controlling interest in Message was $86 million on 1 June 20X8. Bravado does not wish to measure the non-controlling interest in subsidiaries on the basis of the proportionate interest in the identifiable net assets, but wishes to use the 'full goodwill' method. The retained earnings of Message were $136 million and other components of equity were $4 million at the date of acquisition. There has been no new issue of capital by Message since the date of acquisition and the excess of the fair value of the net assets is due to an increase in the value of non-depreciable land.

(ii) On 1 June 20X7, Bravado acquired 6% of the ordinary shares of Mixted. Bravado had treated this as an investment in equity instruments at fair value in the financial statements to 31 May 20X8, and had made an irrevocable election (see Note (d)) to recognise changes in fair value in other comprehensive income. There were no changes in the fair value of Mixted in the year to 31 May 20X9. On 1 June 20X8, Bravado acquired a further 64% of the ordinary shares of Mixted and gained control of the company. The consideration for the acquisitions was as follows:

	Holding %	Consideration $m
1 June 20X7	6	10
1 June 20X8	64	118
	70	128

Under the purchase agreement of 1 June 20X8, Bravado is required to pay the former shareholders 30% of the profits of Mixted on 31 May 20Y0 for each of the financial years to 31 May 20X9 and 31 May 20Y0. The fair value of this arrangement was measured at $12 million at 1 June 20X8 and at 31 May 20X9 this value had not changed. This amount has not been included in the financial statements.

At 1 June 20X8, the fair value of the equity interest in Mixted held by Bravado before the business combination was $15 million, and the fair value of the non-controlling interest in Mixted was $53 million. The fair value of the identifiable net assets at 1 June 20X8 of Mixted was $170 million (excluding deferred tax assets and liabilities), and the retained earnings and other components of equity were $55 million and $7 million respectively. There has been no new issue of share capital by Mixted since the date of acquisition and the excess of the fair value of the net assets is due to an increase in the value of property, plant and equipment (PPE).

The fair value of the PPE at acquisition was provisional pending receipt of the final valuations for these assets. These valuations were received on 1 December 20X8 and they resulted in a further increase of $6 million in the fair value of the net assets at the date of acquisition. This increase does not affect the fair value of the non-controlling interest. PPE is depreciated on the straight-line basis over seven years. The tax base of the identifiable net assets of Mixted was $166 million at 1 June 20X8. The tax rate of Mixted is 30%.

(iii) Bravado acquired a 10% interest in Clarity, a public limited company, on 1 June 20X7 for $8 million. The investment was accounted for as an investment in equity instruments and at 31 May 20X8, its value was $9 million. On 1 June 20X8, Bravado acquired an additional 15% interest in Clarity for $11 million and achieved significant influence. Clarity made profits after dividends of $6 million and $10 million for the years to 31 May 20X8 and 31 May 20X9. An irrevocable election was made to take changes in fair value through other comprehensive income (items that will not be reclassified to profit or loss).

(iv) Bravado has made an irrevocable election to hold its investments in Message, Mixted and Clarity at fair value with changes in fair value recognised in other comprehensive income. There were no changes in fair value during the year ended 31 May 20X9.

(v) On 1 June 20X7, Bravado purchased an equity instrument of 11 million dinars which was its fair value. On that date an election was made to hold it at fair value through other comprehensive income. The relevant exchange rates and fair values were as follows:

	$ to dinars	Fair value of instrument – dinars
1 June 20X7	4.5	11
31 May 20X8	5.1	10
31 May 20X9	4.8	7

Bravado has not recorded any change in the value of the instrument since 31 May 20X8. The reduction in fair value as at 31 May 20X9 is deemed to be as a result of impairment.

(vi) There is no impairment of goodwill arising on the acquisitions.

Required

(a) Prepare a consolidated statement of financial position as at 31 May 20X9 for the Bravado Group. **(25 marks)**

(b) Calculate and explain the impact on the calculation of goodwill if the non-controlling interest was calculated on a proportionate basis for Message and Mixted. **(5 marks)**

(Total = 30 marks)

15 Jocatt

68 mins

P2 12/10, amended

The following draft group financial statements relate to Jocatt, a public limited company.

JOCATT GROUP
STATEMENT OF FINANCIAL POSITION AS AT 30 NOVEMBER

	20X2 $m	20X1 $m
Assets		
Non-current assets		
Property, plant and equipment	327	254
Investment property	8	6
Goodwill	48	68
Other intangible assets	85	72
Investment in associate	54	–
Investments in equity instruments	94	90
	616	490

	20X2 $m	20X1 $m
Current assets		
Inventories	105	128
Trade receivables	62	113
Cash and cash equivalents	232	143
	399	384
	1,015	874
Equity and liabilities		
Equity attributable to the owners of the parent:		
Share capital	290	275
Retained earnings	351	324
Other components of equity	15	20
	656	619
Non-controlling interest	55	36
Total equity	711	655
Non-current liabilities		
Long-term borrowings	67	71
Deferred tax	35	41
Long-term provisions: pension obligation	25	22
Total non-current liabilities	127	134
Current liabilities		
Trade payables	144	55
Current tax payable	33	30
Total current liabilities	177	85
Total liabilities	304	219
Total equity and liabilities	1,015	874

JOCATT GROUP
STATEMENT OF PROFIT OR LOSS AND OTHER COMPREHENSIVE INCOME
FOR THE YEAR ENDED 30 NOVEMBER 20X2

	$m
Revenue	432.0
Cost of sales	(317.0)
Gross profit	115.0
Other income	25.0
Distribution costs	(55.5)
Administrative expenses	(36.0)
Finance costs	(6.0)
Gains on property	10.5
Share of profit of associate	6.0
Profit before tax	59.0
Income tax expense	(11.0)
Profit for the year	48.0
Other comprehensive income after tax (items that will not be reclassified to profit or loss)	
Gain on investments in equity instruments (IEI)	2.0
Losses on property revaluation	(7.0)
Remeasurement losses on defined benefit pension plan	(6.0)
Other comprehensive income for the year, net of tax	(11.0)
Total comprehensive income for the year	37.0

	$m
Profit attributable to:	
Owners of the parent	38.0
Non-controlling interest	10.0
	48.0
Total comprehensive income attributable to:	
Owners of the parent	27.0
Non-controlling interest	10.0
	37.0

JOCATT GROUP
STATEMENT OF CHANGES IN EQUITY FOR THE YEAR ENDED 30 NOVEMBER 20X2

	Share capital $m	Retained earnings $m	Investments in equity instruments $m	Revaluation surplus (PPE) $m	Total $m	Non-controlling interest $m	Total equity $m
Balance at 1 December 20X1	275	324	4	16	619	36	655
Share capital issued	15				15		15
Dividends		(5)			(5)	(13)	(18)
Rights issue						2	2
Acquisitions						20	20
Total comprehensive income for the year		32	2	(7)	27	10	37
Balance at 30 November 20X2	290	351	6	9	656	55	711

The following information relates to the financial statements of Jocatt.

(i) On 1 December 20X0, Jocatt acquired 8% of the ordinary shares of Tigret. Jocatt had treated this as an investment in equity instruments in the financial statements to 30 November 20X1 with changes in fair value taken to profit or loss for the year. There were no changes in fair value in the year to 30 November 20X1. On 1 January 20X2, Jocatt acquired a further 52% of the ordinary shares of Tigret and gained control of the company. The consideration for the acquisitions was as follows.

	Holding %	Consideration $m
1 December 20X0	8	4
1 January 20X2	52	30
	60	34

At 1 January 20X2, the fair value of the 8% holding in Tigret held by Jocatt at the time of the business combination was $5 million and the fair value of the non-controlling interest in Tigret was $20 million. The purchase consideration at 1 January 20X2 comprised cash of $15 million and shares of $15 million.

The fair value of the identifiable net assets of Tigret, excluding deferred tax assets and liabilities, at the date of acquisition comprised the following.

	$m
Property, plant and equipment	15
Intangible assets	18
Trade receivables	5
Cash	7

The tax base of the identifiable net assets of Tigret was $40 million at 1 January 20X2. The tax rate of Tigret is 30%.

(ii) On 30 November 20X2, Tigret made a rights issue on a 1 for 4 basis. The issue was fully subscribed and raised $5 million in cash.

(iii) Jocatt purchased a research project from a third party including certain patents on 1 December 20X1 for $8 million and recognised it as an intangible asset. During the year, Jocatt incurred further costs, which included $2 million on completing the research phase, $4 million in developing the product for sale and $1 million for the initial marketing costs. There were no other additions to intangible assets in the period other than those on the acquisition of Tigret.

(iv) Jocatt operates a defined benefit pension scheme. The current service costs for the year ended 30 November 20X2 are $10 million. Jocatt enhanced the benefits on 1 December 20X1. The total cost of the enhancement is $2 million. The net interest on net plan assets was $8 million for the year and Jocatt recognises remeasurement gains and losses in accordance with IAS 19.

(v) Jocatt owns an investment property. During the year, part of the heating system of the property, which had a carrying amount of $0.5 million, was replaced by a new system, which cost $1 million. Jocatt uses the fair value model for measuring investment property.

(vi) Jocatt had exchanged surplus land with a carrying amount of $10 million for cash of $15 million and plant valued at $4 million. The transaction has commercial substance. Depreciation for the period for property, plant and equipment was $27 million.

(vii) Goodwill relating to all subsidiaries had been impairment tested in the year to 30 November 20X2 and any impairment accounted for. The goodwill impairment related to those subsidiaries which were 100% owned.

(viii) Deferred tax of $1 million arose in the year on the gains on investments in equity instruments where the irrevocable election was made to take changes in fair value through other comprehensive income.

(ix) The associate did not pay any dividends in the year.

Required

Prepare a consolidated statement of cash flows for the Jocatt Group using the indirect method under IAS 7 *Statement of Cash Flows*.

Note. Ignore deferred taxation other than where it is mentioned in the question.   **(35 marks)**

16 Warrburt   **59 mins**

P2 12/08, amended

The following draft group financial statements relate to Warrburt, a public limited company:

WARRBURT GROUP

STATEMENT OF FINANCIAL POSITION AS AT 30 NOVEMBER 20X8

	20X8	20X7
	$m	$m
Assets		
Non-current assets		
Property, plant and equipment	354	360
Goodwill	80	100
Other intangible assets	228	240
Investment in associate	100	–
Investment in equity instruments	142	150
	904	850

	20X8 $m	20X7 $m
Current assets		
Inventories	135	198
Trade receivables	92	163
Cash and cash equivalents	284	323
	511	684
Total assets	1,415	1,534
Equity and liabilities		
Equity attributable to owners of the parent		
Share capital	650	595
Retained earnings	367	454
Other components of equity	49	20
	1,066	1,069
Non-controlling interest	46	53
Total equity	1,112	1,122
Non-current liabilities		
Long-term borrowings	20	64
Deferred tax	28	26
Retirement benefit obligation	100	96
Total non-current liabilities	148	186
Current liabilities:		
Trade payables	115	180
Current tax payable	35	42
Short-term provisions	5	4
Total current liabilities	155	226
Total liabilities	303	412
Total equity and liabilities	1,415	1,534

WARRBURT GROUP

STATEMENT OF PROFIT OR LOSS AND OTHER COMPREHENSIVE INCOME FOR THE YEAR
ENDED 30 NOVEMBER 20X8

	$m
Revenue	910
Cost of sales	(886)
Gross profit	24
Other income	7
Distribution costs	(40)
Administrative expenses	(35)
Finance costs	(9)
Share of profit of associate	6
Loss before tax	(47)
Income tax expense	(29)
Loss for the year	(76)

	$m
Other comprehensive income for the year (after tax, not reclassified to P/L)	
Investment in equity instruments (IEI)	27
Gains on property revaluation	2
Remeasurement losses on defined benefit plan	(4)
Other comprehensive income for the year (after tax)	25
Total comprehensive income for the year	(51)
Profit/(loss) attributable to:	
Owners of the parent	(74)
Non-controlling interest	(2)
	(76)
Total comprehensive income attributable to:	
Owners of the parent	(49)
Non-controlling interest	(2)
	(51)

WARRBURT GROUP

STATEMENT OF CHANGES IN EQUITY FOR THE YEAR ENDED 30 NOVEMBER 20X8

	Share capital $m	Retained earnings $m	IEI $m	Revaluation surplus $m	Total $m	Non-controlling interest $m	Total equity $m
Balance at 1 December 20X7	595	454	16	4	1,069	53	1,122
Share capital issued	55				55		55
Dividends		(9)			(9)	(5)	(14)
Total comprehensive income for the year		(78)	27	2	(49)	(2)	(51)
Balance at 30 November 20X8	650	367	43	6	1,066	46	1,112

NOTE TO STATEMENT OF CHANGES IN EQUITY

	$m
Profit/(loss) attributable to owners of parent	(74)
Remeasurement losses on defined benefit pension plan	(4)
Total comprehensive income for year – retained earnings	(78)

The following information relates to the financial statements of Warrburt.

(i)   Warrburt holds investments in equity instruments (IEI) which are owned by the parent company. At 1 December 20X7, the total carrying amount of those investments was $150 million. In respect of $112 million of this $150 million, Warrburt had made an irrevocable election under IFRS 9 for changes in fair value to go through other comprehensive income (items that will not be reclassified to profit or loss). The remaining $38 million related to an investment in the shares of Alburt, in respect of which changes in fair value had been taken to profit or loss for the year. During the year, the investment in Alburt was sold for $45 million, with the fair value gain shown in 'other income' in the financial statements. The following schedule summarises the changes:

	Alburt $m	Other $m	Total $m
Carrying amount at 1 December 20X7	38	112	150
Add gain on derecognition/revaluation of IEI	7	30	37
Less sales of IEI at fair value	(45)	–	(45)
Carrying amount at 30 November 20X8	–	142	142

Deferred tax of $3 million arising on the $30 million revaluation gain above has been taken into account in 'other comprehensive income' for the year.

(ii) The retirement benefit obligation shown in the statement of financial position comprises the following:

	$m
Liability at 1 December 20X7	96
Expense for period	10
Contributions to scheme (paid)	(10)
Remeasurement losses	4
Liability at 30 November 20X8	100

Warrburt recognises remeasurement gains and losses in other comprehensive income in the period in which they occur, in accordance with IAS 19. The benefits paid in the period by the trustees of the scheme were $3 million. There is no tax impact with regards to the retirement benefit obligation.

(iii) The property, plant and equipment (PPE) in the statement of financial position comprises the following:

	$m
Carrying amount at 1 December 20X7	360
Additions at cost	82
Gains on property revaluation	4
Disposals	(56)
Depreciation	(36)
Carrying amount at 30 November 20X8	354

Plant and machinery with a carrying amount of $1 million had been destroyed by fire in the year. The asset was replaced by the insurance company with new plant and machinery which was valued at $3 million. The machines were acquired directly by the insurance company and no cash payment was made to Warrburt. The company included the net gain on this transaction in 'additions at cost' and as a deduction from administrative expenses.

The disposal proceeds were $63 million. The gain on disposal is included in administrative expenses. Deferred tax of $2 million has been deducted in arriving at the 'gains on property revaluation' figure in 'other comprehensive income (items that will not be reclassified to profit or loss)'.

The remaining additions of PPE comprised plant and equipment purchased on 30 June 20X8. The cost of the PPE was $80 million with $60 million being paid on 31 October 20X8 and the balance to be paid on 31 December 20X8.

(iv) Warrburt purchased a 25% interest in an associate for cash on 1 December 20X7. The net assets of the associate at the date of acquisition were $300 million. The associate made a profit after tax of $24 million and paid a dividend of $8 million out of these profits in the year ended 30 November 20X8.

(v) An impairment test was carried out at 30 November 20X8 on goodwill and other intangible assets. The result showed that goodwill was impaired by $20 million and other intangible assets by $12 million.

(vi)   The short-term provisions relate to finance costs which are payable within six months.

Required

(a)   Prepare a group statement of cash flows for Warrburt for the year ended 30 November 20X8 in accordance with IAS 7 *Statement of Cash Flows*, using the indirect method.   **(25 marks)**

(b)   Discuss the key issues which the statement of cash flows highlights regarding the cash flow of the company.   **(5 marks)**

(Total = 30 marks)

Section 3 – Exam-standard questions

PART A: Apply fundamental ethical and professional principles to ethical dilemmas and discuss the consequences of unethical behaviour

17 Jarvis   39 mins

Jarvis is a public limited company involved in manufacturing raw materials. Acting responsibly is a key focus for the company's board. Given the nature of its operations, Jarvis has recently set up an innovation initiative in order to find new ways to solve environmental challenges. The finance director takes the view that by investing in innovative technology the company will be able to find solutions to environmental issues, thereby enhancing the environment for future generations. He believes that all expenditure on this newly created initiative can be immediately classified as a non-current asset.

Required

(a)   Advise the finance director of Jarvis on the considerations necessary in order to apply the proposed accounting treatment to the innovation initiative.   **(5 marks)**

(b)   Discuss what is meant by corporate responsibility and in particular the factors which should encourage companies to disclose social and environmental information.   **(10 marks)**

(c)   A recent survey has indicated that there has been a vast increase in narrative reporting by FTSE 350 companies on the subject of corporate responsibility; however, only a very small proportion of companies identify corporate responsibilities as strategic issues or provide key performance indicators in this area.

   Required

   Discuss the ethical issues of narrative reporting without reference to strategy and the lack of key performance indicators to support the narrative disclosures.   **(3 marks)**

   Professional marks will be awarded in part (c) for the application of ethical principles.

                                                                                        (2 marks)

                                                                              (Total = 20 marks)

18 Columbus   39 mins

P2 6/14, amended

(a)   The directors of Columbus have strong views on the usefulness of the financial statements after their move to International Financial Reporting Standards (IFRSs). They are of the opinion that although IFRSs implement a fair value model, IFRSs are failing users of financial statements as they do not reflect the financial value of an entity.

   Required

   Discuss the directors' views above as regards the use of fair value in IFRSs and the fact that IFRSs do not reflect the financial value of an entity.   **(10 marks)**

(b)   Columbus plans to update its production process and the directors feel that technology-led production is the only feasible way in which the company can remain competitive. On 1 May 20X3, Columbus entered into a lease for a property and the leasing arrangement was established in order to maximise taxation benefits. However, the financial statements have not shown a lease asset or liability to date.

   A new financial controller joined Columbus shortly before the financial year end of 30 April 20X4 and is presently reviewing the financial statements to prepare for the upcoming audit and to begin making a loan application to finance the new technology. The financial controller feels that the lease relating to both the property should be recognised in the

statement of financial position, but the managing director, who did a brief accountancy course ten years ago, strongly disagrees. The managing director wishes to charge the rental payments to profit or loss. The managing director feels that the arrangement does not meet the criteria for recognition in the statement of financial position, and has made it clear that showing the lease in the statement of financial position could jeopardise both the company's upcoming loan application and the financial controller's future prospects at Columbus.

Required

Discuss the ethical and accounting issues which face the financial controller in the above situation and advise on the appropriate accounting treatment for the lease. **(8 marks)**

Professional marks will be awarded in part (b) for the application of ethical principles.

(2 marks)

Note. In your answer, assume that IFRS 16 *Leases* is effective.

(Total = 20 marks)

19 Casino
49 mins

P2 12/11, amended

(a) Casino has three distinct business segments. Management has calculated the net assets, revenue and profit before common costs, which are to be allocated to these segments. However, they are unsure as to how they should allocate certain common costs and whether they can exercise judgement in the allocation process. They wish to allocate head office management expenses; pension expense; the cost of managing properties and interest and related interest-bearing assets. They also are uncertain as to whether the allocation of costs has to conform to the accounting policies used in the financial statements.

Required

Advise the management of Casino on the points raised in the above paragraph. **(7 marks)**

(b) Segmental information reported externally is more useful if it conforms to information used by management in making decisions. The information can differ from that reported in the financial statements. Although reconciliations are required, these can be complex and difficult for the user to understand. Additionally, there are other standards where subjectivity is involved and often the profit motive determines which accounting practice to follow. The directors have a responsibility to shareholders in disclosing information to enhance corporate value but this may conflict with their corporate social responsibility.

Required

Discuss how the ethics of corporate social responsibility disclosure are difficult to reconcile with shareholder expectations. **(7 marks)**

(c) Casino's directors feel that they need a significant injection of capital in order to modernise plant and equipment as the company has been promised new orders if it can produce goods to an international quality. The bank's current lending policies require borrowers to demonstrate good projected cash flow, as well as a level of profitability which would indicate that repayments would be made. However, the current projected statement of cash flows would not satisfy the bank's criteria for lending. The directors have told the bank that the company is in an excellent financial position, the financial results and cash flow projections will meet the criteria and the chief accountant will forward a report to this effect shortly. The chief accountant has only recently joined Casino and has openly stated that he cannot afford to lose his job because of his financial commitments.

Required

Discuss the potential ethical conflicts which may arise in the above scenario and the ethical principles which would guide how the chief accountant should respond in this situation.

(9 marks)

Professional marks will be awarded in parts (b) and (c) for the application of ethical principles.

(2 marks)

(Total = 25 marks)

20 Presdon

39 mins

P2 Mar/Jun 16, amended

(a) The directors of Presdon have been reviewing the International Integrated Reporting Council's *Framework for Integrated Reporting*. The directors believe that International Financial Reporting Standards are already extensive and provide stakeholders with a comprehensive understanding of an entity's financial position and performance for the year. In particular, statements of cash flows enable stakeholders to assess the liquidity, solvency and financial adaptability of a business. They are concerned that any additional disclosures could be excessive and obscure the most useful information within a set of financial statements. They are therefore unsure as to the rationale for the implementation of a separate, or combined, integrated report.

Required

Discuss the extent to which statements of cash flows provide stakeholders with useful information about an entity and whether this information would be improved by the entity introducing an Integrated Report. **(10 marks)**

(b) Presdon has a year end of 31 January. Shortly before 31 January 20X6, Presdon gave a $5 million, zero interest, short-term loan to its subsidiary, Mielly. Mielly repaid the loan in full during February 20X6. Since the loan was repaid within Presdon's usual credit terms of 30 days, it was classified as a trading item as at 31 January 20X6. Consequently Presdon included the balance within trade and other receivables and Mielly included it within trade and other payables at the year end. Mielly has several bank loans with substantial debt covenants linked to both interest cover and its gearing ratio. The bank loans would become immediately repayable should Mielly breach any of the terms of the covenants. Before receiving the loan, Mielly had a bank overdraft balance of $4.5 million.

Required

Discuss the impact which the $5 million loan would have on the debt covenants of Mielly and whether there are any ethical implications arising from the situation. **(8 marks)**

Professional marks will be awarded for the application of ethical principles. **(2 marks)**

(Total = 20 marks)

21 Chippin

29 mins

P2 12/10, amended

Chippin, a public limited company, operates in the energy industry and undertakes complex natural gas trading arrangements, which involve exchanges in resources with other companies in the industry. Chippin is entering into a long-term contract for the supply of gas and is raising a loan on the strength of this contract. The proceeds of the loan are to be received over the year to 30 November 20X3 and are to be repaid over four years to 30 November 20X7. Chippin wishes to report the loan proceeds as operating cash inflow because it is related to a long-term purchase contract. The directors of Chippin receive a bonus if the operating cash flow exceeds a predetermined target for the year and feel that the indirect method is more useful and informative to users of financial statements than the direct method.

Required

(a)   Comment on the directors' view that the indirect method of preparing statements of cash flows is more useful and informative to users than the direct method. **(7 marks)**

(b)   Discuss the reasons why the directors may wish to report the loan proceeds as an operating cash flow rather than a financing cash flow and whether there are any ethical implications of adopting this treatment. **(6 marks)**

Professional marks will be awarded for the application of ethical principles. **(2 marks)**

(Total = 15 marks)

22 Egin Group
39 mins

ACR 6/06, amended

On 1 June 20X5, Egin, a public limited company, was formed out of the reorganisation of a group of companies with foreign operations. The directors are reluctant to disclose related party information as they feel that such transactions are a normal feature of business and need not be disclosed.

Under the new group structure, Egin owns 80% of Briars, 60% of Doye, and 30% of Eye. Egin exercises significant influence over Eye. The directors of Egin are also directors of Briars and Doye but only one director of Egin sits on the management board of Eye. The management board of Eye comprises five directors. Originally the group comprised five companies but the fifth company, Tang, which was a 70% subsidiary of Egin, was sold on 31 January 20X6. There were no transactions between Tang and the Egin Group during the year to 31 May 20X6. 30% of the shares of Egin are owned by another company, Atomic, which exerts significant influence over Egin. The remaining 40% of the shares of Doye are owned by Spade, which exerts significant influence over Doye.

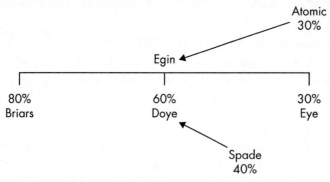

During the current financial year to 31 May 20X6, Doye has sold a significant amount of plant and equipment to Spade at the normal selling price for such items. The directors of Egin have proposed that where related party relationships are determined and sales are at normal selling price, any disclosures will state that prices charged to related parties are made on an arm's length basis.

One of the directors of Briars who is not on the management board of Egin owns the whole of the share capital of a company, Blue, that sells goods at market price to Briars. The director is in charge of the production at Briars and also acts as a consultant to the management board of the group.

Required

(a)   Discuss why it is important to disclose related party transactions, explaining the criteria which determine a related party relationship. **(7 marks)**

(b)   Describe the nature of any related party relationships and transactions which exists:

(i)   Within the Egin Group including Tang; **(5 marks)**
(ii)   Between Spade and the Egin Group; **(3 marks)**
(iii)   Between Atomic and the Egin Group; **(3 marks)**

commenting on whether transactions should be described as being at 'arm's length'.

Professional marks will be awarded for the application of ethical principles. **(2 marks)**

(Total = 20 marks)

PART B: Evaluate the appropriateness of the financial reporting framework and critically discuss changes in accounting regulation

23 Conceptual framework   49 mins

P2 12/07, amended

The International Accounting Standards Board (IASB) is working on a project to update its conceptual framework for financial accounting and reporting. The goals of the project are to provide a more complete, clear and updated set of concepts to use when IFRS Standards are revised or developed. The first phase, a joint project with the US Financial Accounting Standards Board (FASB), has been published as the *Conceptual Framework for Financial Reporting*.

Required

(a) Discuss why it is beneficial to develop an agreed international conceptual framework and the extent to which an agreed international conceptual framework can be used to resolve practical accounting issues.   **(10 marks)**

(b) In 2015, the IASB issued Exposure Draft ED/2015/3: *Conceptual Framework for Financial Reporting*, which addresses areas found to be deficient in the existing *Conceptual Framework*.

Discuss the changes proposed in the ED in respect of the following matters:

(i)   Derecognition of assets and liabilities
(ii) The reintroduction of prudence   **(6 marks)**

(c) What criticisms could be made of the proposed changes in the Exposure Draft on the *Conceptual Framework*?   **(9 marks)**

(Total = 25 marks)

24 Lizzer   49 mins

(a) The directors of Lizzer have decided not to disclose any information concerning the two matters below.

(i)   Lizzer is a debt issuer whose business is the securitisation of a portfolio of underlying investments and financing their purchase through the issuing of listed, limited recourse debt. The repayment of the debt is dependent upon the performance of the underlying investments. Debt-holders bear the ultimate risks and rewards of ownership of the underlying investments. Given the debt specific nature of the underlying investments, the risk profile of individual debt may differ.

Lizzer does not consider its debt-holders as being amongst the primary users of the financial statements and, accordingly, does not wish to provide disclosure of the debt-holders' exposure to risks in the financial statements, as distinct from the risks faced by the company's shareholders, in accordance with IFRS 7 *Financial Instruments: Disclosures*.

Required

Discuss the reasons why the debt-holders of Lizzer may be interested in its financial statements and advise the directors whether their decision not to provide disclosure of the debt-holders exposure to risks is consistent with the principles of IFRS 7. **(6 marks)**

(ii) At the date of the financial statements, 31 January 20X3, Lizzer's liquidity position was quite poor, such that the directors described it as 'unsatisfactory' in the management report. During the first quarter of 20X3, the situation worsened with the result that Lizzer was in breach of certain loan covenants at 31 March 20X3. The financial statements were authorised for issue at the end of April 20X3. The directors' and auditor's reports both emphasised the considerable risk of not being able to continue as a going concern.

35

The notes to the financial statements indicated that there was 'ample' compliance with all loan covenants as at the date of the financial statements. No additional information about the loan covenants was included in the financial statements. Lizzer had been close to breaching the loan covenants in respect of free cash flows and equity ratio requirements at 31 January 20X3.

The directors of Lizzer felt that, given the existing information in the financial statements, any further disclosure would be excessive and confusing to users.

Required

Critique, from the perspective of the investors and potential investors of Lizzer, the decision of the directors not to include further disclosure about the breach of loan covenants. **(6 marks)**

(b) The directors of Lizzer have read various reports about excessive disclosure in annual reports. Some reports suggested that excessive disclosure is burdensome and can overwhelm users. However, other reports argued that there is no such thing as too much 'useful' information for users.

Required

(i) Discuss why it is important to ensure the optimal level of disclosure in annual reports, describing the reasons why users of annual reports may have found disclosure to be excessive in recent years and the actions taken by the IASB to address this issue.

(9 marks)

(ii) Describe the barriers, which may exist, to reducing excessive disclosure in annual reports. **(4 marks)**

(Total = 25 marks)

25 Accounting standards and disclosure 49 mins

P2 12/08, amended

Whilst acknowledging the importance of high quality corporate reporting, the recommendations to improve it are sometimes questioned on the basis that the marketplace for capital can determine the nature and quality of corporate reporting. It could be argued that additional accounting and disclosure standards would only distort a market mechanism that already works well and would add costs to the reporting mechanism, with no apparent benefit. It could be said that accounting standards create costly, inefficient, and unnecessary regulation. It could be argued that increased disclosure reduces risks and offers a degree of protection to users. However, increased disclosure has several costs to the preparer of financial statements.

Required

(a) Explain why accounting standards are needed to help the market mechanism work effectively for the benefit of preparers and users of corporate reports. **(9 marks)**

(b) Discuss the benefits to the users of financial statements and relative costs to the preparer of increased disclosure of information in financial statements. **(14 marks)**

Professional marks will be awarded for quality of discussion and reasoning. **(2 marks)**

(Total = 25 marks)

PART C: Apply professional judgement in the reporting of the financial performance of a range of entities

26 Tang

49 mins

P2 Sep/Dec 15, amended

IFRS 15 *Revenue from Contracts with Customers* provides detailed and consistent guidance regarding revenue recognition. IFRS 15 sets out a five-step model, which applies to revenue earned from a contract with a customer with limited exceptions, regardless of the type of revenue transaction or the industry. Step one in the five-step model requires the identification of the contract with the customer and is critical for the purpose of applying the Standard. The remaining four steps in the Standard's revenue recognition model are irrelevant if the contract does not fall within the scope of IFRS 15.

Required

(a) (i) Discuss the criteria which must be met for a contract with a customer to fall within the scope of IFRS 15. **(5 marks)**

(ii) Discuss the four remaining steps which lead to revenue recognition after a contract has been identified as falling within the scope of IFRS 15. **(9 marks)**

(b) (i) Tang enters into a contract with a customer to sell an existing printing machine such that control of the printing machine vests with the customer in two years' time. The contract has two payment options. The customer can pay $240,000 when the contract is signed or $300,000 in two years' time when the customer gains control of the printing machine. The interest rate implicit in the contract is 11.8% in order to adjust for the risk involved in the delay in payment. However, Tang's incremental borrowing rate is 5%. The customer paid $240,000 on 1 December 20X4 when the contract was signed. **(4 marks)**

(ii) Tang enters into a contract on 1 December 20X4 to construct a printing machine on a customer's premises for a promised consideration of $1,500,000 with a bonus of $100,000 if the machine is completed within 24 months. At the inception of the contract, Tang correctly accounts for the promised bundle of goods and services as a single performance obligation in accordance with IFRS 15. At the inception of the contract, Tang expects the costs to be $800,000 and concludes that it is highly probable that a significant reversal in the amount of cumulative revenue recognised will occur. Completion of the printing machine is highly susceptible to factors outside of Tang's influence, mainly issues with the supply of components.

At 30 November 20X5, Tang has satisfied 65% of its performance obligation on the basis of costs incurred to date and concludes that the variable consideration is still constrained in accordance with IFRS 15. However, on 4 December 20X5, the contract is modified with the result that the fixed consideration and expected costs increase by $110,000 and $60,000 respectively. The time allowable for achieving the bonus is extended by six months with the result that Tang concludes that it is highly probable that the bonus will be achieved and that the contract still remains a single performance obligation. Tang has an accounting year end of 30 November. **(7 marks)**

Required

Discuss how the above two contracts should be accounted for under IFRS 15. (In the case of (b)(i), the discussion should include the accounting treatment up to 30 November 20X6 and in the case of (b)(ii), the accounting treatment up to 4 December 20X5.)

Note. The mark allocation is shown against each of the items above.

(Total = 25 marks)

27 Blochberger   49 mins

(a)   Blochberger is a manufacturer of consumer goods. On 30 November 20X7, Blochberger
      entered into a one-year contract to sell goods to a large global chain of retail stores. The
      customer committed to buy at least $30 million of products over the one year contract. The
      contract required Blochberger to make a non-refundable payment of $3 million to the customer
      at the inception of the contract. The $3 million payment is to compensate the customer for the
      changes required to its shelving to accommodate Blochberger's products. Blochberger duly
      paid this $3 million to the customer on 30 November 20X7.

      In December 20X7, Blochberger transferred goods to the customer worth $4 million to the
      customer and invoiced them for this amount.   **(6 marks)**

(b)   On 1 July 20X7, Blochberger entered into a contract with another customer to sell Product A
      for $200 per unit. If the customer purchases more than 1,000 units of Product A in a
      12-month period, the contract specifies that the price per unit is retrospectively reduced to
      $180 per unit.

      For the quarter ended 30 September 20X7, Blochberger sold 75 units of Product A to the
      customer. At that date, Blochberger estimated that the customers' purchases would not exceed
      the 1,000-unit threshold required for the volume discount.

      In October 20X8, the customer acquired another company and in the quarter ended
      31 December 20X7, Blochberger sold an additional 500 units of Product A to the customer. In
      light of this, Blochberger now estimates that the customer's purchases will exceed the 1,000-
      unit threshold (in the 12 months to 30 June 20X8) and therefore, it will be required to
      retrospectively reduce the price per unit to $180.   **(7 marks)**

(c)   On 31 December 20X7, Blochberger sold Product B to a customer for $12,100 payable
      24 months after delivery. The customer obtained control of the product at contract inception.
      However, the contract permits the customer to return the product within 90 days. The product
      is new and Blochberger has no relevant historical evidence of product returns or other
      available market evidence.

      The cash selling price of Product B is $10,000, which represents the amount that the customer
      would pay upon delivery of the same product sold under otherwise identical terms and
      conditions as at contract inception. The cost of the product to Blochberger is $8,000.
                                                                               (7 marks)

(d)   On 1 September 20X7, Blochberger purchased a new machine for use in its factory. The
      directors have capitalised the purchase price but are unsure how to treat the following related
      costs. $400,000 was spent on testing whether the machine was functioning properly. During
      the testing period (September–October 20X7), samples were produced and sold for a total of
      $75,000. $300,000 was also spent on training existing employees how to operate the new
      machine. The machine is being used to manufacture a new product, Product C and $1 million
      was spent of advertising this new product. Testing was completed and commercial production
      of Product C commenced on 31 October 20X7.   **(5 marks)**

Required

Advise Blochberger on how the above transactions should be dealt with in its financial statements for
the year ended 31 December 20X7 (and up to 31 March 20X8 for part (c)).

Note. The mark allocation is shown against each of the four issues above.   **(Total = 25 marks)**

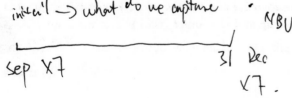

38

BPP
LEARNING MEDIA

28 Minco   49 mins

P2 6/14, amended

(a)   Minco is a major property developer. On 1 June 20X3, Minco entered into a contract with Holistic Healthco for the sale of a building for $3 million. Holistic Healthco intends to use the building as a fitness and leisure centre. The building is located in a busy city, where there are many gyms and leisure centres. Holistic Healthco's experience to date has been in stores selling health foods and aromatherapy oils, and it has no experience of the fitness industry.

Holistic Healthco paid Minco a non-refundable deposit of $150,000 on 1 June 20X3 and entered into a long-term financing agreement with Minco for the remaining 95% of the promised consideration. The terms of the financing arrangement are that if Holistic Healthco defaults, Minco can repossess the building, but cannot seek further compensation from Holistic Healthco, even if the collateral does not cover the full value of the amount owed. The building cost Minco $1.8 million to construct. Holistic Healthco obtained control of the building on 1 June 20X3.

Minco argues that this contract falls within the scope of IFRS 15 *Revenue from Contracts with Customers*, and that the non-refundable deposit should be recognised as revenue. **(8 marks)**

(b)   Minco often sponsors professional tennis players in an attempt to improve its brand image. At the moment, it has a three-year agreement with a tennis player who is currently ranked in the world's top ten players. The agreement is that the player receives a signing bonus of $20,000 and earns an annual amount of $50,000, paid at the end of each year for three years, provided that the player has competed in all the specified tournaments for each year. If the player wins a major tournament, she receives a bonus of 20% of the prize money won at the tournament. In return, the player is required to wear advertising logos on tennis apparel, play a specified number of tournaments and attend photo/film sessions for advertising purposes. The different payments are not interrelated. **(5 marks)**

(c)   Minco leased its head office during the current accounting period and the agreement terminates in six years' time.

There is a clause in the lease relating to the internal condition of the property at the termination of the lease. The clause states that the internal condition of the property should be identical to that at the outset of the lease. Minco has improved the building by adding another floor to part of the building during the current accounting period. There is also a clause which enables the landlord to recharge Minco for costs relating to the general disrepair of the building at the end of the lease. In addition, the landlord can recharge any costs of repairing the roof immediately. The landlord intends to replace part of the roof of the building during the current period. **(5 marks)**

(d)   On 1 June 20X1, Minco acquired a property for $5 million and annual depreciation of $500,000 is charged on the straight-line basis with no residual value. At the end of the previous financial year of 31 May 20X3, when accumulated depreciation was $1 million, a further amount relating to an impairment loss of $350,000 was recognised, which resulted in the property being valued at its estimated value in use. On 1 October 20X3, as a consequence of a proposed move to new premises, the property was classified as held for sale. At the time of classification as held for sale, the fair value less costs to sell was $3.4 million. At the date of the published interim financial statements, 1 December 20X3, the property market had improved and the fair value less costs to sell was reassessed at $3.52 million and at the year end on 31 May 20X4 it had improved even further, so that the fair value less costs to sell was $3.95 million. The property was sold on 5 June 20X4 for $4 million. **(7 marks)**

Required

Discuss how the above items should be dealt with in the financial statements of Minco.

Note. The mark allocation is shown against each of the four issues above.

(Total = 25 marks)

29 Havanna
49 mins

You are the newly appointed financial controller of Havanna and have been asked to give advice to the board of directors on the following transactions it entered into in the year ended 30 November 20X3.

(a)   Havanna owns a chain of health clubs and has entered into binding contracts with sports organisations, which earn income over given periods. The services rendered in return for such income include access to Havanna's database of members, and admission to health clubs, including the provision of coaching and other benefits. These contracts are for periods of between 9 and 18 months. Havanna's accounting policy for revenue recognition is to recognise the contract income in full at the date when the contract is signed. The rationale is that the contracts are binding and at the point of signing the contract, the customer gains access to Havanna's services. The directors are reluctant to change their accounting policy.

Required

Advise the directors, with reference to the underlying principles of IFRS 15 *Revenue from Contracts with Customers*, how the revenue in relation to the contracts should be recognised.

(10 marks)

(b)   In May 20X3, Havanna decided to sell one of its regional business divisions through a mixed asset and share deal. The decision to sell the division at a price of $40 million was made public in November 20X3 and gained shareholder approval in December 20X3. It was decided that the payment of any agreed sale price could be deferred until 30 November 20X5. It is estimated that the cost of allowing the deferred payment is $0.5 million and that legal and other professional fees associated with the disposal will be around $1 million. The business division was identified correctly as 'held for sale' and was presented as a disposal group in the statement of financial position as at 30 November 20X3. At the initial classification of the division as held for sale, its net carrying amount was $90 million. In writing down the disposal group's carrying amount, Havanna accounted for an impairment loss of $30 million which represented the difference between the carrying amount and value of the assets measured in accordance with applicable International Financial Reporting Standards (IFRS).

Required

Advise the directors how to account for the disposal group in the financial statements for the year ended 30 November 20X3.   **(5 marks)**

(c)   Havanna has decided to sell its main office building to a third party for $5 million and lease it back on a ten-year lease. The current fair value of the property is $5 million and the carrying amount of the asset is $4.2 million. The present value of the lease payments has been calculated as $3.85 million. The remaining useful life of the building is 15 years. The transaction constitutes a sale in accordance with IFRS 15 *Revenue from Contracts with Customers*. The CEO of Havanna believes this represents a very good deal for Havanna and has told you that the profit on disposal of $0.8 million must be reported in the statement of profit or loss as it will help to ensure that the company meets the covenants imposed by the bank in respect of Havanna's interest cover ratio. He reminded you that you are new to your role and that recording a profit on this transaction will be of benefit to your future success and the business as a whole.

(i) Advise the directors of Havanna on how to account for this sale at the start of the lease, including any gain on the sale, with reference to the principles of relevant IFRSs. **(5 marks)**

(ii) Comment on the effect of the transaction on Havanna's interest cover ratio and briefly discuss the impact on bank covenants of the introduction of IFRS 16 *Leases*. **(3 marks)**

(iii) In your role as financial controller, prepare notes for a discussion with Havanna's whistleblowing helpline in respect of any potential ethical issues that arise from the above scenario, with reference to ACCA's *Code of Ethics and Conduct*. **(2 marks)**

(Total = 25 marks)

30 Alexandra

49 mins

Alexandra, a public limited company, designs and manages business solutions and infrastructures.

(a) In November 20X0, Alexandra defaulted on an interest payment on an issued bond loan of $100 million repayable in 20X5. The loan agreement stipulates that such default leads to an obligation to repay the whole of the loan immediately, including accrued interest and expenses. The bondholders, however, issued a waiver postponing the interest payment until 31 May 20X1. On 17 May 20X1, Alexandra felt that a further waiver was required, so requested a meeting of the bondholders and agreed a further waiver of the interest payment to 5 July 20X1, when Alexandra was confident it could make the payments. Alexandra classified the loan as long-term debt in its statement of financial position at 30 April 20X1 on the basis that the loan was not in default at the end of the reporting period as the bondholders had issued waivers and had not sought redemption.

Required

(i) Explain, with reference to the principles of relevant IFRSs, the appropriate accounting treatment for the above issue in Alexandra's financial statements for the year ended 30 April 20X1. **(5 marks)**

(ii) Discuss, in respect of the above issue, any ethical implications and any potential impact on the analysis of Alexandra's financial statements by its investors. **(5 marks)**

(b) Alexandra enters into contracts with both customers and suppliers. The supplier solves system problems and provides new releases and updates for software. Alexandra provides maintenance services for its customers. In previous years, Alexandra recognised revenue and related costs on software maintenance contracts when the customer was invoiced, which was at the beginning of the contract period. Contracts typically run for two years.

During 20X0, Alexandra had acquired Xavier Co, which recognised revenue, derived from a similar type of maintenance contract as Alexandra, on a straight-line basis over the term of the contract. Alexandra considered both its own and the policy of Xavier Co to comply with the requirements of IFRS 15 *Revenue from Contracts with Customers* but it decided to adopt the practice of Xavier Co for itself and the group. Alexandra concluded that the two recognition methods did not, in substance, represent two different accounting policies and did not, therefore, consider adoption of the new practice to be a change in policy.

In the year to 30 April 20X1, Alexandra recognised revenue (and the related costs) on a straight-line basis over the contract term, treating this as a change in an accounting estimate. As a result, revenue and cost of sales were adjusted, reducing the year's profits by some $6 million.

Required

Explain, with reference to the principles of relevant IFRSs, the appropriate accounting treatment for the above issue in Alexandra's financial statements for the year ended 30 April 20X1. **(5 marks)**

(c)   Alexandra has a two-tier board structure consisting of a management and a supervisory board. Alexandra remunerates its board members as follows:

- Annual base salary
- Variable annual compensation (bonus)
- Share options

In the consolidated financial statements, within the related parties note under IAS 24 *Related Party Disclosures*, Alexandra disclosed the total remuneration paid to directors and a total for each of these boards. No further breakdown of the remuneration was provided.

The management board comprises both the executive and non-executive directors. The remuneration of the non-executive directors, however, was not included in the key management disclosures as the board believed the amounts involved to be immaterial. Some members of the supervisory and management boards are of a particular nationality. Alexandra was of the opinion that in that jurisdiction, it is not acceptable to provide information about remuneration that could be traced back to individuals. Consequently, the finance director of Alexandra explained that the board had instructed him to provide the related party information in the annual report in an ambiguous way to prevent users of the financial statements from tracing remuneration information back to specific individuals.

Required

(i)   Explain, with reference to the principles of relevant IFRSs, how the transactions above should be dealt with in Alexandra's financial statements, and the reasons why this treatment is important to investors.   **(7 marks)**

(ii)   Discuss any ethical issues arising in relation to this scenario.   **(3 marks)**

(Total = 25 marks)

31 Verge   **49 mins**

P2 6/13, amended

(a)   In its annual financial statements for the year ended 31 March 20X3, Verge, a public limited company, had identified the following operating segments.

(i)   Segment 1 local train operations
(ii)   Segment 2 inter-city train operations
(iii)   Segment 3 railway constructions

The company disclosed two reportable segments. Segments 1 and 2 were aggregated into a single reportable operating segment. Operating segments 1 and 2 have been aggregated on the basis of their similar business characteristics, and the nature of their products and services. In the local train market, it is the local transport authority which awards the contract and pays Verge for its services. In the local train market, contracts are awarded following a competitive tender process, and the ticket prices paid by passengers are set by and paid to the transport authority. In the inter-city train market, ticket prices are set by Verge and the passengers pay Verge for the service provided.   **(6 marks)**

(b)   Verge entered into a contract with a government body on 1 April 20X1 to undertake maintenance services on a new railway line. The total revenue from the contract is $5 million over a three-year period. The contract states that $1 million will be paid at the commencement of the contract but although invoices will be subsequently sent at the end of each year, the government authority will only settle the subsequent amounts owing when the contract is completed. The invoices sent by Verge to date (including $1 million above) were as follows:

Year ended 31 March 20X2 $2.8 million
Year ended 31 March 20X3 $1.2 million

The balance will be invoiced on 31 March 20X4. Verge has only accounted for the initial payment in the financial statements to 31 March 20X2 as no subsequent amounts are to be paid until 31 March 20X4. The amounts of the invoices reflect the work undertaken in the period. Verge wishes to know how to account for the revenue on the contract in the financial statements to date.

The interest rate that would be used in a separate financing transaction between Verge and the government agency is 6%. This reflects the credit characteristics of the government agency.

(6 marks)

(c) In February 20X2, an inter-city train did what appeared to be superficial damage to a storage facility of a local company. The directors of the company expressed an intention to sue Verge but in the absence of legal proceedings, Verge had not recognised a provision in its financial statements to 31 March 20X2. In July 20X2, Verge received notification for damages of $1.2 million, which was based upon the estimated cost to repair the building. The local company claimed the building was much more than a storage facility as it was a valuable piece of architecture which had been damaged to a greater extent than was originally thought. The head of legal services advised Verge that the company was clearly negligent but the view obtained from an expert was that the value of the building was $800,000. Verge had an insurance policy that would cover the first $200,000 of such claims. After the financial statements for the year ended 31 March 20X3 were authorised, the case came to court and the judge determined that the storage facility actually was a valuable piece of architecture. The court ruled that Verge was negligent and awarded $300,000 for the damage to the fabric of the facility. **(6 marks)**

(d) Verge was given a building by a private individual in February 20X2. The benefactor included a condition that it must be brought into use as a train museum in the interests of the local community or the asset (or a sum equivalent to the fair value of the asset) must be returned. The fair value of the asset was $1.5 million in February 20X2. Verge took possession of the building in May 20X2. However, it could not utilise the building in accordance with the condition until February 20X3 as the building needed some refurbishment and adaptation and in order to fulfil the condition. Verge spent $1 million on refurbishment and adaptation.

On 1 July 20X2, Verge obtained a cash grant of $250,000 from the government. Part of the grant related to the creation of 20 jobs at the train museum by providing a subsidy of $5,000 per job created. The remainder of the grant related to capital expenditure on the project. At 31 March 20X3, all of the new jobs had been created. **(7 marks)**

Required

Advise Verge on how the above accounting issues should be dealt with in its financial statements for the years ending 31 March 20X2 (where applicable) and 31 March 20X3.

Note. The mark allocation is shown against each of the four issues above.

(Total = 25 marks)

32 Formatt   49 mins

(a) On 30 November 20X4, Formatt loaned $8 million to a third party at an agreed interest rate. At the same time, it sold the third party loan to Window whereby, in exchange for an immediate cash payment of $7 million, Formatt agreed to pay to Window the first $7 million plus interest collected from the third party loan. Formatt retained the right to $1 million plus interest. The 12-month expected credit losses are $300,000 and Formatt has agreed to suffer all credit losses. A receivable of $1 million has been recognised in the financial statements at 30 November 20X4. As a result of the agreement with Window, the directors of Formatt are unsure as to whether they should recognise any part of the interest bearing loan of $8 million in the statement of financial position at 30 November 20X4. They understand that the *Conceptual Framework* and the ED/2015/3: *Conceptual Framework for Financial Reporting*

both mention 'control' as one of the criteria for recognition of an asset but do not understand the interaction between the *Conceptual Framework* and IFRS 9 *Financial Instruments* as regards the recognition of a financial asset.

Required

Advise the directors of Formatt on how the above arrangement should be dealt with in its financial statements with reference to relevant IFRSs and pronouncements on the *Conceptual Framework*. **(8 marks)**

(b) Formatt has a subsidiary, Key, which has a significant amount of non-current assets. There are specific assets on which the directors of Key wish to seek advice.

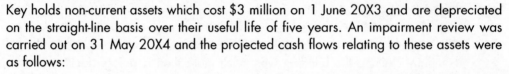

(i) Key holds non-current assets which cost $3 million on 1 June 20X3 and are depreciated on the straight-line basis over their useful life of five years. An impairment review was carried out on 31 May 20X4 and the projected cash flows relating to these assets were as follows:

Year to	31 May 20X5	31 May 20X6	31 May 20X7	31 May 20X8
Cash flows ($'000)	280	450	500	550

The company used a discount rate of 5%. At 30 November 20X4, the directors used the same cash flow projections and noticed that the resultant value in use was above the carrying amount of the assets and wished to reverse any impairment loss calculated at 31 May 20X4. The government has indicated that it may compensate the company for any loss in value of the assets up to 20% of the impairment loss.

(ii) Key holds a non-current asset, which was purchased for $10 million on 1 December 20X1 with an expected useful life of ten years. On 1 December 20X3, it was revalued to $8.8 million. At 30 November 20X4, the asset was reviewed for impairment and written down to its recoverable amount of $5.5 million.

(iii) Key committed itself at the beginning of the financial year to selling a property that is being under-utilised following the economic downturn. As a result of the economic downturn, the property was not sold by the end of the year. The asset was actively marketed but there were no reasonable offers to purchase the asset. Key is hoping that the economic downturn will change in the future and therefore has not reduced the price of the asset.

Required

Discuss, with suitable computations and reference to the principles of relevant IFRSs, how to account for any potential impairment of the above non-current assets in Key's individual financial statements for the year ended 30 November 20X4.

(17 marks)

Note. The following 5% discount factors may be relevant.

Year 1	0.9524
Year 2	0.9070
Year 3	0.8638
Year 4	0.8227

(Total = 25 marks)

33 Emcee
49 mins

P2 Mar/Jun 16, amended

Emcee, a public limited company, is a sports organisation which owns several football and basketball teams. It has a financial year end of 31 May 20X6.

(a) Emcee needs a new stadium to host sporting events which will be included as part of Emcee's property, plant and equipment. Emcee commenced construction of a new stadium on 1 February 20X6, and this continued until its completion which was after the year end of 31 May 20X6. The direct costs were $20 million in February 20X6 and then $50 million in each month until the year end. Emcee has not taken out any specific borrowings to finance the construction of the stadium, but it has incurred finance costs on its general borrowings during the period, which could have been avoided if the stadium had not been constructed. Emcee has calculated that the weighted average cost of borrowings for the period 1 February to 31 May 20X6 on an annualised basis amounted to 9% per annum. Emcee needs advice on how to treat the borrowing costs in its financial statements for the year ended 31 May 20X6.

(6 marks)

(b) Emcee purchases and sells players' registrations on a regular basis. Emcee must purchase registrations for that player to play for the club. Player registrations are contractual obligations between the player and Emcee. The costs of acquiring player registrations include transfer fees, league levy fees, and player agents' fees incurred by the club. Often players' former clubs are paid amounts which are contingent upon the performance of the player whilst they play for Emcee. For example, if a contracted basketball player scores an average of more than 20 points per game in a season, then an additional $5 million may become payable to his former club. Also, players' contracts can be extended and this incurs additional costs for Emcee.

At the end of every season, which also is the financial year end of Emcee, the club reviews its playing staff and makes decisions as to whether they wish to sell any players' registrations. These registrations are actively marketed by circulating other clubs with a list of players' registrations and their estimated selling price. Players' registrations are also sold during the season, often with performance conditions attached. Occasionally, it becomes clear that a player will not play for the club again because of, for example, a player sustaining a career threatening injury or being permanently removed from the playing squad for another reason. The playing registrations of certain players were sold after the year end, for total proceeds, net of associated costs, of $25 million. These registrations had a net book value of $7 million.

Emcee would like to know the financial reporting treatment of the acquisition, extension, review and sale of players' registrations in the circumstances outlined above. **(11 marks)**

(c) Emcee uses the revaluation model to measure its stadiums. The directors have been offered $100 million from an airline for the property naming rights of all the stadiums for three years. There are two directors who are on the management boards of Emcee and the airline. Additionally, there are regulations in place by both the football and basketball leagues which regulate the financing of the clubs. These regulations prevent capital contributions from a related party which 'increases equity without repayment in return'. The aim of these regulations is to promote sustainable business models. Sanctions imposed by the regulator include fines and withholding of prize monies. Emcee wishes to know how to take account of the naming rights in the valuation of the stadium and the potential implications of the financial regulations imposed by the leagues. **(8 marks)**

Required

Discuss how the above events would be shown in the financial statements of Emcee under International Financial Reporting Standards.

Note. The mark allocation is shown against each of the three issues above.

(Total = 25 marks)

34 Scramble

Scramble, a public limited company, is a developer of online computer games.

(a) At 30 November 20X1, 65% of Scramble's total assets were mainly represented by internally developed intangible assets comprising the capitalised costs of the development and production of online computer games. These games generate all of Scramble's revenue. The costs incurred in relation to maintaining the games at the same standard of performance are expensed to profit or loss for the year. The accounting policy note states that intangible assets are valued at historical cost. Scramble considers the games to have an indefinite useful life, which is reconsidered annually when the intangible assets are tested for impairment. Scramble determines value in use using the estimated future cash flows which include maintenance expenses, capital expenses incurred in developing different versions of the games and the expected increase in revenue resulting from the cash outflows mentioned above. Scramble does not conduct an analysis or investigation of differences between expected and actual cash flows. Tax effects were also taken into account. **(7 marks)**

(b) Scramble has two cash generating units (CGU) which hold 90% of the internally developed intangible assets. Scramble reported a consolidated net loss for the period and an impairment charge in respect of the two CGUs representing 63% of the consolidated profit before tax and 29% of the total costs in the period. The recoverable amount of the CGUs is defined, in this case, as value in use. Specific discount rates are not directly available from the market, and Scramble estimates the discount rates, using its weighted average cost of capital. In calculating the cost of debt as an input to the determination of the discount rate, Scramble used the risk-free rate adjusted by the company specific average credit spread of its outstanding debt, which had been raised two years previously. As Scramble did not have any need for additional financing and did not need to repay any of the existing loans before 20X4, Scramble did not see any reason for using a different discount rate. Scramble did not disclose either the events or circumstances that led to the recognition of the impairment loss or the amount of the loss recognised in respect of each cash-generating unit. Scramble felt that the events and circumstances that led to the recognition of a loss in respect of the first CGU were common knowledge in the market and the events and the circumstances that led to the recognition loss of the second CGU were not needed to be disclosed. **(8 marks)**

(c) Scramble wished to diversify its operations and purchased a professional football club, Rashing. In Rashing's financial statements for the year ended 30 November 20X1, it was proposed to include significant intangible assets which related to acquired players' registration rights comprising registration and agents' fees. The agents' fees were paid by the club to players' agents either when a player is transferred to the club or when the contract of a player is extended. Scramble believes that the registration rights of the players are intangible assets but that the agent's fees do not meet the criteria to be recognised as intangible assets as they are not directly attributable to the costs of players' contracts. Additionally, Rashing has purchased the rights to 25% of the revenue from ticket sales generated by another football club, Santash, in a different league. Rashing does not sell these tickets nor has any discretion over the pricing of the tickets. Rashing wishes to show these rights as intangible assets in its financial statements. **(10 marks)**

Required

Discuss the validity of the accounting treatments proposed by Scramble in its financial statements for the year ended 30 November 20X1.

Note. The mark allocation is shown against each of the three accounting treatments above.

(Total = 25 marks)

35 Estoil

49 mins

P2 12/14

(a) An assessment of accounting practices for asset impairments is especially important in the context of financial reporting quality in that it requires the exercise of considerable management judgement and reporting discretion. The importance of this issue is heightened during periods of ongoing economic uncertainty as a result of the need for companies to reflect the loss of economic value in a timely fashion through the mechanism of asset write-downs. There are many factors which can affect the quality of impairment accounting and disclosures. These factors include changes in circumstance in the reporting period, the market capitalisation of the entity, the allocation of goodwill to cash generating units, valuation issues and the nature of the disclosures.

Required

Discuss the importance and significance of the above factors when conducting an impairment test under IAS 36 *Impairment of Assets*. **(15 marks)**

(b) (i) Estoil is an international company providing parts for the automotive industry. It operates in many different jurisdictions with different currencies. During 20X4, Estoil experienced financial difficulties marked by a decline in revenue, a reorganisation and restructuring of the business and it reported a loss for the year. An impairment test of goodwill was performed but no impairment was recognised. Estoil applied one discount rate to all cash flows for all cash generating units (CGUs), irrespective of the currency in which the cash flows would be generated. The discount rate used was the weighted average cost of capital (WACC) and Estoil used the 10-year government bond rate for its jurisdiction as the risk-free rate in this calculation. Additionally, Estoil built its model using a forecast denominated in the functional currency of the parent company. Estoil felt that any other approach would require a level of detail which was unrealistic and impracticable. Estoil argued that the different CGUs represented different risk profiles in the short term, but over a longer business cycle, there was no basis for claiming that their risk profiles were different.

(ii) Fariole specialises in the communications sector with three main CGUs. Goodwill was a significant component of total assets. Fariole performed an impairment test of the CGUs. The cash flow projections were based on the most recent financial budgets approved by management. The realised cash flows for the CGUs were negative in 20X4 and far below budgeted cash flows for that period. The directors had significantly raised cash flow forecasts for 20X5 with little justification. The projected cash flows were calculated by adding back depreciation charges to the budgeted result for the period with expected changes in working capital and capital expenditure not taken into account.

Required

Discuss the acceptability of the above accounting practices under IAS 36 *Impairment of Assets*. **(10 marks)**

(Total = 25 marks)

36 Evolve

49 mins

P2 Sep/Dec 16, amended

(a) Evolve is a real estate company, which is listed on the stock exchange and has a year end of 31 August. On 21 August 20X6, Evolve undertook a scrip (bonus) issue where the shareholders of Evolve received certain rights. The shareholders are able to choose between:

(i) Receiving newly issued shares of Evolve, which could be traded on 30 September 20X6; or

(ii) Transferring their rights back to Evolve by 10 September 20X6 for a fixed cash price which would be paid on 20 September 20X6.

In the financial statements at 31 August 20X6, Evolve believed that the criteria for the recognition of a financial liability as regards the second option were not met at 31 August 20X6 because it was impossible to reliably determine the full amount to be paid, until 10 September 20X6. Evolve felt that the transferring of the rights back to Evolve was a put option on its own equity, which would lead to recording changes in fair value in profit or loss in the next financial year. Evolve disclosed the transaction as a non-adjusting event after the reporting period. **(9 marks)**

(b) At 31 August 20X6, Evolve controlled a wholly owned subsidiary, Resource, whose only assets were land and buildings, which were all measured in accordance with International Financial Reporting Standards. On 1 August 20X6, Evolve published a statement stating that a binding offer for the sale of Resource had been made and accepted and, at that date, the sale was expected to be completed by 31 August 20X6. The non-current assets of Resource were measured at the lower of their carrying amount or fair value less costs to sell at 31 August 20X6, based on the selling price in the binding offer. This measurement was in accordance with IFRS 5 *Non-Current Assets Held for Sale and Discontinued Operations*. However, Evolve did not classify the non-current assets of Resource as held for sale in the financial statements at 31 August 20X6 because there were uncertainties regarding the negotiations with the buyer and a risk that the agreement would not be finalised. There was no disclosure of these uncertainties and the original agreement was finalised on 20 September 20X6. **(10 marks)**

(c) Evolve operates in a jurisdiction with a specific tax regime for listed real estate companies. Upon adoption of this tax regime, the entity has to pay a single tax payment based on the unrealised gains of its investment properties. Evolve purchased Monk whose only asset was an investment property for $10 million. The purchase price of Monk was below the market value of the investment property, which was $14 million, and Evolve chose to account for the investment property under the cost model. However, Evolve considered that the transaction constituted a 'bargain purchase' under IFRS 3 *Business Combinations*. As a result, Evolve accounted for the potential gain of $4 million in profit or loss and increased the 'cost' of the investment property to $14 million. At the same time, Evolve opted for the specific tax regime for the newly acquired investment property and agreed to pay the corresponding tax of $1 million. Evolve considered that the tax payment qualifies as an expenditure necessary to bring the property to the condition necessary for its operations, and therefore was directly attributable to the acquisition of the property. Hence, the tax payment was capitalised and the value of the investment property was stated at $15 million. **(6 marks)**

Required

Advise Evolve on how the above transactions should be correctly dealt with in its financial statements with reference to relevant International Financial Reporting Standards.

Note. The mark allocation is shown against each of the three issues above.

(Total = 25 marks)

37 Gasnature
49 mins

P2 Sep/Dec 15, amended

(a) Gasnature is a publicly traded entity involved in the production and trading of natural gas and oil. Gasnature jointly owns an underground storage facility with another entity, Gogas. Both parties extract gas from offshore gas fields, which they own and operate independently from each other. Gasnature owns 55% of the underground facility and Gogas owns 45%. They have agreed to share services and costs accordingly, with decisions regarding the storage facility requiring unanimous agreement of the parties. The underground facility is pressurised so that the gas is pushed out when extracted. When the gas pressure is reduced to a certain level, the remaining gas is irrecoverable and remains in the underground storage facility until it is decommissioned. Local legislation requires the decommissioning of the storage facility at the end of its useful life. Gasnature wishes to know how to treat the agreement with Gogas including any obligation or possible obligation arising on the underground storage facility and the accounting for the irrecoverable gas. **(9 marks)**

(b) Gasnature has entered into a ten-year contract with Agas for the purchase of natural gas. Gasnature has made an advance payment to Agas for an amount equal to the total quantity of gas contracted for ten years which has been calculated using the forecasted price of gas. The advance carries interest of 6% per annum, which is settled by way of the supply of extra gas. Fixed quantities of gas have to be supplied each month and there is a price adjustment mechanism in the contract whereby the difference between the forecasted price of gas and the prevailing market price is settled in cash monthly. If Agas does not deliver gas as agreed, Gasnature has the right to claim compensation at the current market price of gas. Gasnature wishes to know whether the contract with Agas should be accounted for under IFRS 9 *Financial Instruments*. **(6 marks)**

(c) Additionally, Gasnature is finalising its financial statements for the year ended 31 August 20X5 and has the following issues.

   (i) Gasnature purchased a major refinery on 1 January 20X5 and the directors estimate that a major overhaul is required every two years. The costs of the overhaul are approximately $5 million which comprises $3 million for parts and equipment and $2 million for labour. The directors proposed to accrue the cost of the overhaul over the two years of operations up to that date and create a provision for the expenditure. **(5 marks)**

   (ii) From October 20X4, Gasnature had undertaken exploratory drilling to find gas and up to 31 August 20X5 costs of $5 million had been incurred. At 31 August 20X5, the results to date indicated that it was probable that there were sufficient economic benefits to carry on drilling and there were no indicators of impairment. During September 20X5, additional drilling costs of $2 million were incurred and there was significant evidence that no commercial deposits existed and the drilling was abandoned. **(5 marks)**

Required

Discuss, with reference to International Financial Reporting Standards, how Gasnature should account for the above agreement and contract, and the issues raised by the directors

Note. The mark allocation is shown against each of the items above.

(Total = 25 marks)

38 Blackcutt

P2 12/12, amended

Blackcutt is a local government organisation whose financial statements are prepared using International Financial Reporting Standards.

(a) Blackcutt wishes to create a credible investment property portfolio with a view to determining if any property may be considered surplus to the functional objectives and requirements of the local government organisation. The following portfolio of property is owned by Blackcutt.

Blackcutt owns several plots of land. Some of the land is owned by Blackcutt for capital appreciation and this may be sold at any time in the future. Other plots of land have no current purpose as Blackcutt has not determined whether it will use the land to provide services such as those provided by national parks or for short-term sale in the ordinary course of operations.

The local government organisation supplements its income by buying and selling property. The housing department regularly sells part of its housing inventory in the ordinary course of its operations as a result of changing demographics. Part of the inventory, which is not held for sale, is to provide housing to low-income employees at below market rental. The rent paid by employees covers the cost of maintenance of the property.   **(8 marks)**

(b)   Blackcutt has outsourced its waste collection to a private sector provider called Waste and Co and pays an annual amount to Waste and Co for its services. Waste and Co purchases the vehicles and uses them exclusively for Blackcutt's waste collection. The vehicles are painted with the Blackcutt local government organisation name and colours. Blackcutt can use the vehicles and the vehicles are used for waste collection for nearly all of the asset's life. If a vehicle breaks down or no longer functions, Waste and Co must provide replacement vehicles fitted with the same waste disposal containers and equipment and painted with the local government organisations name and colours.   **(6 marks)**

(c)   Blackcutt owns a warehouse. Chemco has leased the warehouse from Blackcutt and is using it as a storage facility for chemicals. The national government has announced its intention to enact environmental legislation requiring property owners to accept liability for environmental pollution. As a result, Blackcutt has introduced a hazardous chemical policy and has begun to apply the policy to its properties. Blackcutt has had a report that the chemicals have contaminated the land surrounding the warehouse. Blackcutt has no recourse against Chemco or its insurance company for the clean-up costs of the pollution. At 30 November 20X6, it is virtually certain that draft legislation requiring a clean up of land already contaminated will be enacted shortly after the year end.   **(4 marks)**

(d)   On 1 December 20X0, Blackcutt opened a school at a cost of $5 million. The estimated useful life of the school was 25 years. On 30 November 20X6, the school was closed because numbers using the school declined unexpectedly. The school is to be converted for use as a library, and there is no expectation that the building will be reopened for use as a school. The current replacement cost for a library of equivalent size to the school is $2.1 million. Because of the nature of the non-current asset, value-in-use and net selling price are unrealistic estimates of the value of the school. The change in use would have no effect on the estimated life of the building.   **(7 marks)**

Required

Discuss how the above events should be accounted for in the financial statements of Blackcutt.

Note. The mark allocation is shown against each of the four events above.

(Total = 25 marks)

39 Lockfine   49 mins

P2 6/11, amended

Lockfine, a public limited company, operates in the fishing industry and has recently made the transition to International Financial Reporting Standards (IFRS). Lockfine's reporting date is 30 April 20X9.

(a)   In the IFRS opening statement of financial position at 1 May 20X7, Lockfine elected to measure its fishing fleet at fair value and use that fair value as deemed cost in accordance with IFRS 1 *First Time Adoption of International Financial Reporting Standards*. The fair value was an estimate based on valuations provided by two independent selling agents, both of whom provided a range of values within which the valuation might be considered acceptable. Lockfine calculated fair value at the average of the highest amounts in the two ranges provided. One of the agents' valuations was not supported by any description of the method adopted or the assumptions underlying the calculation. Valuations were principally based on discussions with various potential buyers. Lockfine wished to know the principles behind the use of deemed cost and whether agents' estimates were a reliable form of evidence on which to base the fair value calculation of tangible assets to be then adopted as deemed cost.

(6 marks)

(b) Lockfine was unsure as to whether it could elect to apply IFRS 3 *Business Combinations* retrospectively to past business combinations on a selective basis, because there was no purchase price allocation available for certain business combinations in its opening IFRS statement of financial position.

As a result of a major business combination, fishing rights of that combination were included as part of goodwill. The rights could not be recognised as a separately identifiable intangible asset at acquisition under the local GAAP because a reliable value was unobtainable for the rights. The fishing rights operated for a specified period of time.

On transition from local GAAP to IFRS, the fishing rights were included in goodwill and not separately identified because they did not meet the qualifying criteria set out in IFRS 1, even though it was known that the fishing rights had a finite life and would be fully impaired or amortised over the period specified by the rights. Lockfine wished to amortise the fishing rights over their useful life and calculate any impairment of goodwill as two separate calculations.

(6 marks)

(c) Lockfine has internally developed intangible assets comprising the capitalised expenses of the acquisition and production of electronic map data which indicates the main fishing grounds in the world. The intangible assets generate revenue for the company in their use by the fishing fleet and are a material asset in the statement of financial position. Lockfine had constructed a database of the electronic maps. The costs incurred in bringing the information about a certain region of the world to a higher standard of performance are capitalised. The costs related to maintaining the information about a certain region at that same standard of performance are expensed. Lockfine's accounting policy states that intangible assets are valued at historical cost. The company considers the database to have an indefinite useful life which is reconsidered annually when it is tested for impairment. The reasons supporting the assessment of an indefinite useful life were not disclosed in the financial statements and neither did the company disclose how it satisfied the criteria for recognising an intangible asset arising from development. **(7 marks)**

(d) The Lockfine board has agreed two restructuring projects during the year to 30 April 20X9:

Plan A involves selling 50% of its off-shore fleet in one year's time. Additionally, the plan is to make 40% of its seamen redundant. Lockfine will carry out further analysis before deciding which of its fleets and related employees will be affected. In previous announcements to the public, Lockfine has suggested that it may restructure the off-shore fleet in the future.

Plan B involves the reorganisation of the headquarters in 18 months' time, and includes the redundancy of 20% of the headquarters' workforce. The company has made announcements before the year end but there was a three month consultation period which ended just after the year end, whereby Lockfine was negotiating with employee representatives. Thus individual employees had not been notified by the year end.

Lockfine proposes recognising a provision in respect of Plan A but not Plan B. **(6 marks)**

Required

Discuss the principles and practices to be used by Lockfine in accounting for the above valuation and recognition issues.

Note. The mark allocation is shown against each of the four items above.

(Total = 25 marks)

40 Coatmin

P2 12/14, amended

(a)   Coatmin is a government-controlled bank. Coatmin was taken over by the government during a financial crisis in the country in which it operates. Coatmin does not directly trade with other government-controlled banks but has underwritten the development of the nationally owned railway and postal service. The directors of Coatmin are concerned about the volume and cost of disclosing its related party interests because they extend theoretically to all other government-controlled enterprises and banks. They wish general advice on the nature and importance of the disclosure of related party relationships and specific advice on the disclosure of the above relationships in the financial statements.   **(5 marks)**

(b)   At the start of the financial year to 30 November 20X3, Coatmin gave a financial guarantee contract on behalf of one of its subsidiaries, a charitable organisation, committing it to repay the principal amount of $60 million if the subsidiary defaulted on any payments due under a loan. The loan related to the financing of the construction of new office premises and has a term of three years. It is being repaid by equal annual instalments of principal with the first payment having been paid. Coatmin has not secured any compensation in return for giving the guarantee, but assessed that it had a fair value of $1.2 million. The guarantee is measured at fair value through profit or loss. The guarantee was given on the basis that it was probable that it would not be called upon. At 30 November 20X4, Coatmin became aware of the fact that the subsidiary was having financial difficulties with the result that it has not paid the second instalment of principal. It is assessed that it is probable that the guarantee will now be called. However, just before the signing of the financial statements for the year ended 30 November 20X4, the subsidiary secured a donation which enabled it to make the second repayment before the guarantee was called upon. It is now anticipated that the subsidiary will be able to meet the final payment. Discounting is immaterial and the fair value of the guarantee is higher than amount of the loss allowance determined in accordance with the IFRS 9 rules on expected credit losses. Coatmin wishes to know the principles behind accounting for the above guarantee under IFRS and how the transaction would be accounted for in the financial records.   **(8 marks)**

(c)   Coatmin's creditworthiness has been worsening but it has entered into an interest rate swap agreement which acts as a hedge against a $2 million 2% bond issue which matures on 31 May 20X6. Coatmin wishes to know the circumstances in which it can use hedge accounting. In particular, it needs advice on hedge effectiveness and whether this can be calculated.   **(8 marks)**

(d)   Coatmin provides loans to customers and funds the loans by selling bonds in the market. The liability is designated as at fair value through profit or loss. The bonds have a fair value decrease of $50 million in the year to 30 November 20X4 of which $5 million relates to the reduction in Coatmin's creditworthiness. The directors of Coatmin would like advice on how to account for this movement.   **(4 marks)**

Required

Discuss, with suitable calculations where necessary, the accounting treatment of the above transactions in the financial statements of Coatmin.

Note. The mark allocation is shown against each of the items above.

(Total = 25 marks)

41 Avco
49 mins

P2 6/14, amended

(a) The difference between debt and equity in an entity's statement of financial position is not easily distinguishable for preparers of financial statements. Some financial instruments may have both features, which can lead to inconsistency of reporting. The International Accounting Standards Board (IASB) has agreed that greater clarity may be required in its definitions of assets and liabilities for debt instruments. It is thought that defining the nature of liabilities would help the IASB's thinking on the difference between financial instruments classified as equity and liabilities.

Required

(i) Discuss the key classification differences between debt and equity under International Financial Reporting Standards.

Note. Examples should be given to illustrate your answer. **(10 marks)**

(ii) Explain why it is important for entities to understand the impact of the classification of a financial instrument as debt or equity in the financial statements. **(5 marks)**

(b) The directors of Avco, a public limited company, are reviewing the financial statements of two entities which are acquisition targets, Cavor and Lidan. They have asked for clarification on the treatment of the following financial instruments within the financial statements of the entities.

Cavor has two classes of shares: A and B shares. A shares are Cavor's ordinary shares and are correctly classed as equity. B shares are not mandatorily redeemable shares but contain a call option allowing Cavor to repurchase them. Dividends are payable on the B shares if, and only if, dividends have been paid on the A ordinary shares. The terms of the B shares are such that dividends are payable at a rate equal to that of the A ordinary shares. Additionally, Cavor has also issued share options which give the counterparty rights to buy a fixed number of its B shares for a fixed amount of $10 million. The contract can be settled only by the issuance of shares for cash by Cavor.

Lidan has in issue two classes of shares: A shares and B shares. A shares are correctly classified as equity. Two million B shares of nominal value of $1 each are in issue. The B shares are redeemable in two years' time. Lidan has a choice as to the method of redemption of the B shares. It may either redeem the B shares for cash at their nominal value or it may issue one million A shares in settlement. A shares are currently valued at $10 per share. The lowest price for Lidan's A shares since its formation has been $5 per share.

Required

Discuss whether the above arrangements regarding the B shares of each of Cavor and Lidan should be treated as liabilities or equity in the financial statements of the respective issuing companies. **(10 marks)**

(Total = 25 marks)

42 Complexity
49 mins

P2 12/09, amended

The definition of a financial instrument captures a wide variety of assets and liabilities including cash, evidence of an ownership interest in an entity, or a contractual right to receive or deliver cash or another financial instrument. Preparers, auditors and users of financial statements have found the requirements for reporting financial assets and liabilities to be very complex, problematic and sometimes subjective. It is important that a standard in this area should allow users to understand the economic substance of the transaction and preparers to properly apply generally accepted accounting principles.

Required

(a) (i)   Discuss, from the perspective of preparers and users of financial statements, how the measurement of financial instruments under International Financial Reporting Standards can create confusion and complexity. **(10 marks)**

(ii) Set out the reasons why using fair value to measure all financial instruments may result in less complexity in accounting for financial instruments, but may lead to uncertainty in financial statements. **(10 marks)**

(b) A company borrowed $47 million on 1 December 20X4 when the market and effective interest rate was 5%. On 30 November 20X5, the company borrowed an additional $45 million when the current market and effective interest rate was 7.4%. Both financial liabilities are repayable on 30 November 20X9 and are single payment notes, whereby interest and capital are repaid on that date.

Required

Discuss the accounting for the above financial liabilities under IFRS 9 using amortised cost, and additionally using fair value as at 30 November 20X5. **(5 marks)**

(Total = 25 marks)

43 Seltec   49 mins

P2 6/10, amended

Seltec, a public limited company, processes and sells edible oils and uses several financial instruments to spread the risk of fluctuation in the price of the edible oils. The entity operates in an environment where the transactions are normally denominated in dollars. The functional currency of Seltec is the dollar.

(a) The entity uses forward and futures contracts to protect it against fluctuation in the price of edible oils. Where forwards are used, the company often takes delivery of the edible oil and sells it shortly afterwards. The contracts are constructed with future delivery in mind but the contracts also allow net settlement in cash as an alternative. The net settlement is based on the change in the price of the oil since the start of the contract. Seltec uses the proceeds of a net settlement to purchase a different type of oil or purchase from a different supplier. Where futures are used these sometimes relate to edible oils of a different type and market than those of Seltec's own inventory of edible oil. The company intends to apply hedge accounting to these contracts in order to protect itself from earnings volatility. Seltec has also entered into a long-term arrangement to buy oil from a foreign entity whose currency is the dinar. The commitment stipulates that the fixed purchase price will be denominated in pounds sterling.

Seltec is unsure as to the nature of derivatives and hedge accounting techniques and has asked your advice on how the above financial instruments should be dealt with in the financial statements. **(15 marks)**

(b) Seltec has decided to enter the retail market and has recently purchased two well-known brand names in the edible oil industry. One of the brand names has been in existence for many years and has a good reputation for quality. The other brand name is named after a famous film star who has been actively promoting the edible oil as being a healthier option than other brands of oil. This type of oil has only been on the market for a short time. Seltec is finding it difficult to estimate the useful life of the brands and therefore intends to treat the brands as having indefinite lives.

In order to sell the oil, Seltec has purchased two limited liability companies from a company that owns several retail outlets. Each entity owns retail outlets in several shopping complexes. The only assets of each entity are the retail outlets. There is no operational activity and at present the entities have no employees.

Seltec is unclear as to how the purchase of the brands and the entities should be accounted for. **(10 marks)**

Required

Discuss the accounting principles involved in accounting for the above transactions and how the above transactions should be treated in the financial statements of Seltec.

Note. The mark allocation is shown against each of the two parts above.

(Total = 25 marks)

44 Carsoon

49 mins

P2 Mar/Jun 17, amended

Carsoon Co is a company which manufactures and retails motor vehicles. It also constructs premises for third parties. It has a year end of 28 February 20X7.

(a)   The entity enters into lease agreements with the public for its motor vehicles. The agreements are normally for a three-year period. The customer decides how to use the vehicle within certain contractual limitations. The maximum mileage per annum is specified at 10,000 miles without penalty. Carsoon is responsible for the maintenance of the vehicle and insists that the vehicle cannot be modified in any way. At the end of the three-year contract, the customer can purchase the vehicle at a price which will be above the market value, or alternatively hand it back to Carsoon. If the vehicle is returned, Carsoon will then sell the vehicle on to the public through one of its retail outlets. These sales of vehicles are treated as investing activities in the statement of cash flows.

The directors of Carsoon wish to know how the leased vehicles should be accounted for, from the commencement of the lease to the final sale of the vehicle, in the financial statements including the statement of cash flows. **(9 marks)**

(b)   On 1 March 20X6, Carsoon invested in a debt instrument with a fair value of $6 million and has assessed that the financial asset is aligned with the fair value through other comprehensive income business model. The instrument has an interest rate of 4% over a period of six years. The effective interest rate is also 4%. On 1 March 20X6, the debt instrument is not impaired in any way. During the year to 28 February 20X7, there was a change in interest rates and the fair value of the instrument seemed to be affected. The instrument was quoted in an active market at $5.3 million but the price based upon an in-house model showed that the fair value of the instrument was $5.5 million. This valuation was based upon the average change in value of a range of instruments across a number of jurisdictions.

The directors of Carsoon felt that the instrument should be valued at $5.5 million and that this should be shown as a Level 1 measurement under IFRS 13 Fair Value Measurement. There has not been a significant increase in credit risk since 1 March 20X6, and expected credit losses should be measured at an amount equal to 12-month expected credit losses of $400,000. Carsoon sold the debt instrument on 1 March 20X7 for $5.3 million.

The directors of Carsoon wish to know how to account for the debt instrument until its sale on 1 March 20X7. **(8 marks)**

(c)   Carsoon constructs retail vehicle outlets and enters into contracts with customers to construct buildings on their land. The contracts have standard terms, which include penalties payable by Carsoon if the contract is delayed, or payable by the customer, if Carsoon cannot gain access to the construction site.

Due to poor weather, one of the projects was delayed. As a result, Carsoon faced additional costs and contractual penalties. As Carsoon could not gain access to the construction site, the directors decided to make a counter-claim against the customer for the penalties and additional costs which Carsoon faced. Carsoon felt that because a counter claim had been made against the customer, the additional costs and penalties should not be included in

contract costs but shown as a contingent liability. Carsoon has assessed the legal basis of the claim and feels it has enforceable rights.

In the year ended 28 February 20X7, Carsoon incurred general and administrative costs of $10 million, and costs relating to wasted materials of $5 million.

Additionally, during the year, Carsoon agreed to construct a storage facility on the same customer's land for $7 million at a cost of $5 million. The parties agreed to modify the contract to include the construction of the storage facility, which was completed during the current financial year. All of the additional costs relating to the above were capitalised as assets in the financial statements.

The directors of Carsoon wish to know how to account for the penalties, counter claim and additional costs in accordance with IFRS 15 *Revenue from Contracts with Customers*.

(8 marks)

Required

Advise Carsoon on how the above transactions should be dealt with in its financial statements with reference to relevant International Financial Reporting Standards.

Note. The mark allocation is shown against each of the three issues above.

(Total = 25 marks)

45 Macaljoy

49 mins

P2 12/07, amended

Macaljoy, a public limited company, is a leading support services company which focuses on the building industry. The company would like advice on how to treat certain items under IAS 19 *Employee Benefits* and IAS 37 *Provisions, Contingent Liabilities and Contingent Assets*. The company operates the Macaljoy Pension Plan B which commenced on 1 November 20X6 and the Macaljoy Pension Plan A, which was closed to new entrants from 31 October 20X6, but which was open to future service accrual for the employees already in the scheme. The assets of the schemes are held separately from those of the company in funds under the control of trustees. The following information relates to the two schemes.

Macaljoy Pension Plan A

The terms of the plan are as follows.

(i)   Employees contribute 6% of their salaries to the plan.

(ii)   Macaljoy contributes, currently, the same amount to the plan for the benefit of the employees.

(iii)   On retirement, employees are guaranteed a pension which is based upon the number of years' service with the company and their final salary.

The following details relate to the plan in the year to 31 October 20X7:

	$m
Present value of obligation at 1 November 20X6	200
Present value of obligation at 31 October 20X7	240
Fair value of plan assets at 1 November 20X6	190
Fair value of plan assets at 31 October 20X7	225
Current service cost	20
Pension benefits paid	19
Total contributions paid to the scheme for year to 31 October 20X7	17

Remeasurement gains and losses are recognised in accordance with IAS 19.

Assume that contributions are paid into the plan and pension benefits are withdrawn from the plan on 31 October 20X7.

56

Macaljoy Pension Plan B

Under the terms of the plan, Macaljoy does not guarantee any return on the contributions paid into the fund. The company's legal and constructive obligation is limited to the amount that is contributed to the fund. The following details relate to this scheme:

	$m
Fair value of plan assets at 31 October 20X7	21
Contributions paid by company for year to 31 October 20X7	10
Contributions paid by employees for year to 31 October 20X7	10

The interest rate on high quality corporate bonds for the two plans are:

1 November 20X6	31 October 20X7
5%	6%

The company would like advice on how to treat the two pension plans, for the year ended 31 October 20X7, together with an explanation of the differences between a defined contribution plan and a defined benefit plan.

Warranties

Additionally, the company manufactures and sells building equipment on which it gives a standard one-year warranty to all customers. The company has extended the warranty to two years for certain major customers and has insured against the cost of the second year of the warranty. The warranty has been extended at nil cost to the customer. The claims made under the extended warranty are made in the first instance against Macaljoy and then Macaljoy in turn makes a counter claim against the insurance company. Past experience has shown that 80% of the building equipment will not be subject to warranty claims in the first year, 15% will have minor defects and 5% will require major repair. Macaljoy estimates that in the second year of the warranty, 20% of the items sold will have minor defects and 10% will require major repair.

In the year to 31 October 20X7, the following information is relevant.

	Standard warranty (units)	Extended warranty (units)	Selling price per unit (both) $
Sales	2,000	5,000	1,000
		Major repair $	Minor defect $
Cost of repair (average)		500	100

Assume that sales of equipment are on 31 October 20X7 and any warranty claims are made on 31 October in the year of the claim. Assume a risk adjusted discount rate of 4%.

Required

Draft a report suitable for presentation to the directors of Macaljoy which:

(a) (i) Discusses the nature of and differences between a defined contribution plan and a defined benefit plan with specific reference to the company's two schemes. **(8 marks)**

(ii) Shows the accounting treatment for the two Macaljoy pension plans for the year ended 31 October 20X7 under IAS 19 *Employee Benefits*. **(8 marks)**

(b) (i) Discusses the principles involved in accounting for claims made under the above warranty provision. **(6 marks)**

(ii) Shows the accounting treatment for the above warranty provision under IAS 37 *Provisions, Contingent Liabilities and Contingent Assets* for the year ended 31 October 20X7. **(3 marks)**

(Total = 25 marks)

46 Panel

ACR 12/05, amended

The directors of Panel, a public limited company, are reviewing the procedures for the calculation of the deferred tax liability for the year ended 31 October 20X5. The directors are unsure how the deferred tax provision will be calculated and have asked for some general advice relating to IAS 12 *Income Taxes*.

The directors wish to know how the provision for deferred taxation would be calculated in the following situations under IAS 12:

(i) *SBP*   On 1 November 20X3, the company had granted ten million share options worth $40 million subject to a two-year vesting period. Local tax law allows a tax deduction at the exercise date of the intrinsic value of the options. The intrinsic value of the ten million share options at 31 October 20X4 was $16 million and at 31 October 20X5 was $46 million. The increase in the share price in the year to 31 October 20X5 could not be foreseen at 31 October 20X4. The options were exercised at 31 October 20X5. The directors are unsure how to account for deferred taxation on this transaction for the years ended 31 October 20X4 and 31 October 20X5.

(ii) *basis*   Panel is leasing plant over a five year period. A right-of-use asset was recorded at the present value of the lease payments of $12 million at the inception of the lease which was 1 November 20X4. The right-of-use asset is depreciated on a straight-line basis over the five years. The annual lease payments are $3 million payable in arrears on 31 October and the effective interest rate is 8% per annum. The directors have not leased an asset before and are unsure as to its treatment for deferred taxation. The company can claim a tax deduction for the annual rental payment as the lease does not qualify for tax relief.

(iii) *PUP*   A wholly owned overseas subsidiary, Pins, a limited liability company, sold goods costing $7 million to Panel on 1 September 20X5, and these goods had not been sold by Panel before the year end. Panel had paid $9 million for these goods. The directors do not understand how this transaction should be dealt with in the financial statements of the subsidiary and the group for taxation purposes. Pins pays tax locally at 30%.

(iv) *Imp*   *C^(w.)*   Nails, a limited liability company, is a wholly owned subsidiary of Panel, and is a cash generating unit in its own right. The value of the property, plant and equipment of Nails at 31 October 20X5 was $6 million and purchased goodwill was $1 million before any impairment loss. The company had no other assets or liabilities. An impairment loss of $1.8 million had occurred at 31 October 20X5. The tax base of the property, plant and equipment of Nails was $4 million as at 31 October 20X5. The directors wish to know how the impairment loss will affect the deferred tax liability for the year. Impairment losses are not an allowable expense for taxation purposes.

Assume a tax rate of 30%.

Required

(a) Explain:

    (i) How IAS 12 *Income Taxes* defines the tax base of assets and liabilities. **(3 marks)**

    (ii) How temporary differences are identified as taxable or deductible temporary differences. **(3 marks)**

    (iii) The general criteria prescribed by IAS 12 for the recognition of deferred tax assets and liabilities. You do **not** need to identify any specific exceptions to these general criteria. **(3 marks)**

(b) Discuss, with suitable computations, how the situations (i) to (iv) above will impact on the accounting for deferred tax under IAS 12 in the consolidated financial statements of Panel.

Note. The situations in (i) to (iv) above carry equal marks. **(16 marks)**

(Total = 25 marks)

47 Kesare

The following statement of financial position relates to Kesare Group, a public limited company, at 30 June 20X6.

	$'000
Assets	
Non-current assets:	
Property, plant and equipment	10,000
Goodwill	6,000
Other intangible assets	5,000
Financial assets (cost)	9,000
	30,000
Current assets	
Trade receivables	7,000
Other receivables	4,600
Cash and cash equivalents	6,700
	18,300
Total assets	48,300
Equity and liabilities	
Equity	
Share capital	9,000
Other reserves	4,500
Retained earnings	9,130
Total equity	22,630
Non-current liabilities	
Long term borrowings	10,000
Deferred tax liability	3,600
Employee benefit liability	4,000
Total non-current liabilities	17,600
Current liabilities	
Current tax liability	3,070
Trade and other payables	5,000
Total current liabilities	8,070
Total liabilities	25,670
Total equity and liabilities	48,300

The following information is relevant to the above statement of financial position:

(i)   The financial assets are classified as 'investments in equity instruments' but are shown in the above statement of financial position at their cost on 1 July 20X5. The market value of the assets is $10.5 million on 30 June 20X6. Taxation is payable on the sale of the assets. As allowed by IFRS 9, an irrevocable election was made for changes in fair value to go through other comprehensive income (not reclassified to profit or loss).

(ii)   The stated interest rate for the long-term borrowing is 8%. The loan of $10 million represents a convertible bond which has a liability component of $9.6 million and an equity component of $0.4 million. The bond was issued on 30 June 20X6.

(iii) The defined benefit plan had a rule change on 30 June 20X6, giving rise to past service costs of $520,000. The past service costs have not been accounted for.

(iv)   The tax bases of the assets and liabilities are the same as their carrying amounts in the draft statement of financial position above as at 30 June 20X6 except for the following:

(1)

	$'000
Property, plant and equipment	2,400
Trade receivables	7,500
Other receivables	5,000
Employee benefits	5,000

(2)   Other intangible assets were development costs which were all allowed for tax purposes when the cost was incurred in 20X5.

(3)   Trade and other payables includes an accrual for compensation to be paid to employees. This amounts to $1 million and is allowed for taxation when paid.

(v)   Goodwill is not allowable for tax purposes in this jurisdiction.

(vi)   Assume taxation is payable at 30%.

Required

(a)   Discuss the conceptual basis for the recognition of deferred taxation using the temporary difference approach to deferred taxation.   **(7 marks)**

(b)   Calculate the deferred tax liability at 30 June 20X6 after any necessary adjustments to the financial statements showing how the deferred tax liability would be dealt with in the financial statements. (Assume that any adjustments do not affect current tax. Candidates should briefly discuss the adjustments required to calculate deferred tax liability.)   **(18 marks)**

(Total = 25 marks)

48 Chemclean   49 mins

P2 Sep/Dec 15, amended

(a)   Chemclean trades in the chemical industry. The entity has development and production operations in various countries. It has entered into an agreement with Jomaster under which Chemclean will licence Jomaster's technology to manufacture a chemical compound, Volut. The technology has a fair value of $4 million. Chemclean cannot use the technology for manufacturing any other compound than Volut. Chemclean has not concluded that economic benefits are likely to flow from this compound but will use Jomaster's technology for a period of three years. Chemclean will have to keep updating the technology in accordance with Jomaster's requirements. The agreement stipulates that Chemclean will make a non-refundable payment of $4 million to Jomaster for access to the technology. Additionally, Jomaster will also receive a 10% royalty from sales of the chemical compound.

Chemclean is also interested in another compound, Yacton, which is being developed by Jomaster. The compound is in the second phase of development. The intellectual property of compound Yacton has been put into a newly formed shell company, Conew, which has no employees. The compound is the only asset of Conew. Chemclean is intending to acquire a 65% interest in Conew, which will give it control over the entity and the compound. Chemclean will provide the necessary resources to develop the compound.   **(10 marks)**

(b)   In the year to 30 June 20X4, Chemclean acquired a major subsidiary. The inventory acquired in this business combination was valued at its fair value at the acquisition date in accordance with IFRS 3 *Business Combinations*. A significant part of the acquired inventory was sold in the post-acquisition period but before 30 June 20X4, the year end.

In the consolidated statement of profit or loss and other comprehensive income, the cost of inventories acquired in the business combination and sold by the acquirer after the business combination was disclosed on two different lines. The inventory was partly shown as cost of goods sold and partly as a 'non-recurring item' within operating income. The part presented under cost of goods sold corresponded to the inventory's carrying amount in the subsidiary's financial statements. The part presented as a 'non-recurring item' corresponded to the fair value increase recognised on the business combination. The 'non-recurring item' amounted to 25% of Chemclean's earnings before interest and tax (EBIT). Chemclean disclosed the accounting policy and explained in the notes to the financial statements that showing the inventory at fair value would result in a fall in the gross margin due to the fair value increase. Further, Chemclean argued that isolating this part of the margin in the 'non-recurring items', whose nature is transparently presented in the notes, enabled the user to evaluate the structural evolution of its gross margin. **(6 marks)**

(c)   In the consolidated financial statements for 20X4, Chemclean recognised a net deferred tax asset of $16 million, which represented 18% of its total equity. This asset was made up of $3 million taxable temporary differences and $19 million relating to the carry-forward of unused tax losses. The local tax regulation allows unused tax losses to be carried forward indefinitely. Chemclean expects that within five years, future taxable profits before tax would be available against which the unused tax losses could be offset. This view was based on the budgets for the years 20X4–20X9. The budgets were primarily based on general assumptions about the development of key products and economic improvement indicators. Additionally, the entity expected a substantial reduction in the future impairment of trade receivables and property which the entity had recently suffered and this would result in a substantial increase in future taxable profit.

Chemclean had recognised material losses during the previous five years, with an average annual loss of $19 million. A comparison of Chemclean's budgeted results for the previous two years to its actual results indicated material differences relating principally to impairment losses. In the interim financial statements for the first half of the year to 30 June 20X4, Chemclean recognised impairment losses equal to budgeted impairment losses for the whole year. In its financial statements for the year ended 30 June 20X4, Chemclean disclosed a material uncertainty about its ability to continue as a going concern. The current tax rate in the jurisdiction is 30%. **(9 marks)**

Required

Discuss how the above items should be dealt with in the financial statements of Chemclean under International Financial Reporting Standards.

Note. The mark allocation is shown against each of the three issues above.

(Total = 25 marks)

49 Ryder   49 mins

ACR 12/05, amended

Ryder, a public limited company, is reviewing the following events which have occurred since its year end of 31 October 20X5. The financial statements were authorised on 12 December 20X5.

(a)   Ryder disposed of a wholly owned subsidiary, Krup, a public limited company, on 10 December 20X5 and made a loss of $9 million on the transaction. As at 31 October 20X5, Ryder had no intention of selling the subsidiary which was material to the group. The directors of Ryder have stated that there were no significant events which have occurred since 31 October 20X5 which could have resulted in a reduction in the value of Krup. The carrying amount of the net assets and purchased goodwill of Krup at 31 October 20X5 were $20 million and $12 million respectively. Krup had made a loss of $2 million in the period 1 November 20X5 to 12 December 20X5. **(6 marks)**

(b)   Ryder acquired a wholly owned subsidiary, Metalic, a public limited company, on 21 January 20X4. The consideration payable in respect of the acquisition of Metalic was 2 million ordinary shares of $1 of Ryder plus a further 300,000 ordinary shares if the profit of Metalic

exceeded $6 million for the year ended 31 October 20X5. The profit for the year of Metalic was $7 million and the ordinary shares were issued on 12 November 20X5. Ryder had included an estimate of the contingent consideration in the cost of the acquisition at 21 January 20X4. The fair value used for the ordinary shares of Ryder at this date including the contingent consideration was $10 per share. The fair value of the ordinary shares on 12 November 20X5 was $11 per share. Ryder also made a one for four bonus issue on 13 November 20X5 which was applicable to the contingent shares issued. The directors are unsure of the impact of the above on earnings per share and the accounting for the acquisition. **(8 marks)**

(c)   The company acquired a property on 1 November 20X4 which it intended to sell. The property was obtained as a result of a default on a loan agreement by a third party and was valued at $20 million on that date which exactly offset the defaulted loan. The property is in a state of disrepair and Ryder intends to complete the repairs before it sells the property. The repairs were completed on 30 November 20X5. The property was sold for $27 million, after costs, on 9 December 20X5. The property was classified as 'held for sale' at the year end under IFRS 5 *Non-current Assets Held for Sale and Discontinued Operations* but shown at the net sale proceeds of $27 million. Property is depreciated at 5% per annum on the straight-line basis and no depreciation has been charged in the year. **(6 marks)**

(d)   The company granted share appreciation rights (SARs) to its employees on 1 November 20X3 based on ten million shares. The SARs provide employees, at the date the rights are exercised, with the right to receive cash equal to the appreciation in the company's share price since the grant date. The rights vested on 31 October 20X5 and payment was made on schedule on 1 December 20X5. The fair value of the SARs per share at 31 October 20X4 was $6, at 31 October 20X5 was $8 and at 1 December 20X5 was $9. The company has recognised a liability for the SARs as at 31 October 20X4 based upon IFRS 2 *Share-based Payment* but the liability was stated at the same amount at 31 October 20X5. **(5 marks)**

Required

Discuss the accounting treatment of the above events in the financial statements of the Ryder Group for the year ended 31 October 20X5, taking into account the implications of events occurring after the end of the reporting period.

Note. The mark allocations are set out after each paragraph above.   **(Total = 25 marks)**

50 Royan   **39 mins**

(a)   Explain the guidance in IAS 37 *Provisions, Contingent Liabilities and Contingent Assets* as regards the recognition and measurement of provisions and discuss any shortcomings of the standard. **(12 marks)**

(b)   Royan, a public limited company, extracts oil and has a present obligation to dismantle an oil platform at the end of the platform's life, which is ten years. Royan cannot cancel this obligation or transfer it. Royan intends to carry out the dismantling work itself and estimates the cost of the work to be $150 million in ten years' time. The present value of the work is $105 million.

A market exists for the dismantling of an oil platform and Royan could hire a third-party contractor to carry out the work. The entity feels that if no risk or probability adjustment were needed then the cost of the external contractor would be $180 million in ten years' time. The present value of this cost is $129 million. If risk and probability are taken into account, then there is a probability of 40% that the present value will be $129 million and 60% probability that it would be $140 million, and there is a risk that the costs may increase by $5 million.

Required

Describe the accounting treatment of the above events under IAS 37.   **(3 marks)**

(c)   The directors of Royan are aware of the requirements of IAS 37, however as prudence is not a concept specifically referred to in the *Conceptual Framework,* they propose that the costs to dismantle the oil platform described above are expensed as incurred, at the end of the platform's life, with no entries or disclosures being made in the latest financial statements.

Required

Discuss whether the directors are acting unethically in the above circumstance and what the group accountant's proposed course of action should be.   **(5 marks)**

(Total = 20 marks)

51 Electron   **49 mins**

P2 Pilot exam

Electron, a public limited company, operates in the energy sector. The company has grown significantly over the last few years and is currently preparing its financial statements for the year ended 30 June 20X6.

Electron buys and sells oil and currently has a number of oil trading contracts. The contracts to purchase oil are treated as non-current assets and amortised over the contracts' durations. On acceptance of a contract to sell oil, 50% of the contract price is recognised immediately with the balance being recognised over the remaining life of the contract. The contracts always result in the delivery of the commodity.   **(4 marks)**

Electron has recently constructed an ecologically efficient power station. A condition of being granted the operating licence by the government is that the power station be dismantled at the end of its useful life which is estimated to be 20 years. The power station cost $100 million and began production on 1 July 20X5. Depreciation is charged on the power station using the straight-line method. Electron has estimated at 30 June 20X6 that it will cost $15 million (net present value) to restore the site to its original condition using a discount rate of 5%. 95% of these costs relate to the removal of the power station and 5% relates to the damage caused through generating energy.   **(8 marks)**

Electron has leased another power station, which was relatively inefficient, to a rival company on 30 June 20X6. The beneficial and legal ownership remains with Electron and in the event of one of Electron's power stations being unable to produce energy, Electron can terminate the agreement. The leased power station is being treated as an operating lease with the net present value of the income of $40 million being recognised in profit or loss. The fair value of the power station is $70 million at 30 June 20X6. A deposit of $10 million was received on 30 June 20X6 and it is included in the net present value calculation.   **(6 marks)**

The company has a good relationship with its shareholders and employees. It has adopted a strategy of gradually increasing its dividend payments over the years. On 1 August 20X6, the board proposed a dividend of 5c per share for the year ended 30 June 20X6. The shareholders will approve the dividend along with the financial statements at the general meeting on 1 September 20X6 and the dividend will be paid on 14 September 20X6. The directors feel that the dividend should be accrued in the financial statements for the year ended 30 June 20X6 as a 'valid expectation' has been created.   **(3 marks)**

The company granted share options to its employees on 1 July 20X5. The fair value of the options at that date was $3 million. The options vest on 30 June 20X8. The employees have to be employed at the end of the three year period for the options to vest and the following estimates have been made:

Estimated percentage of employees leaving during vesting period at:

Grant date 1 July 20X5   5%
30 June 20X6   6%   **(4 marks)**

Required

Draft a report suitable for presentation to the directors of Electron which discusses the accounting treatment of the above transactions in the financial statements for the year ended 30 June 20X6, including relevant calculations.

(Total = 25 marks)

52 William

49 mins

P2 6/12, amended

William is a public limited company and would like advice in relation to the following transactions.

(a) William owned a building on which it raised finance. William sold the building for $6 million, its fair value, to a finance company on 1 June 20X2 when the carrying amount was $3.6 million. The same building was leased back from the finance company for a period of 20 years. The remaining useful life of the building is 25 years. The lease rentals for the period are $441,000 payable annually in arrears. The interest rate implicit in the lease is 7%. The present value of the lease payments is $5 million. The transaction constitutes a sale in accordance with IFRS 15 *Revenue from Contracts with Customers*.

William wishes to know how to account for the above transaction for the year ended 31 May 20X3. **(8 marks)**

(b) William operates a defined benefit pension plan for its employees. Shortly before the year end of 31 May 20X3, William decided to relocate a division from one country to another, where labour and raw material costs are cheaper. The relocation is due to take place in December 20X3. On 13 May 20X3, a detailed formal plan was approved by the board of directors. Half of the affected division's employees will be made redundant in July 20X3, and will accrue no further benefits under William's defined benefit pension plan. The affected employees were informed of this decision on 14 May 20X3. The resulting reduction in the net pension liability due the relocation is estimated to have a present value of $15 million as at 31 May 20X3. Total relocation costs (excluding the impact on the pension plan) are estimated at $50 million.

William requires advice on how to account for the relocation costs and the reduction in the net pension liability for the year ended 31 May 20X3. **(8 marks)**

(c) On 1 June 20X0, William granted 500 share appreciation rights to each of its twenty managers. All of the rights vest after two years' service and they can be exercised during the following two years up to 31 May 20X4. The fair value of the right at the grant date was $20. It was thought that three managers would leave over the initial two-year period and they did so. The fair value of each right was as follows.

Year	Fair value at the year-end
	$
31 May 20X1	23
31 May 20X2	14
31 May 20X3	24

On 31 May 20X3, seven managers exercised their rights when the intrinsic value of the right was $21.

William wishes to know what the liability and expense will be at 31 May 20X3. **(5 marks)**

(d) William acquired another entity, Chrissy, on 1 May 20X3. At the time of the acquisition, Chrissy was being sued as there is an alleged mis-selling case potentially implicating the entity. The claimants are suing for damages of $10 million. William estimates that the fair value of any contingent liability is $4 million and feels that it is more likely than not that no outflow of funds will occur.

William wishes to know how to account for this potential liability in Chrissy's entity financial statements and whether the treatment would be the same in the consolidated financial statements. **(4 marks)**

Required

Discuss, with suitable computations, the advice that should be given to William in accounting for the above events.

Note. The mark allocation is shown against each of the four events above.

(Total = 25 marks)

53 Leigh

49 mins

ACR 6/07

(a) Leigh, a public limited company, purchased the whole of the share capital of Hash, a limited company, on 1 June 20X6. The whole of the share capital of Hash was formerly owned by the five directors of Hash and under the terms of the purchase agreement, the five directors were to receive a total of three million ordinary shares of $1 of Leigh on 1 June 20X6 (market value $6 million) and a further 5,000 shares per director on 31 May 20X7, if they were still employed by Leigh on that date. All of the directors were still employed by Leigh at 31 May 20X7.

Leigh granted and issued fully paid shares to its own employees on 31 May 20X7. Normally share options issued to employees would vest over a three-year period, but these shares were given as a bonus because of the company's exceptional performance over the period. The shares in Leigh had a market value of $3 million (one million ordinary shares of $1 at $3 per share) on 31 May 20X7 and an average fair value of $2.5 million (one million ordinary shares of $1 at $2.50 per share) for the year ended 31 May 20X7. It is expected that Leigh's share price will rise to $6 per share over the next three years. **(10 marks)**

(b) On 31 May 20X7, Leigh purchased property, plant and equipment for $4 million. The supplier has agreed to accept payment for the property, plant and equipment either in cash or in shares. The supplier can either choose 1.5 million shares of Leigh to be issued in six months' time or to receive a cash payment in three months' time equivalent to the market value of 1.3 million shares. It is estimated that the share price will be $3.50 in three months' time and $4 in six months' time.

Additionally, at 31 May 20X7, one of the directors recently appointed to the board has been granted the right to choose either 50,000 shares of Leigh or receive a cash payment equal to the current value of 40,000 shares at the settlement date. This right has been granted because of the performance of the director during the year and is unconditional at 31 May 20X7. The settlement date is 1 July 20X8 and the company estimates the fair value of the share alternative is $2.50 per share at 31 May 20X7. The share price of Leigh at 31 May 20X7 is $3 per share, and if the director chooses the share alternative, they must be kept for a period of four years. **(9 marks)**

(c)   Leigh acquired 30% of the ordinary share capital of Handy, a public limited company, on 1 April 20X6. The purchase consideration was one million ordinary shares of Leigh which had a market value of $2.50 per share at that date and the fair value of the net assets of Handy was $9 million. The retained earnings of Handy were $4 million and other reserves of Handy were $3 million at that date. Leigh appointed two directors to the Board of Handy, and it intends to hold the investment for a significant period of time. Leigh exerts significant influence over Handy. The summarised statement of financial position of Handy at 31 May 20X7 is as follows.

	$m
Share capital of $1	2
Other reserves	3
Retained earnings	5
	10
Net assets	10

There had been no new issues of shares by Handy since the acquisition by Leigh and the estimated recoverable amount of the net assets of Handy at 31 May 20X7 was $11 million.

(6 marks)

Required

Discuss with suitable computations how the above share-based transactions should be accounted for in the financial statements of Leigh for the year ended 31 May 20X7.

(Total = 25 marks)

54 Fair values and IFRS 13   49 mins

Financial statements have seen an increasing move towards the use of fair values in accounting. Advocates of 'fair value accounting' believe that fair value is the most relevant measure for financial reporting, whilst others believe that historical cost provides a more useful measure. Issues have been raised over the reliability and measurement of fair values, and over the nature of the current level of disclosure in financial statements in this area.

The objective of IFRS 13 *Fair Value Measurement* is to define fair value, set out in a single IFRS a framework for measuring fair value and require disclosure about fair value measurements.

Required

(a)   Discuss the view that fair value is a more relevant measure to use in corporate reporting than historical cost. **(12 marks)**

(b)   (i)   Fairview acquired a research and development project as part of a business combination. Fairview does not intend to complete the project, but instead acquired the project to prevent its competitors from accessing the technology. Therefore the project principally provides defensive value to Fairview by improving the prospects for the output of its own project and preventing competitor access to the developed technology.

Required

How might the highest and best use of the project be determined for the purpose of measuring fair value in order to apply IFRS 13 *Fair Value Measurement*? **(6 marks)**

(ii)   Fairview and Westway individually entered into legal obligations to each pay $200,000 to Brownfield in seven years in exchange for some goods.

Fairview has a very good credit rating and can borrow at 4%. Westway's credit rating is lower and it can borrow at 8%.

Required

What is the fair value of the legal obligation that Fairview and that Westway must record in their financial statements? **(3 marks)**

(iii) Fairview holds shares in Greenfield, which it treats as an equity instrument (a financial asset). Sale of this financial asset is restricted by contract to qualifying investors.

Required

How would the fair value of this instrument be measured? **(4 marks)**

(Total = 25 marks)

55 Mehran

49 mins

P2 Mar/Jun 16 amended

The directors of Mehran, a public limited company, have seen many different ways of dealing with the measurement and disclosure of the fair value of assets, liabilities and equity instruments. They feel that this reduces comparability among different entities' financial statements. They would like advice on how IFRS 13 *Fair Value Measurement* should be applied to several transactions.

(a) Mehran has just acquired a company, which comprises a farming and mining business. Mehran wishes advice on how to place a fair value on some of the assets acquired.

One such asset is a piece of land, which is currently used for farming. The fair value of the land if used for farming is $5 million. If the land is used for farming purposes, a tax credit arises annually, which is based upon the lower of 15% of the fair market value of land or $500,000 at the current tax rate. The current tax rate in the jurisdiction is 20%.

Mehran has determined that market participants would consider that the land could have an alternative use for residential purposes. The fair value of the land for residential purposes before associated costs is thought to be $7.4 million. In order to transform the land from farming to residential use, there would be legal costs of $200,000, a viability analysis cost of $300,000 and costs of demolition of the farm buildings of $100,000. Additionally, permission for residential use has not been formally given by the legal authority and because of this, market participants have indicated that the fair value of the land, after the above costs, would be discounted by 20% because of the risk of not obtaining planning permission.

In addition, Mehran has acquired the brand name associated with the produce from the farm. Mehran has decided to discontinue the brand on the assumption that it will gain increased revenues from its own brands. Mehran has determined that if it ceases to use the brand, then the indirect benefits will be $20 million. If it continues to use the brand, then the direct benefit will be $17 million. **(7 marks)**

(b) Mehran wishes to place a fair value on the inventory of the entity acquired. There are three different markets for the produce, which are mainly vegetables. The first is the local domestic market where Mehran can sell direct to retailers of the produce. The second domestic market is one where Mehran sells directly to manufacturers of canned vegetables. There are no restrictions on the sale of produce in either of the domestic markets other than the demand of the retailers and manufacturers. The final market is the export market but the government limits the amount of produce which can be exported. Mehran needs a licence from the government to export its produce. Farmers tend to sell all of the produce that they can in the export market and, when they do not have any further authorisation to export, they sell the remaining produce in the two domestic markets.

It is difficult to obtain information on the volume of trade in the domestic market where the produce is sold locally direct to retailers but Mehran feels that the market is at least as large as the domestic market – direct to manufacturers. The volumes of sales quoted below have been taken from trade journals.

	Domestic market – direct to retailers	Domestic market – direct to manufacturers	Export market
Volume – annual	Unknown	20,000 tonnes	10,000 tonnes
Volume – sales per month	10 tonnes	4 tonnes	60 tonnes
Price per tonne	$1,000	$800	$1,200
Transport costs per tonne	$50	$70	$100
Selling agents' fees per tonne	–	$4	$6

(10 marks)

(c)   Mehran owns a non-controlling equity interest in Erham, a private company, and wishes to measure the interest at its fair value at its financial year end of 31 March 20X6. Mehran acquired the ordinary share interest in Erham on 1 April 20X4. During the current financial year, Erham has issued further equity capital through the issue of preferred shares to a venture capital fund.

As a result of the preferred share issue, the venture capital fund now holds a controlling interest in Erham. The terms of the preferred shares, including the voting rights, are similar to those of the ordinary shares, except that the preferred shares have a cumulative fixed dividend entitlement for a period of four years and the preferred shares rank ahead of the ordinary shares upon the liquidation of Erham. The transaction price for the preferred shares was $15 per share.

Mehran wishes to know the factors which should be taken into account in measuring the fair value of their holding in the ordinary shares of Erham at 31 March 20X6 using a market-based approach. **(8 marks)**

Required

Discuss the way in which Mehran should measure the fair value the above assets with reference to the principles of IFRS 13 *Fair Value Measurement*.

Note. The mark allocation is shown against each of the three issues above.

(Total = 25 marks)

56 Yanong

49 mins

P2 6/15 amended

The directors of Yanong, a public limited company, would like advice, with reference to IFRS 13 *Fair Value Measurement*, on several transactions.

(a)   Yanong owns several farms and also owns a division which sells agricultural vehicles. It is considering selling this agricultural retail division and wishes to measure the fair value of the inventory of vehicles for the purpose of the sale. Three markets currently exist for the vehicles. Yanong has transacted regularly in all three markets. At 30 April 20X5, Yanong wishes to find the fair value of 150 new vehicles, which are identical. The current volume and prices in the three markets are as follows:

Market	Sales price – per vehicle $	Historical volume – vehicles sold by Yanong	Total volume of vehicles sold in market	Transaction costs – per vehicle $	Transport costs to the market – per vehicle
Europe	40,000	6,000	150,000	500	400
Asia	38,000	2,500	750,000	400	700
Africa	34,000	1,500	100,000	300	600

Yanong wishes to value the vehicles at $39,100 per vehicle as these are the highest net proceeds per vehicle, and Europe is the largest market for Yanong's product. Yanong would like advice as to whether this valuation would be acceptable under IFRS 13 *Fair Value Measurement*. **(6 marks)**

(b) The company uses quarterly reporting for its farms as they grow short-lived crops such as maize. Yanong planted the maize fields during the quarter to 31 October 20X4 at an operating cost of $10 million. The fields originally cost $20 million. There is no active market for partly grown fields of maize and therefore Yanong proposes to use a discounted cash flow method to value the maize fields. As at 31 October 20X4, the following were the cash flow projections relating to the maize fields:

	3 months to 31 January 20X5 $m	3 months to 30 April 20X5 $m	Total $m
Cash inflows		80	80
Cash outflows	(8)	(19)	(27)
Notional rental charge for land usage	(1)	(1)	(2)
Net cash flows	(9)	60	51

In the three months to 31 January 20X5, the actual operating costs amounted to $8 million and at that date Yanong revised its future projections for the cash inflows to $76 million for the three months to April 20X5. At the point of harvest at 31 March 20X5, the maize was worth $82 million and it was sold for $84 million (net of costs to sell) on 15 April 20X5. In the measurement of fair value of the maize, Yanong includes a notional cash flow expense for the 'rent' of the land where it is self-owned.

The directors of Yanong wish to know how they should have accounted for the above biological asset at 31 October 20X4, 31 January 20X5, 31 March 20X5 and when the produce was sold. Assume a discount rate of 2% per quarter as follows:

	Factor
Period 1	0.980
Period 2	0.961

(7 marks)

(c) On 1 May 20X2, Yanong granted 500 share appreciation rights (SARs) to its 300 managers. All of the rights vested on 30 April 20X4 but they can be exercised from 1 May 20X4 up to 30 April 20X6. At the grant date, the value of each SAR was $10 and it was estimated that 5% of the managers would leave during the vesting period. The fair value of the SARs is as follows:

	Fair value of SAR $
30 April 20X3	9
30 April 20X4	11
30 April 20X5	12

All of the managers who were expected to leave employment did leave the company as expected before 30 April 20X4. On 30 April 20X5, 60 managers exercised their options when the intrinsic value of the right was $10.50 and were paid in cash.

Yanong is confused as to whether to account for the SARs under IFRS 2 *Share-based Payment* or IFRS 13 *Fair Value Measurement,* and would like advice as to how the SARs should have been accounted for from the grant date to 30 April 20X5. **(7 marks)**

(d)   Yanong uses the revaluation model for its non-current assets. Yanong has several plots of farmland which are unproductive. The company feels that the land would have more value if it were used for residential purposes. There are several potential purchasers for the land but planning permission has not yet been granted for use of the land for residential purposes. However, preliminary enquiries with the regulatory authorities seem to indicate that planning permission may be granted. Additionally, the government has recently indicated that more agricultural land should be used for residential purposes.

Yanong has also been approached to sell the land for commercial development at a higher price than that for residential purposes.

Yanong would like advice on how to measure the fair value of the land in its financial statements.   **(5 marks)**

Required

Advise Yanong on how the above transactions should be dealt with in its financial statements with reference to relevant International Financial Reporting Standards.

Notes

1   The mark allocation is shown against each of the four issues above.
2   Ignore any deferred tax implications of the transactions above.

(Total = 25 marks)

57 Canto   **49 mins**

P2 Mar/Jun 17

Canto Co is a company which manufactures industrial machinery and has a year end of 28 February 20X7. The directors of Canto require advice on the following issues:

(a)   On 1 March 20X4, Canto acquired a property for $15 million, which was used as an office building. Canto measured the property on the cost basis in property, plant and equipment. The useful life of the building was estimated at 30 years from 1 March 20X4 with no residual value. Depreciation is charged on the straight-line basis over its useful life. At acquisition, the value of the land content of the property was thought to be immaterial.

During the financial year to 28 February 20X7, the planning authorities approved the land to build industrial units and retail outlets on the site. During 20X7, Canto ceased using the property as an office and converted the property to an industrial unit. Canto also built retail units on the land during the year to 28 February 20X7. At 28 February 20X7, Canto wishes to transfer the property at fair value to investment property at $20 million. This valuation was based upon other similar properties owned by Canto. However, if the whole site were sold including the retail outlets, it is estimated that the value of the industrial units would be $25 million because of synergies and complementary cash flows.

The directors of Canto wish to know whether the fair valuation of the investment property is in line with International Financial Reporting Standards and how to account for the change in use of the property in the financial statements at 28 February 20X7.   **(9 marks)**

(b)   On 28 February 20X7, Canto acquired all of the share capital of Binlory, a company which manufactures and supplies industrial vehicles. At the acquisition date, Binlory has an order backlog, which relates to a contract between itself and a customer for ten industrial vehicles to be delivered in the next two years.

In addition, Binlory requires the extensive use of water in the manufacturing process and can take a pre-determined quantity of water from a water source for industrial use. Binlory cannot manufacture vehicles without the use of the water rights. Binlory was the first entity to use water from this source and acquired this legal right at no cost several years ago. Binlory has the right to continue to use the quantity of water for manufacturing purposes but any unused

water cannot be sold separately. These rights can be lost over time if non-use of the water source is demonstrated or if the water has not been used for a certain number of years. Binlory feels that the valuation of these rights is quite subjective and difficult to achieve.

The directors of Canto wish to know how to account for the above intangible assets on the acquisition of Binlory. **(8 marks)**

(c)   Canto acquired a cash-generating unit (CGU) several years ago but, at 28 February 20X7, the directors of Canto were concerned that the value of the CGU had declined because of a reduction in sales due to new competitors entering the market. At 28 February 20X7, the carrying amounts of the assets in the CGU before any impairment testing were:

	$m
Goodwill	3
Property, plant and equipment	10
Other assets	19
Total	32

The fair values of the property, plant and equipment and the other assets at 28 February 20X7 were $10 million and $17 million respectively and their costs to sell were $100,000 and $300,000 respectively.

The CGU's cash flow forecasts for the next five years are as follows:

Date year ended	Pre-tax cash flow	Post-tax cash flow
	$m	$m
28 February 20X8	8	5
28 February 20X9	7	5
28 February 20Y0	5	3
28 February 20Y1	3	1.5
28 February 20Y2	13	10

The pre-tax discount rate for the CGU is 8% and the post-tax discount rate is 6%. Canto has no plans to expand the capacity of the CGU and believes that a reorganisation would bring cost savings but, as yet, no plan has been approved.

The directors of Canto need advice as to whether the CGU's value is impaired. The following extract from a table of present value factors has been provided.

Year	Discount rate 6%	Discount rate 8%
1	0.9434	0.9259
2	0.8900	0.8573
3	0.8396	0.7938
4	0.7921	0.7350
5	0.7473	0.6806

(8 marks)

Required

Advise the directors of Canto on how the above transactions should be dealt with in its financial statements with reference to relevant International Financial Reporting Standards.

Note. The mark allocation is shown against each of the three issues above.

(Total = 25 marks)

58 Ethan

P2 6/12 amended

Ethan, a public limited company, develops, operates and sells investment properties.

(a) Ethan focuses mainly on acquiring properties where it foresees growth potential, through rental income as well as value appreciation. The acquisition of an investment property is usually realised through the acquisition of the entity, which holds the property.

In Ethan's consolidated financial statements, investment properties acquired through business combinations are recognised at fair value, using a discounted cash flow model as approximation to fair value. There is currently an active market for this type of property. The difference between the fair value of the investment property as determined under the accounting policy, and the value of the investment property for tax purposes results in a deferred tax liability.

Goodwill arising on business combinations is determined using the measurement principles for the investment properties as outlined above. Goodwill is only considered impaired if and when the deferred tax liability is reduced below the amount at which it was first recognised. This reduction can be caused both by a reduction in the value of the real estate or a change in local tax regulations. As long as the deferred tax liability is equal to, or larger than, the prior year, no impairment is charged to goodwill. Ethan explained its accounting treatment by confirming that almost all of its goodwill is due to the deferred tax liability and that it is normal in the industry to account for goodwill in this way.

Since 20X0, Ethan has incurred substantial annual losses except for the year ended 31 May 20X3, when it made a small profit before tax. In year ended 31 May 20X3, most of the profit consisted of income recognised on revaluation of investment properties. Ethan had announced early in its financial year ended 31 May 20X4 that it anticipated substantial growth and profit. Later in the year, however, Ethan announced that the expected profit would not be achieved and that, instead, a substantial loss would be incurred. Ethan had a history of reporting considerable negative variances from its budgeted results. Ethan's recognised deferred tax assets have been increasing year-on-year despite the deferred tax liabilities recognised on business combinations. Ethan's deferred tax assets consist primarily of unused tax losses that can be carried forward which are unlikely to be offset against anticipated future taxable profits. **(13 marks)**

(b) Ethan wishes to apply the fair value option rules of IFRS 9 *Financial Instruments* to debt issued to finance its investment properties. (Ethan's argument for applying the fair value option is based upon the fact that the recognition of gains and losses on its investment properties and the related debt would otherwise be inconsistent.) Ethan argued that there is a specific financial correlation between the factors, such as interest rates, that form the basis for determining the fair value of both Ethan's investment properties and the related debt. **(7 marks)**

Mismatch

(c) Ethan has an operating subsidiary, which has in issue A and B shares, both of which have voting rights. Ethan holds 70% of the A and B shares and the remainder are held by shareholders external to the group. The subsidiary is obliged to pay an annual dividend of 5% on the B shares. The dividend payment is cumulative even if the subsidiary does not have sufficient legally distributable profit at the time the payment is due.

NCI

In Ethan's consolidated statement of financial position, the B shares of the subsidiary were accounted for in the same way as equity instruments would be, with the B shares owned by external parties reported as a non-controlling interest. **(5 marks)**

Required

Discuss how the above transactions and events should be recorded in the consolidated financial statements of Ethan.

Note. The mark allocation is shown against each of the three transactions above.

(Total = 25 marks)

59 IFRSs and SMEs

49 mins

ACR 6/06, amended

In 2009, the IASB published the *IFRS for Small and Medium-Sized Entities* (IFRS for SMEs) which is based on the principles in full IFRS, but tailored to the needs of small companies.

Required

(a) Discuss whether it was necessary to develop a separate Standard specifically for SMEs.
(7 marks)

(b) Discuss the purpose of the IFRS for SMEs and the type of entity to which it should apply. Your answer should consider the issues surrounding the development of the IFRS for SMEs.
(7 marks)

(c) Explain the key recognition and measurement simplifications under the IFRS for SMEs compared to full IFRS. **(6 marks)**

(d) Explain how items not dealt with by the IFRS for SMEs should be treated. **(5 marks)**

(Total = 25 marks)

60 Whitebirk

43 mins

P2 12/10, amended

(a) The main argument for separate accounting standards for small and medium-sized entities is the undue cost burden of reporting, which is proportionately heavier for smaller firms.

Required

Discuss the main differences and modifications to IFRS which the IASB made when it published the *IFRS for Small and Medium-Sized Entities* (IFRS for SMEs), giving specific examples where possible and include in your discussion how the Board has dealt with the problem of defining an SME. **(11 marks)**

(b) Whitebirk has met the definition of a SME in its jurisdiction and wishes to comply with the IFRS for SMEs. The entity wishes to seek advice on how it will deal with the following accounting issues in its financial statements for the year ended 30 November 20X2. The entity already prepares its financial statements under full IFRS.

   (i) Whitebirk purchased 90% of Close, an SME, on 1 December 20X1. The purchase consideration was $5.7 million and the value of Close's identifiable assets was $6 million. The value of the non-controlling interest at 1 December 20X1 was measured at $0.7 million. Whitebirk has used the full goodwill method to account for business combinations and the life of goodwill cannot be estimated with any accuracy. Whitebirk wishes to know how to account for goodwill under the IFRS for SMEs.

   (ii) Whitebirk has incurred $1 million of research expenditure to develop a new product in the year to 30 November 20X2. Additionally, it incurred $500,000 of development expenditure to bring another product to a stage where it is ready to be marketed and sold.

   (iii) Whitebirk purchased some properties for $1.7 million on 1 December 20X1 and designated them as investment properties under the cost model. No depreciation was charged as a real estate agent valued the properties at $1.9 million at the year end.

   (iv) Whitebirk has an intangible asset valued at $1 million on 1 December 20X1. The asset has an indefinite useful life, and in previous years had been reviewed for impairment. As at 30 November 20X2, there are no indications that the asset is impaired.

Required

Discuss how the above transactions should be dealt with in the financial statements of Whitebirk, with reference to the IFRS for SMEs. **(11 marks)**

(Total = 22 marks)

61 Zack

P2 12/13 amended

(a)   Due to the complexity of International Financial Reporting Standards (IFRS), often judgements used at the time of transition to IFRS have resulted in prior period adjustments and changes in estimates being disclosed in financial statements. The selection of accounting policy and estimation techniques is intended to aid comparability and consistency in financial statements. However, IFRS also place particular emphasis on the need to take into account qualitative characteristics and the use of professional judgement when preparing the financial statements. Although IFRS may appear prescriptive, the achievement of all the objectives for a set of financial statements will rely on the skills of the preparer. Entities should follow the requirements of IAS 8 *Accounting Policies, Changes in Accounting Estimates and Errors* when selecting or changing accounting policies, changing estimation techniques, and correcting errors.

However, the application of IAS 8 is additionally often dependent upon the application of materiality analysis to identify issues and guide reporting. Entities also often consider the acceptability of the use of hindsight in their reporting.

Required

(i)   Discuss how judgement and materiality play a significant part in the selection of an entity's accounting policies.

(ii)   Discuss the circumstances where an entity may change its accounting policies, setting out how a change of accounting policy is applied and the difficulties faced by entities where a change in accounting policy is made.

(iii) Discuss why the current treatment of prior period errors could lead to earnings management by companies, together with any further arguments against the current treatment.

Credit will be given for relevant examples.

Note. The total marks will be split equally between each part.   **(15 marks)**

(b)   In 20X3, Zack, a public limited company, commenced construction of a shopping centre. It considers that in order to fairly recognise the costs of its property, plant and equipment, it needs to enhance its accounting policies by capitalising borrowing costs incurred whilst the shopping centre is under construction. A review of past transactions suggests that there has been one other project involving assets with substantial construction periods where there would be a material misstatement of the asset balance if borrowing costs were not capitalised. This project was completed in the year ended 30 November 20X2. Previously, Zack had expensed the borrowing costs as they were incurred. The borrowing costs which could be capitalised are $2 million for the 20X2 asset and $3 million for the 20X3 asset.

A review of the depreciation schedules of the larger plant and equipment not affected by the above has resulted in Zack concluding that the basis on which these assets are depreciated would better reflect the resources consumed if calculations were on a reducing balance basis, rather than a straight-line basis. The revision would result in an increase in depreciation for the year to 30 November 20X2 of $5 million, an increase for the year end 30 November 20X3 of $6 million and an estimated increase for the year ending 30 November 20X4 of $8 million.

Additionally, Zack has discovered that its accruals systems for year end creditors for the financial year 30 November 20X2 processed certain accruals twice in the ledger. This meant that expenditure services were overstated in the financial statements by $2 million. However, Zack has since reviewed its final accounts systems and processes and has made appropriate changes and introduced additional internal controls to ensure that such estimation problems are unlikely to recur.

All of the above transactions are material to Zack.

Required

Discuss how the above events should be shown in the financial statements of Zack for the year ended 30 November 20X3. **(10 marks)**

(Total = 25 marks)

62 Pod   49 mins

P2 Mar/Jun 16 amended

The introduction of a new accounting standard can have significant impact on an entity by changing the way in which financial statements show particular transactions or events. In many ways, the impact of a new accounting standard requires the same detailed considerations as is required when an entity first moves from local Generally Accepted Accounting Practice to International Financial Reporting Standards (IFRS).

A new or significantly changed accounting standard often provides the key focus for examination of the financial statements of listed companies by national enforcers who issue common enforcement priorities. These priorities are often highlighted because of significant changes to accounting practices as a result of new or changed standards or because of the challenges faced by entities as a result of the current economic environment. Recent priorities have included recognition and measurement of deferred tax assets and impairment of financial and non-financial assets.

Required

(a) (i)   Discuss the key practical considerations, and financial statement implications which an entity should consider when implementing a move to a new IFRS. **(7 marks)**

     (ii) Discuss briefly the reasons why regulators might focus on the impairment of non-financial assets and deferred tax assets in a period of slow economic growth, setting out the key areas which entities should focus on when accounting for these elements.
(9 marks)

(b)   Pod is a listed company specialising in the distribution and sale of photographic products and services. Pod's statement of financial position included an intangible asset which was a portfolio of customers acquired from a similar business which had gone into liquidation. Pod changed its assessment of the useful life of this intangible asset from 'finite' to 'indefinite'. Pod felt that it could not predict the length of life of the intangible due to a number of factors such as technological evolution, and changing consumer behaviour.

         Pod has a significant network of retail branches. In its financial statements, Pod changed the determination of a cash generating unit (CGU) for impairment testing purposes at the level of each major product line, rather than at each individual branch. The determination of CGUs was based on the fact that each of its individual branches did not operate on a standalone basis as some income, such as volume rebates, and costs were dependent on the nature of the product line rather than on individual branches. Pod considered that cash inflows and outflows for individual branches did not provide an accurate assessment of the actual cash generated by those branches. Pod, however, has daily sales information and monthly statements of profit or loss produced for each individual branch and this information is used to make decisions about continuing to operate individual branches.

Required

Discuss whether the changes to accounting practice suggested by Pod are acceptable under International Financial Reporting Standards. **(9 marks)**

(Total = 25 marks)

63 Lucky Dairy

49 mins

ACR 6/02, amended

The Lucky Dairy, a public limited company, produces milk for supply to various customers. It is responsible for producing 25% of the country's milk consumption. The company owns 150 farms and has 70,000 cows and 35,000 heifers which are being raised to produce milk in the future. The farms produce 2.5 million kilograms of milk per annum and normally hold an inventory of 50,000 kilograms of milk (Extracts from the draft accounts to 31 May 20X2).

The herds comprise at 31 May 20X2:

70,000 – 3-year old cows (all purchased on or before 1 June 20X1)
25,000 – heifers (average age 1½ years old – purchased 1 December 20X1)
10,000 – heifers (average age 2 years – purchased 1 June 20X1)

There were no animals born or sold in the year. The per unit values less estimated point of sale costs were as follows.

	$
2-year old animal at 1 June 20X1	50
1-year old animal at 1 June 20X1 and 1 December 20X1	40
3-year old animal at 31 May 20X2	60
1½-year old animal at 31 May 20X2	46
2-year old animal at 31 May 20X2	55
1-year old animal at 31 May 20X2	42

The company has had a difficult year in financial and operating terms. The cows had contracted a disease at the beginning of the financial year which had been passed on in the food chain to a small number of consumers. The publicity surrounding this event had caused a drop in the consumption of milk and as a result the dairy was holding 500,000 kilograms of milk in storage.

The government had stated, on 1 April 20X2, that it was prepared to compensate farmers for the drop in the price and consumption of milk. An official government letter was received on 6 June 20X2, stating that $1.5 million will be paid to Lucky on 1 August 20X2. Additionally on 1 May 20X2, Lucky had received a letter from its lawyer saying that legal proceedings had been started against the company by the persons affected by the disease. The company's lawyers have advised them that they feel that it is probable that they will be found liable and that the costs involved may reach $2 million. The lawyers, however, feel that the company may receive additional compensation from a government fund if certain quality control procedures had been carried out by the company. However, the lawyers will only state that the compensation payment is 'possible'.

The company's activities are controlled in three geographical locations, Dale, Shire and Ham. The only region affected by the disease was Dale and the government has decided that it is to restrict the milk production of that region significantly. Lucky estimates that the discounted future cash income from the present herds of cattle in the region amounts to $1.2 million, taking into account the government restriction order. Lucky was not sure that the fair value of the cows in the region could be measured reliably at the date of purchase because of the problems with the diseased cattle. The cows in this region amounted to 20,000 in number and the heifers 10,000 in number. All of the animals were purchased on 1 June 20X1. Lucky has had an offer of $1 million for all of the animals in the Dale region (net of point of sale costs) and $2 million for the sale of the farms in the region. However, there was a minority of directors who opposed the planned sale and it was decided to defer the public announcement of sale pending the outcome of the possible receipt of the government compensation. The board had decided that the potential sale plan was highly confidential but a national newspaper had published an article saying that the sale may occur and that there would be many people who would lose their employment. The board approved the planned sale of Dale farms on 31 May 20X2.

The directors of Lucky have approached your firm for professional advice on the above matters.

Required

Advise the directors on how the biological assets and produce of Lucky should be accounted for under IAS 41 *Agriculture* and discuss the implications for the published financial statements of the above events.

Note. Candidates should produce a table which shows the changes in value of the cattle for the year to 31 May 20X2 due to price change and physical change excluding the Dale region, and the value of the herd of the Dale region as at 31 May 20X2. Ignore the effects of taxation. Heifers are young female cows, whilst "cattle" refers to both cows and heifers.   **(25 marks)**

64 Coate   49 mins

P2 12/12 amended

Coate, a public limited company, is a producer of ecologically friendly electrical power (green electricity).

(a)   Coate's revenue comprises mainly the sale of electricity and green certificates. Coate obtains green certificates under a national government scheme. Green certificates represent the environmental value of green electricity. The national government requires suppliers who do not produce green electricity to purchase a certain number of green certificates. Suppliers who do not produce green electricity can buy green certificates either on the market on which they are traded or directly from a producer such as Coate. The national government wishes to give incentives to producers such as Coate by allowing them to gain extra income in this way.

Coate obtains the certificates from the national government on satisfactory completion of an audit by an independent organisation, which confirms the origin of production. Coate then receives a certain number of green certificates from the national government depending on the volume of green electricity generated. The green certificates are allocated to Coate on a quarterly basis by the national government and Coate can trade the green certificates.

Coate is uncertain as to the accounting treatment of the green certificates in its financial statements for the period ended 30 November 20X2 and how to treat the green certificates which were not sold at the end of the reporting period.   **(8 marks)**

(b)   During the year ended 30 November 20X2, Coate acquired an overseas subsidiary whose financial statements are prepared in a different currency to Coate. The amounts reported in the consolidated statement of cash flows included the effect of changes in foreign exchange rates arising on the retranslation of its overseas operations. Additionally, the group's consolidated statement of cash flows reported as a loss the effect of foreign exchange rate changes on cash and cash equivalents as Coate held some foreign currency of its own denominated in cash.

                                                                            (5 marks)

(c)   Coate also sold 50% of a previously wholly owned subsidiary, Patten, to a third party, Manis. Manis is in the same industry as Coate. Coate has continued to account for the investment in Patten as a subsidiary in its consolidated financial statements. The main reason for this accounting treatment was the agreement that had been made with Manis, under which Coate would exercise general control over Patten's operating and financial policies. Coate has appointed three out of four directors to the board. The agreement also stated that certain decisions required consensus by the two shareholders.

Under the shareholder agreement, consensus is required with respect to:

(i)   Significant changes in the company's activities

(ii)   Plans or budgets that deviate from the business plan

(iii)   Accounting policies; acquisition of assets above a certain value; employment or dismissal of senior employees; distribution of dividends or establishment of loan facilities

Coate feels that the consensus required above does not constitute a hindrance to the power to control Patten, as it is customary within the industry to require shareholder consensus for decisions of the types listed in the shareholders' agreement. **(7 marks)**

(d)   In the notes to Coate's financial statements for the year ended 30 November 20X2, the tax expense included an amount in respect of 'Adjustments to current tax in respect of prior years' and this expense had been treated as a prior year adjustment. These items related to adjustments arising from tax audits by the authorities in relation to previous reporting periods.

The issues that resulted in the tax audit adjustment were not a breach of tax law but related predominantly to transfer pricing issues, for which there was a range of possible outcomes that were negotiated during 20X2 with the taxation authorities. Further, at 30 November 20X1, Coate had accounted for all known issues arising from the audits to that date and the tax adjustment could not have been foreseen as at 30 November 20X1, as the audit authorities changed the scope of the audit. No penalties were expected to be applied by the taxation authorities. **(5 marks)**

Required

Discuss how the above events should be accounted for in the individual or, as appropriate, the consolidated financial statements of Coate.

Note. The mark allocation is shown against each of the four events above.

(Total = 25 marks)

PART D: Prepare the financial statements of groups of entities

65 Marrgrett   49 mins

P2 12/08, amended

Marrgrett, a public limited company, is considering purchasing additional shares in its associate, Josey, a public limited company, which will increase its holding from 30% to 70%. Marrgrett will offer the shareholders of Josey cash and shares in Marrgrett as consideration.

Marrgrett anticipates that it will pay $5 million in transaction costs to lawyers and bankers. Josey had previously been the subject of a management buyout. In order that the current management shareholders may remain in the business, Marrgrett is going to offer them share options in Josey subject to them remaining in employment for two years after the acquisition of the additional shares. Additionally, Marrgrett will also offer the same shareholders shares in the holding company which are contingent upon a certain level of profitability being achieved by Josey. Each shareholder will receive shares of the holding company up to a value of $50,000, if Josey achieves a pre-determined return on capital employed for the next two years.

Josey has several intangible assets that are used primarily in marketing or promotion of its products. These include trade names, internet domain names and non-competition agreements. These are not currently recognised in Josey's financial statements.

Marrgrett wishes to use the 'full goodwill' method on the acquisition. Marrgrett is unsure as to whether this method is mandatory, or what the effects are of recognising 'full goodwill'. Additionally, the company is unsure as to whether the nature of the consideration would affect the calculation of goodwill.

To finance the acquisition of Josey, Marrgrett intends to partially dispose of an interest in two subsidiaries. Marrgrett will retain control of the first subsidiary but will sell the controlling interest in the second subsidiary, which will become an associate. Because of its plans to change the overall structure of the business, Marrgrett wishes to recognise a re-organisation provision at the date of the business combination.

Marrgrett has a new financial controller whose knowledge of group accounting is not up to date. She has asked you for advice on how to apply the IFRSs relevant to group accounting in the light of the proposed acquisition and partial disposals.

Required

Explain the principles and the nature of the accounting treatment of the above plans under International Financial Reporting Standards.   **(25 marks)**

66 Marchant   59 mins

30 April X4.

P2 6/14, amended

The following information is relevant to the preparation of the group financial statements of Marchant, a public limited company, for the year ended 30 April 20X4:

(i)   On 1 May 20X2, Marchant acquired 60% of the equity interests of Nathan, a public limited company, for cash of $80 million. The fair value of the identifiable net assets acquired was $110 million at that date. The fair value of the non-controlling interest (NCI) in Nathan was $45 million on 1 May 20X2. Marchant uses the 'full goodwill' method for all acquisitions. The share capital and retained earnings of Nathan were $25 million and $65 million respectively and other components of equity were $6 million at the date of acquisition. The excess of the fair value of the identifiable net assets at acquisition was due to non-depreciable land.

Goodwill has been tested for impairment annually and as at 30 April 20X3 had reduced in value by 20%. However, at 30 April 20X4, the impairment of goodwill had reversed and goodwill was valued at $2 million above its original value. This upward change in value has

already been included in above draft financial statements of Marchant prior to the preparation of the group accounts.

(ii) Marchant disposed of an 8% equity interest in Nathan on 30 April 20X4 for a cash consideration of $18 million and accounted for the gain or loss on disposal in profit or loss. The carrying amount of the net assets of Nathan at 30 April 20X4 was $120 million before any adjustments on consolidation. Marchant accounts for investments in its individual financial statements using IFRS 9 *Financial Instruments,* and has made an election to show gains and losses in other comprehensive income. The carrying amount of the investment in Nathan was $90 million at 30 April 20X3 and $95 million at 30 April 20X4 before the disposal of the equity interest.

(iii) Marchant acquired 60% of the equity interests of Option, a public limited company, on 30 April 20X2 for cash of $70 million. Option's identifiable net assets had a fair value of $86 million and the NCI had a fair value of $28 million at the date of acquisition. On 1 November 20X3, Marchant disposed of a 40% equity interest in Option for a cash consideration of $50 million. Option's identifiable net assets were $90 million and the value of the NCI was $34 million at the date of disposal. The remaining equity interest had a fair value of $40 million. After the disposal, Marchant exerts significant influence over Option. Any increase in net assets since acquisition has been reported in profit or loss and the carrying value of the investment in Option had not changed since acquisition. Goodwill has not been impaired. No entries have been made in the financial statements of Marchant for this transaction other than to record the cash received.

(iv) Marchant sold inventory to Nathan at its fair value of $12 million. Marchant made a loss on the transaction of $2 million and Nathan still holds $8 million in inventory at the year end.

(v) Ignore the taxation effects of the above adjustments.

Required

(a) (i) Explain, including relevant calculations, how goodwill should have been calculated on the acquisition of Nathan and Option and subsequently treated in the consolidated financial statements of Marchant. **(8 marks)**

(ii) Explain, with supporting workings, the adjustments needed to the consolidated financial statements to correctly reflect intergroup trading. **(3 marks)**

(iii) Discuss, with suitable workings, how the disposal of Option and the resulting gain should have been treated in Marchant's consolidated financial statements. **(4 marks)**

(iv) Advise, with suitable calculations, how the gain on the investment in Nathan under IFRS 9 and the gain on the disposal of the equity interest in Nathan, included in Marchant's separate financial statements, should be adjusted for in preparation for incorporation into the consolidated financial statements. **(9 marks)**

(b) Explain, with suitable calculations, how the sale of the 8% interest in Nathan should be dealt with in the consolidated statement of financial position at 30 April 20X4. **(6 marks)**

(Total = 30 marks)

67 Traveler

Traveler, a public limited company, operates in the manufacturing sector. The draft statements of financial position of the group companies are as follows at 30 November 20X1.

	Traveler $m	Data $m	Captive $m
Assets			
Non-current assets			
Property, plant and equipment	439	810	620
Investment in subsidiaries:			
Data	820		
Captive	541		
Financial assets	108	10	20
	1,908	820	640
Current assets	1,067	781	350
Total assets	2,975	1,601	990
Equity and liabilities			
Share capital	1,120	600	390
Retained earnings	1,066	442	169
Other components of equity	60	37	45
Total equity	2,246	1,079	604
Total liabilities	729	522	386
Total equity and liabilities	2,975	1,601	990

The following information is relevant to the preparation of the consolidated financial statements:

(i) On 1 December 20X0, Traveler acquired 60% of the equity interests of Data, a public limited company for cash of $600 million. At acquisition, the fair value of the non-controlling interest in Data was $395 million. Traveler wishes to use the 'full goodwill' method for recognising the goodwill of Data. On 1 December 20X0, the fair value of the identifiable net assets acquired was $935 million, retained earnings of Data were $299 million and other components of equity were $26 million. The excess in fair value of the identifiable assets is due to land which is not depreciated.

On 30 November 20X1, Traveler acquired a further 20% interest in Data for a cash consideration of $220 million.

(ii) On 1 December 20X0, Traveler acquired 80% of the equity interests of Captive for a consideration of $541 million. The consideration comprised cash of $477 million and the transfer of non-depreciable land with a fair value of $64 million. The carrying amount of the land at the acquisition date was $56 million. At the year end, this asset was still included in the non-current assets of Traveler and the sale proceeds had been credited to profit or loss.

At the date of acquisition, the identifiable net assets of Captive had a fair value of $526 million, retained earnings were $90 million and other components of equity were $24 million. The excess in fair value is due to non-depreciable land. The acquisition of Captive was accounted for using the 'partial goodwill' method.

(iii) Goodwill was tested for impairment after the additional acquisition in Data on 30 November 20X1. The recoverable amount of Data was $1,099 million and that of Captive was $700 million.

(iv)   Included in the financial assets of Traveler is a ten-year 7% loan provided to a company external to the group. Traveler's business model is to collect the contractual cash flows associated the loan. Traveler has adopted IFRS 9 *Financial Instruments* and the loan asset is currently held at an amortised cost of $31 million. This is net of an allowance, including interest, at 30 November 20X0 for 12 months' expected credit losses of $2 million. At 30 November 20X1, the borrower was in financial difficulties and its credit rating had been downgraded such that the loan may be considered to be in Stage 2 according to the IFRS 9 expected credit loss model. Lifetime expected credit losses are $9.9 million. This reflects the difference between the carrying amount and the revised expected receipts of three annual amounts of $8 million, starting in one year's time and discounted at the original effective interest rate of 6.7%. Rather than recognise lifetime expected credit losses, Traveler now wishes to value the loan at fair value using current market interest rates. Current market interest rates are 8%.

Required

(a)   (i)   Advise the directors of Traveler, with suitable workings, how the loan should be accounted for in Traveler's financial statements 30 November 20X1.   **(5 marks)**

(ii)   Explain to the directors of Traveler, with appropriate calculations, how goodwill should be calculated on the acquisition of Data and Captive, showing any adjustments which need to be made to the financial statements to correct any errors made.   **(10 marks)**

(iii)   Calculate the retained earnings for inclusion in the consolidated financial statements of the Traveler Group at 30 November 20X1.   **(3 marks)**

(iv)   Calculate the non-controlling interests for inclusion in the consolidated statement of financial position of the Traveler Group as at 30 November 20X1.   **(4 marks)**

(b)   Captive sold goods to Traveler during the year at a 60% mark-up. Similar goods are usually sold to other parties at a mark-up of 20%. The directors of Traveler believe that no ethical issues arise as such transactions will be eliminated within the consolidated financial statements. On 31 March 20X2, Traveler announced its intention to sell its shareholding in Captive to the highest bidder.

Required

Identify the accounting principles which should be considered when accounting for intra-group transactions in the consolidated financial statements and identify any ethical issues which may arise from the scenario.   **(8 marks)**

(Total = 30 marks)

68 Angel   59 mins

P2 12/13, amended

The following draft consolidated financial statements relate to Angel, a public limited company.

Angel's new finance director has explained that he is used to preparing cash flow statements using the direct method and requires some advice on the indirect method as used by his predecessor for the Angel Group.

ANGEL GROUP: EXTRACTS FROM STATEMENT OF FINANCIAL POSITION
AS AT 30 NOVEMBER 20X3

	30 Nov 20X3 $m	30 Nov 20X2 $m
Assets		
Non-current assets		
Property, plant and equipment	475	465
Investment in associate	80	–
Financial assets	215	180
Current assets		
Inventories	155	190
Trade receivables	125	180
Cash and cash equivalents	465	355
	745	725
Current liabilities:		
Trade payables	155	361
Current tax payable	49	138
Total current liabilities	204	499

ANGEL GROUP: EXTRACT FROM STATEMENT OF PROFIT OR LOSS AND OTHER
COMPREHENSIVE INCOME FOR THE YEAR ENDED 30 NOVEMBER 20X3

	$m
Revenue	1,238
Cost of sales	(986)
Gross profit	252
Other income	30
Administrative expenses	(45)
Other expenses	(54)
Operating profit	183
Finance costs	(11) — not
Share of profit of associates	12
Profit before tax	184

The following information relates to the financial statements of the Angel Group:

(i) Angel decided to renovate a building which had a carrying amount of $nil at 1 December 20X2. As a result, $3 million was spent during the year on its renovation. On 30 November 20X3, Angel received a cash grant of $2 million from the government to cover some of the renovation cost and the creation of new jobs which had resulted from the use of the building. The grant related equally to both job creation and renovation. The only elements recorded in the financial statements were a charge to revenue for the renovation of the building and the receipt of the cash grant, which has been credited to additions of property, plant and equipment (PPE).

Angel treats grant income on capital-based projects as deferred income.

(ii) On 1 December 20X2, Angel acquired all of the share capital of Sweety for cash of $30 million. The fair values of the identifiable assets and liabilities of Sweety at the date of acquisition are set out below. There were no other acquisitions in the period. The fair values in the table below have been reflected in the year end balances of the Angel Group.

	Fair values
	$m
Property, plant and equipment	14
Inventories	6
Trade receivables	3
Cash and cash equivalents	2
Total assets	25
Trade payables	(5)
Net assets at acquisition	20

(iii) Angel's property, plant and equipment (PPE) comprises the following.

	$m
Carrying amount at 1 December 20X2	465
Additions at cost including assets acquired on the purchase of subsidiary	80
Gains on property revaluation	8
Disposals	(49)
Depreciation	(29)
Carrying amount at 30 November 20X3	475

Angel has constructed a machine which is a qualifying asset under IAS 23 *Borrowing Costs* and has paid construction costs of $4 million, which has been charged to other expenses. Angel Group paid $11 million in interest in the year, recorded as a finance cost, which includes $1 million of interest which Angel wishes to capitalise under IAS 23. There was no deferred tax implication regarding this transaction.

The proceeds on disposal of PPE were $63 million. The gain on disposal is included in administrative expenses.

Note. Ignore the effects of any depreciation required on the construction costs.

(iv) Angel purchased a 30% interest in an associate for cash on 1 December 20X2. The associate reported a profit for the year of $40 million and paid a dividend of $10 million out of these profits in the year ended 30 November 20X3.

(v) An impairment test carried out at 30 November 20X3 showed that goodwill and other intangible assets were impaired by $26.5 million and $90 million, respectively. The impairment of goodwill relates to 100% owned subsidiaries.

(vi) The finance costs were all paid in cash in the period.

Required

(a) (i) Explain to the finance director why the building renovation has been incorrectly recorded, setting out the correcting entries. **(4 marks)**

(ii) Explain, showing supporting calculations, the adjustments that need to be made to calculate the correct profit before tax figure for inclusion in a consolidated statement of cash flows for the Angel Group for the year ended 30 November 20X3, prepared using the indirect method. **(4 marks)**

(iii) Prepare the cash generated from operations figure for inclusion in a consolidated statement of cash flows for the Angel Group for the year ended 30 November 20X3, using the indirect method, in accordance with the requirements of IAS 7 *Statement of Cash Flows*. For each line item, explain to the finance director of Angel Group the reason for its inclusion in the reconciliation. **(14 marks)**

(b) The directors of Angel are confused over several issues relating to IAS 7 *Statement of Cash Flows*. They wish to know the principles utilised by the International Accounting Standards Board in determining how cash flows are classified, including how entities determine the nature of the cash flows being analysed.

Angel decided after the year end to deposit some funds with the bank in two term deposit accounts as follows:

(i) $3 million into a 12-month term account, earning 3.5% interest. The cash can be withdrawn by giving 14 days' notice to the bank, but Angel will incur a penalty, being the loss of all interest earned.

(ii) $7 million into a 12-month term account earning 3% interest. The cash can be withdrawn by giving 21 days' notice. Interest will be paid for the period of the deposit but if money is withdrawn, the interest will be at the rate of 2%, which is equivalent to the bank's stated rate for short-term deposits.

Angel is confident that it will not need to withdraw the $3 million cash from the higher-rate deposit within the term, but wants to keep easy access to the remaining $7 million to cover any working capital shortfalls which might arise.

Required

Discuss the principles behind the classifications in the statement of cash flows whilst advising Angel on how to treat the two transactions above. **(8 marks)**

(Total = 30 marks)

69 Weston

59 mins

P2 Mar/Jun 16, amended

Weston Group, a public limited company, operates a chain of pizza restaurants and has a factory which supplies its restaurants with pizza bases. It has grown by acquiring and rebranding a number of competitor businesses, operating in different regions. The following information relates to the financial statements of the Weston Group.

WESTON GROUP
EXTRACT FROM STATEMENT OF FINANCIAL POSITION AS AT 31 JANUARY

	20X6 $m	20X5 $m
Assets		
Non-current assets		
Other non-current assets	393	432
Investment in associate	102	–
Total non-current assets	495	432
Total current assets	253	312
Total assets	748	744
Equity and liabilities		
Total equity	565	476
Total non-current liabilities	100	135
Total current liabilities	83	133
Total liabilities	183	268
Total equity and liabilities	748	744

WESTON GROUP
EXTRACT FROM STATEMENT OF PROFIT OR LOSS AND OTHER COMPREHENSIVE INCOME
FOR THE YEAR ENDED 31 JANUARY 20X6

	$m
Operating profit	190
Finance costs	(23)
Share of profit of associate	16
Profit before tax	183
Income tax expense	(40)
Profit for the year from continuing operations	143
Discontinued operations	
Loss for the year from discontinued operations (Note (i))	(25)
Profit for the year	118

The following information relates to the financial statements of Weston:

(i) On 31 July 20X5, Weston disposed of its entire 80% equity holding in Northern for cash. The shares had been acquired on 31 July 20X1 for a consideration of $132 million when the fair value of the net assets was $124 million. This included an increase of $16 million in the fair value of land which had a remaining useful life of eight years. Deferred tax at 25% on the fair value adjustment was also correctly provided for in the consolidated accounts and is included within the fair value of net assets. The fair value of the non-controlling interest at acquisition was $28 million. Goodwill, calculated under the full fair value method, was impaired by 75% at 31 January 20X5. There has been no further impairment of Northern in the current year.

The carrying amounts of assets and liabilities in the individual accounts of Northern at disposal are listed below.

	Carrying amount $m
Property, plant and equipment	80
Inventory	38
Trade receivables	23
Trade and other payables	(10)
Deferred tax liability	(6)
Bank overdraft	(2)

(ii) The loss for the period from discontinued operations in the consolidated statement of profit or loss and other comprehensive income relates to Northern and can be analysed as follows:

	$m
Profit before tax	6
Income tax expense	(2)
Loss on disposal	(29)
	(25)

The directors have stated that they expect the loss on disposal to be disclosed in the statement of cash flows as a non-cash adjustment to cash generated from operations. They are optimistic that this will display the results of the continuing group in a more positive light, increasing the cash generated from operations.

(iii) Weston purchased a 40% interest in an associate, Southland, for cash on 1 February 20X5. Southland paid a dividend of $10 million in the year ended 31 January 20X6. Weston does not have an interest in any other associates.

(iv) Weston Group prepares its statement of cash flows using the indirect method.

Required

(a) (i) Explain to the directors the effect of the disposal of Northern on the consolidated statement of cash flows for the Weston Group for the year ended 31 January 20X6. You should prepare the relevant extracts and workings to support your explanation.

(16 marks)

(ii) Explain to the directors the effect of the acquisition of Southland on the consolidated statement of cash flows for the Weston Group for the year ended 31 January 20X6. You should prepare the relevant extracts and workings to support your explanation.

(8 marks)

Note. Marks will be allocated in (a) for a suitable discussion of the principles involved as well as the accounting treatment.

(b) Weston's directors are planning to dispose of some surplus machinery and small investments (not subsidiaries) that are no longer considered core to the business. They want to include proceeds of the sale of property, plant and equipment and the sale of investments in equity instruments in 'cash generated from operations'. The directors are concerned about the importance of meeting targets in order to ensure job security and feel that this treatment for the proceeds would enhance the 'cash health' of the business.

Required

Discuss the ethical responsibility of Weston's company accountant in ensuring that manipulation of the statement of cash flows, such as that suggested by the directors, does not occur.

(6 marks)

(Total = 30 marks)

70 Kayte

49 mins

P2 12/14 amended

(a) Kayte operates in the shipping industry and owns vessels for transportation. In June 20X4, Kayte acquired Ceemone whose assets were entirely investments in small companies. The small companies each owned and operated one or two shipping vessels. There were no employees in Ceemone or the small companies. At the acquisition date, there were only limited activities related to managing the small companies as most activities were outsourced. All the personnel in Ceemone were employed by a separate management company. The companies owning the vessels had an agreement with the management company concerning assistance with chartering, purchase and sale of vessels and any technical management. The management company used a shipbroker to assist with some of these tasks.

Kayte accounted for the investment in Ceemone as an asset acquisition. The consideration paid and related transaction costs were capitalised as a non-current asset. Kayte argued that the vessels were only passive investments and that Ceemone did not own a business, since all activities regarding commercial and technical management were outsourced to the management company. As a result, the acquisition was accounted for as if the vessels were acquired as assets on a stand-alone basis.

Additionally, Kayte had borrowed heavily to purchase some vessels and was struggling to meet its debt obligations. Kayte had sold some of these vessels but in some cases, the bank did not wish Kayte to sell the vessel. In these cases, the vessel was transferred to a new entity, in which the bank retained a variable interest based upon the level of the indebtedness. Kayte's directors felt that the entity was a subsidiary of the bank and are uncertain as to whether they have complied with the requirements of IFRS 3 *Business Combinations* and IFRS 10 *Consolidated Financial Statements* as regards the above transactions. **(13 marks)**

(b)   Kayte's vessels constitute a material part of its total assets. The economic life of the vessels is estimated to be 30 years, but the useful life of some of the vessels is only 10 years because Kayte's policy is to sell these vessels when they are 10 years old. Kayte estimated the residual value of these vessels at sale to be half of acquisition cost and this value was assumed to be constant during their useful life. Kayte argued that the estimates of residual value used were conservative in view of an immature market with a high degree of uncertainty and presented documentation which indicated some vessels were being sold for a price considerably above carrying amount. Broker valuations of the residual value were considerably higher than those used by Kayte. Kayte argued against broker valuations on the grounds that it would result in greater volatility in reporting.

Kayte keeps some of the vessels for the whole 30 years and these vessels are required to undergo an engine overhaul in dry dock every 10 years to restore their service potential, hence the reason why some of the vessels are sold. The residual value of the vessels kept for 30 years is based upon the steel value of the vessel at the end of its economic life. At the time of purchase, the service potential which will be required to be restored by the engine overhaul is measured based on the cost as if it had been performed at the time of the purchase of the vessel. Normally, engines last for the 30-year total life if overhauled every 10 years. Additionally, one type of vessel was having its funnels replaced after 15 years, but the funnels had not been depreciated separately.   **(12 marks)**

Required

Discuss the accounting treatment of the above transactions in the financial statements of Kayte.

Note. The mark allocation is shown against each of the elements above.

(Total = 25 marks)

71 Bubble   59 mins

P2 Sep/Dec 15, amended

The following draft financial statements relate to Bubble Group, a public limited company and two other companies in which it owns investments.

DRAFT STATEMENTS OF FINANCIAL POSITION AS AT 31 OCTOBER 20X5

	Bubble	Salt	Tyslar
	$m	$m	Dinars m
Assets			
Non-current assets:			
Property, plant and equipment	280	105	390
Investment in Salt	110	–	–
Investment in Tyslar	46	–	–
Financial assets	12	9	98
	448	114	488
Current assets			
Inventories	20	12	16
Trade and other receivables	30	25	36
Cash and cash equivalents	14	11	90
	64	48	142
Total assets	512	162	630

	Bubble	Salt	Tyslar
	$m	$m	Dinars m
Equity			
Ordinary share capital	80	50	210
Retained earnings	230	74	292
Other components of equity	40	12	–
Total equity	350	136	502
Non-current liabilities	95	7	110
Current liabilities	67	19	18
	162	26	128
Total equity and liabilities	512	162	630

The following information is relevant to the Bubble Group.

(a) Bubble acquired 80% of the equity shares of Salt on 1 November 20X3 when Salt's retained earnings were $56 million and other components of equity were $8 million. The fair value of the net assets of Salt were $120 million at the date of acquisition. This does not include a contingent liability which was disclosed in Salt's financial statements as a possible obligation of $5 million. The fair value of the obligation was assessed as $1 million at the date of acquisition and remained unsettled as at 31 October 20X5. Any remaining difference in the fair value of the net assets at acquisition relates to non-depreciable land. The fair value of the non-controlling interest at acquisition was estimated as $25 million. Bubble always adopts the full goodwill method under IFRS 3 *Business Combinations*.

(b) Bubble owns 60% of the equity shares of Tyslar, a company located overseas, which uses the dinar as its functional currency. The shares in Tyslar were acquired on 1 November 20X4 at a cost of 368 million dinars. At the date of acquisition, retained earnings were 258 million dinars and Tyslar had no other components of equity. No fair value adjustments were deemed necessary in relation to the acquisition of Tyslar. The fair value of the non-controlling interest was estimated as 220 million dinars at acquisition. No dividend was paid by Tyslar in the year ended 31 October 20X5.

(c) An impairment review of goodwill was undertaken as at 31 October 20X5. No impairment was necessary in relation to Salt, but the goodwill of Tyslar is to be impaired by 20%. Neither Bubble, Salt nor Tyslar has issued any equity shares since acquisition.

(d) On 1 February 20X5, Bubble gave an interest-free loan to Tyslar for $10 million. Tyslar recorded this correctly in its financial statements using the spot rate of exchange. Tyslar repaid $5 million on 1 July 20X5 when the spot exchange rate was $1 to 10 dinars. Tyslar therefore reduced its non-current liabilities by 50 million dinars. No further entries were made in Tyslar's financial statements. The outstanding balance remains within the financial assets of Bubble and the non-current liabilities of Tyslar.

(e) The following exchange rates are relevant to the preparation of the group financial statements:

	Dinars to $
1 November 20X4	8
1 February 20X5	9
31 October 20X5	9.5
Average for year to 31 October 20X5	8.5

Required

(a) (i) Explain, with supporting calculations, the entries Tyslar needs to make in its individual financial statements as at 31 October 20X5 in order to correctly reflect the loan from Bubble. **(5 marks)**

(ii) Translate Tyslar's statement of financial position at 31 October 20X5 into dollars for inclusion in the consolidated statement of financial position and explain your calculations to the directors, including how to incorporate the translated figures into Bubble's consolidated financial statements. **(8 marks)**

(iii) Explain, including suitable calculations, and reference to the principles of relevant IFRSs how goodwill should have been calculated on the acquisitions of Salt and Tyslar and subsequently recorded in the consolidated financial statements of Bubble as at 31 October 20X5. **(8 marks)**

(b) The directors of Bubble are not fully aware of the requirements of IAS 21 *The Effects of Changes in Foreign Exchange Rates* in relation to exchange rate differences. They would like advice on how exchange differences should be recorded on both monetary and non-monetary assets in the individual financial statements and how these differ from the requirements for the translation of an overseas entity. The directors also wish to be advised on what would happen to the exchange differences if Bubble were to sell all of its equity shares in Tyslar, and any practical issues which would arise on monitoring exchange differences if the remaining balance on the loan from Bubble to Tyslar was not intended to be repaid.

Required

Provide a brief memo for the directors of Bubble which identifies the correct accounting treatment for the various issues raised. **(9 marks)**

(Total = 30 marks)

72 Aspire
49 mins

P2 6/14 amended

Aspire, a public limited company, operates many of its activities overseas. The directors have asked for advice on the correct accounting treatment of several aspects of Aspire's overseas operations. Aspire's functional currency is the dollar.

(a) Aspire has created a new subsidiary, which is incorporated in the same country as Aspire. The subsidiary has issued 2 million dinars of equity capital to Aspire, which paid for these shares in dinars. The subsidiary has also raised 100,000 dinars of equity capital from external sources and has deposited the whole of the capital with a bank in an overseas country whose currency is the dinar. The capital is to be invested in dinar denominated bonds. The subsidiary has a small number of staff, who are paid in dollars, and its operating expenses, which are low, are incurred in dollars. The profits are under the control of Aspire. Any income from the investment is either passed on to Aspire in the form of a dividend or reinvested under instruction from Aspire. The subsidiary does not make any decisions as to where to place the investments.

Aspire would like advice on how to determine the functional currency of the subsidiary. **(8 marks)**

(b) Aspire has a foreign branch which has the same functional currency as Aspire. The branch's taxable profits are determined in dinars. On 1 May 20X3, the branch acquired a property for 6 million dinars. The property had an expected useful life of 12 years with a zero residual value. The asset is written off for tax purposes over eight years. The tax rate in Aspire's jurisdiction is 30% and in the branch's jurisdiction is 20%. The foreign branch uses the cost model for valuing its property and measures the tax base at the exchange rate at the reporting date.

Aspire would like an explanation (including a calculation) as to why a deferred tax charge relating to the asset arises in the group financial statements for the year ended 30 April 20X4 and the impact on the financial statements if the tax base had been translated at the historical rate. **(7 marks)**

(c)   On 1 May 20X3, Aspire purchased 70% of a multi-national group whose functional currency was the dinar. The purchase consideration was $200 million. At acquisition, the carrying amount of the net assets were 1,000 million dinars. The fair values of the net assets were 1,100 million dinars and the fair value of the non-controlling interest was 250 million dinars. Aspire uses the full goodwill method.

Aspire wishes to know how to account for goodwill arising on the above acquisition in the group financial statements for the year ended 30 April 20X4.   **(5 marks)**

(d)   Aspire took out a foreign currency loan of 5 million dinars at a fixed interest rate of 8% on 1 May 20X3. The interest is paid at the end of each year. The loan will be repaid after two years on 30 April 20X5. The interest rate is the current market rate for similar two-year fixed interest loans.

Aspire requires advice on how to account for the loan and interest in the financial statements for the year ended 30 April 20X4.   **(5 marks)**

Aspire has a year end of 30 April 20X4 and the average currency exchange rate for the year is not materially different from the actual rate.

EXCHANGE RATES

	$1 = dinars
1 May 20X3	5
30 April 20X4	6
Average exchange rate for year ended 30 April 20X4	5.6

Required

Advise the directors of Aspire on their various requests above, showing suitable calculations where necessary.

Note. The mark allocation is shown against each of the four issues above.

(Total = 25 marks)

73 Plans   29 mins

X, a public limited company, owns 100% of companies Y and Z which are both public limited companies. The X group operates in the telecommunications industry and the directors are considering two different plans to restructure the group.

The statements of financial position of X and its subsidiaries Y and Z at 31 May 20X7 are as follows:

	X	Y	Z
	$m	$m	$m
Property, plant and equipment	600	200	45
Cost of investment in Y	60		
Cost of investment in Z	70		
Net current assets	160	100	20
	890	300	65
Share capital – ordinary shares of $1	120	60	40
Retained earnings	770	240	25
	890	300	65

X acquired the investment in Z on 1 June 20X1 when the company's retained earnings balance was $20 million. The fair value of the net assets of Z on 1 June 20X1 was $60 million. Company Y was incorporated by X and has always been a 100% owned subsidiary. The fair value of the net assets of Y at 31 May 20X7 is $310 million and of Z is $80 million. The fair values of the net current assets of both Y and Z are approximately the same as their carrying amounts.

The directors are unsure as to the impact or implications that the following plans are likely to have on the individual financial statements of each company and on the consolidated financial statements.

Local companies' legislation requires that the amount at which share capital is recorded is dictated by the nominal value of the shares issued and if the value of the consideration received exceeds that amount, the excess is recorded in the share premium account. Shares cannot be issued at a discount. In the case of a share for share exchange, the value of the consideration can be deemed to be the carrying amount of the investment exchanged.

The plan to restructure the group involves Y purchasing the whole of X's investment in Z. There are two alternatives relating to the purchase consideration.

Plan 1

The purchase consideration would be 50 million $1 ordinary shares of Y.

Plan 2

The purchase consideration would be a cash amount of $75 million.

Required

Discuss the key considerations and the accounting implications of the above plans for the X group. Your answer should show the potential impact on the individual financial statements of X, Y and Z and the consolidated financial statements after each plan has been implemented. **(15 marks)**

74 Decany
49 mins

P2 12/11, amended

Decany owns 100% of the ordinary share capital of Ceed and Rant. All three entities are public limited companies. The group operates in the shipbuilding industry, which is currently a depressed market. Rant has made losses for the last three years and its liquidity is poor. The view of the directors is that Rant needs some cash investment. The directors have decided to put forward a restructuring plan as at 30 November 20X1. Under this plan:

(a) Ceed is to purchase the whole of Decany's investment in Rant. The purchase consideration is to be $98 million payable in cash to Decany. The $98 million will then be loaned by Decany on a long-term unsecured basis to Rant.

(b) Ceed will purchase land with a carrying amount of $10 million from Rant for a total purchase consideration of $15 million. The land has a mortgage outstanding on it of $4 million. The total purchase consideration of $15 million comprises both five million $1 nominal value non-voting shares issued by Ceed to Rant and the $4 million mortgage liability which Ceed will assume.

(c) A dividend of $25 million will be paid from Ceed to Decany to reduce the accumulated retained earnings of Ceed.

The statements of financial position of Decany and its subsidiaries at 30 November 20X1 are summarised below.

	Decany $m	Ceed $m	Rant $m
Non-current assets			
Property, plant and equipment at cost/valuation	600	170	45
Investment in Ceed (at cost)	130		
Investment in Rant (at cost)	95		
Current assets	155	130	20
	980	300	65

	Decany $m	Ceed $m	Rant $m
Equity and reserves			
Share capital	140	70	35
Retained earnings	750	220	5
	890	290	40
Non-current liabilities			
Long-term loan	5		12
Current liabilities			
Trade payables	85	10	13
	980	300	65

As a result of the restructuring, several of Ceed's employees will be made redundant. According to the detailed plan, the costs of redundancy will be spread over two years with $4 million being payable in one year's time and $6 million in two years' time. The market yield of high quality corporate bonds is 3%. The directors feel that the overall restructure, excluding the redundancy costs, will cost $2 million.

Required

(a) (i) Prepare the individual statements of financial position for Decany, Ceed and Rant after the proposed restructuring plan. **(13 marks)**

(ii) Explain the requirements of IAS 27 *Separate Financial Statements* as regards the reorganisation and payment of dividends between group companies, discussing any implications for the restructuring plan. **(6 marks)**

(b) Discuss the key implications of the proposed plans for the restructuring of the group.

(6 marks)

(Total = 25 marks)

75 Moorland
49 mins

(a) Moorland is a listed entity with several subsidiaries. The directors of Moorland are reviewing their annual report and wish to understand more about the changing nature of financial reporting.

Required

Discuss the importance of published financial statements as a source of information for the investor, giving examples of the changing nature of the performance measures being utilised by investors. **(11 marks)**

(b) Tybull is Moorland's only overseas subsidiary and Moorland has always disclosed Tybull as an operating segment within the consolidated financial statements. The directors of Moorland are considering how the company identifies its operating segments and the rationale for disclosing segmental information. In particular, they are interested in whether it is possible to reclassify their operating segments and whether this may impact on the usefulness of segmental reporting for the business. There have been no internal organisational changes at Moorland for the past five years.

The CEO of Moorland has proposed to report 'underlying earnings per share' in its annual report, calculated by adjusting earnings for various items that are considered to be non-recurring, divided by the weighted average number of ordinary shares outstanding during the period. A similar performance measure is disclosed by several companies in the same industry as Moorland. The CEO believes that presenting underlying earnings per share will aid investors in their analysis of Moorland's performance, and therefore it should be presented prominently. In calculating underlying earnings per share, one item the CEO wishes to exclude from earnings is a large impairment loss relating to the goodwill of a subsidiary. He believes that this cost can be excluded as it is unlikely to reoccur.

Required

(i) Advise the directors as to how operating segments are identified and whether they can be reclassified. Include in your discussion whether Tybull should be treated as a separate segment and how it may impact on the usefulness of the information if its results were not separately disclosed in accordance with IFRS 8 *Operating Segments*.
(8 marks)

(ii) Discuss the usefulness to investors of Moorland's plan to report underlying earnings per share, and suggest ways in which the directors could improve its usefulness to investors.
(6 marks)

(Total = 25 marks)

76 Tufnell
49 mins

Tufnell, a public limited company, operates in the fashion sector and has undertaken a group re-organisation during the current financial year to 30 September 20X7. As a result, the following events occurred.

(a) (i) Tufnell identified two manufacturing units, North and South, which it had decided to dispose of in a single transaction. These units comprised non-current assets only. One of the units, North, had been impaired prior to 30 September 20X7 and it had been written down to its recoverable amount of $35 million. The criteria in IFRS 5 *Non-current Assets Held for Sale and Discontinued Operations*, for classification as held for sale had been met for North and South at 30 September 20X7. The following information related to the assets of the cash generating units at 30 September 20X7:

	Depreciated historical cost	Fair value less costs of disposal and recoverable amount	Carrying amount under IFRS 5
	$m	$m	$m
North	50	35	35
South	70	90	70
	120	125	105

The fair value less costs of disposal had risen at the year end to $40 million for North and $95 million for South. The increase in the fair value less costs of disposal had not been taken into account by Tufnell. **(7 marks)**

(ii) As a consequence of the re-organisation, and a change in government legislation, the tax authorities have allowed a revaluation of the non-current assets of the holding company for tax purposes to market value at 30 September 20X7. There has been no change in the carrying amounts of the non-current assets in the financial statements. The tax base and the carrying amounts after the revaluation are as follows:

	Carrying amount at 30 September 20X7	Tax base at 30 September 20X7 after revaluation	Tax base at 30 September 20X7 before revaluation
	$m	$m	$m
Property	50	65	48
Vehicles	30	35	28

Other taxable temporary differences amounted to $5 million at 30 September 20X7. Assume income tax is paid at 30%. The deferred tax provision at 30 September 20X7 had been calculated using the tax values before revaluation. **(6 marks)**

(iii) A subsidiary company had purchased computerised equipment for $4 million on 30 September 20X6 to improve the manufacturing process. Whilst re-organising the group, Tufnell had discovered that the manufacturer of the computerised equipment was now selling the same system for $2.5 million. The projected cash flows from the equipment are:

	Cash flows
	$
Year ended 30 September 20X8	1.3
20X9	2.2
20Y0	2.3

The residual value of the equipment is assumed to be zero. The company uses a discount rate of 10%. The directors think that the fair value less costs of disposal of the equipment is $2 million. The directors of Tufnell propose to write down the non-current asset to the new selling price of $2.5 million. The company's policy is to depreciate its computer equipment by 25% per annum on the straight line basis. **(5 marks)**

(iv) The directors are worried about the impact that the above changes will have on the value of its non-current assets and its key performance indicator which is 'Return on Capital Employed' (ROCE). ROCE is defined as net profit before interest and tax divided by share capital, other reserves and retained earnings. The directors have calculated ROCE as $30 million divided by $220 million, ie 13.6% before any adjustments required by the above. **(2 marks)**

Required

(a) Discuss the accounting treatment of the above transactions and the impact that the resulting adjustments to the financial statements would have on ROCE.

   Note. Your answer should include appropriate calculations where necessary and a discussion of the accounting principles involved.

(b) The directors are considering alternative methods for measuring the performance of its subsidiaries, including residual income.

   Required

   Explain what is meant by alternative performance measures and how residual income could be used to measure the relative performance of each subsidiary from the point of view of the shareholders. **(3 marks)**

Professional marks will be awarded in this question for clarity and quality of presentation.

(2 marks)

(Total = 25 marks)

77 Cloud

49 mins

P2 6/15 amended

(a) IAS 1 *Presentation of Financial Statements* defines profit or loss and other comprehensive income. The purpose of the statement of profit or loss and other comprehensive income is to show an entity's financial performance in a way which is useful to a wide range of users so that they may attempt to assess the future net cash inflows of an entity. The statement should be classified and aggregated in a manner which makes it understandable and comparable. However, the International Integrated Reporting Council (IIRC) is calling for a shift in thinking more to the long term, to think beyond what can be measured in quantitative terms and to think about how the entity creates value for its owners. Historical financial statements are essential in corporate reporting, particularly for compliance purposes, but it can be argued that they do not provide meaningful information. Preparers of financial statements seem to be unclear about the interaction between profit or loss and other comprehensive income (OCI) especially regarding the notion of reclassification, but are equally uncertain about whether the IIRC's *Integrated Reporting Framework* constitutes suitable criteria for report preparation. The International Accounting Standards Board (IASB) has tried to clarify what distinguishes recognised items of income and expense which are presented in profit or loss from items of income and expense presented in OCI.

   Required

   (i) Describe the current presentation requirements relating to the statement of profit or loss and other comprehensive income. **(4 marks)**

   (ii) Discuss, with examples, the nature of a reclassification adjustment and the arguments for and against allowing reclassification of items to profit or loss.

   Note. A brief reference should be made in your answer to the IASB's Exposure Draft on the *Conceptual Framework*. **(5 marks)**

   (iii) Discuss the principles and key components of the IIRC's *Integrated Reporting Framework*, and any concerns which could question the Framework's suitability for assessing the prospects of an entity. **(8 marks)**

   Professional marks will be awarded in the question for clarity and quality of presentation.

   (2 marks)

(b) Cloud, a public limited company, regularly purchases steel from a foreign supplier and designates a future purchase of steel as a hedged item in a cash flow hedge. The steel was purchased on 1 May 20X4 and at that date, a cumulative gain on the hedging instrument of $3 million had been credited to other comprehensive income. At the year end of 30 April 20X5, the carrying amount of the steel was $8 million and its net realisable value was $6 million. The steel was finally sold on 3 June 20X5 for $6.2 million. On a separate issue, Cloud purchased an item of property, plant and equipment for $10 million on 1 May 20X3. The asset is depreciated over five years on the straight-line basis with no residual value. At 30 April 20X4, the asset was revalued to $12 million. At 30 April 20X5, the asset's value has fallen to $4 million. The entity makes a transfer from revaluation surplus to retained earnings for excess depreciation, as the asset is used.

Required

Show how the above transactions would be dealt with in the financial statements of Cloud from the date of the purchase of the assets.

Note. Ignore any deferred taxation effects. **(6 marks)**

(Total = 25 marks)

78 Amster

49 mins

P2 Sep/Dec 17

When an entity issues a financial instrument, it has to determine its classification either as debt or as equity. The result of the classification can have a significant effect on the entity's reported results and financial position. An understanding of what an entity views as capital and its strategy for capital management is important to all companies and not just banks and insurance companies. There is diversity in practice as to what different companies see as capital and how it is managed.

Required

(a) (i) Discuss why the information about the capital of a company is important to investors, setting out the nature of the published information available to investors about a company's capital.

Note. Your answer should briefly set out the nature of financial capital in integrated reports. **(8 marks)**

(ii) Discuss the importance of the classification of equity and liabilities under International Financial Reporting Standards and how this classification has an impact on the information disclosed to users in the statement of profit or loss and other comprehensive income and the statement of financial position. **(6 marks)**

(b) Amster has issued two classes of preference shares. The first class was issued at a fair value of $50 million on 30 November 20X7. These shares give the holder the right to a fixed cumulative cash dividend of 8% per annum of the issue price of each preferred share. The company may pay all, part or none of the dividend in respect of each preference share. If the company does not pay the dividend after six months from the due date, then the unpaid amount carries interest at twice the prescribed rate subject to approval of the management committee. The preference shares can be redeemed but only on the approval of the management committee.

The second class of preference shares was issued at a fair value of $25 million and is a non-redeemable preference share. The share has a discretionary annual dividend which is capped at a maximum amount. If the dividend is not paid, then no dividend is payable to the ordinary shareholders. Amster is currently showing both classes of preference shares as liabilities.

On 1 December 20X6, Amster granted 250 cash-settled share awards to each of its 1,500 employees on the condition that the employees remain in its employment for the next three

years. Cash is payable at the end of three years based on the share price of the entity's shares on that date. During the year to 30 November 20X7, 65 employees left and, at that date, Amster estimates that an additional 115 employees will leave during the following two years. The share price at 30 November 20X7 is $35 per share and it is anticipated that it will rise to $46 per share by 30 November 20X9. Amster has charged the expense to profit or loss and credited equity with the same amount.

The capitalisation table of Amster is set out below:

Amster Group – capitalisation table

	30 November 20X7
	$m
Long-term liabilities	81
Pension plan deficit	30
Cumulative preference shares	75
Total long-term liabilities	186
Non-controlling interest	10
Shareholders equity	150
Total group equity	160
Total capitalisation	346

Required

Discuss whether the accounting treatment of the above transactions is acceptable under International Financial Reporting Standards including any adjustment which is required to the capitalisation table and the effect on the gearing and the return on capital employed ratios.

(9 marks)

Professional marks will be awarded in this question for clarity and quality of presentation.

(2 marks)

(Total = 25 marks)

Part F: Communicate the impact of changes and potential changes in accounting regulation on financial reporting

79 Sanchera

49 mins

P2 Sep/Dec 16, amended

The International Accounting Standards Board (IASB) has been undertaking number of projects to explore how disclosures in IFRS financial reporting can be improved. The Disclosure Initiative is made up of a number of implementation and research projects. One project centres on a discussion on whether the definition of materiality should be changed and whether IAS 1 *Presentation of Financial Statements* should include additional guidance which clarifies the key characteristics of materiality. The IASB issued an Exposure Draft ED/2015/8 of a proposed practice statement to provide guidance on the application of materiality to financial statements. Materiality is a matter which has been debated extensively in the context of many forms of reporting, including the International Integrated Reporting Framework. There are difficulties in applying the concept of materiality in practice when preparing the financial statements and it is thought that these difficulties contribute to a disclosure problem, namely, that there is both too much irrelevant information in financial statements and not enough relevant information. Further, the IASB has published amendments to IAS 7 *Statement of Cash Flows* to improve information provided to the users of financial statements regarding an entities financing activities.

Required

(a) (i)   Discuss the current definition of materiality, how the current application of the concept of materiality has led to concerns regarding the clarity and understandability of financial statements and comment on the proposed guidance under ED/2015/8.

(9 marks)

(ii) Discuss how the concept of materiality would be used in applying the International Integrated Reporting Framework. **(4 marks)**

(iii) Discuss the issues with IAS 7 *Statement of Cash Flows* prior to the amendments as a result of the Disclosure Initiative and briefly outline the improvements following the amendments. **(7 marks)**

(b) Sanchera, a listed company, has prepared a statement of cash flows for the year ended 31 August 20X6. At 1 September 20X5, Sanchera had shown in its financial statements long-term borrowings of $50 million and the capital element of lease liabilities at $5 million. At 31 August 20X6, the long-term borrowings had increased to $140 million and the capital element of lease liabilities to $17 million. During the financial year, Sanchera had taken out a long-term loan with a financial institution of $55 million and had acquired Pecuna, a listed company, for $150 million on 1 July 20X6. Pecuna had a long-term loan of $35 million at acquisition. Further, Sanchera had entered into new lease arrangements with liabilities totalling $15 million and had paid $3 million off the capital element of the lease liabilities. Sanchera showed interest paid on lease liabilities of $5 million in the operating activities section of the statement of cash flows. Finally, Sanchera had an overdraft with the bank of $2 million.

Required

Prepare a note to the Statement of Cash Flows, which reconciles opening and closing balances relating to liabilities arising from financing activities. **(5 marks)**

(Total = 25 marks)

Answer Bank

Section 1 – Preparation questions

1 Financial instruments

(a) STATEMENT OF PROFIT OR LOSS AND OTHER COMPREHENSIVE INCOME

	$
Finance income (441,014 × (W1) 8%)	35,281

STATEMENT OF FINANCIAL POSITION

	$
Non-current assets Financial asset (441,014 + 35,281)	476,295

Working: Effective interest rate

$$\frac{600,000}{441,014} = 1.3605 \therefore \text{from tables interest rate is 8\%}$$

(b) **Compound instrument**

	$
Presentation	
Non-current liabilities	
Financial liability component of convertible bond (Working)	1,797,467
Equity	
Equity component of convertible bond (2,000,000 – (Working) 1,797,467)	202,533

Working: Fair value of equivalent non-convertible debt

	$
Present value of principal payable at end of 3 years	1,544,367

$$(4,000 \times \$500 = \$2m \times \frac{1}{(1.09)^3})$$

	$
Present value of interest annuity payable annually in arrears for 3 years [(5% × $2m) × 2.531]	253,100
	1,797,467

2 Leases

(a) **Interest rate implicit in the lease**

PV = annuity × cumulative discount factor (CDF)

250,000   = 78,864 × CDF

$$\therefore \text{CDF} = \frac{250,000}{78,864}$$

$$= 3.170$$

∴ Interest rate is 10%

BPP
LEARNING MEDIA

(b) At the inception of the lease, Sugar Co recognises a right-of-use asset and a lease liability. The right-of-use asset is measured at the amount of the lease liability, which is the present value of the future lease payments discounted at the rate of interest implicit in the lease, here $250,000. At 31 December, the right-of-use asset is measured at cost less accumulated depreciation: $250,000 – $(250,000/4) = $187,500. The lease liability is measured by increasing the carrying amount to reflect interest on the lease liability and reducing the carrying amount to reflect the lease payments made.

STATEMENT OF FINANCIAL POSITION AS AT 31 DECEMBER 20X1 (EXTRACT)

	$
Property, plant and equipment	
Right-of-use asset	187,500
Non-current liabilities	
Lease liabilities (W)	136,886
Current liabilities	
Lease liabilities (W) (196,136 – 136,886)	59,250

STATEMENT OF PROFIT OR LOSS AND OTHER COMPREHENSIVE INCOME
FOR THE YEAR ENDED 31 DECEMBER 20X1 (EXTRACT) (PROFIT OR LOSS SECTION)

Depreciation on right-of-use asset	62,500
Finance charges	25,000

Working: Lease liability

		$
Year ended 31 December 20X1:		
1.1.X1	Liability b/d	250,000
1.1.X1 – 31.12.X1	Interest at 10%	25,000
31.12.X1	Instalment in arrears	(78,864)
31.12.X1	Liability c/d	196,136
Year ended 31 December 20X2:		
1.1.X2 – 31.12.X2	Interest at 10%	19,614
31.12.X2	Instalment in arrears	(78,864)
31.12.X2	Liability c/d	136,886

3 Defined benefit plan

NOTES TO THE STATEMENT OF PROFIT OR LOSS AND OTHER COMPREHENSIVE INCOME

Defined benefit expense recognised in profit or loss

	$m
Current service cost	11
Past service cost	10
Net interest on the net defined benefit asset (10% × (110 + 10)) – (10% × 150)	(3)
	18

Other comprehensive income (items that will not be reclassified to profit or loss)
Remeasurement of defined benefit plans

	$m
Remeasurement gain on defined benefit obligation	17
Remeasurement loss on plan assets	(22)
	(5)

NOTES TO THE STATEMENT OF FINANCIAL POSITION

Net defined benefit asset recognised in the statement of financial position

	31 December 20X1 $m	31 December 20X0 $m
Present value of pension obligation	116	110
Fair value of plan assets	(140)	(150)
Net asset	(24)	(40)

Changes in the present value of the defined benefit obligation

	$m
Opening defined benefit obligation	110
Interest on obligation (10% × (110 + 10))	12
Current service cost	11
Past service cost	10
Benefits paid	(10)
Gain on remeasurement through OCI (balancing figure)	(17)
Closing defined benefit obligation	116

Changes in the fair value of plan assets

	$m
Opening fair value of plan assets	150
Interest on plan assets (10% × 150)	15
Contributions	7
Benefits paid	(10)
Loss on remeasurement through OCI (balancing figure)	(22)
Closing fair value of plan assets	140

Tutorial note.

The interest on the defined benefit obligation is calculated on the balance at the start of the year ($110 million) plus the increase in obligation of $10 million due to past service costs. Interest is charged on the increase in obligation due to past service costs because the $10 million given in the question is the present value at the start of the year (if it were the present value at the end of the year, no interest would be required).

4 Sundry standards

> **Workbook reference.** Employee benefits are covered in Chapter 4 of the SBR Workbook, embedded derivatives in covered in Chapter 7.

(a)   NOTES TO THE STATEMENT OF PROFIT OR LOSS AND OTHER COMPREHENSIVE INCOME

Defined benefit expense recognised in profit or loss

	$'000
Current service cost	275
Net interest on the net defined benefit liability (318 – 306)	12
Curtailment cost	58
	345

Other comprehensive income (items that will not be reclassified to profit or loss)
Remeasurement of defined benefit plans

	$'000
Remeasurement loss on defined benefit obligation	(19)
Remeasurement gain on plan assets	89
	70

NOTES TO THE STATEMENT OF FINANCIAL POSITION

Net defined benefit liability recognised in the statement of financial position

	31 January 20X8 $m	31 January 20X7 $'000
Present value of pension obligation	4,640	4,300
Fair value of plan assets	(4,215)	(3,600)
Net liability	425	700

Changes in the present value of the defined benefit obligation

	$'000
Opening defined benefit obligation	4,300
Benefits paid	(330)
Interest on obligation (4,300 – 330) × 8%	318
Curtailment	58
Current service cost	275
Loss on remeasurement through OCI (balancing figure)	19
Closing defined benefit obligation	4,640

Changes in the fair value of plan assets

	$'000
Opening fair value of plan assets	3,600
Contributions	550
Benefits paid	(330)
Interest on plan assets ((3,600 + 550 – 330) × 8%)	306
Gain on remeasurement through OCI (balancing figure)	89
Closing fair value of plan assets	4,215

(b) **Settlement**

(i) *Calculation of net defined benefit liability*

Changes in the present value of the defined benefit obligation

20X8

	$'000
Opening defined benefit obligation (1.1.X8)	40,000
Interest on obligation (40,000 × 8%)	3,200
Current service cost	2,500
Past service cost	2,000
Benefits paid	(1,974)
	45,726
Loss on remeasurement through OCI (bal. fig.)	274
Closing defined benefit obligation (31.12.X8)	46,000

20X9

	$'000
Opening defined benefit obligation (1.1.X9)	46,000
Interest on obligation (46,000 × 9%)	4,140
Current service cost	2,860
Settlement	(11,400)
Benefits paid	(2,200)
	39,400
Loss on remeasurement through OCI (bal. fig.)	1,400
Closing defined benefit obligation (31.12.X9)	40,800

Changes in the fair value of plan assets

20X8

	$'000
Opening fair value of plan assets (1.1.X8)	40,000
Interest on plan assets (40,000 × 8%)	3,200
Benefits paid	(1,974)
Contributions paid	2,000
	43,226
Loss on remeasurement through OCI (bal. fig.)	(226)
Closing fair value of plan assets (31.12.X8)	43,000

	$'000
Opening fair value of plant assets (1.1.X9)	43,000
Interest on plan assets (43,000 × 9%)	3,870
Settlement	(10,800)
Benefits paid	(2,200)
Contributions paid in	2,200
	36,070
Loss on remeasurement through OCI (bal. fig.)	(390)
Closing fair value of plan assets (31.12.X9)	35,680

- During 20X8, there is an improvement in the future benefits available under the plan and as a result there is a past service cost of $2 million, being the increase in the present value of the obligation as a result of the change.

- During 20X9, Sion sells part of its operations and transfers the relevant part of the pension plan to the purchaser. This is a settlement. The overall gain on settlement is calculated as:

	$'000
Present value of obligation settled	11,400
Fair value of plan assets transferred on settlement	(10,800)
Cash transferred on settlement	(400)
Gain	200

(ii) *Financial statements extracts*

STATEMENT OF FINANCIAL POSITION

	20X8 $'000	20X9 $'000
Net defined benefit liability:		
(46,000 – 43,000)/(40,800 – 35,680)	3,000	5,120

STATEMENT OF PROFIT OR LOSS AND OTHER COMPREHENSIVE INCOME

	20X8 $'000	20X9 $'000
Profit or loss		
Current service cost	2,500	2,860
Past service cost	2,000	–
Gain on settlement	–	(200)
Net interest: (3,200 – 3,200)/(4,140 – 3,870)	–	270
Other comprehensive income		
Remeasurement loss on defined benefit pension plan:		
(274 + 226)/(1,400 +390)	500	1,790

(c) **Classification of financial assets**

Bed's deposit is a **financial asset**. According to IFRS 9 *Financial Instruments*, financial assets are classified as measured at either **amortised cost or fair value**.

A financial asset is measured at **amortised cost** where:

(i) The asset is held within a **business model** where the objective is to hold financial assets in order to **collect contractual cash flows**; and

(ii) The contractual terms of the financial asset give rise on specified dates to **cash flows that are solely payments of principal and interest** on the principal amount outstanding.

All other financial assets are measured at fair value.

Deposit with Em Bank

At first glance, it appears that this deposit **may meet the criteria to be measured at amortised cost** because Bed will receive cash flows comprising the principal amount ($10 million) and interest (2.5%). However, IFRS 9 requires the **cash flows to be consistent with a basic lending arrangement**, where the **time value of money and credit risk** are typically the most significant elements of interest. **Contractual terms** that **introduce exposure to risk or volatility in the contractual cash flows** that is

unrelated to a basic lending arrangement, such as exposure to changes in exchange rates, **do not give rise to contractual cash flows that are solely payments of principal and interest**.

The **additional 3% interest** Bed will receive if the exchange rate target is reached, exposes Bed to **risk in cash flows** that are **unrelated to a basic lending arrangement** (movement in exchange rates). Therefore, the contract with Em Bank does not give rise to contractual cash flows that are purely payments of principal and interest and as a result, it should not be measured at amortised cost. This type of contract is referred to as a 'hybrid contract'.

This **additional 3%** dependent on exchange rates is an **embedded derivative**. Derivatives embedded within a **host** which is a **financial asset** within the scope of IFRS 9 are **not separated out** for accounting purposes. Instead the **usual IFRS 9 measurement** requirements should be applied to the entire hybrid contract.

Since the **contract with Em Bank** does **not** meet the criteria to be measured at **amortised cost**, the **entire contract** (including the term entitling Bed to an additional 3% if the exchange rate target is met) should be **measured at fair value through profit or loss**.

5 Control

(a) IFRS 10 states that an investor **controls** an investee if and only if it has all of the following.

(1) **Power** over the investee

(2) Exposure, or rights, to **variable returns** from its involvement with the investee, and

(3) The **ability to use its power** over the investee to affect the amount of the investor's returns.

Power is defined as **existing rights that give the current ability to direct the relevant activities of the investee**. There is no requirement for that power to have been exercised.

Relevant activities may include:

- Selling and purchasing goods or services
- Managing financial assets
- Selecting, acquiring and disposing of assets
- Researching and developing new products and processes
- Determining a funding structure or obtaining funding

In some cases assessing power is straightforward, for example, where power is obtained directly and solely from having the majority of voting rights or potential voting rights, and as a result the ability to direct relevant activities.

(b)

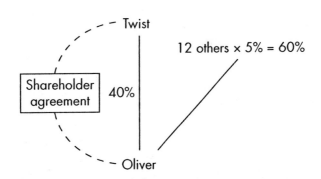

The absolute size of Twist's holding and the relative size of the other shareholdings alone are not conclusive in determining whether the investor has rights sufficient to give it power. However, the fact that Twist has **a contractual right to appoint, remove and set the remuneration of management** is sufficient to conclude that it **has power over Oliver**. The fact that Twist has not exercised this right is not a determining factor when assessing whether Twist has power. In conclusion, Twist does control Oliver, and should consolidate it.

(c)

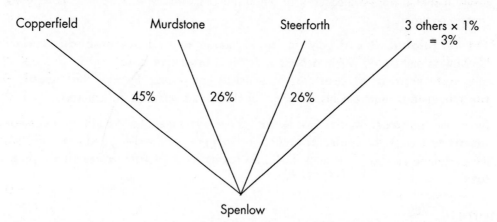

In this case, the size of Copperfield's voting interest and its size relative to the other shareholdings are sufficient to conclude that Copperfield **does not have power**. Only two other investors, Murdstone and Steerforth, would need to co-operate to be able to prevent Copperfield from directing the relevant activities of Spenlow.

(d)

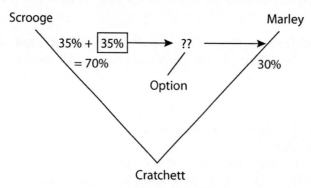

Scrooge holds a majority of the current voting rights of Cratchett, so is likely to meet the power criterion because it appears to have the current ability to direct the relevant activities. Although Marley has currently exercisable options to purchase additional voting rights (that, if exercised, would give it a majority of the voting rights in Cratchett), the terms and conditions associated with those options are such that the options are not considered substantive.

Thus voting rights, even combined with potential voting rights, may not be the deciding factor. Scrooge should consolidate Cratchett.

6 Associate

J GROUP CONSOLIDATED STATEMENT OF FINANCIAL POSITION AS AT 31 DECEMBER 20X5

Assets	$'000
Non-current assets	
Freehold property (1,950 + 1,250 + 370 (W7))	3,570
Plant and equipment (795 + 375)	1,170
Investment in associate (W3)	480
	5,220
Current assets	
Inventories (575 + 300 – 20 (W6))	855
Trade receivables (330 + 290))	620
Cash at bank and in hand (50 + 120)	170
	1,645
	6,865
Equity and liabilities	
Equity attributable to owners of the parent	
Issued share capital	2,000
Retained earnings	1,785
	3,785
Non-controlling interests (W5)	890
Total equity	4,675
Non-current liabilities	
12% debentures (500 + 100)	600
Current liabilities	
Bank overdraft	560
Trade payables (680 + 350)	1,030
	1,590
Total liabilities	2,190
	6,865

Workings

1   Group structure

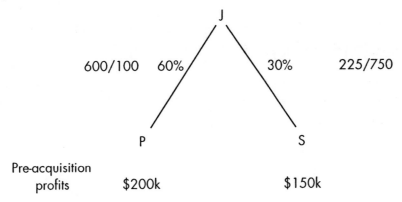

2   Goodwill

	$'000	$'000
Consideration transferred		1,000
NCI (at 'full' FV: 400 × $1.65)		660
Net assets acquired:		
Share capital	1,000	
Retained earnings at acquisition	200	
Fair value adjustment (W7)	400	
		(1,600)
		60
Impairments to date		(60)
Year-end value		–

3   Investment in associate

	$'000
Cost of associate	500.0
Share of post-acquisition retained reserves (W4)	72.0
Less impairment of investment in associate	(92.0)
	480.0

4   Retained earnings

	J Co $'000	P Co $'000	S Co $'000
Retained earnings per question	1,460	885	390
Unrealised profit (W6)		(20)	
Fair value adjustment movement (W6)		(30)	
Retained earnings at acquisition		(200)	(150)
		635	240
P Co: share of post-acquisition retained earnings 60% × 635	381		
S Co: share of post-acquisition retained earnings 30% × 240	72		
Goodwill impairments to date			
P Co: 60 (W2) × 60%	(36)		
S Co	(92)		
	1,785		

5   Non-controlling interests

	$'000
NCI at acquisition (W2)	660
NCI share of post-acquisition retained earnings ((W4) 635 × 40%)	254
NCI share of impairment losses ((W2) 60 × 40%)	(24)
	890

6   Unrealised profit on inventories

P Co ⟶ J Co $100k × 25/125 = $20,000

7   Fair value adjustment table

	At acquisition $'000	Movement $'000	At reporting date $'000
Land	200		200
Buildings	200	(30)	170 (200 × 34/40)
	400	(30)	370

7 Part disposal

(a)   ANGEL GROUP
       CONSOLIDATED STATEMENT OF FINANCIAL POSITION AS AT 31 DECEMBER 20X8

	$'000
Non-current assets	
Property, plant and equipment	200.00
Investment in Shane (W3)	133.15
	333.15
Current assets (890 + 120 (cash on sale))	1,010.00
	1,343.15
Equity attributable to owners of the parent	
Share capital	500.00
Retained reserves (W4)	533.15
	1,033.15
Current liabilities	310.00
	1,343.15

ANGEL GROUP
CONSOLIDATED STATEMENT OF PROFIT OR LOSS AND OTHER COMPREHENSIVE INCOME
FOR THE YEAR ENDED 31 DECEMBER 20X8

	$'000
Profit before interest and tax [100 + (20 × 6/12)]	110.00
Profit on disposal of shares in subsidiary (W6)	80.30
Share of profit of associate (12 × 35% × 6/12)	2.10
Profit before tax	192.40
Income tax expense [40 + (8 × 6/12)]	(44.00)
Profit for the year	148.40
Other comprehensive income (not reclassified to P/L) net of tax [10 + (6 × 6/12)]	13.00
Share of other comprehensive income of associate (6 × 35% × 6/12)	1.05
Other comprehensive income for the year	14.05
Total comprehensive income for the year	162.45

	$'000
Profit attributable to:	
Owners of the parent	146.60
Non-controlling interests (12 × 6/12 × 30%)	1.80
	148.40
Total comprehensive income attributable to:	
Owners of the parents	159.75
Non-controlling interests (18 × 6/12 × 30%)	2.70
	162.45

ANGEL GROUP
CONSOLIDATED RECONCILIATION OF MOVEMENT IN RETAINED RESERVES

	$'000
Balance at 31 December 20X7 (W5)	373.40
Total comprehensive income for the year	159.75
Balance at 31 December 20X8 (W4)	533.15

Workings

1 *Timeline*

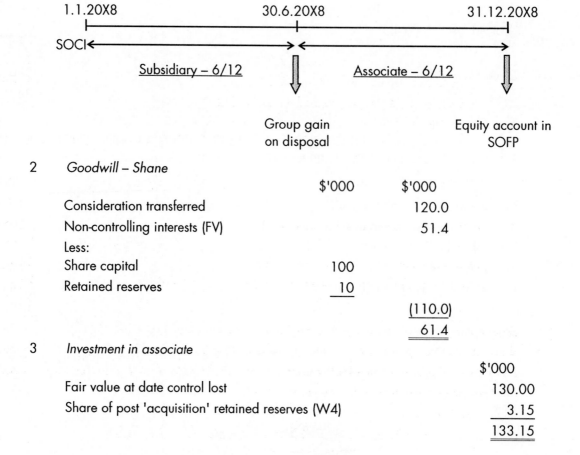

2 *Goodwill – Shane*

	$'000	$'000
Consideration transferred		120.0
Non-controlling interests (FV)		51.4
Less:		
Share capital	100	
Retained reserves	10	
		(110.0)
		61.4

3 *Investment in associate*

	$'000
Fair value at date control lost	130.00
Share of post 'acquisition' retained reserves (W4)	3.15
	133.15

4   *Group retained reserves*

	Angel	Shane 70%	Shane 35% retained
Per question/date of disposal (90 – (18 × 6/12))	400.00	81	90
Group profit on disposal (W4)	80.30		
Less retained reserves at acquisition/date of disposal		(10)	(81)
		71	9
Shane: 70% × 71	49.70		
Shane: 35% × 9	3.15		
	533.15		

5   *Retained reserves b/f*

	Angel $'000	Shane $'000
Per question	330.0	72
Less pre-acquisition retained reserves		(10)
	330.0	62
Shane – Share of post-acquisition ret'd reserves (62 × 70%)	43.4	
	373.4	

6   *Group profit on disposal of Shane*

	$'000	$'000
Fair value of consideration received		120.0
Fair value of 35% investment retained		130.0
Less share of carrying amount when control lost		
Net assets 190 – (18 × 6/12)	181.0	
Goodwill (W2)	61.4	
Less non-controlling interests (W7)	(72.7)	
		(169.7)
		80.3

7   *Non-controlling interests at date of disposal*

	$'000	$'000
Non-controlling interest at acquisition (FV)		51.4
NCI share of post-acq'n retained earnings (30% × 71(W4))		21.3
		72.7

(b)   **Angel disposes of 10% of its holding**

If Angel disposes of 10% of its holding in Shane, Shane goes from being a 70% subsidiary to a 60% subsidiary. In other words **control is retained**. No accounting boundary has been crossed, and the event is treated as a transaction between owners.

The accounting treatment is as follows:

Statement of profit or loss and other comprehensive income

(i)   The subsidiary is **consolidated in full** for the whole period.

(ii)   The **non-controlling interest in the statement of profit or loss and other comprehensive income** will be based on percentage before and after disposal, ie time apportion.

(iii)   There is **no profit or loss on disposal**.

Statement of financial position

(i)   The **change (increase) in non-controlling interests** is shown as an **adjustment to the parent's equity**.

(ii)   **Goodwill** on acquisition **is unchanged** in the consolidated statement of financial position.

In the case of Angel and Shane you would time apportion the non-controlling interest in the statement of profit or loss and other comprehensive income, giving 30% for the first half the year and 40% for the second half. You would also calculate the adjustment to the parent's equity as follows:

	$'000
Fair value of consideration received	X
Increase in NCI in net assets and goodwill at disposal	(X)
Adjustment to parent's equity	X

8 Step acquisition

(a)   Prior to the acquisition of 20% on 1 March 20X1, **SD already controls KL** with its 60% investment, so **KL is already a subsidiary** and would be fully consolidated. In substance, this is **not an acquisition**. Instead, it is treated in the group accounts as a **transaction between the group shareholders** ie the parent has purchased a 20% shareholding from the non-controlling interests (NCI). No goodwill is calculated on the additional investment.

The value of the NCI needs to be worked out at the date of the additional investment (1 March 20X1), and the **proportion purchased by the parent needs to be removed from NCI**. The difference between the consideration transferred and the amount of the reduction in the NCI is included as an **adjustment to equity**.

KL must be **consolidated** in the group **statement of profit or loss and other comprehensive income** for the **full year** but **NCI will be pro-rated** with 40% for the first eight months and 20% for the following four months. In the **consolidated statement of financial position**, KL will be **consolidated with a 20% NCI**.

(b)   (i)   Goodwill $1,450,000 (W2)
        (ii)   Group retained earnings $9,843,999 (W3)
        (iii)   Non-controlling interests $1,096,001 (W4)

Workings

1   *Group structure*

SD

	1.7.X0	60%
	1.3.X1	20%
		80%

KL   Pre-acquisition retained earnings $2,760,000

Timeline

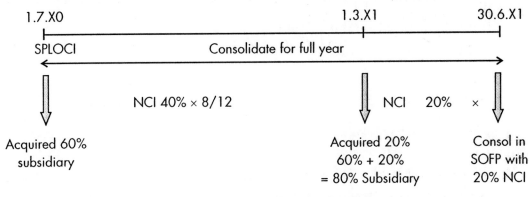

2   *Goodwill (calculated at date when control was originally obtained)*

		$	$
Consideration transferred			3,250,000
NCI at fair value			1,960,000
Less net assets at acquisition:			
Share capital		1,000,000	
Pre-acquisition retained earnings (W1)		2,760,000	
			(3,760,000)
Goodwill			1,450,000

3   *Consolidated retained earnings*

	SD	KL 60%	KL 80%
	$	$	$
At year end/step acquisition	9,400,000	3,186,667	3,400,000
Unrealised profit (W5)			(60,000)
At acquisition/step acquisition		(2,760,000)	(3,186,667)
		426,667	153,333
Group share (60% × 426,667)	256,000		
(80% × 153,333)	122,666		
Adjustment to parent's equity W6)	65,333		
	9,843,999		

KL's retained earnings for the year to 30 June 20X1 (3,400,000 – 2,760,000) = $640,000
KL's retained earnings for the 8 months to 28 February 20X1 (640,000 × 8/12) = $426,667
KL's retained earnings as at 28 February 20X1 (2,760,000 + 426,667 = $3,186,667

4   *Non-controlling interest*

	$
NCI at acquisition	1,960,000
NCI share of post-acquisition retained earnings to 28.2.X1	
(40% × 426,667 (W3))	170,667
	2,130,667
Decrease in NCI on further acquisition (20%/40% × 2,130,667)	(1,065,333)
NCI share of post-acquisition retained earnings to 30.6.X1	
(20% × 153,333 (W3))	30,667
	1,096,001

5   *Provision for unrealised profit*

Intragroup sales by KL $750,000

Mark-up ($750,000 × $\frac{25}{125}$) × 40% = $60,000

(adjust in KL's retained earnings for the period **after** 1 March 20X1)

6   *Adjustment to equity on acquisition of further 20% of KL*

	$
Fair value of consideration paid	(1,000,000)
Decrease in NCI (W4)	1,065,333
Adjustment to equity	65,333

Adjustment would be:

	$	$
DEBIT (↓) Non-controlling interest	1,065,333	
CREDIT (↑) Group equity		65,333
CREDIT (↓) Cash (consideration)		1,000,000

9 Foreign operation

CONSOLIDATED STATEMENT OF FINANCIAL POSITION

	$'000
Property, plant and equipment (1,285 + 543 (W2))	1,828
Goodwill (W4)	240
	2,068
Current assets (410 + 247 (W2))	657
	2,725
Share capital	500
Retained earnings (W5)	1,260
Other components of equity – translation reserve (W8)	98
	1,858
Non-controlling interest (W6)	131
	1,989
Loans (200 + 37 (W2))	237
Current liabilities (400 + 99 (W2))	499
	736
	2,725

CONSOLIDATED STATEMENT OF PROFIT OR LOSS AND OTHER COMPREHENSIVE INCOME

	$'000
Revenue (1,125 + 619 (W3))	1,744
Cost of sales (410 + 274 (W3))	(684)
Gross profit	1,060
Other expenses (180 + 108 (W3))	(288)
Goodwill impairment loss (W4)	(18)
Profit before tax	754
Income tax expense (180 + 76 (W3))	(256)
Profit for the year	498

Other comprehensive income
Items that may subsequently be reclassified to profit or loss

Exchange difference on translating foreign operations (W9)	69
Total comprehensive income for the year	567

Profit attributable to:	
Owners of the parent (balancing figure)	466
Non-controlling interests (W7)	32
	498

Total comprehensive income attributable to:	
Owners of the parent	525
Non-controlling interests (W7)	42
	567

Workings

1   *Group structure*

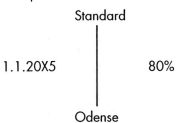

Standard

1.1.20X5   80%

Odense   Pre-acquisition retained earnings = 2,500,000 krone

2   *Translation of Odense – Statement of financial position*

	Kr'000	Rate	$'000
Property, plant and equipment	4,400	8.1	543
Current assets	2,000	8.1	247
	6,400		790
Share capital	1,000	9.4	106
Pre-acquisition retained earnings	2,500	9.4	266
Post-acquisition retained earnings:			
– 20X5 profit	1,200	9.1	132
– 20X5 dividend	(345)	8.8	(39)
– 20X6 profit	1,350	8.4	161
– 20X6 dividend	(405)	8.1	(50)
Exchange difference on net assets		Bal fig	78
	5,300		654
Loans	300	8.1	37
Current liabilities	800	8.1	99
	1,100		136
	6,400		790

The bracketed lines (266 through 78) total 470.

3 Translation of Odense – statement of profit or loss and other comprehensive income

	Odense Kr'000	Rate	Odense $'000
Revenue	5,200	8.4	619
Cost of sales	(2,300)	8.4	(274)
Gross profit	2,900		345
Other expenses	(910)	8.4	(108)
Profit before tax	1,990		237
Income tax expense	(640)	8.4	(76)
Profit/Total comprehensive income for the year	1,350		161

4 Goodwill

	Kr'000	Kr'000	Rate	$'000
Consideration transferred (520 × 9.4)		4,888		520
Non-controlling interests (3,500 × 20%)		700		74
Share capital	1,000		9.4	
Retained earnings	2,500			
		(3,500)		(372)
		2,088		222
Exchange differences 20X5		–	β	15
At 31.12.X5		2,088	8.8	237
Impairment losses 20X6		(148)	8.1	(18)
Exchange differences 20X6		–	β	21
At 31.12.X6		1,940	8.1	240

5 Consolidated retained earnings

	Standard $'000	Odense $'000
At year end	1,115	470
At acquisition		(266)
		204
Group share of post-acquisition retained earnings (204 × 80%)	163	
Less: impairment losses to date (W4)	(18)	
	1,260	

6 Non-controlling interests (statement of financial position)

	$'000
NCI at acquisition (W4)	74
NCI share of post-acquisition retained earnings of Odense (204 (W5) × 20%)	41
NCI share of exchange differences on net assets (78 (W2) × 20%)	16
	131

7 Non-controlling interests (statement of profit or loss and other comprehensive income)

	PFY $'000	TCI $'000
Profit/Total comprehensive income for the year (W3)	161	161
Other comprehensive income: exchange differences on net assets (W9)	–	48
	161	209
NCI share	× 20%	× 20%
	= 32	= 42

8   *Consolidated translation reserve*

	$'000
Exchange differences on net assets (78 (W2) × 80%)	62
Exchange differences on goodwill (15 + 21 (W4))	36
	98

9   *Exchange differences*

	$'000
On translation of net assets:	
Closing NA @ CR (W2)	654
Opening NA @ OR (1,000 + 3,355 = 4,355* @ 8.8)	(495)
Less retained profit as translated (PFY – dividends)(161 (W3) – 405 @ 8.1)	(111)
	48
On goodwill (W4)	21
	69

* The opening net assets have been calculated as share capital (from Odense's statement of financial position) plus opening retained earnings (from Odense's statement of changes in equity extract). Alternatively, they could have been calculated as closing net assets less total comprehensive income for the year plus dividends: Kr(5,300,000 – 1,350,000 + 405,000).

Tutorial note.

As Standard chose to measure the non-controlling interest in Odense at the proportionate share of net assets at acquisition, the partial goodwill method has been adopted. This means that only group goodwill is recognised in the consolidated statement of financial position and therefore, no goodwill is recognised for the non-controlling interests (NCI). Therefore, there are no exchange differences on goodwill relating to NCI. This is why only the exchange differences on net assets (and not the exchange differences on goodwill) are included in the NCI workings ((W6) and (W7)). Since all the recognised goodwill relates to the group, in the consolidated translation reserve working (W8), the exchange differences on goodwill are not multiplied by the group share.

If Standard had measured NCI at fair value at acquisition (the full goodwill method), both group goodwill and goodwill relating to the NCI would have been recognised. Therefore, in the NCI workings, the exchange differences on goodwill would be included. In the consolidated translation reserve working, the exchange differences on goodwill would be multiplied by the group share (in the same way as the exchange differences on net assets have been treated).

It might help if you think about the treatment of exchange differences on goodwill as being the same as the treatment for impairment losses on goodwill. So under the partial goodwill method, as all of the recognised goodwill relates to the group, all of the impairment losses and exchange differences on goodwill belong to the group so they should be recognised in full in the consolidated retained earnings and translation reserve workings respectively and neither would be included in NCI workings. Whereas for the full goodwill method, impairment losses and exchange differences on goodwill are apportioned between the group (in the retained earnings and translation reserve workings) and the NCI (in the NCI workings).

10 Consolidated statement of cash flows

STATEMENT OF CASH FLOWS FOR THE YEAR ENDED 31 DECEMBER 20X5

	$'000	$'000
Cash flows from operating activities		
Profit before tax	16,500	
Adjustments for:		
Depreciation	5,800	
Impairment losses (W1)	240	
	22,540	
Increase in trade receivables (W4)	(1,700)	
Increase in inventories (W4)	(4,400)	
Increase in trade payables (W4)	1,200	
Cash generated from operations	17,640	
Income taxes paid (W3)	(4,200)	
Net cash from operating activities		13,440
Cash flows from investing activities		
Acquisition of subsidiary net of cash acquired	(600)	
Purchase of property, plant and equipment (W1)	(13,100)	
Net cash used in investing activities		(13,700)
Cash flows from financing activities		
Proceeds from issue of share capital (W2)	2,100	
Dividends paid (W2)	(900)	
Dividends paid to non-controlling interest (W2)	(40)	
Net cash from financing activities		1,160
Net increase in cash and cash equivalents		900
Cash and cash equivalents at the beginning of the period		1,500
Cash and cash equivalents at the end of the period		2,400

Workings

1   Assets

	Property, plant and equipment $'000	Goodwill $'000
b/d	25,000	–
OCI (revaluation)	500	
Depreciation/Impairment	(5,800)	**(240)** β
Acquisition of sub/associate	2,700	1,640 (W5)
Cash paid/(rec'd) β	**13,100**	–
c/d	35,500	1,400

2   Equity

	Share capital $'000	Share premium $'000	Retained earnings $'000	Non-controlling interest $'000
b/d	10,000	2,000	21,900	–
SPLOCI			11,100	350
Acquisition of subsidiary	1,500	2,500		1,440 (W5)
Cash (paid)/rec'd β	**800**	**1,300**	**(900)***	**(40)**
c/d	12,300	5,800	32,100	1,750

*Dividend paid is given in question but working shown for clarity.

3   Liabilities

	Tax payable
	$'000
b/d	4,000
P/L	5,200
Acquisition of subsidiary	200
Cash (paid)/rec'd	**(4,200)** β
c/d	5,200

4   Working capital changes

	Inventories	Receivables	Payables
	$'000	$'000	$'000
Balance b/d	10,000	7,500	6,100
Acquisition of subsidiary	1,600	600	300
	11,600	8,100	6,400
Increase/(decrease) (balancing figure)	**4,400**	**1,700**	**1,200**
Balance c/d	16,000	9,800	7,600

5   Purchase of subsidiary

	$'000
Cash received on acquisition of subsidiary	400
Less cash consideration	(1,000)
Cash outflow	(600)

Note. Only the **cash** consideration is included in the figure reported in the statement of cash flows. The **shares** issued as part of the consideration are reflected in the share capital working (W2) above.

Goodwill on acquisition (before impairment):

	$'000
Consideration: 55 + 695 (W3) + 120 (W2) + 216	5,000
Non-controlling interest: 4,800 × 30%	1,440
Net assets acquired	(4,800)
Goodwill	1,640

11 Current issues

Top tips. This is a multi-part question covering a number of aspects of current issues in financial reporting. Ensure you split your time so that you spend adequate time on each part to maximise marks.

Easy marks. There are elements such as in Part (a) on leases, Part (e) on the Disclosure Initiative and materiality Exposure Draft and Part (f) on the *Conceptual Framework* Exposure Draft where straightforward knowledge is required.

(a) (i) **Key changes in IFRS 16 *Leases***

    (1) The most important change from its predecessor, IAS 17 *Leases*, is that nearly **all leases must be reported in the statement of financial position.** The distinction between finance and operating leases no longer applies for lessees, where a single lessee accounting modem now applies, although it does for lessors.

    (2) There are exceptions for leases of low value and leases of under twelve months duration.

    (3) A lessee must measure the **lease liability** similarly to other financial liabilities and recognise **interest** on the liability.

    (4) Lease assets (right-of-use assets) and liabilities are initially measured on a **present value** basis. Generally, assets must subsequently be depreciated under the cost model in IAS 16 *Property, Plant and Equipment*.

    (5) Requirements for **lessors** are essentially **unchanged.**

    (6) There are **extensive disclosure requirements** for both lessees and lessors.

(ii) **Key likely effects of IFRS 16**

    (1) Companies will be required to report **larger amounts of assets and liabilities** in their statements of financial position. This will particularly affect companies that currently have much of their leasing commitment off-balance sheet in the form of operating leases. An example of this is airlines, many of which do not show any asset or liability in respect of their aircraft. Under IFRS 16, an airline entering into a lease for an aircraft would show an asset for the 'right to use' the aircraft and an equal liability based on the current value of the lease payments it has promised to make.

    (2) As a result of bringing lease liabilities onto the statement of financial position, **loan covenants may be breached** and need to be renegotiated.

    (3) For companies that currently hold material operating leases, the **pattern of expenses will change**. Specifically, the **lease expense will be 'front-loaded'**. This is because IFRS 16 replaces the IAS 17 straight-line operating lease expense with a depreciation charge for leased assets, included within operating costs and an interest expense on lease liabilities included within financing costs which is usually higher in the early years of the lease. The total expense will generally be the same but there will be a **difference in expense profile** between IFRS 16 and IAS 17, with a consequent effect on EBITDA and operating profit.

    (4) With regard to the statement of cash flows, IFRS 16 will generally change the **presentation of cash flows** in respect of leases previously accounted for as operating leases.

        Operating cash outflows, which is where operating lease payments are reported under IAS 17, will **reduce**. However, there will be a corresponding **increase in financing cash outflows**. This is because repayments of the capital component of a lease liability are included within financing activities.

(b) IFRS 16 *Leases* requires entities to **account for the lease component of the contract separately from the non-lease component.** The entity must split the rental or lease payment and:

- Account for the lease component under IFRS 16; and
- Account for the service element separately, generally as an expense in profit or loss.

The consideration in the contract is **allocated on the basis of the stand-alone prices** of the lease component(s) and the non-lease component(s).

On-Ice Co should allocate $25,313, ($30,000 × $27,000 ÷ $(27,000 + 5,000) to the lease element and account for that as a lease under IFRS 16.

On-Ice Co should allocate $4,687 ($30,000 × $5,000 ÷ $(27,000 + 5,000) to the servicing element and recognise it in profit or loss as an expense.

(c) **Classification of liabilities under the proposed amendments to IAS 1** *Presentation of Financial Statements*

Exposure draft ED 2015/1 aims to clarify that the classification of liabilities as current or non-current should be based on the entity's **rights** at the end of the reporting period. It provides criteria as to when a liability should be classified as current and all liabilities not meeting this criteria should be classified as non-current. The key change under the proposals is that prior to the ED, an entity needed to have an unconditional right to defer settlement of an obligation for at least 12 months in order to classify a liability as non-current. The ED removes the term 'unconditional'. This is seen as a positive step by the IASB as in the real world rights are rarely unconditional because they often depend on compliance in the future with loan covenants.

The Exposure Draft also clarifies that 'settlement' of a liability refers to 'the transfer to the counterparty of cash, equity instruments, other assets or services that results in the extinguishment of the liability.'

(d) **Additional performance measures**

Additional performance measures (APMs) can take the form of additional key performance indicators or providing more information on the individual items within the financial statements. Users have driven the demand for APMs because financial statements, prepared in accordance with applicable financial reporting standards, have been restricted in the amount of information that can be provided.

Preparers of financial statements may wish to report **'sustainable' (or 'underlying') earnings**. This means, in effect, that certain items of income and expense are excluded because they are considered irrelevant as regards their impact on future years' performance. Examples of such items include fair value gains or losses on financial instruments.

Common APMs include the following:

(i) **Normalised profit.** This may be defined in various ways, but principally means profit per IFRS (or other applicable standards) excluding non-recurring items such as disposals of businesses, and other items such as amortisation of intangibles.

(ii) **EBIT.** This means earnings before interest and tax.

(iii) **EBITDA.** This stands for earnings before interest, tax, depreciation and amortisation.

(iv) **Net financial debt.** This is gross financial debt less cash and cash equivalents and other financial assets, and is a useful indicator of an entity's ability to meet its financial obligations.

In general, APMs are any measures of financial performance not specifically defined by the applicable financial reporting framework.

The **problematic nature** of some APMs may be seen in the case of EBITDA. This is a proxy for operating cash flows, although it is not the same. It takes operating profit and strips out depreciation, amortisation and (normally) any separately-disclosed items such as exceptional items.

EBITDA is not a cash flow ratio as such, but it is a widely used, and sometimes misused, approximation. Particular reservations include:

(i)   EBITDA is not a cash flow measure and, while it excludes certain subjective accounting practices, it is still subject to accounting manipulation in a way that cash flows would not be. Examples would include revenue recognition practices and items that have some unusual aspects but are not disclosed separately and, therefore, not added back.

(ii)   EBITDA is not a sustainable figure as there is no charge for capital replacement such as depreciation in traditional profit measures or CAPEX (capital expenditure) as in free cash flow.

More generally, APMs are sometimes used by issuers to present an **overly favourable picture** of an entity's financial performance by stripping out the negative aspects.

(e)   (i)   The IASB's Disclosure Initiative is a broad-based undertaking exploring how disclosures in IFRS financial reporting can be improved. It is made up of a number of projects, the second of which was completed in January 2016.

The Disclosure Initiative was formally begun in 2012. Subsequently the IASB undertook a constituent survey on disclosure and held a disclosure forum designed to bring together securities regulators, auditors, investors and preparers. This led to the issue of Feedback Statement Discussion Forum – Financial Reporting Disclosure in May 2013, which outlined the IASB's intention to consider a number of further initiatives, including short-term and research projects.

The disclosure initiative is intended to **complement the work being done on the Conceptual Framework project.**

(ii)   In October 2015, a Draft Practice Statement was issued as part of the Disclosure Initiative. The Statement was developed in response to concerns with the level of uncertainty over the application of the concept of materiality, which can result in excessive disclosure of immaterial information while important information can be obscured or even missed out of the financial statements. Its objective was to help preparers, auditors and regulators use judgement when applying the concept of materiality in order to make financial reports more meaningful. It provides non-mandatory guidance to assist with the application of the concept of materiality to financial statements prepared in accordance with IFRS. The Statement is divided into the following three key areas:

(1)   Characteristics of materiality

(2)   How to apply the concept of materiality when making decisions about presenting and disclosing information in the financial statements

(3)   How to assess **whether omissions and misstatements of information are material** to the financial statements.

Note that whilst not examinable, it is worth stating that the IASB issued IFRS Practice Statement *Making Materiality Judgements* on 14 September 2017. It proposes a four-step process entities may find useful to apply when making materiality judgements. It is not mandatory and may be applied with immediate effect.

(f)   In the IASB's May 2015 Exposure Draft: Conceptual Framework for Financial Reporting, it proposes, for the first time, conceptual guidance on whether to present income and expenses in profit and loss or in other comprehensive income (OCI).

The ED considers the purpose of the statement of profit or loss is to:

(a)   Depict the return that an entity has made on its economic resources during the period; and

(b)   Provide information that is helpful in assessing prospects for future cash flows and in assessing management's stewardship of the entity's resources.

The ED does not define profit or loss, although it does require a total, but states that it is the primary source of information about a company's financial performance. The ED suggests a rebuttable presumption that all income and expenses are to be included in profit and loss and that income and expenses should only be classified as OCI if it results in enhanced relevance of the profit or loss, or, if they relate to assets or liabilities remeasured to current value.

A presumption that income and expenses included in OCI in one period will be subsequently reclassified to profit or loss (sometimes known as recycling) is also introduced, again with the requirement that their inclusion will enhance the relevance of the information in the statement of profit or loss for the period. The presumption that a future reclassification will occur could be rebutted if there is no clear basis for identifying the period in which reclassification would enhance the relevance of the information in the statement of profit or loss. If no such basis can be identified, this may indicate that the income or expenses should not be included in OCI.

Section 2 – Groups preparation questions

12 Ejoy

> **Workbook references.** Discontinued operations are covered in Chapter 13 of your Workbook. Joint arrangements are covered in Chapter 14. Financial instruments are covered in Chapter 7.
>
> **Top tips.** This question required the production of a consolidated statement of profit or loss and other comprehensive income (SPLOCI) of a group. You were expected to calculate and impairment test the investment in a subsidiary, to account for a joint venture, to deal with impairment and hedging of financial assets, and account for a discontinued operation. Make sure you draw up the group structure before you start detailed work on your answer. As this is a consolidated SPLOCI and both acquisitions occurred partway through the year, you might find it helpful to also draw up a timeline. The next step should be to aggregate the parent and subsidiaries income and expenses on the face of your proforma before going on to tackle the adjustments. Once you have completed your answer, make sure that you carefully review the approach to calculating the impairment loss under the partial goodwill method when you are given the recoverable amount of the subsidiary – it is complex but is likely to be regularly tested. You should also review the financial instruments adjustments as it can be tricky applying your knowledge to a scenario.
>
> **Easy marks.** Do not spend too long on the discontinued operation. You would not be penalised too heavily if you got this wrong and there are easy marks to be gained for adding across and other basic consolidation aspects.

Marking scheme

	Marks
Goodwill	7
Joint venture	2
Financial assets	7
Statement of profit or loss and other comprehensive income	8
Tbay	4
Non-controlling interest	2
Maximum	30

EJOY: CONSOLIDATED STATEMENT OF PROFIT OR LOSS AND OTHER COMPREHENSIVE INCOME FOR THE YEAR ENDED 31 MAY 20X6

	$m
Continuing operations	
Revenue (2,500 + 1,500)	4,000
Cost of sales (1,800 + 1,200 + 34 (W8))	(3,034)
Gross profit	966
Other income (70 + 10 – 3 (W11)	77
Distribution costs (130 + 120)	(250)
Administrative expenses (100 + 90)	(190)
Finance income (W6)	9
Finance costs (W7)	(137)
Profit before tax	475
Income tax expense (200 + 26)	(226)
Profit for period from continuing operations	249

	$m
Discontinued operations	
Profit for the year from discontinued operations $((30 \times ^6/_{12}) - 2 \text{ (W8)})$	13
Profit for the year	262
Other comprehensive income for the year (not reclassified to P/L):	
Gain on property revaluation net of tax: $80 + 10 + (8 \times ^6/_{12})$	94
Total comprehensive income for the year	356
Profit attributable to:	
Owners of the parent	257
Non-controlling interest (W2)	5
	262
Total comprehensive income for the year attributable to:	
Owners of the parent (bal. fig.)	348
Non-controlling interest (W2)	8
	356

Workings

1 Group structure

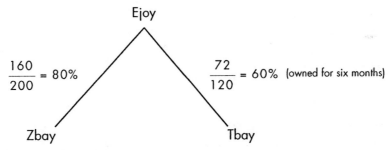

Tbay is a discontinued operation (IFRS 5).

Timeline

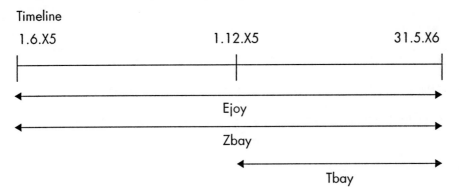

2 Non-controlling interest

	Profit for the year		Total comp income	
	Zbay $m	Tbay $m	Zbay $m	Tbay $m
PFY/TCI per question	34.0		44	
$(30 \times 6/12)/(38 \times 6/12)$		15		19
Interest income on loan asset held by Zbay (W4)	4.5		4.5	
Interest on loss allowance during the year (Loan held by Zbay) (W4)	(0.1)		(0.1)	

Less impairment loss (loan asset) (W4)	(45.5)		(45.5)		
	(7.1)	15	2.9	19	
	× 20%	× 40%	× 20%	× 40%	
	(1.4)	6	0.6	7.6	

4.6   8.2

3 Goodwill

		Zbay $m		Tbay $m
Consideration transferred		520		192
Non-controlling interests	(600 × 20%)	120	(310 × 40%)	124
Fair value of net assets at acquisition		(600)		(310)
		40		6

4 Loan held by Zbay

On 31 May 20X5, Zbay will have recognised, in accordance with IFRS 9, an allowance equivalent to twelve months' expected credit losses. This is the lifetime expected credit losses multiplied by the probability of default in the next twelve months: 10% × $25m = $2.5m. This is the brought down loss allowance at 1 June 20X5.

Interest of 4% will be recognised on this allowance of $2.5m during the year ended 31 May 20X6, which is the unwinding of the discount. This interest will be recognised in profit or loss for the year, and will increase the loss allowance by the same amount:

DEBIT   Profit or loss (4% × $2.5m) $0.1m
CREDIT   Loss allowance $0.1m

The loss allowance at 31 May 20X6 is therefore $2.6m.

Interest income must also be recognised in profit or loss for the year ended 31 May 20X6 on the gross carrying amount of $100m: 4.5% × $100m = $4.5m.

By 31 May 20X6 there is objective evidence of impairment. Stage 3 of the IFRS 9 has been reached, and lifetime expected credit losses, now revised to $48.1m, must be recognised in full. This means that the loss allowance, including interest, of $2.6m must be increased to $48.1m, and the difference charged to profit or loss for the year ended 31 May 20X6:

DEBIT   Profit or loss ($48.1m – $2.6m) $45.5m
CREDIT   Loss allowance $45.5m

5 Hedged bond (Ejoy)

	$m
1.6.X5	50.0
Interest income (5% × 50)	2.5
Interest received	(2.5)
Fair value loss (balancing figure)	(1.7)
Fair value at 31.5.X6 (per question)	48.3

Because the interest rate swap is 100% effective as a fair value hedge, it exactly offsets the loss in value of $1.7 million on the bond. The bond is classified at fair value through profit or loss. Both the gain on the swap and the loss on the bond are recognised in profit or loss as income and expense. The net effect on profit or loss is nil.

6 *Finance income*

	$m
Interest income on loan asset held by Zbay (W4)	4.5
Interest receivable on bond held by Ejoy (W5)	2.5
Interest received on interest rate swap held by Ejoy	0.5
Fair value gain on interest rate swap	1.7
	9.2

7 *Finance costs*

	$m
Per draft statements of profit or loss and other comprehensive income (50 + 40)	90.0
Interest on loss allowance during the year (Loan held by Zbay) (W4)	0.1
Increase in loss allowance (Loan held by Zbay) (W4)	45.5
Fair value loss on hedged bond (W5)	1.7
	137.3

8 *Impairment losses*

	Zbay $m	Tbay $m
Notional goodwill (40 × 100%/80%) (6 × 100%/60%) (W3)	50.0	10.0
Carrying amount of net assets (W9)/(W10)	622.9	329.0
	672.9	339.0
Recoverable amount	(630.0)	
Fair value less costs of disposal (344 – (5 × 100%/60%))		(335.7)
Impairment loss: gross	42.9	3.3
Impairment loss recognised: all allocated to goodwill (80% × 42.9)/(60% × 3.3)	34.3	2.0

9 *Carrying amount of net assets at 31 May 20X6 (Zbay)*

	$m
Fair value of identifiable assets and liabilities acquired (1 June 20X4)	600.0
TCI for year to 31 May 20X5	20.0
TCI for year to 31 May 20X6 per draft statement of profit or loss and other comprehensive income	44.0
Interest income on loan asset held by Zbay (W4)	4.5
Interest on loss allowance during the year (Loan held by Zbay) (W4)	(0.1)
Less impairment loss (loan asset) (W4)	(45.5)
	622.9

10 *Carrying amount of net assets (Tbay)*

	$m
Carrying amount of investment in Tbay at 31 May 20X6:	
Fair value of net assets at acquisition (1 December 20X5)	310
Post-acquisition TCI (38 × 6/12)	19
	329

11 *Joint venture*

	$m	$m
Elimination of Ejoy's share of gain on disposal (50% × 6)		3
DEBIT Other income	3	
CREDIT Investment in joint venture		3

13 Zippy

Workbook references. Disposals are covered in Chapter 12 of your Workbook. Pensions are covered in Chapter 4 and revenue is covered in Chapter 1. Fair value is covered in Chapters 3 and 10.

Top tips. This question was a consolidated statement of profit or loss and other comprehensive income with a disposal part-way through the year in which control is lost but significant influence retained. It is important to get the group structure right. Adjustments were required for the disposal (including goodwill and loss on disposal calculations), fair values, investment property, defined benefit pension plan and revenue recognition. You also needed to 'work backwards' with regard to the goodwill on the other subsidiary to determine what the net assets acquired would have been, and then move on to calculate what goodwill should have been.

Easy marks. Once you have established the group structure, there are some very easy marks to be had for aggregating the income and expenses of the three companies on a line by line basis and for Ginny, multiplying the numbers given in the question by $\frac{9}{12}$.

	Marks
Revenue	5
Cost of sales	1
Investment income	4
Administrative costs	4
Ginny disposal	4
Ginny associate	2
Boo and impairment	3
Retirement benefits	4
Non-controlling interest	2
Presentation of OCI into reclassified/not reclassified to profit or loss	1
	30

ZIPPY
GROUP STATEMENT OF PROFIT OR LOSS AND OTHER COMPREHENSIVE INCOME FOR THE YEAR ENDED 30 JUNE 20X6

	$m
Revenue: $420 + (132 \times \frac{9}{12}) + 90 + 6.6$ (W8)	615.60
Cost of sales: $304 + (76 \times \frac{9}{12}) + 72 + 2$ (W4)	(435.00)
Gross profit	180.60
Investment income: $36 + (19 \times \frac{9}{12}) + 5 - 14$ (W3) + 4.8 (W6)	46.05
Administrative costs: $22 + (12 \times \frac{9}{12}) + 18 + 1.2$ (W6) + 10 (W7)	(60.20)
Other expenses: $31 + (18 \times \frac{9}{12}) + 15 + 1.8$ (W4)	(61.30)
Operating profit	105.15
Net finance costs: $2 + (6 \times \frac{9}{12}) + 9 + 1.4$ (W7)	(16.90)
Loss on disposal of subsidiary (W3)	(8.00)
Share of profit of associate: $32 \times \frac{3}{12} \times 40\%$	3.20

	$m
Profit before tax	83.45
Income tax expense: $30 + (7 \times \frac{9}{12}) - 3$	(32.25)
Profit for the year	51.20

Other comprehensive income (items that will not be reclassified to profit or loss)

Gain on property revaluation: $14 + (16 \times \frac{9}{12}) + 2.4$ (W6)	28.40
Remeasurement of defined benefit pension plan (W7)	4.00
Share of profit of other comprehensive income of associate: $16 \times \frac{3}{12} \times 40\%$	1.60
Other comprehensive income for the year	34.00
Total comprehensive income for the year	85.20

Profit attributable to:
Owners of the parent (bal. fig.)	45.60
Non-controlling interests (W2)	5.60
	51.20

Total comprehensive income attributable to:
Owners of the parent	74.80
Non-controlling interests (W2)	10.40
	85.20

Workings

1   Group structure

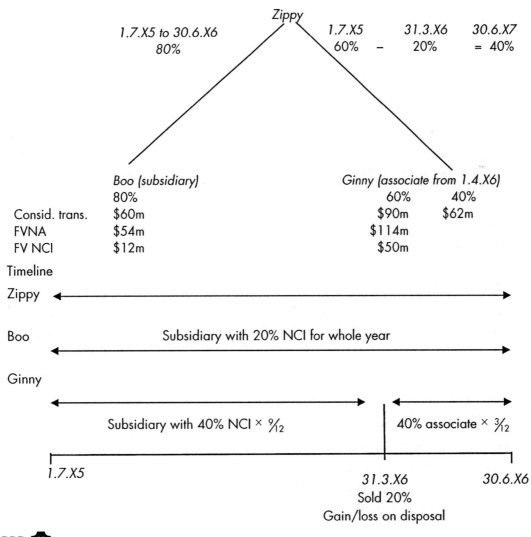

2   Non-controlling interests

	Ginny		Boo	
	Profit for year	TCI	Profit for year	TCI
	$m	$m	$m	$m
Per question			(16.0)	(16.0)
$32 \times \frac{9}{12}$	24.0			
$48 \times \frac{9}{12}$		36.0		
Depreciation of fair value adjustment (W4)			(2.0)	(2.0)
Impairment of full goodwill (W4)	–	–	(1.8)	(1.8)
	24.0	36.0	(19.8)	(19.8)
NCI share	× 40%	× 40%	× 20%	× 20%
	9.6	14.4	(4.0)	(4.0)

$5.6m $10.4m

3   Gain/(loss) on disposal of Ginny (control lost)

	$m	$m
Fair value of consideration received		44
Fair value of 40% investment retained		62
Less share of consolidated carrying amount at date control lost		
Net assets: $118m + ($48m × $\frac{9}{12}$)	154	
Goodwill (W4)	26	
Less non-controlling interests (W5)	(66)	
		(114)
		(8)

Note. The gain on disposal in the individual financial statements of Zippy would have been $44m – ($90m × 20%/60%) = $14m. This was included in Zippy's investment income and must be removed in arriving at consolidated investment income.

4   Goodwill

	Ginny	Boo
	$m	$m
Consideration transferred	90	60.0
Fair value of non-controlling interest	50	12.0
Fair value of net assets	(114)	(44.0)β
	26	28.0 (per qu.)
Effect of finalisation of fair value of net assets:		
$54m (per qu.) – $44m*	–	(10.0)
	–	18.0
Impairment loss: 10%	–	(1.8)
	26	16.2

*Note. The final fair value of the identifiable net assets is $10m higher than the carrying amount of net assets that was used in the initial goodwill calculation. Therefore, goodwill is reduced by $10m. Additional depreciation should be charged to cost of sales of ($10m/5) = $2m. Note that the fair values were finalised within the initial accounting period (a maximum of 12 months from acquisition) so the adjustment is treated retrospectively. Goodwill impairment of $1.8m is to be charged to other expenses.

5   Non-controlling interests of Ginny (SOFP) at disposal

	$m
Non-controlling interest at acquisition (W4)	50
NCI share of post acq'n retained earnings to 31 March 20X6:	
($154m (W3) – $114m) × 40%	16
	66

6   Investment property: ten-floor office block

	Investment property $m	Owner occupied $m	Total $m
1 July 20X5: 90 × 8/10	72.0	18.0	90.0
90 × 2/10			
Depn. $18m/15 years	–	(1.2) (P/L)	(1.2)
	72.0	16.8	88.8
Fair value gain β	4.8 (P/L)	2.4 (OCI)	7.2
Fair value at 30 June 20X6:	76.8		
96 × 8/10		19.2	
96 × 2/10			96.0

*Note. Depreciation of $1.2m should be charged to administrative costs. The fair value gain on investment property of $4.8m should be recorded in investment income. The fair value gain on owner-occupied property of $2.4m should be recorded in other comprehensive income.

7   Defined benefit pension plan

	$m
Net obligation b/d 1 July 20X5	(14.0)
Service costs for y/e 30 June 20X6	(10.0) (P/L)
Net interest on net defined benefit obligation: 14 × 10%	(1.4) (P/L)
Contributions to scheme	8.0
Remeasurement gains	4.0 (OCI)
Net obligation c/d 30 June 20X6	(13.4)

Service costs and interest will be charged to profit or loss for the year, service costs to administrative costs and interest to finance costs. Remeasurement gains will be credited to other comprehensive income for the year.

8   Revenue recognition: Whizoo

Manufacturing defects:

The $40 credit per unit is a revision to the transaction price for the first 6,000 units sold. Therefore, there should be a reduction in revenue equal to (6,000 × $40) $0.24m for the first 6,000 units sold.

DEBIT	Revenue (6,000 × $40)	$0.24m	
CREDIT	Trade receivables		$0.24m

Further 7,000 units:

The negotiated price of $950 per unit is dependent on the purchase of the initial 10,000 units. Therefore, it does not meet the conditions to be accounted for as a separate contract. Instead it is treated as a cancellation of the old contract together with the creation of a new contract. The revenue attributable to the further 7,000 units manufactured will therefore be calculated using a weighted average price based on the remaining 4,000 units under the original contract (at $1,000 per unit) and the 5,000 units under the new contract (at $950 per unit). This is calculated as follows:

$$\frac{(4,000 \times \$1,000) + (5,000 \times \$950)}{(4,000 + 5,000)} = \$972 \text{ per item}$$

The additional revenue to be accrued for these 7,000 units is (7,000 × $972) = $6.8m.

DEBIT	Receivables (7,000 × $972)	$6.8m	
CREDIT	Revenue		$6.8m

No revenue can yet be included for the 2,000 units which have not been manufactured as at 30 June 20X6 as Zippy has not satisfied its performance obligation. The net increase to the revenue of Zippy should be ($6.8m − $0.24m) $6.6m.

14 Bravado

Workbook references. Step acquisitions are covered in Chapter 11. The full and partial goodwill methods are covered in Chapter 10, financial instruments in Chapter 7 and foreign transactions in Chapter 15.

Top tips. This question required the preparation of a consolidated statement of financial position where the non-controlling interest on acquisition was at fair value. This is often called the full goodwill method. There was also a calculation and explanation of the impact on the calculation of goodwill if the non-controlling interest was calculated on a proportionate basis (or the 'partial goodwill' method). The main body of the question requires you to deal with the calculation of goodwill in a simple situation, the calculation of goodwill where there was a prior holding in the subsidiary and contingent consideration, an investment in an associate, a foreign currency transaction, deferred tax and impairment of inventory. Don't be put off by the fact that the goodwill on Message is negative (gain on a bargain purchase). This is unusual, and can sometimes mean your calculation is wrong, but you don't lose many marks for arithmetical mistakes.

Easy marks. In part (a), easy marks are available for aggregating the parent's and subsidiaries' assets and liabilities on a line by line basis. If you're pushed for time you should ignore the foreign currency investment, as it's fiddly and only carries two marks.

Part (b) has a generous mark allocation, since the calculation is similar to that in part (a) – you just need the NCI share of the subsidiary's net assets.

		Marks
(a)	Property, plant and equipment	3
	Goodwill	4
	Investment in associate	3
	Investment in equity instrument	2
	Current assets	1
	Retained earnings	4
	Other components of equity	3
	Share capital and long-term borrowings	1

	Marks
Deferred tax	1
Current liabilities	1
Non-controlling interest	2
	25
(b) Message	1
Mixted	1
Explanation	3
	5
	30

(a) BRAVADO GROUP
CONSOLIDATED STATEMENT OF FINANCIAL POSITION AS AT 31 MAY 20X9

	$m
Non-current assets	
Property, plant and equipment: 265 + 230 + 161 + 40 (W7) + 12 (W7)	708.0
Goodwill (W2)	25.0
Investment in associate (W3)	22.5
Investment in equity instruments: 51 + 6 + 5 – 17.4 (W8)	44.6
	800.1
Current assets	
Inventories: 135 + 55 + 73	263.0
Trade and other receivables: 91 + 45 + 32	168.0
Cash and cash equivalents: 102 + 100 + 8	210.0
	641.0
	1,441.1
Equity attributable to owners of the parent	
Share capital	520.0
Retained earnings (W4)	284.1
Other components of equity (W5)	(0.4)
	803.7
Non-controlling interests (W6)	148.8
	952.5
Non-current liabilities	
Long-term borrowings: 120 + 15 + 5	140.0
Deferred tax: 25 + 9 + 3 + 2.6 (W7)	39.6
	179.6
Current liabilities	
Trade and other payables: 115 + 30 + 60 + 12 (W2)	217.0
Current tax: 60 + 8 + 24	92.0
	309.0
	1,441.1

Workings

1 *Group structure*

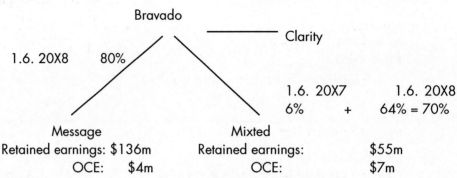

	1.6.X7			1.6.X8
	10%	+	15%	= 25%

Bravado

———— Clarity

1.6. 20X8   80%

	1.6. 20X7		1.6. 20X8
	6%	+	64% = 70%

Message	Mixted	
Retained earnings: $136m	Retained earnings:	$55m
OCE: $4m	OCE:	$7m

2 *Goodwill*

	Message		Mixted	
	$m	$m	$m	$m
Consideration transferred				
Cash		300		118
Contingent (at FV)		–		12
		300		130
Non-controlling interest (at fair value)		86		53
Fair value of previously held equity interest				15
Less fair value of net assets at acquisition				
Per question/170 + 6	400		176	
Deferred tax liability (W7)	–		(3)	
		(400)		(173)
Negative goodwill (Gain on bargain purchase)/Goodwill		(14)*		25

*Note. This is a gain on a bargain purchase and should be recorded in profit or loss for the year attributable to the parent (W4).

3 *Investment in associate*

	$m
Cost = fair value at date significant influence achieved: $9m + $11m	20.0
Share of post 'acquisition' retained earnings $10m* × 25%	2.5
	22.5

*Note. The profit for the year to 31 May 20X9 is the relevant figure, as the investment only became an associate at the beginning of that year.

4 *Retained earnings*

	Bravado	Message	Mixted
	$m	$m	$m
At year end	240.0	150	80.0
Fair value movement (W7)			(1.6)
Gain on bargain purchase (W2)	14.0		
At acquisition		(136)	(55.0)
		14	23.4
Group share			
Message: 80% × 14	11.2		
Mixted: 70% × 23.4	16.4		
Clarity: 25% × 10*	2.5		
	284.1		

*Note. The $10m profit for the year to 31 May 20X9 is the post-acquisition figure as Clarity became an associate on 1 June 20X8.

5   Other components of equity

	Bravado $m	Message $m	Mixted $m
At year end	17.0	4	7
Foreign IEI (W9)	(17.4)		
At acquisition		(4)	(7)
Group share post acq'n: Message	0.0	0	0
Mixted	0.0		
	(0.4)		

6   Non-controlling interests

	Message $m	Mixted $m
NCI at date of control (FV/W2)	86.0	53
NCI share of post-acquisition reserves		
Message: 14 (W4) × 20%	2.8	
Mixted: 23.4 (W4) × 30%		7
	88.8	60

148.8

Note. The NCI share of post-acquisition reserves should include all relevant reserves (eg retained earnings, other components of equity). However, as neither subsidiary has any post-acquisition other components of equity, the only post-acquisition reserves to include here are retained earnings.

7   Fair value adjustments

Message:

	At acq'n 1.6.X8 $m	Movement $m	At year end 31.5 X9 $m
Land: 400 – (220 + 136 + 4)	40	–	40

Mixted:

	At acq'n 1.6.X8	Movement $\frac{1}{7}$	At year end 31.5 X9
Property, plant & equipment:			
170 + 6 – (100 + 55 + 7)	14	(2.0)	12.0
Deferred tax liability: (176 – 166) × 30%	(3)	0.4	(2.6)
	11	(1.6)	9.4

8   Foreign currency investment in equity instrument

	$m
Value on initial recognition: 11m dinars × 4.5	49.50
Value at 31 May 20X8: 10m dinars × 5.1	51.00
Gain	1.50

At 31 May 20X8, this gain would be recorded in other comprehensive income (not reclassified to profit or loss).

	DEBIT	Investment in equity instrument	$1.5m	
	CREDIT	Other components of equity (via OCI)		$1.5m

	$m
Value at 31 May 20X8	51.00
Value at 31 May 20X9: 7m dinars × 4.8	(33.60)
Impairment	17.40

This is recorded as follows

DEBIT	Other components of equity (via OCI)	$17.4m	
CREDIT	Investment in equity instrument		$17.4m

(b) **Goodwill if non-controlling interest is calculated on a proportionate basis**

	Message		Mixted	
	$m	$m	$m	$m
Consolidated transferred				
Cash		300		118.0
Contingent (at FV)		–		12.0
		300		130.0
Non-controlling interest (20% × 400)/(30% × 173)		80		51.9
Fair value of previously held equity interest				15.0
Less fair value of net assets at acquisition				
Per question	400		176	
Deferred tax liability (W7)	–		(3)	
		(400)		(173.0)
Negative goodwill (Gain on bargain purchase)/goodwill		(20)		23.9

The proportionate basis results in only the parent's share of goodwill being incorporated into the goodwill calculation. This is sometimes referred to as the 'partial goodwill' method. Whereas the 'full goodwill' or fair value method incorporates the parent's share and the non-controlling interest's share of goodwill into the calculation.

In the case of **Message**, if non-controlling interest is valued on a **proportionate basis**, the **gain on the bargain purchase is greater** which **would increase the reported income**. The reason for this is that under the full goodwill method, the goodwill relating to non-controlling interests (calculated as fair value of NCI $86m less NCI share of net assets: 20% × $400m) is positive goodwill of $6m which has been netted off against the parent's gain on bargain purchase. Therefore, excluding this positive goodwill under the proportionate method results in a greater gain on the bargain purchase.

In the case of **Mixted**, the **goodwill is less** under the proportionate method which would result in **lower net assets** in the consolidated statement of financial position with the result that **impairment of goodwill** may be **less**.

15 Jocatt

Workbook references. Group statements of cash flow are covered in Chapter 16, step acquisitions in Chapter 11, deferred tax in Chapter 6, non-current assets in Chapter 3 and pension plans in Chapter 4.

Top tips. In tackling this statement of cash flows question, remember that time management is the key. Set out your proforma and workings and do not spend too long on the fiddly bits. The question required you to understand how a step acquisition would work under IFRS 3 – you need to know that the fair value of the previously held interest in Tigret, and the fair value of the non-controlling interest in Tigret as a subsidiary, go in the goodwill calculation. Other complications include a retirement benefit scheme and a rights issue. Be careful to ensure that the purchase of the subsidiary is dealt with in calculating cash flows across the range of assets and liabilities.

Easy marks. These are available for basic cash flow aspects – working capital calculations, non-controlling interest, tax and investment property additions. Follow our order for the workings – the easy ones come first.

	Marks
Net profit before tax	1
Retirement benefit expense	2
Depreciation on PPE	1
Depreciation on investment property	1
Amortisation of intangible assets	1
Profit on exchange of land	1
Loss on replacement of investment property	1
Associate's profit	1
Impairment of goodwill	4
Gain on revaluation of investment in equity instruments (Tigret) prior to derecognition	1
Finance costs	1
Decrease in trade receivables	1
Decrease in inventories	1
Increase in trade payables	1
Cash paid to defined benefit pension plan	1
Interest paid	1
Income taxes paid	2
Purchase of associate	1
Purchase of PPE	2
Purchase of subsidiary	1
Additions – investment property	1
Proceeds from sale of land	1
Intangible assets	1
Purchase of investments in equity instruments	1
Repayment of long-term borrowings	1
Rights issue NCI	1
Non-controlling interest dividend	1
Dividends paid	1
Net increase in cash and cash equivalents	1
	35

JOCATT GROUP
STATEMENT OF CASH FLOWS FOR YEAR ENDED 30 NOVEMBER 20X2

	$m	$m
Cash flows from operating activities		
Profit before taxation	59.0	
Adjustments for:		
Depreciation (per question)	27.0	
Amortisation (W1)	17.0	
Impairment of goodwill (W1)	31.5	
Profit on exchange of land*: 15 + 4 – 10	(9.0)	
Gain on investment property* (W1)	(1.5)	
Loss on replacement of investment property*	0.5	
Gain on revaluation of investment in equity instruments		
(Tigret – fair value on derecognition less fair value at		
1 December 20X1:5 – 4)	(1.0)	
Retirement benefit expense (W7)	4.0	
Cash paid to defined benefit pension plan (W3)	(7.0)	
Share of profit of associate (per question)	(6.0)	
Interest expense (per question)	6.0	
	120.5	
Decrease in trade receivables (W4)	56.0	
Decrease in inventories (W4)	23.0	
Increase in trade payables (W4)	89.0	
Cash generated from operations	288.5	
Interest paid (per question)	(6.0)	
Income taxes paid (W3)	(16.5)	
Net cash from operating activities		266
Investing activities		
Acquisition of subsidiary, net of cash acquired: 15 – 7	(8.0)	
Acquisition of associate (W1)	(48.0)	
Purchase of property, plant and equipment (W1)	(98.0)	
Purchase of investment property (per question)	(1.0)	
Purchase of intangible assets (W6)	(12.0)	
Purchase of investments in equity instruments (W1)	(5.0)	
Proceeds from sale of land	15.0	
Net cash used in investing activities		(157)
Financing activities		
Proceeds from issue of share capital (W2)	0.0	
Repayment of long-term borrowings (W3)	(4.0)	
Rights issue to non-controlling shareholders (from SOCIE)	2.0	
Dividends paid (from SOCIE or (W2))	(5.0)	
Dividends paid to non-controlling interest shareholders	(13.0)	
(from SOCIE or (W2))		
Net cash used in financing activities		(20)
Net increase in cash and cash equivalents		89
Cash and cash equivalents at the beginning of the year		143
Cash and cash equivalents at the end of the year		232

*Note. The statement of profit or loss and other comprehensive income in the question shows 'gains on property' of $10.5m, which need to be added back to profit in arriving at cash generated from operations. This is made up of $1.5m gain on investment property (W1) and $9m gain on the exchange of surplus land for cash and plant (Note (vi) of the question). The double entry for the exchange is:

DEBIT	Cash	$15m	
DEBIT	Plant	$4m	
CREDIT	Land		$10m
CREDIT	Profit or loss		$9m

Separate from this, also shown in W1, is an impairment loss on the old heating system (Note (v) of the question), for which the double entries are:

DEBIT	Profit or loss (old heating system)	$0.5m	
CREDIT	Investment property (old heating system)		$0.5m
DEBIT	Investment property (new heating system)	$1m	
CREDIT	Cash		$1m

Workings

1   Assets

	PPE	Investment property	Goodwill	Other intangible assets	Associate	Investments in equity instruments
	$m	$m	$m	$m	$m	$m
b/d	254	6.0	68.0	72	0	90
P/L		**1.5 β**			6	1
OCI	(7)					3 *
Dep'n/ Amort'n/ Impairment	(27)		**(31.5)** β	**(17)** β		
Acquisition of sub/assoc	15		(W5)11.5	18	48 β	
Non-cash additions	4					
Disposals/ derecognition	(10)	(0.5)				(W5) (5)
Cash paid/ (rec'd) β	**98**	1.0	0.0	(W6) 12	(0)	**5**
c/d	327	8.0	48.0	85	54	94

*Grossed up for related tax: $2m + $1m

2   Equity

	Share capital $m	Retained earnings $m	NCI $m
b/d	275	324	36
P/L		38	10
OCI		(6)	
Acquisition of subsidiary	15		20
Rights issue (5 × 40%)			2
Cash (paid)/rec'd β	**0**	**(5)** *	**(13)** *
c/d	290	351	55

*Note. Cash flow given in question, but working shown for clarity.

3   Liabilities

	Long-term borrowings $m	Tax payable $m (41 + 30)	Pension obligation $m
b/d	71	71.0	22
P/L		11.0	(W7) 4
OCI		1.0	6
Acquisition of subsidiary		(W5)1.5	
Cash (paid)/rec'd β	**(4)**	**(16.5)**	**(7)**
c/d	67	68.0 (35 + 33)	25

4   Working capital changes

	Inventories $m	Trade receivables $m	Trade payables $m
b/d	128	113	55
Acquisition of subsidiary		5	
∴ **Increase/(decrease)**	**(23)**	**(56)**	**89**
c/d	105	62	144

5   Goodwill on acquisition of Tigret

	$m	$m
Consideration transferred: $15m + $15m		30.0
Fair value of non-controlling interests		20.0
Fair value of previously held investment		5.0
		55.0
Identifiable net assets:		
($15m + $18m + $5m + $7m)	45.0	
Deferred tax: ($45m – $40m) × 30%	(1.5)	
		(43.5)
		11.5

6   Intangible assets

The research costs of $2m and the marketing costs of $1m are charged to profit or loss for the year.

The $8m cost of the patents and the $4m development costs = $12m are cash outflows to acquire intangible assets.

7   Retirement benefit expense

The total net pension cost charged to profit or loss is:

	$m
Current service cost	10
Past service cost (recognised immediately)	2
Net interest income on net plan assets	(8)
	4

16 Warrburt

> **Workbook references.** Group statements of cash flow are covered in Chapter 16, financial instruments in Chapter 7, employee benefits in Chapter 4 and non-current assets in Chapter 3.
>
> **Top tips.** There are many straightforward, non-group aspects to this group statement of cash flows, so make sure you don't get bogged down in the detailed adjustments at the expense of these. The adjustments to the net loss before tax include some more unusual ones, such as the profit on the investment in equity instruments. We have set up workings for impairment on goodwill and intangibles, even though the amounts are given to you in the question. It is good practice to set up standard workings in case there is something missing from the information in the question, or you have to calculate the figures from scratch. In part (b), use the information in the first part of the question in answering this part to make your answer applied. Don't just give general advantages and disadvantages of statements of cash flows – this would not score a pass. Don't skimp on part (b) – it has five marks. Our answer is longer than you would need to produce in the exam, and credit will be given for each valid point even if they are not included in our suggested solution.
>
> **Easy marks.** These are available for setting out the proforma and workings, downloading figures from the financial statements given in the question and also for valid points made in part (b) on interpretation. Do not spend too much time on the fiddly workings at the expense of these much easier marks.

Marking scheme

		Marks
(a)	Net loss before tax	1
	Investment in equity instruments	2
	Retirement benefit	2
	Property, plant and equipment	3
	Profit on insurance claim	1
	Associate	3
	Goodwill and intangibles	1
	Interest expense and interest paid	2
	Taxation	3
	Working capital	3
	Proceeds of share issue	1
	Repayment of borrowings	1
	Dividends	1
	Non-controlling interest	1
		25
(b)	Key issues highlighted by statement of cash flows: discussion – 1 mark per valid point which may include:	
	Statement of cash flows is indicator of company's liquidity	1
	Loss before tax compared to net cash from operating activities	1
	Cash from sale of investments not sustainable in long term	1
	Working capital is being used for investing activities	1
	Discussion of ratios (current ratio, quick ratio, gearing)	1
		5
		30

(a)   WARRBURT GROUP
       STATEMENT OF CASH FLOWS FOR THE YEAR ENDED 30 NOVEMBER 20X8

	$m	$m
Operating activities		
Net loss before tax	(47)	
Adjustments for		
Gain on revaluation of investment in equity instruments (W1)	(7)	
Retirement benefit expense	10	
Depreciation	36	
Profit on sale of property plant and equipment: $63m – $56m	(7)	
Profit on insurance claim: $3m – $1m	(2)	
Share of profit of associate	(6)	
Impairment losses: $20m + $12m (W1)	32	
Interest expense	9	
	18	
Decrease in trade receivables (W4)	71	
Decrease in inventories (W4)	63	
Decrease in trade payables (W4)	(85)	
Cash generated from operations	67	
Retirement benefit contributions*	(10)	
Interest paid (W5)	(8)	
Income taxes paid (W3)	(39)	
Net cash from operating activities		10
Investing activities		
Purchase of property, plant and equipment (per qu/(W1))	(60)	
Proceeds from sale of property, plant and equipment	63	
Proceeds from sale of investments in equity instruments (W1)	45	
Acquisition of associate (W1)	(96)	
Dividend received from associate: (W1)	2	
Net cash used in investing activities		(46)
Financing activities		
Proceeds from issue of share capital (W2)	55	
Repayment of long-term borrowings (W3)	(44)	
Dividends paid	(9)	
Dividends paid to non-controlling shareholders (W3)	(5)	
Net cash used in financing activities		(3)
Net decrease in cash and cash equivalents		(39)
Cash and cash equivalents at beginning of year		323
Cash and cash equivalents at end of year		284

*Note. Only the contributions paid are reported in the cash flow, because this is the only movement of cash. The amounts paid by the trustees are not included, because they are not paid by the company.

Workings

1   *Assets*

	PPE $m	Goodwill $m	Intangible assets $m	Associate $m	Investment in equity instruments $m
b/d	360	100	240	0	150
P/L				6	
OCI (revaluation)	4				30*
Fair value gain on investment in Alburt					7**
Dep'n/Impairment/	(36)	**(20)** β	**(12)** β		
Acquisition of associate				**96** β	
Asset destroyed	(1)				
Replacement from insurance company (at fair value)	3				
Disposals	(56)				
Non-cash additions (on credit)($80m – $60m(W4))	20				
				8 × 25%	
Cash paid/(rec'd)	**60**	0	0	(2)	**(45)**
c/d	354	80	228	100	142

* This is the gain on revaluation, which is shown in the statement of profit or loss and other comprehensive income net of deferred tax of $3m (W3), that is at $27m. The gross gain is therefore $30m and is the amount reflected in this working.

** This is fair value on disposal less fair value at 1 December 20X7.

2   *Equity*

	Share capital $m	Retained earnings $m	NCI $m
b/d	595	454	53
P/L		(74)	(2)
OCI		(4)*	
Cash (paid)/rec'd	**55** β	(9) **	(5) **
c/d	650	367	46

*Actuarial loss

**Cash flow given in question, but working shown for clarity

3   *Liabilities*

	Long-term borrowings $m	Tax payable $m	Retirement benefit obligation $m
b/d	64	(26 + 42) 68	96
P/L		29	10
OCI		3 + 2 (W1)* 5	4
Cash (paid)/rec'd	**(44)** β	**(39)** β	**(10)****
c/d	20	63 (28+ 35)	100

* On revaluation gain on PPE + revaluation gain on investments in equity interests

** Only the contributions paid are reported in the cash flow, because this is the only movement of cash. The amounts paid by the trustees are not included, because they are not paid by the company.

4   Working capital changes

	Inventories $m	Trade receivables $m	Trade payables $m
b/d	198	163	180
PPE on credit ($80m – $20m (W1))			20
∴ **Increase/(decrease)**	**(63)** β	**(71)** β	**(85)** β
c/d	135	92	115

5   Interest payable

	$m
b/d (short-term provisions)	4
Profit or loss for year	9
Cash paid (balancing figure)	**(8)**
c/d (short-term provisions)	5

(b) **Key issues arising from the statement of cash flows**

The statement of financial position and the statement of profit or loss and other comprehensive income, and the ratios associated with these statements, can provide useful information to users, but it is the **statement of cash flows** which gives the **key insight** into a company's liquidity. Cash is the lifeblood of business, and less able to be manipulated than profit. It is particularly important to look at where the cash has come from. If the cash is from trading activity, it is a healthy sign.

Although Warrburt has made a loss before tax of $47m, net cash from operating activities is a modest but healthy $10m. Before working capital changes, the cash generated is $18m. The question arises, however, as to **whether this cash generation can continue if profitability does not improve**.

Of some concern is the fact that **a large amount of cash has been generated by the sale of investments in equity instruments**. This source of cash generation is not sustainable in the long term.

Operating cash flow **does not compare favourably with trading liabilities** ($115m). In the long-term, operating cash flow should finance the repayment of long-term debt, but in the case of Warrburt, working capital is being used to **for investing activities,** specifically the purchase of an associate and of property, plant and equipment. It remains to be seen whether these investments generate future profits that will sustain and increase the operating cash flow.

The company's **current ratio** (511/155 = 3.3) and **acid test ratio** (376/155 = 2.43) are **sound;** it appears that cash is tied up in long-term, rather than short-term investment. An encouraging sign, however, is that the cash used to repay long-term loans has been more than replaced by cash raised from the issue of share capital. This means that **gearing will reduce**, which is particularly important in the light of possible problems sustaining profitability and cash flows from trading activities.

Section 3 – Exam-standard questions

17 Jarvis

Workbook references. Ethics are covered in Chapter 2, non-current assets in Chapter 3 and social and environmental reporting in Chapter 17.

Top tips. Part (a) requires a discussion of possible capitalisation of innovation project spend as non-current assets. This is a fundamental topic you should be familiar with technically and able to demonstrate straightforward knowledge as well as discuss.

Part (b) requires a discussion of corporate responsibility and in particular social and environmental reporting. Part (c) requires consideration of the ethical factors involved in companies disclosing large amounts of narrative information in these areas but not viewing corporate responsibility as part of corporate strategy. Both of these topics are likely to appear on a recurring basis so make sure you are comfortable with answering discussion type questions. Revisit Skills Checkpoint 5 in the Workbook for a recap on the necessary exam technique.

Easy marks. Part (a) contains some easy marks for knowledge and you can gain further marks by demonstrating an ability to link your accounting knowledge to the particular scenario. Part (b) is straightforward knowledge and part (c) allows scope for interpretation – it is more important that you show awareness of the issues than come up with a 'correct' answer.

Marking scheme

		Marks
(a)	Accounting treatment for innovation initiative – discussion 1 mark per point to a maximum of 5 marks. Points may include:	
	Definition of an asset	1
	IAS 16 or IAS 38	1
	Research or development	2
	Impairment risk	1
		5
(b)	Corporate responsibility and factors encouraging disclosure – discussion 1 mark per point to a maximum of 10 marks. Points may include:	

Corporate responsibility

To stakeholders and society		2
Wider consequences of strategic decisions		2
Disclosure		1

Factors encouraging disclosure

Public interest		2
Shareholder value		1
Government and professional bodies		1
Published guidelines		1
		10

(c)   Ethical issues – discussion 1 mark per point to a maximum of 5 marks.
        Points may include:

Lack of supporting quantitative disclosures	1
Corporate responsibility not a strategic priority	1
Risk of just being public relations exercise/manipulation	<u>1</u>
	3
Professional marks	<u>2</u>
	<u><u>20</u></u>

(a)   **Definition of an asset**

In order to determine the appropriate accounting treatment for Jarvis' innovation initiative, consideration must be given as to the **nature of the spend** by the new team and whether it meets the **definition of an asset** in accordance with the IASB's *Conceptual Framework*. To be recognised it must be 'a resource **controlled** by the entity as a result of **past events** and from which **future economic benefits** are expected to flow to the entity' (*Conceptual Framework*: para. 4.4(a), emphasis BPP). To be classified as a non-current asset, Jarvis must have the intention to use the asset on a continuing basis and it should not be intended for resale.

IAS 16 or IAS 38

A review of the **type of spend** must be completed as well as discussion regarding the intended use for the knowledge created going forward. For example, if Jarvis is to invent new systems and processes, or perhaps new machinery, will the potential technology be retained for use within the company only, or will the ideas be patented and made available for use by other entities?

This will assist in determining whether IAS 16 *Property, Plant and Equipment* or IAS 38 *Intangible Assets* is relevant.

Research or development

It is likely that, at least **initially**, the expenditure will be categorised as **research** under IAS 38 because in the early stages of the initiative, the costs are likely to relate to investigation rather than a specific product or process. Per IAS 38, the research costs must be **expensed** to profit and loss as incurred because at this stage, Jarvis will be unable to demonstrate future economic benefits. When Jarvis' innovation team has created some new ideas and is in a position to move forward with project development (of a specific process or product), an **intangible asset** can only be recognised if the appropriate **IAS 38 criteria** for **capitalising development costs** have been met.

An example of potentially capitalisable costs is the employee benefit expense of the team. The element that is directly attributable to an internally generated intangible asset may be included.

Impairment risk

Jarvis will need to closely monitor the nature and treatment of the spend it incurs on various innovation projects, in order to ensure ongoing treatment remains appropriate. Following capitalisation there will be a risk of impairment **if** there is a **change in the direction of a project or the external environment**.

(b)   **Corporate responsibility**

To stakeholders and society

Increasingly, as well as being profitable, businesses are increasingly expected to have a **responsibility** to those groups and individuals that they can affect, ie, its **stakeholders**,

and to **society** at large. Stakeholders are usually defined as customers, suppliers, employees, communities and shareholders or other financiers.

Wider consequences of strategic decisions

Strategic decisions by businesses, especially global businesses, nearly always have **wider social and environmental consequences**. In fact, it could be argued that a company produces two outputs, the goods or services that it provides and the social and environmental consequences of its activities. These latter aspects are what is meant by corporate responsibility and two of the main areas are social reporting and environmental reporting.

Disclosure

There are no standards that apply when making social or environmental disclosures although there are a variety of published guidelines that entities may follow if they wish. Therefore, social and environmental disclosures are **voluntary** which means that companies are free to disclose information that they believe is relevant. This is often a criticism of social and environmental disclosures as there is a **risk** that companies only **report information that is favourable**.

Disclosure often encompasses areas that can be monitored: such as the level of the entity's carbon emissions or carbon 'footprint' as it is now often called, the level of community support, and the use of sustainable inputs, such as buying paper from suppliers that plant new trees.

Factors encouraging disclosure

There are many factors which should encourage companies to disclose information on their levels of corporate responsibility in terms of social and environmental reporting in their financial statements.

Public interest

Probably the most important factor however is public interest, which is increasing rapidly. It is now widely recognised that although financial statements are primarily produced for investors there are also many other **stakeholders** in a company. All of these stakeholders are potentially interested in the way in which the company's business affects the community and the environment. Increasingly the end user customer is concerned about how the product is made and concerned about the use of cheap labour and the poor working conditions that are often associated with it. Equally the customer will be concerned about packaging and waste and the effects of this on the environment. If a company has a good reputation for care of its employees and care for the environment this will be an important marketing tool.

Shareholder value

As investors become more aware of social and environmental issues affecting society, companies now appreciate that their attitude to **corporate responsibility** can have a **direct effect on shareholder value**. Their social and environmental policies are an important part of their overall performance and responsible practices in these areas and the provision of information in the annual report on these areas will have a positive effect on shareholder value if the company is perceived to be a good investment.

Government and professional bodies

A further factor is the **increasing influence of governments and professional bodies** in their **encouragement of disclosure** and sustainable practices. In some countries there are awards for environmental and social reporting and the disclosures provided in the financial statements. In the UK, the Prince of Wales set up the 'Accounting for Sustainability' project which is designed to develop systems that will help both public and private sector organisations account more accurately for the wider social and environmental costs of their activities. Voluntary disclosures often encourage good practise which can help to keep companies ahead of the curve when new regulations are introduced by government.

Published guidelines

There are also a variety of **published guidelines and codes of practice** designed to encourage the practices of social and environmental reporting, such as the **International Integrated Reporting <IR> Framework and Global Reporting Initiative.**

However, what is missing is any substantial amount of legislation or accounting requirements in this area. The disclosure that is taking place is largely driven by the factors considered above, but the level and type of disclosure is then at the discretion of the company.

(c)   **Ethical issues**

Lack of supporting quantitative disclosures

The problem that has been noted with companies' disclosures regarding corporate responsibility is that although there is now widespread **narrative disclosure** in the annual report, this tends **not** to be **backed up with quantitative disclosures** in the form of key performance indicators. This can make is difficult for stakeholders to understand the impact of company actions and make comparisons between companies.

Corporate responsibility not a strategic priority

One of the reasons for this is that **few companies** identify aspects of corporate responsibility as **strategic priorities.** The ethical problem here is that the narrative reports are of extensive amounts of information that are not necessarily being actively managed within the business, giving perhaps a false impression of the extent of corporate responsibility at board level. The reporting itself often has no clear links to the business performance and strategy and is therefore not necessarily a clear reflection of the company's thinking on these areas.

Risk of just being a public relations exercise

If social and environmental issues do not genuinely affect strategic and operational decisions such as the types of products developed, supply chain issues, brand positioning and corporate culture then it could be argued that these corporate responsibility disclosures are **little more than a public relations exercise.** There is a risk that the disclosures are manipulated by reporting only favourable information to present the company in the best possible light. This could at worst **mislead stakeholders** in the company.

18 Columbus

Workbook references. Ethics are covered in Chapter 2, fair value in Chapter 3 and leases in Chapter 8.

Top tips. Part (a) required a discussion of the extent to which fair values are used in IFRS and the impact of this on the usefulness of financial statements. Part (b) contained an ethical issue. The issue concerned the tension between judgement and conflict of interest, in the context of recognising a lease in the statement of financial position. It is important to tailor your answer to the requirements in discussion parts of questions – the ACCA examining team has criticised candidates in the past for failure to **apply** their knowledge.

Easy marks. Part (a) allows for flexibility in the arguments made. This question provides an opportunity to answer across a range of standards and not just focus on IFRS 13. In part (b), you must make reference to more than simply the rules by including comments on the fact that subjectivity and professional judgement are involved. There are marks allocated for the ethical discussion so be careful not to solely discuss the rules about leasing rather than using ethical insight. Selecting the threats and fundamental principles from the ACCA *Code of Ethics and Conduct* that are relevant to the scenario will help you generate points for your answer.

Marking scheme

		Marks
(a)	Use of fair value in IFRS – discussion 1 mark per point to a maximum of 10 marks. Points may include:	
	Treatment under IFRS	2
	Advantages of historical cost	1
	Definition of fair value	2
	Examples of use of fair value in IFRS	4
	Financial value of an entity	1
		10
(b)	Ethical and accounting issues – discussion 1 mark per point to a maximum of 10 marks. Points may include:	
	Accounting issues	
	Recognition in statement of financial position	1
	IFRS 16 definition of a lease	1
	Initial recognition and measurement	2
	Ethical issues	
	Threats to fundamental principles	2
	Professional competence	1
	Appropriate action	1
		8
	Professional marks	2
		20

(a) **Use of fair value in IFRSs**

Treatment under IFRS

It is not entirely accurate to say that IFRS implement a fair value model. While IFRS use fair value (and present value) more than other accounting frameworks, and more than they, and the old IAS did in the past, it is **not a complete fair value system.** IFRS are often based on the **business model of the entity** and on the probability of realising the asset- and liability-related cash flows through operations or transfers.

In fact the IASB favours a mixed measurement system, with some items being measured at fair value and others at historical cost.

Advantages of historical cost

Historical cost has a number of **advantages** over fair values, mainly as regards reliability.

(i) It is **easy to understand**.

(ii) It is grounded in **real transaction amounts**, and is therefore **objective** and objectively verifiable.

(iii) There is **less scope for manipulation**.

There are however **disadvantages** of historical cost accounting such as potentially **understating** the **value** of assets and liabilities, particularly in times of rising prices and **cost bases of assets** being very **different** depending on when the asset was purchased. Fair value accounting can help to overcome these issues.

Definition of fair value

Before the publication of IFRS 13 *Fair Value Measurement*, there were a number of definitions of fair value, and there was considerable inconsistency. IFRS 13 was developed to solve some of these problems. IFRS 13 defines fair value as **'the price that would be received to sell an asset or paid to transfer a liability in an orderly transaction between market participants at the measurement date' (IFRS 13: Appendix A)**. The price which would be received to sell the asset or paid to transfer (not settle) the liability is described as the **'exit price'**.

IFRS 13 has brought consistency to the definition and application of fair value, and this consistency is applied across other IFRS, which are generally required to measure fair value 'in accordance with IFRS 13'. This **does not mean, however, that IFRS requires all assets and liabilities to be measured at fair value**. On the contrary, many entities measure most items at depreciated historical cost, a notable exception being in the case of business combinations, where assets and liabilities are recorded at fair value at the acquisition date. In other cases, the use of fair value is restricted.

Examples of use of fair values in IFRS

Examples include:

(i)   IAS 16 *Property, Plant and Equipment* **allows revaluation** through other comprehensive income, provided it is **carried out regularly**.

(ii)   While IAS 40 *Investment Property* allows the **option** of measuring investment properties **at fair value** with corresponding changes in profit or loss, and this arguably reflects the business model of some property companies, **many companies still use historical cost.**

(iii) IAS 38 *Intangible Assets* **permits the measurement of intangible assets at fair value** with corresponding changes in equity, but **only** if the assets can be measured reliably through the existence of an **active market** for them.

(iv)   IFRS 9 *Financial Instruments* requires some financial assets and liabilities to be measured at **amortised cost** and others at **fair value**. The measurement basis is largely determined by the **business model** for that financial instrument. For financial instruments measured at fair value, depending on the category and the circumstances, gains or losses are recognised either in profit or loss or in other comprehensive income.

Financial value of an entity

While IFRS makes some use of fair values in the measurement of assets and liabilities, **financial statements prepared under IFRS are not,** as is sometimes believed, **intended to reflect the aggregate value of an entity.** On the contrary, the IASB's *Conceptual Framework for Financial Reporting* specifically states that general purpose financial reports are not designed to show the financial value of a reporting entity. Such an attempt would be incomplete, **since IFRS disallows the recognition of certain internally generated intangibles**. Rather, the objective identified by the IASB is to provide financial information about a reporting entity which is useful to existing and potential investors, lenders and other creditors in making decisions about providing resources to the entity.

It is only when an entity is **acquired by another entity and consolidated** in group accounts that an entity's **net assets are reported at market value.**

(b) **Accounting issues**

Recognition in statement of financial position

IFRS 16 *Leases* is the result of an IASB project to **end off-balance sheet accounting** for leases and it requires **recognition of nearly all leases of over 12 months** duration in the statement of financial position, moving to a single lessee accounting model. (There is an exception for low value leases, but as this is a property lease, it will not be of low value.)

IFRS 16 definition of a lease

The arrangement meets the IFRS 16 criteria for a lease in that there is an identifiable asset and the contract conveys the right to control the use of that asset for a period of time in exchange for consideration.

Initial recognition and measurement

Columbus must recognise a right-of-use asset representing its right to use the property and a lease liability representing its obligation to make lease payments. At the commencement date, Columbus should recognise the right-of-use asset at cost. This will include:

(a) The amount of the initial measurement of the lease liability;

(b) Any lease payments made or incentives received before the start date;

(c) Any initial direct costs; and

(d) Any costs to be incurred for dismantling or removing the underlying asset or restoring the site at the end of the lease term.

Columbus must initially recognise the liability at the present value of the future lease payments including any payments expected at the end of the lease discounted using the rate implicit in the lease.

Ethical issues

If the managing director is trying to compel the financial controller to change what would be the appropriate treatment because of business pressures, then this presents the financial controller with an ethical dilemma. The pressure will be greater because the financial controller is new.

Threats to fundamental principles

As the financial controller's future position at Columbus has been threatened if the managing director's proposed accounting treatment is not adopted, there has been an **intimidation threat** to the fundamental principles of **objectivity and integrity** from the ACCA *Code of Ethics and Conduct.*

Furthermore, as the managing director has flagged the risk that Columbus may not secure its future loan finance if the lease is recorded is the statement of financial position, there is an **advocacy threat** because the financial controller may feel compelled to follow an incorrect accounting treatment to maximise the changes of obtaining the loan. The pressure will be greater because the financial controller is new

Professional competence

When preparing the financial statements, the financial controller should adhere to the fundamental principle of **professional competence** which requires preparing accounts that **comply with IFRS**.

Thus, if the arrangement meets the IFRS 16 criteria for a lease, which it appears to, the lease should not be kept out of the statement of financial position in order to understate the liabilities of the entity for the purposes of raising a loan and future job security of the financial controller. If the financial controller were to **accept the managing director's proposed**

treatment, this would contravene IFRS 16 and **breach the fundamental principle of professional competence**.

Appropriate action

The ACCA *Code of Ethics and Conduct* will be an essential point of reference in this situation, since it sets out boundaries outside which accountants should not stray. If the managing director refuses to allow the financial controller to apply the IFRS 16 treatment, then the financial controller **should disclose this to the appropriate internal governance authority**, and thus feel confident that their actions were ethical.

The difference of opinion that has arisen between the financial controller and the managing director best resolved by the **financial controller seeking** professional advice from the ACCA and legal advice if required.

19 Casino

> **Workbook references.** Segment reporting and corporate social responsibility are covered in Chapter 17. Ethical issues are covered in Chapter 2.
>
> **Top tips.** Remember that you **must** apply the principles to the scenario. This applies particularly to parts (a) and (c) but the narrative paragraph preceding the discussion requirement in part (b) is useful in generating ideas for your answer.
>
> **Easy marks.** All three parts of the question allow a variety of valid points to be made and there is scope for marks to be gained for how well the scenario is discussed rather than simply stating the 'right' answer.

		Marks
(a)	Allocation of common costs – discussion 1 mark per point to a maximum of 7 marks. Points may include:	
	Impact on profit/net assets of allocation	1
	IFRS 8 guidance on allocation	1
	Suggested basis for allocation for each cost in scenario	3
	Differing amounts in segment report to financial statements	<u>2</u>
		7
(b)	Reconciliation of ethics of CSR disclosure to shareholder expectations – discussion 1 mark per point to a maximum of 7 marks. Points may include:	
	Expectation for businesses to be socially and environmentally responsible	1
	Responsibility to all stakeholders, not just shareholders	1
	Reasons for not wanting to disclose information	1
	Good CSR can result in increased shareholder value	2
	Many companies now providing disclosures beyond those required by IFRS	<u>2</u>
		7

(c)   Ethical conflicts and ethical principles – discussion 1 mark per point to a maximum of 9 marks. Points may include:

Ethical conflicts

Pressure to obtain finance	1
Personal circumstances	1
Duty to shareholders, employees and bank	2

Ethical principles

Self-interest threat	1
Advocacy threat	1
Potential breach of objectivity, integrity, professional competence	2
Appropriate action	1
	9

Professional marks for (b) and (c)	2
	25

(a)   **Allocation of common costs under IFRS 8 *Operating Segments***

If segment reporting is to fulfil a useful function, costs need to be appropriately assigned to segments. Centrally incurred expenses and central assets can be significant, and the basis chosen by an entity to allocate such costs **can therefore have a significant impact** on the financial statements. In the case of Casino, head office management expenses, pension expenses, the cost of managing properties and interest and related interest-bearing assets could be material amounts, whose misallocation could mislead users.

IFRS 8 *Operating Segments* **does not prescribe a basis** on which to allocate common costs, but it does require that that basis should be **reasonable**. For example, it would not be reasonable to allocate the head office management expenses to the most profitable business segment to disguise a potential loss elsewhere. Nor would it be reasonable to allocate the pension expense to a segment with no pensionable employees.

A reasonable basis on which to allocate common costs for Casino might be as follows:

(i)   **Head office management costs**. These could be allocated on the basis of revenue or net assets. Any allocation might be criticised as arbitrary – it is not necessarily the case that a segment with a higher revenue requires more administration from head office – but this is a fairer basis than most.

(ii)   **Pension expense**. A reasonable allocation might be on the basis of the number of employees or salary expense of each segment.

(iii)   **Costs of managing properties**. These could be allocated on the basis of the value of the properties used by each business segment, or the type and age of the properties (older properties requiring more attention than newer ones).

(iv)   **Interest and interest-bearing assets**. These need not be allocated to the same segment – the interest receivable could be allocated to the profit or loss of one segment and the related interest-bearing asset to the assets and liabilities of another. IFRS 8 calls this asymmetrical allocation.

The **amounts reported under IFRS 8 may differ from those reported in the consolidated financial statements** because IFRS 8 requires the information to be presented on the same basis as it is reported internally, even if the accounting policies are not

the same as those of the consolidated financial statements. For example, segment information may be reported on a cash basis rather than an accruals basis or different accounting policies may be adopted in the segment report when allocating centrally incurred costs if necessary for a better understanding of the reported segment information.

IFRS 8 requires **reconciliations** between the segments' reported amounts and those in the consolidated financial statements. Entities must disclose the nature of such differences, and of the basis of accounting for transactions between reportable segments.

(b) **Reconciliation of ethics of corporate social responsibility disclosure with shareholder expectations**

Increasingly businesses are expected to be **socially and environmentally responsible as well as profitable**. Strategic decisions by businesses, particularly global businesses nearly always have wider social and environmental consequences. It could be argued that a company produces two outputs: goods and services, and the social and environmental consequences of its activities, such as pollution.

The requirement to be a **good corporate citizen goes beyond the normal duty of ethical behaviour** in the preparation of financial statements. To act ethically, the directors must put the interests of the company and its shareholders first, for example they must not mislead users of financial statements and must exercise competence in their preparation. Corporate citizenship, on the other hand, is concerned with a company's **accountability to a wide range of stakeholders**, not just shareholders. There may well be a **conflict of interest between corporate social responsibility and maximising shareholder wealth**; for example it may be cheaper to outsource abroad, but doing so may have an adverse effect on the local economy.

However, the two goals **need not conflict**. It is possible that being a good corporate citizen can **improve business performance. Customers may buy from a company that they perceive as environmentally friendly,** or which avoids animal testing, and **employees may remain loyal** to such a company, and both these factors are likely to increase shareholder wealth in the long term. If a company engages constructively with the country or community in which it is based, it may be seen by shareholders and potential shareholders as being a **good long-term investment** rather than in business for short-term profits.

As regards disclosure, a company that makes **detailed disclosures,** particularly when these go beyond what is required by legislation or accounting standards, will be seen as **responsible and a good potential investment,** provided they are clear, concise, relevant and understandable. For example, many quoted companies now prepare social and environmental disclosures following guidelines such as the International Integrated Reporting <IR> Framework or the Global Reporting Initiative. The IASB have also provided guidance in the form of an IFRS Practice Statement for entities preparing a management commentary.

(c) **Ethical conflicts**

In this scenario, there is a **twofold conflict of interest:**

(i) *Pressure to obtain finance and chief accountant's personal circumstances*

The chief accountant is under pressure to provide the bank with a projected cash flow statement that will meet the bank's criteria when in fact the actual projections do not meet the criteria. The chief accountant's financial commitments mean that that he cannot afford to lose his job. **The ethical and professional standards required of the accountant are at odds with the pressures of his personal circumstances.**

(ii)   *Duty to shareholders, employees and bank*

The **directors have a duty to act in the best interests of the company's shareholders and employees, and a duty to present fairly any information the bank may rely on**. Although the injection of capital to modernise plant and equipment might appear in the shareholders' and employees' best interests through generation of future profits, if the new finance is obtained on the basis of misleading information, it could actually be detrimental to the survival of the company.

It could be argued that there is a **conflict between the short-term and medium term interests of the company** (the need to modernise) **and its long-term interests** (the detriment to the company's reputation if its directors do not act ethically).

Ethical principles guiding the accountant's response

Specifically here, there is a **self-interest threat** in the form of the risk of the chief accountant losing his job and an **advocacy threat** in the form of disclosing favourable information in order to obtain the loan finance.

The chief accountant's financial circumstances and pressure from the directors could result in him knowingly disclosing incorrect information to the bank which means that the fundamental principles of **objectivity, integrity and professional competence** from ACCA's *Code of Ethics and Conduct* may be compromised.

In the case of **objectivity**, the chief accountant is likely to be **biased** due to the **risk of losing his job** if he does not report a favourable cash flow forecast to the bank. **Disclosing the incorrect information knowingly** would compromise his **integrity** as he would not be acting in a straightforward and honest manner is his professional and business relationships. Although forecasts, unlike financial statements, do not typically specify that they have been prepared in accordance with IFRS, the principle of **professional competence** requires the accountant to prepare cash flow projections to the **best of his professional judgement** which would not be the case if the projections showed a more positive position than is actually anticipated.

Appropriate action

The **chief accountant is faced with an immediate ethical dilemma** and must apply his moral and ethical judgement. As a professional, he has a responsibility to present the truth fairly, and not to indulge in 'creative accounting' in response to pressure.

The chief accountant should therefore put the interests of the company and professional ethics first, and insist that the report to the bank is an honest reflection of the current financial position. As an advisor to the directors he must not allow a deliberate misrepresentation to be made to the bank, no matter what the consequences are to him personally. The accountant must not allow any undue influence from the directors to override his professional judgement or undermine his integrity. This is in the long-term interests of the company and its survival.

The chief accountant should try to persuade the directors to accept the submission of the correct projected statement of cash flows to the bank. If they refuse, he should consider consulting ACCA for professional advice and if necessary, seek legal counsel.

20 Presdon

Workbook references. Group statements of cash flow are covered in Chapter 16. Integrated Reporting is covered in Chapter 17. Ethics is covered in Chapter 2.

Top tips. Don't skimp on either part (a) on the usefulness of statements of cash flows versus integrated reporting or part (b) on ethics. You should aim to generate one point per mark. There are marks for valid points in both areas and some flexibility within the discussion. In a discussion question like part (a), it is helpful to consider both benefits and limitations then come to a conclusion at the end of your answer.

Easy marks. Part (a) on the usefulness of the statement of cash flows and the integrated report is a good source of marks. You should be able to demonstrate an understanding of the limitations of corporate reporting as well as the nature of it. The various elements of corporate reporting are not distinct but are interrelated. Thus, the information content of a statement of cash flows can be compared to the information content of an Integrated Report, and you should be able to give a view on the two. In part (b), be careful not to focus on only the reporting issues to the detriment of the ethical issues. It is key to link your comments to the scenario presented and the ethical implications.

Marking scheme

	Marks

(a) Usefulness of statement of cash flows and the Integrated Report
– Discussion 1 mark per point to a maximum of 10 marks.
Points may include:

Usefulness of statement of cash flows

Liquidity, solvency, financial adaptability	1
IAS 7 Amendment: additional disclosures on financing activities	1
Comparison of cash flows and profit	1
Predictive value	1
Link to rest of financial statements	1

Integrated Report

Limitations of financial statements	1
Aim of integrated reporting	1
Problems with integrated reporting	1
Benefits of integrated reporting	1

Conclusion

	1
	10

(b) Impact on debt covenants and ethical implications
– Discussion 1 mark per point to a maximum of 8 marks.
Points may include:

Impact on debt covenants

Interest cover	1
Gearing	1

Ethical implications

Not unusual for group companies to provide financial assistance	1
Aim and disclosure of loan	1
Loan improves liquidity and avoids breach of gearing covenant	1

Responsibility of accountants not to mislead stakeholders	1
Suspicious timing and nature of loan	1
Appropriate action	1
	8
Professional marks	2
	20

(a)   Usefulness of statements of cash flows

Liquidity, solvency and financial adaptability

Statements of cash flows provide valuable information to stakeholders on the entity's **liquidity** (its ability to pay its short-term obligations), **solvency** (its ability to meet its long-term financial commitments) and **financial adaptability** (its ability to take effective action to alter the amount and timing of its cash flows to respond to unexpected needs or opportunities). Information about cash flows helps stakeholders understand the entity's operations and evaluate its investing and financing activities.

Financing activities

IAS 7 *Statement of Cash Flows* was amended in January 2016 as part of the IASB's Disclosure Initiative to provide **additional disclosures** to enable **users** of financial statements to **evaluate changes in liabilities arising from financing activities**.

This amendment requires entities to disclose the following changes arising from financing activities (to the extent necessary): (i) changes from financing cash flows; (ii) changes arising from obtaining or losing control of subsidiaries or other businesses; (iii) the effect of changes in foreign exchange rates; (iv) changes in fair values; and (v) other changes.

This should improve the usefulness of the statement of cash flows although there is a risk that the increase in disclosures might overwhelm stakeholders.

Comparison of cash flows and profit

Cash flows are objective and **verifiable** and so are more easily understood than profits. Profits can be manipulated through the use of judgement or by the choice of a particular accounting policy. Operating cash flows are therefore useful at highlighting the differences between cash and profits. The **cash generated from operations** is a useful **indication of the quality of the profits** generated by a business. Good quality profits will generate cash and increase the financial adaptability of an entity.

Predictive value

Cash flow information will also **have some predictive value**. Information about an entity's cash flows during a period can help users to assess the entity's ability to generate future net cash inflows. Therefore, it may assist stakeholders in making judgements on the amount, timing and degree of certainty of future cash flows.

Link to rest of the financial statements

Cash flow information should be **used in conjunction with the rest of the financial state**ments. The adjustment of non-cash flow items within operating activities may not be easily understood. The classification of cash flows can be manipulated between operating, investing and financing activities. It is important therefore not to examine the cash flow information in isolation. It is only through an analysis of the statement of financial position, statement of comprehensive income and notes, together with the cash flow, that a more comprehensive picture of the entity's position and performance develops.

Integrated Report

Limitations of financial statements

It is true that International Financial Reporting Standards are extensive and their required disclosures very comprehensive. This has led to criticism that the usefulness of financial statements may be limited where the most **relevant information** is **obscured by immaterial disclosures**.

Aim of integrated reporting

Integrated reporting is designed to convey a **wider message** on organisational performance, covering **all of an entity's resources** and **how it uses these 'capitals' to create value** over the short-, medium- and long-term, not only its financial resources.

Benefits of integrated reporting

Integrated reporting will provide **stakeholders** with **valuable information** which would not be immediately accessible from an entity's financial statements.

Financial statements are based on **historical information** and may **lack predictive value**. They are essential in corporate reporting, particularly for compliance purposes but do not provide meaningful information regarding business value.

The **primary purpose** of an **integrated report** is to **explain** to providers of capital **how the organisation generates value over time**. This is summarised through an examination of the key activities and outputs of the organisation whether they be financial, manufactured, intellectual, human, social or natural.

An integrated report seeks to **examine the external environment** which the entity operates within and to provide an insight into the entity's resources and relationships to generate value. It is **principles based** and should be **driven by materiality**, including how and to what extent the entity understands and responds to the needs of its stakeholders. This would include an analysis of **how the entity has performed within its business environment**, together with a description of **prospects and challenges for the future**. It is this strategic direction which is lacking from a traditional set of financial statements and will be invaluable to stakeholders to make a more informed assessment of the organisation and its prospects.

Problems with integrated reporting

An integrated reporting system would **increase disclosure** as well as imposing **additional time and cost constraints** on the reporting entity. It may require changes to IT systems in order to capture the data, as well as the initial use of an external consultancy to design the report.

Conclusion

Arguably, an Integrated Report may give improved information to stakeholders and therefore provide a coherent story about the business which **goes above and beyond that provided by the statement of cash flows** regarding liquidity, solvency and the financial adaptability of a business. It may help the entity to think holistically about its strategy and manage key risks, as well as make informed decisions and **build investor confidence**.

However, the entity must assess **whether** it believes those **benefits outweigh the potential disadvantages** of the extra cost and administration it may incur as the report remains voluntary.

(b) **Impact on debt covenants**

Interest cover

With regard to debt covenants, since the loan is **interest free**, it will have **no impact on the interest cover** of Mielly. Neither profits nor finance costs will be affected.

Gearing

The **impact** on the **gearing ratio** of Mielly is unclear and would **depend on how debt was classified** within the terms of the covenants. Should the overdraft be included within debt, the loan would substantially improve the gearing ratio through the elimination of the Mielly overdraft.

In any case, the **classification** of the loan within the trade and other receivables and trade and other payables balances would be **misleading**. The loan is not believed to be for trading purposes and a **fairer representation** would to be to include the loan within the **current asset investments of Presdon** and as a **short-term loan within the current liabilities of Mielly**. This would ensure that the loan would be treated as debt within the gearing calculation of Mielly and would not be misleading for the bank when assessing whether a breach of the debt covenants had taken place.

Ethical implications

It is not unusual for members of a group to provide financial assistance in the form of loans or to act as a guarantor between one another. Provided that the loan was **not issued to manipulate the financial statements** and that there was **full disclosure** as a related party transaction, then **no ethical issues may arise**. However, this would appear to be unlikely in this scenario.

Accountants have the **responsibility** to issue **financial statements** which **do not mislead the stakeholders** of the business. It would appear that the financial statements are being **deliberately misrepresented**, which would be **deemed unethical**. The cash received would improve the liquidity of Mielly and may enable the company to avoid a breach on the debt covenants. Accountants should be guided by the ACCA's *Code of Ethics and Conduct*. Deliberate enhancement of the entity's liquidity position would **contravene the principles of integrity, objectivity and professional behaviour**.

The **timing and nature** of the loan may provide **further evidence** that the rationale for the loan was to ensure **no breach of the covenants** took place.

It is unclear what the business purpose of the loan was, but the substance of the transaction appears to be primarily to alter the appearance of the statement of financial position. The loan was for an **unusually short period** given that it was repaid within 30 days. It is **unlikely that Mielly would be in a position to repay the loan so quickly**, if, having used the cash received for a legitimate reason, it were to repay it from cash generated from its operations.

In addition, the **timing is very suspicious** given that it was issued just prior to the 31 January 20X6 year end. The loan thereby being reflected in the financial position of the company as reported externally conceals the overdraft in Mielly's books.

Appropriate action

To avoid the financial statements of Mielly being misleading to stakeholders, the directors should consider **reclassifying** the loan receivable in Presdon's statement of financial position from trade receivables to current asset investments and the loan payable in Mielly's statement of financial position from trade payables to a short-term loan within current liabilities. Both companies must also ensure the transaction is disclosed in their individual financial statements as a related party transaction.

21 Chippin

Marking scheme

		Marks
(a)	Indirect versus direct method – discussion 1 mark per point to a maximum of 7 marks. Points may include:	
	Direct method	
	Explanation	1
	Advantages to users	1
	Disadvantages to users	1
	Indirect method	
	Explanation	1
	Advantages	1
	Disadvantages	1
	Apply to context of Chippin	$\frac{1}{7}$
(b)	Reporting loan proceeds as an operating cash flow – discussion 1 mark per point to a maximum of 6 marks. Points may include:	
	Incentive to increase operating cash flow to receive extra income	1
	Motivation for using indirect method – reduce clarity for users	1
	Objective for IAS 7's flexibility in cash flow classification is fair presentation	1
	Ethical behaviour important in financial statements preparation	1
	Directors must put company's and stakeholder's interests first	1
	Classify as 'financing' not 'operating'	$\frac{1}{6}$
	Professional marks	$\frac{2}{15}$

(a) **Preparing statements of cash flows: indirect method versus direct method**

Direct method

The **direct method** of preparing cash flow statements reports cash flows from operating activities as **major classes of gross cash receipts and gross cash payments**. It shows the items that affected cash flow and the size of those cash flows. Cash received from, and cash paid to, specific sources such as customers, suppliers and employees are presented separately. This contrasts with the indirect method, where accruals-basis net profit/(loss) before tax is converted to cash flow information by means of add-backs and deductions.

An important **advantage** of the direct method is that it is easier for the users to understand as they can see and understand the actual **cash flows,** and how they relate to items of income or expense. For example, payments of expenses are shown as cash disbursements and are deducted from cash receipts. In this way, the **user is able to recognise the cash receipts and payments** for the period.

From the point of view of the **user, the direct method is preferable**, because it discloses information, not available elsewhere in the financial statements, which could be of use in estimating future cash flow.

However, where the user is an investor, the direct method may reduce shareholder returns because preparation of **the direct method is typically more time-consuming and expensive** than the indirect method due to the extra workings required to ascertain gross cash receipts and payments relating to operating activities.

Indirect method

The **indirect method** involves **adjusting the net profit or loss** for the period for:

(1) Changes during the period in inventories, operating receivables and payables;

(2) Non-cash items, eg depreciation, movements in provisions, deferred taxes and unrealised foreign currency gains and losses;

(3) Other items, the cash flows from which should be classified under investing or financing activities, eg profits or losses on sales of assets, investment income.

From the point of view of the **preparer of accounts, the indirect method is easier to use,** and **nearly all companies use it in practice**. The main argument companies have for using the indirect method is that the **direct method is too costly**. 'The **indirect method** is cheaper for the company to prepare and will result in **higher shareholder returns**.

The **disadvantage** of the indirect method is that **users find it difficult to understand** and it is therefore more **open to manipulation**. This is particularly true with regard to classification of cash flows. Companies may wish to classify cash inflows as operating cash flows and cash outflows as non-operating cash flows.

The directors' proposal to report the loan proceeds as operating cash flow may be an example of such manipulation. For Chippin, the indirect method would **not,** as is claimed, **be more useful and informative to users** than the direct method. IAS 7 *Statement of Cash Flows* allows both methods, however, so the indirect method would still be permissible. Because users find the indirect method less easy to understand, it can be more open to manipulation by misclassifying cash flows.

(b) **Reporting the loan proceeds as operating cash flow**

The directors of Chippin have an **incentive to enhance operating cash flow**, because they receive a bonus if operating cash flow exceeds a predetermined target. This represents a **self-interest threat** under ACCA's *Code of Ethics and Conduct*. Accordingly, their proposal to classify the loan proceeds as operating cash flow should come under scrutiny.

Their proposal should first of all be considered in the light of their claim that the indirect method is more useful to users than the direct method. The opposite is the case, so while both methods are allowed, the directors' **motivation for wishing to use the method that is less clear to users** should be questioned.

IAS 7 *Statement of Cash Flows* allows some leeway in classification of cash flows under the indirect method. For example, dividends paid by the entity can be shown as financing cash flows (showing the cost of obtaining financial resources) or operating cash flows (so that users can assess the entity's ability to pay dividends out of operating cash flows). However, the **purpose of such flexibility is to present the position as fairly as possible**. Classifying loan proceeds as operating cash flow does not do this.

Ethical behaviour in the preparation of financial statements, and in other areas, is of **paramount importance**. Directors act unethically if they use 'creative' accounting in accounts preparation to make the figures look better, in particular if their presentation is determined not by finding the best way to apply International Financial Reporting Standards in order to report the cash flow position fairly to stakeholders, but, as here, by **self-interest**.

To act ethically, the directors must put the interests of the company and its shareholders first, and must also have regard to other stakeholders such as the loan provider. Accordingly, the **loan proceeds should be reported as cash inflows from financing activities,** not operating activities.

22 Egin Group

Workbook reference. Related parties and ethics are covered in Chapter 2.

Top tips. In part (a), make sure you identify both sub-requirements:

(1) Discuss why it is important to disclose related party transactions
(2) Explain the criteria which determine a related party relationship.

The second sub-requirement is asking you to state IAS 24 *Related Party Disclosures*'s definition of a related party (for both persons and entities). The first sub-requirement requires deeper thought as to why related party transactions need to be disclosed.

The best way to approach part (b) is to prepare a plan on your question paper by adding to the group structure provided any entities or individuals who are not shown as well as any transactions between the entities and individuals involved. Then you need to apply the IAS 24 related party definitions.

Easy marks. Easy marks are available in part (a) for listing as the criteria for determining a related party relationship as this is basic knowledge. However, make sure you do not overlook the additional sub-requirement to discuss why it is important to disclose related party transactions. Part (b) is trickier but looking for relationships of significant influence and control should help you to identify any related parties.

Marking scheme

		Marks
(a)	Reasons	4
	Criteria which determine a related party relationship	3
(b)	Egin Group	5
	Spade	3
	Atomic	3
	Professional marks	2
		20

(a) Why it is important to disclose related party transactions

The directors of Egin are correct to say that related party transactions are a normal feature of business. However, where entities are members of the same group, for example parent and subsidiary, the **financial performance and position of both entities can be affected** by these transactions. An obvious instance of this is where one group company sells goods to another at artificially low prices which can have a detrimental impact on the stakeholders of the selling company.

In the absence of other information, users of the financial statements **assume that a company pursues its interests independently** and undertakes transactions on an **arm's length basis** on terms that could have been obtained in a transaction with a third party.

Knowledge of related party relationships and transactions affects the way in which users assess a company's operations and the risks and opportunities that it faces. Therefore, **details of an entity's controlling party and transactions with related parties should be disclosed**. Even if the company's transactions and operations have not been affected by a related party relationship, **disclosure puts users on notice that they may be affected in future**.

It is essential to the **stakeholders' positive view of a company's moral and ethical behaviour** that **controls** are in place to **capture related party disclosures** that are accurate and complete. This serves to **minimise the risk of unethical** or fraudulent **behaviour**.

Criteria which determine a related party relationship

Under IAS 24 *Related Party Disclosures* a related party is a person or entity that is related to the entity that is preparing its financial statements (the 'reporting entity').

Persons

IAS 24 states that a person or a close member of that person's family is related to a reporting entity if that person:

(1) Has **control** or **joint control** over the reporting entity;

(2) Has **significant influence** over the reporting entity; or

(3) Is a member of the **key management personnel** of the reporting entity or of a parent of the reporting entity.

Entities

An entity is related to a reporting entity if any of the following conditions apply:

(1) The entity and the reporting entity are **members of the same group** (which means that each parent, subsidiary and fellow subsidiary is related to the others).

(2) One entity is an **associate* or joint venture*** of the other entity (or an associate or joint venture of a member of a group of which the other entity is a member).

(3) Both entities are **joint ventures* of the same third party**.

(4) One entity is a **joint venture* of a third entity** and the other entity is an **associate of the third entity**.

(5) The entity is a **post-employment benefit plan** for the benefit of employees of either the reporting entity or an entity related to the reporting entity.

(6) The entity is **controlled** or **jointly controlled** by a person identified in the definition above.

(7) A person identified above as having control or joint control over the reporting entity has **significant influence** over the entity or is a member of the **key management personnel** of the entity (or of a parent of the entity).

(8) The entity, or any member of a group of which it is a part, provides key management personnel services to the reporting entity or to the parent of the reporting entity.

*Including subsidiaries of the associate or joint venture.

(b) **Nature of related party relationships**

Within the Egin Group

Briars and Doye are related parties of Egin because they are **members of the same group** (both subsidiaries of Egin). For the same reason, as fellow subsidiaries, **Briars and Doye** are also **related parties of each other. Eye is also a related party of Egin** because it is an **associate of Egin.** (Egin has **significant influence** over Eye.)

Briars and Doye may be related parties of Eye. There is only one director in common and IAS 24 states that entities are not necessarily related simply because they have a director (or other member of key management personnel) in common, or because a member of key management personnel of one entity has significant influence over the other entity. However, **Eye is an associate of Egin**, and therefore **a member of the group** that Briars and Doye are members of (see (2) under 'Entities' above).

Although Tang was sold several months before the year end it was a **related party of Egin, Briars and Doye until then**. Therefore, the related party relationship between Tang and the Egin group **should be disclosed** even though there were no transactions between them during the period.

Blue is a related party of Briars as a **director of Briars controls it.** Because the director is not on the management board of Egin it is **not clear whether Blue is also a related party of Egin group**. This would depend on whether the director is considered key management personnel at a group level. The director's services as a consultant to the group may mean that a related party relationship exists. The issue would depend on whether this role meant that this person was directing or controlling a major part of the group's activities and resources.

Between Spade and the Egin Group

Spade is a related party of Doye because it exerts **significant influence** over Doye. This means that the **sale** of plant and equipment **to Spade must be disclosed. Egin is not necessarily a related party of Spade** simply because both have an investment in Doye. A related party relationship will only exist if one party **exercises influence** over another **in practice**.

The directors have proposed that disclosures should state that prices charged to related parties are set on an **arm's length basis**. Because the transaction took place **between related parties** by definition it **cannot have taken place on an arm's length basis** and this description cannot be substantiated and would be **misleading**. Doye sold plant and equipment to Spade at **normal selling prices** and this is the information that should be disclosed, provided the terms can be substantiated.

Between Atomic and the Egin Group

Atomic is a related party of Egin because it can exercise **significant influence** over it. Atomic's significant influence over Egin gives it **significant influence over Briars and Doye** as they are controlled by Egin. **Eye is not a related party of Atomic** as Atomic has no ability to exercise control or significant influence over Eye.

23 Conceptual framework

Workbook reference. The IASB's *Conceptual Framework for Financial Reporting* is covered in Chapter 1.

Top tips. Although this question is rather general, it is a good idea to mention the IASB documents, covered in your BPP Workbook. The IASB sees the conceptual framework project as being a key current development, and there has been a significant amount of coverage in the accountancy press. Students should read the accountancy press in order to gain an insight into current issues. This question and answer has been amended since it was set.

Easy marks. As part (a) is fairly open ended, it gives scope for different approaches and credit will be given for valid points well expressed. This does not mean you can waffle. You should think about the practical use of a conceptual framework and consider the reasons for differences in accounting.

Marking scheme

Marks

(a)   Discussion 1 mark per point to a maximum of 10 marks. Points may
        include:

Need for a conceptual framework

Useful for decision making	1
Theoretical in nature but practical aims	1
No framework results in haphazard approach	1
Needed for consistency in accounting standards	1
Rules-based approach open to manipulation	1

Resolve practical accounting issues

Framework cannot provide all the answers	1
Variety of users of accounts	1
Focus on some users at expense of other users	1
Provides definitions for use in accounting standards	1
Provides guidance in absence of a relevant IAS/IFRS	1
	10

(b)   Discussion 1 mark per point to a maximum of 6 marks. Points may include:

Derecognition of assets and liabilities
Driven by faithful representation (of assets/liabilities retained and changes in assets/liabilities)   1

Derecognise when transferred, consumed, collected, fulfilled expired

                                                                                        1

Continue to recognise any retained assets/liabilities   1
Control approach   1

The reintroduction of prudence
Importance for neutrality and faithful representation   1
Works for both overstatement and understatement of assets and liabilities

                                                                                        1
                                                                                   _____
                                                                                        6

(c)   Discussion 1 mark per point to a maximum of 9 marks. Points may include:

Criticisms of proposed changes in ED
Objective of general purpose financial reporting   1
Qualitative characteristics of useful information   1
Financial statements and the reporting entity   1
Classify as 'financing' not 'operating'   1
Elements   1
Recognition   1
Measurement   1
Presentation and disclosure   2
                                                                                   _____
                                                                                        9
                                                                                   _____
                                                                                       25
                                                                                   _____

(a)   **The need for a conceptual framework**

The financial reporting process is concerned with providing information that is **useful in the business and economic decision-making process**. Therefore, a conceptual framework will form the theoretical basis for determining which events should be accounted for, how they should be measured and how they should be communicated to the user.

Although it is theoretical in nature, a conceptual framework for financial reporting has **highly practical final aims**.

The **danger of not having a conceptual framework** is demonstrated in the way some countries' standards have developed over recent years; standards tend to be produced in a **haphazard and fire-fighting approach**. Where an agreed framework exists, the standard-setting body act as an architect or designer, rather than a fire-fighter, building accounting rules on the foundation of sound, agreed basic principles.

The lack of a conceptual framework also means that **fundamental principles are tackled more than once in different standards**, thereby producing **contradictions and inconsistencies** in basic concepts, such as those of prudence and matching. This leads to ambiguity and it affects the true and fair concept of financial reporting.

Without a conceptual framework, there is a **risk** that a financial reporting environment becomes governed by specific rules rather than general principles. A **rules-based approach** is much **more open to manipulation** than a principles-based one. For

example, a rule requiring an accounting treatment based on a transaction reaching a percentage threshold, might encourage unscrupulous directors to set up a transaction in such a way to deliberately to achieve a certain accounting effect (eg keep finance off the statement of financial position).

A conceptual framework can also **bolster standard setters against political pressure** from various 'lobby groups' and interested parties. Such pressure would only prevail if it was acceptable under the conceptual framework.

Can it resolve practical accounting issues?

A framework cannot provide all the answers for standard setters. It can provide **basic principles** which can be used when deciding between alternatives, and can narrow the range of alternatives that can be considered. The IASB's *Conceptual Framework* has provided **definitions that have formed the basis of definitions in accounting standards** in areas such as financial instruments and provisions. A framework can also provide guidance in the absence of an accounting standard. For example, there is no IFRS dealing specifically with off balance sheet finance, so the IASB's *Conceptual Framework* must form the basis for decisions.

However, a conceptual framework is **unlikely**, on past form, to **provide all** the **answers to practical accounting problems**. There are a number of reasons for this:

(i)   Financial statements are intended for a variety of users, and it is not certain that a single conceptual framework can be devised which will suit all users.

(ii)   Given the diversity of user requirements, there may be a need for a variety of accounting standards, each produced for a different purpose (and with different concepts as a basis).

(iii)   It is not clear that a conceptual framework makes the task of preparing and then implementing standards any easier than without a framework.

The IASB's *Conceptual Framework for Financial Reporting* was criticised by the UK Accounting Standards Board at least partly on grounds of practical utility – it is thought to be **too theoretical,** and also for focusing on **some users (decision makers) at the expense of others (shareholders)**. Perhaps it is not possible to satisfy all users.

(b)   **ED/2015/3 *Conceptual Framework for Financial Reporting***

(i)   **Derecognition of assets and liabilities**

Guidance on derecognition is new to this proposed version of the *Conceptual Framework*. The **guidance is driven by the requirement of faithful representation.** A faithful representation must be provided of:

(1)   The **assets and liabilities retained after a transaction** or other event that led to derecognition, and

(2)   The **change in the entity's assets and liabilities as a result of that transaction** or other event.

These aims are normally achieved by:

(a)   **Derecognising** any **assets or liabilities** that have been **transferred, consumed, collected or fulfilled,** or have **expired** and recognising any resulting income or expense.

(b)   **Continuing to recognise the assets or liabilities retained**, if any, which become a separate unit of account. Accordingly, no income or expenses are recognised on the retained component as a result of the derecognition of the transferred component.

Decisions about derecognition are generally straightforward. If an entity disposes of an entire asset or an entire liability and retains no exposure to that asset or liability, then normally there is no issue. However, in **some cases the two aims** described above **conflict** with each other, making the decisions more difficult. For example, if an entity disposes of only part of an asset or a liability, the accounting treatment may be less apparent. The **discussion in the Exposure Draft focuses on these cases**.

In most cases, an entity will achieve the best result if it applies the control approach, that is, by derecognising an asset or a liability when it no longer meets the recognition criteria.

(ii) **Prudence**

Chapter 2 *The Qualitative Characteristics of Useful Financial Information* was finalised in the 2010 version of the *Conceptual Framework,* and so there are generally only limited changes from that version. However, one change that could be regarded as important is the introduction of an **explicit reference to the idea of prudence**. Prudence is described as the **exercise of caution when making judgements under conditions of uncertainty**. It is explicitly stated that prudence is important in achieving **neutrality,** and therefore in achieving **faithful representation**. Prudence had been removed from the *Conceptual Framework* in 2010 on the grounds that it conflicted with neutrality, carrying a bias in favour of caution.

The IASB has further clarified that prudence works both ways: assets and liabilities should be neither overstated nor understated.

(c) **Possible criticisms of the proposals**

The IASB has summarised the feedback on its *ED/2015/3 Conceptual Framework for Financial Reporting*. As well as positive feedback, the summary includes the following criticisms:

Objective of general purpose financial reporting

The ED has added to the objective the importance of providing information needed to assess management's **stewardship** of the entity's resources. Some respondents want **more guidance** on stewardship, specifically:

- How 'stewardship' relates to 'accountability'

- The impact on future standard-setting decisions

- The link between the discussion of buy, sell and hold decisions and the discussion of stewardship

Others want stewardship included as an **additional objective** in its own right whereas others disagree with giving more prominence to stewardship.

There are **mixed views** about the **description of the primary user group** (existing and potential lenders and other creditors) with some wanting to expand it and others wanting to narrow it down.

Qualitative characteristics of useful information

(i) **Prudence**. Some respondents believe that the ED does not sufficiently reflect the notion of 'asymmetric prudence' – the recognition of losses and liabilities at a lower level of likelihood (and hence often earlier) than gains and assets. This notion is mentioned in the Basis for Conclusions, but some believe it ought to be part of the *Conceptual Framework* itself. Whereas others believe that prudence should not be reintroduced in any form.

(ii) **Measurement uncertainty**. The ED introduces measurement uncertainty under the qualitative characteristic of 'relevance'. There are three alternative views of what measurement uncertainty should be an aspect of:

- Faithful representation;
- Relevant and faithful representation; or
- Reliability (reintroduced as a qualitative characteristic).

Financial statements and the reporting entity

The ED introduces the concept of the boundary of a reporting entity in the form of direct control ('unconsolidated' financial statements) and both direct and indirect control ('consolidated' financial statements).

Some respondents are **critical** of the **terms 'direct control' and 'indirect control'** especially since they are not used by IFRS 10 *Consolidated Financial Statements* and many **disagree that consolidated financial statements are more likely to provide useful information** than unconsolidated financial statements.

The elements of financial statements

There is some **concern** that changes in definition and recognition criteria would mean that more **'low probability' assets and liabilities would be recognised**.

Banks broadly disagree with the proposed new description of a 'present obligation' in the ED's explanation of the definition of a liability.

Recognition

Some respondents **disagree with the removal of the 'probability criterion'** and would prefer to keep the existing recognition criteria because the new approach is too abstract and subjective and could result in recognition of assets and liabilities with low probability of inflow or outflow of future economic benefits.

Measurement

The ED categorises measurement bases into historical cost and current value (including fair value, value in use for assets and fulfilment value for liabilities). Some respondents feel that **only two measurement bases** should be included – historical cost and fair value.

Others believe that **clear guidance and principles** need to be added to the ED as to **when a particular measurement basis should be selected in a standard**.

A few user groups feel that a **different measurement basis** should be used in the **statement of financial position** and the **statement of profit or loss** with the remaining balance being included in other comprehensive income (OCI) but others believe this would be too complicated and not understood by users.

Presentation and disclosure

Many would like **further guidance** on which items to include in **profit or loss (P/L)**, which items to include in **other comprehensive income (OCI)** and **the basis for recycling**.

The ED includes a rebuttable presumption that all items included in OCI should be reclassified to P/L in future periods. Some believe that only **some items should be reclassified to P/L** whereas others believe OCI items should **never be reclassified**.

24 Lizzer

Marking scheme

			Marks
(a)	(i)	Reasons for debt-holders interest/advise directors – discussion 1 mark per point to a maximum of	6
	(ii)	Critique of directors' decision – discussion 1 mark per point to a maximum of	6
(b)	(i)	Optimal level of disclosure – discussion 1 mark per point to a maximum of	9
	(ii)	Barriers to reducing disclosure – discussion 1 mark per point to a maximum of	4
			25

(a) (i) **Disclosure of debt risk**

Users of financial statements

It is not for Lizzer alone to determine who the primary users of financial statements are and what disclosures are necessary. The entity **needs to consider the requirements of IFRS 7** *Financial Instruments: Disclosures,* and apply them more broadly to include debt-holders as well as just shareholders. More generally, IAS 1 *Presentation of Financial Statements* states that the objective of financial statements is to provide information about an entity's financial performance, financial position and cash flows that is useful to a wide range of users in making economic decisions. These users are defined by the *Conceptual Framework* (and the revised *Conceptual Framework*) as 'existing and potential investors, lenders and **other creditors**' (*Conceptual Framework*: para. OB1).

The debt-holders of Lizzer are creditors of the entity. They have provided funds to the entity from which they expect to receive a return, based on the performance of the underlying investments. The debt holders ultimately bear the risks and rewards associated with the investments Lizzer has made. They will be interested in the financial statements of Lizzer in order to understand the risks associated with the underlying investments and assess the impact on their own risk and return.

IFRS 7 requirements

The objective of IFRS 7 is to require entities to provide disclosures in their financial statements that enable users to evaluate:

(1) The significance of financial instruments for the entity's financial position and performance

(2) The nature and extent of risks arising from financial instruments to which the entity is exposed during the period and at the reporting date, and how the entity manages those risks

The key requirement of IFRS 7 is to **show the extent to which an entity is exposed to different types of risk,** relating to both recognised and unrecognised financial instruments. The risk disclosures required by IFRS 7 are given from the perspective of management which should allow the users of financial statements to better understand how management perceives, measures and manages the risks associated with financial instruments.

Credit risk is one such risk, defined by the Standard as:

'The risk that one party to a financial instrument will cause a financial loss for the other party by failing to discharge an obligation' (IFRS 7: Appendix A).

Clearly disclosures about credit risk are important to debt-holders. Such disclosures are **qualitative** (exposure to risk and objectives, policies and processes for managing risk) and **quantitative**, based on the information provided internally to management personnel, enhanced if this is insufficient.

More important in this context is **market risk**. The debt-holders are exposed to the risk of the underlying investments whose value could go up or down depending on market value. Market risk is defined as:

'The risk that the fair value or future cash flows of a financial instrument will fluctuate because of changes in market prices. Market risk comprises three types of risk: currency risk, interest rate risk and other price risk' (IFRS 7: Appendix A).

Disclosures required in connection with market risk are:

(1) **Sensitivity analysis**, showing the effects on profit or loss of changes in each market risk

(2) If the sensitivity analysis reflects interdependencies between risk variables, such as interest rates and exchange rates the method, **assumptions and limitations** must be disclosed

(ii) **Potential breach of loan covenants**

The applicable standards here are IFRS 7 *Financial Instruments: Disclosures*, and IAS 10 *Events after the Reporting Period*.

The directors of Lizzer are not correct in their decision not to disclosure additional information about the breach of loan covenants after the year end date. According to IFRS 7, Lizzer **should have included additional information** about the loan covenants **sufficient to enable the users of its financial statements to evaluate the nature and extent of risks arising from financial instruments** to which the entity is exposed at the end of the reporting period. Such disclosure is particularly important in Lizzer's case because there was considerable risk at the year end (31 January 20X3) that the loan covenants would be breached in the near future, as indicated by the directors' and auditors' doubts about the company continuing as a going concern. Although the breach of loan covenants does not directly impact the investors as they have not provided borrowings to Lizzer, there are implications in terms of the ability of Lizzer to continue as a going concern as this will have negative consequences for the returns they receive on their investments. Potential investors are unlikely to invest in a company that is a going concern risk due to the uncertainty around its future.

Information should have been given about the **conditions attached to the loans and how close the entity was at the year end to breaching** the covenants. IFRS 7 requires disclosure of additional information about the covenants relating to each loan or group of loans, including headroom (the difference between the amount of the loan facility and the amount required).

The **actual breach of the loan covenants** at 31 March 20X3 was a **material event after the reporting period** as defined in IAS 10. The breach, after the date of the financial statements but before those statements were authorised, represents a material **non-adjusting event**, which should have given rise to further disclosures in accordance with IAS 10.

Although the breach is a non-adjusting event, there appears to be some **inconsistency** between the information in the directors' and auditor's reports (which express going-concern doubts) and the information in the financial statements, which are prepared on a going-concern basis. **If any of the figures** in the statement of financial position are **affected,** these will **need to be adjusted.**

(b) (i) **Optimal level of disclosure**

It is important to ensure the optimal level of disclosure in annual reports because excessive disclosure can **obscure relevant information** and make it harder for users to find the key points about the performance of the business and its prospects for long-term success. It is important that financial statements are **relevant, reliable** and can be **understood**.

However, it is equally important that useful information is **presented in a coherent way** so that users can find what they are looking for and gain an understanding of the company's business and the opportunities, risks and constraints that it faces.

There has been a gradual increase in the length of annual reports over time. This, often, **has not resulted in better information for the users of financial statements, but more confusion** as to the reason for the disclosure.

Causes of excessive disclosure

Requirements of different regulators and standard-setters

A significant cause of excessive disclosure in annual reports is the vast array of requirements imposed by laws, regulations and financial reporting standards. **Regulators and standard setters have a key role to play in reducing excessive disclosure**, both by cutting the requirements that they themselves already impose and by guarding against the imposition of unnecessary new disclosures. A listed company may have to comply with listing rules, company law, international financial reporting standards and the corporate governance codes. Thus **a major source of excessive disclosure is the fact that different parties require differing disclosures for the same matter.**

Furthermore, many disclosure requirements have been introduced in new or revised international financial reporting standards in previous years without any review of their overall impact on the length or usefulness of the resulting financial statements.

Consideration of other stakeholders

Preparers now have to consider many other stakeholders including employees, unions, environmentalists, suppliers, customers, etc. **The disclosures required to meet the needs of this wider audience have contributed to the increased volume of disclosure.** The growth of previous initiatives on going concern, sustainability, risk, the business model and others that have been identified by regulators as 'key' has also expanded the annual report size.

Inappropriate use of 'checklists'

A problem that seems to exist is that **disclosures are being made because a disclosure checklist suggests it may need to be made**, without assessing **whether the disclosure is necessary** in a company's particular circumstances. This requires the application of materiality to disclosures and therefore requires judgement.

Response of IASB

The IASB launched the Disclosure Initiative in 2013 in response to feedback that there is a need to improve the effectiveness of disclosures in financial statements. It includes:

- *Materiality implementation projects.* The IASB believe that uncertainty on behalf of the preparers of financial statements as to how the concept of materiality should be applied has compounded the disclosure issue. An Exposure Draft (ED/2015/8) on the application of materiality to financial statements has therefore been issued. In a separate project (ED/2017/6) the IASB is proposing to amend the definition of materiality to make it clearer that information is material if omitting, misstating or *obscuring it* could reasonably be expected to influence the decisions of users of the financial statements, addressing the issue that too much information can be just as problematic as the omission of information.

- *Research projects.* A Discussion Paper *Disclosure Initiative – Principles of Disclosure* has been issued with the aim of encouraging entities to apply better judgement and communicate more effectively in making disclosures. Disclosure principles will also help the IASB improve disclosure requirements. A further project, the Standards-level Review of Disclosures, will consider how to improve disclosure requirements in Standards.

(ii) **Barriers to reducing disclosure**

Entities are sometimes reluctant to reduce the level of disclosure. These barriers are behavioural and include the following:

(1) **The perception that disclosing everything will satisfy all interested parties.** Many of the disclosures will not be applicable to the needs of any one user.

(2) **The threat of criticism or litigation.** Preparers of financial statements err on the side of caution rather than risk falling foul of the law by omitting a required disclosure. Removing disclosures is seen as creating a risk of adverse comment and regulatory challenge.

(3) **Cut and paste mentality.** If items were disclosed in last year's annual report and the issue is still ongoing, there is a tendency to copy the disclosures into this year's report. It is thought that, if such disclosures are removed, stakeholders may wonder whether the financial statements still give a true and fair view. Disclosure is therefore the safest option and the default position.

(4) **Checklist approach.** While materiality should determine what is disclosed, because what is material is what may influence the user, the assessment of what is material can be a matter of judgement. The purpose of checklists is to include all possible disclosures that could be material. Users may not know which of the checklist disclosures is actually material in the context of their specific needs.

25 Accounting standards and disclosure

Workbook references. Issues covered here are covered in Chapters 1, 17 and 19.

Top tips. This is an open-ended question. Part (a) asked why accounting standards help the 'market mechanism'. Your answer should deal with matters of consistency and comparability, which make the information more transparent than would be the case in a 'free for all'. Part (b), on the costs and benefits of disclosure, continues to be topical in the light of the IASB's ongoing work on its Disclosure Initiative. Arguments both for and against disclosure could be made, as well as the case that too much disclosure means that the user cannot see the wood for the trees.

You are advised to do a quick answer plan before you start, otherwise there is danger of rambling. Remember that the *Conceptual Framework* is always a useful reference point for answers to discursive questions.

Easy marks. There are no easy marks as such; the trick is to focus your answer on the specific requirements, aim to generate one point per mark and fully explain everything you say, but do not be tempted to waffle.

Marking scheme

		Marks
(a)	Common understanding	2
	Neutral, unbiased	2
	Comparability	1
	Credibility	2
	Consistency	2
		9

	Marks
(b) Investment process	4
Risk	2
Protection	2
Costs	2
Competitive disadvantage	2
Other criteria	2
	14
Professional marks	2
	25

(a) Accounting standards and the market mechanism

Independently from financial reporting standards, the marketplace for capital encourages entities to invest time and thought into the quality of their reports. Companies have a vested interest in providing quality reports to potential lenders and investors, and if such information is not forthcoming, the cost of capital will be higher. However, **accounting standards play a key role in the effective functioning of the market mechanism** in the following ways:

(i) **Consistency.** Accounting standards are generally developed in accordance with an agreed conceptual framework. For example International Financial Reporting Standards use definitions of assets and liabilities that are found in the IASB's *Conceptual Framework for Financial Reporting*. In consequence, there is consistency in the presentation of financial information, and a common understanding of terms used for the elements of financial statements. This aids efficiency and decision making, since users do not need to learn a new set of concepts for each reporting entity.

(ii) **Neutrality.** While companies have an incentive to provide information in order to gain access to capital, they do not necessarily have an incentive to be unbiased. On the contrary, they may wish to portray their financial performance and position in a misleadingly favourable light. Users are aware of the potential bias, but if accounting standards are in place, compelling a company to present the information fairly, they can have more confidence in the financial statements. This increased trust helps decision making and efficiency, while too much scepticism is as bad as too little.

(iii) **Comprehensiveness.** Reports prepared in accordance with, say, International Financial Reporting Standards are required to contain certain information. As a minimum, certain primary financial statements and accompanying notes are required, for example a statement of cash flows. Potential lenders and companies are aware of these requirements, and therefore know that reports prepared under accounting standards will meet certain of their information needs. In the absence of accounting standards, lenders would have to request information on an *ad hoc* basis, or speculate as to why certain information was missing.

(iv) **Comparability.** If accounting standards are in force, the financial statements of companies can be compared effectively, which makes the decision-making process more efficient. Without them, companies could use very different bases for the preparation of accounts, and the user would not be comparing like with like. This is particularly important in the context of a global economy, where comparisons cross

national borders, and was one of the main reasons why International Financial Reporting Standards were developed.

(v) **Verification.** Auditors verify that financial statements have been prepared in accordance with applicable accounting standards. While an audit report is not a guarantee of a good investment, it lends credibility to the financial statements in a report.

(b) **Costs and benefits of increased disclosure**

Benefits to users of disclosure

Users of financial statements need **as much relevant information as possible** in order to make or retain wise investments and to avoid less prudent uses of capital. Companies also benefit from providing this information as it means that they do not take on debt that they cannot afford. There are, then, obvious advantages to increased disclosure.

(i) **Lenders** need to know if a company has **liquidity problems**. Disclosure of reasons for a large bank overdraft, or changes in gearing, may help allay any concerns, or alternatively may help the lender avoid a bad decision.

(ii) Users need to know the full extent of **any risk** they are taking on in investing in, trading with or lending to a company. Risk is not automatically a bad thing, if potential returns are good, and information on both profitability and gearing can help the decision-making process along. A venture capitalist may be more willing to take on risk than a high street bank, but both will need full disclosure of relevant information. A better understanding of risk may lower the cost of capital.

(iii) **Investors** and potential investors will need to know which companies are the most **profitable**, and whether those profits are sustainable. Their job is to maximise returns. It is not in the long-term interests of either companies or potential investors to withhold information.

Effective disclosure is **particularly important** in times of **economic uncertainty** particularly around risk and going concern assessments. For example, European (especially British) companies are facing uncertainty around Brexit. The EY July 2017 report *The impact of Brexit on corporate reporting* states:

'The consequences of Brexit could have an impact on the significant judgements made in preparing financial statements as well as the sensitivity of key accounting estimates, especially where markets have experienced higher volatility. Therefore, companies should focus on the adequacy of their disclosures around judgements, estimates and associated sensitivities and consider whether additional or different information should be given'.   (2017: p3)

The key to ensuring disclosure is beneficial is to make it **relevant** and **targeted to the needs of users**. It is possible to increase disclosures beyond the point of usefulness. In 2013, in response to feedback that there is a **need to improve the effectiveness of disclosures** in financial statements, the IASB launched its **'Disclosure Initiative'**. The project began in response to criticisms about disclosure overload in order to explore opportunities to see how those applying IFRS can improve and simplify disclosures within existing disclosure requirements.

There are currently four ongoing projects:

(1) Discussion Paper *Disclosure Initiative – Principles of Disclosure* which sets out the IASB's preliminary views on disclosure principles that should be included in a general disclosure standard or in non-mandatory guidance on the topic.

(2) The Materiality Practice Statement project – the IASB finalised a Practice Statement in 2017 containing non-mandatory guidance to help entities making materiality judgements when preparing IFRS general purpose financial statements.

(3)   The Definition of Material project – the IASB has issued an Exposure Draft of proposed amendments to IAS 1 and IAS 8 to refine the definition of materiality and clarify its application.

(4)   The Standards-level Review of Disclosures project – this research project will considered how to improve disclosure requirements in Standards.

It is telling that for the years **2017 to 2021**, the IASB has chosen **'better communication'** as its central theme. This widens the IASB's remit to refocus their activities in response to requests from investors to make financial information more relevant to them and improve the communication of that information.

Costs to preparers of disclosure

Companies are sometimes reluctant to increase the level of disclosure, not because they have anything to hide, but because of the associated costs. These include the following:

(i)   **Costs to collate and prepare the required information.** These costs are principally time costs of senior and junior staff, but may include fees to external consultants or lawyers. Training of staff – for example, in new methods of data collection – may be required, or staff may need to be moved from other, revenue-generating projects.

(ii)   **Costs of disseminating information.** This may simply mean a thicker annual report; for example, increasing printing costs or the cost of more time to present the information on the web. The annual report and accounts may not be adequate, and additional reports may be used.

(iii) **Cost of lost competitive advantage.** Extra information on marketing strategies, planned products or locations for expansion can give competitors an advantage that they might not otherwise have had. In particular, disclosure of problems, weaknesses and strategies for improvement may give the competitor an idea of areas to target. This disadvantage should not be overstated, however. A company does not need to give away trade secrets, and if the competitor is, for the benefits outlined above, also providing increased disclosure, there is no advantage to either party.

(iv)   **Potential litigation.** The additional information disclosed needs to be accurate, as misleading disclosure runs the risk of litigation. Time – and therefore money – needs to be spent checking the information to avoid this risk. That said, there is also a risk of litigation arising from incomplete or inadequate disclosure, so potential litigation should not, in itself, be a reason to avoid increased disclosure.

Even in times of economic uncertainty, **enhanced disclosures are arguably worth the extra cost.** Even if the news is bad, it is better that users know, rather than be surprised later when it gets worse. A company with a reputation for full disclosure will earn the trust of potential investors. There are indeed costs to increased disclosure, but the **cost of non-disclosure may be greater**.

Disclosure now often **goes beyond what is required by IFRS** and national legislation. Many companies voluntarily produce an **integrated report** prepared in accordance with the guidelines of the International Integrated Reporting Council's *International Integrated Reporting <IR> Framework*. The focus of an integrated report is on the organisation's ability to create value in the short, medium and long term and focuses on capitals beyond the financial (manufactured capital, intellectual capital, human capital, social and relationship capital and natural capital). A **social and environmental report** is also becoming increasingly commonplace. There is a **cost** associated with this extra reporting but it is often considered worth it in order to **better engage with the company's stakeholders**.

26 Tang

Marking scheme

			Marks
(a)	(i)	Definition of a contract	1
		Contract approved and committed to perform obligations	1
		Can identify each party's rights and payment terms	1
		Contract has commercial substance	1
		Probable consideration	1
			5
	(ii)	Identify performance obligations in the contract	2
		Determine the transaction price	3
		Allocation the transaction price to the performance obligations	2
		Recognise revenue when or as entity satisfies performance obligations	2
		Competitive disadvantage	9
(b)	(i)	Contract contains significant financing component	1
		Separate into revenue and loan components	1
		Discussion of correct discount rate	1
		Contract liability and subsequent interest	1
			4
	(ii)	Bonus is variable consideration	1
		Exclude bonus from transaction price at contract inception/end of first year	1
		Satisfy performance obligation over time so recognise revenue over time	1
		Recognise 65% of fixed consideration as revenue in first year	1
		4 December 20X5: contract modified – include bonus in transaction price	1
		Not an adjusting event after reporting period – account for in second year	1
		Update percentage complete and estimates of revenue and costs	1
			7
			25

(a) (i) **Criteria for a contract under IFRS 15**

Definition of a contract

The definition of what constitutes a contract for the purpose of applying IFRS 15 is critical. A contract exists when an **agreement** between **two or more parties** creates **enforceable rights and obligations** between those parties. The agreement **does not need to be in writing** to be a contract but the decision as to whether a contractual right or obligation is enforceable is considered within the **context of the relevant legal framework** of a jurisdiction. Thus, whether a contract is enforceable will vary across jurisdictions. The performance obligation could **include promises** which result in a **valid expectation** that the entity will transfer goods or services to the customer even though those promises are not legally enforceable.

An entity should only account for a contract with a customer within the scope of IFRS 15 when all of the following five criteria have been met.

(1) *Contract approved and committed to perform obligations*

The first criteria set out in IFRS 15 is that the parties should have **approved the contract** and are **committed to perform their respective obligations**. It would be questionable whether that contract is enforceable if this were not the case. In the case of **oral or implied contracts**, this may be **difficult** but **all relevant facts and circumstances should be considered** in assessing the parties' commitment.

The parties **need not** always be **committed to fulfilling all of the obligations** under a contract. IFRS 15 gives the example where a customer is required to purchase a minimum quantity of goods but past experience shows that the customer does not always do this and the other party does not enforce their contract rights. The IFRS 15 criterion could still be satisfied in this example if there is evidence that the parties are substantially committed to the contract.

(2) *Entity can identify each party's rights*

It is essential that each party's **rights** can be **identified** regarding the goods or services to be transferred. Without this criterion, an entity would not be able to assess the transfer of goods or services and therefore, the point at which revenue should be recognised.

(3) *Entity can identify each party's payment terms*

It is essential that each party's **payment terms** can be **identified** regarding the goods or services to be transferred. This requirement is the key to determining the transaction price.

(4) *Contract has commercial substance*

The contract must have **commercial substance** before revenue can be recognised, as without this requirement, entities might artificially inflate their revenue and it would be questionable whether the transaction has economic consequences.

The contract is deemed to have commercial substance when the **risk, timing or amount of the entity's future cash flows** is expected to **change** as a result of the contract.

(5) *Probable consideration*

It should be **probable** that the entity will **collect the consideration due** under the contract. An **assessment** of a **customer's credit risk** is an important

element in **deciding whether a contract has validity** but customer credit risk **does not affect** the **measurement or presentation** of revenue.

The **consideration may** be **different** to the **contract price** because of discounts and bonus offerings. The entity should **assess** the **ability of the customer to pay** and the **customer's intention to pay** the consideration.

Reassessment

If a contract with a customer does not meet these criteria, the entity can continually re-assess the contract to determine whether it subsequently meets the criteria.

Combination of contracts

Two or more contracts which are entered into around the **same time** with the **same customer** may be **combined** and accounted for as a **single contract**, if they meet the specified criteria.

Contract modifications

The Standard provides **detailed requirements** for contract modifications. A modification may be accounted for as a **separate contract or a modification** of **the original contract**, depending upon the **circumstances** of the case.

(ii) **Four remaining IFRS 15 steps**

As explained in part (a)(i), step one in the five-step model requires the identification of the contract with the customer. After a contract has been determined to fall under IFRS 15, the following steps are required before revenue can be recognised.

Step 2: Identify the performance obligations in the contract

This step requires the **identification** of the **separate performance obligations** in the contract. This is often referred to as 'unbundling', and is done at the beginning of a contract. The key factor in identifying a separate performance obligation is the **distinctiveness of the good or service**, or a **bundle** of goods or services. A good or service is **distinct** if the **customer can benefit from the good or service** on its own or together with other readily available resources and is **separately identifiable** from other elements of the contract.

IFRS 15 requires a **series of distinct goods or services** which are **substantially the same** with the same pattern of transfer, to be regarded as a **single performance obligation**. A **good or service**, which has been **delivered**, may **not** be **distinct** if it **cannot be used without another good or service** which has not yet been delivered. Similarly, goods or services which are **not distinct** should be **combined with other goods or services** until the entity identifies a **bundle** of goods or services which is **distinct**.

IFRS 15 provides **indicators** rather than criteria to determine when a good or service is distinct within the context of the contract. This allows management to apply judgement to determine the separate performance obligations which best reflect the economic substance of a transaction.

Step 3: Determine the transaction price

This step requires the entity to **determine the transaction price**, which is **the amount of consideration which an entity expects to be entitled to in exchange for the promised goods or services**. This amount excludes amounts collected on behalf of a third party, for example, government taxes. An entity must determine the amount of consideration to which it expects to be entitled in order to recognise revenue.

The transaction price **might include variable** or **contingent consideration**. **Variable consideration** should be estimated as either the **expected value** or the **most likely amount**. Management should use the approach which it expects will **best predict the amount** of consideration and should be **applied consistently** throughout the contract.

An entity can **only include variable consideration** in the transaction price to the extent that it is **highly probable** that a subsequent change in the estimated variable consideration will **not** result in a **significant revenue reversal**. If it is not appropriate to include all of the variable consideration in the transaction price, the entity should assess whether it should include part of the variable consideration. However, this latter amount still has to pass the 'revenue reversal' test.

Additionally, an entity should estimate the transaction price taking into account **non-cash consideration**, **consideration payable to the customer** and the **time value of money** if a significant financing component is present. The latter is not required if the time period between the transfer of goods or services and payment is less than one year.

If an entity anticipates that it may ultimately accept an amount lower than that initially promised in the contract due to, for example, past experience of discounts given, then revenue would be estimated at the lower amount with the collectability of that lower amount being assessed. Subsequently, if revenue already recognised is not collectable, impairment losses should be taken to profit or loss.

Step 4: Allocate the transaction price to the performance obligations in the contract

This step requires the **allocation of the transaction price to the separate performance obligations**. When a contract contains more than one distinct performance obligation, an entity allocates the transaction price to each distinct performance obligation on the **basis of the relative standalone selling prices** of the goods or services promised. This allocation is made at inception of the contract. It is not adjusted to reflect subsequent changes in the standalone selling prices of those goods or services.

The **best evidence** of **standalone selling price** is the **observable price** of a good or service when the entity **sells that good or service separately**. If that is **not available**, an **estimate** is made by using an approach which maximises the use of observable inputs. For example, expected cost plus an appropriate margin or the assessment of market prices for similar goods or services adjusted for entity-specific costs and margins or in limited circumstances a residual approach.

Where the transaction price includes **a variable amount and discounts**, consideration needs to be given as to **whether** these **amounts relate to all or only some of the performance obligations** in the contract. Discounts and variable consideration will typically be allocated proportionately to all of the performance obligations in the contract. However, if certain conditions are met, they can be allocated to one or more separate performance obligations.

Step 5: Recognise revenue when (or as) the entity satisfies a performance obligation

This final step requires revenue to be recognised **as each performance obligation is satisfied**. An entity satisfies a performance obligation by **transferring control of a promised good or service** to the customer, which could occur **over time** or **at a point in time**. The definition of control includes the ability to prevent others from directing the use of and obtaining the benefits from the asset.

Where an entity satisfies its **performance obligation over time, revenue** is recognised over time **in line with the pattern of transfer**.

If an entity does not satisfy its performance obligation over time, it satisfies it at a **point in time** and revenue will be recognised **when control is passed** at that point in time. Factors which may indicate the passing of control include the present right to payment for the asset or the customer has legal title to the asset or the entity has transferred physical possession of the asset.

(b) (i) **Existing printing machine**

The contract contains a **significant financing component** because of the **length of time between when the customer pays for the asset and when Tang transfers the asset to the customer**, as well as the **prevailing interest rates** in the market. This is a slightly unusual situation in which the customer is paying Tang in advance (24 months before the finished machine is ready for use) but the principles of the treatment of significant financing components prevail.

A contract with a customer which has a significant financing component should be **separated into a revenue component** (for the notional cash sales price) and a **loan component.** Consequently, the accounting for a sale arising from a contract which has a significant financing component should be comparable to the accounting for a loan with the same features.

An entity should use the **discount rate** which would be reflected in a **separate financing transaction** between the **entity and its customer** at contract inception. The **interest rate implicit** in the transaction may be **different** from the rate to be used to **discount** the cash flows, which should be the entity's **incremental borrowing rate.** IFRS 15 would therefore dictate that the rate which should be used in adjusting the promised consideration is 5%, which is the entity's incremental borrowing rate, and not 11.8%. As the customer is paying Tang in advance, in substance, Tang is borrowing $240,000 from the customer which makes Tang's incremental borrowing rate the most appropriate rate to use.

Tang would account for the significant financing component as follows:

Recognise a **contract liability** for the **$240,000** payment received on 1 December 20X4 at the contract inception.

During the two years from contract inception (1 December 20X4) until the transfer of the printing machine, Tang adjusts the amount of consideration and accretes the contract liability by recognising **interest** on $240,000 at **5%** for two years.

This would result in interest of $12,000 ($240,000 × 5%) in the year ended 30 November 20X5.

Contract liability would stand at $252,000 ($240,000 + $12,000) at 30 November 20X5. Therefore, interest in the year ended 30 November 20X6 would be $12,600 ($252,000 × 5%).

This would bring the contract liability up to $264,600.

Contract **revenue would be recognised** on the **transfer of the printing machine to the customer** on 30 November 20X6 by debiting the contract liability and crediting revenue with $264,600.

(ii) **Constructed printing machine**

Tang accounts for the promised bundle of goods and services as a single performance obligation satisfied over time in accordance with IFRS 15. At the inception of the contract, Tang expects the following:

Transaction price	$1,500,000
Expected costs	$800,000
Expected profit (46.7%)	$700,000

The $100,000 **bonus** constitutes **variable consideration** under IFRS 15. At contract inception, Tang **excludes the $100,000 bonus** from the transaction price because it **cannot conclude** that it is **highly probable that a significant reversal in the amount of cumulative revenue recognised will not occur**. Completion of the printing machine is highly susceptible to factors outside the entity's influence.

This is a contract where Tang **satisfied its performance obligation over time**. Therefore, **revenue** should also be recognised **over time** by measuring the **progress towards complete satisfaction** of that performance obligation. By the end of the first year, the entity has satisfied 65% of its performance obligation on the basis of costs incurred to date. Costs incurred to date are therefore $520,000 ($800,000 × 65%) and Tang reassesses the **variable consideration of $100,000** and concludes that the amount is still constrained which means that it **may not yet be recognised**. Therefore, at 30 November 20X5, only the **portion of the fixed consideration of $1,500,000** related to **progress to date** may be recognised as revenue. This results in revenue of $975,000 ($1,500,000 × 65%). The following amounts would therefore be included in the statement of profit or loss:

Revenue $975,000
Costs $520,000
Gross profit $455,000

However, on 4 December 20X5, the contract is **modified**. As a result, the fixed consideration and expected costs increase by $110,000 and $60,000, respectively. This increases the fixed consideration to $1,610,000 ($1,500,000 + $110,000) and the expected costs to $860,000 ($800,000 + $60,000).

The total potential consideration after the modification is $1,710,000 which is $1,610,000 fixed consideration + $100,000 completion bonus as Tang has concluded that receipt of the bonus is highly probable and that including the bonus in the transaction price will **not result in a significant reversal in the amount of cumulative revenue recognised in accordance with IFRS 15**. Tang also concludes that the contract remains a **single performance obligation**. Thus, Tang accounts for the **contract modification as if it were part of the original contract**. Therefore, Tang **updates its estimates** of costs and revenue as follows:

Tang has satisfied 60.5% of its performance obligation ($520,000 actual costs incurred compared to $860,000 total expected costs). The entity recognises additional revenue of $59,550 [(60.5% of $1,710,000) – $975,000 revenue recognised to date] at the date of the modification as a cumulative catch-up adjustment. As the **contract amendment** took place **after the year end,** the additional revenue would **not** be treated as an **adjusting event** after the reporting period. Therefore, it would be accounted for in the year ended 30 November 20X6 rather than as an adjustment in the year ended 30 November 20X5.

27 Blochberger

Marking scheme

		Marks
(a)	$3m is not in exchange for distinct good or service	1
	Treat $3m as a reduction of the transaction price	1
	Recognise revenue on transfer of control – delivery in December 20X7	1
	Recognise contract asset on payment on $3 million	1
	Compensation is 10% of transaction price	1
	On delivery, recognise revenue of $3.5m ($4 million invoiced less 10%)	1
		6
(b)	Sales price depends on volume of sales – element of variable consideration	1
	Recognise if highly probable that significant reversal will not occur	1
	Quarter ended 30 September 20X7: use full sales price of $200 as volume discount target unlikely to be met	2
	Quarter ended 31 December 20X7: use discounted sales price of $180 as volume discount target likely to be met	2
	Also recognise $20 discount retrospectively on units sold in previous quarter	1
		7
(c)	No revenue on transfer of product – right of return; lack of evidence	1
	Recognise revenue in following year when right of return lapses	1
	On transfer of goods, recognise asset for right to recover the product and reduce inventory	1
	Recognise receivable/revenue in subsequent year when right of return lapses	1
	Record cost of sales and derecognise asset for right to recover product	1

	Marks
Contract contains considerable financing component	1
Recognise interest on receivable over contract period once right of return lapses	1
	7

(d)

Capitalise directly attributable costs	1
Capitalise costs of testing less net proceeds from samples	1
Do not capitalise training costs – recognise as an expense	1
Do not capitalise advertising costs – recognise as an expense	1
Begin depreciation when asset is available for use	1
	5
	25

(a) **One-year contract**

IFRS 15 *Revenue from Contracts with Customers* is relevant here. The **$3 million compensation** that Blochberger must pay its customer under the contract is referred to as **'consideration payable to a customer'** by IFRS 15 (para. 48). Blochberger must **assess** whether the payment is **in exchange for a distinct good or service** that transfers to Blochberger. As Blochberger will not obtain control of any rights to the customer's shelves, the payment is **not** in exchange for a distinct good or service that transfers to Blochberger. Consequently, IFRS 15 requires the $3 million payment to be treated as a **reduction of the transaction price** rather than a purchase from a supplier.

The revenue from the sale of the goods would be treated as satisfaction of a performance obligation at a point in time which means that Blochberger should recognise **revenue** when it **transfers control** of the goods to the customer which will be at the point of delivery in December 20X7.

The **$3 million compensation** payable by Blochberger should **not be recorded as a reduction in the transaction price** until Blochberger recognises revenue from the sale of the goods.

Therefore, on 30 November 20X7, Blochberger should treat the $3 million compensation paid as a **contract asset** within current assets (since it is a one year contract) with the following accounting entry:

DEBIT	Contract asset	$3m
CREDIT	Cash	$3m

This compensation amounts to 10% ($3 million/$30 million) of the contract price. Consequently, as Blochberger **transfers goods to the customer**, the **transaction price must be reduced by 10%**. Therefore, in December 20X7, Blochberger should **recognise $3.6 million of revenue** being the $4 million invoiced less $0.4 million of the consideration payable to the customer. The accounting entry would be as follows:

DEBIT	Trade receivable	$4m
CREDIT	Revenue	$3.6m
CREDIT	Contract asset	$0.4m

(b)   **Contract to sell Product A**

As the sales price could either be $200 or $180 per unit depending on the volume of units sold, there is an element of **variable consideration** in this contract. This is referred to as a **volume discount incentive** by IFRS 15 whereby Blochberger's customer will receive a discount of $20 per unit ($200 – $180) of Product A if it purchases more than 1,000 units in a 12 month period. This type of variable consideration should be measured at its most likely amount, namely $200 per unit if the 1,000-unit threshold is unlikely to be met and $180 per unit if it is highly probable that the 1,000-unit threshold will be met.

Some or all of the **variable consideration** should only be **included in the transaction price** to the extent that it is **highly probable** that a **significant reversal in the cumulative revenue recognised will not occur** when the uncertainty associated with the variable consideration is subsequently resolved (ie when the total amount of units purchased is known). This means that revenue should be recognised at the undiscounted amount of $200 per unit unless it is highly probable that the 1,000-unit target will be reached.

For the **quarter ended 30 September 20X7**, Blochberger uses the purchasing pattern of the customer to conclude that the **1,000-unit target is unlikely to be reached**. This is because when extrapolated, the customer would only purchase 300 units in the year rather than the 1,000 required for the discount. Therefore, the **volume discount incentive** should **not** be **recognised** and **revenue** should be recognised at the **full sales price of $200**, resulting in total revenue of $15,000 (75 units sold × $200 per unit) as at this point in time, it is highly unlikely that any of the $200 revenue per unit will reverse.

For the **quarter ended 31 December 20X8**, due the customer's acquisition, there has a significant increase in demand with a sale of 500 units for the quarter, implying that it is highly probable that the **1,000-unit threshold will be reached** and the **discounted price earned**. Therefore, the **$20 volume discount incentive** should now be **recognised**, both for the 500 units sold in the current quarter and for the 75 units sold in the previous quarter. Consequently, revenue of $88,500 should be recognised for the quarter ended 31 December 20X7 being $90,000 for the sale of 500 units (500 units × $180 per unit) less the change in transaction price of $1,500 (75 units × $20 price reduction) for the reduction of revenue relating to units sold for the quarter ended 30 September 20X7.

(c)   **Contract to sell Product B**

Blochberger should **not recognise revenue** on transfer of the product to the customer on 31 December 20X7. This is because the existence of the **right of return** (within 90 days) and the **lack of historical evidence** (since this is a new product) mean that Blochberger **cannot conclude that it is highly probable** that a **significant reversal** in the amount of cumulative revenue recognised **will not occur**. Consequently, revenue may only be recognised in the next accounting period (the year ended 31 December 20X8), after three months when the right of return lapses (provided the customer has not returned the goods).

Therefore, on transfer of the goods on 31 December 20X7, an **asset** should be recorded for the **right to recover the product** and the item should be **removed from inventory** at the amount of $8,000 (the cost of the inventory):

DEBIT	Asset for right to recover product to be returned	$8,000
CREDIT	Inventory	$8,000

A **receivable and revenue of $10,000** will be recognised in the following accounting period when the **right of return lapses** on 31 March 20X8 provided the product is not returned. The **'asset for right to recover product to be returned'** will also be **transferred to cost of sales**. This will result in the following accounting entries:

DEBIT	Receivable	$10,000	
CREDIT	Revenue		$10,000
DEBIT	Cost of sales	$8,000	
CREDIT	Asset for right to recover product to be returned		$8,000

The contract also includes a **significant financing component** since there is a **difference** between the amount of the **promised consideration** of $12,100 and the **cash selling price** of $10,000 at the date the goods are transferred to the customer.

During the three-month **right of return period** (1 January 20X8 – 31 March 20X8) **no interest** is recognised because **no contract asset or liability** is recognised.

Interest revenue on the receivable should then be recognised at the **effective interest rate** (based on the remaining contractual term of 21 months) in accordance with IFRS 9 *Financial Instruments*.

(d) **New machine**

IAS 16 *Property, Plant and Equipment* requires **capitalisation** of any costs **directly attributable** to bringing the asset to the location and condition necessary for it to be capable of operating in the manner intended by management. Testing of the machine to ensure that it is functioning properly is required before the machine can be used in commercial production. Therefore, under IAS 16, Blochberger should **capitalise** $325,000 being the $400,000 **costs of testing** the asset's functionality **less the net proceeds** of $75,000 from selling items produced while bringing the asset to its required location and condition.

However, the **training costs** of $300,000 must be **expensed** in profit or loss as they are not considered a direct cost. Equally the $1 million **advertising costs** of the new product (Product C) manufactured by the new machine must also be treated as an **expense**. IAS 16 specifically prohibits capitalisation of the costs of introducing a new product or service.

Under IAS 16, **depreciation** should begin **when the asset is available for use** ie when it is in the location and condition necessary for it to be capable of operating in the manner intended by management. Therefore, depreciation on the new machine should begin on 31 October 20X7 when the functionality testing is completed and commercial production begins.

28 Minco

Workbook references. Revenue recognition and interim financial reporting are covered in Chapter 1. Intangible assets, property, plant and equipment, and impairment are covered in Chapter 3. IFRS 5 *Non-current Assets Held for Sale and Discontinued Operations* is covered in Chapter 13.

Top tips. The question covered a number of standards and issues (revenue, interim reporting, asset held for sale, provisions, intangibles and the treatment of an annual retainer). The best approach to this type of question is to allow time for planning – once you have identified and interpreted the requirement, you should actively read through the question scenario, trying to identify the relevant accounting standard(s) for each of items (a), (b), (c) an (d). You should aim to draw up a plan either by annotating the question paper or creating your own mind map or list of bullet-points – the key here is to draw out the relevant rules or principles from the IAS or IFRS and apply them to the scenario. Without discussion of the principles and application, you will not score enough marks to pass the question.

Easy marks. There are some easy marks to be had in part (a) for showing knowledge of the criteria for identifying the contract with a customer but you must apply this knowledge to the scenario to score enough marks to pass. Part (b) is more challenging but easier marks are to be had for applying the accruals concept when determining the correct point at which to recognise the expense.

The easier marks in part (c) related to trying to identify whether an obligation existed and whether a provision should be recognised. In part (d), you should have been able to apply the IFRS 5 accounting treatment for non-current assets held for sale even if you were unfamiliar with IAS 34.

Marking scheme

		Marks
(a)	Discussion of IFRS 15 criteria for identifying the contract	2
	Probability of collection of consideration in doubt	1
	Evidence that probability of collection in doubt	1
	Minco has not substantially transferred consideration nor terminated contract	1
	Do not recognise revenue	1
	Account for non-refundable payment as a deposit liability	1
	Continue to reassess IFRS 15 criteria	1
		8
(b)	Signing bonus	2
	Annual retainer	2
	Performance bonus	1
		5
(c)	Additional floor	2
	General disrepair of building	2
	Roof repair	1
		5
(d)	Follow same accounting policies as for annual financial statements	1
	Measure asset at lower of carrying amount and fair value less costs to sell	1
	1.10.20X3: recognise impairment loss of $100,000	1
	1.12.20X4: reverse impairment loss of $120,000 as less than cumulative impairment losses to date of $45,000	1
	31.5.20X4: can only recognise $330,000 of the $430,000 increase in fair value less costs to sell (up to remaining cumulative impairment losses to date)	1
	5.6.20X4: recognise gain on disposal	1
	Gain on disposal is non-adjusting event after the reporting period	1
		7
		25

(a)   **Contract for sale of the building**

Revenue from a contract may be recognised in accordance with IFRS 15 *Revenue from Contracts with Customers* when all of the following criteria (IFRS 15: para. 9) are met.

(i)   The **parties** to the contract have **approved the contract**.

(ii)   **Each party's rights** in relation to the goods or services to be transferred **can be identified**.

(iii)   The **payment terms and conditions** for the goods or services to be transferred **can be identified**.

(iv)   The contract has **commercial substance**.

(v)   The **collection of an amount of consideration** to which the entity is entitled to in exchange for the goods or services is **probable**.

Criteria (i) to (iv) have been met, but **criterion (v),** relating to Holistic Healthco's ability and intention to pay, is **in doubt.** The following factors need to be taken into consideration.

(i) Holistic Healthco's liability under the loan is limited because the **loan is non-recourse**. If the customer defaults Minco is not entitled to full compensation for the amount owed, but only has the right to repossess the building.

(ii) Holistic Healthco intends to repay the loan (which has a significant balance outstanding) primarily from income derived from its fitness and leisure centre. This is a **business facing significant risks** because of high competition in the industry and because of the customer's limited experience.

(iii) Holistic Healthco has **no other income or assets** that could be used to repay the loan.

It is therefore **not probable that Minco will collect the consideration** to which it is entitled in exchange for the transfer of the building and so the IFRS 15 (Paragraph 9) criteria have not been met. Minco must then consider whether either of the criteria in IFRS 15 Paragraph 15 have been met, that is:

(a) Has Minco has received **substantially all** of the consideration?
(b) Has Minco **terminated the contract?**

The answer to both of these is **no,** therefore, in accordance with Paragraph 16 of the standard, **Minco must account for the non-refundable $150,000 payment as a deposit liability**. Minco must continue to account for the initial deposit, as well as any future payments of principal and interest, as a deposit liability, until such time that the company concludes that the criteria in Paragraph 9 are met, specifically that it will recover the consideration owing, or until it has received substantially all of it, or terminated the contract. Minco must **continue to assess the situation** to see if these changes have occurred.

(b) **Promotional expenditure**

There are three types of payment involved in the arrangement with the tennis player. The question states that the payments are not interrelated, so the interactions between them do not need to be examined and the expense recognition pattern may be different for each.

Signing bonus

The contract is for advertising and promotional expenditure to improve Minco's brand image. IAS 38 *Intangible Assets* requires **that these costs must be expensed when the services are received**. The signing bonus is paid in advance of the services being received, those services being wearing Minco's logo, taking part in a specified number of tournaments and attending photo/film sessions for advertising. The signing bonus of $20,000 is paid to the player at the start of the contract, but relates to the full three-year contract term. It must therefore be treated as a **prepayment at the start of the contract and expensed on a straight-line basis** over the three-year contract period.

If the **contract is terminated** before the end of the three-year period, Minco should **expense immediately any amount not recovered** from the player.

It has been assumed in specifying the above treatment that separate services cannot be identified. However, **if the terms of the contract allow separate services to be identified and measured reliably**, then Minco should **recognise the expense once the separate service is rendered.**

Annual retainer

Minco has also contracted to pay the player an annual retainer of $50,000 provided she has competed in all the specified tournaments for that year. IFRS 9 *Financial Instruments* requires this arrangement to be treated as a **financial liability** because Minco has a **contractual**

obligation to deliver cash to the player. The financial liability is recognised at the **present value of the expected cash flows.**

Minco incurs this obligation on the date **when the player has competed in all the specified tournaments** and it is at this point that the **liability should be recognised.**

Performance bonus

Minco must also pay a performance bonus to the player whenever she wins a tournament. These payments are **related to specific events,** and therefore they are treated as **executory contracts.** (An executory contract is a contract in which something remains to be done by one or both parties.) They are **accrued and expensed when the player has won** a tournament.

(c) **Head office**

Additional floor

IAS 16 *Property, Plant and Equipment* is the relevant standard here. The standard requires that Minco should capitalise the costs of the extra floor, which is an improvement to the building, and amortise these costs over the six-year lease period.

IAS 16 states that the initial cost of an asset **should include** the initial estimate of the **costs of dismantling and removing the item and restoring the site** where the entity has an obligation to do so. This is the case here: Minco has an obligation to remove the floor at the end of the lease because of the clause in the lease requiring the building's condition to be identical at the end of the lease to its condition at the beginning of the lease. A **present obligation exists**, as defined by IAS 37 *Provisions, Contingent Liabilities and Contingent Assets* and therefore the entity should also **recognise a provision** for that amount. The provision should be **discounted to its present value** and the unwinding of the discount recognised in profit or loss.

This arrangement is, in substance, a decommissioning liability. The **asset** recognised for the cost of removal should be **amortised over the six-year period of the lease**. Minco may recover the cost from the benefits generated by the new floor over the remainder of the lease.

General disrepair of the building

A **present obligation** arises for the repair costs under IAS 37 because the lease agreement states that the landlord can re-charge these costs to Minco. The **obligating event is the wear and t**ear to the building, which arises gradually over the period of the lease and which will result in an outflow of economic benefits. The **estimated costs should be spread over the six-year lease** period. A **reliable estimate** of the yearly obligation can be made, although this may not necessarily be one sixth per year, for example if exceptional wear and tear arises in any given year.

Roof repair

The lease states clearly that the landlord can re-charge any costs of repairing the roof immediately. Accordingly, **an obligation exists** and a **provision needs to be made for the whole of the roof repair work** on the date on which the requirement was identified.

(d) **Property**

IAS 34 requirement

In accordance with IAS 34 *Interim Financial Reporting*, an entity must apply the same accounting policies in its interim financial statements as in its annual financial statements. Measurements should be made on a 'year to date' basis. Minco's interim financial statements are for the six months to 30 November 20X3.

Minco must apply the provisions of IFRS 5 *Non-Current Assets Held for Sale and Discontinued Operations* to the valuation of the property.

Application of IFRS 5

In accordance with IFRS 5, an asset held for sale should be measured at the **lower of** its **carrying amount** and **fair value less costs to sell**. Immediately before classification of the asset as held for sale, the entity must recognise impairment in accordance with applicable IFRS. Any impairment loss is generally recognised in profit or loss, but if the asset has been measured at a revalued amount under IAS 16 or IAS 38 the impairment will be treated as a revaluation decrease. **Once** the asset has been **classified as held for sale**, any **impairment loss** will be based on the **difference between the adjusted carrying amounts and the fair value less cost to sell**. The impairment loss (if any) will be **recognised in profit or loss**.

A **subsequent increase** in fair value less costs to sell may be **recognised** in profit or loss **only to the extent of any impairment previously recognised**. To summarise:

Step 1   Calculate carrying amount under the applicable accounting standard, here IAS 16:

Depreciation of $500,000 per year implies a useful life of 10 years, of which 8 years are remaining at 1 June 20X3. Depreciation must then be charged for the four months to 1 October 20X3, the date of classification as held for sale is calculated on the carrying amount net of the impairment loss incurred on 31 May 20X3, over the remaining useful life of eight years: '

$$\frac{\$5\text{m cost} - \$1\text{m accumulated depreciation} - \$0.35\text{m impairment}}{8\text{-year remaining useful life}} \times 4/12$$

= $152,083 (rounded to $0.15 million)

So the carrying amount at 1 October 20X3 is $5m – $1m – $0.35m – $0.15m = $3.5 million

Step 2   Classified as held for sale. Compare the carrying amount ($3.5 million) with fair value less costs to sell ($3.4 million). Measure at the lower of carrying amount and fair value less costs to sell, here $3.4 million, giving an initial write-down of $100,000. Cease depreciation.

Step 3   Determine fair value less costs to sell at the date of the interim financial statements, 1 December 20X3, here given as $3.52 million and compare with carrying amount of $3.4 million. This gives a gain of $120,000.

The impairment previously recognised is: $350,000 + $100,000 = $450,000. The gain of $120,000 is less than this, and may therefore be credited to profit or loss, and the property is carried at $3.52 million.

Step 4   On 31 May 20X4, fair value less costs to sell is $3.95 million. The change in fair value less cost to sell is recognised but the gain recognised cannot exceed any impairment losses to date. Impairment losses to date are $350,000 + $100,000 – $120,000 = $330,000, and this is less than the change in fair value less costs to sell of $430,000 ($3.95m – $3.52m). This restricted gain of $330,000 is recognised, and the property is carried at $3.85 million ($3.52m + $330,000).

Step 5   On 5 June 20X4, the property is sold for $4 million, at which point a gain of $150,000 is recognised. If material, this sale would be a non-adjusting event under IAS 10 *Events After the Reporting Period*.

29 Havanna

(a) **Contracts with sports organisations**

The applicable standard relating to the contracts is IFRS 15 *Revenue from Contracts with Customers*. The core principle of IFRS 15 is that the amount of revenue recognised reflects the amount of consideration an entity expects to receive in exchange for the delivery of promised goods or services. IFRS 15 has a five-step process that can be used for all types of revenue transaction and all industries, which gives preparers of financial information a process to undertake in order to achieve this core principle.

Five-step process

(i)   Identify the contract with the customer

(ii)   Identify the separate performance obligations – this helps the preparer to identify the promised goods or services

(iii)   Determine the transaction price – this helps the preparer to determine the amount of consideration receivable

(iv)   Allocate the transaction price to the performance obligations

(v)   Recognise revenue when (or as) a performance obligation is satisfied

In this case, it is assumed that (i) and (iii) are satisfied – the contracts are binding, and there is no indication in the question that the transaction price is undetermined.

Identify the separate performance obligations

Step (ii) **'identify the separate performance obligations'** needs to be considered. Havanna has treated the services provided under the contracts as a single performance obligation satisfied at a point in time, when the customer signs the contract.

However, there are **potentially at least three separate performance obligations** in the form of the different services provided by Havanna to the sports organisations. These are access to Havanna's database of members, admission to health clubs and provision of coaching (and other benefits).

At contract inception, IFRS 15 requires entities to assess the goods or services promised in a contract with a customer to identify as a performance obligation each promise to transfer to the customer either:

(1)   A good or service that is distinct; or

(2)   A **series of distinct goods or services** that are **substantially the same** and have the **same pattern of transfer** to the customer.

A series of distinct goods or services have the same pattern of transfer to the customer if both of the following criteria are met:

(1)   Each distinct good or service in the series that the entity promises to transfer to the customer would **meet the criteria to be a performance obligation satisfied over time**; and

(2)   **The same method** would be used to **measure the entity's progress towards complete satisfaction of the performance obligation** to transfer each distinct good or service in the series to the customer.

According to IFRS 15, a performance obligation is satisfied over time when the **customer simultaneously receives and consumes the benefits** provided by the entity's performance as the entity performs. This is the case with all three of the services offered by Havanna to the sports organisations. Furthermore, the same method would be used to measure Havanna's progress to towards complete satisfaction over time – the most appropriate measure would be a time-based measure as Havanna has an obligation to provide their services on a continuous basis over the 9 to 18 month contract.

Therefore, **Havanna's services** qualify as a **series of distinct goods and services that are substantially the same** which should be grouped together as a **single performance obligation**. This issue then is to identify when this performance obligation is satisfied to determine the point of revenue recognition.

Satisfaction of the performance obligation

Havanna's accounting policy treats the performance obligation as being satisfied at a point in time (when the customer signs the contract). However, as explained above, because the sports organisations simultaneously receive and consume the benefits provided by Havanna, per IFRS 15, the **performance obligation is satisfied over time**.

For each performance obligation satisfied over time, IFRS 15 requires an entity to recognise revenue over time by measuring progress towards complete satisfaction of that performance obligation.

As the sports organisation will benefit from access to Havanna's database, access to health clubs and provision of coaching evenly throughout the contract, the best measure of progress towards complete satisfaction of the performance obligation over time is a **time-based measure** and Havanna should recognise revenue on a **straight-line basis over the period of the contract** rather than when the customer signs the contract.

It is important that IFRS 15 is appropriately applied to these contracts because failing to do so would not be in line with applicable accounting standards. The fundamental principle of professional behaviour in ACCA's *Code of Ethics and Conduct* includes compliance with law and regulations. Thus not applying IFRS 15 would be a breach of this fundamental principle.

(b)   (i)   **Sale of division**

Impairment loss

The division to be sold meets the criteria in IFRS 5 *Non-current Assets Held for Sale and Discontinued Operations* to be classified as held for sale, and has been classified as a **disposal group** under IFRS 5.

A disposal group that is held for sale should be measured at the **lower of** its **carrying amount** and **fair value less costs to sell**. Immediately before classification of a disposal group as held for sale, the entity must recognise impairment in accordance with applicable IFRS. Any impairment loss is generally recognised in profit or loss, but if the asset has been measured at a revalued amount under IAS 16 *Property, Plant and Equipment* or IAS 38 *Intangible Assets,* the impairment will be treated as a revaluation decrease.

Once the disposal group has been **classified as held for sale**, any further **impairment loss** will be based on the **difference between the adjusted carrying amounts and the fair value less cost to sell**. The impairment loss (if any) will be **recognised in profit or loss**. For assets carried at fair value prior to initial classification, the requirement to deduct costs to sell from fair value will result in an immediate charge to profit or loss.

Havanna has calculated the impairment as $30m, being the difference between the carrying amount at initial classification and the value of the assets measured in accordance with IFRS. However, applying the treatment described above:

Step 1   Calculate carrying amount under applicable IFRS: $90m – $30m = $60m

Step 2   Classified as held for sale. Measure at the **lower** of the adjusted carrying amount under applicable IFRS ($60m) and fair value less costs to sell of $38.5m ($40m expected sales prices less expected costs of $1.5m). Therefore, an **additional impairment loss of $21.5m is required** to write down the carrying amount of $60m to the fair value less costs to sell of $38.5m.

(c) **Sale and leaseback**

(i) This is a sale and leaseback transaction which should be accounted for in accordance with IFRS 16 *Leases*. IFRS 16 requires an **initial assessment** to be made regarding **whether** or not the **transfer constitutes a sale**. This is done by determining when the performance obligation is satisfied **in accordance with IFRS 15** *Revenue from Contracts with Customers* (IFRS 16: para.99).

In this case, we are told in the question that the **IFRS 15 criteria have been met**. IFRS 16 therefore requires that Havanna should **derecognise the carrying amount** of the asset ($4.2m) and **recognise a right-of-use asset** at the proportion of the previous carrying amount that relates to the right-of-use asset retained. A **gain or loss** should then be recognised in relation to the **rights transferred** to the buyer-lessor. Although there is a gain to be recognised in profit or loss, this will not be the $0.8 million (being sales price of $5m – carrying amount of $4.2m) the CEO has calculated. Havanna should also recognise a **lease liability** at the present value of lease payments of $3.85m.

The right-of-use asset at the start of the leaseback should be calculated as:

Carrying amount × present value of lease payments/Fair value
= $4.2m × $3.85m/$5m = $3,234,000.

Havanna should only recognise the amount of gain that relates to the rights transferred. The gain on sale of the building is $800,000 ($5,000,000 – $4,200,000), of which:

($800,000 × $3.85m/$5m) = $616,000 relates to the rights retained.

The balance, $184,000 ($800,000 – $616,000), relates to the rights transferred to the buyer and should be recognised as a gain.

At the start of the lease Havanna should account for the transaction as follows:

	Debit	Credit
	$	$
Cash	5,000,000	
Right-of-use asset	3,234,000	
Building		4,200,000
Lease liability		3,850,000
Gain on rights transferred		184,000
	8,234,000	8,234,000

The **right-of-use asset** should be **depreciated over ten years** (being the shorter of the lease term and the remaining useful life of the asset). The **gain will be recognised in profit or loss** and the **lease liability** will be **increased** each year by the **interest charge** and **reduced by the lease payments**.

(ii) **Interest cover and effect on covenants**

The interest cover ratio in its most simple form is an entity's earnings before interest and tax divided by its interest expense for the period. In stating that the transaction will help to ensure that the interest cover covenant will be met, the CEO has failed to take into account the additional finance cost that will arise as a result of the lease liability. Furthermore, earnings will be increased by the gain on the rights transferred of $0.184m, but this is far less than the $0.8m gain expected by the CEO. More information would be required as to the interest payable on the lease in order to quantify whether the interest cover will indeed improve as a result of the sale and leaseback.

The move from IAS 17 *Leases* to IFRS 16 *Leases* has had a significant impact on the reported profits, assets and liabilities of companies and has therefore had a resultant impact on covenants. Companies and their lenders have had to reconsider whether they

will be able to meet their covenants when IFRS 16 is applied and have had to renegotiate the terms on which borrowings have been provided. This is particularly the case for companies which report significantly increased liabilities because IFRS 16 has brought all lease obligations on to the statement of financial position. This has had a significant commercial implication for the borrowers and lenders.

(iii) **Notes for discussion with whistleblowing helpline**

Professional competence and due care – reporting the profit of $0.8m would not be in keeping with the required accounting treatment under IFRS 16. I would not be acting with professional competence and due care if I recorded the profit as $0.8m.

Intimidation – the CEO is placing me under undue pressure by stating that there would be benefit to the company and to 'my future success' by recording the profit of $0.8m. I imply from this that he is expecting me to report $0.8m as profit, whether or not I believe it to be correct. I am fearful of whether my job is at risk if I do not do as he has asked. I, as a professional accountant, should be able to operate objectively without undue actual or perceived pressure.

Self-interest – the CEO has stated that recording the $0.8m profit would be of personal benefit to my future success. This concerns me as it puts me in a situation where my objectivity is compromised by a self-interest threat. As a professional accountant, my behaviour should not be influenced by perceived financial or other benefits offered. I believe appropriate safeguards to combat this threat are not in place at Havanna.

30 Alexandra

Workbook references. IAS 1 *Presentation of Financial Statements* and IFRS 15 *Revenue from Contracts with Customers* are covered in Chapter 1. IAS 8 *Accounting Policies, Changes in Accounting Estimates and Errors* and related parties and ethics are covered in Chapter 2.

Top tips. Part (a) was on reclassification of long-term debt as current – make sure you are familiar with IAS 1 as it is not a difficult standard but is often overlooked by students – IAS 1 requires a liability to be classified as current if it is due to be settled within 12 months after the date of the statement of financial position. Part (b) had a correction of an error (IAS 8) arising from an incorrect application of IFRS 15. Thus you have the interaction of two standards, so don't just concentrate on one. Part (c) was on related party disclosures for key management personnel, which needed to be broken down by category.

Easy marks. Part (c) has some easy marks for reproducing definitions from IAS 24 although these must then be applied to the scenario to pass this part of the question.

Marking scheme

			Marks
(a)	(i)	Loan – accounting treatment – 1 mark per point up to	5
	(ii)	Ethical implications	2
	(iii)	Impact on investors analysis	3
			10
(b)		Correction of revenue error	5
(c)	(i)	Directors remuneration accounting treatment – 1 mark per point up to	5
		Importance of disclosure to investors – 1 mark per point up to	2
	(ii)	Ethical implications – 1 mark point up to	3
			10
			25

(a) **Default on loan**

Under IAS 1 *Presentation of Financial Statements*, a **long-term financial liability** due to be **settled within 12 months** of the year end date should be classified as a **current liability**. Furthermore, a **long-term financial liability** that is payable on **demand** because the entity **breached** a **condition** of its loan agreement should be classified as **current** at the year end even if the **lender** has agreed **after the year end**, and **before** the financial statements are **authorised for issue**, **not** to **demand payment** as a consequence of the breach.

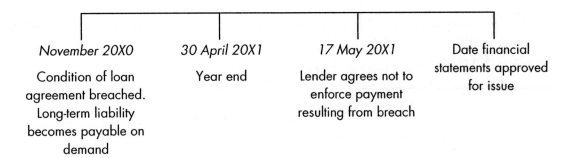

November 20X0	30 April 20X1	17 May 20X1	Date financial statements approved for issue
Condition of loan agreement breached. Long-term liability becomes payable on demand	Year end	Lender agrees not to enforce payment resulting from breach	

However, if the **lender** has **agreed** by the **year end** to provide a **period of grace** ending **at least twelve months after the year end** within which the entity can rectify the breach and during that time the lender cannot demand immediate repayment, the liability is classified as **non-current**.

In the case of Alexandra, the waiver was given before the year end, but only for the loan to be repaid a month after the year end, then a further waiver was agreed, but again only for a few weeks. It would **not therefore be appropriate for Alexandra to classify the bond as long-term debt** in the statement of financial position as at 30 April 20X1.

The fact that Alexandra has defaulted and sought two loan waivers may cast doubt on its ability to continue as a going concern, especially as the loan waivers may not be renewed. If there is uncertainty regarding Alexandra's going concern status, IAS 1 requires Alexandra to disclose these uncertainties. If Alexandra ceases to be a going concern, then the financial statements would need to be prepared on a break-up basis.

Ethical implications

Presentation of the loan as non-current is unethical as it does not faithfully represent the financial position of Alexandra at the year end.

The motivation of the directors in presenting the loan as non-current should be questioned. It may be that they have presented the loan as such to deliberately mislead their investors, lenders and other creditors as to the precarious financial position they find themselves in. This represents a threat to ACCA's *Code of Ethics and Conduct* fundamental principle of integrity, which requires professional accountants to be honest.

Impact on investors' analysis

Alexandra's incorrect presentation of this loan could have a serious impact on investors as they seek to analyse the financial statements. Investors need information to help them assess the prospects for future net cash inflows to an entity. Given that the bond obligation may become repayable immediately in this case, Alexandra's ability to continue as a going concern and be able to generate any future cash flows is clearly at risk.

According to the *Conceptual Framework*, the objective of financial reporting is to provide financial information about the entity that is useful to investors (and certain other stakeholders) in making decisions about providing resources to the entity. In Alexandra's case, reporting the loan as non-current is not useful to investors, it is misleading. In fact, it is materially misleading

as it could quite feasibly influence the economic decisions Alexandra's investors make on the basis of its financial statements.

(b) **Maintenance contracts**

There are two aspects to consider:

(i)   What is the correct way to recognise the revenue from the maintenance contracts?

(ii)   What adjustments does Alexandra need to make, having changed its method of recognition?

Correct IFRS 15 treatment

IFRS 15 *Revenue from Contracts with Customers* has a five-stage process for recognising revenue:

(i)   Identify the contract with the customer.
(ii)   Identify the separate performance obligations.
(iii)   Determine the transaction price.
(iv)   Allocate the transaction price to the performance obligations.
(v)   Recognise revenue when (or as) a performance obligation is satisfied

Step (ii) would classify the performance obligations in Alexandra's contracts with customers as the promise to transfer maintenance services to its customers.

Step (v) of the IFRS 15 process requires the entity to recognise revenue when or as a performance obligation is satisfied. IFRS 15 would treat the maintenance services as a **performance obligation satisfied over time** because the customer simultaneously receives and consumes the benefits as the performance takes place. Therefore, IFRS 15 requires Alexandra to recognise revenue over time by measuring the progress towards complete satisfaction of that performance obligation. This means that **revenue should be recognised as the services are provided** (step (v)).

IFRS 15 mentions various methods of measuring progress including output and input methods. In the case of the maintenance contracts, the best measure of progress towards complete satisfaction of the performance obligation over time is a **time-based measure** and Alexandra should recognise revenue on a **straight-line basis over the specified period.**

Accordingly, **the new treatment**, and the one used to date by Xavier Co, is the **correct** accounting treatment under IFRS 15, and the **previous treatment,** of recognising the revenue on invoicing at the beginning of the contract, was **incorrect**.

Adjustments under IAS 8

The accounting treatment previously used by Alexandra was incorrect because it did not comply with IFRS 15 *Revenue from Contracts with Customers*. Consequently, the change to the new, correct policy is **the correction of an error rather than a change of accounting policy**.

IAS 8 *Accounting Policies, Changes in Accounting Estimates and Errors* states that changes in accounting estimates result from changes in circumstances, new information or more experience, which is not the case here. This is a prior period error, which **must be corrected retrospectively**. This involves **restating the opening balances** for that period so that the financial statements are presented as if the error had never occurred.

In the opening balance of retained earnings, the maintenance contract income that was recognised in full in the year ended 30 April 20X0 must be split between the revenue due for that year (on an IFRS 15 basis as described above) and that which should be deferred to subsequence periods. There will be less revenue recognised in the prior year, resulting in a **net debit to opening retained earnings**.

In the year ended 30 April 20X1, the correct accounting policy has been applied. Since the maintenance contracts typically run for two years, it is likely that most of the **income deferred from the prior year relating to this period will also be recognised** in the current period. The effect of this for the year ended 30 April 20X1 is that the reduction in profits of $6m will be mitigated by the recognition of income deferred from last year.

(c) **Directors' remuneration**

The disclosures that Alexandra has provided are insufficient to comply with IAS 24 *Related Party Disclosures* on two counts:

(i) No breakdown of directors' remuneration
(ii) Exclusion of remuneration of non-executive directors

Breakdown of directors' remuneration

IAS 24 *Related Party Disclosures* requires that entities should **disclose** key management personnel compensation **not only in total** but also **for each of the** following **categories:**

- Short-term employee benefits
- Post-employment benefits
- Other long-term benefits
- Termination benefits
- Share-based payment

The remuneration for the directors of Alexandra fits into the categories of 'short-term benefits' (ie salary and bonus) and 'share-based payment' (ie share options), and should be disclosed accordingly. Only totals for each category need to be disclosed, not the earnings of individual board members, so no cultural protocol will be breached by these disclosures. However, Alexandra is a public limited company, and so local legislation and corporate governance rules may require more detailed disclosure.

Non-executive directors

By excluding the non-executive directors from the remuneration disclosures, **Alexandra is in breach of IAS 24**.

IAS 24 defines **key management personnel** as those persons having authority and responsibility for planning, directing and controlling the activities of the entity, directly or indirectly, including any director (**whether executive or otherwise**) of that entity. Transactions with directors are material by their very nature, not their size, so this cannot be used as an excuse not to disclose the required information.

Thus, the remuneration of the non-executive directors, who are key management personnel, should have been disclosed along with that of the executive directors.

Importance of disclosure to investors

Disclosures about related parties are necessary to draw attention to the possibility that the entity's financial position and profit or loss may have been affected by the existence of related parties and by transactions and outstanding balances with such parties.

Director's remuneration disclosures are particularly contentious. Public concern about excessive director remuneration has existed for some time. Investors want to know how much of an entity's income is being spent on its directors and whether this represents good value for money. Given the default on the bond and waivers to postpone interest payments, it is likely that the company would come under criticism if payments to directors were considered particularly high.

The disclosure of individual components of remuneration is important because it could influence the performance of a director – eg a high early termination payment may be seen to be rewarding poor performance.

Ethical issues

A fundamental principle of ACCA's *Code of Ethics and Conduct* is that of professional behaviour, which includes compliance with relevant regulation. It would therefore be unethical not to disclose all the information required by IAS 24.

The finance director should be fully aware of the requirements of IAS 24 and whether information is material. If he is not aware of these requirements, then this is a serious threat to the fundamental principle of professional competence and due care, as the knowledge and skill of the finance director is questionable.

If the finance director is aware of these requirements, his motivation as to why adequate disclosure was not provided should be investigated further. It may be that his objectivity has been compromised by pressure from the other board members to report the directors' remuneration in this way.

31 Verge

Workbook references. Segment reporting is covered in Chapter 17, and both IAS 1 *Presentation of Financial Statements* and revenue recognition are covered in Chapter 1. Provisions and contingencies are covered in Chapter 5 and government grants in Chapter 3.

Top tips. Part (a) requires you to apply the criteria in IFRS 8 to determine whether the company was correct in aggregating two reportable segments. There is plenty of information in the scenario to suggest otherwise. Part (b) needs some thought as possible confusion may arise about the $1m payment in advance, which is also included in an invoice. However, even if you missed this, you could still get good marks for seeing that the payments needed to be discounted in order that revenue should be recognised at fair value, and for seeing that the incorrect accounting treatment applied needed to be corrected retrospectively following IAS 8. You have met provisions (Part (c)) in your earlier studies, but in SBR, questions are likely to go into more depth. The information you require is in the scenario, but you need to think about applying the standard. Part (d) asks you to consider the interaction of two property-related standards you have met before in your previous studies, but again in a less straightforward context.

In this type of question, as well as providing a written explanation of the correct accounting treatment, you should also show the accounting entries where this is possible (parts (c) and (d) in this question).

Easy marks. These are available for identifying which standards apply and outlining the principles applicable, and you will gain these marks whether or not you come to the correct conclusion about the accounting treatment. There are also some easy marks for definitions in parts (a) and (c).

		Marks
(a)	Segment explanation up to	6
(b)	IFRS 15 explanation and calculation	6
(c)	IAS 37 explanation and calculation	6
(d)	IAS 1/16/20 explanation and calculation	7
		25

(a) **Operating segments**

IFRS 8 *Operating Segments* requires operating segments as defined in the standard to be reported separately if they exceed at least one of certain qualitative thresholds. Two or more operating segments **below** the thresholds may be **aggregated** to produce a reportable segment if the segments have **similar economic characteristics,** and the segments are similar in a **majority** of the following aggregation criteria:

(i) The nature of the products and services
(ii) The nature of the production process
(iii) The type or class of customer for their products or services
(iv) The methods used to distribute their products or provide their services
(v) If applicable, the nature of the regulatory environment

Verge has aggregated segments 1 and 2, but this aggregation may not be permissible under IFRS 8. While the products and services are similar, the **customers for those products and services are different.** Therefore the fourth aggregation criteria has not been met.

In the local market, the decision to award the contract is in the hands of the local authority, which also sets prices and pays for the services. The **company is not exposed to passenger revenue risk**, since a contract is awarded by competitive tender. It could be argued that the local authority is the major customer in the local market.

By contrast, in the inter-city train market, the **customer ultimately determines whether a train route is economically viabl**e by choosing whether or not to buy tickets. Verge sets the ticket prices, but will be influenced by customer behaviour or feedback. The **company is exposed to passenger revenue risk**, as it sets prices which customers may or may not choose to pay.

It is possible that the fifth criteria, regulatory environment, is not met, since the local authority is imposing a different set of rules to that which applies in the inter-city market.

In conclusion, the two segments have different economic characteristics and so **should be reported as separate segments** rather than aggregated.

(b) **Maintenance contract**

The applicable standards here are IFRS 15 *Revenue from Contracts with Customers* and IAS 8 *Accounting Policies, Changes in Accounting Estimates and Errors.*

Recognition of revenue from the maintenance contract

IFRS 15 states that the entity must **determine the transaction price** (Step (iii) of the IFRS 15 five-step process for revenue recognition). The transaction price is the amount of consideration a company expects to be entitled to from the customer in exchange for transferring goods or services and must take account of the time value of money, if material.

Under IFRS 15, an entity must **adjust the promised amount of consideration for the effects of the time value of money if the timing of payments** agreed to by the parties to the contract (either explicitly or implicitly) **provides the customer or the entity with a significant benefit of financing** the transfer of goods or services to the customer. In those circumstances, the contract contains a **significant financing component**. A significant financing component may exist regardless of whether the promise of financing is explicitly stated in the contract or implied by the payment terms agreed to by the parties to the contract.

Where the inflow of cash or cash equivalents is **deferred,** the amount of the inflow must be **discounted** because the fair value is less than the nominal amount. In effect, this is partly a financing transaction, with Verge providing interest-free credit to the government body. IFRS 15 requires the use of the **discount rate** which would be reflected in a **separate financing transaction** between the entity (Verge) and its customer (the government agency). This rate has been provided in the question as 6%. This 6% must be used to calculate the discounted amount, and the difference between this and the cash eventually received recognised as **interest income**.

IFRS 15 revenue recognition process (Step (v)) would treat this as a **performance obligation satisfied over time** because the customer simultaneously receives and consumes the benefits as the performance takes place. Verge must therefore **recognise revenue from the contract as the services are provided,** that is **as work is performed** throughout the contract's life, and not as the cash is received. The invoices sent by Verge reflect the work performed in each year, but the amounts must be **discounted in order to report the revenue at fair value**. The exception is the $1 million paid at the beginning of the contract. This is paid in advance and therefore not discounted, but it is invoiced and recognised in the year ended 31 March 20X2. The remainder of the amount invoiced in the year ended 31 March 20X2 ($2.8m – $1m = $1.8m) is discounted at 6% for two years.

In the year ended 31 March 20X3, the invoiced amount of $1.2m will be discounted at 6% for only one year. There will also be interest income of $96,000, which is the **unwinding of the discount** in 20X2.

Recognised in y/e 31 March 20X2

	$m
Initial payment (not discounted)	1.0
Remainder invoiced at 31 March 20X2: $1.8 \times \dfrac{1}{1.06^2}$	1.6
Revenue recognised	2.6

Recognised in y/e 31 March 20X3

Revenue: $\$1.2m \times \dfrac{1}{1.06} = \$1.13m$

Unwinding of the discount on revenue recognised in 20X2 $1.6m \times 6\% = \$96,000$

Correction of prior period error

The accounting treatment previously used by Verge was incorrect because it did not comply with IFRS 15 *Revenue from contracts with customers*. Consequently, the change to the new, correct policy is **the correction of an error rather than a change of accounting policy**.

Prior period errors, under IAS 8 *Accounting Policies, Changes in Accounting Estimates and Errors*, result from failure to use or misuse of information that:

(i) Was available when financial information for the period(s) in question was available for issue; and

(ii) Could reasonably be expected to have been obtained and taken into account in the preparation and presentation of those financial statements.

IAS 8 includes the effects of mistakes in applying accounting policies, mathematical mistakes and oversights. Only including $1m of revenue in the financial statements for the year ended 31 March 20X2 is clearly a mistake on the part of Verge. As a prior period error, it **must be corrected retrospectively**. This involves **restating the comparative figures** in the financial statements for 20X3 (ie, the 20X2 figures) and **restating the opening balances** for 20X3 so that the financial statements are presented as if the error had never occurred.

(c)   **Legal claim**

A **provision** is defined by IAS 37 *Provisions, Contingent Liabilities and Contingent Assets* as **a liability of uncertain timing or amount.** IAS 37 states that a provision should only be recognised if:

- There is a **present obligation** as the result of a **past event**
- An **outflow of resources embodying economic benefits is probable**; and
- A **reliable estimate** of the amount can be made.

If these conditions apply, a provision must be recognised.

The past event that gives rise, under IAS 37, to a present obligation, is known as the **obligating event.** The obligation may be legal, or it may be constructive (as when past practice creates a valid expectation on the part of a third party). The entity must have **no realistic alternative but to settle** the obligation.

Year ended 31 March 20X2

In this case, the obligating event is the damage to the building, and it took place in the year ended 31 March 20X2. As at that date, no legal proceedings had been started, and the damage appeared to be superficial. While Verge should recognise an obligation to pay damages, at 31 March 20X2 **the amount of any provision would be immaterial**. It would a best estimate of the amount required to settle the obligation at that date, taking into account all relevant risks and uncertainties, and at the year end the amount does not look as if it will be substantial.

Year ended 31 March 20X3

IAS 37 requires that **provisions should be reviewed at the end of each accounting period for any material changes** to the best estimate previously made. The legal action will cause such a material change, and Verge will be required to reassess the estimate of likely damages. While the local company is claiming damages of $1.2m, Verge is not obliged to make a provision for this amount, but rather should **base its estimate on the legal advice** it has received and the opinion of the expert, both of which put the value of the building at $800,000. This amount should be provided for as follows.

DEBIT   Profit or loss for the year $800,000
CREDIT   Provision for damages $800,000

Some or all of the expenditure needed to settle a provision may be expected to be recovered form a third party, in this case the insurance company. If so, the **reimbursement should be recognised only when it is virtually certain that reimbursement will be received if the entity settles the obligation**.

- The reimbursement should be treated as a **separate asset,** and the amount recognised should **not be greater than the provision itself**.

- The provision and the amount recognised for reimbursement **may be netted off in profit or loss** for the year.

There is no reason to believe that the insurance company will not settle the claim for the first $200,000 of damages, and so the company **should accrue for the reimbursement** as follows.

DEBIT   Receivables $200,000
CREDIT   Profit or loss for the year $200,000

Verge lost the court case and is required to pay $300,000. This was after the financial statements were authorised, however, and so it is **not an adjusting event** per IAS 10

Events after the reporting period. Accordingly the amount of the provision as at 31 March 20X3 does not need to be adjusted.

(d) **Gift of building**

The applicable standards here are IAS 16 *Property, Plant and Equipment,* and IAS 20 *Accounting for Government Grants and Disclosure of Government Assistance,* within the framework of IAS 1 *Presentation of Financial Statements.* IAS 1 requires that all items of income and expense recognised in a period should be included in profit or loss for the period unless a standard or interpretation requires or permits a different treatment.

IAS 16: recognition of building

IAS 16 states that the **cost** of an item of property, plant and equipment should be **recognised when two conditions** have been fulfilled:

- It is probable that future economic benefits associated with the item will flow to the entity.

- The cost of the item can be measured reliably.

These conditions are normally fulfilled when the risks and rewards have transferred to the entity, and they may be assumed to transfer **when the contract is unconditional and irrevocable**. As at 31 March 20X2, the condition of use has **not been complied** with and Verge has not taken possession of the building.

The building may, however, be recognised in the year ended 31 March 20X3, as the conditions of donation were met in February 20X3. The **fair value** of the building of $1.5m must be recognised as income in **profit or loss** for the year, as it was a gift. The **refurbishment and adaptation cost must also be included** as part of the cost of the asset in the statement of financial position, because, according to IAS 16, the cost includes **directly attributable costs of bringing the asset to the location and condition necessary** for it to be capable of operating in a manner intended by management. The transactions should be recorded as follows.

DEBIT	Property, plant and equipment	$2.5m	
CREDIT	Profit or loss for the year		$1.5m
CREDIT	Cash/payables		$1m

In addition, the building would be depreciated in accordance with the entity's accounting policy, which could (depending on the policy) involve time-apportioning over one or two months (February and March 20X3), depending on when in February the building came into use as a museum.

IAS 20: Government grant

The principle behind IAS 20 is that of accruals or matching: the **grant received must be matched with the related costs** on a systematic basis. Grants receivable as compensation for costs already incurred, or for immediate financial support with no future related costs, should be recognised as income in the period in which they are receivable.

Government grants are assistance by government in the form of transfers of resources to an entity in return for past or future compliance with certain conditions relating to the operating activities of the entity.

There are two main types of grants:

(i) **Grants related to assets**: grants whose primary condition is that an entity qualifying for them should purchase, construct or otherwise acquire long-term assets.

(ii) **Grants related to income**: These are government grants other than grants related to assets.

It is not always easy to match costs and revenues, but in this case the terms of the grant are explicit about the expense to which the grant is meant to contribute. **Part of the grant** relates to the **creation of jobs** and this amount (20 × $5,000 = $100,000) should be **taken to income.**

The **rest of the grant** ($250,000 – $100,000 = $150,000) should be recognised as **capital-based grant** (grant relating to assets). IAS 20 would **two possible approaches** for the capital-based portion of the grant.

(i)   Match against the depreciation of the building using a deferred income approach.

(ii)   Deduct from the carrying amount of the building, resulting in a reduced depreciation charge.

The double entry would be:

DEBIT   Cash $250,000
CREDIT   Profit or loss $100,000
CREDIT   Deferred income/PPE (depending on the accounting policy) $150,000

If a deferred income approach is adopted, the **deferred income would be released over the life of the building and matched against depreciation**. Depending on the policy, both may be time-apportioned because conditions were only met in February 20X3.

32 Formatt

> **Workbook references.** The *Conceptual Framework* and related Exposure Draft are covered in Chapter 1. Financial instruments are covered in Chapter 7. Impairments are covered in Chapter 3.
>
> **Top tips.** In part (a) you are asked to relate your answer to both IFRSs and pronouncements on the *Conceptual Framework*. Being able to relate and/or critique an accounting treatment in the light of the *Conceptual Framework* is a key skill required for SBR. You must ensure your knowledge of the *Conceptual Framework* and related Exposure Draft is up to date. In part (b), you must make sure that you explain the calculations you provide and the principles of the accounting standard on which they are based. Do not make the mistake of expecting the calculations to speak for themselves. SBR is preparation for the accountant's role as advisor – and explanations will be just as important in this role as computations so ensure the key issues are discussed in sufficient depth.
>
> **Easy marks.** These are available for the calculation of value in use and recoverable amount in part (b).

Marking scheme

		Marks
(a)	Financial asset – discussion 1 mark per point up to	8
(b)	Non-current asset at cost	8
	Non-current asset at valuation	6
	Non-current asset held for sale	3
		25

(a)   The *Conceptual Framework* defines an asset as 'a resource controlled by the entity as a result of past events and from which future economic benefits are expected to flow to the entity' (Conceptual Framework: para. 4.4(a))'. The existing *Conceptual Framework* does not define control. The ED/2015/3 *Conceptual Framework for Financial Reporting* defines an asset as 'a present economic resource controlled by the entity as a result of past events' (ED/2015/3: para. 4.4). It goes on to say that control links the economic resource to the entity and that

assessing control helps to identify what economic resource the entity should account for. For example, if an entity has a proportionate share in a property without controlling the entire property, the entity's asset is its share in the property, which it controls, not the property itself, which it does not. An entity controls an economic resource if it has the present ability to direct the use of the economic resource and obtain the economic benefits which flow from it. However, risks and rewards can be a helpful factor to consider when determining the transfer of control.

The entity should consider whether the contractual rights to the cash flows from the asset have expired as, if so, the asset should be derecognised. Secondly, if the contractual rights to the cash flows have not expired, as is the case with Formatt, the entity should consider whether it has transferred the financial asset. When an entity transfers a financial asset, it should evaluate the extent to which it retains the risks and rewards. IFRS 9 *Financial Instruments* provides three examples of when an entity has transferred substantially all the risks and rewards of ownership, these are: an unconditional sale of a financial asset, sale of a financial asset with an option to repurchase the financial asset at its fair value and sale of a financial asset which is deeply 'out of the money'. Thus in this case, even though most of the cash flows which are derived from the loan are passed on to Window (up to a maximum of $7 million), Formatt is essentially still in 'control' of the asset as the risks and rewards have not been transferred because of the subordinated retained interest. Formatt's residual interest also absorbs the potential credit losses.

If Formatt has neither retained nor transferred substantially all of the risks and rewards of ownership, the assessment of control is important. If control has been retained, the entity would continue to recognise the asset to the extent of its continuing involvement.

However, as Formatt has retained the risks and rewards, it should recognise the financial asset in the statement of financial position and the 12-month expected credit losses.

(b) **Principles of IAS 36 *Impairment of Assets***

The basic principle of IAS 36 is that an asset should be carried at no more than its recoverable amount, that is, the greater of amount to be recovered through use or sale of the asset. If an **asset's carrying amount** is **higher than its recoverable amount**, an **impairment loss** has occurred. The impairment loss should be **written off** against profit or loss for the year.

An asset's **recoverable amount** is **defined** as the **higher** of:

(1) The **asset's fair value less costs of disposal**. This is the price that would be received to sell the asset in an orderly transaction between market participants at the measurement date under current market conditions, net of costs of disposal.

(2) The asset's **value in use**. This is the present value of estimated future cash flows (inflows minus outflows) generated by the asset, including its estimated net disposal value (if any) at the end of its useful life. A number of factors must be reflected in the calculation of value in use (variations, estimates of cash flows, uncertainty), but the most important is the **time value of money** as value in use is based on **present value calculations**.

(i) **Impairment loss at 31 May 20X4**

The carrying amount of the non-current assets of Key at 31 May 20X4 is cost less accumulated depreciation:

$3m – ($3m/5) = $2.4m.

This needs to be compared to value in use at 31 May 20X4, which, using a discount rate of 5%, is calculated as:

Year ended	31 May 20X5	31 May 20X6	31 May 20X7	31 May 20X8	Total
Cash flows ($'000)	280	450	500	550	
Discount factors	0.9524	0.9070	0.8638	0.8227	
Discounted cash flows ($'000)	267	408	432	452	1,559

The value in use of $1,559,000 is below the carrying amount, so the carrying amount must be written down, giving rise to an **impairment loss**:

$2,400,000 – $1,559,000 = $841,000

Value in use at 30 November 20X4

The directors wish to reverse the impairment loss calculated as at 31 May 20X4, on the grounds that, using the same cash flows, the value in use of the non-current assets is now above the carrying amount. However, while IAS 36 requires an assessment at each reporting date of whether an impairment loss has decreased, this does not apply to the unwinding of the discount (or goodwill). Since the **same cash flows** have been used, the increase in value in use is **due to the unwinding of the discount, and so cannot be reversed**.

Government reimbursement

The treatment of compensation received in the form of reimbursements is governed by IAS 37 *Provisions, Contingent Liabilities and Contingent Assets*. Reimbursements from governmental indemnities are **recorded** as an asset and in profit or loss for the year when, and only when, it is **virtually certain** that reimbursement will be received if the entity settles the obligation. In practice, this will be **when the compensation becomes receivable,** and the receipt is **treated as a separate economic event** from the item it was intended to compensate for. In this particular case, receipt is by no means certain, since the government has merely indicated that it may compensate.

Thus, **no credit can be taken** for compensation of 20% of the impairment loss.

(ii) **Revalued asset**

When an **impairment loss occurs** for a **revalued asset**, the **impairment loss** should be first be charged to other comprehensive income (that is, treated as a **revaluation decrease**). Any **excess** is then charged to **profit or loss**.

The revaluation gain and impairment loss will be accounted for as follows:

	Revalued carrying amount $m
1 December 20X1	10.0
Depreciation (10 × 2/10)	(2.0)
Revaluation (bal. fig.)	0.8
1 December 20X3	8.8
Depreciation (1 year) (8.8 × 1/8)	(1.1)
Impairment loss (bal. fig.)	(2.2)
Recoverable amount at 30 November 20X4	5.5

The impairment loss of $2.2m is charged to **other comprehensive income** until the revaluation surplus has been eliminated, and the rest is charged to profit or loss. Therefore, the impairment **loss charged to other comprehensive income** will be **$0.8m**. The **remainder**, $2.2m – $0.8m = $1.4m will be **charged to profit or loss**.

It is possible that the company would have transferred an amount from revaluation surplus to retained earnings to cover the excess depreciation of $0.1m. If so, the impairment loss charged to OCI would be $(0.8 – 0.1m) = $0.7m.

(iii) **Property to be sold**

The fact that management plans to sell the property because it is being under-utilised may be an **indicator** of **impairment**. Such assets (or cash-generating units) must be tested for impairment when the decision to sell is made.

IFRS 5 *Non-current Assets Held for Sale and Discontinued Operations* may apply in such cases, but the decision to sell the asset is generally made well before the IFRS 5 criteria are met. IFRS requires an asset or disposal group to be classified as held for sale where it is **available for immediate sale** in its **present condition** subject only to **terms that are usual** and customary and the sale is **highly probable**. For a sale to be highly probable:

- Management must be **committed** to the sale;
- An **active programme to locate a buyer** must have been initiated;
- The **market price** must be **reasonable** in relation to the asset's current fair value; and
- The sale must be **expected to be completed within one year** from the date of classification.

An asset (or disposal group) that is held for sale should be measured at the **lower of** its **carrying amount** and **fair value less costs to sell**. Immediately before classification of the asset as held for sale, the entity must update any impairment test carried out. **Once** the asset has been **classified as held for sale**, any **impairment loss** will be based on the **difference between the adjusted carrying amounts and the fair value less cost to sell**. The impairment loss (if any) will be **recognised in profit or loss**.

A **subsequent increase** in fair value less costs of disposal may be **recognised** in profit or loss **only to the extent of any impairment previously recognised**.

In the case of the property held by Key, it is likely that **IFRS 5 would not apply** because **not all the criteria for a highly probable sale** have been met. Management is committed to the sale, and there is an active programme to locate a buyer. However, **Key has not reduced the price of the asset, which is in excess of its market value** – one of the IFRS 5 criteria is that the market price must be reasonable in relation to the asset's current fair value. In addition, the asset has remained unsold for a year, so it **cannot be assumed that the sale will be completed within one year** of classification.

The property does not meet the IFRS 5 criteria, so it **cannot be classified as held for sale**. However, an **impairment** has taken place and, in the circumstances, the **recoverable amount** would be **fair value less costs to sell**.

33 Emcee

> **Workbook references**. IAS 38 *Intangible Assets*, IAS 23 *Borrowing Costs* and IFRS 13 *Fair Value Measurement* are covered in Chapter 3. IFRS 5 *Non-current Assets Held for Sale and Discontinued Operations* is covered in Chapter 13 and IAS 24 *Related Party Disclosures* in Chapter 2.
>
> **Top tips.** This is a multi-standard question in which the three parts are independent. You should scan read all parts of the question and attempt the part you feel most comfortable with first. The issues covered are borrowing costs (part (a)), intangible assets, non-current assets held for sale and impairment of assets (part (b)) and fair value measurement and related party transactions (part (c)). The recommended approach is to discuss the general principles of the relevant standards and then apply them to the scenario. Part (b) is broken down into four elements so ensure you provide an answer to each.
>
> **Easy marks.** No parts of this question are particularly easy – the main way to get the marks is to break down the scenario into its constituent parts and make sure you deal with each relevant standard.

Marking scheme

		Marks
(a)	Discussion of IAS 23 requirements and calculation of capitalised interest – 1 mark per point to a maximum	6
(b)	Discussion of IAS 38 recognition requirements, applicability of IFRS 5 and impairment under IAS 26 – 1 mark per point to a maximum	11
(c)	Discussion of IFRS 13 and IAS 24 – 1 mark per point to a maximum	8
		25

(a) **Borrowing costs**

IAS 23 *Borrowing Costs* requires borrowing costs incurred on acquiring or constructing an asset to be **capitalised** if the asset takes a substantial period of time to be prepared for its intended use or sale. Borrowing costs should be capitalised during construction and include the costs of general borrowings which would have been avoided if the expenditure on the asset had not occurred. The general borrowing costs are determined by applying the weighted average of the borrowing costs applicable to the general pool

The weighted-average carrying amount of the stadium during the period is:

$(20 + 70 + 120 + 170)m/4$, that is \$95m.

The capitalisation rate of the borrowings of Emcee during the period of construction is 9% per annum, therefore the total amount of borrowing costs to be capitalised is the weighted-average carrying amount of the stadium multiplied by the capitalisation rate.

That is ($95m × 9% × 4/12) $2.85m.

(b) **Players' registrations**

Acquisition

IAS 38 *Intangible Assets* states that an entity should recognise an intangible asset where it is probable that future economic benefits will flow to the entity and the cost of the asset can be measured reliably. Therefore, the **costs** associated with the acquisition of players' registrations should be **capitalised at the fair value of the consideration payable**.

Costs would include transfer fees, league levy fees, agents' fees incurred by the club and other directly attributable costs. Costs also **include the fair value of any contingent consideration**, which is primarily payable to the player's former club with associated league levy fees, once payment becomes probable. Subsequent reassessments of the amount of contingent consideration payable would be also included in the cost of the player's registration. The estimate of the fair value of the contingent consideration payable requires management to assess the likelihood of specific performance conditions being met, which would trigger the payment of the contingent consideration. This assessment would be carried out on an individual player basis. The additional amount of contingent consideration potentially payable, in excess of the amounts included in the cost of players' registrations, would be disclosed. Amounts capitalised would be fully amortised over the period covered by the player's contract.

Extension

Where a playing contract is extended, any **costs associated with securing the extension are added to the unamortised carrying amount** at the date of the extension and the revised carrying amount is amortised over the remaining revised contract life.

Sale of registrations

Player registrations would be classified as assets held for sale under IFRS 5 *Non-Current Assets Held for Sale and Discontinued Operations* when their **carrying amount is expected to be recovered principally through a sale** transaction and a sale is considered to be highly probable. Additionally, the registrations should be actively marketed by Emcee, which it appears that they are. It would appear that in these circumstances that management is committed to a plan to sell the registration, that the asset is available for immediate sale, that an active programme to locate a buyer is initiated by circulating clubs. IFRS 5 requires that it is unlikely that the plan to sell the registrations will be significantly changed or withdrawn. In order to fulfil the last criteria of IFRS 5, it may be prudent to only class these registrations as held for sale where unconditional offers have been received prior to a period end.

However, because of the subjectivity involved, in the case of player registrations these assets would be stated at the lower of the carrying amount and fair value less costs to sell, as the carrying amount will already be stated in accordance with IFRSs.

Gains and losses on disposal of players' registrations would be determined by comparing the fair value of the consideration receivable, net of any transaction costs, with the carrying amount and would be recognised in profit or loss within profit on disposal of players' registrations. Where a part of the consideration receivable is contingent on specified performance conditions, this amount is recognised in profit or loss when the conditions are met.

The player registrations disposed of, subsequent to the year end, for $25m, with an associated net book value of $7m, would be disclosed as events after the reporting date.

Impairment review

IAS 36 *Impairment of Assets* states that entities should annually **test their assets for impairment**. An asset is impaired if its carrying amount exceeds its recoverable amount which is the higher of the asset's fair value less costs of disposal and its value in use. It is difficult to determine the value in use of an individual player in isolation as that player (unless via a sale or insurance recovery) cannot generate cash flows on his own. Whilst any individual player cannot really be separated from the single cash generating unit (CGU), being the basketball or football team, there may be certain circumstances where a player is taken out of the CGU, when it becomes clear that they will not play for the club again. If such circumstances arise, the **carrying amount of the player should be assessed against**

the best estimate of the player's fair value less any costs to sell and an impairment charge made in profit or loss, which reflects any loss arising.

(c)   **Valuation of stadiums**

IFRS 13 *Fair Value Measurement* would value the stadiums at the **price which would be received to sell the asset in an orderly transaction between market participants** at the measurement date. The price would be the one which **maximises the value of the asset** or the group of assets using the principal of the highest and best use. The price would essentially use Level 2 inputs which are inputs other than quoted market prices included within Level 1 which are observable for the asset or liability, either directly or indirectly. Property naming rights present complications when valuing property. The status of the property dictates its suitability for inviting sponsorship attached to its name. It has nothing to do with the property itself but this can be worth a significant amount. Therefore, Emcee could **include the property naming rights in the valuation** of the stadiums and write it off over three years.

IAS 24 *Related Party Disclosures* sets out the criteria for two entities to be treated as related parties. Such criteria include being members of the same group or where a person or a close member of that person's family is related to a reporting entity if that person has control or joint control over the reporting entity. IAS 24 deems that parties are not related simply because they have a director or key manager in common. In this case, there are **two directors in common** and it appears as though the **entities are not related**. However, the regulator will need to establish whether the **sponsorship deal is a related party transaction** (RPT) for the purpose of the financial control provisions. There would need to be demonstrated that the airline may be expected to influence, or be influenced by, the club or a related party of the club. If the deal is deemed to be an RPT, the regulator will consider whether the sponsorship is at fair value.

34 Scramble

Workbook references. Intangible assets and impairment are covered in Chapter 3. IFRS 9 *Financial Instruments* is covered in Chapter 7.

Top tips. Parts (a) and (b) were on impairment testing. You may have found part (b), requiring determination of the discount rate to be used, rather difficult, and you may have needed to draw on your financial management studies. Part (c) was on intangible assets (agents' fees on transfer of players to the club and extension of players' contracts) and an IFRS 9 financial asset (rights to ticket sales of another football club).

Easy marks. There are no obvious easy marks in this question.

Marking scheme

		Marks
(a)	Intangible assets – subjective assessment	7
(b)	Cash generating units – subjective assessment	8
(c)	Intangible assets – subjective assessment	10
		25

(a) **Internally developed intangibles**

IAS 38 *Intangible Assets* **allows internally developed intangibles to be capitalised** provided certain criteria (technological feasibility, probable future benefits, intent and ability to use or sell the software, resources to complete the software, and ability to measure cost) are met. It is assumed, in the absence of information to the contrary, that they have; accordingly Scramble's treatment is correct in this respect.

Scramble is also correct in expensing the maintenance costs. These should not be capitalised as they do not enhance the value of the asset over and above the original benefits.

As regards subsequent measurement, IAS 38 requires that **an entity must choose either the cost model or the revaluation** model for each class of intangible asset. Scramble has chosen cost, and this is acceptable as an accounting policy.

Intangible assets **may have a finite or an indefinite useful life**. IAS 38 states that an entity may treat an intangible asset as having an indefinite useful life, when, having regard to all relevant factors there is no foreseeable limit to the period over which the asset is expected to generate net cash inflows for the entity.

'Indefinite' is not the same as 'infinite'. Computer software is mentioned in IAS 38 as an intangible that is prone to technological obsolescence and whose life may therefore be short. Its **useful life should be reviewed each reporting period** to determine whether events and circumstances continue to support an indefinite useful life assessment for that asset. If they do not, the change in the useful life assessment from indefinite to finite should be accounted for as a change in an accounting estimate.

The asset should also be **assessed for impairment in accordance with IAS 36** *Impairment of Assets*. Specifically, the entity must test the intangible asset for impairment annually, and whenever there is an indication that the asset may be impaired. The asset is tested by **comparing its recoverable amount with its carrying amount**.

The **cash flows** used by Scramble to determine value in use for the purposes of impairment testing **do not comply with IAS 36**. Scramble does not analyse or investigate the differences between expected and actual cash flows, but this is an important way of testing the reasonableness of assumptions about expected cash flows, and IAS 36 requires such **assumptions to be reasonable and supported by evidence**.

Scramble is also **incorrect** to include in its estimate of future cash flows those **expected to be incurred in improving the games and the expected increase in revenue** resulting from that expense. IAS 36 requires cash flow projections to relate to the asset in its current condition. Nor should cash flow estimates include tax payments or receipts as here.

(b) **Discount rate for impairment**

While the cash flows used in testing for impairment are specific to the entity, the **discount rate is supposed to appropriately reflect the current market assessment of the time value of money and the risks specific to the asset or cash generating unit**. When a specific rate for an asset or cash generating unit is not directly available from the market, which is usually the case, an estimated discount rate may be used instead. An estimate should be made of a **pre-tax rate that reflects the current market assessment of the time value of money and the risks specific to the asset** that **have not been adjusted** for in the estimate of future cash flows. According to IAS 36, this rate is the return that the investors would require if they chose an investment that would generate cash flows of amounts, timing and risk profile equivalent to those that the entity expects to derive from the assets.

Rates that should be considered are the entity's weighted average cost of capital, the entity's incremental borrowing rate or other market rates. The objective must be to obtain a rate which is sensible and justifiable. Scramble should not use the risk-free rate adjusted by the company specific average credit spread of outstanding debt raised two years ago. Instead the credit

spread input applied **should reflect the current market assessment of the credit spread at the time of impairment testing**, even though Scramble does not intend raising any more finance.

Disclosures

With regard to the impairment loss recognised in respect of each cash generating unit, IAS 36 requires disclosure of:

- The amount of the loss
- The events and circumstances that led to the loss
- A description of the impairment loss by class of asset

It is **no defence** to maintain that this information was **common knowledge in the market**. The disclosures are still needed. It should be noted that IAS 1 requires disclosure of material items, so this information needs to be disclosed if the loses are **material,** with materiality determined using a suitable measure such as percentage of profit before tax.

(c) **Recognition of intangible assets**

Registration rights and agents' fees

The relevant standard here is IAS 38 *Intangible Assets*. An **intangible asset may be recognised** if it is controlled by the entity (it gives the entity the power to benefit from the asset), if it meets the identifiability criteria in IAS 38, if it is probable that future economic benefits attributable to the asset will flow to the entity and if its fair value can be measured reliably. For an intangible asset to be identifiable the asset must be separable or it must arise from contractual or other legal rights. It appears that these **criteria have been met**:

(i) The registration rights are contractual.

(ii) Scramble has control, because it may transfer or extend the rights.

(iii) Economic benefits will flow to Scramble in the form of income it can earn when fans come to see the player play.

IAS 38 specifies the items that make up the **cost** of separately acquired assets:

(i) Its purchase price, including import duties and non-refundable purchase taxes, after deducting trade discounts and rebates; and

(ii) Any directly attributable cost of preparing the asset for its intended use.

IAS 38 specifically mentions, as an example of directly attributable costs, 'professional fees arising directly from bringing the asset to its working condition'. In this business**, the players' registration rights meet the definition of intangible assets**. In addition, **Scramble is incorrect** in believing that the **agents' fees** paid on extension of players' contracts do not meet the criteria to be recognised as intangible assets. The fees are incurred to service the player registration rights, and **should therefore be capitalised as intangible assets**.

Rights to revenue from ticket sales

Whether Rashing can show these rights as intangible assets depends on whether the IAS 38 criteria have been met. Since Rashing has no discretion over the pricing of the tickets and cannot sell them, it cannot be said to control the asset. Accordingly, the rights **cannot be treated as an intangible asset**.

The entity is only entitled to cash generated from ticket sales, so the issue is one of a **contractual right to receive cash**. The applicable standard is therefore not IAS 38 but IFRS 9 *Financial Instruments,* under which the rights to ticket revenue represent a **financial asset**.

IFRS 9 has two classifications for financial assets: amortised cost and fair value. Financial assets are classified as being at **amortised cost** if **both** of the following apply.

(i) The asset is held within a business model whose objective is to hold the assets to collect the contractual cash flows.

(ii) The contractual terms of the financial asset give rise, on specified dates, to cash flows that are solely payments of principal and interest on the principal outstanding.

All other financial assets are measured at fair value.

Rashing's receipts are regular cash flows, but they are based on ticket revenues, which are determined by match attendance. Therefore, they are not solely payments of principal and interest, and **do not meet the criteria for classification at amortised cost**. Consequently, the financial asset should be classified as being **at fair value** under IFRS 9.

35 Estoil

Workbook reference. Impairment is covered in Chapter 3 of your Workbook.

Top tips. This question dealt with a problematic issue rather than a current issue. While IAS 36 is brought forward knowledge from earlier studies, the depth of discussion required is greater, and the scenario requires more thought. Part (a) required a discussion of factors to take account of in conducting an impairment test. There are five factors provided in the question and you should use these as headings under which to structure your answer. The discussion required drew on your financial management knowledge (eg WACC).

Easy marks. There are no obvious easy marks in this question.

Marking scheme

		Marks
(a)	Changes in circumstances	3
	Market capitalisation	2
	Allocating goodwill	2
	Valuation issues	6
	Disclosures	2
		15
(b)	Discount rate	5
	Cash flow forecast	5
		10
		25

(a) Entities must determine, **at each reporting date**, whether there are any indications that impairment has occurred. Indicators of impairment may be internal or external. The following factors need to be considered when conducting an impairment test under IAS 36 *Impairment of Assets*.

(i) **Changes in circumstances in the reporting period**

Circumstances may change due to internal factors, for example matters as physical damage, adverse changes to the methods of use of the asset, management restructuring and over-estimation of cash flows, and external factors, such as **adverse changes** in the **markets** or **business** in which the asset is used, or adverse changes to the **technological, economic or legal environment** of the business.

If such indicators come to light between the date of the impairment test and the end of the next reporting period, **more than one impairment test may be required** in the accounting period. In addition, tests for impairment of goodwill and some other intangible assets may be performed at any time during the accounting period, provided it is performed at the same time each year. Not all goodwill is tested at the year end – some entities test it at an interim period. Should impairment indicators arise after the annual impairment test has been performed, it may be necessary to test goodwill for impairment again at the year end.

A possible indicator of impairment is volatility in the market, for example, sharp changes in commodity prices may cause the assets of mining and energy companies to be impaired. In such cases, the assets affected should be tested in the interim period.

(ii) **Market capitalisation**

A strong indicator of impairment is when the **carrying amount** of an entity's assets exceeds the entity's **market capitalisation,** suggesting that the entity is overvalued. However, there **may not be a direct correlation** between the market capitalisation and the impairment loss arising from a lower return generated on the entity's assets –the market may have taken other factors into account. The discrepancy does, however, **highlight the need for the entity to examine its cash-generating units, and possibly to test goodwill for impairment**. The reason for the shortfall must be examined and understood, even though IAS 36 does not require a formal reconciliation between an entity's market capitalisation, its fair value less costs to sell and its value in use.

(iii) **Allocating goodwill to cash-generating units**

Goodwill arising on an acquisition is required to be allocated to each of the acquirer's cash-generating units (CGUs), or to a group of CGUs, that are expected to benefit from the synergies of the combination. **If CGUs are subsequently revised or operations disposed of, IAS 36 requires goodwill to be reallocated, based on relative values, to the units affected.**

The difficulty with this is that IAS 36 **does not give guidance as to what is meant by relative value.** While **fair value less costs to sell** (FVLCS) could be used, this is not mandated by the standard. However, the entity may still need to carry out a valuation process on the part retained. **Value in use** (VIU) is a possibility, but the measure needs to be one that can be applied equally to both the part retained and the part disposed of. VIU has the obvious problem that it will be much the same as FVLCS for the operations disposed of, but there could be significant differences between VIU and FVLCS for the part retained. Alternatively, there could be reasonable ways of estimating relative value by using an **appropriate industry or business surrogate**, for example revenue, profits, industry KPIs.

(iv) **Valuation issues**

The basic principle of IAS 36 is that an asset should be carried at no more than its recoverable amount, that is the amount to be recovered through use or sale of the asset. If an **asset's value** is **higher than its recoverable amount,** an **impairment loss** has occurred. The impairment loss should be **written off** against profit or loss for the year.

The **recoverable amount** is **defined** as the **higher** of the **asset's fair value less costs of disposal** and the asset's **value in use**. Measuring both of these requires the use of **estimates and assumptions,** some of which **may be problematic**.

(1) **Fair value less costs of disposal** is defined as the price that would be received to sell the asset in an orderly transaction between market participants at the measurement date under current market conditions, net of costs of disposal. IAS 36 gives a 'hierarchy of evidence' for this, with 'price in a binding sale agreement' at the top, only likely to be available if the asset is held for sale, and allowing, in the absence of any active market, estimates based on **a discounted cash flow (DCF) model, which may not be reliable.**

(2) Determining the types of **future cash flows which should be included in the measurement of VIU can also be difficult.** Under IAS 36 an asset or CGU must be tested in its current status, not the status that management wishes it was in or hopes to get it into in the near future. Therefore, the standard requires VIU to be measured at the net present value of the future cash flows the entity expects to derive from the asset or CGU in its current condition over its remaining useful life. This means that it is not appropriate to take account of management plans for enhancing the performance of the asset or CGU, even though these may bring about an increase in value.

(3) While the cash flows used in testing for impairment are specific to the entity, the **discount rate is supposed to appropriately reflect the current market assessment of the time value of money and the risks specific to the asset or cash generating unit**. When a specific rate for an asset or cash generating unit is not directly available from the market, which is usually the case, the discount rate to be used is a surrogate. An estimate should be made of a **pre-tax rate that reflects the current market assessment of the time value of money and the risks specific to the asset** that have **not been adjusted** for in the estimate of future cash flows. According to IAS 36, this rate is the return that the investors would require if they chose an investment that would generate cash flows of amounts, timing and risk profile equivalent to those that the entity expects to derive from the assets.

Rates that should be considered are the entity's weighted average cost of capital (WACC), the entity's incremental borrowing rate or other market rates. The objective must be to obtain a rate which is sensible and justifiable.

(4) The test is further complicated by the **impact of taxation**. IAS 36 requires that VIU be measured using pre-tax cash flows and a pre-tax discount rate, but WACC is a post-tax rate, as are most observable equity rates used by valuers.

(5) There is a need for **consistency in determining the recoverable amount and carrying amount which are being compared**. For example, in the case of pensions, there can be significant differences between the measurement basis of the pension asset or (more likely) liability and the cash flows that relate to pensions.

(6) IAS 36 requires that **corporate assets** must be allocated to a cash-generating unit on a 'reasonable and consistent basis, but does not expand on this.

(v) **Disclosures**

With regard to the impairment loss recognised in respect of each cash generating unit, IAS 36 would disclosure of:

(1) The amount of the loss
(2) The events and circumstances that led to the loss
(3) A description of the impairment loss by class of asset

It is **no defence** to maintain that this information was **common knowledge in the market**. The disclosures are still needed.

(b)   (i)   **Discount rate**

Estoil has **not complied with IAS 36** *Impairment of Assets* in its use of one discount rate for all cash-generating units (CGUs) regardless of the currency of the country in which the cash flows are generated. IAS 36 requires that **future cash flows must be estimated in the currency in which they will be generated** and then discounted using a discount rate appropriate for that currency. The present value thus calculated must be **translated using the spot exchange rate at the date of the value in use calculation.**

The currency in which the estimated cash flows are denominated has an impact on many of the inputs to the weighted average cost of capital (WACC) calculation, including the risk-free interest rate. **Estoil was incorrect in using the ten-year government bond rate for its own jurisdiction** as the risk-free rate because government bond rates differ between countries due to different expectations about future inflation, and so there may be a discrepancy between the expected inflation reflected in the estimated cash flows and the risk-free rate.

IAS 36 requires that the **discount rate should appropriately reflect the current market assessment of the time value of money and the risks specific to the asset or cash generating unit**. Applying one discount rate for all the CGUs does not achieve this. The WACC of the CGU or of the company of which the CGU is currently part should generally be used to determine the discount rate. The company's WACC may only be used for all CGUs if the risks associated with the individual CGUs do not materially diverge from the remainder of the group, and this is **not evident** in the case of Estoil.

(ii)   **Cash flow forecasts**

IAS 36 requires that any cash flow projections are based upon **reasonable and supportable assumptions** over a maximum period of five years unless it can be proven that longer estimates are reliable. The assumptions should **represent management's best estimate of the range of economic conditions expected to obtain over the remaining useful life of the asset**. Management must also assess the reasonableness of the assumptions by examining the reasons for any differences between past forecasted cash flows and actual cash flows. **The assumptions that form the basis for current cash flow projections must be consistent with past actual outcomes.**

Fariole has **failed to comply** with the requirements of IAS 36 in the preparation of its cash flow forecasts. Although the realised cash flow **forecasts for 20X4 were negative** and well below projected cash flows, **the directors significantly increased budgeted cash flows for 20X5**. This increase was **not justified**, and casts doubts on Fariole's ability to budget realistically.

IAS 36 requires estimates of future cash flows to include:

(1)   Projections of cash inflows from the continuing use of the asset

(2)   Projections of cash outflows which are necessarily incurred to generate the cash inflows from continuing use of the asset

(3)   Net cash flows to be received (or paid) for the disposal of the asset at the end of its useful life.

Forecast cash outflows must include those relating to the day-to-day servicing of the asset. This will **include future cash outflows needed to maintain the level of economic benefits expected to be generated by the asset in its current condition.** Fariole has not taken into account expected changes in working capital and capital expenditure, but it is very likely that investments in working capital and

capital expenditure would be necessary to maintain the assets of the CGUs in their current condition.

In conclusion, the **cash flow forecasts used by Fariole are not in accordance with IAS 36.**

36 Evolve

> **Workbook references.** IAS 32 *Financial Instruments: Presentation* and IFRS 9 *Financial Instruments* are covered in Chapter 7. IFRS 5 *Non-current Assets Held for Sale and Discontinued Operations* is covered in Chapter 13. IAS 16 *Property, Plant and Equipment* and IAS 40 *Investment Property* are covered in Chapter 3 and IAS 12 *Income Taxes* in Chapter 6.
>
> **Top tips.** Part (a) is tricky. It asks how the potential payment of cash in the future to equity shareholders should be classified. It had to be classified as a financial liability as there was a contractual obligation to deliver cash as a result of a put option to sell the rights back to the company. An event after the reporting period provided additional evidence of the valuation and should therefore be treated as an adjusting event. Part (b) is more mainstream. The directors had not classified the assets of a subsidiary as held for sale, even though the IFRS 5 criteria were met, on the grounds that they did not have a binding agreement to sell. However, this is not required for a sale to be considered 'highly probable' under IFRS 5, and so the assets should have been classified as held for sale. Part (c) required consideration of three issues. First, a gain arising where a subsidiary which was purchased at less than the market value of its sole asset should not be treated as a bargain purchase because this treatment is only available for a business combination, and the substance of the transaction was the purchase of an asset rather than a business combination. Second, the company wishes to use the cost model, the asset should have been recorded at cost, even if this is less than market value, so the potential gain should not have been recorded in profit or loss or added to the cost of the asset. Third, the deferred tax liability arising on the difference from market value should not be capitalised as it is not linked to bringing the asset to the condition necessary for its operations,
>
> **Easy marks.** There are no easy marks in this question. Marks are not as difficult to earn in part (b), as opposed to parts (a) or (c).

> **Marking scheme**
>
> | | | Marks |
> |---|---|---|
> | (a) | 1 mark per point up to maximum | 9 |
> | (b) | 1 mark per point up to maximum | 10 |
> | (c) | 1 mark per point up to maximum | 6 |
> | | | 25 |

(a) **Obligation to purchase own equity instruments**

A financial liability for the present value of the maximum amount payable to shareholders should be recognised in the financial statements as of 31 August 20X6. At 31 August 20X6, the rights are equivalent to a written put option because they represent for Evolve a purchase obligation which gives shareholders the right to sell the entity's own equity instruments for a fixed price. The fundamental principle of IAS 32 *Financial Instruments: Presentation* is that a financial instrument should be classified as either a financial liability or an equity instrument according to the substance of the contract, not its legal form, and the definitions of financial liability and equity instrument. IAS 32 states that a contract which contains an entity's obligation to purchase its own equity instruments gives rise to a financial liability, which

should be recognised at the present value of its redemption amount. IAS 32 also states that a contractual obligation for an entity to purchase its own equity instruments gives rise to a financial liability for the present value of the redemption amount even if the obligation is conditional on the counterparty exercising a right to redeem, as is the case with the scrip issue of Evolve.

Evolve had set up the conditions for the share capital increase in August 20X6 and, therefore, the contract gave rise to financial liabilities from that date and Evolve should have recognised a financial liability for the present value of the maximum amount payable to shareholders in its financial statements for the year ended 31 August 20X6. A non-adjusting event under IAS 10 *Events After the Reporting Period* is an event after the reporting period which is indicative of a condition which arose after the end of the reporting period. However, it could be argued that the transferring of the free allocation rights back to Evolve is in fact an adjusting event as it is an event after the reporting period which provides further evidence of conditions which existed at the end of the reporting period.

(b) **Classification as held for sale**

The non-current assets of Resource should have been presented as held for sale in the financial statements, in accordance with IFRS 5 *Non-Current Assets Held for Sale and Discontinued Operations*, as at 31 August 20X6. IFRS 5 states that the appropriate level of management must be committed to a plan to sell the asset for the sale to be probable. Evolve's acceptance of a binding offer in August 20X6 and the publication of this information indicated a high probability of sale. Despite the uncertainties surrounding the sale, the transaction remained highly probable at 31 August 20X6. IFRS 5 requires an entity to classify a non-current asset as held for sale if its carrying amount will be recovered principally through sale rather than through continuing use.

IFRS 5 does not require the existence of a binding sales agreement in order to classify a non-current asset as held for sale but only a high probability of its occurrence. The acceptance of an offer by Evolve indicates that the transaction met the criteria to be classified as held for sale at 31 August 20X6. The finalisation of the agreement on 20 September 20X6 only confirmed the situation existing at 31 August 20X6. Further, Evolve cannot apply IFRS 5 measurement criteria without classifying the item as held for sale in its statement of financial position particularly as a profit or impairment may arise when using such criteria. IFRS 5 also states that immediately before the initial classification of the asset as held for sale, the carrying amount of the asset should be measured in accordance with applicable IFRSs. This was already the case as regards the non-current assets of Resource.

Other criteria which indicate that the non-current assets should be shown as held for sale include the fact that a buyer for the non-current assets has been found, the sale occurred within 12 months of classification as held for sale, the asset was actively marketed for sale at a sales price which has been accepted, and despite the uncertainties at 31 August 20X6, events after the reporting period indicate that the contract was not significantly changed or withdrawn. The fact that the information regarding the uncertainties was not publicly disclosed is irrelevant.

Thus as the non-current assets met the criteria to be classified as held for sale, they should have been measured and presented as such in the financial statements. Assets classified as held for sale must be presented separately on the face of the statement of financial position.

(c) **Investment property**

IFRS 3 *Business Combinations* must be applied when accounting for business combinations, but does not apply where the acquisition is not of a business. In this case, the acquisition was essentially that of an asset and therefore the measurement requirements of IFRS 3 would not apply.

IAS 40 *Investment Property* states that the cost of an investment property comprises its purchase price and any directly attributable expenditure, such as professional fees for legal

services. IAS 16 *Property, Plant and Equipment* states that the cost of an item of PPE comprises any cost directly attributable to bringing the asset to the condition necessary for it to be capable of operating in the manner intended by management. Hence if Evolve wishes to use the cost basis for accounting for the investment property, the potential gain should not have been recorded in profit or loss or added to the cost of the asset.

Evolve should have recognised the tax payment as an expense in the statement of profit or loss and other comprehensive income. Administrative and other general overhead costs are not costs of an item of PPE according to IAS 16. The specific fiscal treatment and the tax to be paid were not linked to bringing the asset to the condition necessary for its operations, as the asset would have been operational without the tax. As such, the tax is a cost linked to the activity of Evolve and should be accounted for as an expense in accordance with IAS 12 *Income Taxes* and included in the profit or loss for the period, unless that tax arises from a transaction recognised outside profit or loss.

37 Gasnature

Workbook references. IFRS 9 *Financial Instruments* is covered in Chapter 7, IFRS 11 *Joint Arrangements* in Chapter 14 and IAS 10 *Events after the Reporting Period* in Chapter 5.

Top tips. Part (a) is a good example of applying mainstream syllabus topics (IAS 16) to an unusual situation ('irrecoverable gas'). Part (b) on 'own use' contracts has come up before, and the case could be argued either way. There were marks available for dealing with fundamental principles of whether the contract is a financial contract or an executory contract. If the arguments seem complex, the good news is that there are only six marks for this part of the question, and you can make up the marks in part (c), which is more mainstream.

Easy marks. Part (c) is relatively straightforward, and you should by now be familiar with the IFRS 11 criteria for distinguishing joint ventures from joint operations.

			Marks
(a)		1 mark per point up to maximum	9
(b)		1 mark per point up to maximum	6
(c)	(i)	1 mark per point up to maximum	5
	(ii)	1 mark per point up to maximum	5
			25

(a) **Joint arrangement**

The classification of a joint arrangement as a joint operation or a joint venture depends upon the rights and obligations of the parties to the arrangement (IFRS 11 *Joint Arrangements*). A joint arrangement occurs where two or more parties have joint control. The contractually agreed sharing of control of an arrangement exists only when decisions about the relevant activities require the unanimous consent of the parties sharing control. The structure and form of the arrangement determines the nature of the relationship. However, regardless of the purpose, structure or form of the arrangement, the classification of joint arrangements depends upon the parties' rights and obligations arising from the arrangement. A joint arrangement which is not structured through a separate vehicle is a joint operation. In such cases, the contractual arrangement establishes the parties' rights and obligations. A joint operator accounts for the assets, liabilities, revenues and expenses relating to its involvement in a joint operation in accordance with the relevant IFRSs. The arrangement with Gogas is a joint

operation as there is no separate vehicle involved and they have agreed to share services and costs with decisions regarding the platform requiring unanimous agreement of the parties. Gasnature should recognise its share of the asset as property, plant and equipment.

Under IAS 16 *Property, Plant and Equipment* (PPE), the cost of an item of property, plant and equipment includes the initial estimate of the present value of dismantling and removing the item and restoring the site on which it is located. IAS 37 *Provisions, Contingent Liabilities and Contingent Assets* contains requirements on how to measure decommissioning, restoration and similar liabilities. Where the effect of the time value of money is material, the amount of a provision should be the present value of the expenditures expected to be required to settle the obligation. Thus costs incurred by an entity in respect of obligations for dismantling, removing and restoring the site on which an item of property, plant and equipment is located are recognised and measured in accordance with IAS 16 and IAS 37. Gasnature should recognise 55% of the cost of decommissioning the underground storage facility. However, because Gasnature is a joint operator, there is also a contingent liability for 45% of the decommissioning costs and there is a possible obligation for the remainder of the costs depending on whether some uncertain future event occurs, that is Gogas goes into liquidation and cannot fund the decommissioning costs. Therefore Gasnature, should also disclose a contingent liability relating to the Gogas's share of the obligation to the extent that it is contingently liable for Gogas's share.

IAS 16 states that property, plant and equipment are tangible items which:

(i)   Are held for use in the production or supply of goods or services, for rental to others, or for administrative purposes; and

(ii)   Are expected to be used during more than one period.

Thus Gasnature should classify and account for its share of the irrecoverable gas as PPE. The irrecoverable gas is necessary for the storage facility to perform its function. It is therefore part of the storage facility and should be capitalised as a component of the storage facility asset. The irrecoverable gas should be depreciated to its residual value over the life of the storage facility. However, if the gas is recoverable in full when the storage facility is decommissioned, then depreciation will be recorded against the irrecoverable gas component only if the estimated residual value of the gas decreases below cost during the life of the facility. When the storage facility is decommissioned and the cushion gas extracted and sold, the sale of the irrecoverable gas is accounted for as the disposal of an item of PPE in accordance with IAS 16 and the gain or loss recognised in profit or loss. The natural gas in excess of the irrecoverable gas which is injected into the facility should be treated as inventory in accordance with IAS 2 *Inventories*.

(b)   **Contract with Agas**

IFRS 9 *Financial Instruments* applies to those contracts to buy or sell a non-financial item which can be settled net in cash with the exception of contracts which are held for the purpose of the receipt or delivery of a non-financial item in accordance with the entity's expected purchase, sale or usage requirements (own use contract). In other words, it will result in physical delivery of the commodity, in this case the extra gas. Contracts which are for an entity's 'own use' are exempt from the requirements of IFRS 9. Such a contract can be irrevocably designated as measured at fair value through profit or loss even if it was entered into for the above purpose. This designation is available only at inception of the contract and only if it eliminates or significantly reduces a recognition inconsistency (sometimes referred to as an 'accounting mismatch') which would otherwise arise from not recognising that contract because it is excluded from the scope of IFRS 9. There are various ways in which a contract to buy or sell a non-financial item can be settled net in cash or another financial instrument or by exchanging financial instruments. These include the following:

(i)   When the terms of the contract permit either party to settle it net in cash.

(ii)   When the ability to settle net in cash is not explicit in the terms of the contract, but the entity has a practice of settling similar contracts net in cash.

(iii)   When, for similar contracts, the entity has a practice of taking delivery of the underlying and selling it within a short period after delivery, for the purpose of generating a profit.

(iv)   When the non-financial item which is the subject of the contract is readily convertible to cash.

A written option to buy or sell a non-financial item which can be settled net in cash is within the scope of IFRS 9. Such a contract cannot be entered into for the purpose of the receipt or delivery of the non-financial item in accordance with the entities expected purchase, sale or usage requirements. Contracts to buy or sell a non-financial item, such as a commodity, which can be settled net in cash or another financial instrument, or by exchanging financial instruments, are within the scope of IFRS 9. They are accounted for as derivatives. A level of judgement will be required in this area as net settlements caused by unique events beyond management's control may not necessarily prevent the entity from applying the 'own use' exemption to all similar contracts.

The contract entered into by Gasnature with Agas seems to be an own use contract which falls outside IFRS 9 and therefore would be treated as an executory contract. However, it could be argued that the contract is net settled because the penalty mechanism requires Agas to compensate Gasnature at the current prevailing market price. Further, if natural gas is readily convertible into cash in the location where the delivery takes place, the contract could be considered net settled. Additionally, if there is volume flexibility, then the contract could be regarded as a written option, which falls within the scope of IFRS 9.

However, the contract will probably still qualify as 'own use' as long as it has been entered into and continues to be held for the expected counterparties' sales/usage requirements. Additionally, the entity has not irrevocably designated the contract as measured at fair value through profit or loss, thus adding weight to the 'own use' designation.

(c)   (i)   It is not acceptable to accrue the costs of the overhaul. The entity does not have a constructive obligation to undertake the overhaul. Under IFRS, costs related to major inspection and overhaul are recognised as part of the carrying amount of property, plant and equipment if they meet the asset recognition criteria in IAS 16 *Property, Plant and Equipment*. The major overhaul component will then be depreciated on a straight-line basis over its useful life (ie over the period to the next overhaul) and any remaining carrying amount will be derecognised when the next overhaul is performed. Costs of the day-to-day servicing of the asset (ie routine maintenance) are expensed as incurred. Therefore the cost of the overhaul should have been identified as a separate component of the refinery at initial recognition and depreciated over a period of two years. This will result in the same amount of expense being recognised in profit or loss over the same period as the proposal to create a provision.

(ii)   Since there were no indicators of impairment at the period end, all costs incurred up to 31 August 20X5 amounting to $5 million should remain capitalised by the entity in the financial statements for the year ended on that date. However, if material, disclosure should be provided in the financial statements of the additional activity during the subsequent period which determined the exploratory drilling was unsuccessful. This represents a non-adjusting event as defined by IAS 10 *Events After the Reporting Period* as an event which is indicative of a condition which arose after the end of the reporting period. The asset of $5 million and additional drilling costs of $2 million incurred subsequently would be expensed in the following year's financial statements.

38 Blackcutt

Workbook references. Investment property and impairment are covered in Chapter 3, leases are covered in Chapter 8 and provisions in Chapter 5.

Top tips. The fact that this is a local government organisation affects the use to which the properties are put in parts (a) and (d). Part (a) requires a basic understanding of IAS 16 and IAS 40 and requires application rather than just knowledge, but the issues are uncontroversial. Part (b) requires knowledge and application of IFRS 16 *Leases*, focusing on whether an arrangement is or contains a lease. Part (c) dealt with a scenario that many accountants face in practice and should have been fairly straightforward. There were three elements to part (d) of the question.

Knowledge of the standard, application of the standard and completion of the calculations. The application of knowledge with reference to the question is essential.

Easy marks. Part (a) on investment property should be familiar to you from your earlier studies, and part (c) is a very straightforward test of IAS 37.

		Marks
(a)	1 mark per point up to maximum	8
(b)	1 mark per point up to maximum	6
(c)	1 mark per point up to maximum	4
(d)	1 mark per point up to maximum	7
		25

(a)   **Investment property**

IAS 40 *Investment Property* applies to the accounting for property (land and/or buildings) **held to earn rentals or for capital appreciation or both**. Examples of investment property given in the standard include, but are not limited to:

(i)   Land held for **long-term capital appreciation**

(ii) Land held for **undetermined future use**

Assets which IAS 40 states are not investment property, and which are therefore **not covered** by the standard include:

(i)   Property held for use in the **production or supply of goods or services** or for administrative purposes

(ii) Property held for **sale in the ordinary course of business** or in the process of construction of development for such sale

Owner-occupied property, property being **constructed on behalf of third parties** and property leased to a third party **under a finance lease** are also specifically **excluded** by the IAS 40 definition. (Note that finance leases still exist for lessors, though not for lessees.)

If the entity provides **ancillary services** to the occupants of a property held by the entity, the appropriateness of classification as investment property is determined by the significance of the services provided. If those services are a relatively insignificant component of the arrangement as a whole (for instance, the building owner supplies security and maintenance services to the lessees), then the entity may treat the property as investment property. **Where**

the services provided are more significant (such as in the case of an owner-managed hotel), the property should be classified as **owner-occupied**.

Applying IAS 40 to Blackcutt's properties, **the land owned for capital appreciation** and which may be sold any time in the future **will qualify as investment property**. Likewise, the **land whose use has not yet been determined** is also covered by the IAS 40 definition of investment property: as it has no current purpose it is deemed to be held for capital appreciation.

Investment property should be recognised as an asset where it is probable that the future economic benefits associated with the property will flow to the entity and the value can be measured reliably. IAS 40 permits an entity to choose between the cost model and the fair value model. Where the fair value model applies, the property is valued in accordance with IFRS 13 *Fair Value Measurement*. Gains or losses arising from changes in the fair value of investment property are recognised in profit or loss for the year.

The **houses routinely bought and sold** by Blackcutt in the ordinary course of its operations will **not qualify as investment property**, but will be treated under IAS 2 *Inventories*.

The **part of the housing inventory** not held for sale but **used to provide housing to low-income employees does not qualify as investment property** either. The properties are **not held for capital appreciation**, and because the rent is **below market rate** and only covers the maintenance costs, **they cannot be said to be held for rentals**. The **rental income is incidental** to the purposes for which the property is held, which is to provide housing services. As with the example of the owner-managed hotel above, the services are significant, and the property should be classified as **owner occupied**. Further indication that it is owner occupied is provided by the fact that it is rented out to **employees of the organisation**. It will be accounted for under IAS 16 *Property, Plant and Equipment*.

(b) **Lease**

The issue here is whether the arrangement with the private sector provider Waste and Co is, or contains, a lease, even if it does not take the legal form of a lease. The **substance of the arrangement should be considered** in connection with the IFRS 16 *Leases*. Key factors to consider are as follows.

(i) Is there an **identifiable asset?**

(ii) Does the customer have the right to **obtain substantially all the economic benefits** from use of the asset throughout the period of use?

(iii) Who has the **right to direct how and for what purpose the asset is used**?

(iv) Does the customer **have the right to operate the asset throughout the period of use** without the supplier having the right to change those operating instructions?

The answer in each case is yes.

(i) The vans are an identifiable asset. Although Waste and Co can substitute another vehicle if one of the existing vehicles needs repairing or no longer works, this substitution right is not substantive because of the significant costs involved in fitting out the vehicle for use by Blackcutt.

(ii) Blackcutt can use the vehicles and uses them exclusively for waste collection for nearly all their life. It therefore has a right to obtain substantially all the economic benefits from the use of the asset.

(iii) Blackcutt controls the vehicles, since it stipulates how they are painted, and ostensibly owns them because they must be painted with Blackcutt's name. It therefore has the right to direct how and for what purpose the asset is used.

228

(iv) As indicated in (ii) above, Blackcutt has the right to operate the asset throughout the period of use, although it has outsourced the driving to Waste and Co.

The arrangement is **a lease**. A **right-of-use asset** should be recorded, and a **lease liability** set up, equal to the present value of the future lease payments. The **service element** relating to the waste collection must be considered as a **separate component** and charged to profit or loss.

(c) **Provision**

Under IAS 37 *Provisions, Contingent Liabilities and Contingent Assets,* provisions must be recognised in the following circumstances, and must not be recognised if they do not apply.

(i) There is a **legal** or **constructive obligation** to transfer benefits as a result of **past events**.

(ii) It is probably that **an outflow of economic resources** will be required to **settle** the **obligation**.

(iii) A **reliable estimate** of the amount required to settle the obligation can be made.

A legal or constructive obligation is one created by an **obligating event.** Here the obligating event is the **contamination of the land**, because of the virtual certainty of legislation requiring the clean-up. As Blackcutt has no recourse against Chemco or its insurance company this past event will certainly give rise to a **transfer of economic benefits from** Blackcutt.

Consequently, Blackcutt **must recognise a provision** for the best estimate of the clean-up costs. It should **not set up a corresponding receivable**, since no reimbursement may be obtained from Chemco or its insurance company.

(d) **Impairment of building**

The basic principle of IAS 36 *Impairment of Assets* is that an asset should be carried at no more than its recoverable amount, that is, the amount to be recovered through use or sale of the asset. If an **asset's value** is **higher than its recoverable amount**, an **impairment loss** has occurred. The impairment loss should be **written off** against profit or loss for the year.

Entities must determine, at each reporting date, whether there are any indications that impairment has occurred. In this case, **impairment is indicated** because the use to which the building is to be put has changed significantly (from a school to a library), a situation which will continue for the foreseeable future.

The **recoverable amount** is **defined** as the **higher** of the **asset's fair value less costs to sell** and the asset's **value in use.** However, these values are unavailable because of the specialised nature of the asset, and the only information available is depreciated replacement cost. Using a **depreciated replacement cost approach**, the impairment loss would be calculated as follows.

Asset	Cost/replacement cost $'000	Accumulated depreciation 6/25 $'000	Carrying amount/ replacement cost $'000
School	5,000	(1,200)	3,800
Library	2,100	(504)	(1,596)
Impairment loss			2,204

Blackcutt should therefore recognise an **impairment loss of $2.204 million** in profit or loss for the year.

39 Lockfine

Marking scheme

		Marks
(a)	1 mark per question up to maximum	6
(b)	1 mark per question up to maximum	6
(c)	1 mark per question up to maximum	7
(d)	1 mark per question up to maximum	6
Maximum		25

(a) **IFRS 1 and deemed cost**

IFRS 1 *First-time Adoption of International Financial Reporting Standards* states that an entity may elect to measure an item of property, plant and equipment at the **date of transition to IFRS** at fair value and **use that fair value as its deemed cost at that date**. Fair value is defined in IFRS 1 as amended by IFRS 13 *Fair Value Measurement* as:

'The price that would be received to sell an asset or paid to transfer a liability in an orderly transaction between market participants at the measurement date.' (IFRS 13; para 9)

An entity adopting IFRS for the first time may, under IFRS 1 as amended by IFRS 13, elect **to use a previous GAAP revaluation** of an item of property, plant and equipment at or before the date of transition to IFRS as deemed cost at the date of the revaluation under the following conditions.

(i) The revaluation was broadly comparable to fair value.

(ii) The revaluation was broadly comparable to cost or depreciated cost in accordance with IFRS, adjusted to reflect, for example, changes in a general or specific price index.

In addition, IFRS 1 does not give detailed rules about determining fair value, and first-time adopters who use fair value as deemed cost **must only provide limited disclosures**, not a full description of the methods and assumptions used.

In the case of Lockfine, the question to be decided is whether the selling agents' estimates can be used as the fair value to be used, in turn, as deemed cost under IFRS 1.

The selling agents' estimates provide only limited information about the valuation methods and assumptions, and it is doubtful that they can be relied upon for determining fair value in accordance with IAS 16 *Property, Plant and Equipment* and IFRS 13 *Fair Value Measurement*. Under IAS 16 measurement of fair value must be **reliable**. While it is correct to use independent valuers, IAS 16 requires that the reporting entity know the **assumptions** that

have been made in assessing reliability. In addition, using the average of the highest amounts may not be prudent.

IFRS 1 allows more latitude than IAS 16. Lockfine is **not in breach of IFRS 1 which does not specify detailed rules for this particular case**, and allows fair value as determined on the basis of selling agents' estimates. This is a cost effective approach for entities that do not perform a full retrospective application of the requirements of IAS 16.

(b)   Fishing rights

IFRS 1 requires that if an entity which is in the process of adopting IFRS decides to apply IFRS 3 retrospectively to a business combination, it **cannot do so selectively,** but must apply IFRS 3 **consistently to all business combinations** that occur between the date on which it decides to adopt IFRS 3 and the date of transition. An entity must have regard to **similar transactions in the period**. When allocating values to the assets and liabilities of the acquired company, the entity needs to have documentation to support its purchase price allocation. Without this, use of other methods of price allocation is not permitted unless the methods are strictly in accordance with IFRS.

Lockfine was **unable to recognise** the fishing rights of the business combination as separately identifiable because it **could not obtain a reliable value** for the rights, so it included the rights within goodwill.

IAS 38 has two criteria, both of which must be met for an entity to recognise an intangible asset, whether purchased or internally generated:

(i)   It is probably that the future economic benefits attributable to the asset will flow to the entity.

(ii)   The cost of the asset can be measured reliably.

The fishing rights **satisfy the first, but not the second of these criteria**. Accordingly the fishing rights were **correctly subsumed within goodwill**. As long as the goodwill presented under the first IFRS financial statements did not require a write down for impairment, it should be the net carrying amount at the date of transition.

Although the fishing rights have a finite life, **they will not be amortised over the period** specified by the rights, because they are included within goodwill. Instead, **the goodwill is reviewed annually for impairment** in accordance with IAS 36 *Impairment of Assets*.

(c)   Electronic map data

The standard that applies here is IAS 38 *Intangible Assets*. Under IAS 38, an intangible asset is an asset with the following characteristics.

(i)   It meets the standard's **identifiability criteria**. This means it must be separable or must arise from contractual or other legal rights

(ii)   It is probable that **future economic benefits** attributable to the asset will flow to the entity. These could be in the form of increased revenues or cost savings.

(iii) The entity has **control**, that is, the power to obtain benefits from the asset.

(iv)   Its cost can be **measured reliably**.

It appears that the capitalised expenses of the acquisition and production of the electronic map data **meet these criteria**.

(i)   The electronic maps are identifiable because they are capable of being separated from the entity as a whole and sold (or transferred or licensed), regardless of whether the entity intends to do this.

(ii)   They are controlled by Lockfine.

(iii) It is probable that benefits attributable to the maps will flow to the entity because the electronic maps will generate revenue when used by the fishing fleet.

(iv) Their value can be measured reliably – Lockfine has a record of the costs.

The **electronic maps** will therefore be **recognised as an intangible asset at cost**. Generally they will subsequently be carried at cost less any amortisation and impairment losses.

Regarding the **database**, Lockfine believes that this has an indefinite useful life and, by implication, should not be amortised but should be tested annually for impairment. IAS 38 regards an intangible asset as having an indefinite useful life when, based on analysis of all the relevant factors, there is no foreseeable limit to the period over which the asset is expected to generate net cash inflows for the entity.

Indefinite does not mean the same as infinite and in the context of IAS 38 has specific implications. In particular, the indefinite useful life should not depend on future planned expenditure in excess of that required to maintain the asset. In this respect, **Lockfine complies with IAS 38**.

In addition, IAS 38 identifies certain factors that may affect the useful life, changing it in this instance from indefinite to finite. These include technological or commercial obsolescence and actions by competitors.

There is no specific requirement for an entity to disclose the IAS 38 criteria for recognition of an intangible asset arising from development, although it does require disclosure of assets which have an indefinite useful life (the carrying amount and reasons for assessing the useful life as indefinite). However, under IAS 1 *Presentation of Financial Statements*, entities **must disclose accounting policies that are relevant for an understanding of their financial statements**. The electronic maps and the data base constitute a material amount of total assets, so the accounting policies, including the IAS 38 criteria for development expenditure, need to be disclosed.

(d) **Restructuring plans**

IAS 37 criteria

IAS 37 *Provisions, Contingent Liabilities and Contingent Assets* **contains specific requirements** relating to **restructuring provisions**. The general recognition criteria apply and IAS 37 also states that **a provision should be recognised** if an entity has a **constructive obligation** to carry out a restructuring. A constructive obligation exists where **management has a detailed formal plan** for the restructuring, identifying **as a minimum:**

(i) The business or part of the business being restructured

(ii) The principal locations affected by the restructuring

(iii) The location, function and approximate number of employees who will be compensated for the termination of their employment

(iv) The date of implementation of the plan

(v) The expenditure that will be undertaken

In addition, the plan must have raised a **valid expectation** in those affected that the entity will carry out the restructuring. To give rise to such an expectation and, therefore, a constructive obligation, the **implementation must be planned to take place as soon as possible**, and the timeframe must be such as to make changes to the plan unlikely.

Plan A

Lockfine proposes recognising a provision in respect of the plan to sell 50% of its off-shore fleet in a year's time and to make 40% of the seamen redundant. However, although the plan has been communicated to the public, the above criteria are not met. **The plan is insufficiently detailed**, and various aspects are not finalised. The figure of 40% is tentative as yet, the **fleets and employees affected have not been identified**, and a decision has not been made on whether the off-shore fleet will be restructured in the future. Some of these issues await further analysis.

The proposal does not, therefore, meet the IAS 37 criteria for a detailed formal plan and an announcement of the plan to those affected by it. Lockfine cannot be said to be committed to this restructuring and so **a provision should not be recognised**.

Plan B

Lockfine has not proposed recognising a provision for the plan to reorganise its headquarters and make 20% of the headquarters' workforce redundant. However, it is likely that this treatment is incorrect, because the plan appears to meet the IAS 37 criteria above:

(i)   The locations and employees affected have been **identified**.

(ii)   An **announcement** has been made and employee representatives notified – it is not necessary to notify individual employees as their representatives have been told.

(iii)   The conclusion of the three month consultation period indicates that the above announcement is sufficiently detailed to give rise to a **valid expectation** that the restructuring will take place, particularly if the discussions have been about the terms of the redundancy.

It will be necessary to **consider the above negotiations** – provided these are about details such as the terms of redundancy rather than about changing the plan, then the IAS 37 criteria have been met. Accordingly, a provision needs to be recognised.

40 Coatmin

> **Workbook references.** Related parties are covered in Chapter 2 and financial instruments are covered in Chapter 7.
>
> **Top tips.** Part (a) tested an exemption from IAS 24 (for government-related activities), rather than the more mainstream aspect. Credit is available for discussion of the principles of IAS 24 so it was possible to score well even if you did not know the specific answer. Part (b) also tested an exemption from the mainstream – financial guarantee contracts, which are not required to be classified as subsequently measured at amortised cost. Pay attention to 'clues' in the question – the fact that the guarantee is being measured at FVTPL suggests that it is a financial instrument rather than a provision. Part (c) on the effectiveness of the interest rate swap is challenging although credit was awarded for textbook knowledge of hedging in general. Part (d) on credit risk is topical and again, marks were available for discussing principles.
>
> **Easy marks.** There are marks for textbook explanations on hedging in part (c), but in general this is a tricky question.

		Marks
(a)	IAS 24	5
(b)	IFRS 9 explanation	4
	Guarantee calculations	4
(c)	Hedging discussion	4
	Effectiveness discussion	4
(d)	Credit risk entries	4
		25

(a) Related parties

The applicable standard relating to the activities is IAS 24 *Related Party Disclosures*. The standard requires disclosure of transactions with related parties. The definition of related parties is very detailed and includes parents, subsidiaries, and key management personnel of the entity or of a parent of the entity. Post-employment benefit plans are also included.

Where related party transactions have taken place, management must disclose the following:

(i) The name of its **parent** and, if different, the **ultimate controlling party** irrespective of whether there have been any transactions.

(ii) Total **key management personnel compensation** (broken down by category)

(iii) **If the entity has had related party transactions**:

    (1) Nature of the related party **relationship**

    (2) Information about the **transactions and outstanding balances, including commitments and bad and doubtful debts** necessary for users to understand the potential effect of the relationship on the financial statements.

No disclosure is required of intragroup related party transactions in the consolidated financial statements (since they are eliminated). Items of a **similar** nature may be disclosed **in aggregate** except where separate disclosure is necessary for understanding purposes.

A **government-related entity** is an entity over which a government has control, joint control or significant influence. In principle, a government-controlled bank such as Coatmin could be required to disclosed details of its transactions, deposits and commitments with the central bank and with other government-controlled banks.

However, an **exemption** is available from full disclosure of transactions, outstanding balances and commitments with the government or with other entities related to the same government.

If the exemption is applied, IAS 24 requires disclosure of:

(a) The **name of the government** and **nature of the relationship**; and

(b) The nature and amount of each **individually significant transaction** (plus a qualitative or quantitative indication of the extent of other transactions which are collectively, but not individually, significant).

These disclosures provide more meaningful information about the nature of the entity's relationship and transactions with government than do the usual IAS 24 disclosures.

(b) **Financial guarantee contract**

IFRS 9 *Financial Instruments* requires entities to classify all financial liabilities as subsequently measured at amortised cost using the effective interest method, with the following exceptions.

(i) Financial liabilities **at fair value through profit or loss**. Such liabilities, including derivatives that are liabilities, must be subsequently measured at fair value.

(ii) Financial liabilities that arise **when a transfer of a financial asset does not qualify for derecognition** or when the continuing involvement approach applies

(iii) **Financial guarantee contracts.** After initial recognition, an issuer of such a contract must subsequently measure it at the higher of:

(1) The amount of the loss allowance determined in accordance with the IFRS 9 rules on expected credit losses; and

(2) The amount initially recognised less, when appropriate, the cumulative amount of income recognised in accordance with the principles of IFRS 15 *Revenue from Contracts with Customers.*

If an entity chooses to measure a financial guarantee contract (or loan commitment) **at fair value through profit or loss,** as here, **all fair value movements go through profit or loss** with no transfer to other comprehensive income. Changes in the credit risk of liabilities relating to financial guarantee contracts are not required to be presented in other comprehensive income under IFRS 9.

Assuming that discounting is not material, the accounting entries will be as follows.

At 1 December 20X2

DEBIT	Profit or loss	$1.2m	
CREDIT	Financial liabilities		$1.2m

To record the loss incurred in giving the guarantee

At 30 November 20X3

DEBIT	Financial liabilities	$0.4m	
CREDIT	Profit or loss		$0.4m

To amortise the initial fair value over the life of the guarantee

This reflects the reduction in exposure arising from the fact that the subsidiary has made the first repayment.

At 30 November 20X4

DEBIT	Profit or loss ($40m – ($1.2m – $0.4m))	$39.2m	
CREDIT	Financial liabilities		$39.2m

To provide for the calling of the guarantee

DEBIT	Financial liabilities ($40m – $0.4m)	$39.6m	
CREDIT	Profit or loss		$39.6m

To record movement from expected credit loss allowance to measurement at amortised initial value

The above change was made in the light of the subsidiary's receipt of the donation enabling it to make the second repayment, which means a change in probability that the guarantee will be called. This is an event after the reporting period which provides further evidence of conditions existing at the end of the reporting period, and so is an adjusting event.

(c)   **Hedging**

IFRS 9 *Financial Instruments* allows hedge accounting but only if **all** of the following **conditions** are met.

(i)   The hedging relationship consists **only of eligible hedging instruments and eligible hedged items**.

(ii) There must be **formal documentation** (including identification of the hedged item, the hedging instrument, the nature of the risk that is to be hedged and how the entity will assess the hedging instrument's effectiveness in offsetting the exposure to changes in the hedged item's fair value or cash flows attributable to the hedged risk).

(iii) The hedging relationship meets all of the IFRS 9 hedge effectiveness criteria.

IFRS 9 defines **hedge effectiveness** as the degree to which changes in the fair value or cash flows of the hedged item attributable to a hedged risk are offset by changes in the fair value or cash flows of the hedging instrument. The directors of Coatmin have asked whether hedge effectiveness can be calculated. IFRS 9 uses an **objective-based assessment** for hedge effectiveness, under which the following criteria must be met.

(i)   There is an **economic relationship** between the hedged item and the hedging instrument, ie the hedging instrument and the hedged item have values that generally move in the opposite direction because of the same risk, which is the hedged risk;

(ii) The **effect of credit risk does not dominate the value** changes that result from that economic relationship, ie the gain or loss from credit risk does not frustrate the effect of changes in the underlying item on the value of the hedging instrument or the hedged item, even if those changes were significant; and

(iii) The **hedge ratio of the hedging relationship** (quantity of hedging instrument vs quantity of hedged item) is the same as that resulting from the quantity of the hedged item that the entity **actually hedges** and the quantity of the hedging instrument that the entity **actually uses** to hedge that quantity of hedged item.

(d)   **Liability**

IFRS 9 *Financial Instruments* requires that financial liabilities which are **designated as measured at fair value through profit or loss are treated differently**. In this case the gain or loss in a period must be classified into:

- Gain or loss **resulting from credit risk**; and
- **Other** gain or loss.

This provision of IFRS 9 was in response to an anomaly regarding changes in the credit risk of a financial liability.

Changes in a financial liability's credit risk affect the fair value of that financial liability. This means that when an entity's creditworthiness deteriorates, the fair value of its issued debt will decrease (and *vice versa*). IFRS 9 requires the gain or loss as a result of credit risk to be recognised in other comprehensive income, unless it creates or enlarges an **accounting mismatch**, in which case it is recognised in profit or loss. The other gain or loss (not the result of credit risk) is recognised in profit or loss.

On derecognition any gains or losses recognised in other comprehensive income are **not** transferred to **profit or loss**, although the cumulative gain or loss may be transferred within equity.

This is a decrease in the fair value of the liability, which is a fair value gain in the books of Coatmin. Coatmin should split the fair value decrease as follows:

STATEMENT OF PROFIT OR LOSS AND OTHER COMPREHENSIVE INCOME (EXTRACT)
FOR THE YEAR ENDED 30 NOVEMBER 20X4

Profit or loss for the year

	$'000
Liabilities at fair value	
Fair value gain not attributable to change in credit risk	45
Profit (loss) for the year	45

Other comprehensive income (not reclassified to profit or loss)

Fair value gain on financial liability attributable to change in credit risk	5
Total comprehensive income	50

41 Avco

Workbook reference. The distinction between debt and equity is covered in Chapter 7.

Top tips. While this question on the distinction between debt and equity was quite narrow in focus, the topic is featured in an article by the examining team and therefore has been flagged by the examining team as topical. The distinction between debt and equity is fundamental to any set of financial statements, and it is essential that you can explain it with reference to such matters as debt being determined where redemption is at the option of the instrument holder, where there is a limited life to the instrument and dividends being non-discretionary. Part (b) required you to apply the principles in part (a) to two scenarios, discussing whether the instruments were debt or equity. It was not possible, therefore, to do part (b) if you could not do part (a), because you need to understand the principles in order to apply them.

Easy marks. It is difficult to find much in the way of easy marks in this challenging question.

Marking scheme

			Marks
(a)	(i)	1 mark per point up to maximum	10
	(ii)	Effects	5
(b)		1 mark per point up to maximum	10
			25

(a)   (i)   **Classification differences between debt and equity**

It is not always easy to **distinguish between debt and equity in an entity's** statement of financial position, partly because many financial instruments have elements of both.

IAS 32 *Financial Instruments: Presentation* brings clarity and consistency to this matter, so that the **classification is based on principles** rather than driven by perceptions of users.

IAS 32 defines an **equity instrument** as: 'any contract that evidences a residual interest in the assets of an entity after deducting all of its liabilities (IAS 32: para. 11). It must first be **established that an instrument is not a financial liability,** before it can be classified as equity.

A key feature of the **IAS 32 definition of a financial liability** is that it **is a contractual obligation to deliver cash or another financial asset to**

another entity. The contractual obligation may arise from a requirement to make payments of principal, interest or dividends. The contractual obligation may be explicit, but it may be implied indirectly in the terms of the contract. An example of a debt instrument is a bond which requires the issuer to make interest payments and redeem the bond for cash.

A financial instrument is an **equity instrument** only if there is no obligation to deliver cash or other financial assets to another entity and if the instrument will or may be settled in the issuer's own equity instruments. An example of an equity instrument is **ordinary shares, on which dividends are payable at the discretion of the issuer.** A less obvious example is preference shares required to be converted into a fixed number of ordinary shares on a fixed date or on the occurrence of an event which is certain to occur.

An instrument may be classified as an equity instrument if it contains a **contingent settlement provision** requiring settlement in cash or a variable number of the entity's own shares **only on the occurrence of an event which is very unlikely to occur** – such a provision is **not considered to be genuine.** If the **contingent payment condition** is **beyond the control of** both the entity and the holder of the instrument, then the instrument is classified as a **financial liability**.

A **contract resulting in the receipt or delivery of an entity's own shares is not automatically an equity instrument.** The classification depends on the so-called **'fixed test'** in IAS 32. A contract which will be settled by the entity receiving or delivering a **fixed number of its own equity instruments in exchange for a fixed amount of cash is an equity instrument**. The reasoning behind this is that by fixing upfront the number of shares to be received or delivered on settlement of the instrument in concern, the holder is exposed to the upside and downside risk of movements in the entity's share price.

In contrast, if the **amount of cash or own equity shares to be delivered or received is variable,** then the contract is a **financial liability or asset.** The reasoning behind this is that using a variable number of own equity instruments to settle a contract can be similar to using own shares as 'currency' to settle what in substance is a financial liability. Such a contract does not evidence a residual interest in the entity's net assets. Equity classification is therefore inappropriate.

IAS 32 gives two **examples** of contracts where the number of own equity instruments to be received or delivered varies so that their fair value equals the amount of the contractual right or obligation.

(1)   A contract to deliver a variable number of own equity instruments equal in value to a fixed monetary amount on the settlement date is classified as a financial liability.

(2)   A contract to deliver as many of the entity's own equity instruments as are equal in value to the value of 100 ounces of a commodity results in liability classification of the instrument.

There are **other factors** which might result in an instrument being **classified as debt.**

(1)   Dividends are non-discretionary.

(2)   Redemption is at the option of the instrument holder.

(3)   The instrument has a limited life.

(4)   Redemption is triggered by a future uncertain event which is beyond the control of both the issuer and the holder of the instrument.

Other factors which might result in an instrument being **classified as equity** include the following.

(1) Dividends are discretionary.

(2) The shares are non-redeemable.

(3) There is no liquidation date.

(ii) **Significance of debt/equity classification for the financial statements**

The distinction between debt and equity is very important, since the classification of a financial instrument as either debt or equity **can have a significant impact on the entity's reported earnings and gearing ratio**, which in turn can affect debt covenants. Companies may wish to classify a financial instrument as **equity,** in order to give a **favourable impression of gearing,** but this may in turn have a **negative effect** on the perceptions of existing shareholders if it is seen **as diluting existing equity interests.**

The distinction is also relevant in the context of a **business combination** where an entity **issues financial instruments as part consideration, or to raise funds to settle a business combination in cash.** Management is often called upon to **evaluate different financing options**, and in order to do so must **understand the classification rules and their potential effects.** For example, **classification as a liability** generally means that **payments are treated as interest** and charged to profit or loss, and this may, in turn, **affect the entity's ability to pay dividends** on equity shares.

(b) (i) **Cavor**

B shares

The classification of Cavor's B shares will be made by applying **the principles-based definitions of equity and liability in IAS 32**, and considering the **substance,** rather than the legal form of the instrument. 'Substance' here relates only to consideration of the contractual terms of the instrument. Factors outside the contractual terms are not relevant to the classification. The following factors demonstrate that Cavor's B shares are **equity instruments.**

(1) **Dividends are discretionary** in that they need only be paid if paid on the A shares, on which there is no obligation to pay dividends. Dividends on the B shares will be paid at the same rate as on the A shares, which will be variable.

(2) Cavor has **no obligation to redeem** the B shares.

Share options

The 'fixed test' must be applied. If the amount of cash or own equity shares to be delivered is variable, then the contract is a debt instrument. Here, however, the contract is to be settled by Cavor issuing a fixed number of its own equity instruments for a fixed amount of cash. Accordingly there is **no variability, and the share options are classified as an equity instrument.**

(ii) **Lidan**

A financial liability under IAS 32 is **a contractual obligation to deliver cash or another financial asset to another entity**. The contractual obligation may arise from a requirement to make payments of principal, interest or dividends. The contractual obligation may be explicit, but it may be implied indirectly in the terms of the contract.

In the case of Lidan, the **contractual obligation is not explicit**. At first glance it looks as if Lidan has a choice as to how much it pays to redeem the B shares. However, the conditions of the financial instrument are such that the value of the **settlement in**

own shares is considerably greater than the cash settlement obligation.
The effect of this is that **Lidan is implicitly obliged to redeem the B shares at for a cash amount of $1 per share**. The own-share settlement alternative is uneconomic in comparison to the cash settlement alternative, and cannot therefore serve as a means of avoiding classification as a liability.

IAS 32 states further that where a derivative contract has settlement options, **all of the settlement alternatives must result in it being classified as an equity instrument**, otherwise it is a financial asset or liability.

In conclusion, **Lidan's B shares must be classified as a liability**.

42 Complexity

Workbook references. Financial instruments are covered in Chapter 7, IFRS 13 is covered in Chapter 3.

Top tips. This is a largely discursive question relating to financial instruments, focusing on the perceived problems with accounting for financial instruments. It requires understanding of IFRS 9 and IFRS 13, as well as an awareness of current issues around financial instruments.

Easy marks. The calculation is a good source of easy marks as it is straightforward. And there are marks for bookwork – listing the problems of complexity and advantages of fair value.

			Marks
(a)	(i)	1 mark per point up to maximum	10
	(ii)	1 mark per point up to maximum	10
(b)		Identical payment	2
		Carrying amount	1
		Fair value	2
			25

(a) (i) Many users and preparers of accounts have found financial instruments to be **complex**.

The main reason for complexity in accounting for financial instruments is the **many different ways in which they can be measured**. The measurement method depends on:

(1) The **applicable financial reporting standard.** A variety of IFRS and IAS apply to the measurement of financial instruments. For example, financial assets may be measured using consolidation for subsidiaries (IFRS 10), the equity method for associates and joint ventures (IAS 28 and IFRS 11) or IFRS 9 for most other financial assets.

(2) The **categorisation of the financial instrument**.

While IFRS 9 classifies financial assets as measured at **amortised cost, fair value through profit or loss or fair value through other comprehensive income** A financial asset may only be classified as measured at amortised cost if the object of the business model in which it is held is to collect

contracted cash flows and its contractual terms give rise on specified dates to cash flows that are solely payments of principal and interest.

(3) Whether **hedge accounting** has been applied. Hedge accounting is **complex**, for example when cash flow hedge accounting is used, gains and losses may be split between profit or loss for the year and other comprehensive income (items that may subsequently be reclassified to profit or loss). In addition, there may be mismatches when hedge accounting applies reflecting the underlying mismatches under the non-hedging rules.

Some measurement methods use an estimate of **current value, and others use historical cost.** Some include impairment losses, others do not.

The different measurement methods for financial instruments creates a number of **problems for preparers and users** of accounts:

(1) The treatment of a particular instrument **may not be the best**, but may be determined by other factors.

(2) Gains or losses resulting from different measurement methods may be combined in the same line item in the statement of profit or loss and other comprehensive income. **Comparability** is therefore compromised.

(3) Comparability is also affected when it is **not clear** what measurement method has been used.

(4) It is **difficult to apply the criteria** for deciding which instrument is to be measured in which way. As new types of instruments are created, the criteria may be applied in ways that are not consistent.

(ii) A single fair value model would be much simpler to apply than the current mixed model. A single measurement method would, it is argued:

(1) Significantly **reduce complexity in classification**. There would be no need to classify financial instruments into the four categories of fair value through profit or loss, available for sale financial assets, loans and receivables and held to maturity. This simplification has already been partially achieved by IFRS 9.

(2) **Reduce complexity in accounting**. There would be no need to account for transfers between the above categories, or to report how impairment losses have been quantified.

(3) **Eliminated measurement mismatches** between financial instruments and reduce the need for fair value hedge accounting.

(4) Eliminate the need to identify and separate **embedded derivatives**.

(5) **Better reflect the cash flows** that would be paid if liabilities were transferred at the re-measurement date.

(6) Make reported information **easier to understand**.

(7) **Improve the comparability** of reported information between entities and between periods.

However, while fair value has some obvious advantages, it has problems too. **Uncertainty** may be an issue for the following reasons

(1) Markets are not all liquid and transparent.

(2) Many assets and liabilities do not have an active market, and methods for estimating their value are more subjective.

(3) Management must exercise judgement in the valuation process, and may not be entirely objective in doing so.

(4) Because fair value, in the absence of an active market, represents an estimate, additional disclosures are needed to explain and justify the estimates. These disclosures may themselves be subjective.

(5) Independent verification of fair value estimates is difficult for all the above reasons.

(b) Different valuation methods bring comparability problems, as indicated in Part (a), and this can be seen with the examples in this part of the question.

Amortised cost

Using amortised cost, both the initial loan and the new loan result in **single payments that are almost identical** on 30 November 20X9:

Initial loan: $47m × 1.05 for 5 years = $59.98m

New loan: $45m × 1.074 for 4 years = $59.89m

However, the **carrying amounts at 30 November 20X5 will be different:**

Initial loan: $47m + ($47m × 5%) = $49.35m

New loan: $45m

Fair value

If the two loans were carried at fair value, both **the initial loan and the new loan would have the same value,** and be carried at $45m. There would be a net profit of $2m, made up of the interest expense of $47m × 5% = $2.35m and the unrealised gain of $49.35m – $45m = $4.35m.

Arguably, since the obligation on 30 November 20X9 will be the same for both loans, fair value is a more appropriate measure than amortised cost.

43 Seltec

Workbook references. Financial instruments are covered in Chapter 7, intangible assets in Chapter 3, and business combinations in Chapters 10 to 16.

Top tips. Embedded derivatives that are financial assets do not need to be separated from their host contract and instead the whole contract is accounted for at fair value through profit or loss. However, the more complex rules still apply to embedded derivatives that are not assets. In part (b), you need to think carefully about what constitutes a business combination – substance is more important than form.

Easy marks. These are available for the definition of embedded derivatives and basic principles of intangible assets.

Marking scheme

	Marks
Hedge accounting	5
Futures	5
Embedded derivative	5
Brands	5
Business combinations	5
	25

(a) **Financial instruments**

Derivatives

IAS 32 *Financial Instruments: Presentation* and IFRS 9 *Financial Instruments* define a **derivative** as a financial instrument or other contract that has all three of the following characteristics.

(i) Its value changes in response to the change in a specified interest rate, financial instrument price, commodity price, foreign exchange rate, index of prices or rates, credit rating or credit index, or other variable (sometimes called the 'underlying').

(ii) It requires no initial net investment or an initial net investment that is smaller than would be required for other types of contracts that would be expected to have a similar response to changes in market factors.

(iii) It is settled at a future date.

A contract is **not considered to be a derivative where its purpose is to take physical delivery** in the normal course of business, unless the entity has a practice of settling the contracts on a net basis.

In the case of Seltec, while the company often takes physical delivery of the edible oil, it does so only to sell shortly afterwards, and usually settles on a net basis. Thus the **contracts will be considered to be derivative** contracts rather than contracts for purchase of inventory. Derivatives are accounted for at fair value through profit or loss, unless hedge accounting applies.

Hedge accounting

The rules on hedge accounting are set out in IFRS 9. Before a hedging relationship qualifies for hedge accounting, **all** of the following **conditions** must be met.

(i) The hedging relationship consists **only of eligible hedging instruments and eligible hedged items**.

(ii) There must be **formal documentation** (including identification of the hedged item, the hedging instrument, the nature of the risk that is to be hedged and how the entity will assess the hedging instrument's effectiveness in offsetting the exposure to changes in the hedged item's fair value or cash flows attributable to the hedged risk).

(iii) The hedging relationship meets all of the following hedge effectiveness criteria

(1) There is an **economic relationship** between the hedged item and the hedging instrument, ie the hedging instrument and the hedged item have values that generally move in the opposite direction because of the same risk, which is the hedged risk;

(2)   The **effect of credit risk does not dominate the value** changes that result from that economic relationship, ie the gain or loss from credit risk does not frustrate the effect of changes in the underlyings on the value of the hedging instrument or the hedged item, even if those changes were significant; and

(3)   The **hedge ratio of the hedging relationship** (quantity of hedging instrument vs quantity of hedged item) is the same as that resulting from the quantity of the hedged item that the entity **actually hedges** and the quantity of the hedging instrument that the entity **actually uses** to hedge that quantity of hedged item.

There are two kinds of hedging that Seltec may consider: fair value hedging and cash flow hedging.

A **fair value hedge** is a hedge of the exposure to changes in the fair value of a recognised asset or liability, or an identified portion of such an asset or liability, that is attributable to a particular risk and could affect profit or loss. The **gain or loss** resulting from **re-measuring** the hedging instrument at fair value is **recognised in profit or loss**. The gain or loss on the hedged item attributable to the **hedged risk** should **adjust the carrying amount** of the hedged item and be **recognised in profit or loss**.

A **cash flow hedge**: a hedge of the exposure to variability in cash flows that:

(i)   Is attributable to a particular risk associated with a recognised asset or liability (such as all or some future interest payments on variable rate debt) or a highly probable forecast transaction (such as an anticipated purchase or sale); and that

(ii)   Could affect profit or loss.

The portion of the gain or loss on the hedging instrument that is determined to be an **effective** hedge must be accounted for in a cash flow reserve and **recognised in other comprehensive income (items that may subsequently be reclassified to profit or loss)** and transferred to profit or loss when the hedged item is recognised in profit or loss. The **ineffective portion** of the gain or loss on the hedging instrument must be **recognised in profit or loss**.

The rules for cash flow hedges are particularly restrictive because it is difficult to isolate and measure the cash flows attributable to the specific risks for the non-financial items. Cash flow hedging results in higher volatility in earnings, so, provided the documentation and other requirements are met, **Seltec may prefer to use fair value hedging**. Seltec must take into account all changes in the price of edible oil of all types and geographical locations that it processes and sells and these must be compared with the changes in the value of the future. The hedge will be ineffective if the contracts have different prices. However, a hedge does not need to be fully effective, and hedge accounting may still be used provided the criteria above are met.

Embedded derivative

Certain contracts that are not themselves derivatives (and may not be financial instruments) include derivative contracts that are 'embedded' within them. These non-derivatives are called **host contracts** IFRS 9 defines an embedded derivative as a derivative instrument that is combined with a non-derivative host contract to form a single hybrid instrument. Some of the cash flows of the instrument vary in a way that is similar to a stand-alone derivative.

Ordinary derivatives must be accounted for at fair value in the statement of financial position with changes recognised through profit or loss.

IFRS 9 treatment

Where the host contract is a financial asset within the scope of the IFRS 9, the classification and **measurement rules of the standard are applied to the entire hybrid**

contract. However, in this case the contract is a financial liability, not a financial asset within the scope of IFRS 9. Accordingly, the following rules apply:

The embedded derivative must be **separated from its host contract** and accounted for as a derivative, provided the following conditions are met.

(i)   The economic characteristics and risks of the embedded derivative are not closely related to the economic characteristics and risks of the host contract.

(ii)   A separate instrument with the same terms as the embedded derivative would meet the definition of a derivative.

(iii)   The hybrid (combined) instrument is not measured at fair value with changes in fair value recognised in the profit or loss (a derivative embedded in a financial asset or financial liability need not be separated out if the entity holds the combined instrument at fair value through profit or loss).

If the embedded derivative is separated from its host contract, the **host contract is accounted for under the applicable IFRS**. A contract denominated in a foreign currency contains an embedded derivative unless:

(i)   The foreign currency denominated in the contract is the currency of one of the parties to the contract.

(ii)   The foreign currency is that commonly used in the market in which such transactions take place.

(iii)   The foreign currency is that in which the related goods or services are denominated in routine commercial transactions.

In the case of Seltec, **none of the above three exceptions apply**. Seltec's trade in edible oil is generally in dollars, not pounds sterling, the pound is not the functional currency of either party, and it is not the currency normally used in transactions in the business environment in which Seltec operates. Finally, the economic characteristics and risks of the embedded derivative are not closely related to the economic characteristics and risks of the host contract, since changes in the price of oil and currency fluctuations have different risks.

In conclusion, IFRS 9 would treat Seltec's contracts as containing an embedded derivative. The currency derivative must be accounted for at fair value through profit or loss.

(b)   **Intangible assets**

An entity should **assess** the useful life of an intangible asset, which may be **finite or indefinite**. An intangible asset has an indefinite useful life when there is **no foreseeable limit** to the period over which the asset is expected to generate net cash inflows for the entity.

Seltec wishes to treat both brands as having indefinite useful lives. However, this may not be appropriate, and there are certain factors that need to be considered:

(i)   Does the brand have long-term potential? The first brand has a proven track record, but the second, named after a famous film star, may last only as long as the film star's popularity, which will not be indefinite.

(ii)   Is Seltec committed to supporting the brand? In the case of the first, it is, but the second is a relatively new product, and it is not clear that Seltec is in for the long haul.

If, as is likely, the **useful life of the second brand is considered to be finite**, its cost less residual value should be amortised on a systematic basis over its useful life, using the straight-line method as an approximation if the pattern of benefits cannot be determined reliably.

The **first brand**, which is correctly said to have an **indefinite useful life**, should not be amortised. Its useful life should be reviewed at each reporting period to determine whether the

assessment of the useful life as indefinite is still applicable. If not, the change, from indefinite to finite would be accounted for as a change in accounting estimate as per IAS 8 *Accounting Policies, Changes in Accounting Estimates and Errors*. It should also be tested for impairment annually in accordance with IAS 36 *Impairment of Assets*, and otherwise accounted for like the second brand.

Purchase of entities

IFRS 3 *Business Combinations* defines a business combination as 'a transaction or event in which an acquirer obtains control of one or more businesses. A business is defined as an integrated set of activities and assets that is capable of being conducted and managed for the purpose of providing a return directly to investors or other owners, members or participants'. Such a return may be in the form of cash, dividends or lower costs.

The two limited liability **companies do not meet the IFRS 3 definition of a business** because they are not self-sustaining and do not generate revenue independently of Seltec. The acquisition **should be treated as a purchase of property**.

44 Carsoon

Workbook references. Leases are covered in Chapter 8, financial instruments in Chapter 7 and revenue in Chapter 1. Fair value is covered in Chapter 3.

Top tips. Allocate your time appropriately across this three-part question. The parts are independent of each other so you should scan read all parts and attempt the one you feel most comfortable with first. The key to part (a) is to understand that Carsoon is the lessor, not the lessee and therefore the distinction between finance leases and operating leases applies. Part (b) asks you to advise on measurement issues for a financial instrument. The calculation is straightforward if you have understood the principles; if not, you would be advised to briefly state the measurement principles of IFRS 13 as far as you can and move on quickly to another part of the question. Part (c) of the question, on contractual revenue, is challenging as it gets into the specific detail of IFRS 15, but it is a topical area you should be familiar with. Ensure you breakdown your response to cover each element.

Easy marks. Part (a) contains generous marks for using the information in the question to explain how to classify Carsoon's vehicle leases in the context of IFRS 16. Parts (b) and (c) are more challenging but part (c) contains some easy marks if you know that the general administration costs and the wasted materials costs should be expensed.

		Marks
(a)	Classification of lease as operating lease not finance lease, accounting requirements for lease payments and assets and cash flow implications – 1 mark per point up to maximum	9
(b)	Type of financial asset, IFRS 13 requirements, account for financial asset – 1 mark per point up to maximum	8
(c)	Discuss each of penalties, counter claim and additional costs 1 mark per point up to maximum	8
		25

(a) Under IFRS 16 *Leases*, **Carsoon is a lessor** and must classify each lease as an operating or finance lease. A lease is classified as a finance lease if it transfers substantially all of the risks and rewards incidental to ownership of the underlying asset. All other leases are classified as operating leases. Classification is made at the inception of the lease. Whether a lease is a finance lease or an operating lease depends on the **substance of the transaction** rather than the form.

In this case, the **leases are operating leases**. The lease is unlikely to transfer ownership of the vehicle to the lessee by the end of the lease term as the option to purchase the vehicle is at a price which is higher than fair value at the end of the lease term. The lease term is not for the major part of the economic life of the asset as vehicles normally have a length of life of more than three years and the maximum unpenalised mileage is 10,000 miles per annum. Additionally, the present value of the minimum lease payments is unlikely to be substantially all of the fair value of the leased asset as the price which the customer can purchase the vehicle is above market value, hence the lessor does not appear to have received an acceptable return by the end of the lease. Carsoon also stipulates the maximum mileage and maintains the vehicles. This would appear to indicate that the risks and rewards remain with Carsoon.

Carsoon should account for the leased vehicles as property, plant and equipment (PPE) under IAS 16 *Property, Plant and Equipment* and depreciate them taking into account the expected residual value. The rental payments should go to profit or loss on a straight-line basis over the lease term. Where an item of PPE ceases to be rented and becomes held for sale, it should be transferred to inventory at its carrying amount. The proceeds from the sale of such assets should be recognised as revenue in accordance with IFRS 15 *Revenue from Contracts with Customers*.

IAS 7 *Statement of Cash Flows* states that payments from operating activities are primarily derived from the principal revenue-producing activities of the entity. Therefore, they generally result from the transactions and other events which enter into the determination of profit or loss. Therefore, cash receipts from the disposal of assets formerly held for rental and subsequently held for sale should be treated as cash flows from operating activities and not investing activities.

(b) For financial assets which are debt instruments measured at fair value through other comprehensive income (FVOCI), both amortised cost and fair value information are relevant because debt instruments in this measurement category are held for both the collection of contractual cash flows and the realisation of fair values. Therefore, debt instruments measured at FVOCI are measured at **fair value** in the **statement of financial position**. In **profit or loss**, interest revenue is calculated using the **effective interest rate method.** The fair value gains and losses on these financial assets are recognised in other comprehensive income (OCI). As a result, the difference between the total change in fair value and the amounts recognised in profit or loss are shown in OCI. When these financial assets are derecognised, the cumulative gains and losses previously recognised in OCI are reclassified from equity to profit or loss. Expected credit losses (ECLs) do not reduce the carrying amount of the financial assets, which remains at fair value. Instead, an amount equal to the ECL allowance which would arise if the asset were measured at amortised cost is recognised in OCI.

The fair value of the debt instrument therefore needs to be ascertained at 28 February 20X7. IFRS 13 *Fair Value Measurement* states that Level 1 inputs are unadjusted quoted prices in active markets for identical assets or liabilities which the entity can access at the measurement date. In-house models are alternative pricing methods which do not rely exclusively on quoted prices. It would seem that a **Level 1 input is available**, based upon activity in the market and further that, because of the active market, there is no reason to use the in-house model to value the debt.

Therefore, the accounting for the instrument should be as follows:

Initial measurement

The bonds will be initially recorded at $6 million and interest of $0.24 million will be received and credited to profit or loss.

Subsequent measurement

At 28 February 20X7, the bonds will be valued at $5.3 million, which recognises 12-month credit losses and other reductions in fair value. The loss of $0.7 million will be charged as an impairment loss of $0.4 million to profit or loss, representing the 12-month expected credit losses and $0.3 million to OCI. When the bond is sold for $5.3 million on 1 March 20X7, the financial asset is derecognised and the loss in OCI ($0.3 million) is reclassified to profit or loss. Also, the fact that the bond is sold for $5.3 million on 1 March 20X7 illustrates that this should have been the fair value on 28 February 20X7.

(c)   IFRS 15 *Revenue from Contracts with Customers* specifies how to account for costs incurred in fulfilling a contract which are not in the scope of another standard. Costs to fulfil a contract which is accounted for under IFRS 15 are divided into those which give rise to an asset and those which are expensed as incurred. Entities will recognise an asset when costs incurred to fulfil a contract meet certain criteria, one of which is that the costs are expected to be recovered.

For costs to meet the 'expected to be recovered' criterion, they need to be either explicitly reimbursable under the contract or reflected through the pricing of the contract and recoverable through the margin.

The penalty and additional costs attributable to the contract should be considered when they occur and Carsoon should have included them in the total costs of the contract in the period in which they had been notified.

As regards the counter claim for compensation, Carsoon accounts for the claim as a contract modification in accordance with IFRS 15. The modification does not result in any additional goods and services being provided to the customer. In addition, all of the remaining goods and services after the modification are not distinct and form part of a single performance obligation. Consequently, Carsoon should account for the modification by updating the transaction price and the measure of progress towards complete satisfaction of the performance obligation. However, on the basis of information available, it is possible to consider that the counter claim had not reached an advanced stage, so that claims submitted to the client should not be included in total revenues.

When the contract is modified for the construction of the storage facility, an additional $7 million is added to the consideration which Carsoon will receive. The additional $7 million reflects the stand-alone selling price of the contract modification. The construction of the separate storage facility is a distinct performance obligation and the contract modification for the additional storage facility is accounted for as a new contract which does not affect the accounting for the existing contract. Therefore the contract is a performance obligation which has been satisfied as assets are only recognised in relation to satisfying future performance obligations. General and administrative costs cannot be capitalised unless these costs are specifically chargeable to the customer under the contract. Similarly, wasted material costs are expensed where they are not chargeable to the customer. Therefore a total expense of $15 million will be charged to profit or loss and not shown as assets.

45 Macaljoy

Workbook reference. Pensions are covered in Chapter 4; provisions in Chapter 5.

Top tips. Part (a)(i) is very straightforward, but make sure you relate your answer to the pension schemes of Macaljoy. In part (a)(ii) it is important that you have an in-depth knowledge of the differences between the two schemes rather than just a general view of the differences.

Similarly, in Part (b)(i), you need to write specifically about warranty provisions, as well as more generally about provisions.

Easy marks. There are marks for straightforward bookwork that you can get even if you don't get all the calculations right.

Marking scheme

				Marks
(a)	Pensions	(i)	Explanation	8
		(ii)	Calculation	8
(b)	Provisions	(i)	Explanation	6
		(ii)	Calculation	3
				25

To: The Directors
          Macaljoy

Date: 1 November 20X7

Subject: **Pension plans and warranty claims**

The purpose of this report is to explain the difference between defined benefit and defined contribution pension plans, and to show the accounting treatment of Macaljoy's pension schemes. It also discusses the principles of accounting for warranty claims and shows the accounting treatment of Macaljoy's warranty claims.

(a)   (i)   **Defined contribution plans and defined benefit plans**

With **defined contribution** plans, the employer (and possibly, as here, current employees too) pay regular contributions into the plan of a given or 'defined' amount each year. The contributions are invested, and the size of the post-employment benefits paid to former employees depends on how well or how badly the plan's investments perform. If the investments perform well, the plan will be able to afford higher benefits than if the investments performed less well.

The B scheme is a defined contribution plan. The employer's liability is limited to the contributions paid.

With **defined benefit** plans, the size of the post-employment benefits is determined in advance, ie the benefits are 'defined'. The employer (and possibly, as here, current employees too) pay contributions into the plan, and the contributions are invested. The size of the contributions is set at an amount that is expected to earn enough investment returns to meet the obligation to pay the post-employment benefits. If, however, it becomes apparent that the assets in the fund are insufficient, the employer will be required to make additional contributions into the plan to make up the expected shortfall. On the other hand, if the fund's assets appear to be larger than they need to be, and in excess of what is required to pay the post-employment benefits, the employer may be allowed to take a 'contribution holiday' (ie stop paying in contributions for a while).

The **main difference** between the two types of plans lies in **who bears the risk**: if the employer bears the risk, even in a small way by guaranteeing or specifying the return, the plan is a defined benefit plan. A defined contribution scheme must give a benefit formula based solely on the amount of the contributions.

A defined benefit scheme may be created even if there is no legal obligation, if an employer has a practice of guaranteeing the benefits payable.

The A scheme is a defined benefit scheme. Macaljoy, the employer, guarantees a pension based on the service lives of the employees in the scheme. The company's liability is not limited to the amount of the contributions. This means that the employer bears the investment risk: if the return on the investment is not sufficient to meet the liabilities, the company will need to make good the difference.

(ii) **Accounting treatment: B scheme**

No assets or liabilities will be recognised for this defined contribution scheme, other than current liabilities to reflect amounts due to be paid to the pension scheme at year end. The **contributions** paid by the company of $10 million will be **charged to profit or loss**. The contributions paid by the employees will not be a cost to the company but will be adjusted in calculating employee's net salary.

Accounting treatment: A scheme

The accounting treatment is as follows:

STATEMENT OF PROFIT OR LOSS AND OTHER COMPREHENSIVE INCOME NOTES

Expense recognised in profit or loss for the year ended 31 October 20X7

	$m
Current service cost	20.0
Net interest on the net defined benefit liability (10 – 9.5)	0.5
Net expense	20.5

Other comprehensive income: remeasurement of defined benefit plans (for the year ended 31 October 20X7)

	$m
Remeasurement gains or losses on defined benefit obligation	(29.0)
Remeasurement gains or losses on plan assets (excluding amounts in net interest)	27.5
	(1.5)

STATEMENT OF FINANCIAL POSITION NOTES

Amounts recognised in statement of financial position

	31 October 20X7 $m	1 November 20X6 $m
Present value of defined benefit obligation	240	200
Fair value of plan assets	(225)	(190)
Net liability	15	10

Change in the present value of the defined benefit obligation

	$m
Present value of obligation at 1 November 20X6	200
Interest on obligation: 5% × 200	10
Current service cost	20
Benefits paid	(19)
Loss on remeasurement through OCI (balancing figure)	29
Present value of obligation at 31 October 20X7	240

Change in the fair value of plan assets

	$m
Fair value of plan assets at 1 November 20X6	190.0
Interest on plan assets: 5% × 190	9.5
Contributions	17.0
Benefits paid	(19.0)
Gain on remeasurement through OCI (balancing figure)	27.5
Fair value of plan assets at 31 October 20X7	225.0

(b) **Warranty provisions**

(i) **Principles**

Under IAS 37 *Provisions, Contingent Liabilities and Contingent Assets,* provisions must be recognised in the following circumstances.

(1) There is a **legal** or **constructive obligation** to transfer benefits as a result of past events.

(2) It is probably that an **outflow of economic resources** will be required to **settle** the **obligation**.

(3) A **reasonable estimate** of the amount required to settle the obligation can be made.

If the company can **avoid expenditure by its future action, no provision** should be recognised. A legal or constructive obligation is one created by an **obligating event**. Constructive obligations arise when an entity is committed to certain expenditures because of a pattern of behaviour which the public would expect to continue.

IAS 37 states that the amount recognised should be the **best estimate of the expenditure required to settle the obligation at the end of the reporting period**. The estimate should **take the various possible outcomes into account** and should be the **amount that an entity would rationally pay** to settle the obligation at the reporting date or to transfer it to a third party. In the case of warranties, the provision will be made at a probability weighted expected value, taking into account the risks and uncertainties surrounding the underlying events.

The amount of the provision should be **discounted to present value** if the time value of money is material using a **risk adjusted rate**. If some or all of the expenditure is expected to be **reimbursed** by a third party, the reimbursement should be **recognised as a separate asset,** but only if it is virtually certain that the reimbursement will be received.

(ii) **Accounting treatment**

In Macaljoy's case, the past event giving rise to the obligation is the sale of the product with a warranty. A provision for the warranty will be made as follows:

	$
Re year 1 warranty	280,000
Re year 2 warranty	350,000
	630,000

If material, the provisions may be discounted:

	$
Re year 1 warranty	269,000
Re year 2 warranty	323,000
	592,000

Calculations are shown below.

Macaljoy may be able to **recognise the asset and income from the insurance claim**, but only if the insurance company has validated the claim and **receipt is virtually certain**. In general contingent assets are not recognised, but disclosed if an inflow of economic benefits is probable.

Calculations

Year 1: warranty

	Expected value $'000	Discounted expected value (4%) $'000
80% × Nil	0	
15% × 7,000 × $100	105	
5% × 7,000 × $500	175	
	280	$280,000/1.04 = $269,000*

Year 2: extended warranty

	Expected value $'000	Discounted expected value (4%) $'000
70% × Nil	0	
20% × 5,000 × $100	100	
10% × 5,000 × $500	250	
	350	$350,000/(1.04)^2 = $323,000*

*Note. These figures are rounded.

46 Panel

Workbook references. Current and deferred tax is covered in Chapter 6. IFRS 2 is covered in Chapter 9 and IFRS 16 in Chapter 3.

Top tips. This is a fairly typical question about IAS 12 containing a written part asking you to explain the requirements of the standard and then a longer part asking you to apply the requirements to four different items including share options, a leasing transaction, an intra company sale and an impairment of property, plant and equipment.

Easy marks. Part (a) contains lots of easy marks, provided you have revised the topic. It is straightforward knowledge, but requires a good understanding of IAS 12 to respond clearly. Part (b) (iii) and (iv) are easier than (i) and (ii), though they carry the same number of marks.

Marking scheme

			Marks
(a)	(i)	Tax base definition	3
	(ii)	Temporary differences	3
	(iii)	Recognition criteria	3
			9
(b)	(i)	Share options	4
	(ii)	Leased plant	4
	(iii)	Intra company	4
	(iv)	Impairment loss	4
			16
			25

(a) (i) **Tax base**

The tax base of an asset is the **tax deduction which will be available in future when the asset generates taxable economic benefits,** which will flow to the entity when the asset is recovered. If the future economic benefits will **not be taxable,** the tax base of an asset is its carrying amount.

The tax base of a liability is its **carrying amount,** less the tax deduction which will be available when the liability is settled in future periods. For revenue received in advance (or deferred income), the tax base is its **carrying amount, less any amount of the revenue which will not be taxable in future periods**.

(ii) **Temporary differences**

Temporary differences occur when items of revenue or expense are included in both accounting profits and taxable profits, but not for the same accounting period.

A **taxable temporary difference** arises when the carrying amount of an asset exceeds its tax base or the carrying amount of a liability is less than its tax base. All taxable temporary differences give rise to a deferred tax liability.

A **deductible temporary difference** arises in the reverse circumstance (when the carrying amount of an asset is less than its tax base or the carrying amount of a liability is greater than its tax base). All deductible temporary differences give rise to a deferred tax asset.

(iii) **Recognition of deferred tax assets and liabilities**

The general requirements of IAS 12 are that deferred tax liabilities should be recognised on all taxable temporary differences (with specific exceptions).

IAS 12 states that a deferred tax asset **should** be recognised for deductible temporary differences if it is **probable** that a taxable profit, or sufficient taxable temporary differences will arise in future **against which the deductible temporary difference can be utilised.**

(b) (i) **Share options**

Under IFRS 2 *Share-based Payment* the company **recognises an expense** for the employee services received in return for the share options granted over the vesting period. The related tax deduction **does not arise until the share options are exercised**. Therefore, a **deferred tax asset arises**, based on the difference between the intrinsic value of the options and their carrying amount (normally zero).

At 31 October 20X4 the tax benefit is as follows:

	$m
Carrying amount of share based payment	–
Less tax base of share based payment (16/2)	(8)
Temporary difference	(8)

The **deferred tax asset is $2.4 million** (30% × 8). This is recognised at 31 October 20X4 provided that taxable profit is available against which it can be utilised. Because the tax effect of the remuneration expense is greater than the tax benefit, the tax benefit is **recognised in profit or loss**. (The tax effect of the remuneration expense is 30% × $40 million ÷ 2 = $6 million.)

At 31 October 20X5 there is **no longer a deferred tax asset** because the options have been exercised. The **tax benefit receivable is $13.8 million** (30% × $46 million). Therefore, the deferred tax asset of $2.4 million is no longer required.

(ii) **Leased plant**

Under IFRS 16 *Leases,* a **right-of-use asset** and a **lease obligation** are recognised.

The lease liability is measured at the **present value of the lease payments** discounted using, if available, the interest rate implicit in the least**.**

The right-of-use asset is measured at the amount of the initial measurement of the lease liability, plus certain other direct costs not incurred in this case, such as legal fees. It is depreciated on a straight-line basis over the five years.

The obligation to pay lease rentals is **recognised as a liability**. Each instalment payable is treated partly as interest and partly as repayment of the liability. The **carrying amount** of the plant for accounting purposes is the **net present value of the lease payments less depreciation**.

A **temporary difference** effectively arises between the value of the plant for accounting purposes and the equivalent of the outstanding obligations, as the annual rental payments quality for the relief. The tax base of the asset is the amount deductable for tax in future, which is zero. The tax base of the liability is the carrying amount less any future tax deductible amounts, which will give a **tax base of zero**.

Therefore at 31 October 20X5 a **net temporary difference** will be as follows:

	$m	$m
Carrying amount in financial statements:		
Asset:		
Net present value of future lease payments at inception of lease	12.00	
Less depreciation (12/5)	(2.40)	
		9.60
Less lease liability		
Liability at inception of lease	12.00	
Interest (8% × 12)	0.96	
Lease rental	(3.00)	
		(9.96)
		0.36
Less tax base		(0.00)
Temporary difference		0.36

A **deferred tax asset of $108,000** (30% × 360,000) arises.

(iii) **Intra-group sale**

Pins has **made a profit of $2 million** on its sale to Panel. Tax is **payable on the profits of individual companies**. Pins is liable for tax on this profit in the current year and will have provided for the related tax in its individual financial statements. However, **from the viewpoint of the group** the profit **will not be realised until the following year**, when the goods are sold to a third party and must be **eliminated** from the consolidated financial statements. Because the group **pays tax before the profit is realised** there is a **temporary difference of $2 million** and a **deferred tax asset of $600,000** (30% × $2 million).

(iv) **Impairment loss**

The impairment loss in the financial statements of Nails **reduces the carrying amount** of property, plant and equipment, but is **not allowable for tax**. Therefore, the **tax base** of the property, plant and equipment **is different from its carrying amount** and there is a **temporary difference**.

Under IAS 36 *Impairment of Assets* the impairment loss is allocated first to goodwill and then to other assets:

	Goodwill	Property, plant and equipment	Total
	$m	$m	$m
Carrying amount at 31 October 20X5	1	6.0	7.0
Impairment loss	(1)	(0.8)	(1.8)
	–	5.2	5.2

IAS 12 states that **no deferred tax should be recognised on goodwill** and therefore **only the impairment loss relating to the property, plant and equipment affects the deferred tax position.**

The effect of the impairment loss is as follows:

	Before impairment	After impairment	Difference
	$m	$m	$m
Carrying amount	6	5.2	
Tax base	(4)	(4.0)	
Temporary difference	2	1.2	0.8
Tax liability (30%)	0.6	0.36	0.24

Therefore the impairment loss reduces deferred the tax liability by $240,000.

47 Kesare

Workbook reference. Deferred tax is covered in Chapter 6.

Top tips. Part (a) can be broken down into its component parts of discussion of the conceptual framework and temporary differences, and credit is available for fairly general discussion of both. The deferred tax calculation is tricky, but there should be some parts that you should be comfortable with. Layout is important to avoid getting muddled.

Easy marks. There are some fairly easy marks in part (a) available for a general discussion about concepts and the conceptual framework. In addition there are some easy marks for adjustments to the financial statements, most of which do not relate to the deferred tax aspects. In general, however, this is not a question that lends itself to easy marks.

		Marks
(a)		
	Conceptual Framework	2
	Temporary difference	3
	Liability	1
	Weakness	$\frac{1}{7}$
(b)	Adjustments: Investment in equity instruments	2
	Convertible bond	2
	Defined benefit plan	2
	Property, plant and equipment	1
	Deferred tax: Goodwill	1
	Other intangibles	1
	Financial assets	1
	Trade receivables	1
	Other receivables	1
	Long-term borrowings	1
	Employee benefits	1
	Trade payables	1
	Calculation	$\frac{3}{18}$
		$\underline{\underline{25}}$

(a) IAS 12 *Income Taxes* is based on the idea that **all changes in assets and liabilities** have **unavoidable tax consequences**. Where the recognition criteria in IFRS are different from those in tax law, **the carrying amount of an asset or liability in the financial statements is different from its tax base** (the amount at which it is stated for tax purposes). These differences are known as **temporary differences**. The practical effect of these differences is that a transaction or event occurs in a different accounting period from its tax consequences. For example, depreciation is recognised in the financial statements in different accounting periods from capital allowances.

IAS 12 requires a company to make **full provision** for the tax effects of temporary differences. Both **deferred tax assets**, and **deferred tax liabilities** can arise in this way.

It may be argued that deferred tax assets and liabilities **do not meet the definition of assets and liabilities** in the IASB *Conceptual Framework for Financial Reporting*. Under the *Conceptual Framework* an asset is the right to receive economic benefits as a result of past events, and a liability is an obligation to transfer economic benefits, again as a result of past events.

Under IAS 12, the tax effect of transactions are recognised in the same period as the transactions themselves, but in practice, tax is paid in accordance with tax legislation when it becomes a legal liability. There is a **conceptual weakness** or inconsistency, in that only one liability, that is tax, is being provided for, and not other costs, such as overhead costs.

256

(b)

	$'000	Adjustments to financial statements $'000	Adjusted financial statements $'000	Tax base $'000	Temporary difference $'000
Property, plant and equipment	10,000		10,000	2,400	7,600
Goodwill	6,000		6,000	6,000	
Other intangible assets	5,000		5,000	0	5,000
Financial assets (cost)	9,000	1,500	10,500	9,000	1,500
Total non-current assets	30,000		31,500		
Trade receivables	7,000		7,000	7,500	(500)
Other receivables	4,600		4,600	5,000	(400)
Cash and cash-equivalents	6,700		6,700	6,700	–
Total current assets	18,300		18,300		
Total assets	48,300		49,800		
Share capital	(9,000)		(9,000)		
Other reserves	(4,500)	(1,500) (400)	(6,400)		
Retained earnings	(9,130)	520	(8,610)		
Total equity	(22,630)		(24,010)		
Long term borrowings	(10,000)	400	(9,600)	(10,000)	400
Deferred tax liability	(3,600)		(3,600)	(3,600)	–
Employee benefits	(4,000)	(520)	(4,520)	(5,000)	480
Current tax liability	(3,070)		(3,070)	(3,070)	–
Trade and other payables	(5,000)		(5,000)	(4,000)	(1,000)
Total liabilities	(25,670)		(25,790)		13,080
Total equity and liabilities	48,300		49,800		

		$'000	$'000
Deferred tax liability			
Liability b/fwd (per draft SOFP)			3,600
Charge: OCI ($1,500 × 30% (Note (1))		450	
P/L (bal. fig)		(126)	
			324
Deferred tax liability c/fwd	14,980 × 30%	4,494	
Deferred tax asset – c/fwd	1,900 × 30%	(570)	
Net deferred tax liability	13,080 × 30%		3,924

Notes on adjustments

1   The investments in equity instruments are shown at cost. However, per IFRS 9, they should instead be valued at fair value, with the increase ($10,500 – $9,000 = $1,500) going to other comprehensive income (items that will not be reclassified to profit or loss) as per the irrevocable election.

2 IAS 32 states that convertible bonds must be split into debt and equity components. This involves reducing debt and increasing equity by $400.

3 The defined benefit plan needs to be adjusted to reflect the change. The liability must be increased by $520,000. The same amount is charged to retained earnings.

4 The development costs have already been allowed for tax, so the tax base is nil. No deferred tax is recognised on goodwill.

5 The accrual for compensation is to be allowed when paid, ie in a later period. The tax base relating to trade and other payables should be reduced by $1 million.

48 Chemclean

Workbook references. IFRS 3 and IFRS 10 are covered in Chapter 10. IAS 12 is covered in Chapter 6 and IAS 38 in Chapter 3.

Top tips. Part (a) deals with standards that should be familiar to you, but the issues require in-depth consideration. In particular, you need to consider how IAS 38 and IFRS 3 interact, focusing on the implications of acquiring technology, outlining the fact that the probability recognition criterion is always considered to be satisfied for intangible assets that are acquired separately or in a business combination. You were expected to discuss that a shell company without employees (and hence without processes required to make it a 'business') is an asset acquisition as opposed to a business combination. Similarly, inventories and cost of sales in Part (b) may seem like basic knowledge but you have to consider it in the context of potential manipulation of the financial statements. Finally deferred tax (part (c)) requires you to question an accounting treatment, which could be aiming at presenting the results in an unrealistically favourable light.

Easy marks. There are marks for knowing the basics of the standards tested, but those marks will not get you a pass on this question.

Marking scheme

		Marks
(a)	1 mark per point up to maximum	10
(b)	1 mark per point up to maximum	6
(c)	1 mark per point up to maximum	9
		25

(a) **Intangible asset**

IAS 38 *Intangible Assets* requires an entity to recognise an intangible asset, whether purchased or self-created (at cost) if, and only if:

(i) It is probable that the future economic benefits which are attributable to the asset will flow to the entity; and

(ii) The cost of the asset can be measured reliably.

This requirement applies whether an intangible asset is acquired externally or generated internally. IAS 38 includes additional recognition criteria for internally generated intangible assets.

The probability of future economic benefits must be based on reasonable and supportable assumptions about conditions which will exist over the life of the asset. The probability recognition criterion is always considered to be satisfied for intangible assets that are acquired separately or in a business combination. If an intangible item does not meet both the definition

of and the criteria for recognition as an intangible asset, IAS 38 requires the expenditure on this item to be recognised as an expense when it is incurred. Research constitutes original and planned investigations undertaken with the prospect of gaining new scientific or technical knowledge and understanding. No intangible assets arising from research should be recognised. Expenditure on research should be recognised as an expense when it is incurred.

In this case, Chemclean should recognise an intangible asset for the use of Jomaster's technology. The right should be measured at its cost of $4m. The intangible asset should be amortised from the date it is available for use. The technology is available for use when the manufacturing of the compound begins. The amortisation should be presented as cost of sales in the statement of profit or loss if expenses are presented by function or as amortisation if expenses are presented by nature, as it is an expense directly related to the production of the compound. At the end of each reporting period, Chemclean is required to assess whether there is any indication that the asset may be impaired, that is its carrying amount may be higher than its recoverable amount.

The price an entity pays to acquire an intangible asset reflects expectations about the probability that the expected future economic benefits from the asset will flow to the entity. The effect of probability is therefore reflected in the cost of the asset.

Due to the nature of intangible assets, subsequent expenditure will only rarely meet the criteria for being recognised in the carrying amount of an asset. Thus, Chemclean continues to expense its own internal development expenditure until the criteria for capitalisation are met and economic benefits are expected to flow to the entity from the capitalised asset. When the drug is sold, the royalty payments are presented in profit or loss.

IFRS 10 *Consolidated Financial Satements* defines control of an investee in terms of the following: 'An investor controls an investee when the investor is exposed, or has rights, to variable returns from its involvement with the investee and has the ability to affect those returns through its power over the investee' (Appendix A). Therefore it appears that Chemclean will control Conew.

IFRS 3 *Business Combinations* defines a 'business' as 'an integrated set of activities and assets that is capable of being conducted and managed for the purpose of providing a return in the form of dividends, lower costs or other economic benefits directly to investors or other owners, members or participants' (Appendix A). A business consists of inputs and processes applied to those inputs which have the ability to create outputs. Although businesses usually have outputs, outputs are not required for an integrated set to qualify as a business. Processes are defined in IFRS 3 as any system, standard, protocol, convention or rule that creates or has the ability to create output. Any transaction in which an entity obtains control of one or more businesses qualifies as a business combination and is subject to the measurement and recognition requirements of IFRS 3. Processes are included in the acquired group when intellectual property (IP) is accompanied by other resources such as assets or employees or other elements such as protocols and plans which will further help develop the IP to the next phase. The formation of a legal entity, which is involved in the transaction, is an irrelevance and the legal form of the transaction does not determine the accounting treatment. Here, the acquisition of an interest in Conew is an asset acquisition and should be accounted for under IAS 38 because Conew does not meet the definition of a business.

(b) **Presentation issues**

IAS 1 *Presentation of Financial Statements* provides little specific guidance on the presentation of line items in financial statements, such as the level of detail or number of line items that should be presented in the financial statements. Furthermore, IAS 1's objective is to set out 'the overall requirements for the presentation of financial statements, guidelines for their structure and minimum requirements for their content'. In doing so, IAS 1 sets out minimum levels of required items in the financial statements by requiring certain items to be presented on the face of, or in the notes to, the financial statements and in other required disclosures. The current

requirements in IFRS do not provide a definition of 'gross profit' or 'operating results' or many other common subtotals. The absence of specific requirements arises from the fact that the guidance in IAS 1 relies on management's judgement about which additional line items, headings and subtotals:

(i)   Are relevant to an understanding of the entity's financial position/financial performance; and

(ii)   Should be presented in a manner which provides relevant, reliable, comparable and understandable information.

IAS 1 allows entities to include additional line items, amend descriptions and the ordering of items in order to explain the elements of financial performance due to various activities, which may differ in frequency and predictability.

In the case of Chemclean, the cost of the inventories sold should be presented as cost of goods sold and not split in the manner set out by Chemclean. IFRS 3 *Business Combinations* requires an acquirer to measure the identifiable assets acquired in a business combination at their fair values at the date of acquisition. Therefore, the carrying amount of the inventories originating from the acquisition of the subsidiary is their acquisition-date fair value.

IAS 2 *Inventories* requires the carrying amount of inventories sold to be recognised as an expense in the period in which the related revenue is recognised. Cost of sales are costs previously included in the measurement of inventory which has now been sold plus unallocated production overheads and abnormal amounts of production costs of inventories. Consequently, the entire carrying amount of inventory, including the effects of the fair value step-up, should be presented as cost of sales. Transactions like business combinations may have a significant impact on profit or loss and these transactions are not necessarily frequent or regular. However, the practice of presenting non-recurring items may be interpreted as a way to present 'Extraordinary items' in the financial statements despite the fact that 'extraordinary items' are not allowed under IAS 1. It can also be argued that additional lines and subtotals, as permitted by IAS 1, may add complexity to the analysis of the financial statements, which may become difficult to understand if entities use sub-totals and additional headings to isolate the effects of non-recurring transactions from classes of expense or income.

(c)   **Deferred tax**

(i)   Chemclean should not have fully recognised the deferred tax asset arising from the carry forward of unused tax losses. It is recognisable only to the extent of its taxable temporary differences. IAS 12 *Income Taxes* states that a deferred tax asset shall be recognised for the carry-forward of unused tax losses to the extent that it is probable that future taxable profit will be available against which unused tax losses can be utilised. IAS 12 explains that the existence of unused tax losses is strong evidence that future taxable profit may not be available. Therefore, when an entity has a history of recent losses, the entity recognises a deferred tax asset arising from unused tax losses only to the extent that the entity has sufficient taxable temporary differences or when there is convincing other evidence that sufficient taxable profit will be available against which the unused tax losses can be utilised by the entity.

Chemclean recognised losses during the previous five years. In order to use the deferred tax asset of $16m, Chemclean would have to recognise a profit of $53.3m at the existing tax rate of 30%. In comparison, the entity recognised an average loss of $19m per year during the five previous years. There should be convincing evidence showing that there would be taxable profits available in the future in order to recognise a deferred tax asset. A comparison of the budgeted results to its actual results for the previous two years indicated material differences relating to impairment losses. In the interim financial statements for the first half of the financial year to 30 June 20X4, Chemclean recognised impairment losses equal to budgeted impairment losses for the whole year. The unused tax losses appear to result from identifiable causes, which are likely to recur. IAS 12 states that in assessing the probability that taxable profit will be available against which the unused tax losses or unused tax credits can be utilised, a consideration is whether the unused tax losses result from identifiable causes which are unlikely to recur.

Chemclean's budgets and assumptions are not convincing other evidence because the entity does not appear to have been capable of making accurate forecasts in the past and there were material differences between the amounts budgeted and realised for the previous two years. Chemclean had presented future budgets primarily based on general assumptions about the development of key products and economic improvement indicators, rather than what was expected to influence the future income and therefore enable the use of the deferred tax asset. Finally, in its financial statements, Chemclean disclosed a material uncertainty about its ability to continue as a going concern. This would be a key factor when considering the recognition of a deferred tax asset.

Therefore no deferred tax asset or liability should be recognised. The liability of $3m relating to temporary differences can be offset against $3m of unused tax losses. No further tax losses should be recognised.

49 Ryder

> **Workbook references.** IAS 10 is covered in Chapter 5, IAS 36 in Chapter 3, IAS 33 in Chapter 17. IFRS 2 is covered in Chapter 9, IFRS 3 in Chapter 10 and IFRS 5 in Chapter 13.
>
> **Top tips.** This is a mixed standards question. The four parts of the question are independent of each other so it is a good idea to scan read all parts first and attempt them in the order in which you feel most comfortable. In most cases there is a correct answer rather than an issue to discuss. Therefore, focus your answers on facts and do not waste time with waffle if you do not know the answer.
>
> **Easy marks.** It is possible to pick up easy marks in all parts of this question, particularly in the numerical aspects. Parts (a) and (b) in particular are fairly straightforward.

Marking scheme

		Marks
(a)	Krup subsidiary – adjusting/non-adjusting discussion, calculation of impairment and discussion of IFRS 5 applicability	6
(b)	Metalic IFRS 3 discussion, calculation of consideration and bonus issue	8
(c)	Property – discussion of held for sale classification and adjustments	6
(d)	Cash-settled share based payment – discussion of SAR, calculation of adjustment to liability	5
		25

(a) **Disposal of subsidiary**

The issue here is the value of the subsidiary at 31 October 20X5. The directors have stated that there has been no significant event since the year end which could have resulted in a reduction in its value. This, taken together with the loss on disposal, indicates that the subsidiary had **suffered an impairment at 31 October 20X5**. IAS 10 *Events After the Reporting Period* requires the sale to be treated as an **adjusting event** as it provides **evidence of a condition that existed at the end of the reporting period**.

The assets of Krup should be **written down to their recoverable amount**. In this case, this is the eventual sale proceeds. Therefore, the value of the net assets and purchased goodwill of Krup should be **reduced by $11 million** (the loss on disposal of $9 million plus the loss of $2 million that occurred between 1 November 2005 and the date of sale). IAS 36 *Impairment of Assets* states that an impairment loss should be allocated to goodwill first and therefore the **purchased goodwill of $12 million is reduced to $1 million**. The impairment loss of $11 million is **recognised in profit or loss**.

Because there was no intention to sell the subsidiary at 31 October 20X5, **IFRS 5 *Non-current Assets Held for Sale and Discontinued Operations* does not apply**. The disposal is **disclosed** in the notes to the financial statements in accordance with IAS 10.

(b) **Issue of shares at fair value**

Contingent consideration

IFRS 3 *Business Combinations* **requires recognition of contingent consideration, measured at fair value, at the acquisition date**.

The treatment of **post-acquisition changes** in the fair value of the contingent consideration **depends on the circumstances**.

(i) If the change is due to **additional information** that affects the position at the acquisition date, **goodwill should be remeasured, as a retrospective adjustment**. The additional information must come to light **within the measurement period**, a maximum of one year after acquisition.

(ii) If the change is **due to events which took place after the acquisition date**, for example meeting an earnings target, an **equity instrument is not remeasured**.

Ryder has **correctly included** an estimate of the amount of consideration in the cost of the acquisition on 21 January 20X4. This would have been based on the fair value of the ordinary shares at that date of $10 per share, giving a total of 300,000 × $10 = $3,000,000:

DEBIT Investment $3,000,000
CREDIT Equity $3,000,000

As the consideration is in the form of shares, and the change is due to an event which took place after the acquisition date (the rise in share price), **the consideration is not remeasured.**

The value of the contingent shares should be included in a **separate category of equity** in the statement of financial position at 31 October 20X5. They should be transferred to share capital and share premium after the actual issue of the shares on 12 November 20X5.

Earnings per share

The other matter is whether the share issue and the bonus issue affect the calculation of earnings per share for the year ended 31 October 20X5. IAS 33 *Earnings per Share* states that contingently issuable shares should be included in the calculation of basic earnings per share only from the date that all the necessary conditions for issue are met. As the conditions were met at 31 October 20X5, the shares should be included in the calculation from that date, even though the shares were not issued until after the year end. IAS 33 also states that if there is a bonus share issue after the year end but before the financial statements are authorised for issue, the bonus shares should be included in the basic and diluted earnings per share calculation (and in the calculation of earnings per share for all previous periods presented).

Both IAS 10 and IAS 33 require **disclosure of all material share transactions** or potential share transactions entered into after the reporting period end, excluding the bonus issue. Therefore, **details of the bonus issue and the issue of the contingent shares should be disclosed** in the notes to the financial statements.

(c) **Property**

The property appears to have been **incorrectly classified** as 'held for sale'. Although the company had always intended to sell the property, IFRS 5 *Non-current Assets Held for Sale and Discontinued Operations* states that in order to qualify as 'held for sale' an asset must be **available for immediate sale in its present condition**. Because **repairs were needed** before the property could be sold and these were **not completed until after the reporting period end**, this was clearly **not the case at 31 October 20X5**.

In addition, the property has been **valued incorrectly**. IFRS 5 requires assets held for sale to be valued at **the lower of their carrying amount or fair value less costs to sell**. The property **should have been valued at its carrying amount of $20 million**, not at the eventual net sale proceeds of $27 million.

The property **must be included within property, plant and equipment** and must be **depreciated**. Therefore, its **carrying amount at 31 October 20X5 is $19 million** ($20 million less depreciation of $1 million). The **gain of $7 million** that the company has previously recognised **should be reversed**.

Although the property cannot be classified as 'held for sale' in the financial statements for the year ended 31 October 2005, it **will qualify for the classification after the end of the reporting period**. Therefore, details of the sale should be **disclosed** in the notes to the financial statements in accordance with IAS 10.

(d) **Share appreciation rights**

The granting of share appreciation rights is a **cash-settled share based payment transaction** as defined by IFRS 2 *Share-based Payment*. IFRS 2 requires these to be **measured at the fair value of the liability** to pay cash. The liability should be **remeasured at each reporting date and at the date of settlement**. Any **changes in fair value** should be **recognised in profit or loss** for the period.

However, the company has **not remeasured the liability since 31 October 20X4**. Because IFRS 2 requires the expense and the related liability to be recognised over the two-year vesting period, as the employees render service, the rights should be measured as follows:

	$m
At 31 October 20X4: ($6 × 10 million × ½)	30
At 31 October 20X5 ($8 × 10 million)	80
At 1 December 20X5 (settlement date) ($9 × 10 million)	90

Therefore, at 31 October 20X5 the liability **should be remeasured to $80 million** and an **expense of $50 million** should be recognised in profit or loss for the year.

The additional expense of $10 million resulting from the remeasurement at the settlement date is not included in the financial statements for the year ended 31 October 20X5, but is recognised the following year.

50 Royan

Marking scheme

		Marks
(a)	Existing guidance and critique	12
(b)	IAS 37 treatment	3
(c)	Ethics	5
		20

(a)   **Guidance in IAS 37**

Under IAS 37 *Provisions, Contingent Liabilities and Contingent Assets,* provisions must be recognised in the following circumstances.

(i)   There is a **legal** or **constructive obligation** to transfer benefits as a result of past events.

(ii)   It is **probable** that **an outflow of economic resources** will be required to **settle the obligation**.

(iii)   The obligation can be **measured reliably**.

IAS 37 considers an outflow to be probable if the event is **more likely than not** to occur.

If the company can **avoid expenditure by its future action, no provision** should be recognised. A legal or constructive obligation is one created by an **obligating event**. Constructive obligations arise when an entity is committed to certain expenditures because of a pattern of behaviour which the public would expect to continue.

IAS 37 states that the amount recognised should be the **best estimate of the expenditure required to settle the obligation at the end of the reporting period**. The estimate should **take the various possible outcomes into account** and should be the **amount that an entity would rationally pay** to settle the obligation at the reporting date or to transfer it to a third party. Where there is **a large population of items,** for example in the case of warranties, the provision will be made at **a probability weighted expected value,** taking into account the risks and uncertainties surrounding the underlying events. Where there is a **single obligation, the individual most likely outcome** may be the best estimate of the liability.

The amount of the provision should be **discounted to present value** if the time value of money is material using a **risk adjusted rate**. If some or all of the expenditure is expected to be **reimbursed** by a third party, the reimbursement should be **recognised as a separate asset,** but only if it is virtually certain that the reimbursement will be received.

Shortcomings of IAS 37

IAS 37 is generally consistent with the *Conceptual Framework*. However there are some issues with IAS 37 that have led to it being criticised:

(i) IAS 37 requires recognition of a liability only if it is **probable,** that is more than 50% likely, that the obligation will result in an outflow of resources from the entity. This is **inconsistent with other standards,** for example IFRS 3 *Business Combinations* and IFRS 9 *Financial Instruments* which do not apply the probability criterion to liabilities. In addition, probability is not part of the *Conceptual Framework* definition of a liability. The definition of a liability is expected to change when the revised version of the *Conceptual Framework* is issued in 2018 and this is likely to have implications for IAS 37.

(ii) There is **inconsistency with US GAAP** as regards how they treat the **cost of restructuring** a business. US GAAP requires entities to recognise a liability for individual costs of restructuring only when the entity has incurred that particular cost, while IAS 37 requires recognition of the total costs of restructuring when the entity announces or starts to implement a restructuring plan.

(ii) The **measurement rules** in IAS 37 are **vague and unclear**. In particular, 'best estimate' could mean a number of things: the most likely outcome, the weighted average of all possible outcomes or even the minimum/maximum amount in a range of possible outcomes. IAS 37 does not clarify which costs need to be included in the measurement of a liability, and in practice different entities include different costs. It is also unclear if 'settle' means 'cancel', 'transfer' or 'fulfil' the obligation. IAS 37 also requires provisions to be discounted to present value but gives no guidance on non-performance risk that is the entity's own credit risk. Non-performance risk can have a lead to a significant reduction in non-current liabilities.

(b) **Treatment under IAS 37**

The IAS 37 criteria for recognising a **provision** have been met as there is a present obligation to dismantle the oil platform, of which the present value has been measured at **$105m**. Because Royan cannot operate the oil without incurring an obligation to pay dismantling costs at the end of ten years, the expenditure also enables it to acquire **economic benefits** (income from the oil extracted). Therefore, Royan should **recognise an asset of $105m** (added to the 'oil platform' in property, plant and equipment) and this should be **depreciated** over the life of the oil platform, which is ten years. In addition, there will be an adjustment charged in profit or loss each year to the present value of the obligation for the **unwinding of the discount.**

(c) **Non-compliance with IAS 37**

The treatment proposed by the directors is non-compliant with IAS 37. It could be due to genuine error and a misunderstanding due to a lack of knowledge, with the directors really believing that the standard is not mandatory. There does not appear to be any motivation to maximise profit to benefit the directors in any way; for example, to increase bonuses or profit related pay, though this could be a consideration. However, in this instance it feels like a deliberate intention to contravene IAS 37 and include a misstatement in the financial statements, rather than a genuine mistake. The directors cannot justify their decision not to apply IAS 37.

If the situation is allowed to continue, one of ACCA's *Code of Ethics and Conduct* fundamental principles will be breached: that of professional behaviour. Members should comply with relevant laws and regulations and should avoid any action that discredits the profession. In knowingly allowing the directors not to apply the requirements of an accounting standard, the accountant would not be acting diligently and in accordance with applicable guidance and would not be demonstrating professional competence and due care.

Despite the potential conflict and likely strong or undue influence from the directors over a sole and more junior employee, the accountant must act with integrity and remain unbiased, recommending to the directors that IAS 37, as it is in issue, must be complied with, and processing the appropriate entries in the financial statements for the year ended 31 July 20X6. A possible approach to achieve resolution may be to discuss the matter with the chairman or a non-executive director, setting out the problem and explaining that the directors have a responsibility to ensure the financial statements are fair and accurate and comply with relevant accounting standards.

51 Electron

> **Workbook references.** Environmental provisions are covered in Chapter 5; leases are in Chapter 8 and share-based payments are in Chapter 9.
>
> **Top tips.** This is a multi-standard question on environmental provisions, leases, proposed dividend and a share option scheme.
>
> **Easy marks.** The proposed dividend is straightforward, as is the explanation (if not the calculations) for the provision. The treatment of share options provides 4 easy marks for nothing much in the way of complications.

Marking scheme

	Marks
Oil contracts	4
Power station	8
Operating leases	6
Proposed dividend	3
Share options	4
	25

REPORT

To: The Directors, Electron   Date: July 20X6
From: Accountant

Accounting treatment of transactions

Oil trading contracts

The first point to note is that the contracts always result in the delivery of the commodity. They are therefore correctly treated as normal sale and purchase contracts, **not financial instruments**.

The adoption of a policy of **deferring recognising revenue and costs is appropriate** in general terms because of the duration of the contracts. Over the life of the contracts, costs and revenues are equally matched. However, there is a mismatch between costs and revenues in the early stages of the contracts.

IFRS 15 *Revenue from Contracts with Customers* should be applied. IFRS 15 has a **five-step process for** recognising revenue, of which Step 5 states: 'Recognise revenue when (or as) a performance obligation is satisfied' (IFRS 15: para. 31). Step 5 would treat this as a **performance obligation satisfied over time** because the oil is delivered over a contract period and therefore control is transferred over time. Revenue should therefore be recognised over the duration of the contract, consistent with the pattern of delivery of oil to the customer.

Power station

IAS 37 *Provisions, Contingent Liabilities and Contingent Assets* states that a provision should be recognised if:

- There is a present obligation as a result of a past transaction or event and

- It is probable that an outflow of resources embodying economic benefits will be required to settle the obligation

- A reliable estimate can be made of the amount of the obligation

In this case, the obligating event is the **installation of the power station**. The **operating licence** has created a **legal obligation** to incur the cost of removal, the expenditure is **probable,** and a **reasonable estimate** of the amount can be made.

Because Electron cannot operate its power station without incurring an obligation to pay for removal, **the expenditure also enables it to acquire economic benefits** (income from the energy generated). Therefore, Electron correctly **recognises an asset** as well as a provision, and **depreciates this asset over its useful life of 20 years**.

Electron should recognise a provision for the cost of removing the power station, but should not include the cost of rectifying the damage caused by the generation of electricity until the power is generated. In this case the cost of rectifying the damage would be 5% of the total discounted provision.

The accounting treatment is as follows:

STATEMENT OF FINANCIAL POSITION AT 30 JUNE 20X6 (EXTRACTS)

	$m
Property, plant and equipment	
Power station	100.0
Decommissioning costs (W)	13.6
	113.6
Depreciation (113.6 ÷ 20)	(5.7)
	107.9
Provisions	
Provision for decommissioning at 1 July 20X5	13.6
Plus unwinding of discount (13.6 × 5%)	0.7
	14.3
Provision for damage (0.7 (W) ÷ 20)	0.1
	14.4

STATEMENT OF PROFIT OR LOSS AND OTHER COMPREHENSIVE INCOME
FOR THE YEAR ENDED 30 JUNE 20X6 (EXTRACTS)

	$m
Depreciation	5.7
Provision for damage	0.1
Unwinding of discount (finance cost)	0.7

Working

	$m
Provision for removal costs at 1 July 20X5 (95% × (15 ÷ 1.05))	13.6
Provision for damage caused by extraction at 30 June 20X6 (5% (15 ÷ 1.05))	0.7

Operating lease

One issue here is the **substance** of the lease agreement. In the case of lessors (but not lessees), IFRS 16 *Leases* classifies leases as either finance leases or operating leases. A finance lease **transfers substantially all the risks and rewards of ownership to the lessee**, while an operating lease does not. The company **retains legal ownership of the equipment** and also **retains the benefits of ownership** (the equipment remains available for use in its operating activities). In addition, the **present value of the lease payments is only 57.1% of the fair value of the leased assets** ($40m/$70m). For a lease to be a finance lease, the present value of the lease payments should be **substantially all** the fair value of the leased assets. Therefore, the lease **appears to be correctly classified as an operating lease**.

A further issue is the **treatment of the fee received**. The company has recognised the whole of the net present value of the future income from the lease in profit or loss for the year to 30 June 20X6, despite the fact that only a deposit of $10 million has been received. In addition, the date of inception of the lease is 30 June 20X6, so **the term of the lease does not actually fall within the current period.** IFRS 16 para. 81 states that **income from operating leases should be recognised on a straight-line basis over the lease term** unless another basis is more appropriate. IFRS 15 *Revenue from Contracts with Customers* applies here. It does not allow revenue to be recognised **before an entity has satisfied its performance obligations under the contract** and therefore **no revenue should be recognised** in relation to the operating leases for the current period.

Proposed dividend

The dividend was **proposed after the end of the reporting period** and therefore IAS 10 *Events After the Reporting Period* applies. This **prohibits the recognition of proposed dividends** unless these are declared before the end of the reporting period. The directors **did not have an obligation** to pay the dividend **at 31 October 20X5** and therefore there **cannot be a liability**. The directors seem to be arguing that their past record creates a constructive obligation as defined by IAS 37 *Provisions, Contingent Liabilities and Contingent Assets*. A constructive obligation may exist as a result of the proposal of the dividend, but this had **not arisen at the end of the reporting period**.

Although the proposed dividend is not recognised it was **approved before the financial statements were authorised for issue** and should be **disclosed** in the notes to the financial statements.

Share options

The share options granted on 1 July 20X5 are **equity-settled transactions**, and are governed by IFRS 2 *Share-based Payment*. The aim of this standard is to recognise the cost of share based payment to employees over the period in which the services are rendered. The options are generally **charged to profit or loss** on the basis of their **fair value at the grant date**. If the equity instruments are traded on an active market, market prices must be used. Otherwise an option pricing model would be used.

The conditions attached to the shares state that the share options will vest in three years' time provided that the employees remain in employment with the company. Often there are other conditions such as growth in share price, but here **employment is the only condition**.

The **treatment** is as follows:

- Determine the fair value of the options at grant date.

- Charge this fair value to profit or loss equally over the three-year vesting period, making adjustments at each accounting date to reflect the best estimate of the number of options that will eventually vest. This will depend on the estimated percentage of employees leaving during the vesting period.

For the year ended 30 June 20X6, the charge to profit or loss is $3m × 94% × 1/3 = $940,000. Shareholders' equity will be increased by an amount equal to this profit or loss charge.

52 William

Marking scheme

		Marks
(a)	Leaseback principle	3
	Accounting	3
	Presentation	2
(b)	Provision for relocation costs	4
	Curtailment (past service cost) of defined benefit pension plan	4
(c)	Cash-settled share-based payments	2
	Calculation	3
(d)	Contingent liability – discussion	4
		25

(a) **Sale and leaseback**

The **form** of this transaction is a **sale and leaseback.** IFRS 16 *Leases* requires an initial assessment to be made regarding whether or not the transfer constitutes a sale. This is done by determining when the performance obligation is satisfied in accordance with IFRS 15 *Revenue from Contracts with Customers* (IFRS 16: para.98). In this case, we are told in the question that the IFRS 15 criteria have been met. IFRS 16 therefore requires that, at the start of the lease, William should measure the right-of-use asset arising from the leaseback of the building at the proportion of the previous carrying amount of the building that relates to the right-of-use retained. This is calculated as carrying amount × discounted lease payments/fair value. The discounted lease payments were given in the question as $5m, which is the lease liability.

For William, the right of use asset is therefore: $3.6m × $5m/$6m = $3m.

William only recognises the amount of gain that relates to the rights transferred. The gain on sale of the building is $2,400,000 ($6,000,000 – $3,600,000), of which:

$(2,400,000 × 5,000,000/6,000,000) = $2,000,000 relates to the rights retained.

The balance, $(2,400,000 – 2,000,000) = $400,000, relates to the rights transferred to the buyer.

At 1 June 20X2, the William should account for the transaction as follows:

	Debit	Credit
	$	$
Cash	6,000,000	
Right-of-use asset	3,000,000	
Building		3,600,000
Financial liability		5,000,000
Gain on rights transferred		400,000
	9,000,000	9,000,000

The right-of-use asset will be depreciated over 20 years, which is the shorter of the lease term and the remaining useful life, $3m ÷ 20 years = $0.15m:

DEBIT Depreciation expense $0.15m
CREDIT Accumulated depreciation $0.15m

The financial liability will be increased each year by the interest charge and reduced by the lease payments.

The finance cost on the lease liability is charged at the implicit rate of 7% to profit or loss for the year ended 31 May 20X3. The amount is calculated as follows:

Lease liability

	$m
1 June 20X2 b/f	5.000
Finance cost: 5m × 7%	0.350
Instalment	(0.441)
31 May 20X3 c/f	4.909
Finance cost: 4.909m × 7%	0.344
Instalment	(0.441)
31 May 20X4 c/f	4.812

The lease liability at 31 May 20X3 is split between current and non-current:

	$m
Non-current liability (owed at 31 May 20X4)	4.812
Current liability (bal. fig.) = instalment (0.441) less finance cost (0.344)	0.097
Total liability at 31 May 20X3	4.909

(b) **Relocation costs and reduction to net pension liability**

A **provision for restructuring** should be recognised in respect of the relocation of the provision during the year ended 31 May 20X3 in accordance with IAS 37 *Provisions, Contingent Liabilities and Contingent Assets*. This is because William's board of directors authorised a **detailed formal plan** for the relocation shortly before the year end (13 May 20X3) and William has **raised a valid expectation in affected employees** that it will carry out the restructuring by informing them of the main features of the plan. As the relocation is due to take within two months of the year end (July 20X3), the time value of money is likely to be immaterial. Therefore, no discounting is required and a provision should be recognised at the estimated relocation costs of $50 million.

The reduction in the net pension liability as a result of the employees being made redundant and no longer accruing pension benefits is a **curtailment** under IAS 19 *Employee Benefits*. IAS 19 defines a curtailment as occurring when an entity significantly reduces the number of employees covered by a plan. It is **treated as a type of past service costs**. The past service cost may be negative (as is the case here) when the benefits are withdrawn so that the present value of the defined benefit obligation decreases. IAS 19 requires the past service cost to be **recognised in profit or loss** at the earlier of:

- When the plan curtailment occurs; and
- When the entity recognises the related restructuring costs.

Here the restructuring costs (and corresponding provision) are recognised in the year ended 31 May 20X3 and the plan curtailment will not take place until after the year end in July 20X3 when the employees are made redundant. Therefore, the **r**eduction in the net pension liability and corresponding income in profit or loss should be recognised at the earlier of these two dates, ie when the restructuring costs are recognised in the year ended 31 May 20X3.

Both the relocation costs and income from the reduction in the net pension liability are likely to require **separate disclosure** in the statement of profit or loss and other comprehensive income or in the notes to the accounts per IAS 1 *Presentation of Financial Statements* due to their materiality.

(c)   **Share-based payment**

Share appreciation rights are **cash-settled share-based-payments**. IFRS 2 *Share-based Payment* requires that the entity should measure the goods or services acquired and the liability incurred at the **fair value of the liability**. The fair value of the liability should be **measured at each reporting date** until the liability is settled and at the date of settlement. Any **changes** in fair value are recognised in profit or loss for the period.

	$
1 June 20X2 liability b/f: (20 – 3 (managers)) × 500 SARS × $14 (fair value) × 2/2 (vested)	119,000
Cash paid on exercise: 7 managers × 500 SARS × $21 (intrinsic value)	(73,500)
Expense (balancing figure)	74,500
31 May 20X3 liability c/f: (20 – 3 – 7 (managers)) × 500 SARS × $24 (fair value)	120,000

The expense for the year is accounted for as follows:

DEBIT	Expense	(P/L)	$74,500	
CREDIT	Cash			$73,500
CREDIT	Liability			$1,000

(d)   **Contingent liability**

The legal claim against Chrissy will be treated differently in Chrissy's individual financial statements as compared with the consolidated accounts of the William group.

Chrissy's individual financial statements

The legal claim against Chrissy **does not meet the definition of a provision** under IAS 37 *Provisions, Contingent Liabilities and Contingent Assets*. One of IAS 37's requirements for a provision is that an outflow of resources embodying economic benefits should be probable, and William believes that it is more likely than not that such an **outflow will not occur**.

However, the possible payment does fall within the IAS 37 definition of a **contingent liability,** which is:

- A possible obligation depending on whether some uncertain future event occurs, or

- A present obligation but payment is not probable or the amount cannot be measured reliably.

Therefore, as **a contingent liability** the details of the claim and the $4 million estimated fair value of the contingent liability would be **disclosed** in the notes to the financial statements.

Consolidated financial statements

Under IFRS 3 *Business Combinations*, an acquirer must allocate the cost of a business combination by recognising the acquiree's identifiable assets, liabilities and contingent

liabilities that satisfy the recognition criteria at their **fair values** at the date of the acquisition. Contingent liabilities where there is only a possible obligation which, under IAS 37, depend on the occurrence or non-occurrence of some uncertain future event are not recognised under IFRS 3. However, the **IAS 37 probability criterion does not apply under IFRS 3**: a contingent liability is recognised **whether or not it is probable that an outflow** of economic benefits will take place, where there is a present obligation and its fair value can be measured reliably.

Consequently, William should **recognise the contingent liability as part of the business combination at its fair value** of $4 million. This will reduce net assets at acquisition, and therefore increase goodwill.

53 Leigh

Workbook reference. Share-based payments are covered in Chapter 9. Associates are covered in Chapter 10.

Top tips. This was a difficult question which dealt with several share-based payment transactions. However, not all such transactions were dealt with by a single accounting standard. Part (a) dealt with the cost of a business combination and the issue of shares as purchase consideration. It also dealt with shares given to employees as remuneration. The events are dealt with under the separate accounting standards IFRS 2 and IFRS 3. Part (b) dealt with the purchase of property, plant and equipment, and the grant of rights to a director when there is a choice of settlement. This part of the question was quite technically demanding. Part (c) dealt with the issue of shares to acquire an associate and the subsequent accounting for the associate.

Easy marks. It is difficult to identify easy marks for this question.

Marking scheme

		Marks
(a)	Hash	7
	Employees	3
(b)	Property, plant and equipment	5
	Director	4
(c)	Handy	6
		25

(a) **Shares issued to the directors**

The 3 million $1 shares issued to the directors **on 1 June 20X6** as part of the **purchase consideration** for Hash are accounted for under **IFRS 3** *Business Combinations* rather than under IFRS 2 *Share-based Payment*. This is because they are not remuneration or compensation, but simply part of the purchase price of the company. The cost of the business combination will be the total of the fair values of the consideration given by Leigh plus any attributable costs. The total fair value here is $6m, of which $3m is share capital and $3m is share premium.

The **contingent consideration** – 5,000 shares per director to be received on 31 May 20X7 if the directors are still employed by Leigh – may, however, be seen as compensation and thus fall to be treated under IFRS 2. The fact that the additional payment of shares is **linked to continuing employment** suggests that it is a compensation arrangement, and therefore **IFRS 2 will apply**.

Under IFRS 2, the fair value used is that at the **grant date,** rather than when the shares vest. The market value of each share at that date is $2. (Three million shares are valued at $6m.) So the total value of the compensation is 5 × 5,000 × $2 = **$50,000.**

The $50,000 is charged to profit or loss with a corresponding increase in equity.

Shares issued to employees

These shares are remuneration and are **accounted for under IFRS 2**.

The fair value used is that at the **date of issue,** as the grant date and issue date are the same, **that is, $3 per share**. Because the shares are given as a bonus they vest immediately and are presumed to be consideration for past services.

The total of $3m would be changed to profit or loss and included in equity.

(b) **Purchase of property, plant and equipment**

Under IFRS 2, the purchase of property, plant and equipment would be treated as a share-based payment in which the counterparty has a **choice of settlement**, in shares or in cash. Such transactions are **treated as cash-settled** to the extent that the entity has incurred a **liability**. It is treated as the issue of a compound financial instrument, with a debt and an equity element.

Similar to IAS 32 *Financial Instruments: Presentation*, IFRS 2 requires the **determination of the liability element and the equity element**. The fair value of the equity element is the fair value of the goods or services (in this case the property) less the fair value of the debt element of the instrument. The fair value of the property is $4m (per question). The share price of $3.50 is the expected share price in three months' time (assuming cash settlement). The fair value of the liability component at 31 May 20X7 is its present value: 1.3 million × $3 = $3.9m.

The journal entries are:

DEBIT	Property, plant and equipment	$4m	
CREDIT	Liability		$3.9m
CREDIT	Equity		$0.1m

In three months' time, the debt component is remeasured to its fair value. Assuming the estimate of the future share price was correct at $3.50, the liability at that date will be 1.3 million × $3.5 = $4.55m. An adjustment must be made as follows:

DEBIT	Expense (4.55 – 3.9)	$0.65m	
CREDIT	Liability		$0.65m

Choice of share or cash settlement

The share-based payment to the new director, which offers a choice of cash or share settlement, is also treated as the issue of a compound instrument. In this case, the **fair value of the services is determined by the fair value of the equity instruments given**. The fair value of the equity alternative is $2.50 × 50,000 = $125,000. The cash alternative is valued at 40,000 × $3 = $120,000. The **difference** between these two values – $5,000 – is deemed to be the **fair value of the equity component**. At the settlement date, the liability element would be measured at fair value and the method of settlement chosen by the director would determine the final accounting treatment.

At 31 May 20X7, the accounting entries would be:

DEBIT	Profit or loss – directors' remuneration	$125,000	
CREDIT	Liability		$120,000
CREDIT	Equity		$5,000

In effect, the director surrenders the right to $120,000 cash in order to obtain equity worth $125,000.

(c) **Investment in Hardy**

The investment in Hardy should be treated as an **associate under** IAS 28 *Investments in Associates and Joint Ventures*. Between 20% and 50% of the share capital has been acquired, and significant influence may be exercised through the right to appoint directors. Associates are accounted for as cost plus post acquisition change in net assets, **generally cost plus share of post-acquisition retained earnings**. The cost is the fair value of the shares in Leigh exchanged for the shares of Handy. However, negative goodwill arises because the fair value of the net assets of Hardy exceeds this. The negative goodwill must be added back to determine the cost to be used for the carrying amount, and, following a reassessment, credited to profit or loss. (Dr Cost 0.2, Cr P/L 0.2)

	$m
Cost: 1m × $2.50	2.5
Add back negative goodwill: (2.5 + (9 × 70% 'NCI') – 9)	0.2
	2.7
Post-acquisition profits: (5 – 4) × 30%	0.3
Carrying amount at 31 May 20X7	3.0

Note. The 0.2 is not part of post-acquisition retained earnings. It is adjustment to the original cost to remove the negative goodwill.

Because negative goodwill has arisen, the investment must be **impairment tested**. A comparison must be made with the estimated recoverable amount of Hardy's net assets. The investment must not be carried above the recoverable amount:

Recoverable amount at 31 May 20X7: $11m × 30% = $3.3m

The recoverable amount is above the carrying amount, so the investment at 31 May 20X7 will be shown at $3m.

54 Fair values and IFRS 13

Workbook references. Fair value is covered in Chapter 3.

Top tips. IFRS 13 was issued a few years ago, but is still very topical. In the exam, you are likely to be given a scenario and asked to apply the standard, it is not enough to just state what it says.

Easy marks. Part (a) is fairly open ended, and credit will be given for valid points if you back up your arguments.

			Marks
(a)		Fair value v historical cost: 1 mark per valid point	12
(b)	(i)	Highest and best use – discussion	6
	(ii)	Fair value and risk profile – discussion	3
	(iii)	Legally restricted financial asset – discussion	4
			25

(a) **Fair value measurement or historical cost**

The debate between historical cost accounting and fair value measurement centres on **reliability versus relevance**. Very broadly speaking, fair values are perceived as relevant but not reliable. Historical cost accounting is perceived as reliable but not relevant.

Fair value can be said to be more relevant than historical cost because it is based on current market values rather than a value that is in some cases many years out of date. Fair values for an entity's assets, it is argued, will be a closer approximation to the value of the entity as a whole, and are more useful to a decision maker or an investor.

If there is **more standardisation in fair valuing** – IFRS 13 *Fair Value Measurement* is a step towards this – then in the future, if not immediately, fair value measurement will have the advantage of being both relevant and reliable.

Historical cost accounting traditionally matches cost and revenue. The objective has been to match the cost of the asset with the revenue it earns over its useful life. It has a number of **disadvantages**.

(i) If the historical cost differs from its fair value on initial recognition, the **matching process in future periods becomes arbitrary**.

(ii) Non-current asset **values are unrealistic**, particularly those of property.

(iii) **Holding gains on inventory are included in profit.** During a period of high inflation the **monetary value of inventories held may increase significantly** while they are being processed. The conventions of historical cost accounting lead to the **realised part of this holding gain** (known as 'inventory appreciation') being **included** in **profit** for the year.

(iv) **Comparisons over time are unrealistic**, because they do not take account of inflation.

(v) **Costs incurred before an asset is recognised are not capitalised.** This is particularly true of development expenditure, and means that the historical cost does not represent the fair value of the consideration given to create the asset.

However, historical cost has a number of **advantages** over fair values, mainly as regards reliability.

(i) It is **easy to understand**.

(ii) It is grounded in **real transaction amounts**, and is therefore **objective** and objectively verifiable.

(iii) There is **less scope for manipulation**.

Until there is **more uniformity and objectivity in fair valuing**, it is likely that historical cost accounting will continue to be used.

(b) (i) The **highest and best use** of the project is determined on the basis of use of the project by market participants, which may be one of the following.

(1) **Continuing with the development**

In this case, market participants continue to develop the project and that use maximises the value of the group of assets or of assets and liabilities in which the project would be used (ie the asset would be used in combination with other assets or with other assets and liabilities).

The fair value of the project would then be measured on the basis of the price that would be received in a current transaction to sell the project, assuming that the R&D would be used with its complementary assets and the associated

liabilities and that those assets and liabilities would be available to market participants.

(2) **Ceasing development for competitive reasons**

In this case, market participants lock up the project and that use maximises the value of the group of assets or of assets and liabilities in which the project would be used.

The fair value of the project would then be measured on the basis of the price that would be received in a current transaction to sell the project, assuming that the R&D would be used (ie locked up) with its complementary assets and the associated liabilities and that those assets and liabilities would be available to market participants.

(3) **Ceasing development**

Market participants discontinue development because the project is not expected to provide the required rate of return and would not provide defensive value through being locked up.

The fair value of the project would be measured on the basis of the price that would be received in a current transaction to sell the project on its own (which might be zero).

Although Fairview intends to cease the R&D project for competitive advantage, it is not necessarily the basis on which it should measure its fair value.

(ii) **Credit ratings**

The fair value of Fairview's promise is approximately $152,000. This is the present value of $200,000 in 7 years at 4% ($200,000 × 1/1.04⁷).

The fair value of Westway's promise is approximately $116,600. This is the present value of $200,000 in 7 years at 8% ($200,000 × 1/1.08⁷).

These two values are different, even though the amount and period are the same, due to the different risk profiles of the two companies.

(iii) **Investment in Greenfield**

IFRS 13 *Illustrative Examples* mentions the case of a financial asset for which sale is legally or contractually restricted for a specified period. The restriction is a characteristic of the instrument and, therefore, would be transferred to market participants. In this case the fair value of the instrument would be measured on the basis of the quoted price for an otherwise identical unrestricted equity instrument of the same issuer that trades in a public market, adjusted to reflect the effect of the restriction. The adjustment would reflect the amount market participants would demand because of the risk relating to the inability to access a public market for the instrument for the specified period. The adjustment will vary depending on:

(1) The nature and duration of the restriction

(2) The extent to which buyers are limited by the restriction (eg there might be a large number of qualifying investors)

(3) Qualitative and quantitative factors specific to both the instrument and the issuer

55 Mehran

Workbook references. IFRS 13 is covered in Chapter 3. IFRS 9 is covered in Chapter 7.

Top tips. Most of this question is on IFRS 13 *Fair Value Measurement*. As well as the fair value hierarchy, it is important to be familiar the principles behind the standard, particularly the 'highest and best use' principle, and that of the 'principal and most advantageous market'. You are expected to understand the nature of the valuation hierarchy and not just quote the requirements. Although financial instruments can be tricky, you can use a similar thought process to more common items; for examples, if a fair valuation were to be placed on a motor car, the market prices for a similar car would be used and adjusted if the mileage on the car was significantly different. The same principle applies to shares.

Easy marks. Working out the most advantageous market is quite straightforward. The numbers are given to you for a reason!

Marking scheme

		Marks
(a)	1 mark per point up to maximum	7
(b)	1 mark per point up to maximum	10
(c)	1 mark per point up to maximum	8
Maximum		25

(a) **Land and brand name**

IFRS 13 *Fair Value Measurement* requires the fair value of a non-financial asset to be measured based on its highest and best use from a market participant's perspective. This requirement does not apply to financial instruments, liabilities or equity. The highest and best use takes into account the use of the asset which is physically possible, legally permissible and financially feasible. The highest and best use of a non-financial asset is determined by reference to its use and not its classification and is determined from the perspective of market participants. It does not matter whether the entity intends to use the asset differently. IFRS 13 allows management to presume that the current use of an asset is the highest and best use unless market or other factors suggest otherwise.

In this case, the agricultural land appears to have an alternative use as market participants have considered its use for residential purposes. If the land zoned for agricultural use is currently used for farming, the fair value should reflect the cost structure to continue operating the land for farming, including any tax credits which could be realised by market participants. Thus, the fair value of the land if used for farming would be $(5 + (20% of 0.5)) million, ie $5.1 million.

If used for residential purposes, the value should include all costs associated with changing the land to the market participant's intended use. In addition, demolition and other costs associated with preparing the land for a different use should be included in the valuation. These costs would include the uncertainty related to whether the approval needed for changing the usage would be obtained, because market participants would take that into account when pricing value of the land if it had a different use. Thus, the fair value of the land if used for residential purposes would be $(7.4 − 0.2 − 0.3 − 0.1) million × 80%, ie $5.44m. Therefore the value of the land would be $5.44m on the highest and best use basis. In this situation, the presumption that the current use is the highest and best use of the land has been overridden by the market factors which indicate that residential development is the highest and

best use. A use of an asset need not be legal at the measurement date, but it must not be legally prohibited in the jurisdiction.

In the absence of any evidence to the contrary, Mehran should value the brand on the basis of the highest and best use. The fair value is determined from the perspective of a market participant and is not influenced by the Mehran's decision to discontinue the brand. Therefore the fair value of the brand is $17m.

(b) **Fair value of inventory**

IFRS 13 sets out the concepts of principal market and most advantageous market. Transactions take place in either the principal market, which is the market with the greatest volume and level of activity for the inventory, or in the absence of a principal market, the most advantageous market. The most advantageous market is the market which maximises the amount which would be received to sell the inventory, after taking into account transaction costs and transportation costs. The price used to measure the inventory's fair value is not adjusted for transaction costs although it is adjusted for transport costs. The principal market is not necessarily the market with the greatest volume of activity for the particular reporting entity. The principle is based upon the importance of the market from the participant's perspective. However, the principal market is presumed to be the market in which the reporting entity transacts, unless there is evidence to the contrary. In evaluating the principal or most advantageous markets, IFRS 13 restricts the eligible markets to only those which can be accessed at the measurement date. If there is a principal market for the asset or liability, IFRS 13 states that fair value should be based on the price in that market, even if the price in a different market is higher. It is only in the absence of the principal market that the most advantageous market should be used. An entity does not have to undertake an exhaustive search of all possible markets in order to identify the principal or most advantageous market. It should take into account all information which is readily available.

There is a presumption in the standard that the market in which the entity normally transacts to sell the asset or transfer the liability is the principal or most advantageous market unless there is evidence to the contrary.

In this case, the greatest volume of transactions is conducted in the domestic market – direct to manufacturers. There is no problem with obtaining data from trade journals but the problem for Mehran is that there is no data to substantiate the volume of activity in the domestic market – direct to retailers even though Mehran feels that it is at least 20,000 tonnes per annum. The most advantageous market is the export market where after transport and transaction costs the price per tonne is $1,094.

	Domestic market – direct to retailers	Domestic market – direct to manufacturers	Export market
	$	$	$
Price per tonne	1,000	800	1,200
Transport costs per tonne	50	70	100
Selling agents' fees per tonne	–	4	6
Net price per tonne	950	726	1,094

It is difficult to determine a principal market because of the lack of information. It could be argued that the domestic market – direct to manufacturers has the highest volume for the produce, and is therefore the principal market by which Mehran should determine fair value of $730 ($800 – $70). However, because of the lack of information surrounding the domestic market – direct to retailers, the principal or most advantageous market will be presumed to be the market in which Mehran would normally enter into transactions which would be the export market. Therefore the fair value would be $1,100 ($1,200 – $100) per tonne.

(c)   **Investment in Erham**

Measuring the fair value of individual unquoted equity instruments which constitute a non-controlling interest in a private company falls within the scope of IFRS 9 *Financial Instruments* in accordance with the principles set out in IFRS 13. There is a range of commonly used valuation techniques for measuring the fair value of unquoted equity instruments and income approaches as well as the adjusted net asset method are acceptable. IFRS 13 states that fair value is a market-based measurement, although it acknowledges that in some cases observable market transactions or other market information might not be available. IFRS 13 does not contain a hierarchy of valuation techniques nor does it prescribe the use of a specific valuation technique for meeting the objective of a fair value measurement. However, IFRS 13 acknowledges that, given specific circumstances, one valuation technique might be more appropriate than another. The market approach takes a transaction price paid for an identical or a similar instrument in an investee and adjusts the resultant valuation. The transaction price paid recently for an investment in an equity instrument in an investee which is similar, but not identical, to an investor's unquoted equity instrument in the same investee would be a reasonable starting point for estimating the fair value of the unquoted equity instrument.

Mehran would take the transaction price for the preferred shares and adjust it to reflect certain differences between the preferred shares and the ordinary shares. There would be an adjustment to reflect the priority of the preferred shares upon liquidation.

Mehran should acknowledge the benefit associated with control. This adjustment relates to the fact that Mehran's individual ordinary shares represent a non-controlling interest whereas the preferred shares issued reflect a controlling interest. There will be an adjustment for the lack of liquidity of the investment which reflects the lesser ability of the ordinary shareholder to initiate a sale of Erham relative to the preferred shareholder. Further, there will be an adjustment for the cumulative dividend entitlement of the preferred shares. This would be calculated as the present value of the expected future dividend receipts on the preferred shares, less the present value of any expected dividend receipts on the ordinary shares. The discount rate used should be consistent with the uncertainties associated with the relevant dividend streams.

Mehran should review the circumstances of the issue of the preferred shares to ensure that its price was a valid benchmark. Mehran must, however, use all information about the performance and operations of Erham which becomes reasonably available to it after the date of initial recognition of the ordinary shares up to the measurement date. Such information can have an effect on the fair value of the unquoted equity instrument at 31 March 20X6. In addition, Mehran should consider the existence of factors such as whether the environment in which Erham operates is dynamic, or whether there have been changes in market conditions between the issue of the preferred shares and the measurement date.

56 Yanong

> **Workbook references.** Agriculture is covered in Chapter 3. Fair value measurement is covered in Chapter 3. Share-based payment is covered in Chapter 9.
>
> **Top tips.** Part (a) required an understanding of the market definitions given in IFRS 13. You are expected to be able to go beyond memorising the valuation inputs. The fair value measurement of the maize (part (b)) was challenging. However, valuation techniques are used extensively in corporate reporting and therefore you must become accustomed to using such techniques in answering questions. Balancing this, the cash-settled share-based payment (part (c)) and valuation of a non-financial asset (the farmland, part (d)) were more straightforward.
>
> **Easy marks.** These could be gained by focusing on the parts of the question you were more familiar with, which is likely to be parts (c) and (d).

		Marks
(a)	1 mark per point up to maximum	6
(b)	1 mark per point up to maximum	7
(c)	1 mark per point up to maximum	7
(d)	1 mark per point up to maximum	5
		25

(a) **Fair value of agricultural vehicles**

IFRS 13 says that fair value is an exit price in the principal market, which is the market with the highest volume and level of activity. It is not determined based on the volume or level of activity of the reporting entity's transactions in a particular market. Once the accessible markets are identified, market-based volume and activity determines the principal market. There is a presumption that the principal market is the one in which the entity would normally enter into a transaction to sell the asset or transfer the liability, unless there is evidence to the contrary. In practice, an entity would first consider the markets it can access. In the absence of a principal market, it is assumed that the transaction would occur in the most advantageous market. This is the market which would maximise the amount which would be received to sell an asset or minimise the amount which would be paid to transfer a liability, taking into consideration transport and transaction costs. In either case, the entity must have access to the market on the measurement date. Although an entity must be able to access the market at the measurement date, IFRS 13 does not require an entity to be able to sell the particular asset or transfer the particular liability on that date. If there is a principal market for the asset or liability, the fair value measurement represents the price in that market at the measurement date regardless of whether that price is directly observable or estimated using another valuation technique and even if the price in a different market is potentially more advantageous.

The principal (or most advantageous) market price for the same asset or liability might be different for different entities and therefore, the principal (or most advantageous) market is considered from the entity's perspective which may result in different prices for the same asset.

In Yanong's case, Asia would be the principal market as this is the market in which the majority of transactions for the vehicles occur. As such, the fair value of the 150 vehicles would be $5,595,000 ($38,000 − $700 = $37,300 × 150). Actual sales of the vehicles in either Europe or Africa would result in a gain or loss to Yanong when compared with the fair value, ie $37,300. The most advantageous market would be Europe where a net price of $39,100 (after all costs) would be gained by selling there and the number of vehicles sold in this market by Yanong is at its highest. Yanong would therefore utilise the fair value calculated by reference to the Asian market as this is the principal market.

IFRS 13 makes it clear that the price used to measure fair value must not be adjusted for transaction costs, but should consider transportation costs. Yanong has currently deducted transaction costs in its valuation of the vehicles. Transaction costs are not deemed to be a characteristic of an asset or a liability but they are specific to a transaction and will differ depending on how an entity enters into a transaction. While not deducted from fair value, an entity considers transaction costs in the context of determining the most advantageous market because the entity is seeking to determine the market which would maximise the net amount which would be received for the asset.

(b) **Accounting treatment of maize**

Where reliable market-based prices or values are not available for a biological asset in its present location and condition, fair value should be measured using a valuation technique. Relevant observable inputs should be maximised whilst unobservable inputs should be minimised. An appropriate valuation technique would be the present value of expected net cash flows from the asset, discounted at a current market-based rate. In the measurement of fair value of growing crops, a notional cash flow expense should be included for the 'rent' of the land where it is owned in order that the value is comparable to an entity which rents its land. The fair value of the biological asset is separate from the value of the land on which it grows.

$m	3 months to 31 January 20X5 $m	3 months to 30 April 20X5 $m	Total $m
Cash inflows		80	80
Cash outflows	(8)	(19)	(27)
Notional rental charge for land	(1)	(1)	(2)
Net cash flows	(9)	60	51
Discounted at 2%	(8.82)	57.67	48.85

Thus in the quarterly accounts at 31 October 20X4, the maize fields should be recognised at $68.85 million ($20 million land plus $48.85 million maize). A fair value gain of $48.85 million should be shown in profit or loss less the operating costs of $10 million.

At 31 January, Yanong has revised its projections for cash inflows to $76 million, which means that the net cash flows at that date were projected to be $(76 – 19 – 1) million, ie $56 million. Discounted at 2%, this amounts to $54.9 million. Thus, a fair value gain of $(54.9 – 48.85) million, ie $6.05 million, should be shown in profit or loss together with the actual operating costs of $8 million.

At the point of harvest, on 31 March 20X5, the maize is valued at $82 million which means that a fair value gain of $(82 – 54.9) million, ie $27.1 million, is recognised in profit or loss and the maize is classified as inventory. The actual operating costs for the quarter would also be shown in profit or loss. When the maize is sold, a further profit of $(84 – 82) million, ie $2 million, is made on sale.

(c) **Share-based payment**

IFRS 13 applies when another IFRS requires or permits fair value measurements or disclosures about fair value measurements (and measurements, such as fair value less costs to sell, based on fair value or disclosures about those measurements). IFRS 13 specifically excludes transactions covered by certain other standards including share-based payment transactions within the scope of IFRS 2 *Share-based Payment*.

For cash settled share-based payment transactions, the fair value of the liability is measured in accordance with IFRS 2 initially, at each reporting date and at the date of settlement using an option pricing model. The measurement reflects all conditions and outcomes on a weighted average basis, unlike equity settled transactions. Any changes in fair value are recognised in profit or loss in the period. Therefore, the SARs would be accounted for as follows:

Year	Expense $	Liability $	Calculation	
30 April 20X3	641,250	641,250	$285 \times 500 \times \$9 \times \frac{1}{2}$	Time-apportioned over vesting period. Using the estimated ($300 \times 95\%$) 285 managers.

Year	Expense $	Liability $	Calculation	
30 April 20X4	926,250	1,567,500	285 × 500 × $11	Expense is difference between liabilities at 30 April 20X4 and 30 April 20X3
30 April 20X5	97,500	1,350,000	225 × 500 × $12	Cash paid is 60 × 500 × $10.50, ie $315,000. The liability has reduced by $217,500 and therefore the expense is the difference of $97,500

The fair value of the liability would be $1,350,000 at 30 April 20X5 and the expense for the year would be $97,500.

(d) **Farmland**

A fair value measurement of a non-financial asset takes into account a market participant's ability to generate economic benefits by using the asset in its highest and best use or by selling it to another market participant who would use the asset in its highest and best use. The maximum value of a non-financial asset may arise from its use in combination with other assets or by itself. IFRS 13 requires the entity to consider uses which are physically possible, legally permissible and financially feasible. The use must not be legally prohibited. For example, if the land is protected in some way by law and a change of law is required, then it cannot be the highest and best use of the land. In this case, Yanong's land for residential development would only require approval from the regulatory authority and that approval seems to be possible, so this alternative use could be deemed to be legally permissible. Market participants would consider the probability, extent and timing of the approval which may be required in assessing whether a change in the legal use of the non-financial asset could be obtained.

Yanong would need to have sufficient evidence to support its assumption about the potential for an alternative use, particularly in light of IFRS 13's presumption that the highest and best use is an asset's current use. Yanong's belief that planning permission was possible is unlikely to be sufficient evidence that the change of use is legally permissible. However, the fact the government has indicated that more agricultural land should be released for residential purposes may provide additional evidence as to the likelihood that the land being measured should be based upon residential value. Yanong would need to prove that market participants would consider residential use of the land to be legally permissible. Provided there is sufficient evidence to support these assertions, alternative uses, for example, commercial development which would enable market participants to maximise value, should be considered, but a search for potential alternative uses need not be exhaustive. In addition, any costs to transform the land, for example, obtaining planning permission or converting the land to its alternative use, and profit expectations from a market participant's perspective should also be considered in the fair value measurement.

If there are multiple types of market participants who would use the asset differently, these alternative scenarios must be considered before concluding on the asset's highest and best use. It appears that Yanong is not certain about what constitutes the highest and best use and therefore IFRS 13's presumption that the highest and best use is an asset's current use appears to be valid at this stage.

57 Canto

> **Workbook references.** Property, plant and equipment, investment properties, intangible assets and impairment of assets are all covered in Chapter 3. Basic groups are covered in Chapter 10.
>
> **Top tips.** Split your time fairly over each part of this three-part question to maximise the marks you gain from the time spent. Parts (a) and (b) both require the discussion of multiple standards to gain the most marks. Part (c) focusses on IAS 36 and the impairment of a CGU. It is more involved, with the selection of appropriate discount rates and the allocation of impairment, but it is not a complicated scenario assuming you have revised IAS 36.
>
> **Easy marks.** Part (a) has generous marks available for a discussion and application of IFRS 13, IAS 16 and IAS 40 knowledge. There also are marks for straightforward calculations in part (c).

Marking scheme

		Marks
(a)	1 mark per point up to maximum	9
(b)	1 mark per point up to maximum	8
(c)	1 mark per point up to maximum	8
		25

(a) **Fair Value**

IFRS 13 *Fair Value Measurement* defines fair value as the price which would be received to sell an asset or paid to transfer a liability in an orderly transaction between market participants at the measurement date. In respect of property:

- The fair value measurement of a non-financial asset such as property takes into account the entity's ability to generate economic benefits by using the asset in its highest and best use or by selling it to another market participant who would use the asset in its highest and best use.

- The highest and best use of property takes into account the use of the asset which is physically possible, legally permissible and financially feasible.

- There are three levels in the IFRS 13 fair value hierarchy, based on the valuation technique used. Due to the lack of an active market for identical assets, it would be rare for property to be classified in Level 1 of the fair value hierarchy. In market conditions where property is actively purchased and sold, the fair value measurement might be classified in Level 2. However, that determination will depend on the facts and circumstances, including the significance of adjustments to observable data. In this regard, IFRS 13 provides a property specific example, stating that a Level 2 input would be the price derived from observed transactions involving similar property interests in similar locations. Accordingly, in active and transparent markets, property valuations may be classified as Level 2, provided that no significant adjustments have been made to the observable data. If significant adjustments to observable data are required, the fair value measurement may fall into Level 3.

PPE to Investment Property

IAS 40 *Investment Property* permits entities to choose between a fair value model and a cost model. One method must be adopted for all of an entity's investment property. A change is permitted only if this results in a more appropriate presentation. IAS 40 notes that this makes it highly unlikely for a change from a fair value model to a cost model to occur. Transfers to or from investment property should only be made when there is a change in use, which is evidenced by the end of owner-occupation, which has occurred in this case. For a transfer from owner-occupied property to investment property carried at fair value, IAS 16 *Property, Plant and Equipment* (PPE) should be applied up to the date of reclassification. Any difference arising between the carrying amount under IAS 16 at that date and the fair value is dealt with as a revaluation under IAS 16.

The aggregate fair value of the site, including the industrial and retail outlets, is higher to market participants than the sum of the fair value of the individual property interests because of synergies and complementary cash flows. Consequently, the fair value of the site as a whole would be maximised as a group of assets. The fair value is determined for the whole site even if the asset is disaggregated when applying IAS 40.

Thus providing that the above criteria have been met, Canto may value the property at $25 million.

Canto will recognise a depreciation expense of $0.5 million in profit or loss in the year to 28 February 20X7 while the property is accounted for using a cost model under IAS 16. At 28 February 20X7, Canto will transfer the property from PPE to investment property. The investment property will be recognised at its fair value of $25 million, the carrying amount of PPE of $13.5 million ($15 million – accumulated depreciation of $1.5 million) will be derecognised and the increase of $11.5 million will be a revaluation surplus.

(b)   IFRS 3 *Business Combinations* states that an acquirer should recognise, separately from goodwill, the identifiable intangible assets acquired in a business combination. An asset is identifiable if it meets either the separability or contractual-legal criteria in IAS 38 *Intangible Assets*.

Customer relationship intangible assets may be either contractual or non-contractual:

(i)   Contractual customer relationships are normally recognised separately from goodwill as they meet the contractual-legal criterion.

(ii)   However, non-contractual customer relationships are recognised separately from goodwill only if they meet the separable criterion.

Consequently, determining whether a relationship is contractual is critical to identifying and measuring both separately recognised customer relationship intangible assets and goodwill, and different conclusions could lead to substantially different accounting outcomes.

Order backlog

The order backlog should be treated as an intangible asset on the acquisition. The fair value of the order backlog is estimated based on the expected revenue to be received, less the costs to deliver the product or service.

Water acquisition rights

The rights are valuable, as Binlory cannot manufacture vehicles without them. The rights were acquired at no cost and renewal is certain at little or no cost. The rights cannot be sold other than as part of the sale of a business as a whole, so there exists no secondary market in the rights. If Binlory does not use the water, then it will lose the rights. In this case, the legal rights cannot be measured separately from the business as a whole and therefore from goodwill. Therefore, the legal rights should not be accounted for as a separate intangible asset acquired in the business combination because the fair value cannot be measured reliably as the legal rights cannot be separated from goodwill.

(c)   IAS 36 *Impairment of Assets* requires that assets be carried at no more than their carrying amount. Therefore, entities should test all assets within the scope of the Standard if indicators of impairment exist. If the recoverable amount (which is the higher of fair value less costs of disposal and value in use) is more than carrying amount, the asset is not impaired. It further

says that in measuring value in use, the discount rate used should be the pre-tax rate which reflects current market assessments of the time value of money and the risks specific to the asset. The discount rate should not reflect risks for which future cash flows have been adjusted and should equal the rate of return which investors would require if they were to choose an investment which would generate cash flows equivalent to those expected from the asset. Therefore pre-tax cash flows and pre-tax discount rates should be used to calculate value in use.

Date year ended	Pre-tax cash flow $m	Discounted cash flows $m at 8%
28 February 20X8	8	7.41
28 February 20X9	7	6.00
29 February 20Y0	5	3.97
28 February 20Y1	3	2.21
28 February 20Y2	13	8.85
Total		28.44

The CGU is impaired by the amount by which the carrying amount of the cash-generating unit exceeds its recoverable amount.

Recoverable amount

The fair value less costs to sell ($26.6 million) is lower than the value in use ($28.44 million). The recoverable amount is therefore $28.44 million.

Impairment

The carrying amount is $32 million and therefore the impairment is $3.56 million.

Allocating impairment losses

Canto will allocate the impairment loss first to the goodwill and then to other assets of the unit pro rata on the basis of the carrying amount of each asset in the cash-generating unit. When allocating the impairment loss, the carrying amount of an asset cannot be reduced below its fair value less costs to sell.

Consequently, the entity will allocate $3 million to goodwill and then allocate $0.1 million on a pro rata basis to PPE (to reduce it to its fair value less costs to sell of $9.9 million) and other assets ($0.46 million to the other assets). This would mean that the carrying amounts would be $9.9 million and $18.54 million respectively.

58 Ethan

Workbook references. Deferred tax is covered in Chapter 6. Investment property and impairment are covered in Chapter 3, financial instruments in Chapter 7 and fair value in Chapter 3.

Top tips. In Part (a), you should focus on IFRS 13. Part (b) required application of the fair value option in IFRS 9 *Financial Instruments*. The option is used where such application would eliminate or significantly reduce a measurement or recognition inconsistency between the debt liabilities and the investment properties to which they were related in this question. In part (c), candidates needed to recognise that, in classifying the B shares as equity rather than as a liability, the entity had not complied with IAS 32 *Financial Instruments: Presentation*. There were pointers to the shares being classified as a liability, in particular the fact that entity was obliged to pay an annual cumulative dividend on the B shares and did not have discretion over the distribution of such dividend.

Easy marks. There are no obviously easy marks in this question.

		Marks
(a)	Fair value of investment properties	13
(b)	Fair value option – IFRS 9	7
(c)	B shares of subsidiary	5
		25

(a) **Fair value of investment properties**

The **fair value** of an asset is the price that would be received to sell an asset or paid to transfer a liability in an orderly transaction between market participants at the measurement date (IFRS 13 *Fair Value Measurement*). IFRS 13 states that valuation techniques must be those which are appropriate and for which sufficient data are available. Entities should maximise the use of relevant **observable inputs** and minimise the use of **unobservable inputs**. The standard establishes a three-level hierarchy for the inputs that valuation techniques use to measure fair value.

Level 1   Quoted prices (unadjusted) in active markets for identical assets or liabilities that the reporting entity can access at the measurement date

Level 2   Inputs other than quoted prices included within Level 1 that are observable for the asset or liability, either directly or indirectly, eg quoted prices for similar assets in active markets or for identical or similar assets in non-active markets or use of quoted interest rates for valuation purposes

Level 3   Unobservable inputs for the asset or liability, ie using the entity's own assumptions about market exit value

Although an active market exists for Ethan's investment properties, Ethan uses a discounted cash flow model to measure fair value. This is **not in accordance with IFRS 13**. As the fair value hierarchy suggests, IFRS 13 favours Level 1 inputs, that is market-based measures, over unobservable (Level 3) inputs such as discounted cash flows.

Goodwill and deferred tax

If the **fair value** of the investment properties **is not measured correctly** in accordance with IFRS 13, this means that the **deferred tax liability** on investment properties **may also be incorrect**. In addition, as goodwill is calculated as consideration transferred less fair value of net assets, **goodwill may be incorrect**. This is because deferred tax is calculated on the difference between the carrying amount of the asset and its tax base. So if the carrying amount is incorrect, the deferred tax will be incorrect. The goodwill calculation uses the fair value of **all** net assets, not just the investment properties and the related deferred tax liability, so it is **incorrect to use an increase in the deferred tax liability** as the **basis** for assessing whether goodwill is impaired.

The reasoning behind Ethan's approach is that as the deferred tax liability decreases, the fair value of net assets increases, thereby decreasing goodwill. However, this method of determining whether goodwill is impaired **does not accord with IAS 36** *Impairment of Assets*. IAS 36 requires that goodwill should be **reviewed for impairment annually** for any indicators of impairment, which may be internal or external, and are not confined to changes in the deferred tax liability. Where it is not possible to measure impairment for individual assets, the loss should be measured for a **cash generating unit**.

The **recoverable amount** is **defined** as the **higher** of:

(i)   The **asset's fair value less costs to sell**. This is the price that would be received to sell the asset in an orderly transaction between market participants at the measurement date under current market conditions, net of costs of disposal.

(ii)   The asset's **value in use**. This is the present value of estimated future cash flows (inflows minus outflows) generated by the asset, including its estimated net disposal value (if any) at the end of its useful life.

If an **asset's carrying amount** is **higher than its recoverable amount**, an **impairment loss** has occurred. The impairment loss should be **written off against profit or loss** for the year, and the corresponding credit (write-off) applied first to goodwill, then to the investment properties, then to other assets pro-rata.

Deferred tax assets on losses

In theory, unused tax losses give rise to a deferred tax asset. However, IAS 12 *Income Taxes* states that **deferred tax assets should only be recognised to the extent that they are regarded as recoverable**. They should be regarded as recoverable to the extent that on the basis of all the evidence available it is **probable that there will be suitable taxable profits against which the losses can be recovered**. It is unlikely that future taxable profits of Ethan will be sufficient to realise all of the tax loss because of:

(i)   The announcement that a substantial loss will be incurred this year instead of the expected profit

(ii)   Considerable negative variances against budgets in the past

Consequently, **Ethan should not recognise the deferred tax asset.**

(b)   **IFRS 9 fair value option**

Generally under IFRS 9 *Financial Instruments*, the debt issued to finance its investment properties would be accounted for using **amortised cost,** while the properties themselves are at fair value. This is an **accounting mismatch,** that is a recognition or measurement inconsistency between the debt liability and the asset to which it relates. The asset and liability, and the gains and losses arising on them, would be measured on different bases.

The IFRS 9 **fair value option** allows an entity to **designate a liability at initial recognition as being at fair value through profit or loss** if using this option would **eliminate or significantly reduce** an accounting mismatch. Ethan has argued that the basis of measurement of the debt and the investment properties is **similar**, particularly as regards **interest rates**. This argument holds good in respect of the interest, and so the **fair value option would be allowed**.

However, IFRS 9 stipulates that if a liability is designated as being at fair value through profit or loss, **changes in the fair value that are due to changes in the liability's credit risk must be recognised directly in other comprehensive income** rather than profit or loss. Such **changes may not be re-classified** to profit or loss in subsequent years, although a **reserves transfer** is permitted from other components of equity to retained earnings. On the other hand**, if changes in the fair value attributable to the credit risk** of the liability **create or enlarge an accounting mismatch in profit or loss**, then all fair value movements are **recognised in profit or loss**.

(c)   **B shares of subsidiary**

Ethan's accounting treatment of the B shares (as equity instruments) does not comply with IAS 32 *Financial Instruments: Presentation*. The IAS 32 definition of a financial liability includes any liability that is **a contractual obligation to deliver cash or another financial asset to another entity**. A financial instrument may only be classified as an equity instrument rather than a liability if the instrument does not include an obligation to deliver cash

or other financial asset to another entity, or to exchange financial instruments with another entity under conditions that are potentially unfavourable.

In the **subsidiary's books,** the B shares would be treated as a **financial liability.** They contain an **obligation** to deliver cash in the form of a fixed dividend. The dividend is cumulative and must be paid whether or not the subsidiary has sufficient legally distributable profits when it is due, and so **the subsidiary cannot avoid this obligation**.

In the **consolidated financial statements,** the B shares would also be treated as a financial liability, **the intragroup element of this liability (70%) would cancel against the investment in B shares in the parent's (Ethan's) statement of financial position.** The shares **owned by external parties would not cancel;** they would remain **a financial liability**. It **is incorrect to treat them as non-controlling interest** because they are **not equity**.

59 IFRSs and SMEs

Workbook reference. The IFRS for SMEs is covered in Chapter 18.

Top tips. This question required you to discuss whether it was necessary to develop the IFRS for SMEs. If you weren't sure on this, then you could make an attempt by considering the differences between large, listed entities and SMEs to come up with a few reasons as to why it might have been considered necessary. The rest of the question was fairly straightforward if you had revised the IFRS for SMEs.

Easy marks. Parts (b) to (d) contained easy marks for stating knowledge of the IFRS for SMEs

Marking scheme

		Marks
(a)	Subjective	7
(b)	Purpose	3
	Definition of entity	4
(c)	Recognition and measurement differences	6
(d)	Items not dealt with	5
Maximum		25

(a)   There were many arguments in favour of the development of a separate Standard for SMEs including the fact that full IFRSs have become very **detailed and onerous** to follow. The **cost** of complying with full IFRSs would likely have **exceeded the benefits** to an SME and the users of its financial statements.

Additionally, SME financial statements are normally **used by a relatively small number of people**. Often, the **investors** are also **involved in day to day management**. The **main external users** of SME financial statements tend to be **lenders and the tax authorities**, rather than institutional investors and their advisers. These users have **different information needs** from those of investors. For these users, the accounting treatments and the detailed disclosures required may sometimes **obscure the picture** given by the financial statements. In some cases, **different, or more detailed information may be needed**. For example, related party transactions are often very significant in the context of SME activities and expanded disclosure may be appropriate.

Furthermore, in many countries, IFRSs are primarily used for large listed companies; however, in some smaller and emerging economies, IFRSs are used as national GAAP for all entities, including SMEs. Before the issue of the IFRS for SMEs, this meant that even very small companies in those countries were required to apply full IFRS. The IASB identified that there were many cases in these countries where companies departed from particular standards and didn't disclose this fact, and that IFRSs were being applied without rigorous enforcement or quality control. This could have been due to **limitations in, and the cost of, accounting expertise** available to smaller companies in applying full IFRSs.

Arguments against the development of a separate SME Standard included the fact that the IASB believed that same concepts of financial reporting are appropriate for all entities regardless of size and that the objectives of general purpose financial statements are fundamentally the same for all entities. On that basis, it is possible to conclude that a single set of accounting standards, (eg full IFRSs) should be suitable for all entities. Additionally, compliance with full IFRSs ensures **comparability** of financial statements with those of other entities.

After reaching out to national standard-setters, the IASB concluded that the majority supported the development of a separate standard for SMEs based on the accounting principles in full IFRSs, but simplified to reduce the cost burden to SMEs and more suited to the users of SME financial statements.

(b) **The purpose of the IFRS for SMEs and type of entity to which it should apply**

Purpose of IFRS for SMEs

The purpose of the IFRS for SMEs is that it should provide the users of SME financial statements with **relevant, reliable and understandable information**.

The Standard is **suitable for SMEs globally** and, while based on the same conceptual framework as full IFRS, **reduces the financial reporting burden** on SMEs by simplifying the accounting and making the requirements less onerous that full IFRS.

Type of entity

The IFRS for SMEs is intended for use by SMEs. The IFRS for SMEs describes an SME as an entity that:

(i) Does not have public accountability; and
(ii) Publishes general purpose financial statements for external users.

Examples of external users include owners who are not involved in managing the business, existing and potential creditors, and credit rating agencies.

The IASB faced a challenge in determining how an SME should be defined. The **definition** of an SME could be based on **size** or on **public accountability** or on a combination of the two. There are several disadvantages of basing the definition on size limits alone. Size limits are **arbitrary** and **different limits are likely to be appropriate in different countries**. Most people believe that SMEs are **not simply smaller versions of listed entities**, but differ from them in more fundamental ways.

The most important way in which SMEs differ from other entities is that they are **not usually publicly accountable**. However, using this as the basis of a definition raised other issues: which types of company are publicly accountable? Obviously the **definition would include** companies which have **issued shares** or other instruments **to the public,** but what about other companies? Should national standard setters define **'publicly accountable'** in a way that is appropriate for their particular jurisdiction? In the end, the IASB concluded that an **entity has public accountability** if its debt or equity instruments are traded in a public market (or are about to be) or the entity **holds assets in a fiduciary**

capacity (eg most banks, credit unions, insurance companies, securities brokers/dealers, mutual funds and investment banks).

(c) **Recognition and measurement simplifications under the IFRS for SMEs**

The IFRS for SMEs allows simplified accounting treatment in a number of areas. The key areas are:

Revenue – revenue is recognised when the risks and rewards of ownership of goods are transferred to the buyer, or when services are performed. This is compared to when performance obligations are satisfied under IFRS 15. Determining and then measuring performance obligations can be complex, hence the approach under IFRS for SMEs is simpler.

Intangible assets (excluding goodwill) – all intangible assets are amortised and a useful life of a maximum useful life of 10 years is used if a reliable useful life cannot be determined. Impairment tests are only required if there are specific indicators of impairment in the year. Under IAS 38, only intangible assets with a finite useful life are amortised and they are required to be reviewed for impairment annually if they do not have a finite useful life or are not yet available for use. Impairment review can be a costly and time consuming exercise for companies, so the IFRS for SMEs promoting amortisation over impairment is easier for companies.

Goodwill – goodwill is amortised under the IFRS for SMEs. It is tested for impairment annually under full IFRS and is not amortised.

Separate financial statements of investors – there is an option to hold investments in subsidiaries, associates or joint ventures at cost, or at fair value through profit or loss, or using the equity method in the IFRS for SMEs. Under full IFRS, the cost option isn't available and fair value can be either through profit or other comprehensive income. The equity method remains an option. Not permitting the cost model and bringing in fair value through other comprehensive income means the full IFRS is more complex than the IFRS for SMEs.

Consolidated financial statements – under the IFRS for SMEs, investments can remain at the same value as in the separate financial statements. Under full IFRS, the equity accounting method must be used. In the IFRS for SMEs, only the partial goodwill method may be used, ie the non-controlling interests are valued at their share of net assets, whereas the full IFRS allows a choice of the partial or full goodwill methods to be used. If there is a foreign subsidiary, the IFRS for SMEs reports translation differences in other comprehensive income with no reclassification to profit or loss, whereas full IFRS does reclassify on disposal.

(d) **How items not dealt with by the IFRS for SMEs should be treated**

The IFRS for SMEs **does not cover all possible transactions** and events and there will be occasions where an SME has to **account for an item that the Standard does not deal with**. There are several alternatives.

(1) The entity is **required to apply the relevant full IFRS**, while still following SME standards otherwise.

(2) Management can **use its judgement** to develop an accounting policy based on the relevant full IFRS, or the *Conceptual Framework*, or other IFRSs for SMEs and the other sources of potential guidance cited in IAS 8.

(3) The entity could continue to follow its **existing practice**.

In practice, the SME should elect the most appropriate accounting treatment to faithfully represent the transactions and events it has entered into. Judgement is required to determine what the appropriate source of reference may be.

60 Whitebirk

Workbook reference. Small and medium-sized entities are covered in Chapter 18 of your Workbook.

Top tips. Part (a) on the main differences between the *IFRS for SMEs* and full IFRS, was reasonably straightforward. Part (b) required you to apply the standard to specific areas: goodwill, research and development expenditure, investment property and impairment. Remember not to use full IFRS!

Easy marks. This was a rich source of easy marks for the well-prepared candidate. Make sure your arguments are well-structured in order to earn those two marks for clarity and quality of discussion.

Marking scheme

			Marks
(a)		Subjective assessment including professional	11
(b)	(i)	Business combination	4
	(ii)	Research and development expenditure	3
	(iii)	Investment property	2
	(iv)	Intangible	2
			22

(a) **Modifications to reduce the burden of reporting for SMEs**

The *IFRS for SMEs* has **simplifications** that reflect the needs of users of SMEs' financial statements and cost-benefit considerations. It is designed to facilitate financial reporting by small and medium-sized entities in a number of ways:

(i)   It provides significantly **less guidance** than full IFRS. A great deal of the guidance in full IFRS would not be relevant to the needs of smaller entities.

(ii) Many of the **principles** for recognising and measuring assets, liabilities, income and expenses in full IFRSs are **simplified**. For example, goodwill and intangibles are always amortised over their estimated useful life (or ten years if it cannot be estimated). Research and development costs must be expensed. With defined benefit pension plans, all actuarial gains and losses are to be recognised immediately in other comprehensive income. All past service costs are to be recognised immediately in profit or loss. To measure the defined benefit obligation, the projected unit credit method must be used.

(iii) Where full IFRSs allow accounting policy choices, the *IFRS for SMEs* **allows only the easier option**. Examples of alternatives not allowed in the *IFRS for SMEs* include: revaluation model for intangible assets and property, plant and equipment, proportionate consolidation for investments in jointly-controlled entities and choice between cost and fair value models for investment property (measurement depends on the circumstances).

(iv) **Topics not relevant** to SMEs are **omitted**: earnings per share, interim financial reporting, segment reporting, insurance and assets held for sale.

(v)   Significantly **fewer disclosures** are required.

(vi) The standard has been written in **clear language** that can easily be translated.

The above represents a considerable reduction in reporting requirements – perhaps as much as 90% – compared with listed entities. Entities will naturally wish to use the *IFRS for SMEs* if they can, but **its use is restricted**.

The restrictions are **not related to size**. There are several disadvantages of basing the definition on size limits alone. Size limits are **arbitrary** and **different limits are likely to be appropriate in different** countries. Most people believe that SMEs are **not simply smaller versions of listed entities**, but differ from them in more fundamental ways.

The most important way in which SMEs differ from other entities is that they are **not usually publicly accountable**. Accordingly, there are **no quantitative thresholds** for qualification as a SME; instead, the scope of the IFRS is determined by a **test of public accountability**. The IFRS is suitable for all entities except those whose securities are publicly traded and financial institutions such as banks and insurance companies.

Another way in which the use of the *IFRS for SMEs* is restricted is that **users cannot cherry pick** from this IFRS and full IFRS. If an entity adopts the *IFRS for SMEs*, it **must adopt it in its entirety**.

(b) (i) **Business combination**

IFRS 3 *Business Combinations* allows an entity to adopt the full or partial goodwill method in its consolidated financial statements. The *IFRS for SMEs* **only allows the partial goodwill method**. This avoids the need for SMEs to determine the fair value of the non-controlling interests not purchased when undertaking a business combination.

In addition, IFRS 3 requires goodwill to be tested annually for impairment. The *IFRS for SMEs* **requires goodwill to be amortised instead**. This is a much simpler approach and the *IFRS for SMEs* specifies that if an entity is unable to make a reliable estimate of the useful life, it is presumed to be ten years, simplifying things even further.

Goodwill on Whitebirk's acquisition of Close will be calculated as:

	$'000
Consideration transferred	5,700
Non-controlling interest: 10% × $6m	600
	6,300
Less fair value of identifiable net assets acquired	(6,000)
Goodwill	300

This goodwill of $0.3m will be amortised over ten years, that is $30,000 per annum.

(ii) **Research and development expenditure**

The *IFRS for SMEs* requires all internally generated research and development expenditure to be **expensed through profit or loss.** This is simpler than full IFRS – IAS 38 *Intangible Assets* requires internally generated assets to be capitalised if certain criteria (proving future economic benefits) are met, and it is often difficult to determine whether or not they have been met.

Whitebirk's total expenditure on research ($0.5m) and development ($1m) must be written off to profit or loss for the year, giving a charge of $1.5m.

(iii) **Investment property**

Investment properties must be held at fair value through profit or loss under the *IFRS for SMEs* where their fair value can be measured without undue cost or effort, which appears to be the case here, given that an estate agent valuation is available. Consequently a gain of $0.2m ($1.9m – $1.7m) will be reported in Whitebirk's profit or loss for the year.

(iv) **Intangible asset**

IAS 36 *Impairment of assets* requires annual impairment tests for indefinite life intangibles, intangibles not yet available for use and goodwill. This is a complex, time-consuming and expensive test.

The *IFRS for SMEs* only requires impairment tests where there are indicators of impairment. In the case of Whitebirk's intangible, there are no indicators of impairment, and so an impairment test is not required.

In addition, IAS 38 *Intangible Assets* does not require intangible assets with an indefinite useful life to be amortised. In contrast, under the *IFRS for SMEs,* all intangible assets must be amortised. If the useful life cannot be established reliably, it must not exceed ten years.

61 Zack

Workbook references. IAS 8 is covered in Chapter 2. IAS 23 is covered in Chapter 3.

Top tips. While IAS 8 is brought forward knowledge from your earlier studies, the depth of discussion required is greater, and the scenario requires more thought. The weighting of the marks is heavily towards the discursive aspect of the question. The preamble to the question gave guidance as to how to answer the question by saying 'entities also often consider the acceptability of the use of hindsight in their reporting'. You should remember to give examples of prior period errors when answering part (a) and could have used those in part (b) as a starting point.

Easy marks. There are marks available for textbook knowledge of IAS 8 and IAS 23, which you should have from your earlier studies, and also the fact that there is much subjectivity in the marking scheme means a variety of valid arguments may be acceptable. Note the word 'valid', however: you **must** apply the knowledge to the scenario and you will get no credit for 'waffle'.

Marking scheme

		Marks
(a)	Subjective discussion	15
(b)	Subjective discussion	10
		25

(a) (i) **Judgement and materiality in selecting accounting policies**

The selection of accounting policies in the preparation of financial statements is important in providing consistency, comparability and clarity to users of those statements. In general entities do not have a great deal of discretion, but must follow the accounting policies required by IFRS that are relevant to the particular circumstances of the entity. In certain circumstances, however, IFRS offers a choice or does not give guidance. In these situations, management should select appropriate accounting policies.

Judgement

Management is required to exercise judgement in developing and applying an accounting policy that results in information that is relevant and reliable. If there is **no IFRS** standard or interpretation that is specifically applicable, management should consider the applicability of the requirements in IFRS on **similar and related issues**, and then the definitions, recognition criteria and measurement concepts for assets, liabilities, income and expenses in the **Conceptual Framework**. Management may also consider the most recent pronouncements of **other standard-setting bodies**

that use a similar conceptual framework to develop accounting standards, other accounting literature and accepted industry practices, to the extent that these do not conflict with IFRS.

Unless a standard permits or requires otherwise, accounting policies should be applied **consistently** to similar transactions and events. For example, it is permissible to carry some items of property, plant and equipment at fair value and some at historical cost, but items within any one class of property, plant and equipment must be treated in the same way.

Management's judgement will be constrained as regards its selection of accounting policies (or changes in accounting policies or estimates) by the need to **follow the requirements of IAS 8** *Accounting Policies, Changes in Accounting Estimates and Errors.*

Materiality

IAS 8 states that omissions or misstatements of items 'are material if they could, by their size or nature, individually or collectively, influence the economic decisions of users taken on the basis of the financial statements'.

In general, IFRS **only apply to material items,** and an accounting policy need not be applied if its effect would be immaterial. Similarly, a **change** in accounting policy or estimate **would only be necessary if the item was material.** Specifically in the context of IAS 8 and errors, materiality 'depends on the size and nature of the omission or misstatement judged in the surrounding circumstances. The size or nature of the item, or a combination of both, could be the determining factor'.

In addition, IAS 8 notes that it is **inappropriate to make, or leave uncorrected, immaterial departures** from IFRSs to **achieve a particular presentation**, so the principle of materiality cannot be abused to present the results in an artificially favourable light.

(ii) **Change in accounting policy**

IAS 8 allows a change in accounting policy **only where required by a standard** or if it results in financial statements providing reliable and **more relevant information** about the effects of transactions, other events or conditions on the entity's financial position, financial performance, or cash flows. Changes in accounting policy **should be very rare,** because IFRS specifies the accounting policies for most of the transactions an entity will make. Changes in accounting **estimates**, on the other hand, will be **more frequent**. A change in accounting estimate is 'an adjustment of the carrying amount of an asset or liability, or related expense, resulting from reassessing the expected future benefits and obligations associated with that asset or liability'. Such changes may be needed to estimate the figures correctly in order to comply with an accounting policy.

IAS 8 notes that changes in accounting policies **do not include applying an accounting policy to a kind of transaction or event that did not occur previously or were immaterial**. Such a policy would be applied **prospectively,** that is prior period figures would not be adjusted. For example, if an entity begins to let out its head office to residents to earn rental income, this change of use of the building would mean that it should be accounted for as an investment property under IAS 40. However, this is not a change of accounting policy, rather it is the application of a standard to an asset to which it did not apply previously, and so there would be no retrospective application.

If a change in accounting policy is required by a new IFRS or interpretation, the change is accounted for as required by that new pronouncement if the new pronouncement

includes specific transition provisions. Not all new standards and interpretations include transition provisions, and if none are included then the change in accounting policy is applied retrospectively.

Retrospective application means that an entity **adjusts the opening balance of each component of equity that is affected for the earliest prior period presented in the financial statements**. It also adjusts the other comparative amounts, that is, amounts in the statement of profit or loss and other comprehensive income, and the statements of financial position, cash flows and changes in equity and related notes. The **comparative amounts** disclosed for each prior period presented **as if the new policy had always applied**. This rule applies except where it is impracticable to determine either the period-specific effects of the change or the cumulative effects of the change.

It is sometimes **difficult to compare** the current period with prior periods because there is **insufficient data** relating to the prior period. Perhaps it was not foreseen that such data would be needed. Even if the data is available, restatement of prior information often requires **complex and detailed estimates** to be made, although this does not mean that reliable adjustments cannot be made.

The further in the past the prior period adjustment relates to, the harder it is for estimates to reflect the circumstances existing at the time. Judgement may be clouded by hindsight, that is influenced by knowledge of events which have occurred since the prior period. **IAS 8 does not permit the use of hindsight** in estimations of amounts to be recognised, measured or disclosed in a prior period, or in making assumptions about management intentions at that time.

If it is impracticable to determine the cumulative effect, at the beginning of the current period, of applying a new accounting policy to all prior periods, an entity must adjust the comparative information to apply the new accounting policy prospectively from the **earliest date practicable**. This may in practice be the current period.

(iii) **IAS 8 and earnings management**

IAS 8 requires the correction of prior period errors to be carried out retrospectively by restating the comparative amounts for the prior period(s) presented in which the error occurred, or if the error occurred before the earliest prior period presented, restating the opening balances of assets, liabilities and equity for the earliest prior period presented. The effect is to restate the comparatives **as if the error had never occurred**. The impact of any prior period errors will not be included in the current period's profit or loss, but will be shown – or perhaps hidden – in retained earnings.

It could be argued that this gives managers an **incentive to use prior period corrections under IAS 8** as a form of **earnings management,** because it allows them to **manipulate current earnings**.

Expenses could be miscalculated and the correction treated as a prior period error in the following year, with an **adjustment through retained earnings rather than profit or loss**. Earnings per share could be miscalculated, or liabilities reported as non-current rather than current. IAS 8 allows such misstatements to be **corrected the following year without any long-term negative effects in the statement of financial position**.

While IAS 8 does not permit **hindsight,** in practice this may be **difficult to prove**, and inappropriate hindsight may be used to relegate bad news to prior periods once the bad news has passed. **Errors are not given the prominence** which users of financial statements might need in order to assess management's competence and integrity, as well as how good the results are. Use of reserves instead of profit or loss has long been seen as undesirable this very reason.

(b) (i) **Borrowing costs**

IAS 23 *Borrowing Costs* requires that borrowing costs directly attributable to the acquisition, construction or production of a 'qualifying asset' (one that necessarily takes a substantial period of time to get ready for its intended use or sale) are included in the cost of the asset. Other borrowing costs are recognised as an expense.

IAS 23 would therefore require capitalisation of the borrowing costs of $3 million incurred while the shopping center is under construction. In the case of the borrowing costs of $2 million incurred on the 20X2 asset, it has been found that there would be a material misstatement of the asset balance if borrowing costs were not capitalised, so IAS 23 requires capitalisation of those borrowing costs.

The accounting treatment previously used by Zack was incorrect because it did not comply with IAS 23. Consequently, the change to the new, correct policy is **the correction of an error rather than a change of accounting policy** as regards the 20X2 asset. This is a prior period error, which **must be corrected retrospectively**. This involves restating the financial statements for the year ended 30 November 20X2, when the contract was completed, and **restating the opening balances** for 20X3 so that the financial statements are presented as if the error had never occurred. In 20X3, the $3 million of borrowing costs should be capitalised in accordance with IAS 23; this is compliance with IFRS rather than a change of accounting policy. It can be assumed that there will be no depreciation, as the asset is under construction.

The **effects of the restatement** for the year ended 30 November 20X2 are:

(1) The carrying amount of property, plant and equipment is **restated upwards** by $2 million, less depreciation for the year.

(2) There is a corresponding **increase in profit or loss** for the year of the same amount.

(3) **Disclosures** are required relating to the prior period error:

- The nature of the prior period error

- For each prior period presented, to the extent practicable, the amount of the correction, for each financial statement line item affected, and for basic and diluted earnings per share

- The amount of the correction at the beginning of the earliest prior period presented

- If retrospective restatement is impracticable, an explanation and description of how the error has been corrected.

(ii) **Change in depreciation method**

Changing from straight line depreciation to reducing balance is a **change in accounting estimate, not a change in accounting policy**. A change in accounting estimate is 'an adjustment of the carrying amount of an asset or liability, or related expense, resulting from reassessing the expected future benefits and obligations associated with that asset or liability.'

Changes in accounting estimates are **not applied retrospectively** and accordingly, financial information presented for prior periods is not restated. Instead, the effect of a change in an accounting estimate is recognised **prospectively** (that is, from the date of change) by including it in profit or loss in the period of change, if the change affects only that period, or in the period of change and future periods, where the change also affects future periods.

Where the effect on future periods is not disclosed because it is not practicable, that fact should be disclosed.

The revision to the depreciation figures calculated by management are not correct, because they include an adjustment of **$5 million for the year to 30 November 20X2**, that is, a **retrospective adjustment.** The carrying amount as at 1 December 20X2 will be depreciated based on **prospective** reducing balance application.

(iii) **Accruals error**

This systems error would be treated as a **prior period error** in accordance with IAS 8. Zack must correct this by **restating the prior period information** for the year ended 30 November 20X2:

(1) Increase profit or loss for 20X2 by $2 million.
(2) Adjust trade payables for 20X2 by $2 million, to eliminate the overstatement.
(3) Restate the movement in reserves note.

This is the correction of an error, not an accounting estimate.

62 Pod

Workbook references. Implementation of a new IFRS is covered in Chapter 19 of the Workbook. Intangible assets and impairment are covered in Chapter 3. Deferred tax is in Chapter 6.

Top tips. Part (a)(i) of this question requires a discussion of the key practical considerations and financial statement implications when implementing a move to a new IFRS. There are a number of valid points that may be made; for example, the impact on performance-related pay, covenants, the need for communication with stakeholders and resourcing issues. Part (a)(ii) is more specific, and students should avoid the temptation to make general points about slow economic growth. The key point with regard to deferred tax assets is whether there will continue to be sufficient profits (otherwise you can't recognise them). An important point to mention with regard to impairment concerns the accuracy of cash flow projections. Part (b) of this question required a discussion of whether two proposed changes were acceptable. The first was a proposal to change the useful life of an intangible asset (a portfolio of customers acquired from a competitor) to 'indefinite', because of an inability to predict the asset's life.

You need to consider the precise meaning of 'indefinite' – it means no foreseeable limit. The second proposal was to alter a cash-generating unit to the product line level rather than individual retail branch level. You needed a thorough knowledge of the criteria for a cash-generating unit and the ability to apply them to the scenario.

Easy marks. Part (a)(i) is fairly open ended when it comes to earning marks.

Marking scheme

			Marks
(a)	(i)	1 mark per point up to maximum	7
	(ii)	1 mark per point up to maximum	9
(b)		1 mark per point up to maximum	9
			25

(a) (i) **Move to a new IFRS**

The entity itself should prepare an impact assessment and project plan relating to the introduction of the new IFRS. There may be significant changes to processes, systems

and controls and management should communicate the impact to investors and other stakeholders. This would include plans for disclosing the effects of new accounting standards which are issued but not yet effective. The entity should chose a path to implementation and establish responsibilities and deadlines. This may help to determine the accountability of the implementation team and allow management to identify gaps in resources.

Further, IFRS-based financial statements are used in contracts or regulation. Banking agreements often specify maximum debt levels or financial ratios which refer to figures prepared in accordance with IFRS. New financial reporting requirements can affect those ratios, with potential breach of those contracts. Many jurisdictions have regulation which restricts the amount which can be paid out in dividends, by reference to accounting profit. Further, some governments use IFRS numbers for statistical and economic planning purposes and the data as evidence to place constraints on profitability in regulated industries.

It is important that the entity communicates the effects of a move to a new IFRS to the markets and analysts. On application of the new IFRS, investors will be provided with different information upon which to base their decisions. Investors' assessment of how management has discharged its stewardship responsibilities may be changed and this could affect the investors' investment decision. Further, new financial reporting requirements may disclose information which is of competitive advantage to third parties and this is a cost to the entity.

A change in an accounting standard could cause some entities to no longer invest in certain assets or it may change how they contract for some activities. For example, now that, under IFRS 16 *Leases*, most leases formerly accounted for as operating leases must be shown on the statement of financial position, this could have adverse economic impacts on certain sectors. Additionally, the new standard could affect the calculation of performance-related pay and impact on any debt covenants in place.

Where there is the introduction of a new accounting standard, the financial statements will need to reflect the new recognition, measurement and disclosure requirements which, in turn, will mean that entities will need to consider the requirements of IAS 8 *Accounting Policies, Changes in Accounting Estimates and Errors*. IAS 8 contains a requirement that changes in accounting policies are fully applied retrospectively unless there are specific transitional provisions. Further, IAS 8 requires the disclosure of a number of matters as regards the new IFRS. Additionally, IAS 1 *Presentation of Financial Statements* requires a third statement of financial position to be presented if the entity retrospectively applies an accounting policy, restates items, or reclassifies items, and those adjustments had a material effect on the information in the statement of financial position at the beginning of the comparative period.

IAS 33 *Earnings per Share* requires basic and diluted EPS to be adjusted for the impacts of adjustments resulting from changes in accounting policies accounted for retrospectively and IAS 8 requires the disclosure of the amount of any such adjustments. Taxation is often calculated on the profit measured for financial reporting purposes. For jurisdictions using IFRS as the basis for income tax, a change in a standard can change the tax base. The economic consequences of the link of accounting with tax liabilities can be significant.

(ii) **Impairment of non-financial and deferred tax asset**

A continuous period of slow economic growth could indicate to regulators that non-financial assets will continue to generate lower than expected cash flows, especially in those industries experiencing a downturn in fortunes. Particular attention should be paid to the valuation of goodwill and intangible assets with indefinite life spans. The entity should focus on certain specific areas including cash flow projections, disclosure of key

assumptions and judgements, and appropriate disclosure of sensitivity analysis for material goodwill and intangible assets with indefinite useful lives.

In measuring value-in-use, cash flow projections should be based on reasonable and supportable assumptions which represent the best estimate of the range of future economic conditions. IAS 36 *Impairment of Assets* points out that greater weight should be given to external evidence when determining the best estimate of cash flow projections. Each key assumption should be consistent with external sources of information, or there should be disclosure of how these assumptions differ from experience or external sources of information. Economic conditions will also impact on the discount rate applied when calculating value in use.

Such an economic climate could result in the recognition of tax losses or the existence of deductible temporary differences where perhaps impairments are not yet deductible for tax purposes. The recognition of deferred tax assets requires detailed consideration of the carry forward of unused tax losses, whether future taxable profits exist, and the need for disclosing judgements made in these circumstances.

IAS 12 *Income Taxes* limits the recognition of a deferred tax asset to the extent that it is probable that future taxable profits will be available against which the deductible temporary difference can be utilised. IAS 12 states that the existence of unused tax losses is strong evidence that future taxable profit might not be available. Therefore, recent losses make the recognition of deferred tax assets conditional upon the existence of convincing other evidence. The probability that future taxable profit will be available to utilise the unused tax losses will need to be reviewed and if convincing evidence is available, there should be disclosure of the amount of a deferred tax asset and the nature of the evidence supporting its recognition. It is particularly relevant to disclose the period used for the assessment of the recovery of a deferred tax asset as well as the judgements made.

(b) Indefinite useful life and cash-generating unit

Under IAS 38 *Intangible Assets,* an intangible asset has an indefinite useful life only if there is no 'foreseeable' limit to its useful life as in the case of a brand name. In the case of Pod, the customer relationship is with individuals and therefore there is by definition a time limit to that relationship. Difficulties in accurately determining an intangible asset's useful life do not provide a basis for regarding that useful life as indefinite. Where the cash flows are expected to continue for a finite period, the useful life of the asset is limited to that period, whereas if the cash flows are expected to continue indefinitely, the useful life is indefinite. The concept of indefinite not meaning infinite life refers to the fact that for intangible assets with an indefinite useful life, maintenance costs are necessary in order that cash inflows may continue for an unlimited period of time. For example, brand names do not have an infinite useful life if no investment is made in them. This argument does not apply to the circumstances of this case and therefore Pod is in contravention of IAS 38.

According to IAS 36 *Impairment of Assets,* a CGU is defined as the smallest identifiable group of assets generating cash inflows which are largely independent of the cash inflows from other assets or groups of assets. In accordance with IAS 36, one factor to be considered is the monitoring of the entity's operations. Pod used the daily sales information and monthly statements of profit or loss of each individual branch to monitor its operations and to make decisions about continuing or disposing of its assets and operations. Each individual branch generates cash inflows which are largely independent of those generated by the other individual branches. Therefore, each branch should be identified as a separate CGU because Pod monitors and makes decisions about its assets and operations at the individual branch level.

63 Lucky Dairy

> **Workbook references.** IAS 41 is covered in Chapter 3 of your workbook. IAS 37 is covered in Chapter 5 and IFRS 5 in Chapter 13.
>
> **Top tips.** In this question you are required to deal with a scenario that had as its main theme IAS 41 *Agriculture*. You should not, however, make the mistake of thinking that this question is just about IAS 41; it requires a knowledge of several other standards including IAS 37 and IFRS 5.

The dairy herd

The dairy herd is a **biological asset** as defined by IAS 41 *Agriculture*. IAS 41 states that a biological asset should be **measured at fair value less estimated point of sale costs** unless its fair value cannot be measured reliably. **Gains and losses** arising from a change in fair value should be **included in profit or loss** for the period.

In this case, fair value is based on market price and point of sale costs are the costs of transporting the cattle to the market. Cattle in the Ham and Shire regions is valued on this basis.

IAS 41 encourages companies to **analyse the change in fair value** between the movement due to **physical changes** and the movement due to **price changes** (see the table below). It also encourages companies to provide a quantified description of each group of biological assets. Therefore the value of the cows and the value of the heifers should be **disclosed separately** in the statement of financial position.

Valuing the dairy herd for the Dale Region is less straightforward as its **fair value cannot be measured reliably at the date of purchase**. In this situation IAS 41 requires the herd to be valued at **cost less any impairment losses**. The standard also requires companies to provide an **explanation of why** fair value cannot be measured reliably and the **range of estimates** within which fair value is likely to fall.

Valuation of cattle, excluding Dale region

	Cows	Heifers	Total
	$'000	$'000	$'000
Fair value of herd at 1 June 20X1 (50,000 × 50)	2,500		2,500
Purchase 1 December 20X1 (25,000 × 40)		1,000	1,000
Increase in fair value less estimated point of sale costs due to price change:			
(50,000 × (55 – 50)/25,000 × (42 – 40))	250	50	300
Increase in fair value less estimated point of sale costs due to physical change:			
(50,000 × (60 – 55)/25,000 × (46 – 42))	250	100	350
Fair value less estimated point of sale costs at			
31 May 20X2 (50,000 × 60/25,000 × 46)	<u>3,000</u>	<u>1,150</u>	<u>4,150</u>

Valuation of cattle in Dale Region

	$'000
Cost at 1 June 20X1	
Cows (20,000 × 50)	1,000
Heifers (10,000 × 40)	400
	1,400
Less impairment loss	(200)
	1,200

Note. The herd is impaired because its recoverable amount is $1.2 million. This is the higher of fair value less costs to sell of $1 million (the amount that the Lucky Dairy has been offered) and value in use of $1.2 million (discounted value of the milk to be produced).

	$'000
Estimated fair value at 31 May 20X2 (for disclosure only):	
Cows (20,000 × 60)	1,200
Heifers (10,000 × 55)	550
	1,750

Milk

The milk is **agricultural produce** as defined by IAS 41 and should normally be measured at **fair value less estimated point of sale costs at the time of milking**. In this case the company is holding ten times the amount of inventory that it would normally hold and it is probable that much of this milk is unfit for consumption. The company should estimate the amount of milk that will not be sold and **write down** the inventory accordingly. The write down should be disclosed separately in the income statement as required by IAS 1 *Presentation of Financial Statements*.

Government grant

Under IAS 41, the government grant should be recognised as income **when it becomes receivable**. As it was only on 6 June 20X2 that the company received official confirmation of the amount to be paid, the income **should not be recognised in the current year**. The amount may be sufficiently material to justify disclosure as a non-adjusting event after the balance sheet date.

Legal proceedings and additional compensation

The lawyers have indicated that the company will probably be found liable for passing on the disease to consumers. There is a **present obligation as the result of a past obligating event** and therefore a **provision for $2 million should be recognised**, as required by IAS 37 *Provisions, Contingent Liabilities and Contingent Assets*.

IAS 37 states that **reimbursement** should only be recognised when it is **virtually certain** to be received. It is **only possible** that the company will receive compensation for the legal costs and therefore this **cannot be recognised**. However, the compensation should be **disclosed** as a contingent asset in the financial statements.

Planned sale of Dale farms

The Board of Directors has **approved the planned closure**, but there has **not yet been a public announcement**. Despite the fact that a local newspaper has published an article on the possible sale, the company **has not created a valid expectation** that the sale will take place and in fact **it is not certain** that the sale will occur. Therefore, there is **no 'constructive obligation'** and under IAS 37 **no provision should be made** for redundancy or any other costs connected with the planned sale.

Under IFRS 5 *Non-Current Assets Held for Sale and Discontinued Operations* Dale must be treated as a **continuing operation** for the year ended 31 May 20X2 as the sale has not taken place. As management are **not yet fully committed** to the sale **neither the operation as a whole nor any of the separate assets of Dale can be classified as 'held for sale'.**

Workbook references. Government grants are covered in Chapter 3, statements of cash flow in Chapter 16, IFRS 10 in Chapter 10, IAS 12 in Chapter 6 and IAS 8 in Chapter 2.

Top tips. Part (a), on the treatment of 'green certificates', effectively tested IAS 20 on government grants, a standard familiar from your earlier studies. It is important to explain **why** the certificates need to be accounted for as government grants. Do not limit your answer to IAS 20. Part (b) was on exchange differences in statements of cash flows. This topic may also be tested as an adjustment in a statement of cash flows question. The key point is that the exchange differences are not cash flows but reconciling items in the movement of cash and cash equivalents. Part (c) tested the issue of control, with the slightly unusual scenario that the parent wished to continue to consolidate an investment that it did not control. Again, the discussion is of more than a single IFRS. There are a number of IFRSs which deal with group accounting and candidates should look at these standards in conjunction with each other. In this question control was determined by looking at IFRS 10 but, additionally, if an entity is not a subsidiary then other standards should be consulted such as IFRS 11 for joint control implications and IAS 28 for equity accounting possibilities. A narrow answer dealing with IFRS 10 would have restricted the marks. Part (d) dealt with the issue of whether a correction to the tax provision in a previous year should be dealt with as a prior period adjustment. It shouldn't, as it is a change in accounting estimate. These items related to adjustments arising from tax audits by the authorities in relation to previous reporting periods. In this and the above part of the question the issues set out in the question were critical to a good answer.

Easy marks. In part (c) you will get marks for textbook knowledge of the definition of control in IFRS 10. Part (d) draws on basic knowledge of the presentation of current tax.

Marking scheme

		Marks
(a)	1 mark per point up to maximum	8
(b)	1 mark per point up to maximum	5
(c)	1 mark per point up to maximum	7
(d)	1 mark per point up to maximum	5
		25

(a) **Green certificates**

The applicable standard relating to the green certificates is IAS 20 *Accounting for Government Grants and Disclosure of Government Assistance.*

The principle behind the Standard is that of accruals or matching: the **grant received must be matched with the related costs**.

Government grants are assistance by government in the form of transfers of resources to an entity in return for past or future compliance with certain conditions relating to the operating activities of the entity. A government grant is recognised only when there is reasonable assurance that the entity will comply with the conditions attaching to it and the grants will be received. In the case of the green certificates, the condition that must be complied with is the environmentally friendly production of electricity, as verified by an independent audit.

There are two main types of grants:

(i) **Grants related to assets.** These are grants whose primary condition is that an entity qualifying for them should purchase, construct or otherwise acquire long-term assets. Subsidiary conditions may also be attached restricting the type or location of the assets or the periods during which they are to be acquired or held.

(ii)   **Grants related to income.** These are government grants other than grants related to assets.

Since Coate can trade the green certificates, they are not long-term assets, and therefore fall into the category of **grants related to income**. They must be matched against the related costs of production of 'green electricity', as they are a form of government compensation for these costs.

There are two possible ways of presenting the grants (green certificates).

(i)   As a credit in profit or loss, either separately or under a general heading such as 'other income'; or

(ii)   As a deduction from the related expense.

The **green certificates** are items held for sale in the ordinary course of business, and therefore should be recognised as **inventories** in accordance with IAS 2 *Inventories*. Green certificates that are unsold at the end of the reporting period are included in inventory and charged to production as **part of the cost of sales**.

A **deferred income approach** is used to match the grant to the related cost as follows:

To record the quarterly receipt of the grant

DEBIT   Certificate (SOFP) $ Fair value of certificate at receipt
CREDIT   Deferred income (SOFP) $ Fair value of certificate at receipt

On the sale of a certificate: contribution to cost of production

When the certificate is sold its fair value may be recognised in profit or loss. It is treated as a deduction from cost of sales because it is a contribution to the cost of generating the 'green electricity'.

DEBIT   Deferred income (SOFP) $ Fair value of certificate at receipt
CREDIT   Cost of sales (SPLOCI) $ Fair value of certificate at receipt

On the sale of a certificate: surplus/deficit

The certificate may be sold for more or less than its fair value at the time it was received from the government. This surplus/deficit is taken to/deducted from revenue in the SPLOCI.

DEBIT   Bank/receivable (SOFP) $ Fair value of trade
CREDIT   Certificate (SOFP) $ Fair value of certificate at receipt
DEBIT/CREDIT Revenue (SPLOCI) $ Balance (deficit/surplus)

Following IAS 1 *Presentation of Financial Statements*, Coate is required to **disclose its accounting policy** in relation to government grants. IAS 20 specifically requires disclosure of **the nature and extent of the government assistance given and any conditions not yet fulfilled or related contingencies**. The disclosures of unfulfilled conditions are unlikely to be extensive because an audit must be completed to show that the conditions have been fulfilled.

(b)   **Foreign exchange and cash flows**

According to IAS 7 *Statement of Cash Flows*, **unrealised foreign exchange gains and losses are not cash flows**. However, IAS 7 requires that the components making up the total opening and closing balances of cash and cash equivalents in the statement of cash flows should be disclosed in order to **reconcile cash and cash equivalents at the beginning and end of the period**.

Individual accounts (foreign cash balances)

Coate holds **foreign currency cash and cash equivalent** balances. As these are **monetary items**, IAS 21 *The Effects of Changes in Foreign Exchange Rates* requires them to

be **retranslated at the closing rate** at the reporting date. Exchange **gains and losses are recorded in profit or loss** in Coate's i**ndividual** financial statements.

Consolidated accounts (overseas subsidiary)

IAS 21 requires the **assets and liabilities** (both monetary and non-monetary) of the overseas subsidiary to be **translated at the closing rate in the consolidated financial statements**. **Income and expenses** are translated at the rate ruling at the date of the transaction or the **average rate** as a close approximation. **Exchange differences** arising on retranslation of opening net assets and retained profit for each peiod are recorded in **other comprehensive income** and held in a translation reserve which is a separate component of equity. **On disposal** of the subsidiary, the gains or losses are **reclassified from other comprehensive income to profit or loss for the year**.

In the **consolidated statement of cash flows**, if the **indirect method** is adopted, these exchange differences are **removed from profit before tax** as an adjustment within 'operating activities'. Instead they are shown at the foot of the consolidated statement of cash flows (as a separate heading from operating, investing and financing activities) as **part of the reconciliation** between opening and closing cash and cash equivalent balances.

As the subsidiary was acquired during the current year, its cash and cash equivalents at the date of acquisition would have been recorded as a **cash flow within 'investing activities'**. As its year end cash and cash equivalents balance would have also been included in the closing cash and cash equivalents balance at the foot of the consolidated statement of cash flows translated at the closing rate, the exchange difference arising from the **movement in exchange rates** between the acquisition date and the year end will have to be shown **separately at the foot of the statement of cash flows** as part of the movement in cash and cash equivalents.

(c) **Treatment of former subsidiary**

Coate wishes to continue to consolidate its investment in Patten, of which it has sold 50% to Manis. The requirement (or in this case permission) to consolidate an investment is determined by **control**, not merely by ownership. In most cases, this will involve the parent company owning a majority of the ordinary shares in the subsidiary (to which normal voting rights are attached). There are circumstances, however, when the parent may own an equal share or only a minority of the voting power in the subsidiary, **but** the parent still has control. Coate is arguing that it still has control over Patten because of the agreement made with Manis that Coate would exercise general control over Patten's operating and financial policies. Whether this is the case will be determined in accordance with IFRS 10 *Consolidated Financial Statements*.

IFRS 10 states that an investor **controls** an investee if and only if it has all of the following:

(i) **Power** over the investee

(ii) Exposure, or rights, to **variable returns** from its involvement with the investee; and

(iii) The **ability to use its power** over the investee to affect the amount of the investor's returns.

Power is defined as **existing rights that give the current ability to direct the relevant activities of the investee**. In some cases assessing power is straightforward, for example, where power is obtained directly and solely from having the majority of voting rights or potential voting rights, and as a result the ability to direct relevant activities. In other cases, assessment is more complex and more than one factor must be considered. Coate has only 50% of the voting rights of Patten, and so other factors come into play here.

IFRS 10 gives the following examples of **rights**, other than voting or potential voting rights, which individually, or alone, can give an investor power.

(i)   Rights to appoint, reassign or remove key management personnel who can direct the relevant activities

(ii) Rights to appoint or remove another entity that directs the relevant activities

(iii) Rights to direct the investee to enter into, or veto changes to transactions for the benefit of the investor

(iv) Other rights, such as those specified in a management contract

Coate does not appear to have these rights over Patten. While the shareholder agreement gives Coate influence over Patten, the requirement for consensus with Manis relates to **decisions made in the ordinary course of business,** such as significant changes in the company's activities or budgets, appointment and dismissal of senior employees. Coate argues that it is customary within the industry to require shareholder consensus for such decisions, but the **extent of the restrictions precludes control by Coate**. Rather, the consensus requirements suggest **joint control,** and indicate that this is a joint arrangement, as per IFRS 11 *Joint Arrangements*. IFRS 11 defines joint control as:

> The contractually agreed sharing of control of an arrangement, which exists only when decisions about the relevant activities require the unanimous consent of the parties sharing control.   (Appendix A)

There are two types of joint arrangements: joint ventures and jointly controlled entities. Patten is a **separate vehicle**. As such, it could be either a joint operation or joint venture, so other facts must be considered.

There are no facts that suggest that Coate and Manis have rights to the assets of Patten in the consolidated financial statements nor an obligation for its liabilities. Therefore, as each party has an interest in the **net assets** of Patten, Patten should be treated as a **joint venture** (rather than a joint operation). Manis must be **de-consolidated from the Coate group,** and **equity accounted for** as a **joint venture** instead.

(d)   **Tax adjustment**

According to IAS 12 *Income Taxes* the tax expense in the statement of profit or loss and other comprehensive income includes the tax charge for the year, any under or overprovision of income tax from the previous year and any increase or decrease in the deferred tax provision:

	$
Current tax expense	X
Under/(over) provisions relating to prior periods	X/(X)
Increases/(decreases) in the deferred tax balance	X/(X)
	X

While the correction of an over- or under-provision relates to a prior period, this is **not a prior period adjustment** as defined in IAS 8 *Accounting Policies, Changes in Accounting Estimates and Errors* as assumed by Coate. Rather, it is a **change in accounting estimate**.

Changes in accounting estimates result from new information or new developments and, accordingly, are **not corrections of errors**. A prior period error, which would require a prior period adjustment is **an omission or misstatement arising from failure to use reliable information** that was available or could have been obtained at the time of the authorisation of the financial statements. This is **not the case here**. Coate had accounted for all known issues at the previous year end (30 November 20X1), and could not have foreseen that the tax adjustment would be required. No penalties were applied by the taxation

authorities, indicating that there were no fundamental errors in the information provided to them. Correction of an over- or under-provision for taxation is routine, since taxation liabilities are difficult to estimate.

The effect of a change in accounting estimate must be **applied by the company prospectively** by including it in profit or loss in the period of change, with separate disclosure of the adjustment in the financial statements.

65 Marrgrett

Workbook references. Basic groups is covered in Chapter 10. Changes in group structure as a result of acquisitions is covered in Chapter 11, and disposals is covered in Chapter 12.

Top tips. This question requires an understanding of IFRS 3 *Business Combinations* in order to provide advice on various aspects of group accounting. Marks are available for discussion and application of the change in accounting treatment from equity accounting for an associate to consolidation of a subsidiary, with reference to control. Marks are also available for discussing the partial disposal of subsidiaries – one in which control is retained and the other in which control is lost but significant influence is retained.

Easy marks. The basic elements of IFRS 3 should be reasonably easy to explain.

Marking scheme

	Marks
IFRS 3 general requirements	3
Increase in holding	4
Consideration	5
Intangible assets	3
NCI	5
Reorganisation provision	2
IFRS 10	3
	25

IFRS 3 General requirements

IFRS 3 *Business Combinations* requires all business combinations to be accounted for as **acquisitions.**

Marrgrett is proposing to purchase additional shares in its associate, Josey. An increase from 30% to 70% will **give control,** as the holding passes the all-important 50% threshold. This is a step-acquisition, which IFRS 3 calls a 'business combination achieved in stages (para. 32(iii)).

Items included in the consideration

All consideration is measured at fair value.

Contingent consideration

The additional shares being offered to Josey's shareholders to the value of $50,000 are part of the consideration contingent on the achievement of a certain level of profitability.

IFRS 3 recognises that, by entering into an acquisition, the acquirer becomes obliged to make additional payments. IFRS 3 **requires recognition of contingent consideration, measured at fair value, at the acquisition date.**

306

The shares worth up to $50,000 meet the IAS 32 *Financial Instruments: Presentation* definition of a financial liability. This contingent consideration will be **measured at fair value,** and any **changes** to the fair value on subsequent re-measurement will be taken to **profit or loss for the year**.

Equity interest already held

Consideration includes cash, assets, contingent consideration, equity instruments, options and warrants. It also includes the **fair value of any equity interest already held.** This means that **the 30% holding must be re-measured to fair value** at the date of the acquisition of the further 40% holding. The revalued 30% stake, together with the consideration transferred in the form of cash and shares, is compared to the fair value of Josey's net assets at the date control was obtained, in order to arrive at a figure for goodwill.

Any **gain or loss** on the revaluation of the associate is taken to **profit or loss for the year**.

Items not included in the consideration

Transaction costs

IFRS 3 requires **costs relating to the acquisition to be recognised as an expense** at the time of the acquisition. They are not regarded as an asset, nor do they form part of the consideration. (Costs of issuing debt or equity are to be accounted for under the rules of IFRS 9.)

Share options

As an incentive to the shareholders and employees of Josey to remain in the business, Marrgrett has offered share options in Josey. These are conditional on them remaining in employment for two years after the acquisition, that is they are contingent on future events. The question arises of whether they are **contingent consideration**, for which the treatment is specified in the revised IFRS 3, **or as compensation** for services after the acquisition, for which the treatment is given in IFRS 2 Share-based payment.

The conditions attached to the share options are employment based, rather than contingent on, say, the performance of the company. Accordingly, the options do not form part of the consideration and must be treated as **compensation and valued under the rules of IFRS 2. The charge will be to post-acquisition earnings**, since the options are given in exchange for services after the acquisition.

Effect of type of consideration

The nature of the consideration transferred – cash, shares, contingent, and so on – **does not affect the goodwill**. However, the structure of the payments may affect post-acquisition profits. For example if part of the consideration is contingent (as here), changes to the fair value will be reflected in profit or loss for the year in future years.

Intangible assets

Josey's intangible assets will be **recognised on acquisition** by Marrgrett of a controlling stake. IFRS 3 requires the acquirer to recognise, separately from goodwill, all identifiable assets of the acquiree. The more intangibles are recognised, the lower the figure for goodwill, which is consideration transferred less fair value of assets acquired and liabilities assumed.

Non-controlling interest

IFRS 3 and IFRS 10 view the group as a single entity in which non-controlling shareholders are also shareholders in the group. This means that goodwill attributable to the non-controlling interest needs to be recognised.

IFRS 3 gives a **choice** as to how to value non-controlling interest:

> For each business combination, the acquirer shall measure any non-controlling interest in the acquiree **either at fair value or at the non-controlling interest's proportionate share of the acquiree's identifiable net assets** (para. 19)

IFRS 3 suggests that the closest approximation to fair value will be the market price of the shares held by the non-controlling shareholders just before the acquisition by the parent.

Non-controlling interest at fair value will be different from non-controlling interest at proportionate share of the acquiree's net assets. The difference is goodwill attributable to non-controlling interest, which may be, but often is not, proportionate to goodwill attributable to the parent.

Partial disposal

The treatment of a partial disposal depends on whether or not control is retained. Generally, control is lost when the holding is decreased to less than 50%.

On disposal of a controlling interest, any retained interest (an associate or trade investment) is measured at fair value on the date that control is lost. This fair value is used in the calculation of the gain or loss on disposal, and also becomes the carrying amount for subsequent accounting for the retained interest.

If the **50%** boundary is **not crossed**, as when the interest in a subsidiary is reduced, the disposal is treated as a **transaction between owners**.

Whenever the 50% boundary is crossed, the existing interest is revalued, and a gain or loss is reported in profit or loss for the year. If the 50% boundary is not crossed, no gain or loss is reported; instead there is an **adjustment to the parent's equity**.

Marrgrett intends to **retain control of the first subsidiary**, so in this case there will be no gain or loss, but an adjustment to the Marrgrett's equity to reflect the increase in non-controlling interest. In the case of the **second subsidiary,** however, **control is lost**. A **gain will be recognised on the portion sold, and also on the portion retained,** being the difference between the fair value and the carrying amount of the interest retained.

Re-organisation provision

IFRS 10 *Consolidated Financial Statements* explains that a plan to restructure a subsidiary following an acquisition is not a present obligation of the acquiree at the acquisition date, unless it meets the criteria in IAS 37 *Provisions, Contingent Liabilities and Contingent Assets*. This is very unlikely to be the case at the acquisition date. Therefore, Marrgrett **should not recognise a liability** for the re-organisation of the group at the date of the acquisition.

This **prevents creative accounting**. An acquirer cannot set up a provision for restructuring or future losses of a subsidiary and then release this to profit or loss in subsequent periods in order to reduce losses or smooth profits.

66 Marchant

Workbook reference. Basic groups are covered in Chapter 10 and disposals are covered in Chapter 12.

Top tips. Part (a) tests several key consolidation principles including relatively straightforward goodwill calculations, an adjustment for intragroup sale of inventory was incorporated (with a 'twist' in that the sale was at fair value so the unrealised loss was genuine) and two disposals, one where control was lost and one in which control was retained. It is important that you know the difference in the treatment, so be sure to revise this if you had difficulty. The impairment of goodwill element of the question requires specific knowledge that the subsequent increase in the recoverable amount of the goodwill is considered to be internally generated rather than a reversal of purchased goodwill impairment. IAS 38 *Intangible Assets* prohibits the recognition of internally generated goodwill, thus any reversal of impairment is not recognised.

Easy marks. There are easy marks available for the calculation of goodwill and for the intragroup part of the question. Remember that marks are given for correct principles with inaccurate calculations.

In Part (b) of the question you are asked to explain, with suitable calculations, how the sale of the 8% interest in a subsidiary should be dealt with in the group statement of financial position at 30 April 20X4. Marks are available for the explanation and the calculation so do not simply show the calculation or you will lose marks.

Marking scheme

			Marks
(a)	(i)	Goodwill Nathan and Option	
		Discussion 1 mark per point to a maximum	4
		Calculation	4
			8
	(ii)	Intra group trading	
		Discussion 1 mark per point to a maximum	3
	(iii)	Disposal of Option	
		Discussion 1 mark per point to a maximum	4
	(iv)	Investment in Nathan in separate financial statements	
		Fair value gain – Discussion 1 mark per point to a maximum	2
		Gain on disposal – Discussion 1 mark per point to a maximum	4
		Calculation	3
			9
(a)		Sale of equity interest in Nathan	
		Discussion 1 mark per point to a maximum	4
		Calculation	2
			6
			30

(a) (i) **Goodwill**

Goodwill on the acquisition of Nathan and Option should have been calculated as follows:

	Nathan $m	Option $m
Fair value of consideration transferred	80.0	70.0
Fair value of non-controlling interest	45.0	28.0
Fair value of identifiable net assets acquired	(110.0)	(86.0)
Goodwill at acquisition date	15.0	12.0
Impairment loss to 30.4.X3: 15 × 20%	(3.0)	–
	12.0	12.0

It is Marchant's policy to apply the 'full goodwill' method and therefore the non-controlling interest should be included in the calculation of goodwill at fair value.

Subsequent to acquisition goodwill should be carried in the statement of financial position at cost less any accumulated impairment losses.

The impairment of the goodwill in Nathan as calculated above had been reversed by Marchant and the goodwill increased to $2m more than its original value, giving an increase of $(3m + 2m) = $5m and a carrying amount of $17m. However, after the goodwill has been impaired, any subsequent increase is considered internally generated goodwill which cannot be recognised. IAS 36 *Impairment of Assets* prohibits the reversal of impairment on goodwill. The $3m uplift and $2m increase cannot be recognised and must be eliminated, so $5m is charged to profit or loss.

DEBIT	Profit or loss	$5m	
CREDIT	Goodwill – Nathan		$5m

Total goodwill is therefore $24m.

(ii) **Intragroup trading**

In order for the consolidated financial statements to display the group as a single economic entity reporting only the transactions which are external to the group, it is necessary to perform a consolidation adjustment to exclude firstly the intra group sale/purchase and secondly to eliminate any unrealised profit.

(1) Cancel intra group sales/purchases:

DEBIT	Revenue	$12m	
CREDIT	Cost of sales (purchases)		$12m

(2) Unrealised profit/loss:

There is an 'unrealised' **loss** on the sale of the inventory. Losses are not cancelled and therefore must remain in the consolidated financial statements as the sale at a loss indicates that the inventory was impaired. No adjustment is required.

(iii) **Group profit on disposal of Option (control lost)**

Marchant has lost control of Option as a result of the sale on 1 November 20X3 of a 40% equity interest. Option's status changes from that of a subsidiary (60% holding) to an associate (20% holding), over which Marchant retains significant influence. An 'accounting boundary' has been crossed because the holding reduces to below 50% and therefore it is appropriate to calculate a gain or loss on disposal, for recognition in profit or loss, under IFRS 3 *Business Combinations*. The effective date of disposal is when control passes, in this case 1 November 20X3. The consolidated financial statements of Marchant the year ended 30 April 20X4 should include the results of Option up to this date with the related non-controlling interest at 40%. The investment should be accounted for as an associate using equity accounting thereafter.

	$m	$m
Fair value of consideration received		50
Fair value of 20% investment retained		40
Less share of consolidated carrying amount when control lost		
Net assets	90	
Goodwill ((a) (ii))	12	
Less non-controlling interests	(34)	
		(68)
		22

(iv) **Investment in Nathan – fair value gain and gain on disposal in separate financial statements**

Marchant has recorded a fair value gain on the investment in Nathan of $95m – $90m = $5m in its individual financial statements for the year ended 30 April 20X4. This gain must be eliminated on consolidation because the calculation of goodwill is based on the fair value of the consideration at the date of acquisition, not at the date of the current financial statements. The double entry for the reversal is:

DEBIT	Other comprehensive income	$5m
CREDIT	Investment in Nathan	$5m

Reversal of fair value gain recognised in parent's separate financial statements

The sale of the 8% equity in Nathan does not result in loss of control (60 – 8 = 52%) and Nathan remains a subsidiary. It represents a decrease in the controlling interest and is accounted for as a transaction between owners under IFRS 3 *Business Combinations*. It is shown as a movement in the parent's equity in the consolidated financial statements, with no profit or loss arising. Accordingly, the gain on the sale recognised in the parent's separate financial statements must be reversed on consolidation:

		$m	$m
DEBIT	Profit or loss (18 – (95 × 8%/60%))	5.33	
DEBIT	Investment in Nathan (95 × 8%/60%)	12.67	
CREDIT	Other components of equity		18

(b) **Sale of 8% interest in Nathan**

When Marchant disposed of 8% of its holding in Nathan, Nathan went from being a 60% subsidiary to a 52% subsidiary. In other words **control is retained**. No accounting boundary has been crossed, and the event is treated as a transaction between owners.

The accounting treatment is as follows:

Statement of profit or loss and other comprehensive income

(1) The subsidiary is **consolidated in full** for the whole period.

(2) The **non-controlling interest in the statement of profit or loss and other comprehensive income** is based on percentage before and after disposal, ie time apportioned. In this case, the sale took place on the last day of the year, so there is a 40% non-controlling interest for the whole year.

(3) There is **no profit or loss on disposal**.

Statement of financial position

(1) The change (increase) in non-controlling interests is shown as an adjustment to the parent's equity in order to represent the reallocation of ownership between the group's equity holders.

(2) The 'closing' non-controlling interest will be based on the year end percentage of 48% (40 + 8 = 48%).

(3) Goodwill on acquisition is unchanged in the consolidated statement of financial position because it is an historical figure unaffected by the change in ownership. The sale may, however, be an indicator of impairment and therefore the directors must test the goodwill for impairment at disposal.

The adjustment to the parent's equity is as follows:

Non-controlling interest at year end:

	$m
Non-controlling interest at acquisition	45.0
NCI share of post-acquisition reserves: 40% × $(120 − (25 + 65 + 6))	9.6
Impairment ($15m x 20% = $3.0m ((a) (ii)) @ 40%)	(1.2)
	53.4

Increase in NCI: $53.4m × 8%/40% = $10.68m

	$m
Fair value of consideration received	18.00
Increase in NCI in net assets and goodwill at disposal	(10.68)
Adjustment to parent's equity	7.32

67 Traveler

Workbook references. Step acquisitions are covered in Chapter 11. Impairment of financial assets is covered in Chapter 7. Fair value adjustments are covered in Chapter 10.

Top tips. For part (a)(i), for the financial asset, you need to identify which of the three stages in the credit loss model is appropriate then apply the relevant accounting treatment. For part (b), perform the calculations first then add the explanations but do not omit the explanations or you will not pass this part of the question. For parts (a)(ii), (iii), and (iv), the key to the calculations is to draw up the relevant proformas for goodwill, retained earnings and non-controlling interests (NCI) then work through the question identifying the relevant numbers and adding them to your proformas. In part (b), discussion of the principles and ethical issues is what is required. This is a good example of what is likely to be tested in group questions in SBR.

Marking scheme

			Marks
(a)	(i)	Loan	
		Classification	2
		Impairment	3
			5
	(ii)	Goodwill	2
		Consideration transferred	2
		Impairment	6
		Fair value adjustments	2
			10
	(iii)	Retained earnings	3
	(iv)	Non-controlling interest	4
(b)		Intra-group transactions and ethics	8
			30

(a) (i) **Loan**

The loan is a **financial asset** held at **amortised cost** under IFRS 9 *Financial Instruments*. Traveler wishes to value the loan at fair value. However, IFRS 9 states that the classification of an instrument is determined on initial recognition and that **reclassifications**, which are not expected to occur frequently, are **permitted** only if the entity's **business model changes**.

Financial assets are subsequently measured at **amortised cost** if **both** of the following apply:

(i) The asset is held within a **business model** whose **objective** is to **hold the assets** to **collect the contractual cash flows**; and

(ii) The contractual terms of the financial asset give rise, on specified dates, to **cash flows** that are **solely payments of principal and interest** on the principal outstanding.

All other financial assets are measured at fair value.

Traveler's **objective** (and therefore its business model) for holding the debt instrument has **not changed**, and so it **cannot measure it at fair value** but must continue to measure it at amortised cost.

As Traveler has adopted IFRS 9 *Financial Instruments*, it must apply the standard's forward-looking impairment model. The financial statements must reflect the deterioration in the credit quality of the financial asset in order to provide users with more useful and timely information.

As the borrower is in financial difficulties, the loan is in **Stage 2**, meaning that the **credit quality of this financial asset has deteriorated significantly** since initial recognition, so **lifetime expected credit losses must be recognised** and the **increase charged to profit or loss**. Traveler is required to record the full value of the increased impairment immediately. The impairment, as shown below, should be calculated at the present value of expected credit shortfalls over the loan's remaining life.

DEBIT   Loss allowance
             (and Traveler's retained earnings 9.9 – 2) $7.9m
CREDIT   Financial assets $7.9m

(ii) **Goodwill on Data and Captive**

Traveler wishes to use the 'full goodwill' method for the calculation of goodwill on the acquisition of Data. This means incorporating the non-controlling interest into the goodwill calculation at fair value. Conversely, for the acquisition of Captive, Traveler has opted to apply the 'partial goodwill' method and this means the non-controlling interest is included in the goodwill calculation at its proportionate share of the acquiree's identifiable net assets.

Goodwill on the acquisition of Data and Captive should have been calculated as follows:

	Full method Data $m	Partial method Captive $m
Consideration transferred – for 60%	600	
Consideration transferred – for 80% (477 + 64) (W1)		541.0
Non-controlling interests		
Fair value (per question/ 526 × 20%)	395	105.2
FV of identifiable net assets at acq'n:	(935)	(526.0)
Goodwill at acquisition date	60	120.2
Impairment losses (W3)	(50)	(61.0)
Goodwill at 30 November 20X1	10	59.2
Total goodwill		69.2

Workings

1   *Group structure*

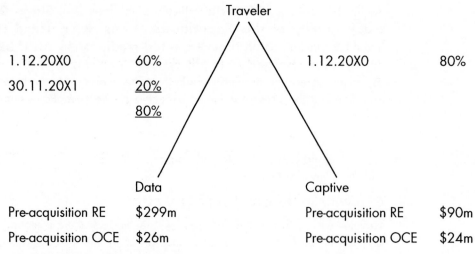

	Data		Captive	
Pre-acquisition RE	$299m		Pre-acquisition RE	$90m
Pre-acquisition OCE	$26m		Pre-acquisition OCE	$24m

2   *Consideration transferred: Captive*

The land transferred as part of the purchase consideration should be valued at its fair value of $64 million at the date of acquisition and included in the goodwill calculation.

This has been incorrectly treated as:

DEBIT	Cost of investment in Captive	$541m	
CREDIT	Profit or loss		$64m
CREDIT	Cash		$477m

The land needs to be removed from non-current assets, the $64m sales proceeds removed from profit or loss and a gain on disposal calculated. The gain is $64m sale consideration, less carrying amount of $56m = $8m. The correct entries should have been:

DEBIT	Cost of investment in Captive	$541m	
CREDIT	Profit or loss (gain on disposal)		$8m
CREDIT	Land		$56m
CREDIT	Cash		$477m

To correct, the entries are:

DEBIT	Profit or loss	$56m	
CREDIT	Land		$56m

3 *Impairment of goodwill*

	Data $m	Captive $m
Net assets at year end (per question)	1,079	604.0
Fair value adjustments (W4)	10	22.0
	1,089	626.0
Goodwill (Data 60, Captive 120.2 × 100%/80% (see Note 2)	60	150.3
	1,149	776.3
Recoverable amount (per question)	(1,099)	(700.0)
Impairment loss gross	50	76.3
Impairment loss recognised (see Note 1): 100%/80%	50	61.0

Notes

1 Because the non-controlling interest in Data is at fair value, goodwill arises on this non-controlling interest, which bears its share of any impairment using the proportions in which profits and losses are shared at the year end when the impairment review arose, that is, 20%. The gross impairment of $50m is taken to the goodwill working and the 20% ($10m) to the NCI working ((a)(iv)). In the case of Captive, where the partial goodwill method is used, only 80% of the impairment is taken to the goodwill working.

2 Because the non-controlling interest in Data is at fair value, the goodwill is already grossed up, but Captive uses the partial goodwill method, so the goodwill needs to be grossed up for an unrecognised NCI of 20%.

4 *Fair value adjustments*

	At acq'n 1.12.20X0 $m	Movement $m	At year end 30.11.20X1 $m
Data:			
Land: 935 – (600 + 299 + 26)	10	–	10
Captive:			
Land: 526 – (390 + 90 + 24)	22	–	22

The land is non-depreciable and therefore the fair value adjustments remain the same as at acquisition.

(iii) Retained earnings

	Traveler $m	Data $m	Captive $m
At year end (per question)	1,066.0	442	169
Loss allowance on loan (a)	(7.9)		
Consideration (W2)	(56.0)		
Pre-acquisition (per question)		(299)	(90)
		143	79

Group share

Data: 143 × 60%	85.8
Captive: 79 × 80%	63.2
Impairment losses (W3)) (50 × 80%) + 61	(101.0)
	1,050.1

(iv) Non-controlling interests

	Data $m	Captive $m
At acquisition (per question/(ii)	395.0	105.2
Post-acquisition share of retained earnings		
Data: 143 (iii) × 40%	57.2	
Captive: 79 (iii) × 20%		15.8
Post-acquisition share of other components of equity		
Data: (37-26)× 40%	4.4	
Captive: (45-24) × 20%		4.2
	456.6	125.2
Acquisition of additional 20% of Data (W1)	(228.3)	–
	228.3	125.2
Impairment losses: 50(W3)) × 20%	(10.0)	–
	218.3	125.2

343.5

Working: Adjustment to parent's equity on acquisition of additional 20% of Data

This is an increase in the controlling interest and therefore a reduction in the non-controlling interest, of 20%/40%:

DEBIT	Non-controlling interest		
	$456.6m × 20%/40%	$228.3m	
CREDIT	Investment		$220m
CREDIT	Parent's equity (other components of equity)		$8.3m

(b) The purpose of group accounts is to show the transactions of the group as if it is a single economic entity. Traveler has control over the economic resources of each subsidiary and therefore a clear picture of the group's position and performance can only be ascertained by combining the financial statements of the parent and all subsidiaries. 100% of the assets, liabilities, income and expenses are added together to reflect the parent entity's control over those resources. Part-ownership is reflected through the inclusion of a non-controlling interest.

Transactions between parent and subsidiaries are a perfectly normal aspect of business relationships. There are no specific rules as to what level of mark-up should be applied to such transactions. Entities are therefore free to determine the sales price which they wish on intra-group transactions and it need not be at arm's length. Intra-group transactions and unrealised profits are eliminated so that the consolidated financial statements best reflect substance and faithfully represent the transactions which pertain to the group. It is true that the mark-up or margin chosen will not alter the profits of the group, however, the impact upon the individual financial statements should still be considered.

A clear self-interest threat arises from the intention to sell the shares in Captive. The directors of Traveler have an incentive to increase the profits of Captive in order to secure as high a price as possible for the sale of the shares. This would be detrimental to the bidder and is a clear ethical issue. The directors should consider the guiding principles of the IASB's *Conceptual Framework* when considering how the mark-up will impact on the profits of the individual group members. The *Conceptual Framework* emphasises that for financial information to be useful, it must be relevant and faithfully represent what it purports to represent. Faithful representation requires accounting policies chosen to be neutral and objective. It could be argued that by deliberately inflating the mark-up, the directors are presenting financial statements which are not neutral or free from bias.

When assessing whether an ethical issue has arisen from the choice of mark-up, consideration of IAS 24 *Related Party Disclosures* is relevant. Traveler and Captive are related parties and the transfer of goods is a related party transaction. Information must be disclosed on related party transactions and balances necessary for users to understand the potential effect of the relationship on the financial statements. This is required since related party transactions are often not carried out on an arm's length basis. Indeed, related party transactions include transfers of resources, services or obligations regardless of whether a price is charged. Provided that the full effects of the transaction were properly disclosed, no ethical issue would arise from selling the goods at an unusually high margin.

68 Angel

Workbook reference. Group statements of cash flow are covered in Chapter 16.

Top tips. There are many straightforward, non-group aspects to this extracts from consolidated statement of cash flows question, so make sure you don't get bogged down in the information provided at the expense of these. We have set up workings for working capital reconciliations even though the movements are straightforward.

Make sure you allocate enough time to part (b) – it has eight marks available for straightforward IAS 7 knowledge.

Easy marks. These are available for the workings in Part (a) (iii) as well as explanations for the adjustments in Part (a), all of which are straightforward, along with valid points made in Part (b) on cash flow. The key point with cash flows is to ensure your understanding of the signage of each adjustment is clear, this will be important not only for your workings but also your explanation to the directors.

Marking scheme

			Marks
(a)	(i)	Building renovation	4
	(ii)	Profit before taxation	4
	(iii)	Cash generated from operations – up to 2 marks per item	14
(b)		Discussion 1 mark per point to a maximum	8
			30

(a) (i) **Building renovation**

The building renovation has been incorrectly accounted for because Angel has debited the cash spent to revenue and this needs to be corrected in order to capitalise the correct amount for the enhancement of the asset. The correcting entries are:

DEBIT	Property, plant and equipment (PPE) $3m	
CREDIT	Revenue	$3m

Being capitalisation of renovation of building and correction of charge to revenue

Angel treats grant income on capital-based projects as deferred income so it should not have credited the cash received from the grant to PPE and it needs to be reclassified to deferred income on the statement of financial position. The grant will then be released in line with future depreciation charges so as to recognise the benefit over the same period as the related costs it is intended to compensate. However, the grant of $2m needs to be split equally between renovation (capital) and job creation (revenue). There do not appear to be any future performance conditions relating to the job creation portion of the grant, so that part may be released immediately to profit and loss at the time the cash has become receivable. The correcting entries for this are:

DEBIT	Property, plant and equipment (PPE) $2m	
CREDIT	Retained earnings – profit or loss	$1m
CREDIT	Deferred income	$1m

Being correction of treatment of grant income

(ii) *Adjustments to profit before tax*

Profit before tax needs to be adjusted to take account of:

(1)   the correcting entries for the building refurbishment and grant in Part (a) (i).

(2)   The $4m construction costs for the machine have been incorrectly charged to other expenses and need to be capitalised as part of property, plant and equipment (information point (iii)).

(3)   The related interest of $1m which is allowable as part of the cost of the asset under IAS 23 *Borrowing Costs* needs to be capitalised (information point (iii)):

Correcting entries for points (2) and (3) are:

DEBIT	Property, plant and equipment $5m	
CREDIT	Profit or loss	$5m

Being correction of construction costs charged to operating expenses and capitalisation of interest under IAS 23.

Therefore, profit before tax may be adjusted as follows to arrive at a correct figure for inclusion in the cash flow statement:

	$m
Per question	184
Correction of renovation costs and grant (a)(i)	4
Correction of construction costs and interest (a)(ii)	5
	193

(iii)   ANGEL GROUP

EXTRACT FROM STATEMENT OF CASH FLOWS FOR THE YEAR ENDED 30 NOVEMBER 20X3

	$m
Operating activities	
Profit before tax (Part (a) (ii))	193.0
Adjustments for:	
Profit on sale of property, plant and equipment: (W1)	(14.0)
Depreciation (per question/W2)	29.0
Impairment of goodwill and intangible assets (per question/W3): $26.5m + $90m	116.5
Share of profit of associate (per question/W4)	(12.0)
Interest expense: $11m per question less $1m capitalised ((a) (ii) (W5)	10.0
	322.5
Decrease in trade receivables (W6)	58.0
Decrease in inventories (W6)	41.0
Decrease in trade payables (W6)	(211.0)
Cash generated from operations	210.5

Workings

1   *Profit on sale of property, plant and equipment (PPE)*

	$m
Proceeds from sale of PPE	63
Less carrying amount of PPE disposed	(49)
Profit on sale of property, plant and equipment	14

This amount needs to be deducted from profit before tax because the profit of $14m is a non-cash credit currently included within profit before tax. The cash proceeds figure of $63m will be included in the investing activities section.

2   *Depreciation*

The depreciation charge of $29m which has been deducted in arriving at the profit before tax figure. It is non-cash and must be added back.

3   *Impairment of goodwill and intangible assets*

The impairment charge of $116.5m, which has been deducted in arriving at the profit before tax figure, is a non-cash movement and, as with depreciation, it must be added back.

4   *Share of profit of associate*

The profit share of $12m recorded in Angel's profit or loss is again a non-cash figure and should therefore be deducted to arrive at a cash figure related to operations. Any dividend received by Angel from its associate during the year will be included as a cash receipt in the investing activities section of Angel's cash flow statement.

5   *Interest expense*

The interest charge of $10m (being the $11m paid less the $1m capitalised) is a cash payment. It is reclassified and shown in the cash flow statement below cash generated from operations as a charge to this figure, along with tax, to arrive at a net cash from operating activities figure.

6   *Working capital changes*

	Inventories $m	Trade receivables $m	Trade payables $m
b/d	190	180	361
Acquisition of subsidiary	6	3	5
∴ **Increase/(decrease)**	**(41)**β	**(58)**β	**(211)**β
c/d	155	125	155

Movements in working capital are brought into the cash generated from operations figure. If the inventories balance has fallen, there is less cash tied up in inventory held and the cash position benefits. The key point here is that Angel acquired a subsidiary, Sweety, during the financial year and gained inventory and trade receivable and payable balances without a related operational movement in cash. Therefore, these amounts must be adjusted when calculating the correct cash flow. The cash payment to acquire Sweety (net of the cash acquired) will be included in the investing activities section of the cash flow statement.

(b)   **Classification of cash flows**

IAS 7 *Statement of Cash Flows* requires the classification of cash flows under three main headings: operating activities, investing activities and financing activities. Operating activities are the principal revenue-producing activities of the entity. Investing activities are the acquisition and disposal of non-current assets and other investments not included in cash equivalents. Financing activities are activities that result in changes in the size and composition of the equity capital and borrowings of the entity.

The classification is, however, **not always straightforward**. Some cash flows which look similar may be **classified differently, depending on the nature of the business**. For example, an investment company might classify dividends received as a cash inflow from operating activities because investment is its operation, whereas a retail company would classify dividends received as an investing activity.

IAS 7 favours classification which **reflects the nature of an entity's activities** over classification in accordance with the underlying item in the statement of financial position.

The statement of cash flows shows the **movement in cash and cash equivalents** between the start and the end of the period. Cash is generally considered to be a straightforward item to determine; cash equivalents less so. IAS 7 defines them as 'short-term, highly liquid investments that are readily convertible to known amounts of cash and which are subject to an insignificant risk of changes in value'. The Standard does not define 'short-term' but does state that 'an investment normally **qualifies as a cash equivalent only when it has a short maturity** of, say, three months or less from the date of acquisition'.

Three months would not generally be long enough for a significant change in value, and is also consistent with the **purpose of meeting short-term cash commitments**. In limited circumstances, a longer-term deposit with an early withdrawal penalty may be treated as a cash equivalent. The terms of the arrangement need to be considered in each case:

(i)   The **$3m** on deposit for twelve months can be withdrawn early, but the penalty – loss of all interest earned – is so significant as to indicate that the cash is not intended to meet short-term cash commitments. Therefore, this investment would **not qualify as a cash equivalent.**

(ii)   The $7m deposit also has a twelve-month maturity period, and can be withdrawn with 21 days' notice. There is a penalty for early withdrawal, but this is much less severe

than the first deposit, being only a reduction in the rate of interest from 3% to 2%. This is normal for short-term deposits, as stated by the bank, indicating that the entity wishes to keep the funds available for short-term needs. Therefore, this deposit **does meet the IAS 7 definition of cash equivalents**.

69 Weston

Workbook reference. Group statements of cash flow are covered in Chapter 16. Ethics is covered in Chapter 2.

Top tips. In Part (a), the proceeds of disposal calculation is a little tricky, but the best way to approach it is to set out the working as for a profit/loss on disposal and find the proceeds as a balancing figure. It is also important to distinguish between cash flows and non-cash flows as well as being clear on signage. In part (b) you should refer to the principles of ACCA's *Code of Ethics and Conduct*.

Easy marks. There are many straightforward cash flows included in this question; the key is to think each transaction through and ensure you include all of the areas of the statement of cash flows affected in your answer. It is usually more than one.

Marking scheme

			Marks
(a)	(i)	Discussion of director's expectation	3
		IAS 7 requirements	2
		IAS 7 extracts	2
		Loss on disposal working	2
		Net assets at disposal working	3
		Goodwill working	2
		NCI at disposal working	2
			16
	(ii)	Discussion of impact of Southland acquisition	4
		IAS 7 extract and workings	4
			8
(b)		Ethical discussion	6
			30

(a) (i) **Effect of Northern disposal on Weston's consolidated statement of cash flow**

The directors' expectation that the loss on disposal of Northern will be added back to the profit before tax figure in the operating cash flows section of the cash flow to arrive at net cash flow from operating activities is incorrect. The profit before tax figure of $183m excludes the results from the discontinued operation, which is presented separately in accordance with IFRS 5 *Non-Current Assets Held for Sale and Discontinued Operations*. The overall discontinued result of $25m must be analysed between the element relating to the trading activities of Northern, which will cease on disposal, and that relating to the disposal transaction, which is a one-off benefit (in the case of disposal proceeds) to the ongoing group.

The 'trading' cash flows of Northern will be included in Weston's consolidated statement of cash flow until the date of disposal. In preparation, the profit before tax from discontinued operations of $6m is initially combined with the Weston Group's

other profits for the year, as are the other line items in the financial statements of Northern, to arrive at a consolidated position.

Subsequently, whether on the face of the cash flow or in the notes, the net cash flows attributable to the operating, investing and financing activities of the Northern discontinued operation must be disclosed, in accordance with IFRS 5, so that a picture of the continuing group can be derived by the user.

In accordance with IAS 7 *Statement of Cash Flows*, the net cash flows arising from losing control of a subsidiary, that is the proceeds on disposal less any cash held in the subsidiary, must be presented separately and classified as investing activities.

In accordance with IAS 7, Weston must disclose each of the following:

(i)   The total consideration received $85.4m (W1);

(ii)   The portion of the consideration consisting of cash and cash equivalents $85.4m;

(iii)   The amount of cash and cash equivalents held by Northern when control is lost $(2)m; and

(iv)   The amount of the assets and liabilities other than cash or cash equivalents in Northern when control is lost, summarised by each major category (see W2 below).

EXTRACT FROM WESTON GROUP STATEMENT OF CASH FLOWS: FOR THE YEAR ENDED 31 JANUARY 20X6: Proceeds on disposal of Northern

Cash flows from investing activities	$m	$m
Proceeds on disposal of Northern: 85.4 (W1) + 2	87.4	
Net cash from investing activities		87.4

The bank overdraft of $2m is added back to the fair value of consideration received of $85.4m, in order to show proceeds net of cash and cash equivalents disposed of as part of the transaction.

Workings

1   *Loss on disposal of Northern*

	$'000	$'000
Fair value of consideration received β		85.4
Less share of carrying amount when control lost:		
Net assets (W2)	129.0	
Goodwill (W3)	9.0	
Less non-controlling interests (W4)	(23.6)	
		(114.4)
Loss on disposal per question		(29.0)

2   *Net assets at date of disposal*

The fair value of the property, plant and equipment at disposal will be $80m as per the question plus the remaining balance of the $16m fair value uplift ($16m less 4/8 years depreciation = $88m). A deferred tax liability on the fair value adjustment would arise of (25% × $16m) = $4m which would be released in line with the extra depreciation, so the carrying amount at disposal will be only $2m ($4m − ($4m × 4/8)). The carrying amount of the entire deferred tax liability at disposal is therefore $8m ($6m per question + $2m).

	$'000
Property, plant and equipment (see Note above)	88
Inventories	38
Trade and other receivables	23
Trade and other payables	(10)
Deferred tax (see Note above)	(8)
Bank overdraft	(2)
	129

3   *Goodwill on acquisition of Northern*

	$m
Consideration transferred	132
Fair value of non-controlling interest	28
	160
Fair value of net assets at acquisition	(124)
Goodwill at acquisition	36
Impairment (75%)	(27)
Carrying amount of goodwill at disposal	9

4   *Non-controlling interests at date of disposal*

	$'000
Non-controlling interest at acquisition (FV)	28.0
NCI share of post-acquisition retained earnings: 20% × (129 (W2) – 124 (W3))	1.0
NCI share of goodwill impairment (20% × 27 (W3))	(5.4)
	23.6

(ii)   **Impact of acquisition of Southland on Weston's consolidated statement of cash flows**

In accordance with IAS 7 *Statement of Cash Flows,* when accounting for an investment in an associate, the statement of cash flows should show the cash flows between the investor and associate, for example, dividends and advances. So, Weston includes in its statement of cash flows the cash flows in respect of its investments in Southland, and distributions and other payments or receipts between it and the associate.

Therefore, the net cash flow from operating activities of the Weston group is determined by adjusting the consolidated profit or loss for the share of profits of the associate, Southland, because it is a non-cash contribution to group profits.

The investing section of the statement of cash flows incorporates:

(i)   The cash outflow on the purchase of the 40% interest in Southland on 1 February 20X5.

(ii)   The cash inflow received by the Weston Group, being its 40% share of the dividend paid out by Southland during the financial year, received in Weston's capacity as an equity shareholder.

EXTRACTS FROM WESTON GROUP STATEMENT OF CASH FLOWS: FOR THE YEAR ENDED 31 JANUARY 20X6: Impact of Southland associate

Cash flow from operating activities
Profit for the year: X
Share of profit of associate   (16)
                                                                                            X

Cash flows from investing activities
Dividends received from associate ($10m × 40%)   4
Purchase of associate (W1)   (90)
Net cash used in investing activities   (86)

Workings

1

	Associate $m
b/d (per question)	0
P/L	16
Acquisition of associate	**90** β
Cash rec'd (div. from associate)	10 × 40%
	(4)
c/d (per question)	102

(b) Ethical responsibility of accountant

Directors may in order to meet targets, wish to **present a company's results in a favourable light.** This may involve manipulation by creative accounting techniques such as window dressing, or, as is proposed by the directors of Weston, an **inaccurate classification**.

If the proceeds of the sale of investments in equity instruments and property, plant and equipment are presented in Weston's cash flow statement as part of 'cash generated from operations', the picture is **misleading**. Operating cash flow is crucial, in the long-term, for the survival of the company, because it derives from trading activities, which is what the company is there to do. Operating cash flows are seen as recurring whereas investing and financing cash flows tend to be more one-off. Weston's operations would not normally see it selling surplus machinery and equity investments as part of its trading operations. **Sales of assets generate short-term cash flow,** and cannot be repeated year-on-year, unless there are to be no assets left to generate trading profits with. This misclassification could be regarded as a deliberate attempt to mislead stakeholders about the performance of Weston, and its potential future performance, which is unethical.

As **a professional, the accountant has a duty,** not only to the **company** he works for, but also to his **professional body,** and to the **stakeholders** in the company. Classification of proceeds from selling machinery and investments should be classified as 'cash flows from **investing activities**' (rather than 'operating activities') according to IAS 7 *Statement of Cash Flows.* Also, IAS 1 *Presentation of Financial Statements* requires fair presentation. Under ACCA's *Code of Ethics and Conduct,* the accountant should adhere to the fundamental principle of **professional competence** and **due care** which includes preparing financial statements that comply with IFRS. Should the accountant permit the directors to proceed with their proposed accounting treatment, he or she would be in breach of this principle of professional competence and due care. There is a danger that the accountant feels pressured to follow the directors' proposed incorrect accounting treatment in order to protect their job security. Therefore, there is a **self-interest threat** in relation to the

directors and an **advocacy threat** in relation to the accountant feeling pressured to act in the directors' best interests.

It is essential that the accountant **tries to persuade the directors not to proceed with the adjustments**, which he or she must know violate IAS 7, and may well go against the requirements of local legislation. If, despite his protests, the directors insist on the misleading presentation, then the accountant has a duty to **bring this to the attention of the auditors**. If unsure of what to do, the accountant should seek professional advice from ACCA.

70 Kayte

Workbook references. IFRS 3 and IFRS 10 (control) are covered in Chapter 10 of your Workbook. IAS 16 is covered in Chapter 3.

Top tips. Part (b) required candidates to consider the IFRS 3 definition of a business. You were expected to base your discussion around the pointers in the scenario which suggested that the accounting treatment was incorrect, and that IFRS 3 principles of control should have been applied. Part (b) was more demanding, covering the application of IAS 16.

Easy marks. The discussion of control should have presented few problems.

Marking scheme

		Marks
(a)	IFRS 3 rather than asset acquisition	3
	Definition of the elements of a business	4
	Outsourced activities	2
	IFRS 10 and control	4
		13
(b)	Vessels sold after 10 years	5
	Vessels kept for 30 years	5
	Funnels	2
		12
		25

(a) **Acquisition of Ceemone**

Compliance with IFRS 3

Kayte has accounted for its investment in Ceemone as an asset acquisition, but this is **incorrect**. The investment **should have been accounted for as a business combination** in accordance with IFRS 3 *Business Combinations*. This has the following implications.

(i) Transaction costs must be expensed.

(ii) The vessels must be recognised at fair value.

(iii) Any deferred tax must be recognised at nominal value.

(iv) Goodwill must be recognised, being the difference between the fair value of the consideration transferred and the fair value of the identifiable assets acquired and the liabilities assumed.

IFRS 3 gives a **definition of a business**, which needs to be applied in determining whether a transaction is a business combination:

> 'An integrated set of activities and assets that is capable of being conducted and managed for the purpose of providing a return in the form of dividends, lower costs or other economic benefits directly to investors or other owners, members or participants.'

> (Appendix A)

A business generally has three elements.

(i)   **Inputs**. Any economic resource (eg non-current assets, intellectual property) that creates, or has the ability to create, outputs when one or more processes are applied to it. In the case of Ceemone, the inputs would be shares in vessel-owning companies, charter arrangements, outsourcing arrangements with a management company and relationships with a shipping broker.

(ii) **Process**. A system, standard, protocol, convention or rule that when applied to an input or inputs creates, or has the ability to create, outputs (eg strategic management, operational processes, resource management). For Ceemone, this would encompass financing the business, purchases and sales of the vessels and activities relating to chartering and operating the vessels.

(iii) **Outputs**. The result of inputs and processes applied to those inputs that provide, or have the ability to provide, a return in the form of dividends, lower costs or other economic benefits. The charter agreements would enable Ceemone to generate revenue and other economic benefits for Kayte. (IFRS 3 states that outputs are not required in order to qualify as a business.)

It is **not relevant that some activities were outsourced** to the management company. IFRS 3 states:

> 'Determining whether a particular set of assets and activities is a business should be based on whether the integrated set is capable of being conducted and managed as a business by a market participant. Thus, in evaluating whether a particular set is a business, it is not relevant whether a seller operated the set as a **business** or whether the acquirer intends to operate the set as a business.'   (para. B11)

Ceemone could choose to conduct and manage the integrated set of assets and activities as a business. In summary, **the acquisition includes all the elements which constitute a business** in accordance with IFRS 3 and must be accounted for as a business combination.

IFRS 10 and control

The directors of Kayte believe that the entity to which the vessels have been transferred and in which the bank holds a variable interest is a **subsidiary of the bank**. In determining this, IFRS 10 *Consolidated Financial Statements* looks at the substance of the transaction rather than its legal form. The key point is whether an investor has **control** over an investee.

IFRS 10 requires an acquirer to be identified in all business combinations, even where the business combination looks like a merger of equals. The acquirer is the entity which obtains **control** of the entity with which it is combined. It is not always easy to determine which party is the acquirer, and IFRS 10 gives guidance on the matter. The key point is **control,** rather than mere ownership, but this may not be easy to assess.

IFRS 10 states that an investor **controls** an investee if and only if it has all of the following.

(i)   **Power** over the investee;

(ii) Exposure, or rights, to **variable returns** from its involvement with the investee; and

(iii) The **ability to use its power** over the investee to affect the amount of the investor's returns.

Power is defined as **existing rights that give the current ability to direct the relevant activities of the investee**. There is no requirement for that power to have been exercised.

It is likely that the bank has power over the entity, and it may be exposed to variable returns from its involvement with the entity. The bank's interest depends on the entity's level of indebtedness, and so it can be said to have the ability to use its power to effect the amount of the investor's returns. The **bank may therefore be regarded as having a measure of control.** However, the extent of this control is not clear and will depend on the constitution of the entity.

(b) **Vessels**

Vessels sold at ten years old

Kayte's estimate of the residual life of these vessels is **based on acquisition cost.** This is **unacceptable** under IAS 16 *Property, Plant and Equipment.* IAS 16 defines residual value as:

> 'The estimated amount that an entity would currently obtain from disposal of the asset, after deducting the estimated costs of disposal, if the asset were already of the age and in the condition expected at the end of its useful life.'   (para. 6)

IAS 16 requires that property, plant and equipment must be depreciated so that its depreciable amount is allocated on a systematic basis over its useful life. Depreciable amount is the cost of an asset less its residual value. IAS 16 stipulates that the **residual value must be reviewed at least each financial year-end** and, if expectations differ from previous estimates, any change is accounted for prospectively as a change in estimate under IAS 8 *Accounting Policies, Changes in Accounting Estimates and Errors.*

Kayte's model implies that the residual value of the vessels remains constant through the vessels' useful life. However, the **residual value should be adjusted,** particularly as the date of sale approaches and the residual value approaches proceeds of disposal less costs of disposal at the end of the asset's useful life.

Following IAS 16, if the residual value is greater than an asset's carrying amount, the depreciation charge is zero until such time as the residual value subsequently decreases to an amount below the asset's carrying amount. The residual value should be the value at the reporting date as if the vessel were already of the age and condition expected at the end of its useful life. Depreciable amount is affected by an increase in the residual value of an asset because of past events, but not by expectation of changes in future events, other than the expected effects of wear and tear.

The **useful life of the vessels (10 years) is shorter than the total life (30 years)** so it is the residual value at the end of the 10-year useful life that must be established.

Vessels kept for 30 years

Kayte **correctly uses a residual value for these vessels based upon the scrap value of steel.** The depreciable amount of the vessels is therefore the cost less the scrap value of steel, and the vessels should be depreciated over the 30-year period.

The engine is a significant part of the asset and should be depreciated separately over its useful life of 10 years until the date of the next overhaul. The cost of the overhaul should be capitalised (a necessary overhaul is not considered a day-to-day servicing cost) and any carrying amount relating to the engine before overhaul should be derecognised. Generally however the depreciation of the original amount capitalised in respect of the engine will be **calculated to have a carrying amount of nil when the overhaul is undertaken.**

Funnels

The funnels should be identified as significant parts of the asset and depreciated across their useful lives of 15 years. As this has not occurred, it will be necessary to **determine what the carrying amount would have been had the funnels been initially separately identified**. The initial cost of the funnels can be determined by reference to replacement cost, and the associated depreciation charge determined using the rate for the vessel (over 30 years). There will therefore be a significant carrying amount to be written off at the time the replacement funnels are capitalised.

71 Bubble

Workbook reference. Foreign exchange is covered in Chapter 15.

Top tips. In Part (a), you are asked to set out and explain various extracts from the preparation of a consolidated statement of financial position for a simple group structure involving an overseas subsidiary with an adjustment for an intra-group loan. It is important to grab the easy marks for basic consolidation workings and not get bogged down in any adjustments you find challenging. Part (a) (ii) requests the translation of Tyslar's statement of financial position, which is very straightforward. It is necessary to provide a brief explanation of the adjustments, in case the figures are wrong.

Part (b) consists mainly in describing the principles of IAS 21. Do not worry too much if you did not know the answer to the last part of the question, relating to the potential disposal of shares in Tyslar – you can score a pass on this part of the question without getting it all right.

Easy marks. These are available in part (a) (ii) for simply translating the statement of financial position at the correct rate. The Salt goodwill calculation is also a straightforward one. Clear workings, referenced logically, are always important.

In part (b), make sure you read the question properly and discuss the treatment of monetary and non-monetary items as well as the elements of the question related to the translation and possible disposal of an overseas entity, with the retention of a loan.

Marking scheme

			Marks
(a)	(i)	Intragroup loan	5
	(ii)	Translation of Tyslar SOFP	
		Discussion	4
		Calculation	4
			8
	(iii)	Goodwill – Salt	3
		Goodwill – Tyslar	5
			8
(b)	1 mark per point up to a maximum		9
		Maximum	30

(a) (i) Intragroup loan

The loan is a foreign currency **monetary item** in Tyslar's financial statements which means it needs to be retranslated at the **closing rate** of exchange. The **exchange differences** should have been recorded through Tyslar's **profit or loss** and will therefore affect **retained earnings**.

	$m	Exchange rate	Dinars m
1 February 20X5	10	9 dinars:$1	90
Cash paid 1 July 20X5	(5)	10 dinars:$1	(50)
			40
Exchange rate loss – balancing figure	—		7.5
31 October 20X5	5	9.5 dinars:$1	47.5

As Tyslar has not retranslated the loan outstanding at year end, a correction is needed to increase Tyslar's **non-current liabilities by 7.5m dinars** and **reduce retained earnings** by a corresponding amount.

DEBIT   Profit or loss (retained earnings)   7.5 dinars (to (a) (ii))
CREDIT   Non-current liabilities   7.5 dinars (to (a) (ii))

In addition, after retranslation, **$5m will be cancelled** from both financial assets and non-current liabilities to **eliminate intragroup balances** on consolidation.

The intragroup loan will be eliminated from the consolidated SOFP.

DEBIT   Non-current liabilities $5m
CREDIT   Financial assets $5m

(ii)   **Translation of Tyslar's SOFP**

In order to covert Tyslar's statement of financial position appropriately in preparation for consolidation into Bubble's financial statements, the **assets and liabilities** shown in the foreign operation's statement of financial position are **translated at the closing rate** at the year end, being 9.5 dinars to the dollar as at 31 October 20X5, regardless of the date on which those items originated. For consolidation purposes, a subsidiary's **share capital and any reserves balances at acquisition** are translated at the **historic rate at the date of acquisition** (being 8 dinars to the dollar on 1 November 20X4 when Bubble acquired its interest).

The **post-acquisition** movements in **retained earnings** are broken down into the profit and dividend for each year post-acquisition (here just one year – the year ended 31 October 20X5). The **profit** for each post-acquisition year is translated at actual rate or **average rate** for that year if it is a close approximation. **Dividends** are translated at the **actual rate**. Tyslar did not pay a dividend in the current year.

The **balancing figure** on translating the statement of financial position represents the **exchange difference** on translating the foreign subsidiary's **net assets**. A further **exchange difference** arises on **goodwill** because it is treated as an asset of the subsidiary and is therefore retranslated at the **closing rate** each year end. The **exchange difference** for the year is reported in **other comprehensive income** in the consolidated statement of profit or loss and other comprehensive income. The group share of **cumulative exchange differences** are recorded in the **translation reserve** and the non-controlling interests' (NCI) share is recorded in the **NCI working**.

The **translated assets and liabilities** must then be **aggregated** with Tyslar's assets and liabilities in the consolidated statement of financial position on a line by line basis.

The **loan correction** calculated in (a)(i) must be **incorporated** into Tyslar's statement of financial position stated in dinars **before the translation** into dollars of the corrected position is performed.

Translation of SOFP of Tyslar at 31 October 20X5

	Dinars (m)	Dinars (m) loan adj (a) (i)	Rate	$m
Property, plant and equipment	390		9.5	41.1
Financial assets	98		9.5	10.3
Inventories	16		9.5	1.7
Trade and other receivables	36		9.5	3.8
Cash and cash equivalents	90		9.5	9.5
	630			66.4
Share capital	210		8	26.3
Retained earnings				
Pre-acquisition	258		8	32.3
Post-acquisition:				
– Profit: y/e 31 October 20X5	34	(7.5) ((a) (i)) = 26.5	8.5	3.1
(292 – 258)*				
Exchange difference (bal.fig)				(9.6)
				52.1
Non-current liabilities	110	7.5((a) (i))	9.5	12.4
Current liabilities	18		9.5	1.9
	630			66.4

* As Bubble has only owned its controlling shareholding in Tyslar for one year and no dividends have been paid in the current year, profit for the year can be calculated as the year end retained earnings less retained earnings at acquisition.

(iii) **Goodwill**

Goodwill: Salt acquired 1 November 20X3

	$m	$m
Consideration transferred (for 80%)		110
Non-controlling interests at fair value		25
Fair value of identifiable assets acquired and liabilities assumed (per Q $120m – $1m)		
Share capital	50	
Retained earnings	56	
Other components of equity	8	
Fair value adjustment re non-depreciable land	6	
(120 – (50 (SC) + 56 (RE) + 8 (OCE)))		
Contingent liability at fair value	(1)	
		(119)
		16

In accordance with IFRS 3 *Business Combinations*, contingent liabilities should be recognised in the goodwill calculation where they are a present obligation arising as the result of a past event and their fair value can be measured reliably even if their settlement is not probable, as in Salt's case where a possible obligation has been disclosed and the fair value has been measured at the acquisition date.

Goodwill: Tyslar acquired 1 November 20X4

	Dinars (m)	Rate	$m
Consideration transferred	368		46.0
Non-controlling interests	220		27.5
	588	8	
Less fair value of net assets at acq'n: $210m + $258m	(468)		(58.5)
At 1 November 20X4	120		15.0
Impairment loss (20% × $120m)	(24)	8.5	(2.8)
			12.2
Exchange loss (bal.fig.)	–		(2.1)
At 31 October 20X5	96	9.5	10.1

Any goodwill arising on the acquisition of Tyslar is treated as an asset of the foreign operation and expressed in its functional currency, here dinars, and is retranslated at the closing rate, here 9.5 as at 31 October 20X5. Since goodwill is under the 'full goodwill' fair value method, both the impairment and the exchange loss will be apportioned 60:40 between the shareholders of the parent and the non-controlling interest respectively.

In summary:

Goodwill for consolidated SOFP will be ($16m + $10.1m) = $26.1m.

The impairment loss is $2.8m of which 60% ($1.7m) will be charged against group retained earnings and 40% ($1.1m) will be charged to the NCI.

Tutorial note.

Here impairment of Tyslar's goodwill has been translated at the average rate of 8.5 but IAS 21 also permits translation at the closing rate rate (9.5 here). Therefore, your answer would also have been marked correct if you had used the closing rate – this would have resulted in an impairment of $2.5 million and an exchange loss of $2.4 million as shown below:

Goodwill: Tyslar acquired 1 November 20X4

	Dinars (m)	Rate	$m
Consideration transferred	368		46.0
Non-controlling interests	220		27.5
	588	8	
Less fair value of net assets at acq'n: (210m share capital + 258m retained earnings)	(468)		(58.5)
At 1 November 20X4	120		15.0
Impairment loss (20% × $120m)	(24)	9.5	(2.5)
			12.5
Exchange loss (bal.fig.)	–		(2.4)
At 31 October 20X5	96	9.5	10.1

(b)   **IAS 21 issues**

Monetary items are units of currency held and assets and liabilities to be received or paid in a **fixed or determinable number of units of currency**. This would include foreign bank accounts, receivables, payables and loans. **Non-monetary** items are **other items** which are in the statement of financial position. For example, non-current assets, inventories and investments.

Monetary items are **retranslated** using the **closing exchange rate** (the year end rate). The exchange differences on retranslation of monetary assets must be recorded in profit or loss. IAS 21 *The Effects of Changes in Foreign Exchange Rates*, is not specific under which heading the exchange gains and losses should be classified.

Non-monetary items which are measured in terms of **historical cost** in a foreign currency are translated using the **exchange rate at the date of the transaction**; and **non-monetary** items which are measured at **fair value** in a foreign currency are translated using the **exchange rates at the date when the fair value was measured**. **Exchange differences** on such items are **recorded consistently** with the recognition of the **movement in fair values**. For example, exchange differences on an investment property, a fair value through profit and loss financial asset, or arising on an impairment, will be recorded in profit or loss. Exchange differences on property, plant and equipment arising from a revaluation gain would be recorded in other comprehensive income.

When translating a **foreign subsidiary**, the **exchange differences on all the net assets**, including goodwill, are recorded within **other comprehensive income**. The proportion belonging to the shareholders of the parent will usually be held in a **separate translation reserve**. The **proportion belonging to the non-controlling interest** is not shown separately but **subsumed within the non-controlling interest figure** in the consolidated financial statements. If Bubble were to **sell all of its equity shares in Tyslar**, the translation reserve will be **reclassified** from equity to profit or loss. In addition, the cumulative exchange differences attributable to the non-controlling interest would be derecognised but would not be reclassified to profit or loss.

When a **monetary item** relating to a **foreign operation** is **not intended to be settled**, the item is treated as **part of the entity's net investment in its subsidiary**. There will be no difference in the accounting treatment in the **individual accounts of Tyslar** and hence exchange differences on the loan would **remain in profit or loss**. However, in the **consolidated financial statements** such differences should initially be recorded in **other comprehensive income**. These will be **reclassified** from equity to profit or loss on subsequent **disposal** of the subsidiary. This can cause practical issues in terms of monitoring all of the individual exchange differences to ensure that they are all correctly classified in the consolidated financial statements.

72 Aspire

Workbook references. Foreign currency transactions are covered in Chapter 15 and deferred tax is covered in Chapter 6.

Top tips. This question dealt with a number of foreign transactions (functional currency, goodwill, deferred tax and a loan), and contained a balanced mixture of discussion and computation. Part (b), on deferred tax issues, was somewhat tricky. The treatment of goodwill (part (c)) is fundamental to the understanding of accounting for an overseas subsidiary. Goodwill arising on acquisition of foreign operations and any fair value adjustments are both treated as the foreign operation's assets and liabilities. They are expressed in the foreign operation's functional currency and translated at the closing rate. Exchange differences arising on the retranslation of foreign entities' financial statements are recognised in other comprehensive income and accumulated in a translation reserve.

> **Easy marks.** There are some easy marks in Part (a) for a discussion of how to determine the functional currency.

		Marks
(a)	1 mark per point up to maximum	8
(b)	1 mark per point up to maximum	7
(c)	1 mark per point up to maximum	5
(d)	1 mark per point up to maximum	5
Maximum		25

(a) **Factors to consider in determining functional currency of Aspire**

IAS 21 *The Effects of Changes in Foreign Exchange Rates* defines functional currency as 'the currency of the primary economic environment in which the entity operates'. Each entity, whether an individual company, a parent of a group, or an operation within a group, should determine its functional currency and **measure its results and financial position in that currency**. If it is not obvious what the functional currency is, management will need to use its judgement in determining the currency which most faithfully represents the economic effects of the underlying transactions, events and conditions.

An entity should generally consider the following factors:

(i) What is the currency that mainly **influences sales prices** for goods and services (this will often be the currency in which sales prices for its goods and services are denominated and settled)?

(ii) What is the currency of the country whose **competitive forces and regulations** mainly determine the sales prices of its goods and services?

(iii) What is the currency that **mainly influences labour, material and other costs** of providing goods or services? (This will often be the currency in which such costs are denominated and settled.)

Other factors may also provide evidence of an entity's functional currency:

(i) It is the currency in which **funds from financing activities** are generated.

(ii) It is the currency in which **receipts from operating activities** are usually retained.

Aspire's subsidiary does not make investment decisions; these are under Aspire's control, and consideration of the currency which influences sales and costs is not relevant. Costs are incurred in dollars, but these are low and therefore not material in determining which is the subsidiary's functional currency. It is necessary, therefore to consider other factors in order to determine the functional currency of the subsidiary and whether its functional currency is the same as that of Aspire.

(i) The **autonomy** of a foreign operation from the reporting entity

(ii) The **level of transactions** between the reporting entity and the foreign operation

(iii) Whether the foreign operation **generates sufficient cash flows** to meet its cash needs

(iv) Whether **its cash flows directly affect those of the reporting entity**

The **subsidiary has issued 2 million dinars of equity to Aspire. Although this is in a different currency from that of Aspire, Aspire has controlled how the proceeds were to be invested** – in dinar-denominated bonds, suggesting that the **subsidiary is merely a vehicle for Aspire to invest in dinar-related investments.** Only 100,000 dinars of equity capital is from external sources, and this amount is insignificant compared to the equity issued to Aspire. The lack of autonomy of the subsidiary is confirmed by the fact that income from investments is either remitted to Aspire, or reinvested on instructions from Aspire, and by the fact that the subsidiary does not have any independent management or significant numbers of staff.

It appears that the subsidiary **is merely an extension of Aspire's activities rather than an autonomous entity.** Its purpose may have been to avoid reporting Aspire's exposure to the dinar/dollar exchange rate in profit or loss – it would be reported in other comprehensive income through the translation of the net investment in the subsidiary. These matters would lead to the conclusion that the **subsidiary's functional currency is the dollar.**

Operations are financed in dinars, and any income not remitted to Aspire is in dinars, and so the dinar represents the currency in which the subsidiary's economic activities are primarily carried out. However, in the absence of the benefit of presenting the dollar/dinar exchange rate fluctuations in other comprehensive income, Aspire could have invested the funds directly, and **so Aspire's functional currency should determine that of the subsidiary**.

(b)   **Deferred tax charge**

Investments in foreign branches (or subsidiaries, associates or joint arrangements) are affected by **changes in foreign exchange rates**. In this case, the branch's taxable profits are determined in dinars, and changes in the dinar/dollar exchange rate may give rise to temporary differences. These differences can arise where the carrying amounts of the non-monetary assets are translated at historical rates and the tax base of those assets are translated at the closing rate. The **closing rate** may be used to translate the tax base because the resulting figure is an **accurate measure of the amount that will be deductible in future periods. The deferred tax is charged or credited to profit or loss.**

The deferred tax arising will be calculated **using the tax rate in the foreign branch's jurisdiction**, that is **20%**.

Property	Dinars ('000)	Exchange rate	Dollars ($'000)
Carrying amount:			
Cost	6,000	5	1,200
Depreciation for the year	(500)		(100)
Carrying amount	5,500		1,100
Tax base:			
Cost	6,000		
Tax depreciation	(750)		
Carrying amount	5,250	6	875
Temporary difference			225
Deferred tax at 20%			45

The **deferred tax charge in profit or loss will therefore increase by $45,000.**

If the tax base had been translated at the historical rate, the tax base would have been $(5.25m ÷ 5m) = $1.05m. This gives a temporary difference of $1.1m – $1.05m = $50,000,

and therefore a deferred tax liability of $50,000 × 20% = $10,000. This is considerably lower than when the closing rate is used.

(c) **Goodwill on acquisition**

Goodwill on acquisition of a foreign subsidiary or group, and any fair value adjustments, are treated as **assets and liabilities of the foreign entity**. They are expressed in the foreign operation's functional currency and translated at the closing rate. This means that an exchange difference will arise between goodwill translated at the opening rate and at the closing rate. Even though the goodwill arose through a consideration paid in dollars, it is treated as a foreign currency asset, which means that it is translated into dinars at the rate ruling on the date of acquisition and then re-translated at the year-end rate.

Any **gain or loss** on translation is taken to **other comprehensive income**.

	Dinars (m)	Rate	$m
Consideration transferred			200
Non-controlling interests translated at 1 May 20X3	250	5	50
Less fair value of net assets at acq'n translated at 1 May 20X3	(1,100)	5	(220)
Goodwill			30
Exchange loss to other comprehensive income	–	ß	(5)
Goodwill as re-translated at 30 April 20X4: 30 × 5 ÷ 6	150	6	25

The exchange loss of $5m is recognised in other comprehensive income with the corresponding credit entries to a separate translation reserve (70%) and non-controlling interest (30%) in the statement of financial position:

DEBIT	Other comprehensive income	$5m	
CREDIT	Translation reserve (SOFP): $5m × 70%		$3.5m
CREDIT	Non-controlling interest (SOFP): $5m × 30%		$1.5m

(d) **Foreign currency loan**

On 1 May 20X3

On initial recognition (at 1 May 20X3), the loan is measured at the transaction price translated into the functional currency (the dollar), because the interest is at a market rate for a similar two-year loan. The loan is translated at the rate ruling on 1 May 20X3.

DEBIT	Cash 5m ÷ 5	$1m	
CREDIT	Financial liability (loan payable)		$1m

Being recognition of loan

As a monetary item, the loan balance at the year-end is translated at the spot rate at the year end.

Year ended 30 April 20X4

Because there are no transaction costs, the effective interest rate is 8%. Interest on the loan is translated at the average rate because this is an approximation for the actual rate

DEBIT	Profit or loss (interest expense): 5m × 8% ÷ 5.6	$71,429	
CREDIT	Financial liability (loan payable)		$71,429

Being recognition of interest payable for the year ended 30 April 20X4

On 30 April 20X4

The interest is paid and the following entry is made, using the rate on the date of payment of $1 = 6 dinars

DEBIT	Financial liability (loan payable) 5m × 8% ÷ 6	$66,667
CREDIT	Cash	$66,667

Being recognition of interest payable for the year ended 30 April 20X4

In addition, as a monetary item, the loan balance at the year-end is translated at the spot rate at the year end: 5m dinars ÷ 6 = $833,333. This gives rise to an exchange gain of £1,000,000 – $833,333 = $166,667. There is a further exchange gain on the interest paid of $71,429 – $66,667 = $4,762. This gives a total exchange gain of $4,762 + $166,667 = $171,429.

73 Plans

> **Workbook reference.** Changes in group structure and group reorganisations are covered in Chapter 12.
>
> **Top tip.** There are marks available for both the individual financial statements and the consolidated position, so even if you are unsure of the answer, you should set out the simpler parts to maximise marks.

Marking scheme

	Marks
Plan 1 – Discussion	3
– Impact of financial statements	6
Plan 2 – Discussion	2
– Impact on financial statements	6
	15

Key considerations and accounting impacts

There are a number of reasons why a group may reorganise, for example:

- Companies may be transferred to another business during a **divisionalisation process**
- To **create efficiencies** of group structure for **tax purposes**
- To address an imbalance in the liquidity of the group
- To transfer resources amongst the group to support borrowings

The impact of each of the proposed plans is discussed below.

Plan 1: share for share exchange

If the purchase consideration is in the form of shares, then a share premium account will need to be set up in the books of Y. This share premium account will reflect the excess of the carrying amount of the investment over the nominal value of the shares issued: $70m – $50m = $20m.

The impact on the individual company accounts and on the consolidated financial statements is as follows:

	Note	X $m	Y $m	Z $m	Group $m
Property, plant and equipment		600	200	45	845
Goodwill					10
Cost of investment in Y	1	130			
Cost of investment in Z	2		70		
Net current assets		160	100	20	280
		890	370	65	1,135
Share capital	3	120	110	40	120
Share premium	4		20		
Retained earnings	5	770	240	25	1,015
		890	370	65	1,135

Notes

1 *Cost of investment in Y*

   This is increased by the total value of the shares issued: $50m nominal + $20m premium = $70m.

2 *Cost of investment in Z*

   Transferred to Y. The carrying amount of the investment is preserved.

3 *Share capital*

   Y's share capital is increased by the nominal value of the shares issued, $50m.

4 *Share premium*

   This is as discussed above.

5 *Retained earnings*

   Goodwill arising on the purchase of Z is $10m ($70m – ($40m + $20m)). The group retained earnings are calculated as follows.

	X $m	Y $m	Z $m
Per question	770	240	25
Retained earnings at acquisition		–	(20)
	770	240	5
Share of post-acquisition retained earnings of Y (240 × 100%)	240		
Share of post-acquisition retained earnings of Z (5 × 100%)	5		
	1,015		

Plan 2: cash purchase

The consolidated financial statements are not affected by the change as the reorganisation is internal. It has no impact on the group as a single entity.

As the purchase consideration is in the form of cash, a gain or loss on the sale of Z will arise in the financial statements of X. This does not count as a distribution as the cash price of $75m is not in excess of the fair value of the net assets of Z, $80m. The effect on the accounts would be as follows:

	Note	X $m	Y $m	Z $m	Group $m
Property, plant and equipment		600	200	45	845
Goodwill					10
Cost of investment in Y		60			
Cost of investment in Z	1		75		
Net current assets	2	235	25	20	280
		895	300	65	1,135
Share capital		120	60	40	120
Retained earnings	3	775	240	25	1,015
		895	300	65	1,135

Notes

1   *Cost of investment in Z*

This is the cash consideration of $75m.

2   *Net current assets*

X's cash increases by $75m and Y's cash decreases by $75m.

3   *Retained earnings*

X's retained earnings have been increased by $5m, being the profit on the sale of the investment in Z. This is eliminated on consolidation as it is an intragroup transaction. The consolidated retained earnings are calculated in exactly the same way as in the share for share exchange.

Summary and conclusion

There are advantages and disadvantages to each of the two plans. Before we could make a recommendation we would need more information about **why** the group wishes to restructure.

Neither plan changes the consolidated financial statements. From an internal point of view it results in a closer relationship between Y and Z. This may be advantageous if Y and Z are close geographically or in terms of similarity of business activities. Alternatively, it might be advantageous for tax or liquidity management reasons.

74 Decany

Workbook references. Group reorganisations are covered in Chapter 12. IAS 37 is covered in Chapter 5.

Top tips. This question tests group reorganisations. In part (a)(i) you have to process the effects of the group reorganisation in the three affected companies of the group, which is straightforward. This part of the question did not require detailed knowledge of IFRS but the ability to apply accounting techniques. The preparation of the consolidated financial statements is not required, and you should not waste time trying to do this. Part (a)(ii) requires a specialist knowledge of IAS 27 *Separate Financial Statements*. The key is to know that the distinction between pre- and post-acquisition profits is no longer required and the payment of such dividends requires the entity to consider whether there is an indicator of impairment. Part (b) requires you to understand that the reconstruction only masked the problem facing the group. It does not solve or alter the business risk currently being faced by the group.

Easy marks. Don't be put off by the fact that this is a reconstruction scheme. There are some fairly straightforward accounts preparation aspects.

Marking scheme

			Marks
(a)	(i)	Decany	5
		Ceed	5
		Rant	3
			13
	(ii)	IAS 27	5
(b)		Discussion – subjective 1 mark per valid point up to maximum	5
		Professional marks	2
			25

(a) (i) **Individual entity statements of financial position after the restructuring plan**

	Note	Decany $m	Ceed $m	Rant $m
Non-current assets				
Property, plant and equipment at depreciated cost/valuation		600	170 + 15 = 185.0	45 – 10 = 35
Cost of investment in Ceed		130		11
Cost of investment in Rant	1		98.0	
Loan receivable	2	98		
Current assets		155 + 25 =	130 – 98 =	20 + 98 =
	2	180	32.0	118
		1,008	315.0	164
Equity and reserves				
Share capital			70 + 5 =	
		140	75.0	35
Share premium	3		6.0	
Retained earnings	5	776	185.5	10
		916	266.5	45
Non-current liabilities				
Long-term loan	6	5	4.0	106
Provisions	7	2	9.5	
Current liabilities				
Dividend payable			25.0	
Trade payables		85	10.0	13
		1,008	315.0	164

Notes

1   *Sale of shares in Rant*

In Ceed's books:

DEBIT	Investment in Rant	$98m	
CREDIT	Cash (current assets)		$98m

This is the cash consideration of $98m.

Decany has made a profit on the sale of rant of $98m – $95m = $3m, which is added to Decany's retained earnings. In Decany's books:

DEBIT	Cash (current assets)	$98m	
CREDIT	Investment in Rant		$95m
CREDIT	Profit or loss (and retained earnings)		$3m

2   *Loan receivable*

Decany now has a loan receivable of $98m and Decany's cash decreases by $98m. In Decany's books:

DEBIT	Loan receivable	$98m	
CREDIT	Cash (current assets)		$98m

In Rant's books:

DEBIT	Cash (current assets)	$98m	
CREDIT	Loan payable		$98m

3   *Sale of land by Rant to Ceed/calculation of share premium*

The value of the shares issued to Decany is the land less the mortgage, ie $11 million. The difference between this and the nominal value is the share premium.

In Ceed's books:

DEBIT	Land	$15m	
CREDIT	Mortgage liability (long-term loan)		$4m
CREDIT	Share capital		$5m
CREDIT	Share premium (balancing figure)		$6m

In Rant's books:

DEBIT	Investment in Ceed	$11m	
DEBIT	Mortgage liability (long-term loan)	$4m	
CREDIT	Land		$10m
CREDIT	Profit or loss (and retained earnings)		$5m

4   *Dividend payable by Ceed to Decany*

In Ceed's books:

DEBIT	Retained earnings	$25m	
CREDIT	Dividend payable		$25m

In Ceed's books:

DEBIT	Dividend receivable (current assets)	$25m	
CREDIT	Profit or loss (and retained earnings)		$25m

5   Retained earnings

	Decany $m	Ceed $m	Rant $m
Per question	750	220.0	5
Dividend from Ceed to Decany (note 4)	25	(25.0)	–
Profit on sale of Rant (note 1)	3	–	–
Profit on sale of land (note 3)			5
Provision for restructuring (note 7)	(2)	(9.5)	–
	776	185.5	10

6   Long-term loan (Rant)

	$m
Per question	12
Loan payable (note 2)	98
Mortgage liability (note 3)	(4)
	106

7   Redundancy costs and provision for restructuring

The fact that there is a detailed plan for restructuring with employees identified for redundancy creates a constructive obligation under IAS 37 *Provisions, Contingent Liabilities and Contingent Assets*, and accordingly a provision should be made for redundancy costs and restructuring. Ceed will incur the redundancy costs, which should be recognised in its financial statements at the present value of the future cash flows:

	$m
$4m × 1/1.03	3.9
$6m × 1/1.03^2	5.6
	9.5

The provision of $9.5m will be shown in Ceed's financial statements, and the overall restructuring provision of $2m in the financial statements of Decany.

(ii) **IAS 27 rules on reorganisation and payment of dividends between group companies**

IAS *27 Separate Financial Statements* effectively allows the **cost of an investment in a subsidiary to be based on the previous carrying amount of the subsidiary rather than on its fair value**. This is only allowed when a new parent (Ceed) is inserted above an existing parent of a group or entity (Rant), and where the following **criteria** are satisfied:

(1)   The new parent (Ceed) obtains control of the original parent or entity (Rant) by issuing equity instruments in exchange for existing equity instruments of the original parent or entity.

(2)   The assets and liabilities of the new group and the original group are the same immediately before and after the reorganisation.

(3)   The owners of the original parent or entity (Decany) before the reorganisation have the same absolute and relative interests in the net assets of the original group and the new group immediately before and after the reorganisation.

The reorganisation of the Decany group appears to meet all the above criteria. (In respect of (3), Rant has not acquired a further interest in Ceed as a result of the transfer of land because the shares in Ceed issued to Rant are non-voting.)

IAS 27 requires all dividends to be recorded **in profit or loss in the parent's separate financial statements when its right to receive the dividend is established**.

If such dividends are paid, the entity is required to consider whether there is has been an **impairment**. Applying IAS 36 *Impairment of Assets,* impairment is indicated in the following cases:

(1) The dividend exceeds the total comprehensive income of the subsidiary, jointly controlled entity or associate in the period the dividend is declared.

(2) The carrying amount of the investment in the separate financial statements exceeds the carrying amounts in the consolidated financial statements of the investee's net assets, including associated goodwill.

Neither of these apply in the case of Ceed, and so there is no indication that Ceed is impaired.

(b) **Impact of reconstruction plan**

The reconstruction plan has no impact on the consolidated financial statements as all the intra-group transactions will be eliminated on consolidation. From an internal point of view it results in **a closer relationship between Ceed and Rant**. This may be advantageous if Ceed and Rant are close geographically or in terms of similarity of business activities.

Regarding the restructuring plan, IAS 37 *Provisions, Contingent Liabilities and Contingent Assets* **contains specific requirements** relating to **restructuring provisions**. The general recognition criteria apply and IAS 37 also states that **a provision should be recognised** if an entity has a **constructive obligation** to carry out a restructuring. A constructive obligation exists where **management has a detailed formal plan** for the restructuring, identifying **as a minimum:**

(i) The business or part of the business being restructured;

(ii) The principal locations affected by the restructuring;

(iii) The location, function and approximate number of employees who will be compensated for the termination of their employment;

(iv) The date of implementation of the plan;

(v) The expenditure that will be undertaken; and

(vi) Those affected, and has raised a valid expectation that it will carry out the restructuring by starting to implement that plan or announcing its main features to those affected by it.

It appears that these criteria have been met. However, the amount of $2m in Decany's financial statements seems rather large, considering that the redundancy is provided separately in the accounts of Ceed, and the restructuring does not involve any relocation. There must be forecasts underpinning the expected cost of $2m and it must meet the criteria above if it is to be provided for in the financial statements.

The plan shows the companies in a **more favourable light** in that Rant's **short-term cash flow problem is eliminated**. Rant now has cash available. However, it is showing a much increased long-term loan. In the financial statements of Rant, the investment in Ceed must be accounted as a financial asset under IFRS 9 *Financial Instruments.*

It is possible that the purchase consideration for Rant of $98m could be seen as **a transaction at an overvalue**. It creates a profit of $3m, which could be seen as artificial. The question also arises as to whether this $3m should be recognised, and whether it should be viewed as a distribution. Should problems arise in connection with local legislation, a share exchange might be a less problematic plan than a cash purchase.

The question may also arise as to whether Ceed has effectively **made a distribution**. This could happen where the purchase consideration was well in excess of the fair value of Rant. An alternative to a cash purchase would be a share exchange. In this case, local legislation would need to be reviewed in order to determine the requirements for the setting up of any share premium account.

75 Moorland

> **Workbook reference.** Chapter 17: Interpretation of financial statements for different stakeholders.
>
> **Top tips.** Part (a) is open ended, and marks will be given for valid points clearly explained.
>
> Part (b)(ii) covers alternative performance measures which is a key topic for SBR. You need to consider Moorland's investors in your answer. Wider reading of articles, particularly those on the ACCA website, will be extremely helpful in being able to answer questions such as this. The ESMA (European Securities and Markets Authority) Guidelines on Alternative Performance Measures and IOSCO's (International Organisation of Securities Commissions) Statement on Non-GAAP Financial Measures, both available online, provide another perspective and will be beneficial to read.
>
> **Easy marks.** Some marks are available for the principles of IFRS 8.

(a)   The objective of published financial statements is to **satisfy the information needs of users.** Some types of user, principally shareholders and credit providers, will always need financial statements as their main source of information about a company. Companies are normally required to file financial statements with the regulatory authorities so that a certain amount of information is available to the general public. The government uses financial statements in order to assess taxation and to regulate the activities of businesses.

Financial reporting has evolved to meet the needs of investors in large public companies and their advisers. Yet published financial statements have **serious limitations:** they are based on historical information and they **only reflect the financial effects** of transactions and events. Investors need to predict a company's future performance, including **changes in shareholder value**.

Traditional **ratio analysis is becoming outdated.** Measures such as earnings per share and the price earnings ratio continue to be important, but analysts now calculate a range of other measures. These include cash flow per share, market value per share and 'consensus earnings per share', which **predicts future performance. Free cash flow** is a key financial performance measure used by analysts to value a company. Free cash flow is cash revenues less cash expenses, taxation paid, cash needed for working capital and cash required for routine capital expenditure. This can be compared with the cost of capital employed to assess whether shareholder value has increased or decreased. It can also be projected and discounted to provide an approximate market value.

Traditional financial statements are **only one of many sources of information used by investors**. There has been an increasing trend in recent years towards non-financial reporting measures. Many companies now produce non-financial reports alongside their traditional financial statements. They will report on factors such as:

- Environment – it is fairly common to see reporting on the carbon emissions of an entity (particularly as governments are now committed to reducing emissions), and an entity's commitment to reducing waste.

- Employees – the satisfaction of employees is essential in ensuring a company's success. As such, many companies will now carry out employee surveys and report on employee satisfaction results, as well as disclose information on social issues such as the gender pay gap within the entity or the difference between the highest and lowest earners.

- Social – many companies report on their commitment to 'giving something back' to their local communities through sponsoring projects or giving staff paid time off to support a good cause.

This type of reporting is no longer considered superfluous to the financial statements but is instead considered an important part in allowing stakeholders to understand more about businesses and the influence they have on our society.

Although there is no mandatory requirement to prepare such non-financial information, there is guidance produced by, for example, the Global Reporting Initiative (relevant for environmental and social reporting) and the International Integrated Reporting Framework (relevant for integrated reporting) that are helping to shape the direction of non-financial reporting.

(b)   (i)   **Operating segment**

IFRS 8 *Operating Segments* describes an operating segment as a component of an entity:

(1)   Which engages in business activities from which it may earn revenues and incur expenses;

(2)   Whose operating results are regularly reviewed by the entity's chief operating decision-maker to make decisions about resources to be allocated to the segment and assess its performance;

(3)   For which discrete financial information is available.

There is a considerable amount of subjectivity in how an entity may apply these criteria to its choice of operating segments. Usually an operating segment would have a segment manager who maintains regular contact with the chief operating decision-maker to discuss operating activities, financial results, forecasts or plans for the segment. Therefore segment managers could have overall responsibility for a particular product, service line or geographical area and so there could be considerable overlap in how an entity may apply the criteria. In such situations the directors of Moorland should consider the core principles of the standard. Information should be disclosed to enable users of its financial statements to evaluate the nature and financial effects of the business activities in which it engages and the economic environments in which it operates.

Since Tybull is the only overseas subsidiary, it is likely that separate disclosure is necessary so that users can better assess the performance of Tybull and its significance to the group. The directors should consider whether there are other segments which exhibit similar long-term financial performance and similar economic characteristics to Tybull. In such circumstances it is possible to aggregate the operating segments into a single segment. For example, the segments should have products of a similar nature and similar methods to distribute their products. The segments should also have similar types of customer, production processes and regulatory environment. The directors of Moorland would need to assess whether such aggregation would limit the usefulness of the disclosures for the users of the financial statements. For example, it would no longer be possible to assess the gross margins and return on capital employed for Tybull on an individual basis, without referring to its individual financial statements.

Operating segments can be reclassified where an entity changes its internal organisational structure. As Tybull has not changed its organisational structure, it is unlikely that it would be able to argue for a reclassification of its operating segments. Should the directors of Moorland decide to reclassify the operating segments and combine Tybull with other segments, IAS 8 *Accounting Policies, Changes in Accounting Estimates and Errors* would need to be applied. A retrospective adjustment would be required to the disclosures and the change would need to be justified. An entity should only change its policy if it enhances the reliability and relevance of the financial statements. This would appear unlikely given the circumstances.

(ii) **Underlying earnings per share**

Underlying earnings per share (underling EPS) is an alternative performance measure (APM). APMs should be provided to enhance the understanding of users of the accounts.

However, APMs can be misleading. Unlike earnings per share, which is defined in IAS 33 *Earnings per Share*, there is no official definition of underlying EPS, so management can choose what items to include or exclude in the underlying earnings. Therefore it is open to bias in its calculation as management could decide to only adjust for items that improve the measure. Furthermore, different companies may define the measure in different ways, which reduces the comparability between entities.

The CEO's wish to exclude impairment on goodwill from the calculation of earnings on the basis that it is unlikely to reoccur is also misleading to investors. An impairment loss on goodwill could quite feasibly re-occur in the future as it is at least partly dependent on circumstances outside of Moorland's control, such as the state of the economy. Therefore, it could be argued that excluding the impairment loss would make the measure of underlying earnings per share less useful to investors.

The CEO wishes to present underlying EPS 'prominently'. It is not clear what is meant by this comment, however, Moorland should ensure that it complies with the requirements of IAS 33 regarding the calculation and presentation of this alternative EPS. IOSCO's (International Organisation of Securities Commissions) Statement on Non-GAAP Financial Measures recommends that APMs are not presented more prominently than GAAP measures, or in a way that confuses or obscures GAAP measures.

Ultimately underlying earnings per share will only provide useful information to Moorland's investors if it is fairly presented.

Moorland could improve the usefulness of underlying EPS by:

- Including an appropriate description of how the measure is calculated
- Ensuring that the calculation of underlying EPS is consistent year on year and that comparatives are presented
- Explaining the reasons for presenting the measure, why it is useful for investors and for what purpose management may use it
- Presenting a reconciliation to the most directly reconcilable measure in the financial statements, for example EPS calculated in accordance with IAS 33
- Not excluding items from underlying EPS that could legitimately reoccur in the future, such as impairment losses on goodwill

76 Tufnell

Workbook references. IFRS 5 is included in Chapter 13, deferred tax in Chapter 6, impairment in Chapter 3 and ROCE and residual income are included in Chapter 17.

Top tips. This question deals with a group re-organisation, deferred tax and revaluation, impairment and re-classification of a lease. These are all linked in with a calculation of the effect on ROCE. In part (a)(i) there is no need to spend time giving the IFRS 5 criteria for classification as held for sale, since we are told in the question that these criteria have been met.

Easy marks. None of this question is easy except for the calculation of ROCE. Do the parts you feel sure about, but have a go at all parts as the first few marks are the easiest to pick up. The professional marks would be awarded for analysing the impact of the information, drawing conclusions and considering the implications for ROCE.

			Marks
(a)	(i)	Discontinuance	7
	(ii)	Deferred tax asset	6
	(iii)	Impairment	5
	(iv)	Formation of opinion of impact on ROCE	2
(b)	APM and residual income		3
Professional marks			2
Maximum			25

(a)   (i)   The criteria in IFRS 5 have been met for North and South. As the assets are to be disposed of in a single transaction, North and South together are deemed to be a **disposal group** under IFRS 5.

The disposal group as a whole is **measured on the basis required for non-current assets held for sale**. Any impairment loss reduces the carrying amount of the non-current assets in the disposal group, the loss being allocated in the order required by IAS 36 *Impairment of Assets*. Before the manufacturing units are classified as held for sale, impairment is tested for on an individual cash generating unit basis. Once classified as held for sale, the impairment testing is done on a **disposal group basis.**

A disposal group that is held for sale should be measured at the **lower of** its **carrying amount** and **fair value less costs to sell**. Any impairment loss is generally recognised in profit or loss, but if the asset has been measured at a revalued amount under IAS 16 *Property, Plant and Equipment* or IAS 38 *Intangible Assets,* the impairment will be treated as a revaluation decrease.

A **subsequent increase** in fair value less costs to sell may be **recognised** in profit or loss **only to the extent of any impairment previously recognised**. To summarise:

Step 1   Calculate carrying amount under the individual standard, here given as $105m.

Step 2   Classified as held for sale. Compare the carrying amount ($105m) with fair value less costs to sell ($125m). Measure at the lower of carrying amount and fair value less costs to sell, here $105m.

Step 3   Determine fair value less costs to sell at the year end (see below) and compare with carrying amount of $105m.

Tufnell has not taken account of the increase in fair value less cost to sell, but only part of this increase can be recognised, calculated as follows.

	$m
Fair value less costs to sell: North	40
Fair value less costs to sell: South	95
	135
Carrying value	(105)
Increase	30

Impairment previously recognised in North: $15m ($50m – $35m)

Step 4 The change in fair value less cost to sell is recognised but the gain recognised cannot exceed any impairment losses to date. Here the gain recognised is $50m – $35m = $15m

Therefore **carrying amount can increase** by $15m to $120m as loss reversals are limited to impairment losses previously recognised (under IFRS 5 or IAS 36).

These adjustments **will affect ROCE**.

(ii) IAS 12 *Income Taxes* requires that deferred tax liabilities must be recognised for all taxable temporary differences. Deferred tax assets should be recognised for deductible temporary differences but only to the extent that taxable profits will be available against which the deductible temporary differences may be utilised.

The differences between the carrying amounts and the tax base represent temporary differences. These **temporary differences are revised** in the light of the revaluation for tax purposes to market value permitted by the government.

Deferred tax liability before revaluation

	Carrying amount	Tax base	Temporary difference
	$m	$m	$m
Property	50	48	2
Vehicles	30	28	2
			4
Other temporary differences			5
			9

Provision: 30% × $9m = $2.7m

Deferred tax asset after revaluation

	Carrying amount	Tax base	Temporary difference
	$m	$m	$m
Property	50	65	15
Vehicles	30	35	5
Other temporary differences			(5)
			15

Deferred tax asset: $1 5m × 30% = $4.5m

This will have a **considerable impact on ROCE**. While the release of the provision of $2.7m and the creation of the asset of $4.5m will not affect profit **before** interest and **tax**, it will **significantly affect the capital employed figure**.

(iii) IAS 36 requires that no asset should be carried at more than its recoverable amount. At each reporting date, Tufnell must **review all assets for indications of impairment,** that is, indications that the carrying amount may be higher than the recoverable amount. Such indications include fall in the market value of an asset or adverse changes in the technological, economic or legal environment of the business. (IAS 36 has an extensive list of criteria.) If **impairment is indicated**, then the asset's **recoverable amount** must be calculated. The manufacturer has reduced the selling price, but this does not automatically mean that the asset is impaired.

The **recoverable amount** is defined as the **higher of the asset's fair value less costs of disposal and its value in use**. If the recoverable amount is less than the carrying amount, then the resulting impairment loss should be charged to profit or loss as an expense (unless the asset was previously revalued).

Value in use is the discounted present value of estimated future cash flows expected to arise from the continuing use of an asset and from its disposal at the end of its useful life. The value in use of the equipment is calculated as follows:

Year ended 30 September	Cash flows	Discounted (10%)
	$m	$m
20X8	1.3	1.2
20X9	2.2	1.8
20Y0	2.3	1.7

The directors are proposing to write the asset down to its fair value of $2.5m. However, its value in use is higher than fair value and also higher than the carrying amount of the asset ($3m). So there has been no impairment and the asset should remain at its carrying amount.

(iv) **Recalculation of ROCE**

	$m
Profit before interest and tax	30.0
Add increase in value of disposal group	15.0
	45.0
Capital employed	220.0
Add increase in value of disposal group	15.0
Add release of deferred tax provision and	
deferred tax asset: 4.5 + 2.7	7.2
	242.2

∴ROCE is 45/242.2 = 13.6%

The directors were concerned that the above changes would adversely affect ROCE. In fact, the effect has been favourable, as **ROCE has risen from 13.6% to 18.6%,** so the **directors' fears were misplaced**.

(b) Alternative performance measures (APMs) report information that is not included on the face of the financial statements. Companies often adjust reported financial information in order to provide helpful additional information for the users of financial statements, telling a clearer story of how the business has performed over the period. They allow the directors of a company more freedom and flexibility to report performance measures that are important to them.

Residual income is one type of APM. Residual income is an entity valuation method that accounts for the cost of equity capital. Performance of the subsidiaries should be measured, in the interests of the group's shareholders, in such a way as to indicate what sort of return each subsidiary is making on the shareholder's investment. Shareholders themselves are likely to be interested in the performance of the group as a whole, measured in terms of return on shareholders' capital, earnings per share, dividend yield, and growth in earnings and dividends. These performance ratios cannot be used for subsidiaries in the group, and so an alternative measure has to be selected, which compares the return from the subsidiary with the value of the investment in the subsidiary.

Residual income would provide a suitable indication of performance from the point of view of the group's shareholders. This could be calculated as:

Profit after debt interest

Minus   A notional interest charge on the value of assets financed by shareholders' capital
Equals   Residual income.

Alternatively, residual income might be measured as:

Profit before interest (controllable by the subsidiary's management)

Minus   A notional interest charge on the controllable investments of the subsidiary
Equals   Residual income.

Each subsidiary would be able to increase its residual income if it earned an incremental profit in excess of the notional interest charges on its incremental investments – ie in effect, if it added to the value of the group's equity.

77 Cloud

Workbook references. Integrated Reporting and other aspects of performance reporting are covered in Chapter 17 of the Workbook. The *Conceptual Framework* and related exposure draft are covered in Chapter 1. Hedging is covered in Chapter 7 and transfers from the revaluation surplus are covered in Chapter 3.

Top tips. This question covered two topics: the issue of recognition of income and expenses in profit or loss vs other comprehensive income, reclassification between the two and integrated reporting. Because the question is fairly open-ended, our answer is much longer than would be needed in an examination where only some of the points would need to be made in order to get the marks.

Easy marks. The Integrated Reporting question is straightforward textbook knowledge.

Marking scheme

			Marks
(a)	(i)	1 mark per point up to maximum	4
	(ii)	1 mark per point up to maximum	5
	(iii)	1 mark per point up to maximum	8
Professional marks			2
(b)	1 mark per point up to maximum		6
			25

(a) (i) **Current presentation requirements**

IAS 1 *Presentation of Financial Statements* defines profit or loss as 'the total of income less expenses, excluding the components of other comprehensive income' (para. 7) and other comprehensive income as comprising 'items of income and expense (including reclassification adjustments) that are not recognised in profit or loss as required or permitted by other IFRSs' (para. 7). IFRS currently requires the statement of profit or loss and other comprehensive income to be presented as either one statement, being a combined statement of profit or loss and other comprehensive income or two statements, being the statement of profit or loss and the statement of comprehensive income. An entity has to show separately in OCI, those items which would be reclassified (recycled) to profit or loss and those items which would never be reclassified (recycled) to profit or loss. The related tax effects have to be allocated to these sections.

IAS 1 states that **profit or loss includes all items of income or expense (including reclassification adjustments) except those items of income or expense which are recognised in OCI as required or permitted by IFRS.** IAS 1 further states that the other comprehensive income section is required to present line items which are classified by their nature, and grouped between those items which will or will not be reclassified to profit or loss in subsequent periods.

(ii)   **Reclassification adjustments**

Reclassification adjustments are **amounts recycled to profit or loss in the current period which were recognised in OCI in the current or previous periods.** An example of items recognised in OCI which may be reclassified to profit or loss are foreign currency gains on the disposal of a foreign operation and realised gains or losses on cash flow hedges. Those items which may not be reclassified are changes in a revaluation surplus under IAS 16 *Property, Plant and Equipment*, and actuarial gains and losses on a defined benefit plan under IAS 19 *Employee Benefits*. However, there is a general lack of agreement about which items should be presented in profit or loss and in OCI. The interaction between profit or loss and OCI is unclear, especially the notion of reclassification and when or which OCI items should be reclassified. A common misunderstanding is that the distinction is based upon realised versus unrealised gains.

There are several **arguments for and against reclassification**. If reclassification ceased, then there would be no need to define profit or loss, or any other total or subtotal in profit or loss, and any presentation decisions can be left to specific IFRSs. It is argued that reclassification protects the integrity of profit or loss and **provides users with relevant information about a transaction which occurred in the period.** Additionally, it can **improve comparability** where IFRS permits similar items to be recognised in either profit or loss or OCI.

Those against reclassification argue that the **recycled amounts add to the complexity of financial reporting,** may lead to earnings management and the reclassification adjustments may not meet the definitions of income or expense in the period as the change in the asset or liability may have occurred in a previous period.

The lack of a consistent basis for determining how items should be presented has led to an **inconsistent use of OCI in IFRS.** Opinions vary but there is a feeling that **OCI has become a home for anything controversial** because of a lack of clear definition of what should be included in the statement. Many users are thought to ignore OCI, as the changes reported are not caused by the operating flows used for predictive purposes.

The **2015 Exposure Draft *Conceptual Framework for Financial Reporting*** brings some clarity to this matter, both on the issue of where items should be recognised and on whether and when they can be reclassified. The ED describes the **statement of profit or loss** as **the 'primary source of information** about an entity's financial performance for the period' (ED/2015/3: para. 7.21), and requires a total or subtotal for profit or loss to be provided. The ED states further that there is a **rebuttable presumption that all income and all expenses will be included in the statement of profit or loss.** This presumption can only be rebutted in the following circumstances:

(1)   The income or expenses relate to assets or liabilities measured at current values.

(2)   Excluding those items from the statement of profit or loss would enhance the relevance of the information in the statement of profit or loss for the period.

Preparers of financial statements cannot make this judgement in applying standards; the **presumption can only be rebutted by the IASB when setting standards.**

Turning to reclassification, the **ED contains a presumption that income and expense items that are included in OCI in one period will be reclassified into the statement of profit or loss in some future period.** (recycled) when doing so **enhances the relevance of the information included in that statement in that period.** However, this presumption **could be rebutted,** for example, if there is no clear basis for identifying the period in which that reclassification would enhance the relevance of the information in the statement of profit or loss. Furthermore, if there is no such basis, this may indicate that the income or expense should not be included in other comprehensive income.

(iii) **Integrated Reporting**

The International Integrated Reporting Council (IIRC) has released a Framework for integrated reporting. The *Framework* establishes principles and concepts which govern the overall content of an integrated report. An integrated report sets out how the organisation's strategy, governance, performance and prospects can lead to the creation of value. The IIRC has set out a principles-based framework rather than specifying a detailed disclosure and measurement standard. This enables each company to set out its own report rather than adopting a checklist approach. The integrated report aims to provide an insight into the company's resources and relationships, which are known as the capitals and how the company interacts with the external environment and the capitals to create value. These capitals can be financial, manufactured, intellectual, human, social and relationship, and natural capital but companies need not adopt these classifications. Integrated reporting is built around the following key components:

(1) Organisational overview and the external environment under which it operates

(2) Governance structure and how this supports its ability to create value

(3) Business model

(4) Risks and opportunities and how they are dealing with them and how they affect the company's ability to create value

(5) Strategy and resource allocation

(6) Performance and achievement of strategic objectives for the period and outcomes

(7) Outlook and challenges facing the company and their implications

(8) The basis of presentation needs to be determined including what matters are to be included in the integrated report and how the elements are quantified or evaluated.

The *Framework* does not require discrete sections to be compiled in the report but there should be a high level review to ensure that all relevant aspects are included. An integrated report should provide insight into the nature and quality of the organisation's relationships with its key stakeholders, including how and to what extent the organisation understands, takes into account and responds to their needs and interests. Further, the report should be consistent over time to enable comparison with other entities.

The IIRC considered the nature of value and value creation. These terms can include the total of all the capitals, the benefit captured by the company, the market value or cash flows of the organisation and the successful achievement of the company's objectives. However, the conclusion reached was that the *Framework* should not define value from any one particular perspective because value depends upon the individual company's own perspective. It can be shown through movement of capital and can be defined as value created for the company or for others. An integrated report should not attempt to quantify value, as assessments of value are left to those using the report.

The report does not contain a statement from those 'charged with governance' acknowledging their responsibility for the integrated report. This may undermine the reliability and credibility of the integrated report. There has been discussion about whether the *Framework* constitutes suitable criteria for report preparation and for assurance. There is a degree of uncertainty as to measurement standards to be used for the information reported and how a preparer can ascertain the completeness of the report. The IIRC has stated that the prescription of specific measurement methods is beyond the scope of a principles-based framework. The *Framework* contains information on the principles-based approach and indicates that there is a need to include quantitative indicators whenever practicable and possible. Additionally, consistency of measurement methods across different reports is of paramount importance. There is outline guidance on the selection of suitable quantitative indicators.

There are additional concerns over the ability to assess future disclosures, and there may be a need for confidence intervals to be disclosed. The preparation of an integrated report requires judgement but there is a requirement for the report to describe its basis of preparation and presentation, including the significant frameworks and methods used to quantify or evaluate material matters. Also included is the disclosure of a summary of how the company determined the materiality limits and a description of the reporting boundaries.

A company should consider how to describe the disclosures without causing a significant loss of competitive advantage. The entity will consider what advantage a competitor could actually gain from information in the integrated report, and will balance this against the need for disclosure.

(b) At 30 April 20X5, Cloud should write down the steel, in accordance with IAS 2 *Inventories*, to its net realisable value of $6 million, therefore reducing profit by $2 million. Cloud should reclassify an equivalent amount of $2 million from equity to profit or loss. Thus there is no net impact on profit or loss from the write down of inventory. The gain remaining in equity of $1 million will affect profit or loss when the steel is sold. Therefore, on 3 June 20X5, the gain on the sale of $0.2 million with be recognised in profit or loss, and the remaining gain of $1 million will be transferred to profit or loss from equity.

As regards the property, plant and equipment, at 30 April 20X4, there is a revaluation gain of $4 million being the difference between the carrying amount of $8 million ($10 million – $2 million) and the revalued amount of $12 million. This revaluation gain is recognised in other comprehensive income.

At 30 April 20X5 the asset's value has fallen to $4 million and the carrying amount of the asset is $9 million ($12 million – $3 million). The entity will have transferred $1 million from revaluation surplus to retained earnings, being the difference between historical cost depreciation of $2 million and depreciation on the revalued amount of $3 million. The revaluation loss of $5 million will be charged first against the revaluation surplus remaining in equity of ($4 million – $1 million), ie $3 million and the balance of $2 million will be charged against profit or loss.

IAS 1 requires an entity to present a separate statement of changes in equity showing amongst other items, total comprehensive income for the period, reconciliations between the carrying amounts at the beginning and the end of the period for each component of equity, and an analysis of other comprehensive income.

78 Amster

> **Workbook references.** Financial instruments are covered in Chapter 7. The *Conceptual Framework* is covered in Chapter 1.
>
> **Top tips.** This question might have alarmed you as you might not have seen a capitalisation table before. However, you must be prepared to encounter disclosures such as this, which are a common feature of published financial statements and useful to investors. You should be able to work out that it requires adjusting in the same way as a statement of financial position would be. For (a)(ii), you need to think about the principles around debt and equity classification for financial instruments and try and relate this to the definitions in the *Conceptual Framework*.

Marking scheme

		Marks
(a)	(i) 1 mark per point up to maximum	8
	(ii) 1 mark per point up to maximum	6
(b)	1 mark per point up to maximum	9
		2
Professional marks		25

(a) (i) **Importance of information concerning an entity's capital**

Essentially there are two classes of capital reported in financial statements, namely debt and equity. However, debt and equity instruments can have different levels of right, benefit and risks. Hence, the details underlying a company's capital structure are absolutely essential to assessing the prospects for changes in a company's financial flexibility, and ultimately, its value.

For investors who are assessing the risk profile of an entity, the management and level of an entity's capital is an important consideration. Disclosures about capital are normally in addition to disclosures required by regulators as their reasons for disclosure may differ from those of the International Accounting Standards Board (IASB). The details underlying a company's capital structure are essential to the assessment of any potential change in an entity's financial standing.

Investors have specific but different needs for information about capital depending upon their approach to their investment in an entity. If their approach is income based, then shortage of capital may have an impact upon future dividends. If ROCE is used for comparing the performance of entities, then investors need to know the nature and quantity of the historical capital employed in the business. Some investors will focus on historical invested capital, others on accounting capital and others on market capitalisation.

Published information

As an entity's capital does not relate solely to financial instruments, the IASB has included these disclosures in IAS 1 *Presentation of Financial Statements* rather than IFRS 7 *Financial Instruments: Disclosures*. Although IFRS 7 requires some specific disclosures about financial liabilities, it does not have similar requirements for equity instruments.

As a result, IAS 1 requires an entity to disclose information which enables users to evaluate the entity's objectives, policies and processes for managing capital. This

objective is obtained by disclosing qualitative and quantitative data. The former should include narrative information such as what the company manages as capital, whether there are any external capital requirements and how those requirements are incorporated into the management of capital. The IASB decided that there should be disclosure of whether the entity has complied with any external capital requirements and, if not, the consequences of non-compliance.

Besides the requirements of IAS 1, the IFRS *Practice Statement, Management Commentary* suggests that management should include forward-looking information in the commentary when it is aware of trends, uncertainties or other factors which could affect the entity's capital resources. Additionally, some jurisdictions refer to capital disclosures as part of their legal requirements.

In addition to the annual report, an investor may find details of the entity's capital structure where the entity is involved in a transaction, such as a sale of bonds or equities. It can be seen that information regarding an entity's capital structure is spread across several documents including the management commentary, the notes to financial statements, interim financial statements and any document required by securities regulators.

Integrated reporting

The capitals identified by the International Integrated Reporting Council (IIRC) are: financial capital, manufactured capital, intellectual capital, human capital, social and relationship capital, and natural capital. Together, they represent stores of value which are the basis of an organisation's value creation. Financial capital is broadly understood as the pool of funds available to an organisation. This includes both debt and equity finance. This description of financial capital focuses on the source of funds, rather than its application which results in the acquisition of manufactured or other forms of capital. Financial capital is a medium of exchange which releases its value through conversion into other forms of capital. It is the pool of funds which is available to the organisation for use in the production of goods or the provision of services obtained through financing, such as debt, equity or grants, or generated through operations or investments.

(ii)   Whether an instrument is classified as either a financial liability or as equity is important as it has a direct effect on an entity's reported results and financial position. The critical feature of a liability is that, under the terms of the instrument, the issuer is or can be required to deliver either cash or another financial asset to the holder and it cannot avoid this obligation. An instrument is classified as equity when it represents a residual interest in the issuer's assets after deducting all its liabilities. If the financial instrument provides the entity an unconditional discretion, the financial instrument is equity.

IAS 32 *Financial Instruments Presentation* sets out the nature of the classification process but the standard is principle based and sometimes the outcomes are surprising to users. IAS 32 focuses on the contractual obligations of the instrument and considers the substance of the contractual rights and obligations. The variety of instruments issued by entities makes this classification difficult with the application of the principles occasionally resulting in instruments which seem like equity being accounted for as liabilities. Recent developments in the types of financial instruments issued have added more complexity to capital structures with the resultant difficulties in interpretation and understanding.

Equity and liabilities are classified separately in the statement of financial position. The *Conceptual Framework* distinguishes the two elements by the obligation of the entity to deliver cash or other economic resources from items which create no such obligation. The statement of profit or loss and other comprehensive income (OCI) includes income and expenses arising from liabilities which is interest and, if applicable, remeasurement and gain or loss on settlement. The statement does not report as income or expense any changes in the carrying amount of the entity's own equity instruments but does include expenses arising from the consumption of services which fall under IFRS 2 *Share-based Payment*. IFRS 2 requires a valuation of the services consumed in exchange for the financial liabilities or equity instruments.

In the statement of financial position, the carrying amount of many financial liabilities changes either with the passage of time or if the liability is remeasured at fair value. However, the amount reported for classes of equity instruments generally does not change after initial recognition except for non-controlling interest.

Liability classification typically results in any payments on the instrument being treated as interest and charged to earnings. This may in turn affect the entity's ability to pay dividends on its equity shares depending upon local legislation.

Equity classification avoids the negative impact which liability classification has on reported earnings, gearing ratios and debt covenants. It also results in the instrument falling outside the scope of IFRS 9 *Financial Instruments*, thereby avoiding the complicated ongoing measurement requirements of that standard.

(b)   In the case of the first class of preference shares, even though there are negative consequences of not paying dividends on the preferred shares as agreed contractually, the company can avoid the obligation to deliver cash. The preferred shares do have redemption provisions but these are not mandatory and are at the sole discretion of the management committee and therefore the shares should be classified as equity.

In the case of the second class, the contractual term requires no dividend to be paid to ordinary shareholders if a payment is not made on the preferred shares. In this case, as Amster can avoid the obligation to settle the annual dividend, the shares are classified as equity. Thus $75 million should be transferred from liabilities to equity.

IFRS 2 *Share-based Payment* states that cash settled share-based payment transactions occur where goods or services are paid for at amounts which are based on the price of the company's equity instruments. The expense for cash settled transactions is the cash paid by the company and any amounts accrued should be shown as liabilities and not equity. Therefore Amster should remove the following amount from equity and show it as a liability.

Expense for year to 30 November 20X7 is:

$$((1,500 - 180 \text{ employees} \times 250 \text{ awards} \times \$35) \times \tfrac{1}{3} = \$3.85 \text{ million}$$

As a result of the adjustments to the financial statements, Amster's gearing ratio will be lowered significantly as the liabilities will drop from 53.8% of total capitalisation to 33.2% of total capitalisation. However, the ROCE may stay the same even though there is an increase in shareholders equity as total capitalisation has not changed. However, this will depend upon the definition used by the entity for capital employed.

Amster Group – capitalisation table

	30 November 20X7 $m	Adjustment $m	30 November 20X7 $m
Long-term liabilities	81	3.85	84.85
Pension plan deficit	30		30.00
Cumulative preference shares	75	(75)	–
Liabilities	186		114.85
Non-controlling interest	10		10.00
Shareholders equity	150	(75 – 3.85)	221.15
Group equity	160		231.15
Total capitalisation	346		346.00

79 Sanchera

Marking scheme

			Marks
(a)	(i)	1 mark per point up to maximum	9
	(ii)	1 mark per point up to maximum	4
	(iii)	1 mark per point up to maximum	7
(b)		1 mark per point up to maximum	5
			25

(a) (i) **Definition of materiality and application of the concept**

Information is **material** if **omitting it or misstating it** could **influence decisions** which users make on the basis of financial information about a specific reporting entity. Materiality is an **entity-specific** aspect of relevance, based on the **nature and/or magnitude** of the items to which it relates in the context of the entity's financial report. It is therefore **difficult to specify a uniform quantitative threshold** for materiality or predetermine what could be material in a particular situation. Materiality should ensure that **relevant information is not omitted or mis-stated** and it should help **filter out obscure information** which is not useful to users of financial statements.

The *Conceptual Framework* describes materiality as an **application** by a particular **entity** of the fundamental **qualitative characteristic of relevance**. When an entity is assessing materiality, it is assessing whether the information is relevant to the readers of its own financial statements. Information relevant for one entity might not be as relevant for another entity. **IAS 1** *Presentation of Financial Statements* says that an entity need **not provide a specific disclosure required by an IFRS** if the **information is not material** and that the application of IFRSs, with additional disclosure when necessary, is presumed to result in financial statements which achieve a fair presentation. In other words, **material information** must be **disclosed irrespective** of whether there is an **explicit disclosure requirement**.

Although **preparers** may understand the concept of materiality, they may be **less certain about how it should be applied**. Preparers may be **reluctant to filter out information which is not relevant** to users as **auditors and regulators may challenge** their reasons for the omissions. The way in which some IFRSs are drafted suggests that their specific requirements override the general statement in IAS 1 that an entity need not provide information which is not material.

There is concern that the application of the concept of materiality to the financial statements **can result in excessive disclosure of immaterial information** while **important information can be obscured or even missed out** of the financial statements.

Proposed guidance under ED/2015/8

ED 2015/8 proposes that **guidance** is provided in the form of a **Practice Statement** in the following areas: characteristics of materiality, presentation and disclosure in financial statements, recognition and measurement, and omissions and misstatements. This will be a **non-mandatory guidance** to assist with the application of the concept of materiality to financial statements prepared in accordance with IFRSs.

Characteristics of materiality

ED/2015/8 **retains** the accepted **notion** that items are **material** if their **omission or misstatement** would **influence the decisions of users** of financial statements. **Judgement** needs to be applied in considering whether inclusion or disclosure of an item would indeed influence the decisions of users. When assessing materiality, preparers need to consider **who the user groups are** and what **types of decisions** they make based on the financial statements, the need for **qualitative and quantitative assessment** and the need to consider items **individually and collectively** with other information.

Presentation and disclosure

Guidance is proposed on how to deal with **immaterial information** and when to **aggregate and disaggregate** information. The IASB suggests that prepares should consider what information to include in the **primary financial statements**, what should be presented in the **notes** and then look at the **financial statements as a whole** to ensure that the financial statements are comprehensive and include the appropriate level of information.

Recognition and measurement

Guidance is proposed relating to the use of **rounding** in the financial statements and materiality in **internal record keeping**.

Omissions and misstatements

The materiality of omissions and misstatements needs to be considered individually and in the financial statements as a whole. Guidance is proposed relating to **current versus prior period misstatement**s and how to deal with **misstatements that are intentionally misleading**.

(ii) **Materiality and the International Integrated Reporting Framework**

Integrated reporting <IR> takes a **broader view of business reporting**, emphasising the need for entities to provide information to help investors **assess the sustainability of their business model**. <IR> is a process which results in communication, through the integrated report, about **value creation over time**.

An integrated report is a **concise communication** about how an organisation's **strategy, governance, performance and prospects** lead to the **creation of value over the short, medium and long term**.

The materiality definition for <IR> purposes would consider that material matters are those which are of such relevance and importance that they could **substantively influence the assessments of the intended report users**. In the case of IR, relevant matters are those which affect or have the **potential to affect the organisation's ability to create value over time**.

For **financial reporting purposes**, the **nature or extent of an omission or misstatement** in the organisation's **financial statements** determines **relevance**. Matters which are considered material for financial reporting purposes, or for other forms of reporting, may also be material for <IR> purposes if they are of such relevance and importance that they could **change the assessments of providers of financial capital with regard to the organisation's ability to create value**. Another feature of materiality for IR purposes is that the definition **emphasises the involvement of senior management and those charged with governance** in the **materiality determination process** in order for the organisation to determine how best to disclose its value creation development in a meaningful and transparent way.

(iii) **Issues with IAS 7 *Statement of Cash flows***

IAS 7 *Statement of Cash Flows* was amended as part of the IASB's Disclosure Initiative. There are many issues with the standard (discussed below) but the amendment focused on providing additional information to the users of financial statements relating to financing activities.

Presentation

The operating activities in the cash flow statement can be presented in one of two ways: the **direct method and the indirect method**. The **direct method is seldom used** as it displays major classes of gross cash receipts and payments and companies' **systems often do not collect this type of data in an easily accessible form**. The **indirect method** is **more commonly used** to present operating activities. The presentation of operating profit under the indirect method of the cash flow statement can start with either profit or loss before or after tax. A user's ability to make comparisons may be affected if entities present reconciliations with different starting points.

Inconsistency of classification

Cash flows from the same transaction may be classified differently. For example, a loan repayment would see the **interest** classified as **operating or financing** activities, whereas the **principal** will be classified as a **financing** activity.

There are concerns over the **flexibility of current classification of** items in the statement of cash flows. For example, dividends and interest paid can be classified as either operating or financing activities. As a result, **users** have to make appropriate **adjustments when comparing different entities**, particularly when calculating free cash flow for valuation purposes. Additionally, when a user is assessing an entity's ability to service debt, interest paid would be reclassified from operating activities to financing activities.

Purpose of cash flows

Sometimes **classification** of certain cash flows may be **inconsistent** with the **purpose** of the cash flows. For example, research expenditure is classified as cash from operating activities but is often considered to be a long-term investment. Some argue that such cash outflows should be included within investing activities, because

they relate to items, which are intended to generate future income and cash flows. IAS 7 takes the view that, to be classified as an investing cash outflow, the expenditure must result in an asset being recognised in the statement of financial position.

Potential for error

Some items of **property, plant and equipment** are purchased from **suppliers on similar credit terms to those for inventory** and for amounts payable to other creditors. As a result, transactions for property, plant and equipment may be **incorrectly included within changes in accounts payable for operating items**. Consequently, unless payments for property, plant and equipment are separated from other payments related to operating activities, they can be allocated **incorrectly to operating activities**.

Differing opinions

There are currently **different views** as to how to show **lessee cash flows** in the statement of cash flows. **Some users** would like the statement of cash flows to reflect lessee cash outflows in a way which is **comparable to those of a financed purchase** where the entity buys an asset and separately finances the purchase. Other users take the view that lease cash payments are **similar in nature to capital expenditure** and should be classified within **investing activities** in the statement of cash flows.

Finally, there is concern about the current **lack of comparability** under IFRS because of the **choice of treatment** currently allowed. A lessee can classify interest payments within operating activities or within financing activities.

Improvements following the amendments to IAS 7

The amendments to IAS 7 address some of these concerns. The **main objective** of the amendment is to **improve information about changes in an entity's liabilities which relate to financing activities.**

The amendments require **disclosure** of how **liabilities** have **changed** as a result of **cash flows in the financing activities** section, changes as a result of **acquiring or disposing of subsidiaries**, the effect of **foreign exchange rates**, the effect of **movements in fair value and other changes**.

An entity is **not required** to provide a **reconciliation** of the **opening and closing amounts in the statement of financial position** for each **liability** for which cash flows are classified as **financing activities**, but IAS 7 does suggest that such a reconciliation may be a **useful way** of ensuring that the **disclosure requirements** are **satisfied**.

Because many entities already voluntarily disclose a net debt reconciliation, the changes should theoretically **not impose any additional burden** on issuers.

(b) **Reconciliation of liabilities from financing activities**

	20X5	Cash flows	Non-cash changes Acquisition	New leases	20X6
	$m	$m	$m	$m	$m
Long-term borrowings	50	55	35		140
Lease liabilities	5	(3)	—	15	17
Long term debt	55	52	35	15	157

Tutorial note.

Sanchera showed interest paid on lease liabilities of $5 million in operating activities. Finally, Sanchera had an overdraft with the bank of $2 million and this would be shown in cash and cash equivalents and not in financing activities.

Mock Exams

ACCA
Strategic Business Reporting (International)

Mock Examination 1

Time allowed: 3 hours 15 minutes

This question paper is divided into two sections:

Section A – BOTH questions are compulsory and MUST be attempted
Section B – BOTH questions are compulsory and MUST be attempted

Do NOT open this question paper until instructed by the supervisor.

Do NOT record any of your answers on the question paper.

This question paper must not be removed from the examination hall.

BPP
LEARNING MEDIA

Section A – BOTH questions are compulsory and MUST be attempted

1 Joey

(a) Joey, a public limited company, operates in the media sector. Joey has investments in two companies, Margy and Hulty. The draft statements of financial position at 30 November 20X4 are as follows:

	Joey $m	Margy $m	Hulty $m
Assets			
Non-current assets			
Property, plant and equipment	3,295	2,000	1,200
Investments in subsidiaries			
Margy	1,675		
Hulty	700		
	5,670	2,000	1,200
Current assets	985	861	150
Total assets	6,655	2,861	1,350
Equity and liabilities			
Share capital	850	1,020	600
Retained earnings	3,340	980	350
Other components of equity	250	80	40
Total equity	4,440	2,080	990
Total liabilities	2,215	781	360
Total equity and liabilities	6,655	2,861	1,350

The following information is relevant to the preparation of the consolidated financial statements:

(1) On 1 December 20X1, Joey acquired 30% of the ordinary shares of Margy for a cash consideration of $600 million when the fair value of Margy's identifiable net assets was $1,840 million. Joey has equity accounted for Margy up to 30 November 20X3. Joey's share of Margy's undistributed profit amounted to $90 million and its share of a revaluation gain amounted to $10 million for the period 1 December 20X1 to 30 November 20X3. On 1 December 20X3, Joey acquired a further 40% of the ordinary shares of Margy for a cash consideration of $975 million and gained control of the company. The cash consideration paid has been added to the equity accounted balance for Margy at 1 December 20X3 to give the carrying amount at 30 November 20X4.

At 1 December 20X3, the fair value of Margy's identifiable net assets was $2,250 million. At 1 December 20X3, the fair value of the equity interest in Margy held by Joey before the business combination was $705 million and the fair value of the non-controlling interest of 30% was assessed as $620 million. The retained earnings and other components of equity of Margy at 1 December 20X3 were $900 million and $70 million respectively. It is group policy to measure the non-controlling interest at fair value.

(2) At the time of the business combination with Margy on 1 December 20X3, Joey included in the fair value of Margy's identifiable net assets, an unrecognised contingent liability with a fair value of $6 million in respect of a warranty claim in progress against Margy, considered to have been measured reliably. In March 20X4, there was a

revision of the estimate of the liability to $5 million. The amount has met the criteria to be recognised as a provision in current liabilities in the financial statements of Margy and the revision of the estimate is deemed to be a measurement period adjustment.

(3) Buildings with a carrying amount of $200 million had been included in the fair value of Margy's identifiable net assets at 1 December 20X3. The buildings have a remaining useful life of 20 years at 1 December 20X3 and are depreciated on the straight-line basis. However, Joey had commissioned an independent valuation of the buildings of Margy which was not complete at 1 December 20X3 and therefore not considered in the fair value of the identifiable net assets at the acquisition date. The valuations were received on 1 April 20X4 and resulted in a decrease of $40 million in the fair value of property, plant and equipment at the date of acquisition. This decrease does not affect the fair value of the non-controlling interest at acquisition and has not been entered into the financial statements of Margy. The excess of the fair value of the net assets over their carrying amount, at 1 December 20X3, is due to an increase in the value of non-depreciable land and the contingent liability.

(4) On 1 December 20X3, Joey acquired 80% of the equity interests of Hulty, a private entity, in exchange for cash of $700 million, gaining control of Hulty from that date. Because the former owners of Hulty needed to dispose of the investment quickly, they did not have sufficient time to market the investment to many potential buyers. The fair value of the identifiable net assets was $960 million. Joey determined that the fair value of the 20% non-controlling interest in Hulty at that date was $250 million. Joey reviewed the procedures used to identify and measure the assets acquired and liabilities assumed and to measure the fair value of both the non-controlling interest and the consideration transferred. After that review, Hulty determined that the procedures and resulting measures were appropriate. The retained earnings and other components of equity of Hulty at 1 December 20X3 were $300 million and $40 million respectively. The excess in fair value is due to an unrecognised franchise right, which Joey had granted to Hulty on 1 December 20X2 for five years. At the time of the acquisition, the franchise right could be sold for its market price. It is group policy to measure the non-controlling interest at fair value.

All goodwill arising on acquisitions has been impairment tested with no impairment being required.

(5) From 30 November 20X3, Joey carried a property in its statement of financial position at its revalued amount of $14 million in accordance with IAS 16 *Property, Plant and Equipment.* Depreciation is charged at $300,000 per year on the straight-line basis. In March 20X4, the management decided to sell the property and it was advertised for sale. On 31 March 20X4, the sale was considered to be highly probable and the criteria for IFRS 5 *Non-current Assets Held for Sale and Discontinued Operations* were met. At that date, the property's fair value was $15.4 million and its value in use was $15.8 million. Costs to sell the property were estimated at $300,000. On 30 November 20X4, the property was sold for $15.6 million. The transactions regarding the property are deemed to be material and no entries have been made in the financial statements regarding this property since 30 November 20X3 as the cash receipts from the sale were not received until December 20X4.

Required

(a) (i)   Explain, showing relevant calculations and with reference to IFRS 3 *Business Combinations*, how the goodwill balance in Joey's consolidated financial statements at 30 November 20X4 should be calculated. **(10 marks)**

(ii) Explain how the transaction described in Note 5 above should be accounted for in Joey's consolidated financial statements at 30 November 20X4. **(6 marks)**

(iii) Prepare, showing required calculations, an extract from Joey's consolidated statement of financial position showing the group retained earnings at 30 November 20X4. *RE* **(4 marks)**

(b) The Joey Group wishes to expand its operations. As part of this expansion, it has granted to the employees of Margy and Hulty, some of whom are considered key management personnel, options over its own shares as at 7 December 20X4. The options vest immediately. Joey is not proposing to make a charge to the subsidiaries for these options.

Joey does not know how to account for this transaction.

Required

Explain to Joey how the above transaction should be dealt with in the subsidiaries' financial statements and Joey's consolidated financial statements, and advise on any disclosures that may be required to ensure external stakeholders are aware of the transaction.   **(5 marks)**

(Total = 25 marks)

2 Jogger

Jogger is a public limited company operating in the retail sector. It has recently appointed a new managing director who is reviewing the draft financial statements for the year ended 30 September 20X9.

(a) The managing director is intrigued by why the annual report and financial statements contains 'more than just numbers' and questions you as to why it is beneficial to Jogger to produce so much information.

Required

Explain the factors which provide encouragement to companies to disclose social and environmental information in their financial statements, briefly discussing whether the content of such disclosure should be at the company's discretion.   **(8 marks)**

(b) The managing director is keen to present the financial results from his first period of leadership in the best possible light. He considers EBITDA to be the most important measure of performance and has suggested that the reported profits under IFRS and alternative measures such as EDITBA can be managed to ensure Jogger reports strong performance. He wants to know whether the finance team have taken advantage of all of the options available to enable this and has reminded the financial controller that he will receive a substantial bonus if earnings targets are met.

Required

Discuss, from the perspective of investors and potential investors, the benefits and shortfalls of reporting EBITDA and comment on the nature of, and incentives for, 'management of earnings' and whether such a process can be deemed to be ethically acceptable.   **(15 marks)**

Professional marks will be awarded in part (b) of this question for the application of ethical principles.   **(2 marks)**

(Total = 25 marks)

Section B – BOTH questions are compulsory and MUST be attempted

3 Klancet

You are the newly appointed finance director of Klancet, a public limited company operating in the pharmaceuticals sector. The company has not had a finance director for several months and the managing director is seeking advice on several financial reporting issues.

(a) Klancet produces and sells its range of drugs through three separate divisions. In addition, it has two laboratories which carry out research and development activities.

In the first laboratory, the research and development activity is funded internally and centrally for each of the three divisions. It does not carry out research and development activities for other entities. Each of the three divisions is given a budget allocation which it uses to purchase research and development activities from the laboratory. The laboratory is directly accountable to the division heads for this expenditure.

The second laboratory performs contract investigation activities for other laboratories and pharmaceutical companies. This laboratory earns 75% of its revenues from external customers and these external revenues represent 18% of the organisation's total revenues.

The performance of the second laboratory's activities and of the three separate divisions is regularly reviewed by the chief operating decision maker (CODM). In addition to the heads of divisions, there is a head of the second laboratory. The head of the second laboratory is directly accountable to the CODM and they discuss the operating activities, allocation of resources and financial results of the laboratory.

Required

(i) Advise the managing director, with reference to IFRS 8 *Operating Segments*, whether the research and development laboratories should be reported as two separate segments. **(6 marks)**

The managing director does not think IFRS 8 provides information that is useful to investors. He feels it just adds more pages to financial statements that are already very lengthy.

Required

(ii) Critique the managing directors' view that IFRS 8 does not provide useful information to investors. **(5 marks)**

(iii) Advise Klancet as to the potential impact, if any, of the IASB's Discussion Paper *Disclosure Initiative – Principles of Disclosure* on the requirements of IFRS 8.
(4 marks)

(b) Klancet is collaborating with Retto, a third party, to develop two existing drugs owned by Klancet.

Project 1

In the case of the first drug, Retto is simply developing the drug for Klancet without taking any risks during the development phase and will have no further involvement if regulatory approval is given. Regulatory approval has been refused for this drug in the past. Klancet will retain ownership of patent rights attached to the drug. Retto is not involved in the marketing and production of the drug. Klancet has agreed to make two non-refundable payments to Retto of $4 million on the signing of the agreement and $6 million on successful completion of the development.

Project 2

Klancet and Retto have entered into a second collaboration agreement in which Klancet will pay Retto for developing and manufacturing an existing drug. The existing drug already has regulatory approval. The new drug being developed by Retto for Klancet will not differ substantially from the existing drug. Klancet will have exclusive marketing rights to the drug if the regulatory authorities approve it. Historically, in this jurisdiction, new drugs receive approval if they do not differ substantially from an existing approved drug.

The contract terms require Klancet to pay an upfront payment on signing of the contract, a payment on securing final regulatory approval, and a unit payment of $10 per unit, which equals the estimated cost plus a profit margin, once commercial production begins. The cost-plus profit margin is consistent with Klancet's other recently negotiated supply arrangements for similar drugs.

Required

Prepare notes for a presentation to the managing director of Klancet as to how to account for the above contracts with Retto in accordance with IFRS and with reference to the *Conceptual Framework* and the related Exposure Draft. **(8 marks)**

Professional marks will be awarded in part (a) for clarity and quality of presentation. **(2 marks)**

(Total = 25 marks)

4 Jayach

(a) IFRS 13 *Fair Value Measurement* defines fair value, establishes a framework for measuring fair value and requires significant disclosures relating to fair value measurement.

IFRS 13 gives guidance regarding fair value measurements in existing standards, although it does not apply to transactions dealt with by certain specific standards. Fair value measurements are categorised into a three-level hierarchy, based on the type of inputs to the valuation techniques used.

Required

Discuss the main principles of fair value measurement as set out in IFRS 13. **(8 marks)**

(b) Jayach, a public limited company, is reviewing the fair valuation of certain assets and liabilities in light of the introduction of IFRS 13.

It carries an asset that is traded in different markets and is uncertain as to which valuation to use. The asset has to be valued at fair value under International Financial Reporting Standards. Jayach currently only buys and sells the asset in the Australasian market. The data relating to the asset are set out below.

Year to 30 November 20X2	Asian market	European market	Australasian market
Volume of market – units	4 million	2 million	1 million
Price	$19	$16	$22
Costs of entering the market	$2	$2	$3
Transaction costs	$1	$2	$2

Additionally, Jayach had acquired an entity on 30 November 20X2 and is required to fair value a decommissioning liability. The entity has to decommission a mine at the end of its useful life, which is in three years' time. Jayach has determined that it will use a valuation technique to measure the fair value of the liability. If Jayach were allowed to transfer the liability to another market participant, then the following data would be used.

Input	Amount
Labour and material cost	$2 million
Overhead	30% of labour and material cost
Third party mark-up – industry average	20%
Annual inflation rate	5%
Risk adjustment – uncertainty relating to cash flows	6%
Risk-free rate of government bonds	4%
Entity's non-performance risk	2%

Jayach needs advice on how to fair value the liability.

Required

Discuss, with relevant computations, how Jayach should fair value the above asset and liability under IFRS 13. **(11 marks)**

(c) The directors of Jayach have received an email from its majority shareholder.

To: Directors of Jayach

From: A Shareholder

Re: Measurement

I have recently seen an article in the financial press discussing the 'mixed measurement approach' that is used by lots of companies. I hope this isn't the case at Jayach because 'mixed' seems to imply 'inconsistent'? Surely it would be better to measure everything in the same way? I would appreciate it if you could you provide further information at the next annual general meeting on measurement bases, covering what approach is taken at Jayach and why, and the potential effect on investors trying to analyse the financial statements.

Required

Prepare notes for the directors of Jayach which discuss the issues raised in the shareholder's email. **(6 marks)**

(Total = 25 marks)

Answers

**DO NOT TURN THIS PAGE UNTIL YOU HAVE
COMPLETED THE MOCK EXAM**

Section A

1 Joey

> **Workbook references.** Basic groups and the principles of IFRS 3 are covered in Chapter 10. Step acquisitions are covered in Chapter 11. IFRS 5 is covered in Chapter 13. Share-based payment is covered in Chapter 9.
>
> **Top tips.** For step acquisitions, it is important to understand the transaction – here you have an associate becoming a subsidiary, so the goodwill calculation for Margy needs to include the fair value of the previously held investments. Remember to discuss the principles rather than just working through the calculations. The examiner has stated that a candidate will not be able to pass the SBR exam on numerical elements alone. The other goodwill calculation is very straightforward, the only unusual aspect being that it is a gain on a bargain purchase.
>
> Don't skimp on part (b) – there are five marks available.
>
> **Easy marks.** There are some easy marks available in part (a) for the standard parts of calculations of goodwill and retained earnings.

Marking scheme

				Marks
(a)	(i)	Goodwill		
		Calculation		4
		Discussion – 1 mark per point up to maximum		6
				10
	(ii)	Asset held for sale		
		Calculation		3
		Discussion – 1 mark per point up to maximum		3
				6
	(iii)	Retained earnings		4
				20
(b)	Subjective assessment of discussion – 1 mark per point up to maximum			5
				25

(a) (i) **Goodwill**

IFRS 3 *Business Combinations* requires goodwill to be recognised in a business combination. A business combination takes place when one entity, the acquirer, obtains control of another entity, the acquiree. IFRS 3 requires goodwill to be calculated and recorded at the acquisition date. Goodwill is the difference between the consideration transferred by the acquirer, the amount of any non-controlling interest and the fair value of the net assets of the acquiree at the acquisition date. When the business combination is achieved in stages, as is the case for Margy, the previously held interest in the now subsidiary must be remeasured to its fair value.

Applying these principles, the goodwill on the acquisition of Hulty and Margy should be calculated as follows:

	Hulty		Margy	
	$m	$m	$m	$m
Consideration transferred		700		975
Non-controlling interest (at fair value)		250		620
Fair value of previously held equity interest (Note (i))				705
Less fair value of net assets at acquisition				
Share capital	600		1,020	
Retained earnings	300		900	
Other components of equity	40		70	
Fair value adjustments:				
Land (Note (ii) and W1)	–		266	
Contingent liability (Note (iii))	–		(6)	
Franchise right (W1)	20		–	
		(960)		(2,250)
Gain on bargain purchase (Note (iv))		(10)		50
Measurement period adjustments:				
Add decrease in FV of buildings (Note (v))				40
Contingent liability: $6m – $5m (Note (iii))				(1)
Goodwill				89

Notes

(i)   Margy is a business combination achieved in stages, here moving from a 30% owned associate to a 70% owned subsidiary on 1 December 20X3. Substance over form dictates the accounting treatment as, in substance, an associate has been disposed of and a subsidiary has been purchased. From 1 December 20X3, Margy is accounted for as a subsidiary of Joey and goodwill on acquisition is calculated at this date. IFRS 3 requires that the previously held investment is remeasured to fair value and included in the goodwill calculation as shown above. Any gain or loss on remeasurement to fair value is reported in consolidated profit or loss.

(ii) IFRS 3 requires the net assets acquired to be measured at their fair value at the acquisition date. The increase in the fair value of Margy's net assets (that are not the result of specific factors covered in Notes (iii) and (v) below) is attributed to non-depreciable land.

(iii) In accordance with IFRS 3, contingent liabilities should be recognised on acquisition of a subsidiary where they are a present obligation arising as the result of a past event and their fair value can be measured reliably (as is the case for the warranty claims) even if their settlement is not probable. Contingent liabilities after initial recognition must be measured at the higher of the amount that would be recognised under IAS 37 *Provisions, Contingent Liabilities and Contingent Assets* and the amount initially recognised under IFRS 3.

(iv) As the goodwill calculation for the acquisition of Hulty results in a negative value, this is a gain on a bargain purchase and should be recorded in profit or loss for the year attributable to the parent. Before doing so, Joey must review the goodwill calculation to ensure that it has correctly identified all of the assets acquired and all of the liabilities assumed, along with verifying that its measurement of the consideration transferred and the non-controlling interest is appropriate. Joey has completed this exercise and thus it is appropriate to record the negative goodwill and related profit.

(v)   As a result of the independent property valuation becoming available during the measurement period, the carrying amount of property, plant and equipment as at 30 November 20X4 is decreased by $40 million less excess depreciation charged of $2 million ($40m/20 years), ie $38 million. This will increase the carrying amount of goodwill by $40 million as IFRS 3 allows the retrospective adjustment of a provisional figure used in the calculation of goodwill at the acquisition date where new information has become available about the circumstances that existed at the acquisition date. Depreciation expense for 20X4 is decreased by $2 million.

Workings

1   *Hulty: Fair value adjustments*

	At acq'n 1 Dec 20X3 $m	Movement (over 4 years) $m	At year end 30 Nov 20X4 $m
Franchise: 960 – (600 + 300 + 40)	20	(5)	15

2   *Margy: Fair value adjustments*

	At acq'n 1 Dec 20X3 $m	Movement (reduced dep'n) $m	At year end 30 Nov 20X4 $m
Land: 2,250 – (1,020 + 900 + 70) + 6*	266	–	266
Property, plant & equipment	(40)	2	(38)

*Contingent liability

(ii)   **Asset held for sale**

At 31 March 20X4, the criteria in IFRS 5 *Non-Current Assets Held for Sale and Discontinued Operations* have been met, and the property should be classified as held for sale. In accordance with IFRS 5, an asset held for sale should be measured at the **lower of** its **carrying amount** and **fair value less costs to sell**. Immediately before classification of the asset as held for sale, the entity must recognise any impairment in accordance with the applicable IFRS. Any impairment loss is generally recognised in profit or loss. The steps are as follows:

Step 1   Calculate carrying amount under applicable IFRS, here IAS 16 *Property, Plant and Equipment*:

At 31 March 20X4, the date of classification as held for sale, depreciation to date is calculated as $300,000 × 4/12 = $100,000. The carrying amount of the property is therefore $13.9 million ($14.0 – $0.1m). The journal entries are:

DEBIT	Profit or loss ((a) (iii))	$0.1m	
CREDIT	Property, Plant & Equipment (PPE)		$0.1m

The difference between the carrying amount and the fair value at 31 March 20X4 is material, so the property is revalued to its fair value of $15.4 million under IAS 16's revaluation model:

DEBIT	PPE ($15.4m – $13.9m)	$1.5m	
CREDIT	Other comprehensive income		$1.5m

Step 2 Consider whether the property is impaired by comparing its carrying amount, the fair value of $15.4 million, with its recoverable amount. The recoverable amount is the higher of value in use (given as $15.8 million) and fair value less costs to sell ($15.4m – $3m = $15.1m.) The property is not impaired because the recoverable amount (value in use) is higher than the carrying amount (fair value). No impairment loss is recognised.

Step 3 Classify as held for sale and cease depreciation under IFRS 5. Compare the carrying amount ($15.4 million) with fair value less costs to sell ($15.1 million). Measure at the lower of carrying amount and fair value less costs to sell, here $15.1 million, giving an initial write-down of $300,000.

DEBIT	Profit or loss ((a) (iii))	$0.3m
CREDIT	PPE	$0.3m

Step 4 On 30 November 20X4, the property is sold for $15.6 million, which, after deducting costs to sell of $0.3 million gives a profit or $0.2 million.

DEBIT	Receivables	$15.3m
CREDIT	PPE	$15.1m
CREDIT	Profit or loss ((a) (iii))	$0.2m

(iii) Retained earnings

JOEY GROUP

CONSOLIDATED STATEMENT OF FINANCIAL POSITION AS AT 30 NOVEMBER 20X4 (EXTRACT)

	$m
Retained earnings (W1)	3,451.7

Workings

W1: Group retained earnings

	Joey $m	Hulty $m	Margy $m
At year end	3,340.0	350	980
FV adjustment: dep'n reduction ((a) (i))			2
FV adjustment: franchise amortisation ((a) (i))		(5)	
Liability adjustment (6–1)* ((a) (i))			5
Gain on bargain purchase ((a) (i))	10.0		
Profit on derecognition of associate (W2)	5.0		
Asset held for sale: (0.2 – 0.1 – 0.3) ((a) (ii))	(0.2)		
At acquisition ((a) (i))		(300)	(900)
		45	87
Group share:			
Hulty: 80% × 45	36.0		
Margy: 70% × 87	60.9		
	3,451.7		

* *The warranty claim provision of $5 million in Margy's financial statements must be reversed on consolidation to avoid double counting. This is because the contingent liability for this warranty claim was recognised in the consolidated financial statements on acquisition of Margy.*

W2: Profit on derecognition of 30% associate

	$m
Fair value of previously held equity interest at date control obtained (per question / ((a) (i))	705
Carrying amount of associate: 600 cost + 90 (post-acq'n RE) + 10 (post acq'n OCE)	(700)
Profit	5

(b) **Share-based payment**

This arrangement will be governed by IFRS 2 *Share-based Payment*, which includes within its scope **transfers of equity instruments of an entity's parent in return for goods or services.** Clear guidance is given in the Standard as to **when to treat group share-based payment transactions as equity settled and when to treat them as cash settled.**

To determine the accounting treatment, the group entity receiving the goods and services must **consider its own rights and obligations as well as the awards granted.** The amount recognised by the group entity receiving the goods and services will not necessarily be consistent with the amount recognised in the consolidated financial statements.

Group share-based payment transactions **must be treated as equity settled** if either of the following apply:

(i)   The entity **grants rights to its own equity instruments**.

(ii)   The entity has **no obligation to settle** the share-based payment transactions.

Treatment in consolidated financial statements

Because the group receives all of the services in consideration for the group's equity instruments, the transaction is treated as **equity settled**. The fair value of the share-based payment at the grant date is **charged to profit or loss over the vesting period with a corresponding credit to equity.** In this case, the options vest immediately on the grant date, the employees not being required to complete a specified period of service and the services therefore being presumed to have been received. The fair value will be taken by reference to the market value of the shares because it is deemed not normally possible to measure directly the fair value of the employee services received.

Treatment in subsidiaries' financial statements

The subsidiaries do not have an obligation to settle the awards, so the grant is treated as an **equity settled** transaction. The fair value of the share-based payment at the grant date is **charged to profit or loss over the vesting period with a corresponding credit to equity.** The parent, Joey, is compensating the employees of the subsidiaries, Margy and Hulty, with no expense to the subsidiaries, and therefore the **credit in equity is treated as a capital contribution**. Because the shares vest immediately, the expense recognised in Margy and Hulty's statement of profit or loss will be the full cost of the fair value at grant date.

IAS 24 disclosures

Some of the employees are considered **key management personnel** and therefore IAS 24 *Related Party Disclosures* should be applied. IAS 24 requires disclosure of the related party relationship, the transaction and any outstanding balances at the year end date. Such disclosures are required in order to provide sufficient information to the users of the financial statements about the potential impact of related party transactions on an entity's profit or loss and financial position. IAS 24 requires that an entity discloses key management personnel compensation in total and for several categories, of which share-based payments is one.

2 Jogger

Marking scheme

		Marks
(a)	Discussion 1 mark per point to a maximum	8
(b)	Reporting EBITDA advantages and disadvantages	5
	Description of management of earnings	5
	Moral/ethical considerations	5
		15
Professional marks		2
		25

(a) **Social and environmental information**

There are a number of factors which encourage companies to disclose social and environmental information in their financial statements. **Public interest** in corporate social responsibility is steadily increasing. Although financial statements are primarily intended for present and potential investors, lenders and other creditors, there is growing recognition that companies actually have **a number of different stakeholders**. These include **customers, employees and the general public,** all of whom are **potentially interested** in the way in which a company's operations affect the natural environment and the wider community. These stakeholders can have a **considerable effect on a company's performance**. As a result, many companies now deliberately attempt to build a **reputation for social and environmental responsibility**. Therefore, the disclosure of environmental and social information is essential. There is also growing recognition that **corporate social responsibility is actually an important part of an entity's overall performance**. Responsible practice in areas such as reduction of damage to the environment and recruitment **increases shareholder value**. Companies that act responsibly and make social and environmental disclosures are **perceived as better investments** than those that do not.

Another factor is **growing interest by governments and professional bodies**. Although there are **no IFRSs** that specifically require environmental and social reporting, it may be required by **company legislation**. There are now a number of **awards for environmental and social reports** and high quality disclosure in financial statements. These provide further encouragement to disclose information.

At present companies are normally able to disclose **as much or as little information as they wish in whatever manner that they wish**. This causes a number of **problems**. Companies tend to disclose information **selectively** and it is difficult for users of the financial statements to **compare the performance of different companies**. However, there are **good arguments** for continuing to allow companies a certain amount of freedom to determine the information that they disclose. If detailed rules are imposed, **companies are likely to adopt a 'checklist' approach** and will **present information in a very general and standardised way**, so that it is of very little use to stakeholders.

(b) **EBITDA and the management of earnings**

EBITDA is a widely used measure of corporate earnings, but it is also a controversial figure. EBITDA attempts to show earnings before tax, depreciation and amortisation. Depreciation and amortisation are expenses that arise from historical transactions over which the company now has very little control, and are often arbitrary in nature as they involve subjectivity in estimating useful lives and residual values. As they are non-cash, it is argued that they do not have any real impact on a company's operations. Companies also argue that they are not in control of tax and it should therefore not be a component of earnings. Interest is the result of financing decisions which are also often historic and influenced by a company's financing decisions. EBITDA is said to eliminate the effect of financing and accounting decisions and therefore gives investors and potential investors better insight into the performance of management and the impact of management decisions.

There are, however, criticisms of EBITDA. The main criticism is that EBITDA is not defined in IFRS and therefore is open to manipulation as companies can choose which items to include/exclude from its calculation. The fact that EBITDA is not defined can also reduce its usefulness to investors and potential investors as comparisons with previous years or to other companies may not be meaningful.

The managing director is proposing EBITDA is managed to report Jogger in a favourable light. 'Earnings management' involves exercising judgement with regard to financial reporting and structuring transactions so as to give a **misleadingly optimistic picture** of a company's performance. Commonly it involves manipulating earnings in order to meet a target predetermined by management.

Earnings management can take place in respect of reported profit under IAS 1, or in alternative performance measures such as EBITDA is as suggested here. Earnings management is done with the intention, whether consciously or not, of **influencing outcomes that depend on stakeholders' assessments**. It is the **intent** to deceive stakeholders that is unethical even if the earnings management remains within the acceptable boundaries of GAAP. For example, a potential investor may decide to invest in a company or an existing investor may be encouraged to increase their shareholding on the basis of a favourable performance or position. A director may wish to delay a hit to profit or loss for the year in order to ensure a particular year's results are well received by investors, or to secure a bonus that depends on profit. Indeed earnings management, sometimes called 'creative accounting', may be described as manipulation of the financial reporting process for private gain.

The directors may also wish to present the company favourably in order to maintain a **strong position within the market**. The motive is not always private gain – he or she may be thinking of the company's stakeholders, such as employees, suppliers or customers – but in the long term, earnings management is not a substitute for sound and profitable business, and cannot be sustained. In this case, the financial controller has been reminded that he will receive a substantial bonus if earnings targets are met. This represents a self-interest threat under ACCA's *Code of Ethics and Conduct* as the financial controller will personally benefit from the management of earnings. The 'reminder' from the managing director could also be interpreted as an intimidation threat if the financial controller feels unduly pressured as a result of the statement.

'Aggressive' earnings management is a form of fraud and differs from reporting error. Nevertheless, all forms of earnings management may be **ethically questionable**, even if not illegal.

The flexibility allowed by IFRSs may cause some variability to occur as a result of the accounting treatment options chosen, but the accounting profession has a responsibility to provide a framework that does not encourage earnings management. For example, the old standard on revenue, IAS 18, was criticised for vagueness and inconsistency in its guidance on the timing of revenue recognition allowing scope for earnings management, allowing directors to act unethically by adopting inappropriate accounting policies to boost revenue. For example, a company's revenue recognition policy could result in improper matching of income and expenses for a transaction, with the income accelerated into the current period while the expenses are accounted for in a future period. The IASB issued IFRS 15 *Revenue from Contracts with Customers* in response.

A more positive way of looking at earnings management is to consider the **benefits of not manipulating earnings:**

(i)   Stakeholders can rely on the data. Word gets around that the company 'tells it like it is' and does not try to bury bad news.

(ii)   It encourages management to safeguard the assets and exercise prudence.

(iii)   Management set an example to employees to work harder to make genuine profits, not arising from the manipulation of accruals.

(iv)   Focus on cash flow rather than accounting profits keeps management anchored in reality.

Earnings management goes against **the principle of corporate social responsibility**. Companies have a duty not to mislead stakeholders, whether their own shareholders, suppliers, employees or the government. Because the temptation to indulge in earnings management may be strong, particularly in times of financial crisis, it is important to have **ethical frameworks** (such as ACCA's *Code of Ethics and Conduct*) **and guidelines** in place. The letter of the law may not be enough.

Section B

3 Klancet

> **Workbook references.** Segment reporting is covered in Chapter 17. Intangible assets are covered in Chapter 3. Financial instruments are covered in Chapter 7. The Disclosure Initiative is covered in Chapter 19.
>
> **Top tips.** In part (a)(i), on segment reporting, the key was to argue that the second laboratory met the definition of an operating segment, while the first one did not. In part (a)(ii) you should consider why segmental information is useful to investors – why would they want this information? What makes this information particularly useful to investors? Part (a)(iii) requires an awareness of current issues in financial reporting, in this case the Disclosure Initiative and the related exposure draft on Improvements to IFRS 8 (which is referenced from the discussion paper *Disclosure Initiative – Principles of Disclosure*). It is crucial that you read widely while studying SBR as questions on current issues will definitely feature in your exam.
>
> In part (b) the key issue was whether the costs could be capitalised as development expenditure, which was the case for the latter, but not the former.
>
> **Easy marks.** These are available for discussing the principles and quantitative thresholds of IFRS 8 in part (a).

Marking scheme

			Marks
(a)	(i)	Requirements of IFRS 8 – 1 mark per point up to maximum	6
	(ii)	Usefulness of IFRS 8 – 1 mark per point up to maximum	5
	(iii)	Impact of Disclosure Initiative – 1 mark per point up to maximum	
			4
(b)		Notes for presentation – 1 mark per point up to maximum	8
			2
Professional marks (part (a))			25

(a)   (i)   Segment reporting

IFRS 8 *Operating Segments* states that an operating segment is a component of an entity which engages in business activities from which it may earn revenues and incur costs. In addition, discrete financial information should be available for the segment and these results should be regularly reviewed by the entity's chief operating decision maker (CODM) when making decisions about resource allocation to the segment and assessing its performance.

Other factors should be taken into account, including the nature of the business activities of each component, the existence of managers responsible for them, and information presented to the board of directors.

According to IFRS 8, an operating segment is one which meets any of the following quantitative thresholds:

(i)   Its reported revenue is 10% or more of the combined revenue of all operating segments.

BPP
LEARNING MEDIA

(ii)   The absolute amount of its reported profit or loss is 10% or more of the greater, in absolute amount, of (1) the combined reported profit of all operating segments which did not report a loss and (2) the combined reported loss of all operating segments which reported a loss.

(iii)   Its assets are 10% or more of the combined assets of all operating segments.

As a result of the application of the above criteria, the first laboratory will not be reported as a separate operating segment. The divisions have heads directly accountable to, and maintaining regular contact with, the CODM to discuss all aspects of their division's performance. The divisions seem to be consistent with the core principle of IFRS 8 and should be reported as separate segments. The laboratory does not have a separate segment manager and the existence of a segment manager is normally an important factor in determining operating segments. Instead, the laboratory is responsible to the divisions themselves, which would seem to indicate that it is simply supporting the existing divisions and not a separate segment. Additionally, there does not seem to be any discrete performance information for the segment, which is reviewed by the CODM.

The second laboratory should be reported as a separate segment. It meets the quantitative threshold for percentage of total revenues and it meets other criteria for an operating segment. It engages in activities which earn revenues and incurs costs, its operating results are reviewed by the CODM and discrete information is available for the laboratory's activities. Finally, it has a separate segment manager.

(ii)   Contrary to the managing directors' views, IFRS 8 provides information that makes the financial statements more relevant and more useful to investors. IFRS financial statements are highly aggregated and may prevent investors from understanding the many different business areas and activities that an entity is engaged in. IFRS 8 requires information to be disclosed that is not readily available elsewhere in the financial statements, therefore it provides additional information which aids an investor's understanding of how the business operates and is managed.

IFRS 8 uses a 'management approach' to report information on an entity's segments and results from the point of view of the decision makers of the entity. This allows investors to examine an entity 'though the eyes of management' – to see the business in the way in which the managers who run the business on their behalf see it. This provides investors with more discrete information on the business segments allowing them to better assess the return being earned from those business segments, the risks that are associated with those segments and how those risks are managed. The more detailed information provides investors with more insight into an entity's longer term performance.

The requirement to disclose information that is actually used by internal decision makers is an important feature of IFRS 8, but is also one of its main criticisms. The fact that the reporting does not need to be based on IFRS makes it difficult to make comparisons with information that was reported in prior periods and with other companies in the sector. The flexibility in reporting can make it easier to manipulate what is reported. IFRS 8 disclosures are often most useful if used in conjunction with narrative disclosures prepared by the directors of the company, such as the Strategic Review in the UK.

(iii)   The IASB's Disclosure Initiative is a series of projects which are focused on how presentation and disclosure can be improved. The discussion paper *Disclosure Initiative – Principles of Disclosure* refers to improvements to IFRS 8 proposed in an exposure draft issued in March 2017. One proposed improvement is to define an entity's 'annual reporting package' as a publicly available set of one or more documents that are published at approximately the same time as the financial statements, and which communicate annual results to the users of financial information. This is a broader term than annual report or financial statements, as these terms are currently used. The ED proposes that the entity is expected to identify the same reportable segments throughout all of its annual reporting package. If this is not the case, then the entity should explain why.

The improvement has been proposed because it seems that some entities are identifying different reportable segments in their financial statements compared to other reports such as the Business Review published at a similar time. This practice is understandably confusing to investors because the identification of reportable segments in IFRS 8 is based on what management uses to make decisions and should therefore reflect how the business is actually managed.

The IASB is considering whether to use the term 'annual reporting package' in its consultations on the principles of disclosure. Specifically whether IFRS required disclosure can be presented in another part of the annual reporting package and cross referenced to the financial statements.

(b)   **Development of drugs**

Notes for presentation to the managing director

1   **Criteria for recognising as an asset**

IAS 38 *Intangible Assets* requires an entity to recognise an intangible asset, whether purchased or self-created (at cost) if, and only if, it is probable that the future economic benefits which are attributable to the asset will flow to the entity and the cost of the asset can be measured reliably.

The *Conceptual Framework* defines an asset as 'a resource controlled by an entity as a result of past events from which future economic benefits are expected to flow to the entity' (para. 4.4(a)).

The Exposure Draft ED/2015/3 *Conceptual Framework for Financial Reporting* proposes to change the definition of an asset to 'a present economic resource controlled by the entity as a result of past events. An economic resource is a right that has the potential to produce economic benefits' (ED/2015/3; Chapter 4).

There is therefore inconsistency in the terminology used by IAS 38 and the *Conceptual Framework* in that IAS 38 refers 'probable economic benefits' and the *Conceptual Framework* says that economic benefits are 'expected' to flow. Neither probable nor expected is defined in IFRSs and therefore there is potential for confusion as to whether the threshold for recognising the future benefits is consistent. The term 'the potential to produce economic benefits' used by the Exposure Draft does not provide any further clarity and therefore the terminology remains inconsistent. There are currently no plans to amend IAS 38 for consistency with the revised *Conceptual Framework*.

2.   **Internally generated intangible assets**

The recognition requirements of IAS 38 apply whether an intangible asset is acquired externally or generated internally. IAS 38 includes additional recognition criteria for internally generated intangible assets.

Development costs are capitalised only after technical and commercial feasibility of the asset for sale or use have been established. This means that the entity must intend and be able to complete the intangible asset and either use it or sell it and be able to demonstrate how the asset will generate future economic benefits, in keeping with the recognition criteria.

If an entity cannot distinguish the research phase from the development phase of an internal project to create an intangible asset, the entity treats the expenditure for that project as if it were incurred in the research phase only.

The price which an entity pays to acquire an intangible asset reflects its expectations about the probability that the expected future economic benefits in the asset will flow to the entity.

3.   **Project 1**

Klancet owns the potential new drug, and Retto is carrying out the development of the drug on its behalf. The risks and rewards of ownership remain with Klancet.

By paying the initial fee and the subsequent payment to Retto, Klancet does not acquire a separate intangible asset. The payments represent research and development by a third party, which need to be expensed over the development period provided that the recognition criteria for internally generated intangible assets are not met.

Development costs are capitalised only after technical and commercial feasibility of the asset for sale or use have been established. This means that the entity must intend and be able to complete the intangible asset and either use it or sell it and be able to demonstrate how the asset will generate future economic benefits. At present, this criterion does not appear to have been met as regulatory authority for the use of the drug has not been given and, in fact, approval has been refused in the past.

4.   **Project 2**

In the case of the second project, the drug has already been discovered and therefore the costs are for the development and manufacture of the drug and its slight modification. There is no indication that the agreed prices for the various elements are not at fair value. In particular, the terms for product supply at cost plus profit are consistent with Klancet's other supply arrangements.

Therefore, Klancet should capitalise the upfront purchase of the drug and subsequent payments as incurred, and consider impairment at each financial reporting date. Regulatory approval has already been attained for the existing drug and therefore there is no reason to expect that this will not be given for the new drug. Amortisation should begin once regulatory approval has been obtained. Costs for the products have to be accounted for as inventory using IAS 2 *Inventories* and then expensed as costs of goods sold as incurred.

4 Jayach

Workbook references. Fair value measurement under IFRS 13 is covered in Chapter 3. The IFRS 13 definition of fair value occurs throughout the Workbook and is relevant to many topics. The Exposure Draft on the *Conceptual Framework* is covered in Chapter 1.

Top tips. Fair value measurement affects many aspects of financial reporting. In part (a), you are asked for the principles of fair value measurement. Part (b) requires application of the principles in the context of the valuation of assets and liabilities. Ensure that you provide explanations to support your workings. Part (c) considers the topic of measurement from a wider perspective. Make sure you relate your answer to the email given in the question. Remember that the examiner has recommended that you read widely, including technical articles and real financial reports, to support your learning.

Easy marks. Credit will be given for textbook knowledge in part (a).

Marking scheme

		Marks
(a)	1 mark per point up to maximum	<u>8</u>
(b)	1 mark per point up to maximum	6
	Calculations	<u>5</u>
		<u>11</u>
(c)	1 mark per point up to maximum	<u>6</u>
		<u><u>25</u></u>

(a) **IFRS 13 principles of fair value measurement**

IFRS 13 *Fair Value Measurement* defines fair value as **'the price that would be received to sell an asset or paid to transfer a liability in an orderly transaction between market participants at the measurement date'** (para. 9).

Fair value is a **market-based measurement,** not an entity-specific measurement. It **focuses on assets and liabilities and on exit (selling) prices**. It takes into account market conditions at the measurement date. In other words, it looks at the amount for which the holder of an asset could sell it and the amount which the holder of a liability would have to pay to transfer it. It can also be used to value an entity's own equity instruments.

It is assumed that the transaction to sell the asset or transfer the liability takes place either:

(1) In the **principal market** for the asset or liability; or

(2) In the absence of a principal market, in the **most advantageous market** for the asset or liability.

The **principal market** is the market which is the **most liquid** (has the greatest volume and level of activity for that asset or liability). The **most advantageous market** is the market which **maximises** the value of an **asset** or **minimises** the **amount** that would be **required to transfer a liability**. In most cases the principal market and the most advantageous market will be the same.

For **non-financial assets**, the fair value measurement is the value for using the asset in its **highest and best use** (the use that would maximise its value) or by selling it to another market participant that would use it in its highest and best use. The **fair value of liabilities** should **reflect the non-performance risk** associated with that liability, ie the risk that the entity will not fulfil its obligation.

Fair value is **not adjusted for transaction costs.** Under IFRS 13, these are **not a feature of the asset or liability,** but may be taken into account when **determining the most advantageous market.**

Fair value measurements are based on an asset or a liability's **unit of account**, which is specified not by IFRS 13, but by each IFRS where a fair value measurement is required. For most assets and liabilities, the unit of account is the individual asset or liability, but in some instances may be a group of assets or liabilities.

IFRS 13 acknowledges that when **market activity declines**, an entity must use a **valuation technique** to measure fair value. In this case the emphasis must be on whether a transaction price is based on an orderly transaction, rather than a forced sale. The technique used must be appropriate in the circumstances and may therefore differ between entities.

The IFRS identifies **three valuation approaches**.

(1) **Market approach.** A valuation technique that uses prices and other relevant information generated by market transactions involving identical or comparable (ie similar) assets, liabilities or a group of assets and liabilities, such as a business.

(2) **Cost approach.** A valuation technique that reflects the amount that would be required currently to replace the service capacity of an asset (often referred to as current replacement cost).

(3) **Income approach.** Valuation techniques that convert future amounts (eg cash flows or income and expenses) to a single current (ie discounted) amount. The fair value measurement is determined on the basis of the value indicated by current market expectations about those future amounts.

(b) **Fair value of asset**

YEAR TO 30 NOVEMBER 20X2

	Asian market	European market	Australasian market
Volume of market – units	4m	2m	1m
	$	$	$
Price	19	16	22
Costs of entering the market	(2)	(2)	n/a*
Potential fair value	17	14	22
Transaction costs	(1)	(2)	(2)
Net profit	16	12	20

Notes

1 Because Jayach currently buys and sells the asset in the Australasian market, the **costs of entering that market** are not incurred and therefore **not relevant**.

2 Fair value is **not adjusted for transaction costs.** Under IFRS 13, these are not a feature of the asset or liability, but may be taken into account when determining the most advantageous market.

3 The **Asian market is the principal market** for the asset because it is the market with the greatest volume and level of activity for the asset. If information about the Asian market is available and Jayach can access the market, then Jayach should base its fair value on this market. Based on the Asian market, the **fair value of the asset would be $17**, measured as the price that would be received in that market ($19) less costs of entering the market ($2) and ignoring transaction costs.

4 If **information** about the Asian market is **not available**, or if Jayach **cannot access the market**, Jayach must measure the fair value of the asset using the price in the **most advantageous market**. The most advantageous market is the market that maximises the amount that would be received to sell the asset, after taking into account both transaction costs and usually also costs of entry, which is the net amount that would be received in the respective markets. The most advantageous market here is therefore the **Australasian market**. As explained above, costs of entry are not relevant here, and so, based on this market, the **fair value would be $22**.

It is assumed that market participants are independent of each other and knowledgeable, and able and willing to enter into transactions.

Fair value of decommissioning liability

Because this is a business combination, Jayach must measure the liability at fair value in accordance with IFRS 13, rather than using the best estimate measurement required by IAS 37 *Provisions, Contingent Liabilities and Contingent Assets*. In most cases there will be no observable market to provide pricing information. If this is the case here, Jayach will use **the expected present value technique** to measure the fair value of the decommissioning liability. If Jayach were contractually committed to transfer its decommissioning liability to a market participant, it would conclude that a market participant would use the inputs as follows, arriving at a **fair value of $3,215,000**.

Input	Amount
	$'000
Labour and material cost	2,000
Overhead: 30% × 2,000	600
Third party mark-up – industry average: 2,600 × 20%	520
	3120
Inflation adjusted total (5% compounded over three years): $3,120 \times 1.05^3$	3,612
Risk adjustment – uncertainty relating to cash flows: 3,612 × 6%	217
	3,829
Discount at risk-free rate plus entity's non-performance risk (4% + 2% = 6%): $3,829/1.06^3$	3,215

(c) A 'mixed measurement' approach means that a company selects a different measurement basis for its various assets and liabilities, rather than using a single measurement basis for all items. The measurement basis selected should reflect the type of entity and sector in which it operates and the business model that the entity adopts.

Some investors have criticised the mixed measurement approach because they think that if different measurement bases are used for assets and liabilities, the resulting totals can have little meaning. Similarly, they believe profit or loss may lack relevance if it reflects a combination of transactions based on historical cost and of value changes for items measured on a current value basis.

However, a single measurement basis may not provide the most relevant information to users. Different information from different measurement bases may be relevant in different circumstances. A particular measurement basis may be easier to understand, more verifiable and less costly to implement. Therefore a mixed measurement approach is not 'inconsistent' but can actually provide more relevant information for stakeholders.

The IASB uses a mixed measurement approach where the measurement method selected is that which is most relevant and which most faithfully represents the information it represents. It seems that most investors feel that this approach is consistent with how they analyse financial statements. The problems of mixed measurement appear to be outweighed by the greater relevance achieved.

Jayach prepares its financial statements under IFRSs, and therefore applies the measurement bases permitted in IFRSs. IFRSs adopt a mixed measurement basis, which includes fair value, historical cost, and net realisable value.

When an IFRS allows a choice of measurement basis, the directors of Jayach must exercise judgment as to which basis will provide the most relevant information for stakeholders. Furthermore when selecting a measurement basis, the directors should consider measurement uncertainty. The Exposure Draft on the *Conceptual Framework* states that for some estimates, a high level of measurement uncertainty may outweigh other factors to such an extent that the resulting information may have little relevance.

ACCA
Strategic Business Reporting (International)

Mock Examination 2

Time allowed:	3 hours 15 minutes

This question paper is divided into two sections:

Section A – BOTH questions are compulsory and MUST be attempted

Section B – BOTH questions are compulsory and MUST be attempted

Do NOT open this question paper until instructed by the supervisor.

Do NOT record any of your answers on the question paper.

This question paper must not be removed from the examination hall.

Section A – BOTH questions are compulsory and MUST be attempted

1 Robby

You work in the finance department of Robby, an entity which has two subsidiaries, Hail and Zinc. Robby has recently appointed two new directors, with limited finance experience, to its board. You have received the following email from the finance director.

To:	**An accountant**
From:	**Finance director**
Subject:	**New directors – help required**

Hi, our two new directors are keen to understand our group financial statements. In particular, they want to understand the effect of acquisitions and joint operations on the consolidated accounts.

I am putting together a briefing document for them and would like you to prepare sections for inclusion in the document on goodwill and on joint operations. Please use the acquisitions of Hail and Zinc (**Attachment 1**) to explain the how the goodwill on acquisition of subsidiaries is accounted for in the group financial statements at 31 May 20X3. Use the gas station joint operation (**Attachment 2**) to explain what a joint operation is and how we account for it in the group financial statements. Make sure you explain the financial reporting principles that underlie both of these.

Attachment 1 – details of acquisitions of Hail and Zinc

cash — Dr Zinc / Cr Cash.

Accounting policy: measure non-controlling interests at acquisition at fair value.

(1) **Hail acquisition.** On 1 June 20X2, acquisition of 80% of the equity interests of Hail. The purchase consideration comprised cash of $50 million payable on 1 June 20X2 and $24.2 million payable on 31 May 20X4. A further amount is payable on 31 August 20X6 if the cumulative profits of Hail for the four-year period from 1 June 20X2 to 31 May 20X6 exceed $150 million. On 1 June 20X2, the fair value of the contingent consideration was measured at $40 million. On 31 May 20X3, this fair value was remeasured at $42 million. → *new est'mate*

On the acquisition date, the fair value of the identifiable net assets of Hail was $130 million. — *NA at acq.*

The notes to the financial statements of Hail at acquisition disclosed a contingent liability. On 1 June 20X2, the fair value of this contingent liability was reliably measured at $2 million. The non-controlling interest at fair value was $30 million on 1 June 20X2. An appropriate discount rate to use is 10% per annum. *NCI* *CL.*

(2) **Zinc acquisition.** On 1 June 20X0, acquisition of 5% of the ordinary shares of Zinc. Robby had treated this investment at fair value through profit or loss.

On 1 December 20X2, acquisition of a further 55% of the ordinary shares of Zinc, obtaining control.

Consideration:

	Shareholding %	Consideration $m
1 June 20X0	5	2
1 December 20X2	55	16
	60	18

At 1 December 20X2, the fair value of the equity interest in Zinc before the business combination was $5 million.

FO

The non-controlling interest at fair value was $9 million on 1 December 20X2. NA

PAR

The fair value of the identifiable net assets at 1 December 20X2 of Zinc was $26 million, and the retained earnings were $15 million. The excess of the fair value of the net assets was due to an increase in the value of property, plant and equipment (PPE), which was provisional pending receipt of the final valuations. These valuations were received on 1 March 20X3 and resulted in an additional increase of $3 million in the fair value of PPE at the date of acquisition. This increase does not affect the fair value of the non-controlling interest at acquisition.

with 12 mth

At 31 May 20X2 the carrying amount of the investment in Zinc in Robby's separate financial statements was $19 million.

Attachment 2 – details of joint operation

Joint operation – 40% share of a natural gas station. No separate entity was set up under the joint operation. Assets, liabilities, revenue and costs are apportioned on the basis of shareholding.

(i)   The natural gas station cost $15 million to construct, was completed on 1 June 20X2 and is to be dismantled at the end of its life of ten years. The present value of this dismantling cost to the joint operation at 1 June 20X2, using a discount rate of 5%, was $2 million.

(ii)   In the year, gas with a direct cost of $16 million was sold for $20 million. Additionally, the joint operation incurred operating costs of $0.5 million during the year.

The revenue and costs are receivable and payable by the other joint operator who settles amounts outstanding with Robby after the year end.

Required

(a)   Prepare for inclusion in the briefing note to the new directors:

(i)   An explanation, with suitable calculations, of how the goodwill on acquisition of Hail and Zinc should be accounted for in the consolidated financial statements at 31 May 20X3. **(16 marks)**

(ii)   An explanation as to the nature of a joint operation and, showing suitable calculations, of how the joint operation should be accounted for in Robby's separate and consolidated statements of financial position at 31 May 20X3. (Ignore retained earnings in your answer.) **(7 marks)**

Note. Marks will be allocated in (a) for a suitable discussion of the principles involved as well as the accounting treatment.

(b)   Robby held a portfolio of trade receivables with a carrying amount of $4 million at 31 May 20X3. At that date, the entity entered into a factoring agreement with a bank, whereby it transferred the receivables in exchange for $3.6 million in cash. Robby has agreed to reimburse the bank for any shortfall between the amount collected and $3.6 million. Once the receivables have been collected, any amounts above $3.6 million, less interest on this amount, will be repaid to Robby. The directors of Robby believe that these trade receivables should be derecognised.

Required

Explain the appropriate accounting treatment of this transaction in the financial statements for the year ended 31 May 20X3, and evaluate this treatment in the context of the *Conceptual Framework for Financial Reporting* and related Exposure Draft. **(7 marks)**

(Total = 30 marks)

2 Ramsbury

The directors of Ramsbury, a public limited company which manufactures industrial cleaning products, are preparing the consolidated financial statements for the year ended 30 June 20X7. In your capacity as advisor to the company, you become aware of the following issues.

In the draft consolidated statement of financial position, the directors have included in cash and cash equivalents a loan provided to a director of $1 million. The loan has no specific repayment date on it but is repayable on demand. The directors feel that there is no problem with this presentation as International Financial Reporting Standards (IFRS) allow companies to make accounting policy choices, and that showing the loan as a cash equivalent is their choice of accounting policy.

On 1 July 20X6, there was an amendment to Ramsbury's defined benefit pension scheme whereby the promised pension entitlement was increased from 10% of final salary to 15%. A bonus is paid to the directors each year which is based upon the operating profit margin of Ramsbury. The directors of Ramsbury are unhappy that there is inconsistency on the presentation of gains and losses in relation to pension scheme within the consolidated financial statements. Additionally, they believe that as the pension scheme is not an integral part of the operating activities of Ramsbury, it is misleading to include the gains and losses in profit or loss. They therefore propose to change their accounting policy so that all gains and losses on the pension scheme are recognised in other comprehensive income. They believe that this will make the financial statements more consistent, more understandable and can be justified on the grounds of fair presentation. Ramsbury's pension scheme is currently in deficit.

Required

Discuss the ethical and accounting implications of the above situations, with reference where appropriate, to International Financial Reporting Standards. **(18 marks)**

Professional marks will be awarded in this question for the application of ethical principles. **(2 marks)**

(Total = 20 marks)

Section B – BOTH questions are compulsory and MUST be attempted

3 Calcula

Calcula is a listed company that operates through several subsidiaries. The company develops specialist software for use by accountancy professionals.

(a) In its annual financial statements for both 20X2 and 20X3 Calcula classified a subsidiary as held for sale and presented it as a discontinued operation. On 1 January 20X2, the shareholders had, at a general meeting of the company, authorised management to sell all of its holding of shares in the subsidiary within the year. In the year to 31 May 20X2, management made the decision public but did not actively try to sell the subsidiary as it was still operational within the group.

Calcula had made certain organisational changes during the year to 31 May 20X3, which resulted in additional activities being transferred to the subsidiary. Also during the year to 31 May 20X3, there had been draft agreements and some correspondence with investment bankers, which showed in principle only that the subsidiary was still for sale.

Required

Discuss whether the classification of the subsidiary as held for sale and its presentation as a discontinued operation is appropriate, making reference to the principles of relevant IFRSs and evaluating the treatment in the context of the *Conceptual Framework for Financial Reporting* and related Exposure Draft. **(9 marks)**

(b) Asha Alexander has recently been appointed as the chief executive officer (CEO) of Calcula. During the last three years, there have been significant senior management changes and organisational restructuring which resulted in confusion among shareholders and employees as to the strategic direction of the company. One investor complained that the annual report made it hard to know where the company was headed.

The specialist software market in which Calcula operates is particularly dynamic and fast changing. It is common for competitors to drop out of the market place. The most successful companies have been particularly focused on enhancing their offering to customers through creating innovative products and investing heavily in training and development for their employees.

The last CEO introduced an aggressive cost-cutting programme aimed at improving profitability. At the beginning of the financial year there were redundancies and the annual staff training and development budget was significantly reduced and has not been reviewed since the change in management.

In response to the confusion surrounding the company's strategic direction, Asha and the board published a new mission, which centres on making Calcula the market leader of specialist accountancy software. In her previous role Asha oversaw the introduction of an integrated approach to reporting performance. This is something she is particularly keen to introduce at Calcula.

During the company's last board meeting, Asha was dismayed by the finance director's reaction when she proposed introducing integrated reporting at Calcula. The finance director made it clear that he was not convinced of the need for such a change, arguing that 'all this talk of integrated reporting in the business press is just a fad, requiring a lot more work, simply to report on things people do not care about. Shareholders are only interested in the bottom line'.

Required

(i)   Discuss how integrated reporting may help Calcula to communicate its strategy to investors and other stakeholders, and improve the company's strategic performance. Your answer should briefly discuss the principles of integrated reporting and make reference to the concerns raised by the finance director.   **(12 marks)**

(ii)   Briefly discuss why the previous CEO's aggressive cost-cutting programme might have led to ethical challenges for Calcula's management team.   **(2 marks)**

Professional marks will be awarded in part (b)(i) for clarity and quality of presentation.
        (2 marks)

        (Total = 25 marks)

4 Janne

Janne is a listed real estate company, which specialises mainly in industrial property. Investment properties constitute more than 60% of its total assets.

(a)   Janne measures its industrial investment property using the fair value method, which is measured using the 'new-build value less obsolescence'. Valuations are conducted by a member of the board of directors. In order to determine the obsolescence, the board member takes account of the age of the property and the nature of its use. According to the board, this method of calculation is complex but gives a very precise result, which is accepted by the industry. There are sales values for similar properties in similar locations available as well as market rent data per square metre for similar industrial buildings.

Required

Discuss whether the above valuation technique is appropriate under IFRSs, making reference to the principles of relevant IFRSs and evaluating the treatment in the context of the *Conceptual Framework for Financial Reporting* and related Exposure Draft.   **(9 marks)**

(b)   Janne has received criticism that its annual report is too detailed, and therefore it is difficult to understand and analyse. In response to the criticism, the managing director has proposed a reduction in disclosures provided in the annual report. This includes, but is not limited to, reducing the accounting policies note, and removing the related party transactions note, which he does not consider important as all transactions are at arm's length. The managing director has recommended that all disclosures that appear irrelevant should be removed.

The finance director has vigorously defended the report, stating that all disclosures made are required by IFRSs, even if some of them appear unnecessary. He has confirmed this by using a 'disclosure checklist' provided by a reputable accountancy firm. He is extremely nervous that the changes proposed risk non-compliance with standards and would not improve the relevance or usefulness of the report for investors.

Required

Discuss the implications of the above in relation to Janne's annual report and its usefulness to investors, with reference to the IASB's Discussion Paper *Disclosure Initiative – Principles of Disclosure*.   **(8 marks)**

(c)   The managing director has also proposed to report a new performance measure 'adjusted net asset value per share', which is defined as net assets calculated in accordance with IFRS, adjusted for various items and then divided by the total number of shares. This would be presented instead of earnings per share as the managing director believes it is more relevant to investors. This performance measure is disclosed by several companies in the same industry as Janne.

Required

Discuss the benefits and drawbacks to investors of Janne's plan to disclose 'adjusted net asset value per share' instead of earnings per share.   **(8 marks)**

(Total = 25 marks)

Answers

DO NOT TURN THIS PAGE UNTIL YOU HAVE COMPLETED THE MOCK EXAM

Section A

1 Robby

> **Workbook references.** The underlying principles of IFRS 3 are covered in Chapter 10. Business combinations achieved in stages are covered in Chapter 11. Joint operations are covered in Chapter 14 and financial instruments in Chapter 7. The *Conceptual Framework* and related Exposure Draft are covered in Chapter 1.
>
> **Top tips.** You must make sure that you explain the principles underlying the accounting for goodwill as you will not be able to pass the exam by only providing calculations. The examining team is looking for an understanding of the accounting involved and not rote learning of consolidation workings.
>
> In part (b), you need to evaluate whether the requirements of IFRS 9 relating to the factoring arrangement are in agreement with the *Conceptual Framework* and the related Exposure Draft. This kind of evaluation in light of the *Conceptual Framework* is likely to be a feature of questions in the SBR examination, so you need to make sure you are familiar enough with the *Conceptual Framework* to be able to answer questions in this way.

Marking scheme

			Marks
(a)	(i)	Goodwill	
		Explanation of IFRS 3 principles	10
		Hail – calculation	3
		Zinc – calculation	3
			16
	(ii)	Joint operation	
		SOFP	3
		Explanation – 1 mark per point up to a maximum	4
			7
(b)		Discussion – 1 mark per point up to a maximum	7
			30

(a) **Sections for inclusion in the finance director's report.**

(i) **Goodwill**

IFRS 3 *Business Combinations* requires goodwill to be recognised in a business combination. A business combination takes place when one entity, the acquirer, obtains control of another entity, the acquiree. IFRS 3 requires goodwill to be calculated and recorded as a non-current asset at the acquisition date.

Goodwill is calculated at the acquisition date as the fair value of the consideration transferred by the acquirer plus the amount of any non-controlling interest less the fair value of the net assets of the acquiree. When the business combination is achieved in stages, as is the case for Zinc, the previously held interest in the new subsidiary must be remeasured to its fair value at the date control is obtained.

Goodwill is not amortised, but instead is tested for impairment at each year end.

Applying these principles, the goodwill on the acquisition of Hail and Zinc for inclusion in the consolidated financial statements at 31 May 20X3 is calculated as follows.

Goodwill related to the acquisition of Hail

	$m	$m
Goodwill at acquisition:		
Consideration transferred for 80% interest		
Cash payable on 1 June 20X1	50	
Deferred cash consideration ($24.2 million/$(1.10)^2$)	20	
Contingent consideration	40	
Fair value of non-controlling interest	30	
		140
Fair value of identifiable net assets acquired	130	
Contingent liability	(2)	
		(132)
		8

The immediate, deferred and contingent consideration transferred should be measured at their fair values at the acquisition date.

Deferred consideration

The fair value of the deferred consideration is the amount payable on 31 May 20X4 discounted to its present value at the acquisition date. The requirement to discount to present value is consistent with other standards. The present value should be unwound in the period to 31 May 20X3 which will increase the carrying amount of the obligation and result in a finance cost in profit or loss. The unwinding of the discount does not affect the goodwill calculation as it is based on the amount payable at the date of acquisition.

Contingent consideration

The fair value of the contingent consideration payable should take into account the various milestones set under the acquisition agreement. At the acquisition date the fair value of the contingent consideration is $40 million.

The contingent consideration payable should be remeasured at 31 May 20X3 to its fair value of $42 million. This remeasurement does not affect the goodwill calculation, but the increase in the fair value of the obligation of $2m should be taken to profit or loss.

Contingent liability

The contingent liability disclosed in Hail's financial statements is recognised as a liability on acquisition in accordance with IFRS 3, provided that its fair value can be reliably measured and it is a present obligation. This is contrary to the normal rules in IAS 37 *Provisions, Contingent Liabilities and Contingent Assets* where contingent liabilities are not recognised but only disclosed.

Conclusion

There is no indication that the goodwill balance is impaired at 31 May 20X3. Thus goodwill related to the acquisition of Hail to be included in the group financial statements at 31 May 20X3 is $8m.

Goodwill related to the acquisition of Zinc

Substance over form drives the accounting treatment for a subsidiary acquired in stages. The legal form is that shares have been acquired, however, in substance:

(1)   The 5% investment has been sold. Per IFRS 3, the investment previously held is remeasured to fair value at the date control is obtained and a gain or loss reported in profit or loss:

	$m
Fair value of 5% at date control achieved (1 December 20X2)	5
Fair value of carrying amount of 5% per SOFP, (ie at 31 May 20X2: $19m per Robby's SOFP adjusted to exclude $16m consideration for 55%)	(3)
Remeasurement gain (1 June 20X2 to 1 December 20X2)	2

(2) A subsidiary has been 'purchased'. The previously held 5% investment is effectively re-acquired at fair value, and so goodwill is calculated including the fair value of the previously held 5% investment.

Goodwill	$m	$m
Consideration transferred – for 55%	16	
Fair value of non-controlling interest	9	
Fair value of previously held interest (for 5% at 1 December 20X2)	5	
		30
Fair value of identifiable net assets at acquisition:		
Provisional measurement	26	
Adjustment to fair value of PPE (within measurement period)	3	
		(29)
		1

Fair value of PPE

The fair value of PPE was provisional at the date of acquisition, with an increase of $3m subsequently identified when the figures were finalised in March 20X3. IFRS 3 permits adjustments to goodwill for adjustments to the fair value of assets and liabilities acquired, provided this adjustment is made within one year of the date of acquisition (the measurement period).

Conclusion

There is no indication that the goodwill balance is impaired at 31 May 20X3. Thus goodwill related to the acquisition of Zinc to be included in the group financial statements at 31 May 20X3 is $1m.

(ii) **Joint operation**

Robby has a joint arrangement with another party in respect of the natural gas station. Under IFRS 11 *Joint Arrangements*, a joint arrangement is one in which two or more parties are bound by a contractual arrangement which gives them joint control over the arrangement.

Joint arrangements can either be joint ventures or joint operations. The classification as a joint venture or joint operation depends on the rights and obligations of the parties to the arrangement. It is important to correctly classify the arrangement as the accounting requirements for joint ventures are different to those for joint operations.

IFRS 11 states that a joint arrangement that is not structured through a separate vehicle is a joint operation. In Robby's case, no separate entity has been set up for the joint arrangement, therefore it is a joint operation. Robby has joint rights to the assets and revenue, and joint obligations for the liabilities and costs of the joint arrangement.

Therefore, Robby, in its capacity as a joint operator, must recognise on a line-by-line basis its own assets, liabilities, revenues and expenses plus its share (40%) of the joint assets, liabilities, revenue and expenses of the joint operation as prescribed by IFRS 11.

This treatment is applicable to both the consolidated and separate financial statements of Robby.

The figures are calculated as follows:

Statement of financial position

	$m
Property, plant and equipment:	
1 June 20X2 cost: gas station (15 × 40%)	6.00
dismantling provision (2 × 40%)	0.80
	6.80
Accumulated depreciation: 6.8/10 years	(0.68)
31 May 20X3 carrying amount	6.12
Trade receivables (from other joint operator): 20 (revenue) × 40%	8.00
Trade payables (to other joint operator): (16 + 0.5) (costs) × 40%	6.60
Dismantling provision:	
At 1 June 20X2	0.80
Finance cost (unwinding of discount): 0.8 × 5%	0.04
At 31 May 20X3	0.84

(b) Accounting treatment

Trade receivables are financial assets and therefore the requirements of IFRS 9 *Financial Instruments* need to be applied. The main question here is whether the factoring arrangement means that Robby should derecognise the trade receivables from the financial statements.

Per IFRS 9, an entity should derecognise a **financial asset** when:

(1) The **contractual rights** to the cash flows from the financial asset **expire**, or

(2) The entity **transfers the financial asset or substantially all the risks and rewards of ownership** of the financial asset to another party.

(IFRS 9: paras. 3.2.3–3.2.6.)

In the case of Robby, the contractual rights to the cash flows have not expired as the receivables balances are still outstanding and expected to be collected. In respect of the risks and rewards of ownership, the substance of the factoring arrangement needs to be considered rather than its legal form. Robby has transferred the receivables to the bank in exchange for $3.6 million cash, but remains liable for any shortfall between $3.6 million and the amount collected. In principle, Robby is liable for the whole $3.6 million, although it is unlikely that the default would be as much as this. **Robby therefore retains the credit risk.** In addition, Robby is entitled to receive the benefit (less interest) of repayments in excess of $3.6 million once the $3.6 million has been collected and therefore retains the potential rewards of full settlement. **Substantially all the risks and rewards** of the financial asset **therefore remain with Robby**, and the receivables should **continue to be recognised.**

The *Conceptual Framework for Financial Reporting* is silent on the matter of derecognition. Consequently different approaches have been adopted in different Standards. The IASB has sought to address this in the Exposure Draft on the *Conceptual Framework* by suggesting that accounting for derecognition should aim to **represent faithfully both** the **asset/liabilities retained** after the event that led to derecognition **and** the **change in the entity's assets/liabilities** as a result of that event.

Meeting both of these aims becomes difficult if the entity disposes of only part of an asset or liability or retains some exposure to that asset or liability, as it can be difficult to faithfully represent the legal form which is the decrease in assets under the factoring arrangement with the substance of retaining the corresponding retention of risks and rewards.

Because of the difficulties in practice in meeting these two aims, the Exposure Draft on the *Conceptual Framework* does not advocate using a control approach or the risks-and-rewards approach to derecognition in every circumstance. Instead, it describes the options available and discusses what factors the IASB would need to consider when developing Standards.

As such, there appears to be no conflict in principles between the Exposure Draft on the *Conceptual Framework* and the requirements of IFRS 9 for derecognition.

2 Ramsbury

> **Workbook references.** The *Conceptual Framework* is covered in Chapter 1 and ethics is covered in Chapter 2. Employee benefits are covered in Chapter 4.
>
> **Top tips.** As with all questions, ensure that you apply your knowledge to the scenario provided and that your answer is in context. It is not enough to simply discuss the accounting requirements. You must draw out the ethical issues. Where relevant, you should identify any threats to the fundamental principles in ACCA's *Code of Ethics and Conduct*.

Marking scheme

	Marks
Accounting issues 1 mark per point to a maximum	9
Ethical issues 1 mark per point to a maximum	9
Professional marks	2
	20

Treatment of loan to director

The directors have included the loan made to the director as part of the cash and cash equivalents balance. It may be that the directors have misunderstood the definition of cash and cash equivalents, believing the loan to be a cash equivalent. IAS 7 *Statement of Cash Flows* defines cash equivalents as "short-term (less than three months), highly liquid investments that are readily convertible to known amounts of cash and which are subject to an insignificant risk of changes in value" (IAS 7: para. 6). However, the loan is not in place to enable Ramsbury to manage its short-term cash commitments, it has no fixed repayment date and the likelihood of the director defaulting is not known. The classification as a cash equivalent is therefore inappropriate.

It is likely that the loan should be treated as a financial asset under IFRS 9 *Financial Instruments*. Further information would be needed, for example, is the $1 million the fair value? A case could even be made that, since the loan may never be repaid, it is in fact a part of the director's remuneration, and if so should be treated as an expense and disclosed accordingly. In addition, since the director is likely to fall into the category of key management personnel, related party disclosures under IAS 24 *Related Party Disclosures* are likely to be necessary.

The treatment of the loan as a cash equivalent is in **breach of the two fundamental qualitative characteristics** prescribed in the IASB's *Conceptual Framework for Financial Reporting*, namely:

(i)   **Relevance.** The information should be disclosed separately as it is relevant to users.

(ii)   **Faithful representation**: Information must be **complete, neutral** and **free from error.** Clearly this is not the case if a loan to a director is shown in cash.

The treatment is also in breach of the *Conceptual Framework's* key **enhancing qualitative characteristics:**

(i) **Understandability.** If the loan is shown in cash, it hides the true nature of the practices of the company, making the financial statements less understandable to users.

(ii) **Verifiability.** Verifiability helps assure users that information faithfully represents the economic phenomena it purports to represent. It means that different knowledgeable and independent observers could reach consensus that a particular depiction is a faithful representation. The treatment does not meet this benchmark as it reflects the subjective bias of the directors.

(iii) **Comparability.** For financial statements to be comparable year-on-year and with other companies, transactions must be correctly classified, which is not the case here. If the cash balance one year includes a loan to a director and the next year it does not, then you are not comparing like with like.

In some countries, loans to directors are **illegal**, with directors being personally liable. Even if this is not the case, there is a potential **conflict of interest** between that of the director and that of the company, which is why separate disclosure is required as a minimum. Directors are responsible for the financial statements required by statute, and thus it is their responsibility to put right any errors that mean that the financial statements do not comply with IFRS. There is generally a legal requirement to maintain proper accounting records, and recording a loan as cash conflicts with this requirement.

In obscuring the nature of the transaction, it is possible that the directors are **motivated by personal interest**, and are thus failing in their duty to act honestly and ethically. There is potentially a self-interest threat to the fundamental principles of the ACCA *Code of Ethics and Conduct*. If one transaction is misleading, it casts doubt on the credibility of the financial statements as a whole.

In conclusion, the treatment is problematic and **should be rectified**.

Ethical implications of change of accounting policy

IAS 8 *Accounting Policies, Changes in Accounting Estimates and Errors* only permits a change in accounting policy if the change is: (i) required by an IFRS or (ii) results in the financial statements providing reliable and more relevant information about the effects of transactions, other events or conditions on the entity's financial position, financial performance or cash flows. A retrospective adjustment is required unless the change arises from a new accounting policy with transitional arrangements to account for the change. It is possible to depart from the requirements of IFRS but only in the extremely rare circumstances where compliance would be so misleading that it would conflict with the overall objectives of the financial statements. Practically this override is rarely, if ever, invoked.

IAS 19 *Employee Benefits* requires all gains and losses on a defined benefit pension scheme to be recognised in profit or loss except for the remeasurement component relating to the assets and liabilities of the plan, which must be recognised in other comprehensive income. So, current service cost, past service cost and the net interest cost on the net defined benefit liability must all be recognised in profit or loss. There is no alternative treatment available to the directors, which, under IAS 8, a change in accounting policy might be applied to move Ramsbury to. The directors' proposals cannot be justified on the grounds of fair presentation. The directors have an ethical responsibility to prepare financial statements which are a true representation of the entity's performance and comply with all accounting standards.

There is a clear self-interest threat arising from the bonus scheme. The directors' change in policy appears to be motivated by an intention to overstate operating profit to maximise their bonus potential. The amendment to the pension scheme is a past service cost which must be expensed to profit or loss during the period the plan amendment has occurred, ie immediately. This would therefore be detrimental to the operating profits of Ramsbury and depress any potential bonus.

Additionally, it appears that the directors wish to manipulate other aspects of the pension scheme such as the current service cost and, since the scheme is in deficit, the net finance cost. The directors are deliberately manipulating the presentation of these items by recording them in equity rather than in profit or loss. The financial statements would not be compliant with IFRS, would not give a reliable picture of the true costs to the company of operating a pension scheme and this treatment would make the financial statements less comparable with other entities correctly applying IAS 19. Such treatment is against ACCA's *Code of Ethics and Conduct* fundamental principles of objectivity, integrity and professional behaviour. The directors should be reminded of their ethical responsibilities and must be dissuaded from implementing the proposed change in policy.

The directors should be encouraged to utilise other tools within the financial statements to explain the company's results such as drawing users attention towards the cash flow where the cash generated from operations measure will exclude the non-cash pension expense and if necessary alternative performance measures such as EBITDA could be disclosed where non-cash items may be consistently stripped out for comparison purposes.

Section B

3 Calcula

> **Workbook reference.** IFRS 5 is covered in Chapter 13. The concept of integrated reporting is covered in Chapter 17.
>
> **Top tips.** In part (a) you are required to provide an analysis of whether the classification of the subsidiary as 'held for sale' and presentation as a discontinued operation is correct in accordance with IFRS 5, so you need to apply your knowledge to the scenario, and not just write down the requirements of IFRS 5. Relating the treatment to the *Conceptual Framework* was not easy, but is likely to be a feature of questions in the SBR exam. Reading the 'Basis for conclusions' accompanying IFRSs provides insight into the decisions of the IASB in developing a standard and often highlights potential conflicts with the *Conceptual Framework*.
>
> To score well in part (b) it is critical that your answer is related to Calcula. The scenario is provided to give you the opportunity to show two things. Firstly, that you understand the theory – ie what integrated reporting is – and secondly, for you to show that can apply your knowledge. A good approach to dealing with such questions is to set the scene by identifying what has gone wrong in the scenario. In this case stakeholders (shareholders and employees) are confused as to the strategic direction that Calcula is trying to pursue.
>
> Next, use your knowledge to explain how integrated reporting can help Calcula to communicate its strategy. Integrated reporting places a strong emphasis on relaying what the company stands for through setting out its objectives and strategy to realise these. The introduction of integrated reporting would therefore provide the company with a great opportunity to convey Asha Alexander's new mission.

Marking scheme

			Marks
(a)	IFRS 5 – 1 mark per valid point up to		9
(b)	(i)	Integrated reporting – 1 mark per valid point up to	12
	(ii)	Cost-cutting programme – 1 mark per valid point up to	2
Professional marks			2
			25

(a)   Subsidiary held for sale

The subsidiary is a disposal group under IFRS 5 *Non-current Assets Held for Sale and Discontinued Operations*. A disposal group is a group of assets and associated liabilities which are to be disposed of together in a single transaction. IFRS 5 classifies a disposal group as held for sale when its carrying amount will be recovered principally through sale rather than use. The held for sale criteria in IFRS 5 are very strict, and often the decision to sell an asset or disposal group is made well before they are met.

IFRS requires an asset or disposal group to be classified as held for sale where it is **available for immediate sale** in its **present condition** subject only to **terms that are usual** and customary and the sale is **highly probable**.

For a sale to be **highly probable:**

- Management must be **committed** to the sale.

- An **active programme to locate a buyer** must have been initiated.

- The asset must be **marketed at a price** that is **reasonable in relation to its own fair value**.

- The sale must be **expected to be completed within one year** from the date of classification.

- It is **unlikely** that **significant changes** will be made to the plan **or the plan withdrawn**.

In **exceptional circumstances**, a disposal group may be classified as held for sale or **discontinued after a period of 12 months**:

(i)   Circumstances arose during the initial 12-month period that were previously considered unlikely, and the disposal group was not sold.

(ii)   During the 12-month period, the entity took steps to respond to the change in circumstances by actively marketing the disposal group at a price that is reasonable in the light of the change in circumstances, and the held-for-sale criteria are met.

The draft agreements and correspondence with bankers are **not specific enough** to prove that the subsidiary met the IFRS 5 criteria at the date it was classified. More detail would be required to confirm that the subsidiary was available for immediate sale and that it was being actively marketed at an appropriate price in order to satisfy the criteria in the year to 31 May 20X2. In addition, the **organisational changes** made by Calcula in the year to 31 May 20X3 are a **good indication that the subsidiary was not available for sale in its present condition at the point of classification**. Additional activities have been transferred to the subsidiary, which is not an insignificant change. The shareholders' authorisation was given for a year from 1 January 20X2. There is **no evidence that this authorisation was extended beyond 1 January 20X3**.

Conclusion

From the information provided, it appears that Calcula should **not classify the subsidiary as held for sale** and should report the results of the subsidiary as a **continuing operation** in the financial statements for the year ended 31 May 20X2 and 31 May 20X3.

Evaluation of treatment in the context of the Conceptual Framework

The *Conceptual Framework* states that the economic decisions that are taken by users of financial statements require an evaluation of the ability of an entity to generate cash and cash equivalents. Separately highlighting the results of discontinued operations provides users with information that is relevant in assessing the ability of the entity to generate future cash flows. If an entity has made a firm decision to sell the subsidiary, it could be argued that the subsidiary should be classified as discontinued, even if the criteria to classify it as 'held for sale' per IFRS 5 have not been met, because this information would be more useful to users. However, the IASB decided against this when developing IFRS 5. This decision could be argued to be in conflict with the *Conceptual Framework*.

(b)   (i)   **Integrated reporting at Calcula**

Confusion

As a result of the recent management changes at Calcula, the company has struggled to communicate its 'strategic direction' to key stakeholders. The company's annual report has made it hard for shareholders to understand Calcula's strategy which in turn has led to confusion. Uncertainty among shareholders and employees is likely to increase the risk of investors selling their shares and talented IT developers seeking employment with competitors.

Integrated reporting

The introduction of integrated reporting may help Calcula to overcome these issues as it places a strong focus on the organisation's future orientation. Integrated reporting is fundamentally concerned with evaluating value creation, and uses qualitative and quantitative performance measures to help stakeholders assess how well an organisation is creating value. In the context of integrated reporting, an entity's resources are referred to as 'capitals'. The International Integrated Reporting Council have identified six capitals which can be used to assess value creation.

Integrated reporting helps to ensure that a balanced view of performance is presented by requiring organisations to report on both positive and negative movements in capital. When preparing an integrated report, management should also disclose matters which are likely to impact on an entity's ability to create value. Internal weaknesses and external threats regarded as being materially important are evaluated and quantified. This provides users with an indication of how management intends to combat such instances should they materialise.

Communicating strategy

An integrated report should detail the entity's mission and values, the nature of its operations, along with features on how it differentiates itself from its competitors.

Including Calcula's new mission to become the market leader in the specialist accountancy software industry would instantly convey what the organisation stands for.

In line with best practice in integrated reporting, Calcula could supplement its mission with how the board intend to achieve this strategy. Such detail could focus on resource allocations over the short to medium term. For example, plans to improve the company's human capital through hiring innovative software developers working at competing firms would help to support the company's long-term mission. To assist users in appraising the company's performance, Calcula should provide details on how it will measure value creation in each capital. 'Human capital' could be measured by the net movement in new joiners to the organisation compared to the previous year.

A key feature of integrated reporting focuses on the need for organisations to use non-financial customer-orientated performance measures (KPI's) to help communicate the entity's strategy. The most successful companies in Calcula's industry are committed to enhancing their offering to customers through producing innovative products. Calcula could report through the use of KPIs how it is delivering on this objective, measures could be set which for example measure the number of new software programs developed in the last two years or report on the number of customer complaints concerning newly released software programs over the period. When reporting on non-financial measures such as KPIs, it is important for Calcula to be consistent in the measures it reports year on year and it should consider reporting similar measures as its competitors as it gives investors a basis on which to compare similar companies.

Improving long-term performance

The introduction of integrated reporting may also help Calcula to enhance its performance. Historically, the company has not given consideration to how decisions in one area have impacted on other areas. This is clearly indicated by the former CEO's cost cutting programme which served to reduce the staff training budget. Although this move may have enhanced the company's short-term profitability, boosting financial capital, it has damaged long term value creation.

The nature of the software industry requires successful organisations to invest in staff training to ensure that the products they develop remain innovative in order to attract customers. The decision to reduce the training budget will most likely impact on future profitability if Calcula is unable to produce the software customers demand.

Finance director's comments

As illustrated in the scenario, the finance director's comments indicate a very narrow understanding of how the company's activities and 'capitals' interact with each other in delivering value. To dismiss developments in integrated reporting as simply being a 'fad', suggest that the finance director is unaware of current developments in financial reporting and the commitment of the ACCA in promoting its introduction. The ACCA's support for integrated reporting may lead to backing from other global accountancy bodies thereby reducing the scope for it be regarded as a passing 'fad'.

However, some critics dispute this and argue that the voluntary nature of integrated reporting increases the likelihood that companies will choose not to pursue its adoption. Such individuals highlight that until companies are legally required to comply with integrated reporting guidelines, many will simply regard it as an unnecessary effort and cost.

The finance director's assertion regarding shareholders is likely to some degree to be correct. Investors looking for short term results from an investment might assess Calcula's performance based on improvements in profitability. However, many shareholders will also be interested in how the board propose to create value in the future. Ultimately, Calcula's aim to appease both groups is its focus on maximising shareholder value, the achievement of which requires the successful implementation of both short and long-term strategies.

Furthermore, unlike traditional annual reports, integrated reports highlight the importance of considering a wider range of users. Key stakeholder groups such as Calcula's customers and suppliers are likely to be interested in assessing how the company has met or not met their needs beyond the 'bottom line'. Integrated reporting encourages companies to report performance measures which are closely aligned to the concepts of sustainability and corporate social responsibility. This is implied by the different capitals used: consideration of social relationships and natural capitals do not focus on financial performance but instead are concerned, for example, with the impact an organisation's activities have on the natural environment.

(ii)   **Cost-cutting programme**

The previous CEO instigated an aggressive cost-cutting programme, designed to increase profitability. This may have put his management team in a difficult position because they were being asked to prioritise profit above all else. Managers have a duty to aim to maximise profit but at the same time they have a duty to guard, preserve and enhance the value of the entity for the good of all affected by it, including employees and the general public. The high management turnover may show evidence of Calcula not treating its employees adequately and them choosing or being made to leave their employment under difficult circumstances. Staff redundancies are a challenging decision for senior managers, who must balance their corporate responsibilities with the individual impacts of sudden unemployment. The cuts to staff training funding may have brought further challenges. Managers have a responsibility to ensure that their own employees are protected from danger. Training cuts may introduce unacceptable risks to health and safety, leading to dangerous working conditions or to inadequate safety standards in products, putting the general public/Calcula's customers at risk.

4 Janne

Marking scheme

		Marks
(a)	Investment properties discussion – 1 mark per valid point up to	9
(b)	Annual report discussion – 1 mark per valid point up to	8
(c)	Alternative performance measure discussion – 1 mark per valid point up to	8
		25

(a) **Investment properties**

IAS 40 *Investment Property* allows two methods for valuing investment property: the fair value model and the cost model. If the fair value method is adopted, **then the investment property must be valued in accordance with IFRS 13** *Fair Value Measurement*. IFRS 13 defines fair value as: 'the price that would be received to sell an asset or paid to transfer a liability in an orderly transaction between market participants at the measurement date' (Appendix A).

Fair value is a market-based measurement rather than specific to the entity, so a company is not allowed to choose its own way of measuring fair value. IFRS 13 states that valuation techniques must be those which are appropriate and for which sufficient data are available. Entities should maximise the use of relevant **observable inputs** and minimise the use of **unobservable inputs**. The standard establishes a three-level hierarchy for the inputs that valuation techniques use to measure fair value.

Level 1   Quoted prices (unadjusted) in active markets for identical assets or liabilities that the reporting entity can access at the measurement date

Level 2   Inputs other than quoted prices included within Level 1 that are observable for the asset or liability, either directly or indirectly, eg quoted prices for similar assets in active markets or for identical or similar assets in non-active markets or use of quoted interest rates for valuation purposes

Level 3   Unobservable inputs for the asset or liability, ie using the entity's own assumptions about market exit value

Although the directors claim that 'new-build value less obsolescence' is accepted by the industry, it **may not be in accordance with IFRS 13**. As the fair value hierarchy suggests, IFRS 13 favours Level 1 inputs, that is market-based measures, over unobservable (Level 3) inputs. Due to the nature of investment property, which is often unique and not traded on a regular basis, fair value measurements are likely to be categorised as Level 2 or Level 3 valuations.

The *Conceptual Framework* provides very little guidance on measurement. However, the Exposure Draft on the *Conceptual Framework* clarifies that a key factor to be considered when selecting a measurement basis is the degree of measurement uncertainty. A high level of measurement uncertainty may result in information that is not relevant. In the case of investment property, IAS 40 allows a choice of cost or fair value, however, if at recognition, fair value is not expected to be reliably measureable on a continuing basis, then the cost model should be used. So to some extent, IAS 40 does include consideration of measurement uncertainty in selecting which measurement basis to use.

There is debate about whether a measurement basis should reflect the entity's business model, so in this case, how the property is used. The Exposure Draft states that how an asset contributes to future cash flows, which in part depends on the entity's business activities, is important in determining an appropriate measurement basis. IAS 40 does not include this criteria for consideration when selecting whether to measure at cost or fair value. However, it does require the inclusion of rentals receivable under current leases to be taken into account in valuations of investment property, which would appear to be in line with the Exposure Draft.

In conclusion, as Janne has chosen to measure its investment property at fair value, it should **apply IFRS 13 to the valuation**, ensuring that the requirements of IAS 40 in measuring fair value are applied. Janne should also disclose in its financial statements the valuation technique used and inputs used to develop those measurements.

(b)   **Annual Report**

Too much information in annual reports can be problematic as it can obscure relevant information and prevent investors from identifying the key issues that are likely to affect their decisions. Removing unnecessary information, or 'clutter', from the annual report is therefore a good idea. However, it must be done carefully to ensure the financial statements still meet their primary objective of satisfying the information needs of existing and potential investors, lenders and other creditors in making decisions about providing resources to the entity.

Disclosures are prescribed by IFRS and therefore are not optional. Management cannot just determine which disclosures appear irrelevant. However, materiality needs to be taken into account when making disclosures. The IASB has issued guidance on the application of materiality to financial statements, which includes the application of materiality when making decisions about presenting and disclosing information. The guidance clarifies that disclosure does not need to be made, even when prescribed by an IFRS, if the resulting information presented is not material. Although the finance director has used a disclosure checklist and determined that all disclosures made were 'necessary', it is not clear whether an assessment has been made as to whether the disclosures are 'material' – would the omission of the disclosure influence the decisions users make on the basis of the financial statements? Therefore there is the potential to reduce disclosure in Janne's financial statements by giving consideration to materiality.

Reducing the size of the accounting policy note is a distinct possibility. Only significant accounting policies are required to be disclosed by IAS 1. Determining what constitutes a significant accounting policy requires judgment and the application of materiality. The IASB's Discussion Paper: *Principles of Disclosure* categorises accounting policies into (1) those always necessary to understand the financial statements, (2) those not in category 1 but necessary to understand the financial statements and (3) not in categories 1 or 2 but used in preparing the financial statements. Only those accounting policies that fall into categories 1 or 2 must be

disclosed. Those in category 3 may be disclosed. Even though this is presently included in a Discussion Paper and not a Standard, Janne could use these principles to help identify the accounting policies which, if not disclosed, would not affect a user's understanding of the financial statements. Janne should ensure that accounting policies that require management judgment or choice are clearly presented, in order that investors have a clear understanding of where management judgement has been applied.

Transactions with related parties are material by their very nature, whether or not they are conducted at arm's length. Disclosures required by IAS 24 in relation to related parties are necessary to draw attention to the possibility that an entity's financial position and profit or loss may have been affected by the existence of related parties and by transactions and outstanding balances with such parties. Janne should not remove these disclosures from its financial statements, as to do so would be misleading to investors and other users of the financial statements and would not be in compliance with IAS 24.

(c)   **Alternative performance measure**

'Adjusted net asset value per share' (adjusted NAV per share) is an alternative performance measure (APM). Entities are increasingly reporting APMs in addition to IFRS performance measures, such as earnings per share, in order to enhance a user's understanding of the financial statements. It is possible for Janne to present this APM, however, it cannot present this measure instead of earnings per share (EPS). EPS is required by IAS 33 which must be applied by listed entities. Therefore, in order to comply with IFRS, EPS and diluted EPS must be presented.

APMs should be provided to enhance the understanding of users of the accounts. Investment properties are likely to form the majority of Janne's assets. Therefore management will be interested in the increase in the value of those properties and related finance (eg loans), both of which are taken into account in adjusted NAV per share. Disclosing adjusted NAV per share should therefore enhance the understanding of investors as it will allow them to evaluate Janne through the eyes of management. Additionally, as adjusted NAV per share is used by other companies in the same industry, disclosing it should allow investors to more effectively compare the performance of Janne with other companies in the same industry.

However, APMs can also be misleading. Unlike EPS, there is no official definition of adjusted NAV per share, so management can choose what items to include in the 'adjustment'. Therefore it is open to bias in its calculation as management could decide to only adjust for items that improve the measure. In order to counter the criticisms, management should provide a description of what is included when arriving at adjusted NAV per share and ideally reconcile the information back to the IFRS information included within the financial statements. Similarly, in order to be useful, the basis of the calculation needs to be consistent from year to year, otherwise comparison between years will be inaccurate. Furthermore, different companies may define the same measure in different ways, which reduces the comparability between entities.

Ultimately adjusted NAV per share will only provide useful information to Janne's investors if it is fairly presented. The European Securities and Markets Authority has developed draft guidelines that address the issues surrounding the use of APMs, which include appropriate description of APMs, consistency from year to year and guidance for presentation. The IASB has also given consideration to this issue in its Discussion Paper on the Principles of Disclosure. This guidance includes not making APMs more prominent than IFRS information and reconciling the APM back to IFRS measures.

It is advisable for Janne's directors to consider this guidance in determining whether to present adjusted NAV per share and how it should be presented. They should also consider whether providing further information in the form of APMs will result in more information being reported in the annual report which they are otherwise attempting to reduce.

ACCA

Strategic Business Reporting (International)

Mock Examination 3

Time allowed: 3 hours 15 minutes

This question paper is divided into two sections:

Section A – BOTH questions are compulsory and MUST be attempted
Section B – BOTH questions are compulsory and MUST be attempted

Do NOT open this question paper until instructed by the supervisor.

Do NOT record any of your answers on the question paper.

This question paper must not be removed from the examination hall.

Section A – BOTH questions are compulsory and MUST be attempted

1 Ashanti

The following financial statement extracts relate to Ashanti, a public limited company.

STATEMENTS OF PROFIT OR LOSS AND OTHER COMPREHENSIVE INCOME (EXTRACTS) FOR THE YEAR ENDED 30 APRIL 20X5

	Ashanti $m	Bochem $m
Profit for the year	41	36
Other comprehensive income for the year, net of tax		
Items that will not be reclassified to profit or loss:		
Gain on investment in equity instruments	6	9
Gains (net) on PPE revaluation	12	6
Other comprehensive income for the year, net of tax	18	15
Total comprehensive income and expense for year	59	51

The following information is relevant to the preparation of the consolidated financial statements:

(i)   On 1 May 20X3, Ashanti acquired 70% of the equity interests of Bochem, a public limited company. The purchase consideration comprised cash of $150 million and the fair value of Bochem's identifiable net assets was $160 million at that date. The fair value of the non-controlling interest in Bochem was $54 million on 1 May 20X3. Ashanti wishes to use the 'full goodwill' method for all acquisitions. The share capital and retained earnings of Bochem were $55 million and $85 million respectively and other components of equity were $10 million at the date of acquisition. The excess of the fair value of the identifiable net assets at acquisition is due to an increase in the value of plant, which is depreciated on the straight-line basis and has a five year remaining life at the date of acquisition.

(ii)   Ashanti disposed of a 10% equity interest in Bochem on 30 April 20X5 for a cash consideration of $34 million. The carrying amount of the net assets of Bochem at 30 April 20X5 was $210 million before any adjustments on consolidation. Goodwill has been tested for impairment annually and as at 30 April 20X4 had reduced in value by 15% and at 30 April 20X5 had lost a further 5% of its original value before the sale of the 10% equity interest.

(iii)   The salaried employees of Ashanti are entitled to 25 days paid holiday each year. The entitlement accrues evenly over the year and unused holiday may be carried forward for one year. The holiday year is the same as the financial year. At 30 April 20X5, Ashanti has 900 salaried employees and the average unused holiday entitlement is three days per employee. 5% of employees leave without taking their entitlement and there is no cash payment in respect of unused holiday entitlement when an employee leaves. There are 255 working days in the year and the total annual salary cost is $19 million. No adjustment has been made in the financial statements for the above and there was no opening accrual required for holiday entitlement.

Required

(a)   (i)   Explain, with suitable workings, how the disposal of the 10% equity interest in Bochem should be accounted for in the consolidated financial statements of Ashanti Group as at 30 April 20X5.   **(10 marks)**

        (ii)   Explain, with supporting calculations, how the non-controlling interest should be accounted for in Ashanti's consolidated statement of profit or loss and other comprehensive income for the year ended 30 April 20X5.   **(6 marks)**

(iii)   Discuss, with suitable workings and reference to the *Conceptual Framework for Financial Reporting,* whether it is appropriate to record an accrual for holiday pay in the consolidated financial statements for the year ended 30 April 20X5.   **(5 marks)**

Note. **Marks will be allocated in (a) for a suitable discussion of the principles involved as well as the accounting treatment.**

(b)   Included in Ashanti's trade receivables is $128.85m due from its customer Kumasi. This relates to a sale which took place on 1 May 20X4, payable in three annual instalments of $50 million commencing on 30 April 20X5 discounted at a market rate of interest, adjusted to reflect the risks of Kumasi, of 8%. Based on previous sales where consideration has been received in annual instalments, the directors of Ashanti estimate a lifetime expected credit loss in relation to this receivable of $75.288 million. The probability of default over next twelve months is estimated at 25%. This assumption has not changed since initial recognition. The $128.85 million was recorded in receivables and revenue, but no other accounting entries have been made.

Required

Discuss, with suitable supporting workings, the options available to Ashanti in the application of the impairment model in IFRS 9 *Financial Instruments* to the balance due from Kumasi.

(9 marks)

(Total = 30 marks)

2 Elevator

(a)   The directors of Elevator, a public limited company, which operates in the UK technology sector, are paid a bonus based on the profit that they achieve in a year. Employees have historically been paid a discretionary bonus based on their individual performance in the year. Elevator's year to date results indicate that it may not achieve the required level of profit to secure a bonus for the directors. Elevator's Chief Executive Officer (CEO) has suggested that one way of managing this is not to pay the employees a bonus in the current year which will keep the wages and salaries expense at a minimum. Elevator reports employee satisfaction scores, staff turnover, gender equality and employee absentee rates as non-financial performance measures in its annual report. The CEO has told the directors in an email that 'no one ever reads the non-financial information anyway' and is therefore not concerned about the impact of his suggestion.

Required

(i)   Comment on the ethical consequences of the proposals made by the CEO and the potential implications for the information given in the annual report.   **(7 marks)**

(ii)   Explain, from the perspective of investors and potential investors, the benefits and potential drawbacks of reporting non-financial performance measures.   **(4 marks)**

(b)   Immediately prior to the 31 May 20X3 year end, Elevator sold land located adjacent to its UK head offices to a third party at a price of $16 million with an option to purchase the land back on 1 July 20X3 for $16 million plus a premium of 3%. On 31 May 20X3 the market value of the land was $25 million and the carrying amount was $12 million. The cash received from this transaction eliminated Elevator's bank overdraft at 31 May 20X3. As instructed by the CEO of Elevator, the finance director has accounted for the transaction as a sale, and has included a profit on disposal in the statement of profit or loss for the year ended 31 May 20X3.

Required

Discuss the financial reporting and ethical implications of the above scenario.   **(7 marks)**

Professional marks will be awarded for the application of ethical principles.   **(2 marks)**

(Total = 20 marks)

Section B – BOTH questions are compulsory and MUST be attempted

3 Glowball

The directors of Glowball, a public limited company are aware that an increasing number of large companies are voluntarily releasing green reports to the public to promote corporate environmental performance and to attract customers and investors. They have heard that their main competitors are applying the 'Global Reporting Initiative' (GRI) in an effort to develop a worldwide format for corporate environmental reporting. However, the directors are unsure as to what this initiative actually means. Additionally, they require advice as to the nature of any legislation or standards relating to environmental reporting, as they are worried that any environmental report produced by the company may not be of sufficient quality and may detract and not enhance their image if the report does not comply with recognised standards. Glowball has a reputation for ensuring the preservation of the environment in its business activities.

Further, the directors have collected information in respect of a series of events but are not sure as to how they would be incorporated in the environmental report or whether they should be accounted for and disclosed in the financial statements.

The events are as follows.

(1)   Glowball is a company that pipes gas from offshore gas installations to major consumers. The company purchased its main competitor during the year and found that there were environmental obligations arising out of the restoration of many miles of farmland that had been affected by the laying of a pipeline. There was no legal obligation to carry out the work but the company felt that there would be a cost of around $150 million if the farmland was to be restored.

(2)   Most of the offshore gas installations are governed by operating licenses which specify limits to the substances which can be discharged to the air and water. These limits vary according to local legislation and tests are carried out by the regulatory authorities. During the year the company was prosecuted for infringements of an environmental law in the USA when toxic gas escaped into the atmosphere. In 20X2 the company was prosecuted five times and in 20X1 eleven times for infringement of the law. The final amount of the fine/costs to be imposed by the courts has not been determined but is expected to be around $5 million. The escape occurred over the seas and it was considered that there was little threat to human life.

(3)   The company produced statistics that measure their improvement in the handling of emissions of gases which may have an impact on the environment. The statistics deal with:

(i)   Measurement of the release of gases with the potential to form acid rain. The emissions have been reduced by 84% over five years due to the closure of old plants.

(ii)   Measurement of emissions of substances potentially hazardous to human health. The emissions are down by 51% on 20W8 levels.

(iii)   Measurement of emissions to water that removes dissolved oxygen and substances that may have an adverse effect on aquatic life. Accurate measurement of these emissions is not possible but the company is planning to spend $70 million on research in this area.

(4)   The company tries to reduce the environmental impacts associated with the siting and construction of its gas installations. This is done in the way that minimises the impact on wild life and human beings. Additionally when the installations are at the end of their life, they are dismantled and are not sunk into the sea. The current provision for the decommissioning of these installations is $215 million and there are still decommissioning costs of $407 million to be provided as the company's policy is to build up the required provision over the life of the installation.

Required

Prepare a report suitable for presentation to the directors of Glowball in which you discuss the following elements:

(a) Current reporting requirements and guidelines relating to environmental reporting.

(10 marks)

(b) The nature of any disclosure which would be required in an environmental report and/or the financial statements for the events (1)–(4) above. **(13 marks)**

Professional marks will be awarded for clarity and quality of presentation. **(2 marks)**

(Total = 25 marks)

4 Suntory

(a) Suntory is a private limited company. On 1 December 20X2, Suntory acquired a trademark, Golfo, for a line of golf equipment for $3 million. Suntory expected to continue marketing and receiving cash flows from the Golfo product-line for 10 years. Suntory therefore decided to amortise the trademark over a 10-year life, using the straight-line method. In December 20X5, a competitor unexpectedly revealed a technological breakthrough which is expected to result in a product which, when launched, will significantly reduce the demand for the Golfo product-line. The demand for the Golfo product-line is expected to remain high until May 20X8, when the competitor is expected to launch its new product.

At 30 November 20X6, the end of the financial year, Suntory assessed the recoverable amount of the trademark at $500,000 and intends to continue manufacturing Golfo products until 31 May 20X8.

The finance director of Suntory has heard that that the concept of materiality in the financial statements is included in an Exposure Draft (ED/2015/8). He has not read the Exposure Draft as materiality is not a new issue in financial reporting so does not understand why an Exposure Draft was issued about it. He does not know if there is anything in the Exposure Draft that is likely to become mandatory when issued.

Required

(i) Explain to the directors, with reference to relevant International Financial Reporting Standards and the principles of the *Conceptual Framework for Financial Reporting*, how to account for the trademark in Suntory's financial statements for the year ended 30 November 20X6. **(9 marks)**

(ii) Explain to the finance director the reason the IASB has issued an Exposure Draft on the application of materiality to financial statements, the key areas the Exposure Draft covers and whether it will give rise to any mandatory requirements. **(4 marks)**

(b) At 30 November 20X6, three people own the shares of Suntory. The finance director owns 60%, and the operations director owns 30%. The third owner is a passive investor who does not help manage the entity. All ordinary shares carry equal voting rights. The wife of the finance director is the sales director of Suntory. Their son is currently undertaking an internship with Suntory and receives a salary of $30,000 per annum, which is normal compensation.

The finance director and sales director have set up an investment company, Baleel. They jointly own Baleel and their shares in Baleel will eventually be transferred to their son when he has finished the internship with Suntory.

In addition, on 1 June 20X6 Suntory obtained a bank loan of $500,000 at a fixed interest rate of 6% per annum. The loan is to be repaid on 30 November 20X7. Repayment of the principal and interest is secured by a guarantee registered in favour of the bank against the private home of the finance director.

The finance director is of the opinion that none of the above should be disclosed in the financial statements. He believes that it is not relevant to the passive investor, and as the finance director and operations director are the other two shareholders, they already have all the information they need.

Required

(i) Advise the directors of Suntory on the identification of related parties and disclosure of related party transactions in the financial statements for the year ending 30 November 20X6. You should refer to the requirements and underlying principles of relevant International Financial Reporting Standards. **(7 marks)**

(ii) Explain to the directors of Suntory why the company's passive investor may be interested in related party disclosures and comment on the finance director's opinion that the information should not be disclosed. **(5 marks)**

(Total = 25 marks)

Answers

**DO NOT TURN THIS PAGE UNTIL YOU HAVE
COMPLETED THE MOCK EXAM**

Section A

1 Ashanti

> **Workbook references.** Subsidiary to subsidiary disposals are covered in Chapter 12. Employee benefits are covered in Chapter 4 and the *Conceptual Framework* in Chapter 1. Financial instruments are covered in Chapter 7.
>
> **Top tips.** In part (a), it is important to clearly understand the sales transaction for Bochem so that you identify that the gain on disposal of the interest in Bochem should not be in the statement of profit or loss and other comprehensive income, but an adjustment to equity. Ensure that you provide explanations where asked for. Part (b) is reasonably flexible, with credit available for sensible comments.
>
> **Easy marks.** There are easy marks available for some straightforward consolidation aspects – goodwill and NCI, although calculations alone will not be sufficient to pass the exam. Then there are some marks for straightforward knowledge in Part (a)(iii) on employee benefits and in part (b) on IFRS 9's impairment model.

Marking scheme

				Marks
(a)	(i)	Sale of 10% of Bochem		
		Calculations		4
		Discussion		6
				10
	(ii)	Non-controlling interest		
		Calculations		3
		Discussion		3
				6
	(iii)	Employee benefits		
		Calculations		2
		Discussion		3
				5
				21
(b)		Trade receivable		
		Calculations		3
		Discussion – 1 mark per point to a maximum		6
				9
				30

(a) (i) **Sale of 10% of Bochem**

Ashanti sold 10% of its 70% equity interest in Bochem on 30 April 20X5, decreasing its interest to 60% but retaining control. IFRS 10 *Consolidated Financial Statements* views the partial disposal of a subsidiary, in which control is retained by the parent company, as an **equity transaction** accounted for directly in equity. The accounting treatment is driven by the concept of **substance over form**. In substance, there has been **no disposal** because the entity is still a subsidiary, so no profit on disposal should be recognised and there is **no effect on the consolidated statement of profit or loss and other comprehensive income**. The transaction is, in effect, a **transfer between the owners** of Bochem (Ashanti and the non-controlling interests).

Ashanti should continue to consolidate Bochem. The sale of the shares should be accounted for in the consolidated financial statements per IFRS 10 by:

(a) Increasing the non-controlling interests (NCI) in the consolidated statement of financial position to reflect the increase in their shareholding of 10%; and

(b) Recognising the difference between the consideration received for the shares and the increase in NCI as an adjustment to equity, attributed to Ashanti.

NCI

The NCI in Bochem should be increased by 10% of the net assets at the date of sale to reflect the transfer of 10% of the shares from Ashanti to the non-controlling interest. The fair value of the net assets of Bochem at the date of sale is calculated as follows.

Net assets of Bochem at date of sale

	$m
Net assets at 30 April 20X5	210.0
Fair value adjustments (W1)	6.0
	216.0
Goodwill (W2)	35.2
	251.2

The NCI will be allocated a 10% share of the net assets, which is **$25.12m** ($251.2m × 10%).

Adjustment to equity

The adjustment to equity is then calculated as:

	$m
Cash consideration	34.00
Increase in NCI	25.12
	8.80

Conclusion

Ashanti should therefore make the following entries in its consolidated financial statements:

DEBIT	Cash (proceeds per question)	$34m	
CREDIT	Non-controlling interest		$25.12m
CREDIT	Adjustment to Ashanti's equity		$8.88m

Workings

1 *Fair value adjustment*

The fair value adjustment on acquisition in respect of plant is a consolidation adjustment only and has not been recorded in the financial statements of Bochem. As such, we must adjust the net assets at 30 April 20X5 to reflect the remaining carrying amount of the fair value adjustment. The increase in the fair value of the plant is depreciated on the straight line basis over the remaining useful life of five years.

Bochem	At acquisition 1 May 20X3	Movement 20X4	20X5	At year end 30 April 20X5
	$m	$m	$m	$m
Plant				
(160 − (55 + 85 + 10))	10	$10/5 = (2)$	(2)	6
		(4)		

2   *Goodwill*

Goodwill is also a consolidation adjustment that is not reflected in the net assets of the subsidiary at 30 April 20X5 and therefore needs to be adjusted when calculating the net assets at disposal. The closing balance of goodwill is calculated after impairment losses have been deducted.

	Bochem
	$m
Consideration transferred (per question)	150.0
Fair value of non-controlling interest (per question)	54.0
Fair value of net assets (per question)	(160.0)
As at 1 May 20X3	44.0
Impairment loss to 30.4.X4: 44 × 15%	(6.6)
	37.4
Impairment loss to 30.4.X5: 44 × 5%	(2.2)
As at 30 April 20X5 (pre-disposal)	35.2

(ii)   Non-controlling interest represents the share of a subsidiary's financial position and performance that is not owned by the parent. For the statement of profit or loss and other comprehensive income, Ashanti should consolidate the results of Bochem for the full year, allocating the non-controlling interest a share of 30%. This is because the 10% disposal transaction, reducing its 70% holding to 60%, did not occur until the final day of the financial year, 30 April 20X5.

There are two adjustments to make to the profit of Bochem on consolidation as a result of the sale of Ashanti's 10% shareholding. The first is to account for the reduction of $2 million in additional annual depreciation which was charged on the fair value uplift of Bochem's plant at acquisition. The second to account for the impairment charge of $2.2 million on goodwill. NCI should be allocated its 30% share of the revised profit and total comprehensive income, which is $9.54 million and $14.04 million respectively.

Working

Non-controlling interests in profit and TCI for the year ended 30 April 20X5

	Bochem	
	Profit for year	TCI
	$m	$m
Per question	36.0	51.0
Depreciation of fair value adjustment ((a) (i) W1)	(2.0)	(2.0)
Impairment of 'full' goodwill ((a) (i) W2)	(2.2)	(2.2)
Revised profit/total comprehensive income	31.8	46.8
	× 30%	× 30%
NCI share of profit/total comprehensive income	9.54	14.04

(iii) **Holiday pay accrual**

IAS 19 *Employee Benefits* classifies this type of holiday pay as a short-term accumulating paid absence as any unused entitlement may be carried forward and utilised in the following year. The obligation arises as the employees render services

that entitle them to future paid absences. The obligation exists even if the employees are not entitled to a cash payment (non-vesting).

This is consistent with the definition of a liability given in the *Conceptual Framework:* 'a liability is a present obligation of the entity arising from past events, the settlement of which is expected to result in an outflow from the entity of resources embodying economic benefits' (para. 4.4(b)). The company has a present obligation, as it needs to provide a paid absence, as a result of past events, as the employee has already undertaken employment and accumulated the benefit from which an outflow of resources is expected. Making payments to employees in respect of absences is considered to be an outflow of benefits.

The measurement of the obligation is affected by Ashanti's estimate of possible leavers (5%). IAS 19 requires that an accrual be made by Ashanti for holiday entitlement carried forward as the current period's entitlement has not been used in full at 30 April 20X5. A corresponding increase in the wages and salaries expense will also be recorded. The current liability is calculated as follows:

Number of days c/fwd: $\quad 900 \times 3 \times 95\% = 2,565$ days

Number of working days: $\quad 900 \times 255 = 229,500$

$$\text{Accrual} = \frac{2,565}{229,500} \times \$19\text{m} = \$0.21\text{m}$$

(b) Trade receivable

The impairment model in IFRS 9 *Financial Instruments* is based on providing for expected credit losses. The financial statements should reflect the general pattern of deterioration or improvement in the credit quality of financial instruments within the scope of IFRS 9. Expected credit losses are the expected shortfall in contractual cash flows, in Ashanti's case the directors have identified this as a figure of $75.288 million.

For trade receivables that do not have an IFRS 15 *Revenue from Contracts with Customers* financing element, the loss allowance is measured at the lifetime expected credit losses, from initial recognition, ie $75.288 million. For trade receivables that do have an IFRS 15 financing element, which the debt due from Kumasi does, (calculated as interest on the trade receivable is $128.85m × 8% = $10.308 million), the entity can choose to apply the 3 stage approach or to recognise an allowance for lifetime expected credit losses from initial recognition.

Option 1: The 3 stage approach

The 12-month expected credit losses are calculated by multiplying the probability of default in the next twelve months by the lifetime expected credit losses that would result from the default. Here this amounts to $18.822million ($75.288m × 25%). Because this allowance is recognised at 1 May 20X4 at initial recognition, the discount must be unwound by one year: $18.822m × 8% = $1.506 million for incorporation in the 30 April 20X5 financial statements.

As the directors' estimate of the probability of default has not changed between the initial recognition and the year end, the trade receivable remains within the stage 1 classification and 12 month expected credit losses are appropriate for the impairment calculation. Were the credit quality of the trade receivable to have significantly deteriorated, or if there had been objective evidence of impairment at the reporting date; the debt would have moved into stage 2 or stage 3 of the impairment model, as appropriate, and Ashanti would have been obliged to record lifetime expected credit losses.

Overall adjustment:

DEBIT   Finance costs (impairment of receivable)

(18.822 + 1.506) $20.328m

CREDIT Loss allowance $20.328m

Option 2: Lifetime expected credit losses

If the IFRS 9 option for the loss allowance for trade receivables with a financing component to always be measured at the lifetime expected losses is taken, Ashanti would need to record the following entries in its financial statements for the year ended 30 April 20X5, incorporating the unwind of 8% as above at $75.288m x 8% = $6.023 million:

Overall adjustment:

DEBIT   Finance costs (impairment of receivable)

(75.288 + 6.023) $81.311m

CREDIT Loss allowance $81.311m

The directors of Ashanti must decide which approach is the most appropriate accounting policy to apply to its trade receivables balance. As demonstrated above, recording lifetime expected credit losses may be simpler but it will also result in a potentially higher finance cost on initial recognition.

2 Elevator

> **Workbook reference**. Ethical issues are specifically covered in Chapter 2 of the Workbook but feature throughout all chapters. Non-financial reporting is covered in Chapter 17.
>
> **Top tips**. Part (a)(i) on the ethical implications of the suggestion combines knowledge of non-financial reporting and ethics. There are marks available for comment on each. Part (a)(ii) discusses the benefits and drawbacks of reporting non-financial information from an investor's perspective, focusing on the employee information given in the question. Part (b) requires discussion of the ethics surrounding the dubious land transaction.
>
> **Easy marks**. In parts (a) and (b), there are plenty of marks available for sensible discussion of ethics as well as marks available in part (b) for straightforward knowledge of ratios and repurchase agreements. Link your answer to the scenario.

Marking scheme

			Marks
(a)	(i)	Ethical considerations	3
		Implications for reported information	4
	(ii)	Comment on non-financial performance measures	4
			11
(b)		Financial reporting – 1 mark per point up to maximum	4
		Ethical issues – 1 mark per point up to maximum	3
			7
Professional marks			2
			20

(a)   (i)   **Ethical considerations**

Ethical behaviour in the fair treatment of employees is important to the long term success of a company, and how it is perceived by stakeholders. The directors of Elevator are considering not paying employees a discretionary bonus in order to achieve profit targets. This will enable the directors to collect their bonus. It is worth noting that there is nothing illegal about the proposal – the bonus paid to employees is discretionary rather than contractual and therefore the company has no legal obligation to pay the bonus. It is the reason behind the non-payment that gives rise to ethical considerations. The suggestion by the CEO would work in reducing expenses and improving profit.

Morally, the suggestion is likely to have negative consequences for the company. The employees will be unhappy that their bonus has been withdrawn, particularly if there has been a past policy of paying annual bonuses. This may have a negative impact on productivity and staff morale, and therefore on employee satisfaction scores and possibly on employee retention rates that are reported as non-financial information within the annual report. It is not clear what the gender composition of the company is to understand whether there would also be implications for the information reported on gender equality, which is a matter being widely reported in the media. Companies are also under increasing pressure to reduce the wage gap between management and employees. Not paying staff a bonus will have a negative impact on this metric.

The comments of the CEO imply that he does not think the negative impact on non-financial reporting will have an impact on the company as the information is not widely read. This type of information is becoming increasingly important to the users of financial statements as they care about companies' treatment of their employees and see it as being important in the long term success of the company. If Elevator did not report employee matters, it may have been able to 'hide' the proposal to not pay the employee bonus from the users of the financial statements, however this additional reporting will bring the issue more to their attention.

(ii)   **Implications for reported information**

Financial performance measures are often criticised for being backward-looking as they report historical information, too focused on short-termism as there are often incentives for achieving, for example, profit or revenue targets and for failing to provide enough relevant information on the factors that drive the success of the business. Whilst some speculative investors may only be interested in short term performance, others will base investment decisions on how a business performs over time and how well the business is expected to perform in the future. Information that can help investors to evaluate this will be valuable. Reporting non-financial performance information such as the staff information reported by Elevator has the benefit of disclosing to the investors the factors that management considers important in ensuring the longer term viability and success of the business. Staff are seen as important assets to businesses and employee satisfaction is an important consideration for companies. Reporting non-financial information can help companies to attract and retain the appropriate level of staff.

There are drawbacks of reporting non-financial information. It is generally more difficult for investors to verify than quantitative information which can lead to concerns about its reliability. As companies decide what information to report, it can be difficult for investors to compare between companies and across different periods. Non-financial information is also more open to manipulation than IFRS-based information as there are no underlying standards or principles which companies must apply. The IASB's Disclosure Initiative project is also concerned as to the volume of information being reported by companies and whether extensive disclosures are clouding the information that is relevant to investors within the financial statements.

(b) **Sale of land**

Accounting treatment

The sale of land is a repurchase agreement under IFRS 15 *Revenue from Contracts with Customers* as Elevator has an option to buy the land back from the third party and, therefore, control has not transferred as the purchaser's ability to use and gain benefit from the land is limited. Elevator must treat the transaction as a financing arrangement and record both an asset (the land) and a financial liability (the cash amount received which is repayable to the third party).

Elevator should not have derecognised the land from the financial statements because the risks and rewards of ownership have not been transferred. The substance of the transaction is a loan of $16 million, and the 3% 'premium' on repurchase is effectively an interest payment.

Recording the transaction as a sale is an attempt to manipulate the financial statements in order to show an improved profit figure and more favourable cash position. The sale must be reversed and the land reinstated at its carrying amount before the transaction. The repurchase, ie the repayment of the loan, takes place one month after the year end, and so this is a current liability:

DEBIT	Property, plant and equipment	$12m	
DEBIT	Retained earnings (to reverse profit on disposal (16 – 12))	$4m	
CREDIT	Current liabilities		$16m

Ethical issues

ACCA qualified accountants are required to comply with the fundamental principles of ACCA's *Code of Ethics and Conduct*. This includes acting with integrity. The integrity of the finance director appears to be compromised in this situation. The effect of the sale just before the year end was to improve profits and to eliminate the bank overdraft, making the cash position look better. However, this is effectively 'window dressing', and is not honest as it does not represent the actual position and performance of Elevator.

Accountants must also act with objectivity, which means that they must not allow bias, conflict of interest or undue influence of others to override professional or business judgments. Therefore, the directors must put the interests of the company and its shareholders before their own interests. The pressure to meet profit targets and achieve a bonus is in the self-interest of the directors and seems to have at least partly driven the transaction and the subsequent accounting, which is clearly a conflict of interest.

Accountants must also comply with the principle of professional behaviour, which requires compliance with relevant laws and regulations. In this case the accounting treatment does not conform to IFRS. It is not clear from the scenario whether the finance director is aware of this or not. If he is aware, but he has applied an incorrect treatment anyway, he has not complied with the principle of professional behavior. It may be that he was under undue pressure from the CEO to record the transaction in this manner, if so there is potentially an intimidation threat. If however, he is not aware that the treatment is incorrect, then he has not complied with the principle of professional competence as his knowledge and skill are not up to date.

3 Glowball

Workbook reference. Environmental reporting is covered in Chapter 17 of the Workbook.

Top tips. This is a comprehensive question covering most aspects of environmental reporting that are likely to come up. Learn our answer and apply it to many questions on this topics.

		Marks
(a)	Current reporting requirements	10
(b)	Restoration	4
	Infringement of law	3
	Emissions	3
	Decommissioning activities	3
Professional marks		2
		25

REPORT

To: The directors
       Glowball

Date: 8 June 20X3

From: An accountant

Environmental Reporting

(a) **Introduction**

The purpose of this report is to provide information about current reporting requirements and guidelines on the subject of environmental reporting, and to give an indication of the required disclosure in relation to the specific events which you have brought to my attention. We hope that it will assist you in preparing your environmental report.

Current reporting requirements and guidelines

Most businesses have generally ignored environmental issues in the past. However, the use and **misuse** of **natural resources** all lead to environmental costs generated by businesses, both large and small.

There are very few rules, legal or otherwise, to ensure that companies disclose and report environmental matters. Any **disclosures tend to be voluntary**, unless environmental matters happen to fall under standard accounting principles. Environmental matters may be reported in the accounts of companies in the following areas.

IFRS and environmental reporting

There are **no required disclosures** under IFRS. However, if environmental matters fall within the scope of specific accounting principles they must be dealt with under the relevant standard. In particular:

- IAS 1 *Presentation of Financial Statements* requires disclosure of facts material to a proper understanding of financial statements.

- IAS 37 *Provisions, Contingent Liabilities and Contingent Assets* requires provisions for environmental damage to be recognised.

National and legal requirements

In the UK, the Companies Act 2006 requires disclosure of environmental matters in the Operating and Financial Review as best practice in Reporting Statement 1. Other countries require environmental reporting under national law.

Voluntary disclosure: sustainability

Most environmental disclosure is voluntary, although lists of companies in particular are under a great deal of pressure to make such disclosures.

The GRI is a long-term, multi-stakeholder international not-for-profit organisation, with many stakeholders. Its aim is to develop and disseminate globally applicable **Sustainability Reporting Guidelines** for voluntary use. These guidelines cover a number of areas (economic, environmental and social), and the latest guidelines (G4) were published in 2013.

The Guidelines set out the **framework of a sustainability report** and offer two options: the **Core option** and the **Comprehensive option**.

(1) The **Core option** contains the **essential elements** of a sustainability report. It provides the background against which an organisation communicates the impacts of its economic, environmental and social and governance performance and impacts.

(2) The **Comprehensive option** builds on the Core option by requiring **additional disclosures**

Organisations choosing the Core option have to disclose **at least one indicator** related to each 'identified material aspect', while organisations choosing the Comprehensive option have to disclose all indicators related to each 'identified material aspect'. For environmental reporting the indicators are: materials; energy; water; biodiversity; emissions; effluents and waste; products and services; compliance; transport; supplier environmental assessment; environmental grievance mechanisms.

(b) **Comments on 'environmental events'**

(1) Of relevance to the farmland restoration is IAS 37 *Provisions, Contingent Liabilities and Contingent Assets*. Provisions for environmental liabilities should be recognised where there is a **legal or constructive obligation** to rectify environmental damage or perform restorative work. The mere existence of the restorative work does not give rise to an obligation and there is no legal obligation. However, it could be argued that there is a constructive obligation arising from the company's approach in previous years, which may have given rise to an **expectation** that the work would be carried out. If this is the case, a provision of $150 million would be required in the financial statements. In addition, this provision and specific examples of restoration of land could be included in the environmental report.

(2) The treatment of the **fine** is straightforward: it is an obligation to transfer economic benefits. An estimate of the fine should be made and a **provision** set up in the financial statements for $5 million. This should be mentioned in the environmental report. The report might also **put the fines in context** by stating how many tests have been carried out and how many times the company has passed the tests. The directors may feel that it would do the company's reputation no harm to point out the fact that the number of prosecutions has been falling from year to year.

(3) These statistics are good news and need to be covered in the environmental report. However, the emphasis should be on **accurate factual reporting** rather than boasting. It might be useful to provide target levels for comparison, or an industry average if available. The emissions statistics should be split into three categories:

- Acidity to air and water
- Hazardous substances
- Harmful emissions to water

As regards the aquatic emissions, the $70 million planned expenditure on **research** should **be mentioned in the environmental report**. It shows a commitment to benefiting the environment. However, **IAS 37 would not permit a provision** to be made for this amount, since an obligation does not exist and the **expenditure is avoidable**. Nor does it qualify as development expenditure under IAS 38.

(4) The environmental report should mention the steps the company is taking to minimise the harmful impact on the environment in the way it sites and constructs its gas installations. The report should also explain the policy of dismantling the installations rather than sinking them at the end of their useful life.

Currently the company builds up a provision for decommissioning costs over the life of the installation. However, IAS 37 does not allow this. Instead, the **full amount must be provided** as soon as there is an **obligation** arising as a result of **past events**, the **settlement** of which is **expected** to result in an **outflow of resources**. The obligation exists right at the beginning of the installation's life, and so the full $407 million must be provided for. A corresponding asset is created.

4 Suntory

Workbook reference. Intangible assets are covered in Chapter 3 and the *Conceptual Framework* is covered in Chapter 1, current issues are in Chapter 19 and related parties in Chapter 2.

Top tips. Part (a)(i) required discussion of the *Conceptual Framework* in reference to the recognition of intangible assets. The examiner has stated that an in-depth knowledge of the *Conceptual Framework* is required to pass the SBR exam. You must be able to discuss the consistency of the *Conceptual Framework* (and related Exposure Draft) with each IFRS that is examined. Ensure you apply this technique in your answers. In part (a)(ii), Exposure draft 2017/6 is mentioned and briefly discussed, indicating the need to read widely to be aware of the current issues. Part (b) is on related parties – identifying the related parties and required disclosures and discussing how such disclosures are useful to investors. You are advised to jot down a plan or diagram of the relationships before launching into your answer. Consideration of the reasons why the finance director does not want to make these disclosures means you can bring ethics into your answer.

Easy marks. The technical requirements in parts (a) and (c) require relatively straightforward knowledge of IAS 38 and IAS 24.

			Marks
(a)	(i)	Discussion of IAS 38, 1 mark per point up to maximum	6
		Consistency with Conceptual Framework and discussion of principles underlying standards, 1 mark per point up to a maximum	3
			9
	(ii)	Discussion of Exposure Draft, 1 mark per point up to a maximum	4
(b)	(i)	Related parties and disclosure requirements per IAS 24, 1 mark per point up to maximum	7
	(ii)	Discussion of investor perspective 1 mark per point up to a maximum	5
			25

(a) (i) **Trademark**

Treatment in financial statements

IAS 38 *Intangible Assets* states that the cost less residual value of an intangible asset with a finite useful life should be amortised on a systematic basis over that life, that the amortisation method should reflect the pattern of benefits and that it should be reviewed at least annually.

If the pattern of consumption of benefits has changed, the amortisation method should be changed prospectively as a change in estimate under IAS 8 *Accounting Policies, Changes in Accounting Estimates and Errors.* The launch of the competitor product in December 20X5 changed the expected useful life of the trademark as expected future reductions in sales indicate a higher rate of consumption of the future economic benefits embodied in the asset. Hence, the trademark should be amortised over the remaining useful life of 2.5 years until May 20X8, as follows.

Cost of trademark $3m ÷ 10 years useful life = $300,000 amortisation per year. Therefore the carrying amount at 1 December 20X5 is ($3 million cost less (($300,000 amortisation per year × 3 years since acquisition)) = $2.1 million.

Amortisation of $840,000 ($2.1m ÷ 2.5 years' remaining useful life = $840,000) for the year to 30 November 20X6 should be expensed to profit or loss and included in the accumulated amortisation of the trademark.

IAS 36 *Impairment of Assets* states that an entity should assess at the end of each reporting period whether there is any indication that an asset may be impaired. The launch of the competitor product in December 20X5 is an external indicator of impairment as the future expected benefits from the asset are reduced as a result of the competitor launch. As such Suntory should test the trademark for impairment. An impairment loss should be recognised if the recoverable amount is less than the carrying amount of the asset. The recoverable amount of an asset is the higher of the fair value less costs of disposal and its value in use.

The carrying amount of the trademark at 30 November 20X6 is $3 million less $900,000 (amortisation for three years as above) less $840,000 (amortisation for current year as above) = $1.26 million.

The recoverable amount of the trademark has been calculated by Suntory as $500,000. Therefore an impairment loss of $760,000 ($500,000 − $1.26m = $760,000) should be recognised at 30 November 20X6.

Conceptual Framework and related Exposure Draft

The requirement of IAS 38 to amortise an intangible asset is in line with the principles of the *Conceptual Framework* for the recognition of expenses. The *Conceptual Framework* states that expenses should be recognised when a decrease in future economic benefits related to an asset has arisen that can be measured reliably. It also states that this recognition of expenses should be on a systematic basis when economic benefits are expected to arise over several accounting periods and the association with income can only be broadly determined. The requirement of IAS 38 to select an amortisation method that reflects the consumption of the economic benefits associated with the intangible asset is in agreement with this principle.

The *Conceptual Framework* does not consider the measurement of assets in any detail. However, the related Exposure Draft does outline that the carrying amount of a (non-financial) asset held at historical cost is adjusted over time to depict the usage (ie amortisation) and any impairment. The requirements of IAS 38 regarding measurement of intangible assets and those of IAS 36 regarding impairment of intangible assets are in line with these proposals.

(ii)   **Materiality**

It is correct to say that materiality is a long-established concept in financial reporting. The definition of materiality is generally well understood – it is an assessment of whether the omission or misstatement of information would impact on the decisions of users of the financial statements. Transactions, items or matters can be material either by their size or their nature. The information needs of users is central to the definition of materiality. The IASB has identified the main users as investors and potential investors, lenders and other creditors, although there are a number of other users of financial statements.

The reason the IASB has issued an Exposure Draft is because it believes there is uncertainty on behalf of the preparers of financial statements as to how the concept of materiality should be applied. There is concern that too much information is being reported in some areas whereas important information is not being reported in other areas, particularly in respect of the notes to the financial statements.

It seems that some companies are unsure about how to make materiality judgements and have therefore used the disclosure requirements in IFRSs as a checklist. The IASB believes this is contributing to the problem of a lack of clarity and excessive volume of information being disclosed in the financial statements. It is hoped that better application of the materiality principles can result in annual reports that are more fair, balanced and relevant.

The Exposure Draft proposed to provide guidance as to how the concept of materiality should be applied. It covers:

- The characteristics of materiality

- How materiality should be applied when making decisions about the presentation and disclosure of information in the financial statements

- How materiality should be applied when recognising and measuring information in the financial statements

- How to assess whether the omission if information is material to financial statements

A Practice Statement has since been issued which provides non-mandatory guidance relating to the above. .

In a separate project (ED 2017/6) the IASB is consulting on the definition of materiality. The current definition of materiality has come under some criticism as it focuses on ensuring that material information is not misstated or omitted, when in fact there is concern that key information is being obscured by immaterial disclosures in the financial statements. The IASB has proposed to amend the definition of materiality to make it clearer that information is material if omitting, misstating or **obscuring** it could reasonably be expected to influence the decisions of users of the financial statements.

(b)   (i)   **Related parties**

IAS 24 *Related Party Disclosures* requires an entity's financial statements to contain the disclosures necessary to draw attention to the possibility that its financial position and profit or loss may have been affected by the existence of related parties and by transactions and outstanding balances with such parties.

The existence of a related party relationship, even if no transactions occur, may be enough to affect the transactions of the entity. Knowledge of an entity's related party relationships may therefore affect a user's assessment of an entity and the risks and opportunities it has – which is why IAS 24 requires this information to be disclosed.

A fundamental principle of ACCA's *Code of Ethics and Conduct* is that of professional behaviour, which includes compliance with relevant regulation. It would therefore be unethical not to disclose the information required by IAS 24. The motivation of the finance director should be considered. It may be that he has other reasons for not wanting to disclose this information which could be dubious.

IAS 24 defines a related party as follows.

"A person or a close member of that person's family is related to a reporting entity if that person:

(i)   Has control or joint control over the reporting entity;

(ii)   Has significant influence over the reporting entity; or

(iii)   Is a member of the key management personnel of the reporting entity or of a parent of the reporting entity." (IAS 24: para. 9(a))

With regards to Suntory, the finance director is a related party, as he owns more than half of the voting power (60%). In the absence of evidence to the contrary, he controls Suntory and is a member of the key management personnel. The sales director is also a related party of Suntory as she is a member of the key management personnel and is a close member (spouse) of the family of the finance director. Their son is a related party of Suntory as he is a close member (son) of their family. The operations director is also a related party as he owns more than 20% of the voting power in Suntory. In the absence of evidence to the contrary, the operations director has significant influence over Suntory and is a member of the key management personnel.

An entity is related to a reporting entity if the entity is controlled or jointly controlled by a person identified as a related party. Hence, Baleel is a related party of Suntory. Baleel is controlled by related parties, the finance and sales directors, for the benefit of a close member of their family, ie their son.

In the absence of evidence to the contrary, the third owner of the shares is not a related party. The person is a passive investor who does not appear to exert significant influence over Suntory. The loan from the bank, which has been guaranteed by the finance director, will be disclosed as such in the financial statements. Disclosure of personal guarantees given by directors in respect of borrowings by the reporting entity should be disclosed in the notes to the financial statements.

(ii)   IAS 24 requires related party disclosures in order to draw attention to the possibility that an entity's financial position and profit or loss may have been affected by the existence of related parties and by transactions and outstanding balances with such parties. In this case, there is a single investor owning 10% of the shares whose investment may be affected by the related party transactions undertaken. Related party transactions are often not undertaken on the same commercial terms as normal 'arms-length' transactions. If the entity, for example, makes purchases or obtains borrowings under a related party transaction, this could be of benefit to the investor as the transaction may be at a discount or a rate of interest that is lower than could be obtained on the open market. If the entity makes a sale or provides a loan to a related party, this may not be of benefit to the investor as the transaction may be at a lower profit level than would otherwise be obtained or the payment terms may be such that the cash flows from the transaction are significantly delayed. Not all related party transactions are undertaken on different terms offered in the normal course of business. An investor will want to understand the related party transactions in order to assess their impact on the entity and its ultimate objective of maximising shareholder wealth.

ACCA

Strategic Business Reporting (International)

Mock Examination 4

Time allowed: 3 hours 15 minutes

This question paper is divided into two sections:

Section A – BOTH questions are compulsory and MUST be attempted

Section B – BOTH questions are compulsory and MUST be attempted

Do NOT open this question paper until instructed by the supervisor.

Do NOT record any of your answers on the question paper.

This question paper must not be removed from the examination hall.

Section A – BOTH questions are compulsory and MUST be attempted

1 Diamond

P2 Mar/Jun 17, amended

The following draft statements of financial position relate to Diamond, Spade and Club, all public listed entities, as at 31 March 20X7.

	Diamond $m	Spade $m	Club $m
Assets			
Non-current assets			
Property, plant and equipment	1,252	1,210	1,265
Investments in subsidiaries			
Spade	1,140		
Club	928		
Investment in Heart	68		
	3,388	1,210	1,265
Current assets	885	782	224
Total assets	4,273	1,992	1,489
Equity and liabilities			
Equity share capital ($1 each)	1,650	720	700
Retained earnings	1,180	880	364
Other components of equity	128	78	59
Total equity	2,958	1,678	1,123
Non-current liabilities	1,143	189	172
Current liabilities	172	125	194
Total liabilities	1,315	314	366
Total equity and liabilities	4,273	1,992	1,489

The following information is relevant to the preparation of the consolidated financial statements:

1   On 1 April 20X6, Diamond acquired 70% of the equity interests of Spade. At 1 April 20X6, the retained earnings and other components of equity of Spade were $780 million and $64 million respectively.

In accounting for the acquisition of Spade, the finance director did not take account of the non-controlling interest, calculating and recording a negative goodwill figure of $460 million on the acquisition, being the purchase consideration of $1,140 million cash less the fair value of the identifiable net assets of Spade at 1 April 20X6 of $1,600 million. However, it is group policy to value non-controlling interests at fair value and, at the date of acquisition, this was $485 million. The excess in fair value of the identifiable net assets is due to non-depreciable land.

2   On 1 April 20X5, Diamond acquired 40% of the equity interests of Club for cash consideration of $420 million. At this date the carrying amount and fair value of the identifiable net assets of Club was $1,032 million. Diamond treated Club as an associate and equity accounted for Club up to 31 March 20X6. On 1 April 20X6, Diamond took control of Club, acquiring a further 45% interest and adding the consideration paid to the carrying amount of its investment in Club. On 1 April 20X6, the retained earnings and other components of equity of Club were $293 million and $59 million respectively. The finance director has calculated a negative goodwill figure of $562 million at acquisition, being the

cash consideration of $500 million less the fair value of the identifiable net assets of $1,062 million. The difference between the carrying amounts and the fair values was in relation to plant with a remaining useful life of five years. The share prices of Diamond and Club were $5.00 and $1.60 respectively on 1 April 20X6. The fair value of the original 40% holding and the fair value of the non-controlling interest should both be estimated using the market value of the shares.

3   Diamond has owned a 25% equity interest in Heart for a number of years. Heart had profits for the year ended 31 March 20X7 of $20 million which can be assumed to have accrued evenly. Heart does not have any other comprehensive income. On 30 September 20X6, Diamond sold a 10% equity interest for cash of $42 million. The finance director of Diamond was unsure of how to treat the disposal and has deducted the proceeds from the carrying amount of the investment at 1 April 20X6 which was $110 million (calculated using the equity accounting method). The fair value of the remaining 15% shareholding was estimated to be $65 million at 30 September 20X6 and $67 million at 31 March 20X7. Diamond no longer exercises significant influence over Heart and has designated the remaining investment as a financial asset at fair value through other comprehensive income.

4   Diamond operates a defined benefit pension scheme. On 31 March 20X7, the company announced that it was to close down a business division and agreed to pay each of its 150 staff a cash payment of $50,000 to compensate them for loss of pension as a result of the closure. It is estimated that the closure will reduce the present value of the pension obligation by $5.8 million. The finance director of Diamond is unsure of how to deal with the settlement and curtailment and has not yet recorded anything within its financial statements.

5   On 1 April 20X6, Diamond acquired a manufacturing unit under an eight-year lease agreement. The lease asset and obligations have been accounted for correctly in the financial statements of Diamond. However, Diamond could not operate effectively from the unit until alterations to its structure costing $6.6 million were completed. The manufacturing unit was ready for use on 31 March 20X7. The alteration costs of $6.6 million were charged to administration expenses. The lease requires Diamond to restore the unit to its original condition at the end of the lease term. Diamond estimates that this will cost a further $5 million. Market interest rates are currently 6%.

Note. The following discount factors may be relevant:

Periods   6%

  7   0.665
  8   0.627

Required

(a)   (i)   Explain to the finance director of Diamond, with appropriate workings, how goodwill should have been calculated on the acquisitions of Spade and Club. Explain any adjustments needed to correct any errors made by the finance director.   **(10 marks)**

      (ii)   Explain to the finance director of Diamond, with supporting calculations, how to record the disposal of Heart in the consolidated financial statements for the year ended 31 March 20X7. Explain any adjustments needed to correct any errors made by the finance director.   **(5 marks)**

      (iii) Discuss, with suitable workings, how the settlement and curtailment of Diamond's defined benefit pension scheme should be reflected in the consolidated financial statements for the year ended 31 March 20X7.   **(3 marks)**

      (iv)   Advise the finance director how the manufacturing unit alteration costs should have been dealt with in the consolidated financial statements for the year ended 31 March 20X7.   **(3 marks)**

(b) Diamond is looking at ways to improve its liquidity. One option is to sell some of its trade receivables to a debt factor. The directors are considering two possible alternative agreements as described below:

(i) Diamond could sell $40 million receivables to a factor with the factor advancing 80% of the funds in full and final settlement. The factoring is non-recourse except that Diamond would guarantee that it will pay the factor a further 9% of each receivable which is not recovered within six months. Diamond believes that its customers represent a low credit risk and so the probability of default is very low. The fair value of the guarantee is estimated to be $50,000.

(ii) Alternatively, the factor would advance 20% of the $40 million receivables sold. Further amounts will become payable to Diamond but are subject to an imputed interest charge so that Diamond receives progressively less of the remaining balance the longer it takes the factor to recover the funds. The factor has full recourse to Diamond for a six-month period after which Diamond has no further obligations and has no rights to receive any further payments from the factor.

Required

Explain the financial reporting principles involved in debt factoring and advise how each of the above arrangements would impact upon the financial statements of future years.

(9 marks)

(Total = 30 marks)

2 Star

P2 Mar/Jun 17, amended

(a) Star, a public limited company supplying oil products globally, has debt covenants attached to some of the loan balances included within liabilities on its statement of financial position. The covenants create a legal obligation to repay the debt in full if Star fails to maintain a liquidity ratio and operating profit margin above a specified minimum. The directors are considering entering into a new five-year leasing arrangement but are concerned about the negative impact which any potential lease obligations may have on these covenants. If they proceed, they are proposing to construct the lease agreement in such a way that it is a series of six ten-month leases rather than a single five-year lease in order to utilise the short-term term lease exemption under IFRS 16 *Leases*. It would then account for the leases in accordance with their legal form. The directors believe that this will meet the requirements of the debt covenant, though they are aware that the proposed treatment may be contrary to accounting standards.

Required

Discuss the ethical issues which arise from the proposal by Star. **(6 marks)**

(b) Star is currently suffering a degree of stagnation in its business development. Its domestic and international markets are being maintained but it is not attracting new customers. Its share price has not increased whilst that of its competitors has seen a rise of between 10% and 20%. Additionally, it has recently received a significant amount of adverse publicity because of its poor environmental record and is to be investigated by regulators in several countries. Although Star is a leading supplier of oil products, it has never felt the need to promote socially responsible policies and practices or make positive contributions to society because it has always maintained its market share. It is renowned for poor customer support, bearing little regard for the customs and cultures in the communities where it does business. It had recently made a decision not to pay the amounts owing to certain small and medium entities (SMEs) as the directors feel that SMEs do not have sufficient resources to challenge the non-payment in a court of law. The management of the company is quite authoritarian and tends not to value employees' ideas and contributions.

Required

Discuss the ethical and social responsibilities of Star and whether a change in the ethical and social attitudes of the management could improve business performance. **(9 marks)**

(c) In many organisations, bonus payments related to annual profits form a significant part of the total remuneration of all senior managers, not just the top few managers. The directors of Star feel that the chief internal auditor makes a significant contribution to the company's profitability, and should therefore receive a bonus based on profit.

Required

Advise Star's directors as to whether this is appropriate. **(3 marks)**

Professional marks will be awarded for the application of ethical principles. **(2 marks)**

(Total = 20 marks)

Section B – BOTH questions are compulsory and MUST be attempted

3 Chesterfield

You have just been appointed financial controller of Chesterfield Co, a family-controlled business which operates a large number of furniture shops, which are located across the country. It also owns a number of factories which manufacture a variety of products, most of which are sold through the shops.

The new managing director, Thomas Conrad, appointed at the same time as you, is very concerned about the limited management information available. The following are regularly prepared:

- Quarterly internal financial accounts
- Daily and weekly sales reports
- Statements comparing ratios of gross profit and expenses to sales

He wishes to introduce better ways of reporting performance as a preliminary step towards:

- Assess the quality of the management of the various operations; and
- Undertaking some rationalisation of the operations.

His initial view is that both management and the operations are very variable in quality.

His first thoughts were that it could be useful to receive reports on the return on capital employed (ROCE) for each operation.

Required

Write a report to the managing director, Thomas Conrad, which:

(a) Explains the problems in measuring return on capital employed (ROCE) and the practical problems this causes in developing and interpreting the ROCE measure for the purposes envisaged **(14 marks)**

(b) Explains the process of determining which financial and non-financial performance measurements are appropriate in this type of business. **(9 marks)**

Professional marks will be awarded in this question for clarity and quality of presentation. **(2 marks)**

(Total = 25 marks)

4 Skye

P2 Mar/Jun 17, amended

(a) The existing *Conceptual Framework* has several notable omissions. It does not include an explicit reference to substance over form nor does it define derecognition or when derecognition should occur. The International Accounting Standards Board has also removed prudence from its framework and has attracted criticism from the academic and practitioner communities for doing so. The Exposure Draft ED 2015/3 on the *Conceptual Framework* attempts to explain the roles of prudence and substance over form in financial reporting whilst putting forward proposals to clarify the aims of the accounting requirements for derecognition.

Required

(i) Discuss the features of the concept of prudence and the arguments for and against its re-introduction into the *Conceptual Framework*. **(6 marks)**

(ii) Explain why it is important for there to be guidance in the *Conceptual Framework* on the role of substance over form, and the principles relating to derecognition set out in the Exposure Draft ED 2015/3 on the *Conceptual Framework*. **(8 marks)**

(b) (i) Skye has B shares in issue which allow the holders to request redemption at specified dates and amounts. The legal charter of Skye states that the entity has a choice whether or not to accept the request for repayment of the B shares. There are no other conditions attached to the shares and Skye has never refused to redeem any of the shares up to the current year end of 31 May 20X7. In all other respects the instruments have the characteristics of equity.

Skye also has preference shares in issue which are puttable by the holders at any time after 31 May 20X7. Under the terms of the shares, Skye has to satisfy the obligation for the preference shares only if it has sufficient distributable reserves. Local legislation is quite restrictive in defining the profits available for distribution as dividends.

The directors of Skye require advice on how to classify the above financial instruments in the company's financial statements at 31 May 20X7. **(6 marks)**

(ii) Skye faces a claim for infringement of the intellectual property rights of a competitor company. On 31 May 20X7, Skye agreed to settle the claim and has paid $15 million to the competitor plus a variable amount of 2% based upon future sales. The variable amount represents compensation for the use of the intellectual property in the past (0.5%) and for its use in the future (1.5%). The directors of Skye have recently heard that the ED 2015/3 on the *Conceptual Framework* has changed the definition of a liability and now feel that there is no future liability arising on the settlement of the claim as it has paid the compensation due to date.

The directors of Skye, however, still require advice on the matter. **(5 marks)**

Required

Advise the directors of Skye on how the above transactions should be dealt with in its financial statements with reference to relevant International Financial Reporting Standards and the Exposure Draft ED 2015/3.

Note. The mark allocation is shown against each of the three issues above.

(Total = 25 marks)

Answers

**DO NOT TURN THIS PAGE UNTIL YOU HAVE
COMPLETED THE MOCK EXAM**

Section A

1 Diamond

Workbook references. Group accounting is covered in chapters 10–14. Employee benefits are covered in Chapter 4, non-current assets in Chapter 3, leasing in Chapter 8 and debt factoring in Chapter 7.

Top tips. This question focuses on the calculation of goodwill and a disposal where significant influence was lost. It is important that you focus on the requirements and ensure that you give advice as well as preparing relevant calculations. Providing the calculations alone will not be sufficient to meet the requirements of the question.

Easy marks. Both the pensions and lease parts of the question also contain easy marks if you are familiar with these areas of the syllabus.

Marking scheme

				Marks
(a)	(i)	Goodwill on acquisition of – Spade	5	
		– Club	5	
				10
	(ii)	Disposal of Heart		5
	(iii)	Pension adjustment		3
	(iv)	Leased manufacturing unit		3
				21
(b)	Debt factoring			9
				30

(a)   Diamond Group

(i)   **Goodwill on acquisition of Spade and Club**

Goodwill on the acquisition of **Spade** should have been calculated as follows:

	$m	$m
Cash consideration		1,140
Non-controlling interest – fair value		485
		1,625
Fair value of identifiable net assets acquired:		
Share capital	720	
Retained earnings	780	
Other components of equity	64	
Fair value adjustment – land	36	
		(1,600)
Goodwill		25

The finance director has not taken into account the fair value of the non-controlling interest in the value of the goodwill. As the finance director had calculated negative goodwill, the resulting gain is a bargain purchase taken directly to profit and loss under IFRS 3 *Business Combinations*, before any gain was taken to profit and loss a review

should have been undertaken to ensure all of the assets and liabilities acquired had been fully recognised and measured appropriately.

The adjustment to the consolidated financial statements would be as follows:

DEBIT	Goodwill	$25 million
DEBIT	Profit or loss	$460 million
CREDIT	NCI	$485 million

Goodwill on the acquisition of **Club** should have been calculated as follows:

Diamond initially has equity accounted for its 40% interest in Club. This would have been accounted for as follows: (Note that the carrying amount of net assets at 31 March 20X6 would be $1,052 million ($700m + $293m + $59m))

	$m
Cost of investment	420
Share of post-acquisition net assets (40% × ($1,052m – $1,032m)	8
	428

When purchasing the extra 45% the $500 million cash has been added, hence the investment in Club is $928 million in Diamond's financial statements. However, on obtaining control in Club, the finance director of Diamond should have restated the value of its original 40% investment to fair value. The fair value is best estimated using the share price of Club and is calculated as (40% × $700m × $1.60) = $448 million. In Diamond's separate financial statements, the investment should have been debited with a further $20 million ($448m – $428m) and the gain on the step acquisition credited to profit or loss. The treatment is driven by Diamond having gained control on 1 April 20X6. The original investment is treated is though it were disposed of and re-acquired at fair value.

Goodwill will be calculated as follows:

	$m	$m
Cash consideration		500
Fair value of original 40% interest		448
		948
Non-controlling interest (15% × $700m × $1.60)		168
		1,116
Fair value of identifiable net assets acquired:		
Share capital	700	
Retained earnings	293	
Other components of equity	59	
Fair value adjustment – plant	10	
		(1,062)
Goodwill		54

The adjustment to the consolidated financial statements would be as follows:

DEBIT	Goodwill	$54 million
DEBIT	Profit or loss	$562 million
CREDIT	NCI	$168 million
CREDIT	Investment in Club	$448 million

Total goodwill is therefore $79 million ($25m + $54m).

Goodwill should be tested for impairment on an annual basis. Any impairment should be charged to profit or loss in the year it is incurred.

(ii) **Disposal of Heart**

Diamond would originally have had significant influence over Heart via its 25% holding. The finance director of Diamond has equity accounted for Heart up to 31 March 20X6 giving an equity value of $110 million. The finance director should have equity accounted right up to 30 September 20X6, at which point significant influence is lost. A further $2.5 million (25% × $20m × 6/12) should have been added to the investment and included within retained earnings.

On losing significant influence, a profit or loss on disposal should be calculated and taken to profit or loss as follows:

	$m
Proceeds	42
Fair value of remaining interest at 30 September 20X6	65
	107
Investment in associate at 30 September 20X6 ($110m + $2.5m)	(112.5)
Loss on disposal	(5.5)

The remaining 15% holding is an investment under IFRS 9 *Financial Instruments* and is restated to fair value of $67 million at 31 March 20X7. A gain is to be recorded in other components of equity of $2 million ($67m – $65m).

The adjustments to Diamond's financial statements would be as follows:

DEBIT	Investment in Heart	$2.5 million	
CREDIT	Retained earnings		$2.5 million

Being Diamond's share of Heart's results from 1 April to 30 September 20X6

CREDIT	Investment in Heart		$47.5 million
DEBIT	Profit or loss	$5.5 million	
DEBIT	Cash	$42 million	

Being loss on disposal of 10% interest in Heart

DEBIT	Investment in Heart	$2 million	
CREDIT	Other components of equity		$2 million

Being gain on restatement of investment to fair value

(iii) **Pension adjustment**

Here a curtailment and settlement are happening together, as Diamond is limiting the future benefits from its defined benefit plan for this group of employees due to the restructuring (curtailment) and compensating them by settling part of the existing expected future obligation with a one-off lump sum payment as part of their termination benefits (settlement). The estimated settlement on the pension liability is $7.5 million (150 × $50,000) and should be included within current liabilities, as it appears to be immediately due to Diamond's employees. As this is $1.7 million more than the estimated curtailment gain of $5.8 million, a loss of $1.7 million should be taken to profit or loss. Non-current liabilities are reduced by the reduction in pension obligations of $5.8 million.

The adjustments to incorporate the transaction into Diamond's financial statements would be as follows:

DEBIT	Profit or loss – settlement loss	$1.7 million	
DEBIT	Retirement benefit obligation	$5.8 million	
CREDIT	Current liabilities		$7.5 million

Being entries to reflect pension settlement and curtailment on closure of division, unrecorded by Diamond

(iv) **Leased manufacturing unit**

The fact that this is a leased asset does not change how the subsequent expenditure on the asset should be treated. The alteration costs of $6.6 million should be capitalised, and not charged as an expense to profit or loss as they have been. A provision for restoration costs of $3.3 million ($5m × 0.665) should also be recognised and capitalised as part of the carrying amount of the asset.

Diamond has a present obligation to incur expenditure as a result of a past event (the structural alterations it has made to the manufacturing unit, which it must restore to original condition under the lease it has signed to return the unit to the lessee). Under IAS 37 *Provisions, Contingent Liabilities and Contingent Assets* a provision should be recognised for the full restoration cost of $3.3 million. Because the structural alterations represent access to future economic benefits, the future cost also represents an asset and this should be recognised.

The adjustments to incorporate the transaction into Diamond's financial statements would be as follows:

	$m	$m
DEBIT Property, plant and equipment	9.9	
CREDIT Profit or loss		6.6
CREDIT Non-current liabilities – restoration cost provision		3.3

Being entries to reflect obligation for restoration of leased asset and capitalisation of alteration costs

The additional property, plant and equipment costs of $9.9 million will require to be depreciated over the remaining 7 years of the lease ($1.4 million per year).

(b) IFRS 9 *Financial Instruments* requires Diamond to consider the commercial substance rather than the legal form of the debt factoring arrangements. IFRS 9 suggests that the trade receivables should be derecognised from the financial statements of Diamond when the following conditions are met:

(i) When Diamond has no further rights to receive cash from the factor

(ii) When the risks and rewards of ownership relating to the receivables have substantially been transferred to the factor

(iii) When Diamond has no further control over the trade receivables

Agreement one

With agreement one there is a sharing of the risks and rewards of ownership as the factoring is non-recourse except that Diamond retains an obligation to refund the factor 9% of irrecoverable debts. It can be seen, however, that substantially all the risks and rewards of ownership have passed to the factor. The probability of an individual default is low given that there is low credit risk and the factor would suffer the vast majority of the loss arising from any default. Diamond also has no further access to the rewards of ownership as the initial $32 million (80% × $40 million) is in full and final settlement. Furthermore, the factor has assumed full control over the collectability of the receivables. The trade receivables should be derecognised from the financial statements of Diamond and $8 million, being the difference between the value of the receivables sold and the cash received, should be charged as an irrecoverable debt expense against the profits of Diamond.

The guarantee should be treated as a separate financial liability in accordance with IFRS 9. This would initially be measured at its fair value of $50,000.

Agreement two

The risks and rewards of ownership do not initially pass to the factor in relation to agreement two. The factor has full recourse to Diamond for a six-month period so the irrecoverable debt risk is still with Diamond. Furthermore, Diamond still has the right to receive further cash payments from the factor, the amounts to be received being dependent on when and if the customers pay the factor. Diamond therefore still has the risks associated with slow payment by their customers. The receivables must not initially be derecognised from the financial statements with the $8 million (20% × $40m) proceeds being treated as a short-term liability due to the factor. The receivables and liability balances would gradually be reduced as the factor recovered the cash from Diamond's customers which would be adjusted for the imputed interest and expensed in profit or loss. Should there be any indication of impairment during the six-month period, the receivables should be credited with a corresponding charge to profit or loss.

Following six months the risks and rewards of ownership have passed to the factor and the balances on the loan and the receivables would be offset. The remaining balance following offset within the receivables of Diamond should be expensed in profit or loss as an irrecoverable debt.

2 Star

> **Workbook references.** Ethics are covered in Chapter 2. Leasing is covered in Chapter 8.
>
> **Top tips.** There are generous marks available for this three-part ethics question. Ensure you split your time appropriately across the parts. Do not waffle. Remember to link your answer to the scenario, the information is given for you to use it. In both parts (a) and (b) you must ensure that your answer demonstrates a good understanding of ethical principles rather than simply the ability to reiterate the ethical codes.
>
> **Easy marks.** Parts (b) and (c) are more generic so there is scope to gain marks for sensible discussion.

Marking scheme

		Marks
(a)	Lease agreement	6
(b)	Ethical and social responsibilities	9
(c)	Internal auditor profit-related bonus	3
Professional marks		2
		20

(a) **Lease agreement substance presentation**

It is of crucial importance that stakeholders of a company can rely on the financial statements in order to make informed and accurate decisions. The directors of Star have an ethical responsibility to produce financial statements which comply with accounting standards, are transparent and free from material error. Lenders will often attach covenants to the terms of an agreement in order to protect their interests in an entity. They would also be of crucial importance to potential debt and equity investors when assessing the risks and returns from any future investment in the entity.

The proposals by Star appear to be a deliberate attempt to circumvent the terms of the covenants. The legal form would be to treat the lease as a series of short-term leases. This would be accounted for as expenses in profit or loss and not recognise the right-of-use asset and the associated lease obligation that the substance of the transaction and IFRS 16 *Leases* requires. This would be a form of 'off-balance sheet finance' and would not report the true assets and obligations of Star. It is likely that liquidity ratios would be adversely misrepresented from the proposed accounting treatment. The operating profit margins are likely to be adversely affected by the attempt to use the short-term exemption, as the expenses associated with the lease are likely to be higher than the depreciation charge if a leased asset was recognised, hence the proposal may actually be detrimental to the operating profit covenant.

Star is aware that the proposed accounting treatment may be contrary to accounting standards. Such manipulation would be a clear breach of the fundamental principles of objectivity and integrity as outlined in the ACCA *Code of Ethics*. It is important that accountants are seen to exercise professional behaviour and due care at all times. The proposals by Star are likely to mislead stakeholders in the entity. This could discredit the profession creating a lack of confidence within the profession. The directors of Star must be reminded of their ethical responsibilities and persuaded that the accounting treatment must fully comply with accounting standards and principles outlined within the framework should they proceed with the debt factoring agreements.

(b)   **Ethical and social responsibilities**

Ethics and corporate social responsibility are important in themselves, but also because they can improve business performance. At present the company is stagnating, because it has focused on maintaining market share and on its own shareholders at the expense of other stakeholders. Corporate social responsibility is concerned with a company's accountability to a wide range of stakeholders, not just shareholders. For Star, the most significant of these include:

(i)   Regulators
(ii)   Customers
(iii)   Creditors
(iv)   Employees

Regulators

The relationship with regulators is not good, mainly because of a poor reputation on environmental matters. Star just does the bare minimum, for example cleaning up contamination only when legally obliged to do so.

Adopting environmentally friendly policies and reporting in detail on these in an environmental report will go some way towards mending the relationship. Litigation costs, which have a direct impact on profit, can be avoided.

Customers

Currently, Star provides poor customer support and makes no effort to understand the customs and cultures of the countries in which it operates. Moreover, it makes no positive contributions and does not promote socially responsible policies. This attitude could easily alienate its present customers and deter new ones. A competitor who does make positive contributions to the community, for example in sponsoring education or environmental programmes, will be seen as having the edge and could take customers away from Star. Corporate social responsibility involves thinking long-term about the community rather than about short-term profits, but in the long-term, profits could suffer if socially responsible attitudes are not adopted.

Creditors

Suppliers are key stakeholders who must be handled responsibly if a reputation in the wider business community is not to suffer. Star's policy of not paying small and medium-sized companies is very shortsighted. While such companies may not be in a position to sue for

payment, the effect on goodwill and reputation will be very damaging in the long-term. Suppliers may be put off doing business with Star. Perhaps a key component can only be sourced from a small supplier, who will not sell to Star if word gets around that it does not pay. This unethical and damaging policy must be discontinued and relationships with all suppliers fostered.

Employees

Employees are very important stakeholders. Star's authoritarian approach to management and its refusal to value employees or listen to their ideas, is potentially damaging to business performance. High staff turnover is costly as new staff must be recruited and trained. Employees who do not feel valued will not work as hard as those who do. In addition, employees may have some good ideas to contribute that would benefit performance; at the moment Star is missing out on these ideas. Acting responsibly and ethically is not just right; it should also lead to the company being more profitable in the long term.

(c) **Internal auditor bonus**

For

The chief internal auditor is an employee of Star, which pays a salary to him or her. As part of the internal control function, he or she is helping to keep down costs and increase profitability. It could therefore be argued that the chief internal auditor should have a reward for adding to the profit of the business.

Against

Conversely, the problem remains that, if the chief internal auditor receives a bonus based on results, he or she may be tempted to allow certain actions, practices or transactions which should be stopped, but which are increasing the profit of the business, and therefore the bonus.

Conclusion

On balance, it is not advisable for the chief internal auditor to receive a bonus based on the company's profit.

3 Chesterfield

> **Workbook references.** The interpretation of financial statements is covered in Chapter 17.
>
> **Top tips.** In part (a) you are given a reasonable amount of information about the specific reasons why better performance measurement is needed, so do try to use this rather than just producing an answer learnt by rote. Part (b) is quite hard: it is about the **process** of selecting measures, not about the measures themselves. Another valid approach would be to talk about critical success factors. Your answer should be tailored to the type of business Chesterfield is involved in.
>
> **Easy marks.** Interpretation questions are generally not easy, but you should consider breaking down the ratio into its component parts and discussing the problems around those as a starting point. Providing appropriate headings and a professional tone in the report should help to gain the professional marks.

Marking scheme

		Marks
(a)	Problems in measuring ROCE	5
	Problems in developing and interpreting ROCE	9
		14
(b)	Explain the process in developing measures	9
Professional marks		2
		25

REPORT

To: Thomas Conrad, Managing Director

From: The Financial Controller   Date: XX.XX.XX

Subject: Return on capital employed and other performance measurements

(a) **The problems with Return on Capital Employed**

Return on capital employed (ROCE) is a simple measure to calculate: it is the percentage given by dividing the operating profit (profit before interest and tax) made by an operation by the amount of capital (total assets less current liabilities) invested in order to make that profit. It is a useful measure of the efficiency of operations. However, both elements of the ROCE fraction present problems in practice.

Problems with profit before interest and tax (PBIT)

Chesterfield has a range of operations, with both manufacturing and retail components in diverse geographical locations In order to calculate ROCE, Chesterfield needs to separately calculate and report on the PBIT for each operation. The management of Chesterfield need to decide what an 'operation' is and ensure that the accounting system can provide the relevant information. It is reasonable to expect that the retail operations would generate a higher profit than the factories, so comparing retail v manufacturing is not a reasonable measure.

Profit is a fairly arbitrary accounting measure. It does not focus on the quality of an operations profits, nor how that operation uses and generates cash. Cash is likely to be an important measure when considering the potential rationalisation of the business.

It is important that the management do not just consider the profit and ROCE for the current year. They will have to obtain historical information in order to do some trend analysis on the returns (which in itself has problems as historical information is not necessarily an indicator of future performance) or calculate ROCE across the next few periods in order to understand the movement over time.

Problems with capital employed

Capital employed is all assets less current liabilities of a business. For the business as a whole these figures may be easy to identify, but when judging the **performance of the separate operations** that make up the business it will be **hard to decide what element of assets shared by several different operations should be taken into account**. For example receivables and payables may be managed centrally by head office, or motor vehicles used by individual shops for deliveries might be part of a pool covering several shops in a region.

Even if the assets used by separate operations can be identified there is the further **problem of ascribing a value to them.**

(i) If assets are valued at historical cost, then an older asset will have a lower value than an identical one acquired more recently, which will result in a higher ROCE. This could mean that shops that have not had recent investment report a better ROCE than newer shops or those that have recently been refitted.

(ii) If the value is restated at current cost, this may disguise the impact of the relative inefficiency of older assets compared with newer ones (for example, repair costs and lack of technological improvements).

(iii) If depreciation is taken into account, are all similar assets being depreciated according to the same accounting policy?

The ROCE measure may, in any case, **not be a reliable guide to the quality of the management of the various operations**.

(i) There is a considerable difference between the return likely to be achievable by a factory on its assets compared with a shop and its, quite different, assets. **Like should be compared with like**, or allowances should be made for differences, otherwise the exercise has no validity.

(ii) If **investment decisions are made centrally** it may not be fair to measure a manager's ability to earn a return on capital that he or she might not have chosen to invest in, in the first place.

(iii) If **managers have control over the assets** in use in their operation, they may be **inclined to under-invest in new assets** in order to keep capital employed figure low which will help to inflate ROCE. This is **unlikely to be in the interests of the company as a whole.**

(b) **Determining which performance measurements are appropriate for particular businesses**

Overriding factors that will determine what performance measures are used in any business are the **costs of setting up information systems to provide them and the benefits of having them**. As Chesterfield is a family-controlled company, performance measurement is likely to be more for management purposes than for external investors and therefore the owners need to consider whether the investment needed to obtain relevant information is necessary to fulfil its stewardship needs.

The process is a matter of looking at **what the business is aiming to achieve (its mission) and what it actually does**. For example, one company may be aiming to be

the biggest player in its market while another aims to corner the niche, luxury end of a market. Speed of delivery may be crucial to the success of one business, whereas quality of the finished product, no matter how long this takes, may be crucial to another.

The **mission of an organisation can be split into four elements and performance measures can be devised to reflect each of these.**

(i) **Purpose**, for example maximising the wealth of the family owners.

(ii) **Strategy**, defining the business the company is in (eg manufacturing and retail of furniture), and the special competences it intends to use to prosper (eg hand built by craftsmen).

(iii) **Policies and standards of behaviour**; for example, customer service standards, employees all paid living wage or above.

(iv) **Values**, related to the organisation's culture. For example, employees who are encouraged to train and develop, no gender pay-gaps, fair treatment of suppliers.

Measures are more likely to compare performance against that of competitors.

It is less easy to generalise about **measures of what the business does**. It is necessary to have a **detailed understanding of how the business operates**, how its production systems or service delivery systems work, what channels it uses for sales, and so on. Measures such as output per machine, number of returns per product sold or sales per region, can then be devised as appropriate.

Signed: Financial Controller

4 Skye

Workbook references. The *Conceptual Framework* and the developments related to it are covered in Chapter 1, financial instruments are covered in Chapter 7.

Top tips. There are four parts to this question so be sure to allocate your time appropriately across the marks. The question is discussion-based so focus your narrative throughout and do not waffle. Part (a) (i) about prudence tests a key concept that you should be familiar with. State the arguments in favour of, and against, the inclusion of prudence in the *Conceptual Framework* logically. Part (b) (i) looks at the classification of equity instruments into liabilities and equity, a narrow focus but one which is fundamental to understanding and interpreting financial statements. If you have revised IAS 32 this is not difficult but you need to use the information given to clearly explain how the instruments fit the criteria. Part (b) (ii) is a little more challenging but even if you do not know the full answer there are marks available for straightforward knowledge of the liabilities definitions, which are fundamental.

Easy marks. Part (a) (i) about prudence contains no 'right' answer and so contains scope for easy marks if you are able to state the arguments for and against clearly. There are generous marks available in Part (a) (ii) on substance over form and derecogition. This is straightforward knowledge but you need to be familiar with the current developments around the *Conceptual Framework*. Part (b) (i) is not difficult is you are familiar with IAS 32 and Part (b) (ii) contains further easy marks for knowledge and application of the definition of a liability.

Marking scheme

				Marks
(a)	(i)	1 mark per point up to maximum		6
	(ii)	1 mark per point up to maximum		8
(b)	(i)	1 mark per point up to maximum		6
	(ii)	1 mark per point up to maximum		5
				25

(a) (i) The preparers of financial statements have to deal with the uncertainties which surround the preparation of financial statements. For example, events such as the collectability of doubtful receivables and the probable useful life of plant and equipment have a degree of uncertainty attached to them. Such uncertainties are recognised by the disclosure and by the exercise of prudence in the preparation of financial statements. Prudence is the inclusion of a degree of caution in the exercise of the judgements needed in making the estimates required under conditions of uncertainty, such that assets or income are not overstated and liabilities or expenses are not understated. However, the exercise of prudence does not allow for deliberate understatement or deliberate overstatement because the financial statements would not be neutral and, therefore, not have the quality of reliability.

Prudence is a term used by different people to mean different things. Some use it to refer to a need to be more cautious when making judgements relating to gains and assets than for those relating to losses and liabilities. Others feel that losses should be recognised at an earlier stage than gains. Faithful representation requires that financial statements are neutral and so an understanding of prudence is linked to an understanding of the term 'neutrality'.

The arguments put forward against the reintroduction of prudence into the *Conceptual Framework* include the fact that there is no common understanding of what prudence means and thus there are different interpretations as to its meaning. This could lead to inconsistent application of the concept.

The exercise of prudence can lead to greater subjectivity in the financial statements, which will affect the evaluation of the entity's performance.

However, the opposite view is that a reference to prudence should be reinstated in the *Conceptual Framework*. Certain Standards are underpinned by the concept of prudence and therefore it is important to explain prudence in the *Conceptual Framework* so that it can be applied consistently. Preparers of financial statements have a natural bias towards optimism and therefore prudence is needed to counteract this bias. Investors are often more concerned with the financial risk relating to potential losses. There are views that some form of conservatism has a role to play in financial reporting even though there are different views about what form this would take. Additionally, the financial crisis has demonstrated the need for prudence when making estimates.

(ii) The existing *Conceptual Framework* does not include an explicit reference to substance over form. However, accounting in accordance with an element's legal form, and not its economic substance, would not result in a faithful representation. The Exposure Draft proposes that a faithful representation should provide information about the substance of an economic phenomenon instead of merely information about its legal form. Accounting for something in accordance with its legal form, even with appropriate disclosures, cannot result in a faithful representation if the economic substance of the item is different.

The existing *Conceptual Framework* does not define derecognition, nor does it describe when derecognition should occur. As a result, different standards have adopted different approaches to derecognition. The derecognition criteria need to reflect how best to portray both an entity's rights and obligations and changes in those rights and obligations. The accounting requirements for derecognition should aim to represent faithfully the assets and the liabilities retained after the derecognition and the changes in the assets and the liabilities as a result of the transaction or event. If an entity disposes of an entire asset or an entire liability and retains no exposure to that asset or liability, then normally there is no issue, but it can be more difficult if an entity disposes of only part of an asset or a liability. In most cases, an entity will achieve the best result if it applies the control approach, that is by derecognising an asset or a liability when it no longer meets the recognition criteria.

(b)   (i)   IAS 32 *Financial Instruments: Presentation* states that a liability is a contractual obligation to deliver cash or another financial asset to another entity and that an equity instrument is any contract which evidences a residual interest in the assets of an entity after deducting all of its liabilities. In this case, Skye has no obligation to transfer cash or another asset to the holders of the instruments and therefore the B shares should be classed as equity. The fact that Skye has not refused redemption in the past does not cause the B shares to be classified as a liability.

The preference shares create an obligation for Skye because of the put option clause in the agreement. The fact that Skye may not be in a position to satisfy the put option feature because of insufficient distributable reserves does not negate the fact that Skye has an obligation.

(ii)   The ED *Conceptual Framework* says that a liability is a present obligation of the entity to transfer an economic resource as a result of past events. A present obligation is an obligation to transfer economic resources which the entity has no practical ability to avoid and has arisen from a past event, that is, economic benefits already received or activities already conducted. The future sales-linked compensation is a mechanism for determining the amount of past and future use of the intellectual property. Therefore, because part of the settlement is a variable amount to pay for past usage (even though this is based on future sales) Skye should recognise a financial liability under IFRS 9 *Financial Instruments* at 31 May 20X7. It is a present obligation as a result of a past event and this principle is the basis of the definition of a liability not only in the ED but also in the existing *Conceptual Framework*. As regards the sales-linked payment relating to future use, the liability arises as new sales are realised and represents an executory contract under IAS 37 *Provisions, Contingent Liabilities and Contingent Assets*. In these circumstances, Skye should not recognise a liability as the variable amount is based upon future sales, unless the executory contract is deemed to be onerous.

ACCA
Strategic Business Reporting (International)

Mock Examination 5 (ACCA Specimen exam)

Time allowed: 3 hours 15 minutes

This question paper is divided into two sections:

Section A – BOTH questions are compulsory and MUST be attempted
Section B – BOTH questions are compulsory and MUST be attempted

Do NOT open this question paper until instructed by the supervisor.

Do NOT record any of your answers on the question paper.

This question paper must not be removed from the examination hall.

Section A – BOTH questions are compulsory and MUST be attempted

1 Kutchen

The following group financial statements relate to the Kutchen Group which comprised Kutchen, House and Mach, all public limited companies.

GROUP STATEMENT OF FINANCIAL POSITION AS AT 31 DECEMBER 20X6

	$m
Assets	
Non-current assets	
Property, plant and equipment	365
Goodwill	–
Intangible assets	23
	388
Current assets	133
Total assets	521
Equity and liabilities	
Share capital of $1 each	63
Retained earnings	56
Other components of equity	26
Non-controlling interest	3
	148
Non-current liabilities	101
Current liabilities	
Trade payables	272
Total liabilities	373
Total equity and liabilities	521

At the time of the internal review of the group financial statements, the following issues were discovered:

(1) On 1 June 20X6, Kutchen acquired 70% of the equity interests of House. The purchase consideration comprised 20 million shares of $1 of Kutchen at the acquisition date and a further 5 million shares on 31 December 20X7 if House's net profit after taxation was at least $4 million for the year ending on that date.

The market price of Kutchen's shares on 1 June 20X6 was $2 per share and that of House was $4.20 per share. It is felt that there is a 20% chance of the profit target being met.

In accounting for the acquisition of House, the finance director did not take into account the non-controlling interest in the goodwill calculation. He determined that a bargain purchase of $8 million arose on the acquisition of House, being the purchase consideration of $40 million less the fair value of the identifiable net assets of House acquired on 1 June 20X6 of $48 million. This valuation was included in the group financial statements above.

After the directors of Kutchen discovered the error, they decided to measure the non-controlling interest at fair value at the date of acquisition. The fair value of the non-controlling interest (NCI) in House was to be based upon quoted market prices at acquisition. House had issued share capital of $1 each, totalling $13 million at 1 June 20X6 and there has been no change in this amount since acquisition.

461

(2)   On 1 January 20X6, Kutchen acquired 80% of the equity interests of Mach, a privately owned entity, for a consideration of $57 million. The consideration comprised cash of $52 million and the transfer of non-depreciable land with a fair value of $5 million. The carrying amount of the land at the acquisition date was $3 million and the land has only recently been transferred to the seller of the shares in Mach and is still carried at $3 million in the group financial statements at 31 December 20X6.

At the date of acquisition, the identifiable net assets of Mach had a fair value of $55 million. Mach had made a net profit attributable to ordinary shareholders of $3.6 million for the year to 31 December 20X5.

The directors of Kutchen wish to measure the non-controlling interest at fair value at the date of acquisition but had again omitted NCI from the goodwill calculation. The NCI is to be fair valued using a public entity market multiple method. The directors of Kutchen have identified two companies who are comparable to Mach and who are trading at an average price to earnings ratio (P/E ratio) of 21. The directors have adjusted the P/E ratio to 19 for differences between the entities and Mach, for the purpose of fair valuing the NCI. The finance director has determined that a bargain purchase of $3 million arose on the acquisition of Mach being the cash consideration of $52 million less the fair value of the net assets of Mach of $55 million. This gain on the bargain purchase had been included in the group financial statements above.

(3)   Kutchen had purchased an 80% interest in Niche for $40 million on 1 January 20X6 when the fair value of the identifiable net assets was $44 million. The partial goodwill method had been used to calculate goodwill and an impairment of $2 million had arisen in the year ended 31 December 20X6. The holding in Niche was sold for $50 million on 31 December 20X6. The carrying amount of Niche's identifiable net assets other than goodwill was $60 million at the date of sale. Kutchen had carried the investment in Niche at cost. The finance director calculated that a gain arose of $2 million on the sale of Niche in the group financial statements being the sale proceeds of $50 million less $48 million being their share of the identifiable net assets at the date of sale (80% of $60 million). This was credited to retained earnings.

(4)   Kutchen has decided to restructure one of its business segments. The plan was agreed by the board of directors on 1 October 20X6 and affects employees in two locations. In the first location, half of the factory units have been closed by 31 December 20X6 and the affected employees' pension benefits have been frozen. Any new employees will not be eligible to join the defined benefit plan. After the restructuring, the present value of the defined benefit obligation in this location is $8 million. The following table relates to location 1.

Value before restructuring	Location 1
	$m
Present value of defined benefit obligation	(10)
Fair value of plan assets	7
Net pension liability	(3)

In the second location, all activities have been discontinued. It has been agreed that employees will receive a payment of $4 million in exchange for the pension liability of $2.4 million in the unfunded pension scheme.

Kutchen estimates that the costs of the above restructuring excluding pension costs will be $6 million. Kutchen has not accounted for the effects of the restructuring in its financial statements because it is planning a rights issue and does not wish to depress the share price. Therefore there has been no formal announcement of the restructuring.

Required

(a) (i) Explain to the directors of Kutchen, with suitable workings, how goodwill should have been calculated on the acquisition of House and Mach showing the adjustments which need to be made to the consolidated financial statements to correct any errors by the finance director. **(10 marks)**

(ii) Explain, with suitable calculations, how the gain or loss on the sale of Niche should have been recorded in the group financial statements. **(5 marks)**

(iii) Discuss, with suitable workings, how the pension scheme should be dealt with after the restructuring of the business segment and whether a provision for restructuring should have been made in the financial statements for the year ended 31 December 20X6. **(7 marks)**

Note. Marks will be allocated in (a) for a suitable discussion of the principles involved as well as the accounting treatment.

(b) When Kutchen acquired the majority shareholding in Mach, there was an option on the remaining non-controlling interest (NCI), which could be exercised at any time up to 31 March 20X7. On 31 January 20X7, Kutchen acquired the remaining NCI in Mach. The payment for the NCI was structured so that it contained a fixed initial payment and a series of contingent amounts payable over the following two years.

The contingent payments were to be based on the future profits of Mach up to a maximum amount. Kutchen felt that the fixed initial payment was an equity transaction. Additionally, Kutchen was unsure as to whether the contingent payments were either equity, financial liabilities or contingent liabilities.

After a board discussion which contained disagreement as to the accounting treatment, Kutchen is preparing to disclose the contingent payments in accordance with IAS 37 *Provisions, Contingent Liabilities and Contingent Assets*. The disclosure will include the estimated timing of the payments and the directors' estimate of the amounts to be settled.

Required

Advise Kutchen on the difference between equity and liabilities, and on the proposed accounting treatment of the contingent payments on acquisition of the NCI of Mach. **(8 marks)**

(Total = 30 marks)

2 Abby

Abby is a company which conducts business in several parts of the world.

The accountant has discovered that the finance director of Abby has purchased goods from a company, Arwight, which the director jointly owns with his wife and the accountant believes that this purchase should be disclosed. However, the director refuses to disclose the transaction as in his opinion it is an 'arm's length' transaction. He feels that if the transaction is disclosed, it will be harmful to business and feels that the information asymmetry caused by such non-disclosure is irrelevant as most entities undertake related party transactions without disclosing them. Similarly, the director felt that competitive harm would occur if disclosure of operating segment profit or loss was made. As a result, the entity only disclosed a measure of total assets and total liabilities for each reportable segment.

When preparing the financial statements for the recent year end, the accountant noticed that Arwight has not paid an invoice for several million dollars and it is significantly overdue for payment. It appears that the entity has liquidity problems and it is unlikely that Arwight will pay. The accountant believes that a loss allowance for trade receivables is required. The finance director has refused to make such an allowance and has told the accountant that the issue must not be discussed with anyone within the trade because of possible repercussions for the credit worthiness of Arwight.

Additionally, when completing the consolidated financial statements, the director has suggested that there should be no positive fair value adjustments for a recently acquired subsidiary and has stated that the accountant's current position is dependent upon following these instructions. The fair value of the subsidiary is $50 million above the carrying amount in the financial records. The reason given for not fair valuing the subsidiary's net assets is that goodwill is an arbitrary calculation which is meaningless in the context of the performance evaluation of an entity.

Finally, when preparing the annual impairment tests of goodwill arising on other subsidiaries, the director has suggested that the accountant is flexible in the assumptions used in calculating future expected cash flows, so that no impairment of goodwill arises and that the accountant should use a discount rate which reflects risks for which future cash flows have been adjusted. He has indicated that he will support a salary increase for the accountant if he follows his suggestions.

Required

Discuss the ethical and accounting implications of the above situations from the perspective of the reporting accountant. **(18 marks)**

Professional marks will be awarded in question 2 for the application of ethical principles. **(2 marks)**

(Total = 20 marks)

Section B – BOTH questions are compulsory and MUST be attempted

3 Africant

(a)   Africant owns several farms and also owns a division which sells agricultural vehicles. It is considering selling this agricultural retail division and wishes to measure the fair value of the inventory of vehicles for the purpose of the sale. Three markets currently exist for the vehicles. Africant has transacted regularly in all three markets.

At 31 December 20X5, Africant wishes to find the fair value of 150 new vehicles, which are identical. The current volume and prices in the three markets are as follows:

Market	Sales price per vehicle $	Historical volume – vehicles sold by Africant	Total volume of vehicles sold in the market	Transaction costs per vehicle $	Transport cost to market per vehicle $
Europe	40,000	6,000	150,000	500	400
Asia	38,000	2,500	750,000	400	700
Africa	34,000	1,500	100,000	300	600

Africant wishes to value the vehicles at $39,100 per vehicle as these are the highest net proceeds per vehicle, and Europe is the largest market for Africant's product.

(i)   Africant wishes to understand the principles behind the valuation of the new vehicles and also whether their valuation would be acceptable under IFRS 13 *Fair Value Measurement*. **(8 marks)**

(ii)   Africant uses the revaluation model for its non-current assets. Africant has several plots of farmland which are unproductive. The company feels that the land would have more value if it were used for residential purposes. There are several potential purchasers for the land but planning permission has not yet been granted for use of the land for residential purposes. However, preliminary enquiries with the regulatory authorities seem to indicate that planning permission may be granted. Additionally, the government has recently indicated that more agricultural land should be used for residential purposes.

Africant has also been approached to sell the land for commercial development at a higher price than that for residential purposes and understands that fair value measurement of a non-financial asset takes into account a market perspective.

Africant would like an explanation of what is meant by a 'market perspective' and advice on how to measure the fair value of the land in its financial statements. **(7 marks)**

Required

Advise Africant on the matters set out above (in (i) and (ii)) with reference to relevant International Financial Reporting Standards.

Note. The mark allocation is shown against each of the two issues above.

(b)   Africant is about to hold its annual general meeting with shareholders and the directors wish to prepare for any potential questions which may be raised at the meeting. There have been discussions in the media over the fact that the most relevant measurement method should be selected for each category of assets and liabilities. This 'mixed measurement approach' is used by many entities when preparing financial statements. There have also been comments in

the media about the impact that measurement uncertainty and price volatility can have on the quality of financial information.

Required

Discuss the impact which the above matters may have on the analysis of financial statements by investors in Africant. **(8 marks)**

Professional marks will be awarded in part (b) for clarity and quality of presentation. **(2 marks)**

(Total = 25 marks)

4 Rationale

The directors of Rationale are reviewing the published financial statements of the group. The following is an extract of information to be found in the financial statements.

Year ended	$m	31 December 20X6 $m	31 December 20X5 $m
Net profit/(loss) before taxation and after the items set out below		(5)	38
Net interest expense		10	4
Depreciation		9	8
Amortisation of intangible assets		3	2
Impairment of property	10		
Insurance proceeds	(7)	3	
Debt issue costs		2	
Share-based payment		3	1
Restructuring charges		4	
Impairment of acquired intangible assets		6	8

The directors use 'underlying profit' to comment on its financial performance. Underlying profit is a measure normally based on earnings before interest, tax, depreciation and amortisation (EBITDA). However, the effects of events which are not part of the usual business activity are also excluded when evaluating performance.

The following items were excluded from net profit to arrive at 'underlying profit'. In 20X6, the entity had to write off a property due to subsidence and the insurance proceeds recovered for this property was recorded but not approved until 20X7, when the company's insurer concluded that the claim was valid. In 20X6, the entity considered issuing loan notes to finance an asset purchase, however, the purchase did not go ahead. The entity incurred costs associated with the potential issue and so these costs were expensed as part of net profit before taxation. The entity felt that the share-based payment was not a cash expense and that the value of the options was subjective. Therefore, the directors wished to exclude the item from 'underlying profit'. Similarly, the directors wish to exclude restructuring charges incurred in the year, and impairments of acquired intangible assets.

Required

(a) (i) Discuss the possible concerns where an entity may wish to disclose additional information in its financial statements and whether the Exposure Draft on the Conceptual Framework for Financial Reporting helps in determining the boundaries for disclosure. **(8 marks)**

(ii) Discuss the use and the limitations of the proposed calculation of 'underlying profit' by Rationale.

Note. Your answer should include a comparative calculation of underlying profit for the years ended 31 December 20X5 and 20X6. **(9 marks)**

(b) The directors of Rationale are confused over the nature of a reclassification adjustment and understand that the IASB has issued pronouncements on the subject.

Required

Discuss, with examples, the nature of a reclassification adjustment and the arguments for and against allowing reclassification of items to profit or loss.

Note. A brief reference should be made in your answer to the IASB's Exposure Draft on the Conceptual Framework. **(8 marks)**

(Total = 25 marks)

Answers

**DO NOT TURN THIS PAGE UNTIL YOU HAVE
COMPLETED THE MOCK EXAM**

Section A

			Marks
(a)	(i)	Discussion 1 mark per point to a maximum	6
		Calculation	4
	(ii)	Discussion 1 mark per point to a maximum	3
		Calculation	2
	(iii)	1 mark for each point to a maximum	7
(b)		1 mark for each point to a maximum	8
			30

1 Kutchen

(a) (i) Goodwill on the acquisition of House and Mach should have been calculated as follows:

House

	$m	$m
Fair value of consideration for 70% interest	42	
Fair value of non-controlling interest	16.38	58.38
Fair value of identifiable net assets acquired		(48)
Goodwill		10.38

Contingent consideration should be valued at fair value and will have to take into account the various milestones set under the agreement. The expected value is (20% × 5 million shares) 1 million shares × $2, ie $2 million. There will be no remeasurement of the fair value in subsequent periods. If this were a liability, there would be remeasurement. The contingent consideration will be shown in OCE. The fair value of the consideration is therefore 20 million shares at $2 plus $2 million (above), ie $42 million.

The fair value of the NCI is 30% × 13 million × $4.20 = $16.38 million.

The finance director has not taken into account the fair value of the NCI in the valuation of goodwill or the contingent consideration. If the difference between the fair value of the consideration, NCI and the identifiable net assets is negative, the resulting gain is a bargain purchase in profit or loss, which may arise in circumstances such as a forced seller acting under compulsion. However, before any bargain purchase gain is recognised in profit or loss, and hence in retained earnings in the group statement of financial position, the finance director should have undertaken a review to ensure the identification of assets and liabilities is complete, and that measurements appropriately reflect consideration of all available information.

The adjustment to the group financial statements would be as follows:

DEBIT	Goodwill	$10.38 million	
DEBIT	Profit or loss	$8 million	
CREDIT	NCI		$16.38 million
CREDIT	OCE		$2 million

Mach

Net profit of Mach for the year to 31 December 20X5 is $3.6 million. The P/E ratio (adjusted) is 19. Therefore the fair value of Mach is 19 × $3.6 million, ie $68.4 million. The NCI has a 20% holding; therefore the fair value of the NCI is $13.68 million.

	$m	$m
Fair value of consideration for 80% interest ($52m + $5m)	57	
Fair value of non-controlling interest	13.68	70.68
Fair value of identifiable net assets acquired		(55)
Goodwill		15.68

The land transferred as part of the purchase consideration should be valued at its acquisition date fair value of $5 million and included in the goodwill calculation. Therefore the increase of $2 million over the carrying amount should be shown in retained earnings.

DEBIT	PPE	$2 million	
CREDIT	Retained earnings		$2 million

The adjustment to the group financial statements would be as follows:

DEBIT	Goodwill	$15.68 million	
DEBIT	Retained earnings	$3 million	
CREDIT	NCI		$13.68 million
CREDIT	PPE		$5 million

Total goodwill is therefore $(15.68 + 10.38) million, ie $26.06 million.

(ii) **Niche**

The finance director had calculated that a gain arose of $2 million on the sale of Niche in the group financial statements being the sale proceeds of $50 million less $48 million which is their share of the identifiable net assets at the date of sale (80% of $60 million). However, the calculation of the gain or loss on sale should have been the difference between the carrying amount of the net assets (including any unimpaired goodwill) disposed of and any proceeds received. The calculation of net assets will include the appropriate portion of cumulative exchange differences and any other amounts recognised in other comprehensive income and accumulated in equity. Additionally, the loss on sale should have been reported as a loss in profit or loss attributable to the parent.

The gain on the sale of Niche should have been recorded as follows:

	$m
Gain/(Loss) in group financial statements on sale of Niche	
Sale proceeds	50
Less	
Share of identifiable net assets at date of disposal (80% × $60 million)	(48)
Goodwill $(40m – (80% of $44m) – impairment $2m)	(2.8)
Loss on sale of Niche recognised in group profit or loss	(0.8)

(iii) After restructuring, the present value of the pension liability in location 1 is reduced to $8 million. Thus there will be a negative past service cost in this location of $(10 – 8) million, ie $2 million. As regards location 2, there is a settlement and a curtailment as all liability will be extinguished by the payment of $4 million. Therefore there is a loss of $(2.4 – 4) million, ie $1.6 million. The changes to the pension scheme in locations 1 and 2 will both affect profit or loss as follows:

Location 1
DEBIT   Pension obligation $2m
CREDIT   Retained earnings $2m

Location 2
DEBIT   Pension obligation $2.4m
DEBIT   Retained earnings $1.6m
CREDIT   Current liabilities $4m

IAS 37 *Provisions, Contingent Liabilities and Contingent Assets* states that a provision for restructuring should be made only when a detailed formal plan is in place and the entity has started to implement the plan, or announced its main features to those affected. A board decision is insufficient. Even though there has been no formal announcement of the restructuring, Kutchen has started implementing it and therefore it must be accounted for under IAS 37.

A provision of $6 million should also be made at the year end.

(b)   The Framework defines a liability as a present obligation, arising from past events and there is an expected outflow of economic benefits. IAS 32 *Financial Instruments: Presentation* establishes principles for presenting financial instruments as liabilities or equity. IAS 32 does not classify a financial instrument as equity or financial liability on the basis of its legal form but on the substance of the transaction. The key feature of a financial liability is that the issuer is obliged to deliver either cash or another financial asset to the holder. An obligation may arise from a requirement to repay principal or interest or dividends.

In contrast, equity has a residual interest in the entity's assets after deducting all of its liabilities. An equity instrument includes no obligation to deliver cash or another financial asset to another entity. A contract which will be settled by the entity receiving or delivering a fixed number of its own equity instruments in exchange for a fixed amount of cash or another financial asset is an equity instrument. However, if there is any variability in the amount of cash or own equity instruments which will be delivered or received, then such a contract is a financial asset or liability as applicable.

The contingent payments should not be treated as contingent liabilities but they should be recognised as financial liabilities and measured at fair value at initial recognition. IAS 37 *Provisions, Contingent Liabilities and Contingent Assets* excludes from its scope contracts which are executory in nature, and therefore prevents the recognition of a liability. Additionally, there is no onerous contract in this scenario.

Contingent consideration for a business must be recognised at the time of acquisition, in accordance with IFRS 3 *Business Combinations*. However, IFRS do not contain any guidance when accounting for contingent consideration for the acquisition of a NCI in a subsidiary. The contract for contingent payments does meet the definition of a financial liability under IAS 32. Kutchen has an obligation to pay cash to the vendor of the NCI under the terms of a contract. It is not within Kutchen's control to be able to avoid that obligation. The amount of the contingent payments depends on the profitability of Mach, which itself depends on a number of factors which are uncontrollable. IAS 32 states that a contingent obligation to pay cash which is outside the control of both parties to a contract meets the definition of a financial liability which shall be initially measured at fair value. Since the contingent payments relate to the acquisition of the NCI, the offsetting entry would be recognised directly in equity.

2 Abby

	Marks
Accounting issues – 1 mark per point up to maximum	10
Ethical issues – 1 mark per point up to maximum	8
Professional	2
	20

The objective of IAS 24 *Related Party Disclosures* is to ensure that an entity's financial statements contain the disclosures necessary to draw attention to the possibility that its financial position and profit or loss may have been affected by the existence of related parties and by transactions and outstanding balances with such parties. If there have been transactions between related parties, there should be disclosure of the nature of the related party relationship as well as information about the transactions and outstanding balances necessary for an understanding of the potential effect of the relationship on the financial statements. The director is a member of the key management personnel of the reporting entity and the entity from whom the goods were purchased is jointly controlled by that director. Therefore a related party relationship exists and should be disclosed.

IFRS 8 *Operating Segments* requires an entity to report financial and descriptive information about its reportable segments. Reportable segments are operating segments or aggregations of operating segments which meet specified criteria. IFRS 8 does not contain a 'competitive harm' exemption and requires entities to disclose the financial information which is provided by the chief operating decision maker (CODM). The management accounts reviewed by the CODM may contain commercially sensitive information, and IFRS 8 might require that information to be disclosed externally. Under IFRS 8, firms should provide financial segment disclosures which enable investors to assess the different sources of risk and income as management does. This sensitive information would also be available for competitors. The potential competitive harm may encourage firms to withhold segment information. However, this is contrary to IFRS 8 which requires information about the profit or loss for each reportable segment, including certain specified revenues and expenses such as revenue from external customers and from transactions with other segments, interest revenue and expense, depreciation and amortisation, income tax expense or income and material non-cash items.

Areas such as impairments of financial assets often involve the application of professional judgement. The director may have received additional information, which has allowed him to form a different opinion to that of the accountant. The matter should be discussed with the director to ascertain why no provision is required and to ask whether there is additional information available. However, suspicion is raised by the fact that the accountant has been told not to discuss the matter. Whilst there may be valid reasons for this, it appears again that the related party relationship is affecting the judgement of the director.

Positive fair value adjustments increase the assets of the acquired company and as such reduce the goodwill recognised on consolidation. However, the majority of positive fair value adjustments usually relate to items of property, plant and equipment. As a result, extra depreciation based on the net fair value adjustment reduces the post-acquisition profits of the subsidiary. This has a negative impact on important financial performance measures such as EPS. Therefore, by reducing fair value adjustments it will improve the apparent performance of new acquisitions and the consolidated financial statements. Accountants should act ethically and ignore undue pressure to undertake creative accounting in preparing such adjustments. Guidance such as IFRS 3 *Business Combinations* and IFRS 13 *Fair Value Measurement* should be used in preparing adjustments and professional valuers should be engaged where necessary.

In measuring value in use, the discount rate used should be the pre-tax rate which reflects current market assessments of the time value of money and the risks specific to the asset. The discount rate should not reflect risks for which future cash flows have been adjusted and should equal the rate of return which investors would require if they were to choose an investment which would generate cash flows equivalent to those expected from the asset. By reducing the impairment, it would have a positive impact on the financial statements. The offer of a salary increase is inappropriate and no action should be taken until the situation is clarified. Inappropriate financial reporting raises issues and risks for those involved and others associated with the company. Whilst financial reporting involves judgement, it would appear that this situation is related to judgement.

There are several potential breaches of accounting standards and unethical practices being used by the director. The director is trying to coerce the accountant into acting unethically. IAS 1 *Presentation of Financial Statements* requires all standards to be applied if fair presentation is to be obtained. Directors cannot choose which standards they do or do not apply. It is important that accountants identify issues of unethical practice and act appropriately in accordance with ACCA's *Code of Ethics*. The accountant should discuss the matters with the director. The technical issues should be explained and the risks of non-compliance explained to the director. If the director refuses to comply with accounting standards, then it would be appropriate to discuss the matter with others affected such as other directors and seek professional advice from the ACCA. Legal advice should be considered if necessary.

An accountant who comes under pressure from senior colleagues to make inappropriate valuations and disclosures should discuss the matter with the person suggesting this. The discussion should try to confirm the facts and the reporting guidance which needs to be followed. Financial reporting does involve judgement but the cases above seem to be more than just differences in opinion. The accountant should keep a record of conversations and actions and discuss the matters with others affected by the decision, such as directors. Additionally, resignation should be considered if the matters cannot be satisfactorily resolved.

3 Africant

			Marks
(a)	1 mark per point up to maximum		15
(b)	1 mark per point up to maximum		8
Professional			2
			25

(a)   (i)   IFRS *13 Fair Value Measurement* says that fair value is an exit price in the principal market, which is the market with the highest volume and level of activity. It is not determined based on the volume or level of activity of the reporting entity's transactions in a particular market. Once the accessible markets are identified, market-based volume and activity determines the principal market. There is a presumption that the principal market is the one in which the entity would normally enter into a transaction to sell the asset or transfer the liability, unless there is evidence to the contrary. In practice, an entity would first consider the markets it can access. In the absence of a principal market, it is assumed that the transaction would occur in the most advantageous market. This is the market which would maximise the amount which would be received to sell an asset or minimise the amount which would be paid to transfer a liability, taking into consideration transport and transaction costs. In either case, the entity must have access to the market on the measurement date. Although an entity must be able to access the market at the measurement date, IFRS 13 does not require an entity to be able to sell the particular asset or transfer the particular liability on that date. If there is a principal market for the asset or liability, the fair value measurement represents the price in that market at the measurement date regardless of whether that price is directly observable or estimated using another valuation technique and even if the price in a different market is potentially more advantageous.

The principal (or most advantageous) market price for the same asset or liability might be different for different entities and therefore, the principal (or most advantageous) market is considered from the entity's perspective which may result in different prices for the same asset.

In Africant's case, Asia would be the principal market as this is the market in which the majority of transactions for the vehicles occur. As such, the fair value of the 150 vehicles would be $5,595,000 ($38,000 – $700 = $37,300 × 150). Actual sales of the vehicles in either Europe or Africa would result in a gain or loss to Africant when compared with the fair value, ie $37,300. The most advantageous market would be Europe where a net price of $39,100 (after all costs) would be gained by selling there and the number of vehicles sold in this market is at its highest. Africant would therefore utilise the fair value calculated by reference to the Asian market as this is the principal market.

The IASB decided to prioritise the price in the most liquid market (ie the principal market) as this market provides the most reliable price to determine fair value and also serves to increase consistency among reporting entities.

IFRS 13 makes it clear that the price used to measure fair value must not be adjusted for transaction costs, but should consider transportation costs. Africant has currently deducted transaction costs in its valuation of the vehicles. Transaction costs are not deemed to be a characteristic of an asset or a liability but they are specific to a

transaction and will differ depending on how an entity enters into a transaction. While not deducted from fair value, an entity considers transaction costs in the context of determining the most advantageous market because the entity is seeking to determine the market which would maximise the net amount which would be received for the asset.

(ii) A fair value measurement of a non-financial asset takes into account a market participant's ability to generate economic benefits by using the asset in its highest and best use or by selling it to another market participant who would use the asset in its highest and best use. The maximum value of a non-financial asset may arise from its use in combination with other assets or by itself. IFRS 13 requires the entity to consider uses which are physically possible, legally permissible and financially feasible. The use must not be legally prohibited. For example, if the land is protected in some way by law and a change of law is required, then it cannot be the highest and best use of the land. In this case, Africant's land for residential development would only require approval from the regulatory authority and as that approval seems to be possible, then this alternative use could be deemed to be legally permissible. Market participants would consider the probability, extent and timing of the approval which may be required in assessing whether a change in the legal use of the non-financial asset could be obtained.

Africant would need to have sufficient evidence to support its assumption about the potential for an alternative use, particularly in light of IFRS 13's presumption that the highest and best use is an asset's current use. Africant's belief that planning permission was possible is unlikely to be sufficient evidence that the change of use is legally permissible. However, the fact the government has indicated that more agricultural land should be released for residential purposes may provide additional evidence as to the likelihood that the land being measured should be based upon residential value. Africant would need to prove that market participants would consider residential use of the land to be legally permissible. Provided there is sufficient evidence to support these assertions, alternative uses, for example, commercial development which would enable market participants to maximise value, should be considered, but a search for potential alternative uses need not be exhaustive. In addition, any costs to transform the land, for example, obtaining planning permission or converting the land to its alternative use, and profit expectations from a market participant's perspective should also be considered in the fair value measurement.

If there are multiple types of market participants who would use the asset differently, these alternative scenarios must be considered before concluding on the asset's highest and best use. It appears that Africant is not certain about what constitutes the highest and best use and therefore IFRS 13's presumption that the highest and best use is an asset's current use appears to be valid at this stage.

(b) Some investors might argue in favour of a single measurement basis for all recognised assets and liabilities as the resulting totals and subtotals can have little meaning if different measurement methods are used. Similarly, profit or loss may lack relevance if it reflects a combination of flows based on historical cost and of value changes for items measured on a current value basis.

However, the majority of investors would tend to favour a mixed measurement approach, whereby the most relevant measurement method is selected for each category of assets and liabilities. This approach is consistent with how investors analyse financial statements. The problems of mixed measurement are outweighed by the greater relevance achieved if the most relevant measurement basis is used for each class of assets and liabilities. The mixed measurement approach is reflected in recent standards; for example, IFRS 9 *Financial Instruments* and IFRS 15 *Revenue from Contracts with Customers*. Historical cost would not have been relevant for all financial assets and has severe limitations for many liabilities; hence, the only viable single measurement method would have been fair value.

IFRS 9 requires the use of cost in some cases and fair value in other cases, while IFRS 15 essentially applies cost allocation. The draft *Conceptual Framework* does not propose a single measurement method for all assets and liabilities, and instead supports the continued use of a mixed measurement approach.

Most accounting measures of assets and liabilities are uncertain and require estimation. While some measures of historical cost are straightforward as it is the amount paid or received, there are many occasions when the measurement of cost can be uncertain – particularly recoverable cost, for which impairment and depreciation estimates are required. In a similar vein, while some measures of fair value can be easily observed because of the availability of prices in an actively traded market (a so-called 'Level 1' fair value), others inevitably rely on management estimates and judgements ('Level 2' and 'Level 3').

High measurement uncertainty might reduce the quality of information available to investors. High price volatility may make analysing an investment in that entity more challenging. If a relevant measure of an asset or liability value is volatile, this should not be hidden from investors. To conceal its volatility would decrease the usefulness of the financial statements. Of course, such volatile gains and losses do need to be clearly presented and disclosed, because their predictive value may differ from that provided by other components of performance.

4 Rationale

Marking scheme

			Marks
(a)	(i)	1 mark per point up to a maximum	8
	(ii)	1 mark per point up to a maximum	9
(b)		1 mark per point up to a maximum	8
			25

(a) (i) There is no specific guidance on information which is not required by an IFRS being disclosed in financial statements. IFRS requires an entity to disclose additional information which is relevant to an understanding of the entity's financial position and financial performance.

A company may disclose additional information where it is felt that an entity's performance may not be apparent from accounts prepared under IFRS. A single standardised set of accounting practices can never be sufficient information to understand an entity's position or performance. Additional information can help users understand management's view of what is important to the entity and the nature of management's decisions.

There are concerns relating to the disclosure of additional information. Such information may not readily be derived or reconciled back to financial statements. There is also difficulty comparing information across periods and between entities because of the lack of standardised approaches. Also the presentation of additional information may be inconsistent with that defined or specified in IFRS and the entity may present an excessively optimistic picture of an entity's financial performance. Non-IFRS information may make it difficult to identify the complete set of financial statements, including whether the information is audited or not. Additionally, the information may be given undue prominence or credibility merely because of its location within the financial statements. Non-IFRS financial information should be clearly labelled in a way that distinguishes it from the corresponding IFRS financial information. Any term used to describe the information should be appropriate having regard to the nature of the

information. The term or label should not cause confusion with IFRS information and should accurately describe the measure.

Disclosure boundaries are not specifically defined in IFRS, but they do derive from the objective of financial statements. According to the proposals in the ongoing Conceptual Framework project, the objective of financial statements is to provide information about an entity's assets, liabilities, equity, income and expenses which is useful to users of financial statements in assessing the prospects for future net cash inflows to the entity and in assessing management's stewardship of the entity's resources. As a result, financial statements provide information about an entity's assets, liabilities and equity which existed at the end of or during the reporting period and about income and expenses which arose during the reporting period. It is directed at users who provide resources to the reporting entity but lack the ability to compel the entity to provide them with the information which they need. The revised Framework limits the range of addressees of general-purpose financial statements to existing or potential investors, lenders and other creditors. The revised Framework continues to acknowledge that general purpose financial statements may not provide information which serves all users' needs.

(ii) The directors of Rationale are utilising a controversial figure for evaluating a company's earnings. Depreciation and amortisation are non-cash expenses related to assets which have already been purchased and they are expenses which are subject to judgement or estimates based on experience and projections. The company, by using EBITDA, is attempting to show operating cash flow since the non-cash expenses are added back.

However, EBITDA can also be misused and manipulated. For example, depreciation schedules can be extended in order to increase profits with the consequential impact on this ratio. It can be argued that because the estimation of depreciation, amortisation and other non-cash items is vulnerable to judgement error, the profit figure can be distorted but by focusing on profits before these elements are deducted, a truer estimation of cash flow can be given. However, the substitution of EBITDA for conventional profit fails to take into account the need for investment in fixed capital items.

There can be an argument for excluding non-recurring items from the net profit figure. Therefore, it is understandable that the deductions for the impairment of property, the insurance recovery and the debt issue costs are made to arrive at 'underlying profit'. However, IAS 1 *Presentation of Financial Statements* states that an entity shall present additional line items, headings and subtotals in the statements presenting profit and loss and other comprehensive income when such presentation is relevant to an understanding of the entity's financial performance (para. 55). This paragraph should not be used to justify presentation of underlying, adjusted and pre-exceptional measures of performance on the face of the income statement. The measures proposed are entity specific and could obscure performance and poor management.

Share-based compensation may not represent cash but if an entity chooses to pay equity to an employee, that affects the value of equity, no matter what form that payment is in and therefore it should be charged as employee compensation. It is an outlay in the form of equity. There is therefore little justification in excluding this expense from net profit. Restructuring charges are a feature of an entity's business and they can be volatile. They should not be excluded from net profit because they are part of corporate life. In the case of Rationale, they have occurred in consecutive years and certainly could not be considered 'one-off'. Severance costs and legal fees are not non-cash items.

Impairments of acquired intangible assets usually reflect a weaker outlook for an acquired business than was expected at the time of the acquisition, and could be considered to be non-recurring. However, the impairment charges are a useful way of holding management accountable for its acquisitions. In this case, it seems as though Rationale has not purchased wisely in 20X6.

It appears as though Rationale wishes to disguise a weak performance in 20X6 by adding back a series of expense items. EBITDA, although reduced significantly from 20X5, is now a positive figure and there is an underlying profit created as opposed to a loss. However, users will still be faced with a significant decline in profit whichever measure is disclosed by Rationale. The logic for the increase in profit is flawed in many cases but there is a lack of authoritative guidance in the area. Many companies adopt non-financial measures without articulating the relationship between themeasures and the financial statements.

Year ended	31 December 20X6 ($m)	31 December 20X5 ($m)
Net profit/(loss) before taxation and after the items set out below	(5)	38
Net interest expense	10	4
Depreciation	9	8
Amortisation of intangible assets	3	2
EBITDA	17	52
Impairment of property	10	
Insurance recovery	(7)	–
Debt issue costs	2	–
EBITDA after non-recurring items	22	52
Share-based payment	3	1
Restructuring charges	4	
Impairment of acquired intangible assets	6	8
Underlying profit	35	61

(b)   Reclassification adjustments are amounts recycled to profit or loss in the current period which were recognised in OCI in the current or previous periods. An example of items recognised in OCI which may be reclassified to profit or loss are foreign currency gains on the disposal of a foreign operation and realised gains or losses on cash flow hedges. Those items which may not be reclassified are changes in a revaluation surplus under IAS 16 *Property, Plant and Equipment*, and actuarial gains and losses on a defined benefit plan under IAS 19 *Employee Benefits*. However, there is a general lack of agreement about which items should be presented in profit or loss and in OCI. The interaction between profit or loss and OCI is unclear, especially the notion of reclassification and when or which OCI items should be reclassified. A common misunderstanding is that the distinction is based upon realised versus unrealised gains.

There are several arguments for and against reclassification. If reclassification ceased, then there would be no need to define profit or loss, or any other total or subtotal in profit or loss, and any presentation decisions can be left to specific IFRSs. It is argued that reclassification protects the integrity of profit or loss and provides users with relevant information about a transaction which occurred in the period. Additionally, it can improve comparability where IFRS permits similar items to be recognised in either profit or loss or OCI.

Those against reclassification argue that the recycled amounts add to the complexity of financial reporting, may lead to earnings management and the reclassification adjustments may not meet the definitions of income or expense in the period as the change in the asset or liability may have occurred in a previous period.

The lack of a consistent basis for determining how items should be presented has led to an inconsistent use of OCI in IFRS. Opinions vary but there is a feeling that OCI has become a home for anything controversial because of a lack of clear definition of what should be included in the statement. Many users are thought to ignore OCI, as the changes reported are not caused by the operating flows used for predictive purposes.

The ED states that it is not feasible to attempt to define in the Conceptual Framework when an item of income or expense should be included in the statement of profit or loss or OCI. Instead, high level guidance on reclassification has been included. The ED proposes that there is a presumption that if income and expenses are included in OCI in one period, they will be reclassified in some future period when including the income in the statement of profit or loss enhances the relevance of the information in that period. The presumption can be rebutted if there is no clear basis for identifying the period in which the reclassification would enhance the relevance of the information in the statement of profit or loss. This may indicate that the income or expense should not have been included in OCI originally. It can be argued that reclassification adjustments do not meet the definition of income and expenses in the period they occur and that, therefore, the IASB should acknowledge in the *Conceptual Framework* those adjustments as items of the statement(s) of performance which do not fulfil the definition of income and expense.

Mathematical tables

Present value table

Present value of $1 = (1+r)^{-n}$ where r = discount rate, n = number of periods until payment.

This table shows the present value of £1 per annum, receivable or payable at the end of *n* years.

Periods	Discount rates (r)									
(n)	1%	2%	3%	4%	5%	6%	7%	8%	9%	10%
1	0.990	0.980	0.971	0.962	0.952	0.943	0.935	0.926	0.917	0.909
2	0.980	0.961	0.943	0.925	0.907	0.890	0.873	0.857	0.842	0.826
3	0.971	0.942	0.915	0.889	0.864	0.840	0.816	0.794	0.772	0.751
4	0.961	0.924	0.888	0.855	0.823	0.792	0.763	0.735	0.708	0.683
5	0.951	0.906	0.863	0.822	0.784	0.747	0.713	0.681	0.650	0.621
6	0.942	0.888	0.837	0.790	0.746	0.705	0.666	0.630	0.596	0.564
7	0.933	0.871	0.813	0.760	0.711	0.665	0.623	0.583	0.547	0.513
8	0.923	0.853	0.789	0.731	0.677	0.627	0.582	0.540	0.502	0.467
9	0.914	0.837	0.766	0.703	0.645	0.592	0.544	0.500	0.460	0.424
10	0.905	0.820	0.744	0.676	0.614	0.558	0.508	0.463	0.422	0.386
11	0.896	0.804	0.722	0.650	0.585	0.527	0.475	0.429	0.388	0.350
12	0.887	0.788	0.701	0.625	0.557	0.497	0.444	0.397	0.356	0.319
13	0.879	0.773	0.681	0.601	0.530	0.469	0.415	0.368	0.326	0.290
14	0.870	0.758	0.661	0.577	0.505	0.442	0.388	0.340	0.299	0.263
15	0.861	0.743	0.642	0.555	0.481	0.417	0.362	0.315	0.275	0.239
16	0.853	0.728	0.623	0.534	0.458	0.394	0.339	0.292	0.252	0.218
17	0.844	0.714	0.605	0.513	0.436	0.371	0.317	0.270	0.231	0.198
18	0.836	0.700	0.587	0.494	0.416	0.350	0.296	0.250	0.212	0.180
19	0.828	0.686	0.570	0.475	0.396	0.331	0.277	0.232	0.194	0.164
20	0.820	0.673	0.554	0.456	0.377	0.312	0.258	0.215	0.178	0.149

Periods	Discount rates (r)									
(n)	11%	12%	13%	14%	15%	16%	17%	18%	19%	20%
1	0.901	0.893	0.885	0.877	0.870	0.862	0.855	0.847	0.840	0.833
2	0.812	0.797	0.783	0.769	0.756	0.743	0.731	0.718	0.706	0.694
3	0.731	0.712	0.693	0.675	0.658	0.641	0.624	0.609	0.593	0.579
4	0.659	0.636	0.613	0.592	0.572	0.552	0.534	0.516	0.499	0.482
5	0.593	0.567	0.543	0.519	0.497	0.476	0.456	0.437	0.419	0.402
6	0.535	0.507	0.480	0.456	0.432	0.410	0.390	0.370	0.352	0.335
7	0.482	0.452	0.425	0.400	0.376	0.354	0.333	0.314	0.296	0.279
8	0.434	0.404	0.376	0.351	0.327	0.305	0.285	0.266	0.249	0.233
9	0.391	0.361	0.333	0.308	0.284	0.263	0.243	0.225	0.209	0.194
10	0.352	0.322	0.295	0.270	0.247	0.227	0.208	0.191	0.176	0.162
11	0.317	0.287	0.261	0.237	0.215	0.195	0.178	0.162	0.148	0.135
12	0.286	0.257	0.231	0.208	0.187	0.168	0.152	0.137	0.124	0.112
13	0.258	0.229	0.204	0.182	0.163	0.145	0.130	0.116	0.104	0.093
14	0.232	0.205	0.181	0.160	0.141	0.125	0.111	0.099	0.088	0.078
15	0.209	0.183	0.160	0.140	0.123	0.108	0.095	0.084	0.074	0.065
16	0.188	0.163	0.141	0.123	0.107	0.093	0.081	0.071	0.062	0.054
17	0.170	0.146	0.125	0.108	0.093	0.080	0.069	0.060	0.052	0.045
18	0.153	0.130	0.111	0.095	0.081	0.069	0.059	0.051	0.044	0.038
19	0.138	0.116	0.098	0.083	0.070	0.060	0.051	0.043	0.037	0.031
20	0.124	0.104	0.087	0.073	0.061	0.051	0.043	0.037	0.031	0.026

Cumulative present value table

This table shows the present value of £1 per annum, receivable or payable at the end of each year for *n* years.

Periods (n)	1%	2%	3%	4%	5%	6%	7%	8%	9%	10%
1	0.990	0.980	0.971	0.962	0.952	0.943	0.935	0.926	0.917	0.909
2	1.970	1.942	1.913	1.886	1.859	1.833	1.808	1.783	1.759	1.736
3	2.941	2.884	2.829	2.775	2.723	2.673	2.624	2.577	2.531	2.487
4	3.902	3.808	3.717	3.630	3.546	3.465	3.387	3.312	3.240	3.170
5	4.853	4.713	4.580	4.452	4.329	4.212	4.100	3.993	3.890	3.791
6	5.795	5.601	5.417	5.242	5.076	4.917	4.767	4.623	4.486	4.355
7	6.728	6.472	6.230	6.002	5.786	5.582	5.389	5.206	5.033	4.868
8	7.652	7.325	7.020	6.733	6.463	6.210	5.971	5.747	5.535	5.335
9	8.566	8.162	7.786	7.435	7.108	6.802	6.515	6.247	5.995	5.759
10	9.471	8.983	8.530	8.111	7.722	7.360	7.024	6.710	6.418	6.145
11	10.37	9.787	9.253	8.760	8.306	7.887	7.499	7.139	6.805	6.495
12	11.26	10.58	9.954	9.385	8.863	8.384	7.943	7.536	7.161	6.814
13	12.13	11.35	10.63	9.986	9.394	8.853	8.358	7.904	7.487	7.103
14	13.00	12.11	11.30	10.56	9.899	9.295	8.745	8.244	7.786	7.367
15	13.87	12.85	11.94	11.12	10.38	9.712	9.108	8.559	8.061	7.606
16	14.718	13.578	12.561	11.652	10.838	10.106	9.447	8.851	8.313	7.824
17	15.562	14.292	13.166	12.166	11.274	10.477	9.763	9.122	8.544	8.022
18	16.398	14.992	13.754	12.659	11.690	10.828	10.059	9.372	8.756	8.201
19	17.226	15.678	14.324	13.134	12.085	11.158	10.336	9.604	8.950	8.365
20	18.046	16.351	14.877	13.590	12.462	11.470	10.594	9.818	9.129	8.514

Periods (n)	11%	12%	13%	14%	15%	16%	17%	18%	19%	20%
1	0.901	0.893	0.885	0.877	0.870	0.862	0.855	0.847	0.840	0.833
2	1.713	1.690	1.668	1.647	1.626	1.605	1.585	1.566	1.547	1.528
3	2.444	2.402	2.361	2.322	2.283	2.246	2.210	2.174	2.140	2.106
4	3.102	3.037	2.974	2.914	2.855	2.798	2.743	2.690	2.639	2.589
5	3.696	3.605	3.517	3.433	3.352	3.274	3.199	3.127	3.058	2.991
6	4.231	4.111	3.998	3.889	3.784	3.685	3.589	3.498	3.410	3.326
7	4.712	4.564	4.423	4.288	4.160	4.039	3.922	3.812	3.706	3.605
8	5.146	4.968	4.799	4.639	4.487	4.344	4.207	4.078	3.954	3.837
9	5.537	5.328	5.132	4.946	4.772	4.607	4.451	4.303	4.163	4.031
10	5.889	5.650	5.426	5.216	5.019	4.833	4.659	4.494	4.339	4.192
11	6.207	5.938	5.687	5.453	5.234	5.029	4.836	4.656	4.486	4.327
12	6.492	6.194	5.918	5.660	5.421	5.197	4.988	4.793	4.611	4.439
13	6.750	6.424	6.122	5.842	5.583	5.342	5.118	4.910	4.715	4.533
14	6.982	6.628	6.302	6.002	5.724	5.468	5.229	5.008	4.802	4.611
15	7.191	6.811	6.462	6.142	5.847	5.575	5.324	5.092	4.876	4.675
16	7.379	6.974	6.604	6.265	5.954	5.668	5.405	5.162	4.938	4.730
17	7.549	7.120	6.729	6.373	6.047	5.749	5.475	5.222	4.990	4.775
18	7.702	7.250	6.840	6.467	6.128	5.818	5.534	5.273	5.033	4.812
19	7.839	7.366	6.938	6.550	6.198	5.877	5.584	5.316	5.070	4.843
20	7.963	7.469	7.025	6.623	6.259	5.929	5.628	5.353	5.101	4.870

Review Form – Strategic Business Reporting (International and United Kingdom) (02/18)

Name: _____   Address: _____

_____

_____

How have you used this Kit?
(Tick one box only)

☐ Home study (book only)

☐ On a course: college _____

☐ With 'correspondence' package

☐ Other _____

Why did you decide to purchase this Kit?
(Tick one box only)

☐ Have used the Workbook

☐ Have used other BPP products in the past

☐ Recommendation by friend/colleague

☐ Recommendation by a lecturer at college

☐ Saw advertising

☐ Other _____

Which BPP products have you used?

Workbook ☐   Other ☐

Kit ☑

During the past six months do you recall seeing/receiving any of the following?
(Tick as many boxes as are relevant)

☐ Our advertisement in *Student Accountant*

☐ Our advertisement in *Pass*

☐ Our advertisement in *PQ*

☐ Our brochure with a letter through the post

☐ Our website www.bpp.com

Which (if any) aspects of our advertising do you find useful?
(Tick as many boxes as are relevant)

☐ Prices and publication dates of new editions

☐ Information on product content

☐ Facility to order books off-the-page

☐ None of the above

Your ratings, comments and suggestions would be appreciated on the following areas.

	Very useful	Useful	Not useful
Passing SBR	☐	☐	☐
Questions	☐	☐	☐
Top Tips etc in answers	☐	☐	☐
Content and structure of answers	☐	☐	☐
Mock exam answers	☐	☐	☐

Overall opinion of this Kit   Excellent ☐   Good ☐   Adequate ☐   Poor ☐

Do you intend to continue using BPP products?   Yes ☐   No ☐

The BPP author of this edition can be e-mailed at: accaqueries@bpp.com

Review Form (continued)

TELL US WHAT YOU THINK

Please note any further comments and suggestions/errors below.